PAUL FISCHER

EURASIA'S EMERGING MEGAMARKETS

Building Your Tomorrow in China, India, and Russia

BOOKSURGE

2010

Copyright © 2010

Paul Fischer

All rights reserved. No reproduction, copy, or transmission of this publication, in part or in full, may be made without written permission.

Cover design and production: BookSurge Publishing, USA (a brand of On-Demand Publishing LLC, a subsidiary of Amazon.com Inc)

Interior page design and layout: BluePencil Infodesign, India (www. bluepencil.in)

ISBN: 1-4392-0664-3

ISBN-13: 9781439206645

Visit www.booksurge.com to order additional copies.

How executives view the megamarkets

Phil Boon, Executive Vice President, Business Operations, INNOSPEC, United Kingdom
So many executives follow the standard business development model in all markets. B-to-B marketing in the emerging markets is more than sales; it is about building partnerships with key accounts.

Dario Cardone, General Manager, Railway Business, SKF, China
Multibillion infrastructure projects in China will offer western players stable order volumes and good profit margins for many years to come. This book offers a viable strategy for tapping the vast potential of Eurasia's rising megamarkets.

Marc Clauss, CEO, ZIEMANN, Germany
Clearly, future growth for capital goods and engineering is in Russia, China, and India, where modernization advances at a fast pace. And we need to be there in order to exploit interlinkages and defend our leadership.

Stefan Durach, Managing Director and Proprietor, DEVELEY, Germany
Acquiring assets and brands of family-owned businesses can be an effective entry mode into Russia's food industry. This book shows how the right concept can help minimize risk and accelerate expansion.

Wolfgang Merkinger, Member of the Board, STRABAG, Austria
The book describes the path through the complexities of the emerging markets and enables managers to make the right strategic choices. These guidelines can help a multinational win tenders and form multicultural teams for serving customers.

Kirill Poltevsky, Head, Strategy Department, JSFC SISTEMA, Russia
For Russian companies, an interconnected Eurasia signifies expanding westward to the EU and eastward to the other big markets—India and China. The book's message is also valid for Russia's business leaders.

Vijay Taparia, Executive Director, SUPREME INDUSTRIES, India
India's companies are diversifying their export markets and investment destinations. They believe that long-term stability warrants a foothold in Europe and Eurasia's emerging megamarkets. The guidelines in this book are useful also for Indian executives.

Zhang Shikun, Director General, DALIAN DEVELOPMENT AREA, China
Dalian has turned into a major hub for manufacturing, logistics, and commodity trading in Northeastern China. The know-how, technology and commitment of foreign investors from other parts of Eurasia were crucial for this achievement.

CONTENTS

Preface. The challenge for Europe and the West   1
    Contents and rationale of the book   6
    Acknowledgements   8

Prologue. From emerging markets to megamarkets   9
A.   Decoupling from the West: Paradigm shift toward emerging economies   9
B.   How new markets emerged   12
    B.1.   Brief history of emerging markets   12
    B.2.   What characterizes an emerging market?   14
    B.3.   The large emerging markets are the megaplayers of tomorrow   16
C.   Implications for Western companies   19
    C.1.   Why invest in an emerging megamarket?   19
    C.2.   How to select an emerging market   21
    C.3.   Foreign direct investment: Positioning for the future   26

PART I: CHINA, INDIA, AND RUSSIA OPEN NEW FRONTIERS FOR BUSINESS

Chapter 1. Why Eurasia holds promise for business   35
1.1.   Eurasia: Diversity in unity   36
    1.1.1.   The world's religions originated in Eurasia   38
    1.1.2.   The world's languages have their roots in Eurasia   40
    1.1.3.   Culture and mentality: The other two soft factors   43
1.2.   Reviving Eurasia's old trade routes   46
1.3.   Eurasia's regional groupings   52

Chapter 2. Eurasia's megamarkets as wealth generators   57
2.1.   Economic performance   57
    2.1.1.   GDP and growth prospects   57
    2.1.2.   Tax revenue and foreign reserves   59
    2.1.3.   Employment and labor costs   62

2.2.	A rising consumer class	64
	2.2.1. Income groups and spending power	64
	2.2.2. Eurasia's new millionaires	66
	2.2.3. Cities and regional markets	68
2.3.	Integration in the global economy	71
	2.3.1. Foreign trade scenario	71
	2.3.2. FDI scenario	73
	2.3.3. Portfolio investments and capital markets	75

Chapter 3. Eurasia's megamarkets as a resource base — 79

3.1.	Human resources	80
	3.1.1. Population trends	80
	3.1.2. Education and literacy	81
	3.1.3. R&D activity and intellectual property	84
3.2.	Agro-resources	88
	3.2.1. Food commodities	91
	3.2.2. Non-food commodities	92
	3.2.3. Animal husbandry and fisheries	95
3.3.	Raw materials, mining, and energy resources	99
	3.3.1. Industrial metals	99
	3.3.2. Precious metals and diamonds	102
	3.3.3. Energy reserves	104

Chapter 4. Eurasia's megamarkets as business platforms for pillar industries — 109

4.1.	Energy	110
	4.1.1. Global energy sector trends	110
	4.1.2. Energy sector trends in the megamarkets	113
	4.1.3. Challenges for foreign energy companies	120
4.2.	Steel	121
	4.2.1. Global steel sector trends	121
	4.2.2. Steel sector trends in the megamarkets	124
	4.2.3. Challenges for foreign steel companies	126
4.3.	Infrastructure and construction	127
	4.3.1. Global construction and infrastructure trends	127
	4.3.2. Infrastructure development in the megamarkets	130
	4.3.3. Trends in housing and building materials	138
	4.3.4. Challenges for foreign construction companies	140
4.4.	Vehicles and transport equipment	141
	4.4.1. Global vehicles and auto components trends	141
	4.4.2. Vehicles and auto components trends in the megamarkets	143
	4.4.3. Trends in other transport equipment segments	150
	4.4.4. Challenges for foreign vehicle companies	154
4.5.	Machinery and equipment	154
	4.5.1. Global machinery trends	154

		4.5.2. Machinery trends in the megamarkets	157
		4.5.3. Challenges for foreign machinery companies	159
	4.6.	Chemicals	161
		4.6.1. Global chemical sector trends	161
		4.6.2. Chemical sector trends in the megamarkets	162
		4.6.3. Challenges for foreign chemical companies	166
	4.7.	Consumer and luxury goods	167
		4.7.1. Global trends in consumer goods	167
		4.7.2. Global trends in luxury goods	172
		4.7.3. Challenges for foreign consumer and luxury goods companies	174

Chapter 5. Eurasia's megamarkets as business platforms for high-tech industries — 177

5.1.	Pharmaceuticals		179
	5.1.1. Global pharmaceutical sector trends		179
	5.1.2. Pharmaceutical sector trends in the megamarkets		181
	5.1.3. Challenges for foreign pharmaceutical companies		185
5.2.	Telecommunications		187
	5.2.1. Global telecommunication sector trends		187
	5.2.2. Telecommunication sector trends in the megamarkets		189
	5.2.3. Challenges for foreign telecommunication companies		195
5.3.	Aerospace		197
	5.3.1. Global aerospace sector trends		197
	5.3.2. Aerospace sector trends in the megamarkets		199
	5.3.3. Challenges for foreign aerospace companies		206
5.4.	Environmental technologies		207
	5.4.1. Global environmental trends		207
	5.4.2. Environmental trends in the megamarkets		210
	5.4.3. Challenges for foreign environmental companies		216

Chapter 6. Eurasia's megamarkets as business platforms for service sectors — 219

6.1.	IT services	219
	6.1.1. Global trends in IT services	219
	6.1.2. IT trends in the megamarkets	221
	6.1.3. Challenges for foreign IT companies	226
6.2.	Financial services	228
	6.2.1. Global trends in financial services	228
	6.2.2. Banking trends in the megamarkets	231
	6.2.3. Insurance trends in the megamarkets	238
	6.2.4. Challenges for foreign banks and insurance companies	243
6.3.	Retailing and commerce	243
	6.3.1. Global retail trends	243
	6.3.2. Retail trends in the megamarkets	246
	6.3.3. Challenges for foreign retail companies	252

6.4.	Logistics and transport	252
	6.4.1. Global logistics trends	252
	6.4.2. Logistics trends in the megamarkets	255
	6.4.3. Challenges for foreign logistics companies	260
6.5.	Tourism and hospitality	261
	6.5.1. Global tourism trends	261
	6.5.2. Tourism trends in the megamarkets	263
	6.5.3. Challenges for foreign tourism and hospitality companies	268

PART II: SECURING LEADERSHIP IN THE NEW MEGAMARKETS

Chapter 7. Internal audit: Prepare for the venture — 275

7.1. Adopting a new logic — 275
 Question 1: What drives the decision to expand in the megamarkets, reality or myths? — 277
 Question 2: What is the company's strategic blueprint for its megamarket venture? — 280
 Question 3: Is opportunity-seeking part of the corporate planning exercise? — 284
 Question 4: Is the projected growth truly profitable? — 286
 Question 5: What are the company's investment intentions for the megamarkets? — 288
 Question 6: What role does senior management play in the megamarket venture? — 290

7.2. Empowering internal resources — 292
 Question 1: Has the company assigned experienced management and support staff to the megamarket operation? — 293
 Question 2: Are physical assets in line with the megamarket venture? — 294
 Question 3: Does the company have leading-edge technology and protect its intellectual property? — 296
 Question 4: Is the company's brand equity projected effectively? — 297
 Question 5: Are financial resources adequate for expansion? — 298
 Question 6: Does the company tap external expertise? — 299

7.3. Mobilizing competencies for competitive advantage — 302
 Strategic tool 1: Strengths and weaknesses analysis — 303
 Strategic tool 2: Portfolio analysis — 306
 Strategic tool 3: Value chain analysis — 308
 Strategic tool 4: Benchmarking — 310
 Strategic tool 5: Customer portfolio analysis — 312
 Strategic tool 6: ABC analysis — 313

Chapter 8. Megamarket intelligence: Scan before the venture — 315

8.1. Understanding the macro drivers — 317
 8.1.1. Politico-legal forces — 319
 8.1.2. Techno-economic forces — 323
 8.1.3. Sociocultural forces — 326

8.2.	Aiming at sector transparency	328
	8.2.1. Market actor analysis	329
	8.2.2. Megamarket segmentation	333
	8.2.3. Megamarket potential analysis	335
8.3.	Screening business partners	337
	8.3.1. Customer reality check	339
	8.3.2. Competitor reality check	340
	8.3.3. Channel reality check	342

Chapter 9. Strategic thrust: Get the fundamentals right — 345

9.1.	Project management	346
9.2.	Expansion principles	351
	9.2.1. Business model for the megamarkets	352
	9.2.2. The bottom and middle of the pyramid	355
	9.2.3. Megamarket synergies and linkages	359
9.3.	Growth path	362
	9.3.1. Consolidation	363
	9.3.2. Integration	366
	9.3.3. Diversification	368
	9.3.4. Globalization	371

Chapter 10. Expansion options: Select a road map — 377

10.1.	Non-equity-based expansion	379
	10.1.1. Export-/sales-driven choices	379
	10.1.2. Licensing and franchising	382
	10.1.3. Procurement-driven choices	384
10.2.	FDI-/equity-based expansion	386
	10.2.1. The strategic alliance route	390
	10.2.2. The greenfield/brownfield route	396
	10.2.3. The M&A route	400
10.3.	Options for combined FDI	406

Chapter 11. Transaction plan: Acquire and integrate — 409

11.1.	Pre-deal assessment	411
	Milestone 1: Nomination of a transaction team	411
	Milestone 2: Target/partner screening	412
	Milestone 3: Determining value drivers	413
	Milestone 4: Preliminary pricing	414
	Milestone 5: Signing of initial agreements	414
11.2.	Deal-making	416
	Milestone 6: Conducting the due diligence in strategic areas	417
	Milestone 7: Selecting a valuation method to determine a price range	421
	Milestone 8: Submitting a purchase offer	426
	Milestone 9: Drafting the agreements	427
	Milestone 10: Ensuring funding and approval	429

11.3. Post-deal integration	430
Milestone 11: Human resources alignment	431
Milestone 12: Financial management and accounting	432
Milestone 13: Marketing and sales	433
Milestone 14: Integration plan	434
Chapter 12. Long-term delivery: Join the top league	**437**
12.1. The governance factor	438
12.1.1. Top-echelon engagement	439
12.1.2. Middle management performance	443
12.1.3. Staff retention	447
12.2. Organizational alignment	454
12.2.1. Traditional organizations: Functional, divisional, and matrix models	455
12.2.2. Intrapreneurial organizations	458
12.2.3. Coordination and communication	460
12.3. Operational excellence	461
12.3.1. Customer relationship management	462
12.3.2. Supplier relationship management	470
12.3.3. Knowledge and innovation management	476
Epilogue	**483**
Bibliography	**487**

LIST OF TABLES AND FIGURES

Prologue. From emerging markets to megamarkets

Table 1.	The rise of the large emerging markets, 2005–2050.	17
Table 2.	Examples of emerging markets, 2008.	22
Table 3.	The next wave of large emerging markets, 2020.	23
Table 4.	Country ratings: Selected indices.	27
Table 5.	Market potential indicators for emerging markets.	29
Figure 1.	Export destinations of emerging economies, 1992–2008.	11
Figure 2.	The world's markets.	16
Figure 3.	The rise of emerging markets in the global economy, 2005–2050.	16
Figure 4.	The large emerging markets and their peripheral markets.	18

Chapter 1. Why Eurasia holds promise for business

Table 1.1.	Christianity and Asian religions.	39
Table 1.2.	Ranking of world languages.	42
Table 1.3.	Eurasia's regional groupings, 2008.	53
Figure 1.1.	Eurasia's six regional blocs.	37
Figure 1.2.	The world's religions originated in Eurasia.	38
Figure 1.3.	Origin and spread of the Indo-European language family.	41
Figure 1.4.	Top Internet languages, 2007.	43
Figure 1.5.	The world's cultural families (examples of countries).	45
Figure 1.6.	Attributes of business culture.	45
Figure 1.7.	Silk Road and major Eurasian trade links (200 BC to AD 1600).	52
Box 1.1.	Chinese cultural characteristics.	43

Chapter 2. Eurasia's megamarkets as wealth generators

Table 2.1.	The world's largest economies by 2020.	58
Table 2.2.	Emerging megamarkets continue to grow, 2006–2020.	58
Table 2.3.	Share of macro sectors in GDP, 2007.	59
Table 2.4.	New job creations by world region, 2007–2020.	62
Table 2.5.	Wages by specialization in selected AMs and EMs, 2007.	63
Table 2.6.	Household income groups in China and India, 2005–2025.	65
Table 2.7.	Private consumption in major economies, 2007.	66
Table 2.8.	Monthly disposable income of a household, Moscow vs. Munich.	66

Table 2.9.	The world's rich, 2006, 2007.	67
Table 2.10.	Main cities and urban areas in megamarkets, 2008.	69
Table 2.11.	Merchandise trade of leading economies, 2007.	72
Table 2.12.	FDI inflows and stock in large emerging economies, 2006–2010.	74
Table 2.13.	Portfolio investments in emerging economies, 2004–2007.	75
Figure 2.1.	Countries with the largest foreign reserves, 2009.	59
Figure 2.2.	State budget in major economies, 2005–2008.	61
Figure 2.3.	Tax revenue in major economies as share of GDP, 2007.	62
Figure 2.4.	Unemployment in major economies, 2007.	63
Figure 2.5.	Mumbai's importance for the Indian economy, 2007.	70
Figure 2.6.	Trilateral trade between Eurasia's megamarkets by 2010.	72
Figure 2.7.	FDI inflows, 1998–2008.	74

Chapter 3. Eurasia's megamarkets as resource base

Table 3.1.	Markets are where people are: Population projections to 2020.	81
Table 3.2.	Youth bulge in emerging economies, 2006.	81
Table 3.3.	Literacy rates in major economies, 2005, 2015.	82
Table 3.4.	Structure of R&D expenditure by mega region, 2007.	87
Table 3.5.	Patents granted and IPR litigation cases in China, 2003–2008.	88
Table 3.6.	Changes in India's food basket, 1983, 2007.	89
Figure 3.1.	Engineering graduates in major economies, 2007–2010.	84
Figure 3.2.	R&D spending in major economies, 2006.	86
Figure 3.3.	Patents filed by Indian entities, 2006.	88
Figure 3.4.	Dynamics of modern agri-chains in megamarkets.	89
Figure 3.5.	Cereal and potato production in major economies, 2006.	91
Figure 3.6.	Cotton and wool production in major economies, 2006.	92
Figure 3.7.	Countries with largest forest cover and plantation areas, 2005.	93
Figure 3.8.	Meat and milk output of major economies, 2006.	96
Figure 3.9.	Livestock in major economies, 2006.	97
Figure 3.10.	Fish catch in major economies, 2006.	98
Figure 3.11.	Production of industrial metals by country, 2006.	100
Figure 3.12.	Production of precious metals and diamonds by country, 2006.	103
Figure 3.13.	Countries with the largest oil and gas reserves, 2006.	105
Box 3.1.	Megamarket scientists focus on high-tech.	85

Chapter 4. Eurasia's megamarkets as business platforms for pillar industries

Table 4.1.	The world's top fifteen energy players, 1/1/2008.	110
Table 4.2.	Primary energy demand in major economies, 2005–2025.	111
Table 4.3.	Russia's top ten companies, 2007.	114
Table 4.4.	India's primary energy mix, 2007.	118
Table 4.5.	India's leading oil and gas companies, 1/1/2008.	118
Table 4.6.	India's renewable energy potential until 2012.	120
Table 4.7.	World steel production by country, 1995–2010.	122
Table 4.8.	World steel demand by country, 1995–2010.	122
Table 4.9.	The world's top twelve steel companies, 1/1/2008.	123

Table 4.10.	China's top ten steel companies, 2007.	124
Table 4.11.	India's top five steel companies, 2007.	125
Table 4.12.	Russia's top five steel companies, 2007.	126
Table 4.13.	Steel capacity expansion plans in the megamarkets by 2010.	127
Table 4.14.	Transport infrastructure in major economies, 2005, 2010.	128
Table 4.15.	The world's top infrastructure and construction companies, 1/1/2008.	129
Table 4.16.	Projected infrastructure investment in India's eleventh five-year plan, 2007–2012.	132
Table 4.17.	Cement production in major economies, 2005, 2010.	139
Table 4.18.	The world's top building materials companies, 1/1/2008.	139
Table 4.19.	The world's top fourteen car companies, 1/1/2008.	141
Table 4.20.	Vehicle production in major economies, 2007, 2015.	142
Table 4.21.	Passenger car penetration in major economies, 2007, 2010.	142
Table 4.22.	Country of origin of cars sold in China, 2007, 2010.	145
Table 4.23.	Vehicle production in India, 2002–2010.	146
Table 4.24.	Russia's leading automakers, 2007, 2010.	149
Table 4.25.	Greenfield projects by foreign carmakers in Russia, 2007–2010.	149
Table 4.26.	Investment in rolling stock by Russian Railways, 2005–2030.	153
Table 4.27.	Car demand in the megamarkets, 2007, 2015.	154
Table 4.28.	The world's top seven machine-tool companies, 2007.	155
Table 4.29.	The world's leading machinery markets, 2007, 2010.	156
Table 4.30.	Technology trends in machining, 2010–2015.	160
Table 4.31.	The world's leading chemical markets, 2004–2010.	161
Table 4.32.	The world's top fourteen chemical companies, 1/1/2008.	162
Table 4.33.	Russia's top six chemical companies, 1/1/2007.	165
Table 4.34.	Demand for big-ticket consumer goods in India, 2005–2015.	170
Table 4.35.	Share of major luxury goods markets, 2007, 2012.	172
Figure 4.1.	The world's leading ten oil and gas producing countries, 2007.	112
Figure 4.2.	Share of world primary energy sources, 2006, 2020.	113
Figure 4.3.	Infrastructure investment in emerging markets, 2008–2017.	128
Figure 4.4.	China's infrastructure projects until 2015.	130
Figure 4.5.	India's Golden Quadrilateral project and main highway corridors, 2005–2010.	134
Figure 4.6.	Main routes on the Eurasian Land Bridge.	136
Figure 4.7.	Vehicles sales in China, 2000–2010.	143
Figure 4.8.	Market share of India's leading automakers, 2008.	147
Figure 4.9.	Russia's truck market and major players, 2002–2008.	152
Figure 4.10.	Share of chemical markets in Asia-Pacific, 2005, 2015.	161
Figure 4.11.	Performance of the world's top fifty chemical companies, 2003–2009.	163
Figure 4.12.	China's global dominance in consumer goods, 2008.	168
Figure 4.13.	Origin of furniture imports into Germany, 2006–2007.	169
Figure 4.14.	Fast fashion market in Europe, 2007.	175
Box 4.1.	Opportunities for construction-related activities in the megamarkets.	129
Box 4.2.	Railway projects in China, 2005–2008.	131
Box 4.3.	Light industry categories: consumer and luxury goods.	167

Chapter 5. Eurasia's megamarkets as business platforms for high-tech industries

Table 5.1.	The world's top fourteen computing and electronics companies, 1/1/2008.	178
Table 5.2.	The world's leading pharmaceutical markets, 2007, 2010.	179
Table 5.3.	The world's top thirteen pharmaceutical companies, 1/1/2008.	179
Table 5.4.	Time frame for launching a new drug.	180
Table 5.5.	India's top five pharmaceutical companies, 2007.	183
Table 5.6.	Cost of drug development and manufacturing in AMs and India, 2007.	183
Table 5.7.	Russia's top pharmaceutical companies, 2007.	185
Table 5.8.	The world's top telecommunication companies, 1/1/2008.	188
Table 5.9.	The world's leading Internet subscriber nations, 2004–2015.	189
Table 5.10.	India's mobile telcos and their subscriber base, 31/1/2008.	192
Table 5.11.	Foreign telecommunication companies aspiring for the Indian market, 2006–2008.	193
Table 5.12.	Russia's top four telecommunication operators, 2000–2008.	194
Table 5.13.	Telephony and Internet subscribers in megamarkets, 2000–2010.	196
Table 5.14.	World's top twelve aerospace companies, 1/1/2008.	197
Table 5.15.	Aircraft market forecast, 2008, 2025.	198
Table 5.16.	Aircraft orders by Indian carriers, 2007–2009.	202
Table 5.17.	Satellite launches in Russia, 2001–2007.	206
Figure 5.1.	Mobile brands and production in China, 2002-2008.	191
Figure 5.2.	Mobile sets sold in Russia, 1999–2010.	195
Figure 5.3.	Air passenger market forecast for 2010.	199
Figure 5.4.	Carbon dioxide emissions in major economies, 2006.	209
Figure 5.5.	Environmental infrastructure expenses in key Chinese cities, 2007.	211
Box 5.1	Reasons for investing in the megamarket pharmaceutical sector.	186
Box 5.2.	Environmental laws in China, 2008.	212

Chapter 6. Eurasia's megamarkets as business platforms for services

Table 6.1.	Expected position of megamarkets in global services by 2015.	219
Table 6.2.	Worldwide IT spending by verticals, 2006–2011.	220
Table 6.3.	IT and BPO exports from the megamarkets, 2002–2010.	220
Table 6.4.	Use of personal computers in leading economies, 2000–2010.	221
Table 6.5.	India's outsourcing professionals, 2001–2010.	223
Table 6.6.	The world's top fifteen banks, 1/1/2008.	229
Table 6.7.	The world's top fifteen insurance companies, 1/1/2008.	231
Table 6.8.	Revenue of Indian banks, 2000–2010.	232
Table 6.9.	Russia's largest banks by assets and profits, 1/11/2008.	235
Table 6.10.	China's leading banks by assets, 2007.	237
Table 6.11.	Banking participations in China, 2005–2007.	238
Table 6.12.	China's insurance market, 2005, 2007.	239
Table 6.13.	India's largest insurers, 2007.	241
Table 6.14.	Insurance markets in Russia and Eastern Europe, 2007.	242

Table 6.15.	Russia's largest insurers, 2007.	242
Table 6.16.	Europe's top ten retail companies, 2007.	245
Table 6.17.	Top retailers in selected Chinese cities, 2007.	247
Table 6.18.	Top players in India's retail sector, 2007–2008.	248
Table 6.19.	Global logistics revenue by region, 2007-2015.	253
Table 6.20.	Share of outsourced logistics expenditure, 2007, 2015.	253
Table 6.21.	The world's top ten logistics companies, 1/1/2008.	253
Table 6.22.	China's main sea ports, 2005–2010.	256
Table 6.23.	Acquisitions of Indian logistics companies, 2006–2008.	258
Table 6.24.	Segments targeted by 3PLs in the megamarkets.	260
Table 6.25.	The world's top ten tourism destination countries, 2006–2007.	262
Table 6.26.	The world's top ten tourism earning countries, 2006–2007.	263
Table 6.27.	India's hospitality and tourism sector, 2002–2008.	264
Figure 6.1.	Main user segments for IT services in Russia, 2007.	226
Figure 6.2.	Number of banks in Russia, 1998–2010.	235
Figure 6.3.	Share of top six container terminal operators, 2007.	254
Box 6.1.	IT-enabled services that are increasingly externalized.	227
Box 6.2.	Profile of ideal 3PL alliance partners.	261

Chapter 7. Internal audit: Prepare for the venture

Table 7.1.	Common megamarket myths.	278
Table 7.2.	Essential skills for investment projects in megamarkets.	301
Table 7.3.	SW-profile for corporate success in the megamarkets.	305
Figure 7.0.	Six steps toward megamarket leadership.	273
Figure 7.1.	Adopting a new megamarket logic (the six building blocks).	276
Figure 7.2.	The company's stakeholder universe.	283
Figure 7.3.	Planning and opportunity-seeking in the megamarkets.	286
Figure 7.4.	From export to FDI in the megamarkets.	289
Figure 7.5.	Getting ready for the megamarkets (the six resources).	293
Figure 7.6.	The five intangibles for the megamarkets.	297
Figure 7.7.	Building sustainable competitive advantages in the megamarkets.	302
Figure 7.8.	Analytical tools for building competitive advantage in the megamarkets.	303
Figure 7.9.	SWOT matrix for the megamarkets.	304
Figure 7.10.	Portfolio matrix for the megamarkets.	307
Figure 7.11.	Dynamic portfolio analysis.	308
Figure 7.12.	Megamarket value chain.	309
Figure 7.13.	Benchmarking categories and phases for the megamarkets.	311
Figure 7.14.	Industry benchmarking with direct competitors.	312
Figure 7.15.	Client portfolio matrix and strategic implications.	313
Figure 7.16.	Megamarket ABC analysis.	314
Box 7.1.	Dimensions of a megamarket strategy.	281
Box 7.2.	Dimensions of excellence for the megamarkets.	288
Box 7.3.	Service portfolio for the megamarkets.	308

Chapter 8. Megamarket intelligence: Scan before the venture

Table 8.1.	Dos and don'ts for intelligence in the megamarkets.	317
Table 8.2.	Entry barriers raised by megamarket actors.	333
Table 8.3.	Megamarket channel typology and analysis.	344
Figure 8.1.	The three levels of megamarket intelligence.	316
Figure 8.2.	The five actors impacting on megamarket investors.	329
Figure 8.3.	Megamarket potential analysis.	338
Box 8.1.	The three macro forces.	320
Box 8.2.	Laws and policies influencing business in the megamarkets.	322
Box 8.3.	Statistical indicators for techno-economic forces.	324
Box 8.4.	Technological indicators.	325
Box 8.5.	Soft factors of the megamarket macro environment.	327
Box 8.6.	Indicators for megamarket industry scan.	328
Box 8.7.	Issues underlying the megamarket actor analysis.	332
Box 8.8.	Segmentation criteria for megamarket expansion.	336
Box 8.9.	Competitor checklist.	342
Box 8.10.	Elements of a megamarket channel check.	343

Chapter 9. Strategic thrust: Get the fundamentals right

Table 9.1.	Composition of a megamarket project management team (example of a greenfield project in India).	347
Table 9.2.	Strategies for the bottom and middle of the pyramid.	358
Table 9.3.	Growth path in the megamarkets.	363
Table 9.4.	Pros and cons of consolidation.	365
Table 9.5.	Pros and cons of integration.	368
Table 9.6.	Pros and cons of diversification.	371
Table 9.7.	Pros and cons of globalization.	376
Figure 9.1.	Cornerstones of strategic thrust in megamarkets.	345
Figure 9.2.	The megamarket project and its subprojects (example of a chemical company).	347
Figure 9.3.	Project management in the megamarkets.	349
Figure 9.4.	Virtuous circle of revenue streams and FDI.	349
Figure 9.5.	Kotler's five steps of market expansion.	350
Figure 9.6.	Elements of a megamarket business model.	352
Figure 9.7.	The megamarket consumer pyramid, 2010.	356
Figure 9.8.	Exploiting geostrategic linkages between megamarkets.	361
Box 9.1.	Project terms of reference (TORs).	348
Box 9.2.	Megamarket expansion principles.	351
Box 9.3.	Two megamarket examples of successful glocalization.	375

Chapter 10. Expansion options: Select a road map

Table 10.1.	Prerequisites for successful alliances in megamarkets.	394
Table 10.2.	Dos and don'ts in implementing strategic alliances in the megamarkets.	395

Table 10.3.	Office leases in megamarket capitals, 2002, 2008.	398
Table 10.4.	Types of M&As in the megamarkets.	401
Table 10.5.	Benefits and risks of megamarket M&As.	403
Table 10.6.	Majority vs. minority acquisitions: Pros and cons.	405
Figure 10.1.	Strategic choices for megamarket expansion.	377
Box 10.1.	Export segments for EU companies.	380
Box 10.2.	Procurement-driven choices.	385
Box 10.3.	Reasons for selecting the FDI route.	387
Box 10.4.	FDI modes for megamarket expansion.	389
Box 10.5.	Types of strategic alliances.	390
Box 10.6.	Risk minimization in megamarket joint ventures.	393
Box 10.7.	Alliance valuation criteria.	395
Box 10.8.	Options for combined FDI.	407
Box 10.9.	Common FDI/M&A errors in the megamarkets.	408

Chapter 11. Transaction plan: Acquire and integrate

Table 11.1.	Due diligence categories for megamarket target evaluation.	420
Table 11.2.	Valuation methods.	423
Table 11.3.	Multiples in advanced and megamarkets for selected industries, 2008.	424
Table 11.4.	Milestones of successful integration in the megamarkets.	435
Figure 11.1.	The three phases of successful transactions in the megamarkets.	410
Figure 11.2.	Candidate selection based on "fits" and value drivers.	413
Figure 11.3.	Post-deal integration options.	431
Box 11.1.	Structure of an LOI for a strategic alliance.	415
Box 11.2.	Legal due diligence issues in the megamarkets.	418
Box 11.3.	Parameters for brand valuation.	425
Box 11.4.	Important provisions of a megamarket transaction agreement.	427
Box 11.5.	Caveats when negotiating a megamarket transaction agreement.	428

Chapter 12. Long-term delivery: Join the top league

Table 12.1.	"Entrepreneur" CEO vs. "manager" CEO.	441
Table 12.2.	Annual salary brackets of managers in the megamarkets, 2008.	450
Table 12.3.	Market share and profit margins determine profitability.	465
Figure 12.1.	The four leadership levels of effective execution.	439
Figure 12.2.	Required talent mix of middle managers.	445
Figure 12.3.	Attrition rates in the advanced markets and emerging megamarkets, 2008.	449
Figure 12.4.	Leadership principles for the megamarkets.	454
Figure 12.5.	Functional and divisional organizations.	456
Figure 12.6.	Matrix organization for global product groups and geographies.	457
Figure 12.7.	Holding structure for megamarket operations.	458
Figure 12.8.	Virtual organization.	459
Figure 12.9.	Transversal domains for higher functional performance in the megamarkets.	462
Figure 12.10.	The four Ps of the marketing mix in the megamarkets.	468

Figure 12.11.	The pricing variable: Four leverage points for profit making.	468
Figure 12.12.	Integrated supply chain (example of an electrical motor company).	474
Figure 12.13.	Supplier portfolio for the megamarkets.	475
Figure 12.14.	Knowledge-building cycle for the megamarkets.	478
Box 12.1.	Causes of execution failure in the megamarkets.	438
Box 12.2.	Eight qualities of senior executives for the megamarkets.	443
Box 12.3.	Middle management to be supervised by the CEO and board.	443
Box 12.4.	Basic rules for retaining specialists in the megamarkets.	450
Box 12.5.	Elements of a compensation package for local managers.	451
Box 12.6.	Leadership styles for the megamarkets.	453
Box 12.7.	Operating principles of networked organizations.	459
Box 12.8.	CRM tasks.	463
Box 12.9.	Efficiency test for CRM/KAM in the megamarkets.	464
Box 12.10.	Lifetime value of a key account.	465
Box 12.11.	Competitive positioning in the megamarkets.	467
Box 12.12.	Promotional mix for the megamarkets.	469
Box 12.13.	Decisions related to SRM.	470
Box 12.14.	SRM tasks.	473
Box 12.15.	Collective and continuous learning.	481

Epilogue

Megamarket hurdles and success factors in the 2010s.   484

PREFACE

The challenge for Europe and the West

The fall of the Berlin wall in 1989, twenty years ago, freed entire populations from the Communist stranglehold, but paradoxically it also stripped European business of its protective cover. Since that historical event, which spurred globalization and ushered in a new era of multi-polar relations and powersharing between civilizations, I have witnessed how Europe's post-war entrepreneurial spirit struggles to confront the influx of new competitors from the emerging economies. Some EU companies have come out stronger, but many have lost their leadership or are struggling to survive; others have closed down or were bought out—a tendency that will intensify as a result of the 2008 financial crisis.

Lulled by an enlarged common market and a buoyant US economy, many EU companies became complacent during the boom years and did not spot the obvious trend beyond their borders: that the billions of people living in the less advanced economies would not remain poor eternally and would one day rise to become the "next-billion" consumers. These potential markets, including the very large ones, were mistakenly neglected. That is how Volkswagen, Peugeot, and Fiat lost India's car market to Suzuki, Hyundai, and Tata, and now they struggle to regain lost terrain. They simply lacked the vision to anticipate events and develop something for India's emerging consumers as Ratan Tata did with the Nano, the world's cheapest car. They also lost opportunities in Russia, where Asian competitors have taken the lead. Similarly, Samsung, LG, and Sony captured Russia's consumer durables markets before EU rivals—dazed in the aftermath of the collapsed Soviet Empire—could react. In China, the EU's construction, energy, engineering, and consumer goods majors are trailing way behind national players who, bolstered by a booming home market, expand to other continents. By 2010, European brands will represent less than 20% of all new car registrations in China compared with more than 70% for Asian (including Chinese) brands. In the early 1990s, EU car makers led by Volkswagen had commanded a market share of 50%. Corporate EU's arrogance and inertia are today costing it revenue and millions of jobs.

Europe's edge in high-tech and services is also under threat as the continent's leading pharma, telecom, aerospace, IT, logistics, and hospitality players contend vigorously to fend off new rivals. "What can we offer them?" asked a member of a high-ranking EU business delegation after visiting, in March 2008, a workshop in Navi Mumbai (India) that was machining high-tech parts for an EU nuclear power plant constructor.

Many leading EU companies started well but eventually failed to build a leadership position in the megamarkets. Some got embroiled in extenuating legal battles (e.g. in China,

Danone vs. Wahaha and OBI vs. local management), lost market share after selecting weak partners (MAN in China and Russia, Unilever in China) or adopted less effective concepts than their competitors (e.g. Siemens Mobile in China, Peugeot in India, Lafarge in Russia). In other cases, excessive resources were wasted to acquire Western rivals, whereas if only a fraction of these funds had been put into the emerging economies, these companies would have created additional profit centers, knowledge pools, or "safety valves" to offset recessions in mature markets. These mistakes became even more manifest with the collapse of the United States housing and stock bubbles in the years 2007–2008. Aggressive players in pursuit of fast expansion based on unwarranted debt finance were forced to reconsider their strategy (syndicated loan for multibillion jumbo bid to acquire a controlling stake in Continental by Schaeffler—both from Germany—in 2008) or were drawn to the brink of default because of financial overstretching (e.g. acquisition of Hanson in the United Kingdom by Germany's Heidelberger Zement for US$15.5 billion in 2007; takeover of America's Anheuser Busch by Belgium's InBev for US$52 billion in 2008). The strategies of many more players will be put to the test as banks become less generous following the widespread liquidity crunch, which began to affect the world economy in the late 2000s.

The problem is aggravated by the lack of foresight of the EU's mainstream political establishment, which gives priority to non-market agendas (European constitution, enlargement, social charta, energy security, climate change, human rights, anti-terrorism, NATO) instead of amplifying its support to the EU business community, which urgently needs flexible labor laws, backing against hostile takeovers, and support in strategic intelligence and lobbying to win international tenders and gain market share through alliances and acquisitions. Commenting on EU enlargement, George Osborne, the British Conservative Party's spokesman, aptly summarized this attitude: "The European Union hasn't understood that today the primary challenge we face is an economic, not a political one. For my generation, the question for Europe is not how to unite, but how to compete—not only within Europe, but with the rest of the world." Russia's leadership seems to take this advice seriously: The country celebrates June 2 as the Day of the Entrepreneur, believing that "everyone who starts a business deserves a medal for bravery" (former president Vladimir Putin, 2005).

Megamarket entrepreneurs, buoyed by close family ties, act with dynamism and ambition to improve. Many EU companies have lost this driving force under the debilitating impact of the welfare system, which remains a major impediment. Deeply entrenched across the European continent and now spreading eastwards to the new member states, it dilutes the enthusiasm of the young and paralyzes family businesses. In Germany, forty thousand companies close down each year, often because the next generation has plans other than carrying on. The other four major EU economies France, Italy, the United Kingdom and Spain face similar problems of devitalized "hidden champions," many of them export-oriented family enterprises that used to form the backbone of the national economy but which have recently sold off their assets or turned into distributors of their former Asian suppliers. The low proportion of entrepreneurs—10%–11% of the working population in countries like France or Germany (the equivalent figure for China and India would be 40%–50%)—partly explains why company closures outnumber start-ups.

Unlike the "star" founders of Africa, Asia, and Latin America, the EU's second- or third-generation owners have in many cases lost interest in the business except for the bottom line. Even when owner-families sit on supervisory boards, there is often little involvement in the daily business and even less vision of where the company should be heading. Profit-based bonus schemes perpetuate a system focused on quick results with little regard to long-term sustainability, which nowadays presupposes engaging in workable alliances with emerging market partners. Managers, paid to increase quarterly gains, are inclined to favor cost-cutting (layoffs, plant closures) over forward strategies aimed at innovative solutions for key accounts in untapped markets. Prominent brands are sold to financial investors, who then offer them to new buyers; with each turnaround precious know-how is lost and the entrepreneurial spirit eroded further. This trend of selling and reselling of corporate assets—partly by using private equity finance—has ground to a halt after the worldwide stock market crash in late 2008, but the aftershocks will reverberate across European industry for many years to come.

Europe's present woes seem to be the result of its past successes. EU politicians share part of the blame. Their immediate concern is to protect their constituencies that are keen on preserving the status quo rather than business-minded, sector-focused concepts of sustainable wealth generation. Any additional revenue is taxed and redistributed to preserve a social superstructure in dire need of sweeping reforms. Strict labor laws punish those who want to work and support those who don't, thus making EU companies uncompetitive and ultimately forcing them out. The EU's thirty-eight-hour week and generous statutory and national holidays slacken growth and, ironically, encourage outsourcing to megamarket companies that offer round-the-clock service. Outsourcing arms global competitors with knowledge, technology, and capital. High costs and unfavorable tax codes discourage EU companies from building equity, weakening them further vis-à-vis their international rivals.

The brain drain, a phenomenon that formerly afflicted the developing world, is reversing and now threatens the erstwhile destination countries. According to the German Statistical Office, 161,000 Germans, most of them qualified engineers and university graduates, left in 2007 (60% more than in the mid 1990s) to seek better career prospects abroad. Departures are expected to be 9–12% higher in 2008–2009. Capital follows people. It is estimated that Germans have stashed away more than €400 billion in foreign bank accounts. The figure for the EU as a whole would be alarmingly high. Switzerland and Liechtenstein, both non-EU members, have been the biggest beneficiaries. Still worse, Europe faces the challenge of an aging population. Its work force will drop by 48–50 million (or 15% of the working population) toward 2040, further burdening the economy. Changing demographics demand adjustments in fiscal and educational policies, flexible labor markets, and a leaner social security system. Immigrants need to be used as a source of talent like in the United States, Australia, or Canada, and not as cheap labor to fund the pensions of the aged.

A snap comparison of media reporting in the EU and emerging economies shows a striking contrast in business confidence. While corporate success stories and ambitious projects make the headlines outside Europe, the EU's media focus on layoffs and closures, a shrinking middle class, and an illusion of grandeur against the backdrop of general powerlessness to stem the tide. Anxiety is mounting about the long-term vulnerability of the world's financial system. In September 2008, an unprecedented subprime crisis led to the renationalization of America's two biggest mortgage lenders, Fannie Mae and Freddie Mac, followed by an historic rescue plan by the US government of AIG and other behemoths. It remains to be seen for how long the US$1 trillion bailout for troubled financial institutions and the leading carmakers will help to avert a general meltdown in the world's largest economy. The real estate bubble did not spare the United Kingdom, Spain, and other EU member states, where overleveraged consumers were unable to service their debt. Business and consumer confidence plunged to their lowest level in Germany and other big industrialized nations (see IFO December 2008 Business Confidence Survey) whereas the emerging megamarkets remained on top of the league table of optimistic countries (see Nielsen January 2009 Global Consumer Confidence Survey). Many of Europe's leading companies—heavily dependent on the battered US and EU economies—issued profit warnings in 2008 amidst plummeting share prices and in anticipation of lower sales. The megamarkets could have compensated part of these losses if they had accounted for a more substantial fraction of corporate sales and profits. Business strategists and financial experts now realize that deep-rooted and lasting crises can also unexpectedly hit the western economies. There are no "safe havens" in a global marketplace; the only sensible way out is to spread risk and generate earnings in as many important markets as possible.

At this critical moment, people with new ideas and fundamental experience should be invited to come to the fore. Instead, the public debate continues to revolve around *déjà-vu* topics proposing old solutions to new problems. Be they supply siders, monetarists, or Keynsianists, economic advisers and central bankers have joined the political class in advocating huge bail-out packages coupled with massive capital infusions into the banking system to avert a financial free-fall. Meant to be implemented at national level, many of these schemes lack the international dimension for multilateral surveillance and risk management, and coordinated solutions to a global phenomenon. By relying essentially on economic forecasting and modeling techniques, such debt-enhancing macro policies (industrialized countries' budget deficits are expected to reach record levels in 2009–2012) miss out on opportunities at sector level. A better alternative would be to devise together with emerging market scholars and business specialists strategies for lifting purchasing power in the "world's less advanced regions" while encouraging higher savings (rather than perpetuating a borrower's mentality to stimulate excessive spending) and enterprise-focused measures in the richer nations. Policies aimed at avant-garde industries, such as renewables, energy saving, recycling, waste management, smart commuting, green building, non-invasive medications, or fast-speed satellite communications, would help create new markets while improving living conditions and sparing the environment across the planet. Instead, as poverty mounts in the "developed" economies, there is a tendency to single out executives, bankers and managers, who are collectively accused of greed and selfishness by populist politicians. Catch-phrases such as "wealth redistribution," "rich tax," and "social justice" may help to win local elections, but such slogans can never replace business-friendly policies to regain lost ground in global markets and restore prosperity among Europe's middle class. After all, governments do not create the type of self-sustaining and productive jobs that business does.

Let us now revert briefly to the three megamarkets that are emerging to the east of the EU: China, India, and Russia. I have been studying and visiting them since the early 1980s. Those were the heydays of Kenichi Ohmae's *Triad* concept, the cornerstones of which were Western Europe, Japan, and the United States. Starting from the early 1990s, it became clear that Eurasia's three megamarkets with their human, energy, and natural resources and pent-up demand would rise rapidly, form their own "strategic triangle," and offer enduring new options for dynamic entrepreneurs. *Foreign Direct Investment in Russia: A Strategy of Industrial Recovery* (Paul Fischer, MacMillan, 2000) and the Russian version (Paul Fischer, Finanzi i Statistiki, 1999) were among the first books to highlight the potential of this mega-economy in key industries and to benchmark it against advanced economies and other emerging powers. The books conceptualized FDI as a vehicle of economic transformation, a policy that was skillfully implemented by the Russian government during 2002–2007, enabling it to achieve fast economic recovery, similar to earlier transformations by China and India. A historical review of investment patterns showed that emerging economies first need to build up inward FDI in order to acquire technologies and become outward investors—a process that can be accelerated with the help of targeted government intervention.

Resisting international pressure to embark on a neo-liberal course, megamarket leaders opted for policies of state guidance backed by five-year plans and national projects. Micro-level industrial policies implemented in close accord with the business elites lifted investments, industrial output, and profits, resulting in higher employment, salaries, and consumption. Foreign investors were invited to join national efforts to raise sector competitiveness and boost monetary reserves that today provide the financial cushion to weather economic downturns. Ideological constraints and lack of curiosity and humility to scrutinize successful models implemented elsewhere have so far impeded EU policymakers from choosing an analogous path. Nero-like, they look on while entire industries are wiped off. More jobs will be lost in the coming years if companies lack the skills and support to conquer the markets of the future. North America and Japan are undergoing a similar "identity" crisis, which in the United States was instrumental in bringing about a landslide electoral victory for the Democratic Party under its presidential nominee Barack Obama on November 4, 2008.

The traditional "EU–USA–Japan Triad" is being outflanked by a group of emerging economies led by China, India, and Russia, which will form a powerful geostrategic bloc that will *nolens volens* shape boardroom decisions in the decades to come. The cards are being dealt now in Eurasia's megamarkets. Many EU companies are taking these markets more seriously today than at the turn of the century, but they must recapture lost terrain. Instead of reacting to competitive pressure, managers must take the initiative and show resolve to be counted among the first in tomorrow's mega-economies. They face growing competition from strengthened megamarket rivals equally eager to stand up, climb the value ladder, and expand internationally. Names such as Bajaj, Haier, and MTS stand for quality, innovation, brand equity, and customer service. Medium-level emerging powers, such as Argentina, Brazil, Chile, Indonesia, Kazakhstan, Mexico, Turkey, Ukraine, and Viet Nam, are producing their own national champions who, in the wake of their megamarket peers, are preparing for a massive assault on "fortress Europe" by 2010–2015.

Fortunately, there are farsighted EU (and US) companies that have written success stories by creating strong brands. They arrived early in the megamarkets, pursued a focused strategy backed by the owners, posted good results, and became deeply rooted in the local business community. Decisions were driven by customer, community, and environmental concerns rather than quick profits, and there was resilient motivation to serve as an example and outperform others. A growing number of Western multinationals already realize higher proportions of their turnover in the megamarkets or plan to do so by 2010–2015, as highlighted on their websites and latest shareholder reports: ABB (20–30% of turnover), BASF (25–35%), Bosch (15–25%), Microsoft (25–30%), Nestlé (20–25%), Procter & Gamble (30–35%), Unilever (25–30%). They use every chance, including economic adjustments during periods of lower growth, to expand through greenfield projects, strategic alliances, and mergers and acquisitions. Many more players can learn from their experiences, sharpen their competitive edge, and aspire to reach the top. This book has been written to help them.

I strongly feel that Europe does not need to face a grim future and that it has the wherewithal to bounce back as it has always done. Europe remains an important source of culture, innovation, and discovery. It plays a fundamental role as political power broker for seeking peaceful solutions to international conflicts (e.g., Middle East, Iran, Caucasus), and its international voice is widely accepted on issues of global concern (e.g., climate change, pollution, human rights, wildlife protection). Despite the gloomy picture drawn by scholars as the "Asian century" dawns, European technological expertise is more sought after than ever, and EU companies, many of them medium-sized, non-listed and family-owned, remain leaders in key industries. Their competence is matchless, and Asia will continue to look to Europe for advice and expertise, just as EU companies need Eurasia's wider space and resources to prosper.

Europe's vitality and its symbiosis with Asia will depend on whether, in the coming years, EU managers, supported by policymakers, can win the battle over Eurasia's megamarkets and their adjacent economies. What matters to Europe also applies to the United States and Japan—the other two old-Triad members—, which host a myriad of innovative entrepreneurs ready to take on new challenges and to reorient their strategies for a better future.

Contents and rationale of the book

This book is about corporate excellence and business expansion in China, India, and Russia—the second, third, and sixth economies in the world by 2020. Their combined GDP in US dollars is today about half that of the United States or the European Union. Starting from the mid 1990s, Russia became the planet's principal supplier of energy and raw materials. Meanwhile China turned into the world's main manufacturing center whereas India strengthened its position as the international hub for IT and other professional services. Excellence in these newly emerged mega-economies makes a company fit for the world market.

The growth trajectory of these megamarkets was belittled throughout the 1990s until they bounced back and moved to center stage, forcing Western companies to react. Two of them—China and Russia—have regained their self-esteem as hosts of the 2008 Summer (Beijing) and 2014 Winter Olympics (Sotchi). Beijing's US$100 million investment in the opening ceremony on August 8, 2008, was the most spectacular and expensive extravaganza ever in Olympic history. India will host the Commonwealth Games in New Delhi in 2010, beating rival contender Hamilton, Canada. Having recaptured their place in the community of leading nations, the three re-emerged powers are creating a connected platform for business to thrive for generations to come. Companies not firmly established in this triangle will have difficulties in achieving or maintaining global leadership.

This book unfolds in two parts following a prologue on emerging markets that have captured the imagination of entrepreneurs, fund managers, and business analysts worldwide. The first part introduces the concept of "Eurasia" (chapter 1), which offers a new strategic perspective to European business leaders. No other continent hosts so many interrelated emerging economies. According to forecasts by the World Bank and IMF, 60% of global growth in the next decade will originate in this space where 70% of the world's consumers live. Modern transport, energy, and communication links will unite Eurasia's economies, and EU companies should profit from geographic proximity.

This book analyzes the restored strength and business potential of the megamarkets compared with the established OECD economies (chapters 2 and 3). They had traditionally supplied abundant labor, raw materials, and commodities, but today they excel in qualified human resources, research, consumerism, industrial platforms for domestic sales and export, and sources of capital and knowledge. The book studies how wealth was accumulated through farsighted policies focused on private enterprise and foreign investment promotion, thus producing a new class of affluent entrepreneurs and millions of emerging consumers.

Surveys of sixteen key industries (chapters 4–6) with projections until 2015 highlight how megamarket firms are closing in on their foreign rivals. The rapid success of some of these companies has raised their capitalization beyond the reach of potential acquirers. Leading Western producers of equipment, components, and finished goods canvass them as potential key accounts. Myriads of medium-sized, family-held businesses in the mega and surrounding markets are developing fast in the trail blazed by these national champions. These "megamarket hidden champions" have improved management methods and quality standards, and they represent attractive candidates for alliances and joint projects.

How can EU companies tap this potential despite the differences and complexities? The second part of the book (chapters 7–12) introduces a blueprint for implementing a winning concept enabling a company to outgrow its rivals. It is based on a six-phase template drawing on a combination of proven steps that can be applied regardless of the company's size, ownership, or origin. The proposed six steps toward megamarket leadership include:

- adopting a strategic logic for the megamarkets by corporate boards and top management while enhancing the company's own resources and building unique competences;
- scanning the environment for greater transparency and decisionmaking power at macro and micro levels;
- pursuing a steady growth path by endorsing milestone projects and reinventing the business model to enlarge customer and market shares;
- picking the most suitable entry or expansion mode after analyzing suitable options;
- scouting the market regularly for acquisition/alliance prospects and devoting time to integrate them and incite them to grow;
- ensuring operational excellence at crucial functional intersections in the organization to guarantee delivery and consolidate the expansion process.

The *modus operandi* highlighted in this book is based on hands-on project work with companies, some of which became leaders in their industries by pursuing a concerted effort, innovative ways, and a structured approach. During 1990–2009, the author participated in more than one hundred intelligence, investment/M&A, and market expansion assignments in China, India, Russia, and the European Union. Case studies based on this frontline experience with client companies (not CEO surveys) describe successful and failed attempts to garner market share and establish profitable operations based on strong brands and customer orientation.

Profitable companies are led by farsighted managers who can see beyond cost savings through offshoring (distribution of processes among subsidiaries) or outsourcing (delegation of work to third parties). They network effectively outside their home markets and avoid hurried, uninformed decisions on crucial investments and recruitment. Their actions are guided by courage rather than fear of failure, also in critical situations.

The book provides valuable guidelines for managers keen on crossing new business frontiers while trying to limit error and to maximize shareholder value. It offers useful tools also for academics, policymakers and specialists working closely with enterprises in the areas of foreign trade, FDI, human resources development, law and international finance.

Acknowledgements

My special thanks go to Mira Shah, who provided precious assistance in editing the text and co-authoring numerous industry chapters; she indefatigably helped to revise the manuscript and coordinate with the publisher. Her experience and knowledge stem from many years of intelligence and consultancy support to our clients in India.

I appreciate the support provided by Guangjie Li and Guangfan Li, who accompanied our China projects over many years and offered research back-up on developments in China's industries and leading companies, and—most importantly—helped interpret the "unwritten rules" of Chinese business and bureaucracy.

I acknowledge the contribution of our Russian team headed by Leonid Umanski, former Vice-President of the USSR Statistical Office and for many years Head of the Information Department of the Intergovernmental CIS Economic Committee. Our joint efforts enabled us to cope with the country's intricacies, issues related to intercultural understanding, and to propose feasible solutions to foreign investors, many of which are featured in the book. Mr Umanski's sudden demise on November 8, 2008 was a tragic loss.

My gratitude goes to John Knight, former Statistician at the UK Office for National Statistics, who provided valuable inputs for various chapters and readily brainstormed with me throughout the writing of the book. The figures and maps were prepared by Mike Ilic, who also brought closer to our teams the newly emerging economies of Southeastern Europe, which have become an integral constituent of the EU's enlargement efforts. Many other team members in the megamarkets, Austria, Germany, Italy, Spain and several Eastern European countries, gave constant marketing, administrative and logistics support for our cross-border projects. They are too numerous to be mentioned individually; I thank them all.

Finally, my high esteem and appreciation go to my father, Dr Albrecht Fischer, who founded FCI, one of Germany's very first post-war business consultancies in 1966. The experience gained with him and his clients in the early days of my career were decisive in forming a cosmopolitan view that allowed me to judge international trends and timely anticipate the emergence of the new economic powers on the Eurasian landmass.

I am particularly indebted to our clients for placing their trust in our team. We are proud that these companies—some of which kindly contributed testimonials for this book—courageously took up the megamarket challenge to become world leaders in their realm of activity.

PROLOGUE

From emerging markets to megamarkets

"The old order changeth, yielding place to new."
—Tennyson

A. Decoupling from the West: Paradigm shift toward emerging economies

Comfort, routine, and limited horizons are the biggest enemies of change. Many executives in the world's leading corporations are driven by old habits and dogmatic beliefs. They may be distressed by the prolonged stagnation and liquidity crunch[1] in the old power Triad EU–USA–Japan, but emotionally they have always preferred to cling to "proven" markets as the main anchor of corporate stability. However, the tectonic shifts in the global economy that are bringing the emerging economies to the fore will move even the most reluctant boardrooms into reflecting on new scenarios. Their task is made more complex by a volatile US dollar, fewer orders from "mature markets" and a tendencial shortage of energy and raw materials, which require urgent action to avert erosion of shareholder value and a downslide in performance. A new generation of young managers with experience outside the erstwhile Triad contends that it is time to reorient corporate strategy toward alternative economies such as the BRICs[2] and their satellite markets to generate sustainable growth and disperse risk.

The argument goes that many emerging economies, especially the larger ones, are "decoupling" from developments in North America and the EU and will not follow them automatically into recession. The chain reaction across global bourses in the aftermath of the subprime crisis in the United States appears to endorse the opposite view (promoted by many columnists and scholars), but strong arguments in favor of the decoupling theory prevail in the medium and long term, at least going by general growth patterns and the trends in the real economy (industry) as opposed to financial markets (bourses). Building materials, dairy, vehicles, chemicals, machine building, telecom equipment and household durables are just a few examples of industries where megamarket companies' sales and profits, supported by strong local demand and investment, have moved anti-cyclically from those in advanced economies. Export-oriented megamarket companies will also gradually reorient their sales and investment strategies toward new emerging markets in Africa, Asia, and Latin America.

---

1. Wall Street plunged, drawing other bourses with it, on September 15, 2008, following the announcement of the bankruptcy of Lehman Brothers and the takeover of Merrill Lynch by Bank of America; both were leading US investment banks.
2. BRICs: Brazil, Russia, India, China.

The financial meltdown caused by the global credit crunch in 2008–2009 as a result of excessive borrowing mainly by Western consumers led to some readjustments in the megamarkets as well. However, in the medium term these economies look less vulnerable and much stronger than their Western counterparts given their future potential (the speed of expansion will still be much faster than in industrialized economies even if GDP growth rates will temporarily drop by 2–3 percentage points[3]), replete state coffers (accumulated foreign reserves offer governments ample room for fiscal stimulus and national projects), huge domestic markets backed by a solid resource base (human and natural resources, broad consumer base), comfortable trade surpluses (especially China and Russia), and— very important—widespread optimism and clairvoyance among national leaders in critical situations[4]. Megamarket governments have a long tradition of economic planning at macro and sector level, intense government–business cooperation[5], and never relied on the "invisible hand" of the market by following the neoliberal course propagated by the West[6]. They seem to be better prepared and poised to come out stronger after the financial crisis. China plans to use more state investment funds to modernize its infrastructure and buy up capacities across the globe, now that share and asset prices have come down to reasonable levels. The Russian government will take more controlling stakes in strategic enterprises in the light of refinancing problems faced by Russia's oligarchs. The Indian government has already engaged in coordinated policy activism with the finance ministry, central bank, and securities board working in concert to increase liquidity required by industry and to enhance business confidence. At corporate level, aggressive megamarket players are well positioned to benefit most from these schemes and may internationally even capitalize on the crisis effect owing to a more favorable cost structure.[7]

Emerging economies enjoyed strong growth and their real estate prices and currencies remained more or less stable during 2005–2008, even as the US economy slowed down and its non-oil imports contracted. As a whole, emerging economies will fail to return to their exceptional growth rates in 2007, but those with high savings and modest debt could recover quickly from the financial crisis. On many measures, such as domestic consumption, investment, and government and external balances, the three largest among

---

3. While most industrialized countries in 2009–2010 will experience a sharp contraction (topped by the United Kingdom with a forecasted fall of national output by more than 5%), the megamarket economies will hold firm with GDP growth rates in the range of 3%–4% for Russia, 6%–7% for India and 7%–8% for China. The megamarkets differ from other emerging economies in that they do not struggle with either twin current-account and budget deficits or excessive foreign debt. See "Emerging markets: stumble of fall? Will the global financial crisis halt the rise of the emerging economies?" *The Economist/The Indian Express.* January 15, 2009.
4. In a recent speech, Russia's Prime Minister V. Putin sees big opportunities for cost reduction and streamlining to raise companies' competitiveness by occupying new niches. "X sezd" [10th session]. *Profil*, November 24, 2008, 12-14.
5. The ministries of the economy in the three megamarkets play an active role in monitoring developments in the major industries. To minimize the consequences of the international financial crisis, Russia's Ministry of the Economy, adjusted its policy framework and initiated concrete steps in 2009 to minimize the negative consequences in industries such as automotive, energy, and chemicals.
6. The exception being Russia which experienced an economic disaster after it was wrongly advised to introduce radical free market reforms including mass privatizations and full-scale price liberalizations following the dissolution of the Soviet Union in 1991.
7. Chinese telecom equipment producer Huawei reported average increases of its contract business of over 40% during 2005–2008. Sales are expected to grow 29% to US$30 billion in 2009. The global economic slowdown has prompted many telecom operators to trim spending and favor more price-competitive candidates. See "Huawei sales rise 46%," *China Daily*, January 8, 2009. In other spheres (e.g. brewery, packaging machinery, standard machine-tools), EU equipment makers expect more competition from Chinese and Indian producers as well.

them—China, India, and Russia—look much sounder than the big rich ones. They accounted for two-fifths of global GDP growth in 2007 and 2008, and are expected to perform equally well throughout 2009–2012. They have become less dependent on the US market and are on the way to becoming a new anchor of stability, both as markets and suppliers, for the international business community. More than 50% of China's exports already go to other emerging economies (2007). Exports to the United States account for 8% of China's, 4% of India's, and 2% of Russia's GDP. India's and Russia's exports to China jumped by 20% and 24%, respectively, in 2007. A slowdown in China would probably hurt their economies more than a US recession. Emerging markets as a group already export more to China (16%) than to the United States (12%). Exports from emerging economies to the United States are growing far less than exports to other emerging economies, which already account for over half of total exports (see figure 1). Because of decoupling, GDP growth rates in emerging economies are expected to drop less sharply than in previous recessions triggered by advanced economies.

A second supporting factor in favor of adjusting corporate focus is domestic consumption and investment, which both accelerated in the megamarkets during 2003–2008. Consumer spending expanded almost three times as fast as in the developed world. About 85%–90% of China's average annual GDP growth of 10% in 2008–2012 will be derived from domestic consumption.[8] Investment fares well if not even better. According to the UK bank HSBC, real capital spending rose by 17% in the emerging economies in 2007, compared with only 1.2% in the advanced economies. Skeptics argue that much of this investment, especially in China, is in export-oriented industries (e.g., textiles, consumer goods, electrical instruments), which will collapse as sales to the United States and the European Union fall. But altogether less than 15% of China's investment is linked to exports; over half of it is in domestic industries (e.g., food, building materials, pharma, consumer goods), infrastructure, and real estate. India and Russia have embarked on similar national infrastructure programs that will guarantee investment growth for several years to come. Meanwhile, more people will join the middle class, providing additional stability because of high consumption but also notoriously high saving rates in the three

Figure 1. Export destinations of emerging economies, 1992–2008.

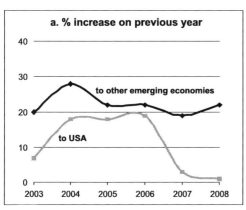
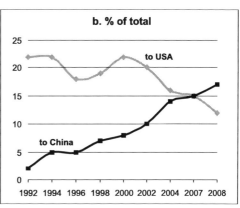

Source: Credit Suisse.

Source: BCA Research.

---

8. See 2.2.1.

megamarkets. Governments will thus be able to use current account surpluses and large foreign reserves to provide fiscal stimulus to the economy, if necessary.

Emerging economies with large external deficits, high debt or geostrategic associations with North America look more vulnerable. Mexico is a case in point. The country's exports to North America accounted for 27% of its GDP in 2007; its GDP grew on average by only 3.8% during 2006–2008 mainly because manufacturing jobs (linked to US exports) and workers' remittances from the United States fell sharply. Mexican authorities now encourage companies to reorient their strategies toward China and the emerging economies of Latin America, Asia, and Africa. The governments of smaller emerging economies (e.g., Colombia, Turkey, South Africa) are adopting similar policies toward less dependence on the United States and deeper regional integration and cooperation, which will probably show lasting impact by the early to mid-2010s.

Perhaps the best evidence of decoupling comes from the multinationals themselves. In 2005–2007, profits of some Fortune 500 and German DAX-listed companies beat all expectations as strong sales and profits growth in emerging markets offset a sharp decline in the EU and North American markets. Non-listed, medium-sized technology leaders followed a similar trend. While companies heavily exposed to the US market issued profit warnings during 2008–2009, those serving alternative markets reported far better results and recovered faster from the adverse effects of the financial crisis, which at the time of writing still weighed heavily on share prices and market capitalization. With luck and perseverance, dynamic EU companies can secure themselves a place in the new megamarkets and thus rise above their competitors in terms of sales and profits.

Decoupling would benefit the EU. Over 60% of its economy is based on inter-EU and transatlantic trade. If the leading EU banks and corporations had been less tilted toward the US economy and more focused on China, India, and Russia, as well as other emerging markets, EU economies would have been more robust to weather the 2008/2009 financial crisis, which had its origin in the United States.

B. How new markets emerged

B.1. Brief history of emerging markets

China, India, and Russia—the three rising powers on the Eurasian continent—need to be viewed in the broader context of emerging markets (EMs), which are a relatively recent phenomenon. *The Economist*, a UK-based business weekly, launched its first emerging-market indicators[9] in 1995, responding to demands by business for more data on these formerly unheard-of economies. Until then, the mainstays of trade and investment had been the "Triad" economies of North America, Western Europe, and Japan. The remaining economies—mostly former colonies in the southern hemisphere—were not of the first immediate interest to Triad businesses, excepting large transnational corporations (TNCs) dealing in lower-end consumer goods or in raw materials and commodities (some

---

9. Emerging-market indicators figure on the last page of the weekly; they usually consist of four headings—overview, economy, financial markets, and GDP growth forecasts—and include other statistics such as foreign trade and FDI.

of them had been established during the colonial era). For much of the twentieth century, many countries belonging to the "South" and located in Africa, Asia, and Latin America were objects of aid, not trade and investment. Lacking inward investment and access to markets, these developing economies (DEs) depended on the goodwill of Western donor countries acting bilaterally or via international organizations such as the UN, the IMF, and the World Bank, which provided public money in the form of loans or grants to strengthen their fledgling economies.

During the five-decade-long Cold War, the socialist economies of Central and Eastern Europe (known collectively as COMECON) limited their trading activities with the West to energy, machinery, and other daily necessities, which were channeled through state-owned import-export agencies until the 1990s. Very few Western companies had the competence and connections to use these possibilities. Cross-border investments by Triad companies were practically inexistent, and neither side encouraged them because of the Cold War. Counter-trading and barter was the order of the day, not payment-based commerce, let alone foreign direct investment.

The end of the Cold War turned the tables. Since the establishment of free market and democratic systems in Central and Eastern Europe, these "transition economies" have experienced record investment inflows from the EU, the United States, and Asia (South Korea, Japan, China, and India). Most former COMECON countries joined the EU in two phases in 2005 and 2007,[10] thus improving business prospects across the continent, especially family-owned companies from the EU. All the former Soviet republics became independent nations as well and, with the exception of the three Baltic states that joined the EU, created the Commonwealth of Independent States (CIS) along with the Russian Federation, which dominates the bloc. The term "transition economies" was gradually replaced by the term "emerging economies or markets" to highlight the surge of business potential in the wake of the ongoing changeover from planned systems to free-market-based democracies.

The "Asian tigers" of Thailand, Malaysia, South Korea, and Taiwan had in fact been the first to break the mold, engaging in state-led industrial restructuring and systematic export promotion in the early 1980s. International donors had found a new definition to describe the dramatic rise of these smaller emerging economies. They called them the "newly industrialized economies" of the Asia-Pacific. But the financial crisis of 1997, which affected most of the countries of East and Southeast Asia, abruptly stopped their growth path, which resumed again only in the new millennium thanks also to the absorptive capacities of the Chinese economy that managed to remain stable during the Asian crisis. With hindsight, the Chinese leadership proved wise by deciding not to devaluate the country's national currency and to act instead as a stability anchor for the neighboring economies, thus absorbing a growing share of their imports.

The most spectacular turnaround in modern economic history was the opening up and economic liberalization in three Eurasian countries of continental dimension: Russia, India, and China, Eurasia's megamarkets (EMMs). These large emerging markets (LEMs),

---

10. 2005: Czech Republic, Estonia, Hungary, Latvia, Lithuania, Poland, Slovakia, and Slovenia. 2007: Bulgaria and Romania.

with their huge populations and abundant natural resources, promise long-term economic growth based on technological progress and farsighted policies. Spurred by an unstoppable trend toward free enterprise and open borders, and against the backdrop of globalization of trading and financial activities, they are the new megamarkets of tomorrow, poised to become the direct competitors of the advanced markets (AMs) belonging to the OECD,[11] which also includes the erstwhile Triad led by the G5 economies of the United States, Japan, Germany, France, and the United Kingdom.

The paradigm shift started in China, which in 1982 launched its first experiment in opening its doors to foreign investors in "special economic zones" (SEZs). Then, the removal of the iron curtain in the early 1990s transformed Russia's economy, which emerged as the leading economy in the region following the breakup of the Soviet Union. Russia opted for convertibility of the ruble coupled with massive privatizations of state assets and price liberalization. Because these measures were implemented radically and without a real "master plan," they triggered a balance of payment crisis in 1998. But sustained reforms and steady oil revenues in the following years have brought the country back on track. Against all odds, Russia has become the fastest growing economy in Europe with annual growth rates expected to be in the range of 7%–8% during 2008–2013.

In 1991, India's foreign exchange reserves sank to a critical level; that severe crisis offered an opportunity to the government to usher in structural reforms, abolish the *license raj*,[12] and gradually open the economy to foreign investors. India's developments are comparable to those in China and Russia: high GDP growth (8%–9%), record FDI, rising incomes, poverty eradication, high literacy, and successful domestic companies.

Stimulated by increasing numbers of educated young people flocking into the labor market who represent a significant buying force on the demand side, LEMs (which include the three EMMs, Brazil, and Mexico) will keep expanding much faster—at least for the next twenty-five years—compared with AMs, where growth has leveled off owing to market saturation and an aging population. LEM growth will be sustained and even compounded by growth of smaller EMs, which will develop strongly in their orbit, offering additional markets and providing a basis for further outsourcing of production and services to lower-cost economies.

B.2. What characterizes an emerging market?

Emerging markets, big and small, have been the subject of many studies. An economy is termed "emerging" when its government pursues clear goals of raising performance levels to those of the world's more advanced nations, engages in all possible efforts to improve living standards, and boasts good performance with an upward tendency. From the plethora of definitions, classifications, and rankings, some typical features of EMs that run common to most publications on the subject can be extracted:

- EMs are not yet members of the rich OECD club.
- They report above-average GDP growth of at least 5% per annum.

---

11. OECD: Organization of Economic Cooperation and Development—the grouping representing the world's most advanced (developed) economies.
12. Previously, enterprises had to apply for a license from the government to start a business.

- Their per capita GDP levels move gradually toward US$10,000 per annum by 2015–2020.
- They offer companies huge potential for future growth owing to an expanding middle class with rising purchasing power and led by consumerism.
- They generally report lower per capita incomes than AMs.
- Corporate tax levels are generally below average to attract foreign investors.
- EM governments seek a higher integration in world markets and rising shares in world trade and FDI stock.
- EMs amass growing foreign currency reserves through private-sector FDI and portfolio investment (PI) inflows, including remittances, which have become more important than public aid from donor countries and multilateral organizations (this factor distinguishes EMs from developing countries, which still depend on foreign aid).
- In EMs, research and development (R&D) expenses (both public and private) are rising.
- The larger EMs can offer TNCs a broad industrial tissue and vast networks of local enterprises as potential key accounts and candidates for alliances and/or acquisitions.
- Many EMs are in transition toward free market systems as national governments are establishing effective institutions and a democratic civic society.
- EMs report visible improvements in public infrastructure, health care, government services, and balanced regional development.
- The larger EMs benefit from a wide-ranging return of talent from their overseas "diaspora" who had earlier settled abroad but now see even greater opportunities back home.[13]

EMs and LEMs (the larger ones among them) are thus situated between AMs and developing economies (DEs), which are much poorer and cannot satisfy certain basic criteria. There are many more EMs today than in the 1980s or 1990s, and their numbers are rising (see figure 2). Countries such as Argentina, Brazil, Chile, China, India, Indonesia, Kazakhstan, Malaysia, Pakistan, Russia, Saudi Arabia, South Africa, UAE, Thailand, Turkey, and Viet Nam have developed very fast in the new millennium and already attract substantial amounts of capital and know-how from AM companies and institutions. Policymakers deploy all possible mechanisms to make these countries as investor-friendly and financially stable as possible. They have learned valuable lessons from earlier crises: Mexico (1994), Russia (1998/1999), China (1989, Tiananmen), India (foreign exchange crisis in 1991), Indonesia (1997), and Argentina (2001).

Emerging economies are sitting on two-thirds of the world's foreign exchange reserves and consume 50% of the world's oil. In the past nine years (2000–2008), their growth has averaged more than 6% compared with only 2% for the rich economies. During 2003–2008, their combined GDP inflated by almost US$1.8 trillion (US$1,800 billion) in current dollar terms, which is comparable to Germany's annual GDP and higher than the US$1.4 trillion (US$1,400 billion) combined increase reported by AMs. The gap in favor of the world's EMs would be even more significant if purchasing power parity (PPP) was used as a measure for GDP calculations.[14] In twenty-five to thirty years, EMs will

---

13. In the 1990s, the US attracted over 650,000 specialists from the EMs. This figure is expected to decrease in this decade as many Asians and Eastern Europeans decide to return to their home countries after their studies or a few years of experience. See *McKinsey Quarterly*, 2001.
14. *Beijing Review*, February 16, 2006.

Figure 2. The world's markets.

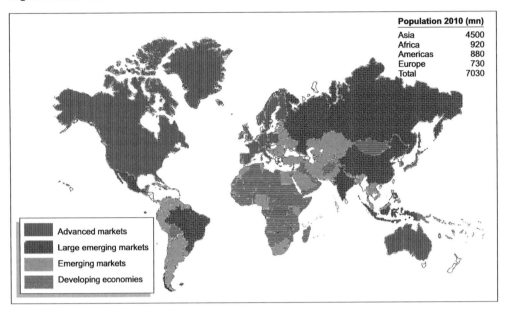

Figure 3. The rise of emerging markets in the global economy, 2005–2050.

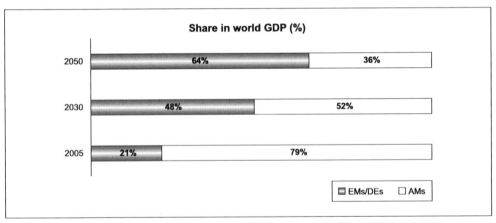

Source: World Bank and Goldman Sachs projections.

emerge as the dominant force in the global economy (see figure 3); their combined GDP will exceed that of the AMs.

B.3. The large emerging markets are the megaplayers of tomorrow

Five large emerging economies—Brazil, China, India, Mexico, and Russia—stand out as they are racing to become the world's next manufacturing, services, technology, financial, and cultural powerhouses. They are speedily moving up the ladder from low to high value-added industries. These countries are transforming the world economic order through increased integration in world markets. In 2007, large emerging markets (LEMs or BEMs[15]) accounted for about 14% of world GDP, 13% of global exports, 12% of global imports, and 19% of global FDI inflows. By 2010, each LEM will have a GDP exceeding US$1 trillion. China's GDP will hover above US$4 trillion,[16] making it the third-largest economy after the United States and Japan. If measured in PPP, the GDP of most LEMs would already be higher than that of most AMs.[17] By 2040, their combined GDP (in US dollars) is projected to touch US$45 trillion, above that of today's largest economies, the G7 (USA, Japan, Germany, UK, France, Italy, Canada), put together (see table 1). As living standards rise, megamarket citizens will quadruple their annual incomes to US$15,000–20,000, thus reaching 60%–70% of the level of AMs but with a much larger population.

Taken as a group, LEMs are becoming as important to world financial stability as the United States, the EU, and Japan. In early 2009, their combined foreign reserves reached almost US$2.5 trillion (US$2,500 billion), far more than the reserves accumulated by the United States, the EU, and Japan together. Megamarket governments can use their newly acquired financial clout to influence the dollar–euro parity. Russia continues to price its raw materials in US dollars, but its central bank has announced that it will increase its euro holdings. Similar shifts were initiated by China's central bank, which intends to reduce its dependence on the volatility of the US economy. These measures have contributed to a drop in the value of the US dollar during 2006–2008.

Besides attracting capital, LEMs are joining the Triad nations as markets absorbing high volumes of imports from other countries and sources of investments and knowledge. Using state enterprises and private "national champions," they are appearing aggressively on the world stage. India's Ranbaxy, Russia's Lukoil, China's Lenovo, Mexico's Cemex, and Brazil's Petrobras are just examples of private LEM companies that have begun to upset the world rankings. Russia's Gazprom (state-owned) reported the third-largest capitalization among Fortune 500 companies in 2007. Each year, the list of foreign takeovers and investments originating from the LEMs continues to grow. Their external FDI spans around the world and now encompasses AMs, EMs, and DEs on all continents, thus making it possible for the poor economies to link up to the world economy and to embark on a growth

Table 1. The rise of the large emerging markets, 2005–2050 (GDP in US$ trillion).

	2005	2015	2030	2040	2050
G 7	27	33	43	47	65
LEM[a]	5	11	30	52	95
EM/DE[a]	9	15	26	46	55
Total	41	59	99	145	215

2005–2030: LEM 5 (Brazil, China, India, Mexico, Russia)
2030–2050: LEM 10 (LEM 5 + Indonesia, Pakistan, Nigeria, Turkey, Viet Nam)
a. LEM: large emerging markets; EM: emerging markets; DE: developing economies.
Source: Adapted from World Bank and Goldman Sachs projections.

---

15. J. E. Garten, *The Big 10: The Big Emerging Markets and How They Will Change Our Lives* (USA: Basic Books, 1998).
16. See 2.1 for more information on the economic performance of the large emerging markets.
17. See chapter 2.

Figure 4. The large emerging markets and their peripheral markets.

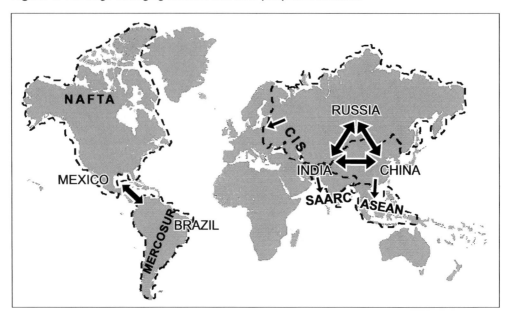

path (see figure 4). China National Petroleum (CNPC), for example, acquired stakes of Petrokazakhstan in Central Asia and is investing in extraction infrastructure in Latin America and Africa (e.g., Sudan).

LEMs attract most investments directed at emerging economies. They succeeded in reducing poverty levels and promoting growing numbers of middle-class consumers leading to higher living standards. China's population segment earning more than US$5,000 per annum already represents 280–300 million people; India's figure is 170–200 million, and Russia's about 50–60 million. Forty-eight percent of India's consumers are aged below twenty-five; in China this category represents 39% of the population (USA: 32%; EU: 29%). The consumption boom has led to a surge in demand for all sorts of raw materials, which triggered price increases on international commodity exchanges. Russia has been a major beneficiary, reinforcing its position as the world's leading "mining center" and "filling station."[18]

Owing to their growing affluence, megamarket governments have been able to increase their political clout in international forums. Since 2005, Brazil, China, India, and South Africa have been invited to join the G8 meetings (Russia was invited for the first time in 1997), which bring together the heads of state and government of the world's richest countries. India and Brazil are contending for permanent membership in the UN Security Council together with Germany. The voice of LEMs can be heard in international organizations (WTO, IMF, World Bank, UN). They rally the support of the smaller emerging and developing countries. During the G20 summit between EMs and AMs in Beijing on October 15, 2005, China and its fellow LEMs pledged to combat poverty and to establish a fairer economic order, taking on the cause of

---

18. See 4.1.

developing countries. The summit participants from EMs agreed to cooperate in four areas:

- The new world order should consist of many socioeconomic models and systems that all have a right to coexist; such a "multipolar" world is preferable to a "monopolar" system oriented toward a single superpower.
- Countries should engage in dialogue, mutual respect, and friendship as a means of overcoming differences; they should resort to peaceful means, not wars and conflicts.
- The world should be guided by a regime of free trade, investments, and financial cooperation and coordination to anticipate crises caused by speculators.
- Advanced countries and the larger emerging economies should provide support to the less developed countries in their fight against poverty, hunger, pollution, and debt relief efforts.

Similar statements were aimed at AMs by the heads of state of the world's emerging markets who gathered in Havana, Cuba, in September 2006 in a symbolic effort to remind the world of the "non-aligned" movement that—headed by Indonesia, India, and Egypt in the 1960s and 1970s—had for the first time voiced concerns about the "double standards" hampering the establishment of a mutually acceptable international order. Today, the world's power architecture is undergoing a radical shift as EMs gain importance.

Eurasia's emerging megamarkets are particularly attractive as they are in the process of forming a geostrategic triangle with interdependent commercial and financial networks involving more and more peripheral emerging markets. These high-growth economies will offer companies from all over the world vast opportunities for long-term expansion.

C. Implications for Western companies

C.1. Why invest in an emerging megamarket?

A TNC with global ambitions and a long-term vision will ignore emerging economies—especially the larger ones—at its peril. When three billion new consumers start moving up the consumption path to catch up with living standards in the West, the opportunity must be seized in the early stages. The CEO of a famous Swiss technology company confirms: "There is no way our company can afford to ignore countries like India and China, which are set to account for half the world's GDP in a not-too-distant future." A local presence from the early stages will enable a company to widen its customer base and to embark on a true learning curve in these new markets. Western firms can gain in many ways from operations in the megamarkets:

- larger sales volumes to achieve scale effects and faster returns on investments
- increased profits through improved competitiveness and cost differentials
- reduced dependence on saturated markets and immunity to cyclical fluctuations
- prolongation of product and service life cycles
- use of local R&D capacity to innovate for the local and world markets

That megamarkets pose a great challenge cannot be denied. Field realities initially prove to be very different from what management had expected, and profits take long to materialize. Political risks due to the state of transition and differences in perception (e.g., Tibet and Caucasus conflicts, which led to visa restrictions for US/EU citizens), economic risks (currency depreciation, extended periods of inflation, real estate and stock exchange bubbles), and business-related risks (know-how pirating, complex partnerships because of mentality-based differences, price dumping due to overcapacities) cannot be excluded. Whereas political and economic risks will decrease with growing economic interdependence between states, business-related risks can be reduced by adopting a correct attitude and a strategic approach based on business intelligence.[19] Negative experiences with partners have led some managers to believe that the best strategy is to withdraw and return to home base. Such decisions are fortunately not the rule and can prove fatal for the future development of a company that strives for global leadership.

In most cases, it is management-related factors and internal constraints that contribute to market failure.[20] Unlike political and economic risks, these problems are avoidable. Business partners and local staff are selected by management, which may make the right or wrong decision. Management is also responsible for showing personal commitment and allocating the human and financial resources needed to expand smoothly. Doing business in non-familiar environments marked by different lifestyles and sociocultural conditions is a new experience for most managers, and mistakes are common. It is important to learn from mistakes and adjust the course, if required. Methods successfully tested in AMs are not necessarily applicable in EMs. Despite technology and transport "convergence" in a global setup, corporate strategies must be tuned to new contexts, making it impossible to adopt "one-way-fits-all" methods across countries.[21] Often, governance methods and organizational setups need to be changed. Project work with companies shows that "divergence" prevails over convergence in emerging markets. "Soft" factors such as culture, religious beliefs, and socializing with the local community determine success as they shape relations with local suppliers, customers, and other business partners. They are more important than perfectly formulated contracts or bonus systems, which may not be sufficient to convince business partners or local managers to "stay on board."

Many companies are ill-prepared to face emerging economies. They lack leaders capable of moving about comfortably in "high-context" environments where networking and personal relations are primordial. Failure to tackle these issues and lack of mental flexibility—compounded by the "not-invented-here" syndrome—leads to negative experiences, personal prejudices, and a return to old practices:

- reorientation to familiar Triad markets;[22]
- postponement of FDI-based decisions and focus on export;
- little interest in understanding the local culture and mastering the language;
- readiness to yield to union pressure at home, which may hamper timely relocation;
- mix-up of priorities in terms of target markets, entry strategy, and time frame.

---

19. See chapter 8.
20. See chapter 7.
21. M. Warner and P. Joynt, eds., *Managing across Cultures: Issues and Perspectives* (UK: Thomson, 2002).
22. Most, even young, CEOs of the world's Fortune 500 companies bring with them experiences from the US or at the most other G7 economies; very rarely have they received their education or spent even a small part of their careers in the LEMs.

To avoid such reversals, it is vital to spend more time on selecting the target market (country, region, industry) based on objective criteria and to generate success stories, which will motivate managers and staff to support the project.

C.2. How to select an emerging market

Companies must be careful when picking new markets. Whereas certain markets can be conquered by exporting to them, others demand consistent strategies of deeper penetration via FDI. Because of the many options available, it is difficult to make the right choice. Following German reunification, most German small and medium-sized enterprises (SMEs) preferred to invest next door in the new *Länder* instead of conquering markets farther away. Companies from EU's core states made similar judgments when deciding to invest in Central European economies after they joined the EU. These markets were selected because they were geographically close, risks were predictable, and "everybody was busy doing it." As a result, many EU companies tied their managerial and financial resources to countries with small domestic markets and rising costs (effects of EU membership and intense competition) while Asian and US competitors went farther offshore, to the larger emerging economies of Asia and Latin America.

Any international expansion plan must be carefully structured and based on an assessment of developments of essential industry parameters in key markets, including qualitative information obtained from field surveys. The real potential can be quite different from what a country's rating might suggest. India has a lower rating than Thailand or Malaysia, but for the foreign retailer or insurer considering entry in 2008–2010, it probably offers more chances as authorities are gradually allowing higher participations in a huge potential market. Russia is attractive for oil and gas-related technologies although in the overall country rating South Korea, Turkey, China, and Brazil may be farther ahead.

General country rankings and ratings focus on macro data, whereas a company needs to know the operational details of its target industry in the new market. Markets that appear at the very top of published ratings may be too small (e.g., Romania after it joined the EU, inciting many SMEs to engage in expensive projects there) or even find themselves downgraded suddenly after a crisis (e.g., Serbia after Kosovo's independence in 2008), which in fact offers a new chance to prepare for entry at low cost. Whether intuitively or intentionally, market size, industry potential, and proximity in terms of geography and culture are the most frequently used criteria for investment decisions.

1. Market size

Market size is based on a combination of parameters. Territorial expanse and population are the most obvious. The area of a market is an indicator of its resource endowment, while its population combined with spending power defines market size or potential.[23] Definitions that include only large territories without population ignore market potential, the third criterion of market size. Three parameters—area, population, and national income (GDP)—should be considered together for a more accurate selection. In this book, we

---

23. Total market potential equals GDP or GDP per capita multiplied by population.

shall draw on our previous definition of a LEM as an EM (non-OECD member) with a population of at least 100 million, a vast land mass, significant raw materials reserves, and a GDP exceeding US$500 billion.[24] Countries below these ceilings can be considered at the most as medium-sized EMs (see table 2). Population is the main size-related criterion because it represents the ultimate source of effective economic power from all perspectives: market, revenue, labor supply, and knowledge. Population, however, must be endowed with purchasing power before it becomes a worthwhile investment criterion for companies. Bangladesh, for example, has a population of 144 million, but it lacks the necessary purchasing power to account for large imports and investment flows. Viet Nam (84 million) has a smaller population but a larger GDP/capita and an expanding market thanks to farsighted policies (special economic zones, FDI promotion, privatization of state-owned companies, tax incentives), which awakened entrepreneurial dynamism and today attracts growing numbers of foreign companies and tourists.

Russia, the biggest country in the world, has an area of almost 17 million square kilometers and qualifies as a LEM or emerging megamarket, even if its population is "only" 144 million. The reason is simple: besides its size and resource endowment, Russia's GDP is approaching US$1 trillion (US$1,000 billion), which is seven to eight times higher than, for example, Pakistan's or Bangladesh's with similar populations. The governments of these two countries will first need to lift national wealth (per capita GDP) to a significantly higher level before they can qualify as large emerging markets. Many European companies have invested in "runner-up economies" like South Africa, Argentina, or Kazakhstan, which may dispose of abundant resources on vast territories but in the long run represent small domestic markets (populations of 42, 39, and 18 million, respectively). Eventually, these investors will have to convert their factories into export platforms and find sales outlets abroad.

Table 2. Examples of emerging markets, 2008.

Large EMs[a]	Medium-sized EMs[b]	Small EMs[c]
Brazil (8.4 mn km², 184 mn persons)	Indonesia (1.8 mn km², 238 mn persons)	Argentina (2.7 mn km², 39 mn persons)
China (9.3 mn km², 1,298 mn persons)	Nigeria (0.9 mn km², 137 mn persons)	Kazakhstan (2.6 mn km², 18 mn persons)
India (2.9 mn km², 1,065 mn persons)	Pakistan (0.7 mn km², 159 mn persons)	Lithuania (0.06 mn km², 3 mn persons)
Mexico (1.9 mn km², 104 mn persons)	Turkey (0.8 mn km², 75 mn persons)	South Africa (1.2 mn km², 42 mn persons)
Russia (16.9 mn km², 144 mn persons)		Ukraine (0.6 mn km², 47 mn persons)

a. Economies with population exceeding 100 million, GDP above US$500 billion and large territories.
b. Economies with population around 100 million, GDP of 200–400 billion, and fairly large area.
c. Economies with population below 100 million and limited market potential (GDP below US$ 200 billion) despite possibly large area.
Source: Based on World Bank figures.

---

24. P. Fischer, *FDI in Russia: A Strategy for Industrial Recovery* (UK: Macmillan/Palgrave, 2000).

Using these combined parameters, LEMs include only five countries by today's measure: Russia in Europe; China and India in Asia; and Mexico and Brazil in Latin America. Africa as a continent is not yet home to any LEM. The Eurasian megamarkets—China, India, and Russia—are a special category, being large and located on one landmass, endowed with natural resources, and having a long tradition of industrial, technological, and military strength. As new economic and political powerhouses, they offer location advantages as manufacturing and distribution hubs for export to neighboring economies, but they also promote partnerships, which will make their economies more interconnected.

Other EMs with relatively large territories mostly in Asia and Africa will arrive on the scene by 2020–2030 as they cross the 100-million-population mark and provided they continue to grow by implementing liberal policies that will help develop entrepreneurship and boost consumer spending (see table 3). Some of these EMs, which fall under the category of "medium-sized" today, are expected to move toward GDP levels above US$400 billion by 2020. By then, as a comparison, Eurasia's three megamarkets (China, India, and Russia) will have GDPs in the range of several trillion US dollars. China is expected to overtake the United States by 2040 with a GDP exceeding US$20 trillion.

Independent of their origin, companies must observe these global trends and position themselves in important economies on time. While a larger economy warrants a capital-intensive investment to cover a larger manufacturing, customer, and supplier base over a longer period, a smaller market can be served more cost-effectively through export, licensing, franchising, or sales-oriented investments (sales office, logistics center).

The conquest of the US market starting from the 1960s, first by European then by Japanese companies, was achieved initially by first pouring resources into the United States, North America's largest market, and later by extending operations to Canada and Mexico. Similarly, investments made in the megamarkets can be used later to penetrate peripheral economies, where their currencies enjoy preferential status, to facilitate cross-border trade and payments.

The Chinese yuan is a reference currency for Southeast Asian economies and is slowly replacing the US dollar as anchor currency. The Indian rupee plays a similar role in the countries of the South Asian Association for Regional Cooperation (SAARC), as does the Russian ruble in the CIS republics.

Large markets tend to overcome a crisis or recession faster than smaller, less dependent economies. Generally speaking, an investment is therefore less at risk there. Russia, for example, suffered an economic downturn throughout the 1990s but has now acquired more stability. Large countries with their large populations are self-sufficient and integrated in the global economy enough to be able to rally support from

Table 3. The next wave of large emerging markets, 2020.

Country	Population 2020 (mn)	GDP 2020 (US$ bn)	GDP growth (%)[a]
Indonesia	280	950	4.6
Pakistan	205	420	4.1
Bangladesh	184	300	5.4
Nigeria	179	480	5.1
Philippines	118	380	4.7
Viet Nam	114	350	7.2
Egypt	105	440	4.0
Turkey	105	1100	4.3
Iran	100	620	5.7
Thailand	90	510	5.2

a. Average GDP growth p.a. in % (2005–2020).
Source: Based on IMF and UN figures.

the world community—bilaterally or with the help of the IMF, World Bank, and other institutions—to minimize negative ramifications. They dispose of considerable natural and human resources for structural adjustment and to launch policies on their own initiative. Their companies have developed a thirst for all sorts of technologies, products, and services and are capable of investing overseas to ensure supplies or the transfer of essential know-how.

2. Geography, language, and culture

Companies have a habit of investing in geographically near and culturally familiar environments. Out of comfort and risk aversion, EU managers prefer the proximity and affinity of neighboring Central and Eastern Europe; US managers are most active in NAFTA and Central American countries; China and India are most active in Asian countries. But these markets may not be large enough to ensure fast returns. Many Italian and French family-owned companies invested in Romania after the fall of the iron curtain. Germans and Austrians went to Poland, Czech Republic, Slovakia, and Hungary. Language affinity helped to establish first contacts and grasp the local culture. Today, as a result of EU membership, these countries suffer from rising costs, making the initial outsourcing strategy far less attractive. As markets, they are too small for future growth, compelling many EU companies to look for other opportunities elsewhere. Many companies had to rethink their strategies and aim at larger markets like Russia, which functions as an entry gate to CIS economies where Russian is the lingua franca. Building materials and consumer goods producers are now expanding in Russia and Ukraine, which most rating agencies still place in the middle or bottom of their league tables (far lower than Slovenia, for example).

Proximity is a practical but not always the best investment consideration. Eurasia's three megamarkets stand out as particularly attractive destinations for EU companies until at least 2040–2050. All three are located on the Eurasian continent, which represents a connected landmass for broader coverage.

Intangible factors such as language, cultural affinity, shared history or experience, similar attitudes, and mindset play a significant role in FDI decisions. Companies from Spain or Portugal lean spontaneously toward Latin American destinations because of the closer cultural ties and more common traditions with these countries than toward Eastern European or Asian countries. The following investment patterns can be observed based on cultural factors:

- Latin: Argentina, Brazil, Chile, Mexico, Romania
- Slav: Belarus, Czech Republic, Poland, Russia, Slovakia, Serbia, Ukraine
- Germanic: Croatia, Hungary, Slovenia
- Indo-European South Asian: India, Pakistan, Sri Lanka
- East Asian: ASEAN countries, China.

Cultural aspects are strongly embedded in business decisions. To avoid risks, managers prefer familiar environments where the blend of climate, religion, language, food, and history do not differ much from their own.[25] Culture determines comfort and trust levels,

---

25. R. D. Lewis, *The Cultural Imperative: Global Trends in the 21st Century* (USA: Intercultural Press, 2003).

which can save time, effort, and possible litigation. Translations, the use of interpreters, access to news and information in a familiar language, and communication between management and staff impact decision-making and costs in a non-negligible way. Some companies prefer India to China because they can communicate in English and understand the legal system, which is based on the British model. It should not be overlooked, however, that the real market potential can be much smaller in a known than in an unfamiliar environment. A pioneer move to "where others hesitate to go or have not been successful" can therefore lead to unexpected discoveries with positive ramifications for future business development.

Many Fortune 500 companies have adopted "BRIC strategies" to take into account the growing importance of these markets, which in most cases represent less than 10% of group sales. Senior executives find it hard, however, to distinguish between markets and determine possible synergies. The BRIC approach[26] is focused on the size of individual markets but lacks "geostrategic" focus based on territorial proximity and rapprochement between countries. Brazil and Mexico, for example, belong to regional groupings (MERCOSUR, NAFTA) but are "culturally" disconnected from the Eurasian heartland including the China–India–Russia triangle.

3. Ranking

The ranting and raving over rankings and ratings needs to be moderated. While there is convergence in assessing market potential and risks of doing business in emerging markets, rankings differ significantly depending on the methodology adopted by reporting agencies. Moody's, Standard & Poor's (S&P), and Fitch IBCA are the three most consulted sovereign credit ratings, which inform investors around the world of a country's creditworthiness; an investment grade signals that a country is viewed as not being a defaulter. Boardroom decisions of corporate, institutional, and financial investors are all too frequently based on such published indicators. But as Moody's top Russia analyst explained regarding an upgrade of Russia's rating: "We're not rating the whole country in some general sense … This is not our job. This was an attempt to assess the risk of default on eurobonds." A business, however, operates at a microeconomic level and needs more detailed information than the narrow assessment base of rankings.

Pause for thought

A board member of a leading cement and building materials group from Europe stated in 2004: "Why should we invest in countries like Russia and India; Moody's has given them low ratings, and we would take unnecessary risk given the rampant corruption in the two countries." The board member had never been personally to either of the two countries for fear of an attempt on his life.

Meanwhile, industrial competitors and venture funds invested huge sums in these markets, leading to higher capacity but leaving the company with little choice but to overpay for potential acquisition candidates. Four years later, it acquired stakes in an Indian entity, which exceeded Western calculations four to five times.

---

26. D. Wilson and R. Purushothaman, "Dreaming with BRICs, The Path to 2050," *Global Economics Paper*, no. 99 (USA: GS Global Economics Web site, 2003). Later adapted by Goldman Sachs.

Consulting and market research companies, business journals, government organizations, and academia regularly update information on countries, pretending to be authoritative sources for companies interested in assessing risk and comparing the potential of various EMs (see table 4). These are ranked according to specific performance criteria, for which macro data are collected from a variety of statistical sources such as the World Bank's World Development Indicators[27] (see table 5). Such rankings are useful for gaining a first impression or preselection of a market. But a corporate investor needs more information on ground realities, which can only be obtained through targeted research in the field.[28] Moreover, the data for rankings is drawn from diverse sources and cannot be strictly comparable. Or, rating agencies can make a wrong call, which they did for practically all financial crises in EMs (Southeast Asia, Russia, Mexico, Argentina) and AMs (e.g., USA/UK 2007–2008 subprime crisis). Companies should remember that a "top-ranking EM" will have high entry costs as it also attracts competitors. Just as winners in the stock market are those who anticipate a trend, so too companies must keep a step ahead when selecting an EM or a respective industry and company in it. TNCs that managed to garner high market shares in Russia, for example, are those that had invested long before the country's ranking moved up. Early entry at low cost enabled a shortened return on investment in an expanding market. The same applies to Brazil and India, which had low rankings throughout the 1990s until 2005 but are now among the fastest growing economies.

C.3. Foreign direct investment: Positioning for the future

Cost-cutting by rationalizing production, restructuring, and shedding staff gives little advantage when competitors worldwide embark on similar strategies while gaining market share through FDI. Also, exports alone will no longer suffice to attain global leadership.[29] To offset the effect of structural recession in the AMs, EU companies need to widen their sphere of influence by outsmarting global competitors and to optimize supply chains by winning over important customers and suppliers in key geographies. The larger emerging economies—taken alone or together—offer an alternative to the EU and US markets, provided companies invest in permanent structures and competent people in these markets and master the local rules.

FDI, which covers overseas manufacturing, cross-border technology transfer, and know-how exchange, is an indicator of the growing connectivity between economies. This recent vehicle of economic integration, which took off at the end of the Cold War, has recorded 10%–12% growth annually ever since—higher than either world trade or world production. Till the early 1990s, world growth was spurred mainly by commerce and aid transfers to developing and transition economies. Today, FDI is the main catalyst for

---

27. As these data are often obtained from national agencies using dissimilar statistical processes, certain data are often not comparable.
28. See chapter 8.
29. New export rules will come into force across the EU starting on July 1, 2009. According to the new provisions, companies residing in the EU will have to obtain electronic approval from customs for each good before it is shipped out. Exports based on monthly declarations will no longer be sufficient—a major impediment for SMEs who will step up their foreign investments outside the EU. "Der exportmeister braucht nachhilfe" [Export champion needs crash course], *Handelsblatt,* October 24–26, 2008, 19.

Table 4. Country ratings: Selected indices.

a. Economic and business indices

Index	Source	Coverage	Web site
Doing Business Ratings	World Bank	Quality of business regulation is surveyed in 155 countries. The variables are broken down into categories: starting a business, labor, contracts, credit, and bankruptcy. It includes size of the informal economy.	www.rru.worldbank.org
FDI Confidence Index	AT Kearney	Annual survey among decision-makers of the thousand leading companies that account for 70% of FDI. Summarizes the impact of likely political, economic, and regulatory changes on their FDI intentions. Covers 65 countries that receive 70% of FDI inflows.	www.atkearney.com
Global Competitiveness Report	World Economic Forum (WEF), Switzerland	117 countries are ranked depending on the macroeconomic environment, state of the country's public institutions, and level of its technological readiness.	www.weforum.org
Global Production Scoreboard	Nova Research, Switzerland	24 countries are ranked according to performance and potential variables: labor cost, skill base, R&D capacity, infrastructure, government, export growth, high-tech exports, and 5 industrial sectors.	www.global-production.com
Global Retail Development Index	AT Kearney	A survey to help retailers prioritize their global development strategies. 30 countries are ranked according to more than 25 variables covering country and business risk, market attractiveness, market saturation, and time pressure.	www.atkearney.com
Globalization Index	AT Kearney, Carnegie Endowment for International Peace	Annual ranking of 62 countries representing 96% of world GDP based on 12 variables concerning economic integration, technological connectivity, personal contact, and political engagement.	www.atkearney.com
Market Potential Indicators for Emerging Markets	Center for International Business Education and Research, Michigan State University, USA	24 emerging market countries are ranked for market size, market growth, market intensity, market consumption capacity, commercial infrastructure, economic freedom, market receptivity, and country risk.	www.globaledge.msu.edu/
Offshore Location Attractiveness Index	AT Kearney	25 countries are shortlisted based on corporate surveys, current and planned BPO activities, and government initiatives. They are then ranked on the basis of financial structure, people skills, and availability; business environment variables to gauge the attractiveness of the countries as locations for offshore services.	www.atkearney.com
World Business Environment Survey	World Bank	Survey of 10,000 companies in 80 countries on the quality of the investment climate as shaped by domestic economic policy; governance; regulatory, infrastructure, and financial impediments; and assessments of the quality of public services.	info.worldbank.org
World Competitiveness Scoreboard	International Institute for Management Development (IMD), Switzerland	55 countries are ranked based on 331 criteria grouped into 4 competitiveness factors: economic performance, government efficiency, business efficiency, and infrastructure.	www.imd.ch

Table 4. Country ratings: Selected indices (cont'd).

b. Other indices

Index	Source	Coverage	Web site
Economic Freedom of the World	The Fraser Institute, Canada	The index measures the degree of economic freedom by examining 21 components related to size of government, legal structures and security of property rights, access to sound money, freedom to trade internationally, and regulation of credit, labor, and business.	www.freetheworld.com
Economic Security Index	International Labour Organization	48,000 workers are surveyed in 90 countries to rank them on 7 measures of work-related security.	www.ilo.org
Failed States Index	The Fund for Peace, USA	Ranking of worst-performing countries based on 12 political, social, and economic variables, by scanning press articles.	www.fundforpeace.org
Freedom in the World	Freedom House, USA	Individual countries are evaluated based on a checklist of questions on political rights and civil liberties that are derived in large measure from the Universal Declaration of Human Rights.	www.freedomhouse.org
Global Corruption Barometer	Transparency International, Germany	64 countries are rated on their level of corruption, based on survey data (50,000 persons). Complements the Corruption Perception Index and Bribe Payers Index.	www.transparency.org
Governance and Democracy Processes; Failed and Fragile States (country rankings)	Country Indicators for Foreign Policy (CIFP) Project, Carleton University, Canada	Country rankings based on democratic participation, government and economic efficiency, accountability, human rights, political stability, and rule of law for Governance ranking and based on fragility index, authority, legitimacy, capacity, governance, economics, security and crime, human development, demography, environment, and gender for Fragile States.	www.carleton.ca/cifp
Governance Research Country Indicator Snapshot	World Bank	160 countries are compared, on the basis of polls and surveys, for governance performance on the basis of 6 dimensions: voice and accountability, political stability, government effectiveness, regulatory framework, rule of law, and corruption control.	www.worldbank.org
Index of Economic Freedom	Heritage Foundation, Wall Street Journal, USA	This index covers 162 countries across 10 specific freedoms such as trade freedom, business freedom, investment freedom, and property rights.	www.heritage.org
Opacity Index	Kurtzmann Group, USA	35 countries are scored for 5 different areas that affect capital markets: corruption, legal system, macroeconomic and fiscal policies, accounting standards and practices (including corporate governance and information release), and regulatory regime.	www.kurtzmangroup.com
Polity IV Country Reports	Integrated Network for Societal Conflict Research (INSCR) program at the Center for Center for Systemic Peace, George Mason University, USA	The country reports for all independent states (with greater than 500,000 total population) in the global state system cover the years since 1800 in an attempt to rate the world's regimes on their level of democracy.	www.systemicpeace.org
State Failure Task Force Report: Phase III Findings	Center for International Development and Conflict Management (CIDCM), University of Maryland, USA	The data set contains 1300 political, demographic, social, economic, environmental variables for all countries of the world from 1955 to 1998 related to 4 kinds of internal conflict: revolutionary wars, ethnic wars, adverse regime changes, and genocides.	www.cidcm.umd.edu

Table 5. Market potential indicators for emerging markets.

Dimension	Weight	Indicators used
Market Size	10/50	Urban population (million)[a] Electricity consumption (billion kwh)[b]
Market Intensity	7/50	GNI per capita estimates using PPP (US$)[a] Private consumption as a percentage of GDP (%)[a]
Commercial Infrastructure	7/50	Telephone mainlines (per 100 habitants)[c] Cellular mobile subscribers (per 100 habitants)[c] Number of PCs (per 100 habitants)[c] Paved road density (km per million people)[a] Internet hosts (per million people)[c] Population per retail outlet (latest year available)[d] Television sets (per 1000 persons)[a]
Market Receptivity	6/50	Per capita imports from USA (US$)[g] Trade as a percentage of GDP (%)[a]
Market Growth Rate	6/50	Average annual growth rate of commercial energy use (%)[a] Real GDP growth rate (%)[a]
Market Consumption Capacity	5/50	Percentage share of middle-class in consumption/income (latest year available)[a]
Economic Freedom	5/50	Economic Freedom Index[e] Political Freedom Index[f]
Country Risk	4/50	Country risk rating[h]

Data used are those available for most recent year.
a. Source: World Bank, World Development Indicators.
b. Source: US Energy Information Administration, International Energy Annual.
c. Source: International Telecommunication Union, ICT Indicators.
d. Source: Euromonitor: European Marketing Data and Statistics; Asian Marketing Data and Statistics.
e. Source: Heritage Foundation, The Index of Economic Freedom.
f. Source: Freedom House, Survey of Freedom in the World.
g. Source: US Census Bureau Foreign Trade Division, Country Data.
h. Source: Euromoney, Country Risk Survey.
Source: Center for International Business Education and Research at Michigan State University (MSU), US. Annual updates.

building global supply, distribution, and knowledge networks. It notably amplifies efforts to boost sales and foreign trade.

Managers who understand this shift will use FDI wisely to link up to other countries' economies, become insiders, and secure sustainable development for their organizations.[30] Mere trading or licensing activities will not suffice to push deep roots in the leading markets of the twenty-first century. Challenged by saturating home markets and rising competition, AM players will be pressed into taking risks and investing in new markets. High performers expand market share by networking and acquiring local brands, a strategy they have applied successfully in their traditional markets. Companies that are not ready to invest in the emerging markets will miss opportunities to be part of a global network that covers fast-growth economies.

The way countries, provinces, cities, industries, enterprises, and people will interact in the coming decades will change significantly. New technologies, open borders, and liberal economic policies of governments will introduce variety in the origin and destination of world trade, investment, and capital flows. Until the 1980s, 90%–95% of FDI was concentrated in the richer OECD economies. Today, the share of emerging and developing economies in world FDI flows has risen to about 30%–35%. The share of these countries

---

30. See chapter 10.

in trade and portfolio investments is also increasing. Some emerging powers have in fact already "emerged"; the spending power of their consumers puts them almost at par with the middle-income OECD economies.

Cross-border FDI will have another positive effect: it will enhance cooperation, pacify tensions, and reduce the risk of wars across Eurasia. FDI in industries and services will thus contribute more to balanced development across the southern hemisphere than foreign aid did.

PART I
CHINA, INDIA, AND RUSSIA OPEN NEW FRONTIERS FOR BUSINESS

"One is not only responsible for what one does, but also for what one does not."
—Laotse, Chinese philosopher

For some Western companies, it has become an inescapable reality, and for others, it will soon be: the need for a strategy specifically designed for the Eurasian megamarkets of China, India, and Russia. Inescapable, because starting from the mid-1990s the three megamarkets have continuously achieved better economic results than any advanced economy. In July 2007, the IMF forecasted that world GDP is expected to show steady increases during 2008–2010 thanks to favorable fundamentals in the three megamarkets: "These countries have replaced the United States and Western Europe as engines of world economic growth." The financial crisis that hit the United States in 2008 will accelerate this trend despite the general slowdown it caused across the world.

The three megamarkets have reached critical mass in most industries, and their companies have started encroaching into the EU/US home markets with adequately priced, highly competitive goods, and—this is a recent but foreseeable phenomenon[1]—via acquisitions of Western companies. To counter this trend, EU/US companies must move into these markets and acquire stakes in local rivals. For technology leaders, it is still not too late to build a profitable business by gaining access to the large consumer and resource bases there. For OECD-based companies, Eurasia's three megamarkets offer manifold assets:

- a fast-growing, vast, and mostly young consumer base that has a heavy "consumption backlog" and strong aspirations to better living standards;
- a talent pool of young, skilled workers, engineers, and managers;
- a broad industrial base with local companies in constant search of technology, know-how, and capital; besides large national champions, they host a myriad of family-run businesses, which as employers, tax payers, and capital investors are important players to reckon with in future decades;
- a supply base for raw materials, components, and finished products for local production and export;
- investment opportunities with high returns in both manufacturing and services;
- an export platform that has well-placed links with Africa, Asia, and Australia;

---

1. For further reading on the phenomenon of outward FDI emerging as a result of successful inward FDI policies, see Paul Fischer, *Foreign Direct Investment in Russia: A Strategy for Industrial Revival* (London: MacMillan/Palgrave, 2000).

- expanding capital markets and various means of financial engineering with local banks, private equity,[2] and venture capital providers to fund acquisitions, alliances, and greenfield projects;
- investor-friendly governments that offer incentives and support to business ventures;
- massive state-led investments in infrastructure, construction, energy, agriculture, and innovation-oriented industries with high R&D components (e.g., IT, telecommunications, aeronautics); dynamic companies can participate in mega projects through public tenders as main contractors or subcontractors.

Unshackled from socialist thinking or collectivist ideology, the megamarkets have progressed steadily over the past two decades. Faster raw materials extraction and higher agricultural, industrial, and service output have boosted economic performance. In most statistical tables, they appear now in the same league as the advanced economies of the United States, the EU, and Japan, and as such they offer invaluable opportunities to Western enterprises for spreading their operations. For decades to come, China's and India's huge urbanizing populations will drive global market growth. The sheer size of the megamarkets makes them political and economic powerhouses to reckon with in the course of the twenty-first century.

In agriculture, India and China have raised productivity and output levels to overcome deficits and become net exporters of food (e.g., India for wheat, rice, seafood, and tea; China for fruit, fish, and meat). While India's green (food crops) and white (milk) revolutions have placed it among the top three for most agricultural products, Russia is converting a downtrodden agricultural sector into a modern supply base for its own people and neighboring populations of Europe, Central Asia, and China.

In raw materials and primary energy extraction (mining, oil drilling, gas recovery), Russia has moved to center stage, controlling a large part of the energy flows to the EU and Central and East Asia. By adding value to its abundant resources, it hopes to become a leading supplier of high-tech base materials, components, and semi-manufactures for high-end industrial applications. Russian oil and gas multinationals are moving downstream by investing in energy processing and distribution at home and through acquisitions abroad. Mining is a very important activity with high growth potential also in China and India, where the domestic economy is consuming more resources than domestically available, forcing large players to invest overseas to ensure supplies (mainly in Africa, Asia, and Latin America).

Industrial output has risen dramatically in all three megamarkets. China has become the "factory of the world" through low-cost and mass production of consumer, industrial, and increasingly high-tech goods. Using fiscal incentives and a policy of investment and industrial promotion, Russia is in the midst of reversing the de-industrialization it faced after the disintegration of the Soviet Union. India's earlier policy of industrial self-reliance has helped to create national champions who are now controlling many industries and selectively acquiring enterprises in foreign countries.

---

2. Foreign private equity companies are increasingly looking at investment opportunities in the megamarkets. Aloe Private Equity from France, for example, targets "green" projects in the field of clean and renewable energy, waste recycling, emissions controls, and eco-processes. See "Private Equity Players Step Up Green Investments in India," *The Hindu Business Line,* January 9, 2008.

In services, India rose rapidly to become an acknowledged world leader in information technology (IT), an advantage that it is converting to occupy a dominant position in knowledge-based industries, particularly for future technologies (biopharma, nanotech, alternative energies). China's service sector is being built around its advanced industrial base, while the Russian government is allocating more oil revenues to develop a modern service infrastructure (banking, insurance, retailing, IT, tourism).

The three countries compete for FDI from advanced economies but are at the same time steadily increasing cross-border FDI and trade among themselves and with other advanced and emerging economies on the Eurasian continent and elsewhere. Reverse FDI from these mega-economies to advanced markets (e.g., Chinese acquisition of the British Rover car factory or Jaguar by India's Tata) is a trend to be taken seriously by EU/US enterprises and governments.

To defend and voice their rising economic power, megamarket politicians are speaking more strongly in international fora such as the WTO, IMF, and UN. Unused to this stance, the industrialized countries feel threatened and are taking defensive, sometimes irrational positions (particularly on agriculture, climate change, and the environment), when they would do better to recognize the new situation and seek partnerships and new opportunities that would benefit their businesses.

Part 1 of this book describes the economic strength of the megamarkets China, India, and Russia through a comparative analysis of key economic indicators, resources, and industry trends so that foreign businesspeople can better capture the opportunities offered by the megamarkets. In its sector surveys (chapters 4–6), it proposes names of leading megamarket companies that have been growing speedily over the past two decades. These players represent important contacts as suppliers, buyers, or alliance partners for joint projects in the megamarkets but also in other world markets.

Before introducing these success stories, we shall dwell on the rising geostrategic and economic importance of the Eurasian continent, to which the three megamarkets and Europe belong.

CHAPTER 1
Why Eurasia holds promise for business

Eurasia's importance is gradually becoming a geostrategic reality for business.[1] Eurasia, the supercontinent composed of the territories of Europe and Asia, is the world's largest landmass, whose peoples have shared a long history. Its richly diverse cultures make it a politically multi-polar entity, nourished by a long tradition of trade and exchange of knowledge. The Black Sea, the Silk Road, the Spice Route, the Khyber Pass, the Indian Ocean, the Malacca Strait, and the South China Sea have for centuries been commercial lifelines linking Europe to Asia. Today, globalization, the opening of markets, and the focus of economic policies on foreign investment and trade are reviving ancient ties and laying the foundation for future progress.

Three emerging megamarkets (China, India, Russia), a unifying Europe, and countries surrounding them can, if taken together, power wealth and employment throughout the contiguous continents of Europe and Asia. For advanced market companies, these emerging markets with annual growth rates of 6%–9% offer extraordinary prospects in the long term for global expansion and leadership through additional revenue, higher profitability, technological innovation, and risk sharing.

But far from all Western business leaders recognize the relevance of these three pillar economies in upholding their companies' global leadership and commit the necessary resources for serving key customers and building adequate supply chains. Not many Fortune 500 corporations and medium-sized technology leaders from the AMs can claim to adopt workable concepts and report sustainable profits in each of the three megamarkets. Continued focus on the familiar markets of North America and Western Europe exposes Western companies to the risk of prolonged recession and isolation while competitors old and new aggressively expand their stance in newly emerging economies and from there start encroaching on their home territories. The megamarkets, on the other hand, offer a gainful alternative, particularly for European investments backed by a strong euro. As long as basic needs of local populations, especially at the middle and bottom of the income pyramid, are not satisfied, these markets will move anti-cyclically from Western economies—where growth rates above 2% have become the exception—thus offering real opportunities provided a company is flexible enough to reorient its strategy.[2]

---

1. So far, the concept of Eurasia has been employed mainly by security analysts and political and military strategists. See Z. Brzezinski, *The Grand Chessboard: American Primacy and Its Geostrategic Imperatives* (Basic Books, 1997) and Myasnikov, *The Strategic Triangle of Russia, China and India: The Eurasian Aspect* (Russian Academy of Science, 2003). As a result of globalization, the notion of Eurasia is going to draw the attention of business strategists, who will have to revert to an interdisciplinary approach by including geostrategic and historical dimensions in their work.

2. See the prologue, section A.

> **Pause for thought**
>
> *For many years, Germany's carmaker Volkswagen decided to focus only on China, where it ranked first for many decades until it was seriously challenged by General Motors, Toyota, and Hyundai.*
>
> *Meanwhile, these competitors had already established themselves in India and Russia, raising an entry barrier for Volkswagen there and threatening Volkswagen's leadership even in Europe because of increased exports from the megamarkets.*

This is not to say that Asia has been completely ignored by Western businesses. The economic rise of first Japan, then Southeast Asia, and now India and China has been reflected in the strategies of the leading companies from advanced economies. But their approach has been fragmented, the focus being mostly on presence (not profits) in single (not all three) countries. The arrival of the three megamarkets calls for a broader perception of Eurasia for formulating coherent strategies that view market developments and competitor moves across the three to identify the right location and time of entry into fast-growing regional markets. Leadership in only one or two of the markets is no longer sustainable as these countries are now interconnected economically, technologically, and politically.

A winning concept for the three megamarkets consists in systematically developing skills around a combination of variables, including committed management, focused investments, and speed in implementing milestone projects.[3] Effective corporate FDI across Eurasia via combinations of mergers and acquisitions (M&As), alliances, and stand-alone projects will make the difference, thus contributing to a company's regional and global leadership. In Asia, high performers from the EU, United States, and Japan have already gained additional market share that now allows them to move further from the megamarkets to the EMs surrounding them (e.g., Kazakhstan, Pakistan, Philippines, Thailand, Ukraine, Viet Nam). Through their megamarket subsidiaries, they dispose of the platforms and contact networks (e.g., overseas Chinese and Indians) needed to close in on even politically sensitive regions such as Cambodia, Iran, Iraq, Laos, Myanmar. Business partners in these economies already feel the positive spillover of being connected to the megamarkets.

1.1. Eurasia: Diversity in unity

Eurasia is considered to be the landmass composed of the adjoining continents of Europe and Asia. It is a simple, neutral, and perennial geographical description that reflects a physical reality. This definition—not ideologically burdened by the more political concept of Eurasianism[4]—offers corporate executives a new perception of the world's largest continent as an extensive space for commercial activity and intercultural exchange.

---

3. More ideas for designing such a concept will be provided in chapters 9–12.
4. Eurasianism, a doctrine that originated in Russia with an anti-Atlanticism or anti-Americanism stance, characterizes a specific Weltanschauung: a political philosophy combining tradition, modernity, and even elements of postmodernism to support the integration of the post-Soviet territories on a democratic, nonviolent, and voluntary basis without the domination of any one religious or ethnic group.

At school and other educational and training institutions, Europe and Asia have traditionally been considered separate continents, owing more to political, economic, and cultural considerations. The geographic dividing line was placed along the Dardanelles, Bosporus, Caucasus Mountains, and Ural Mountains. The political divide between the two has been constantly shifted by historical events (e.g., Mongol invasions, Soviet supremacy in Central Europe) and has ultimately been blurred with the fall of the iron curtain. No country highlights this anomaly better than Russia, which is considered European although about 70% of it lies in Asia—i.e., beyond the Ural mountain range. Russia alone occupies 20% of the Eurasian landmass. As a comparison, the EU as a political and economic entity represents hardly 5% of Eurasia's total area; it can therefore only continue playing in the big league if it keeps politically united and technologically advanced in key industries, which presupposes that EU companies position themselves successfully in Eurasia's major markets.

According to the broader definition, Eurasia has the world's widest territorial extent. Its vast space is richly endowed with a diversity of plant, animal, and mineral resources. Many different civilizations could develop and progress by exchanging knowledge on discoveries and inventions. Interestingly, people from Eurasia reached out to and peopled the Americas, Australia, and southern Africa, but they were never conquered by people from other continents. Geographically, the Eurasian landmass encompasses six large regional blocs—East Asia, Southeast Asia, South Asia, the Middle East, and Europe in the West that surround the interior core of Central Asia (the sixth one) with its vast plains and steppes— corresponding to a large extent to the territory of today's CIS countries (see figure 1.1). Each region brought about highly evolved civilizations, which despite regular conflicts and mutual conquests over centuries finally merged and coexisted even with different religious beliefs and languages, many of which share the same roots.

Figure 1.1. Eurasia's six regional blocs.

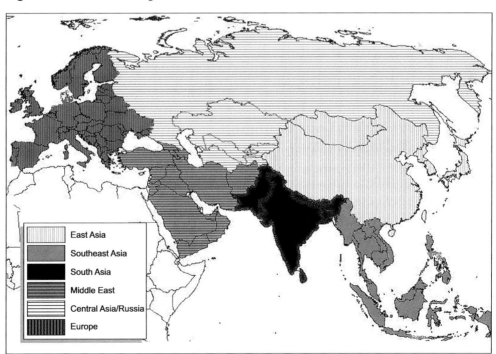

Unlike other continents, Eurasia is basically self-sufficient in food, minerals, fuels, and other resources (wood, fisheries, water), and in consumer and industrial goods, which makes it economically less vulnerable. In absolute terms, Eurasia represents about 70% of the world's human population and a great part of its raw materials reserves, making it economically far more powerful than any other continent, with about 90% of the world's reported foreign reserves (US$2.5 trillion) enabling it to influence the monetary, fiscal, and trade policies of the United States, as of today the world's most powerful economy. Eurasia is not a unified economic grouping, let alone a political one, but intensifying commercial and cultural exchanges via regional cooperation are pointing toward closer partnerships among nations starting from this continent. European enterprises should actively participate in these positive developments to secure their future.

1.1.1. The world's religions originated in Eurasia

The world's major religions all have their roots in Eurasia. Christianity (2.1 billion adherents; 33% of the world's population),[5] Islam (1.3 billion; 21%), and Judaism (12 million or only 0.22% of the world's population)—whose adherents form almost half of the world's population—originated in the western part of Eurasia now known as the Middle East (see figure 1.2). Europe became the center from which Christianity spread across the globe. Orthodoxy, a branch of Christianity, became the religious anchor in Russia, eastern Romania, and Bulgaria. The earlier religions like Jainism (5000 BC), Hinduism (900 million adherents; 14% of the world's population),[6] and Buddhism (600 BC) sprang from India and greatly influenced later Western religions and Asian philosophical thought. While Buddhism spread to Tibet, Southeast Asia, China, Mongolia, and Japan, Hinduism extended southwards and eastwards via the sea route out to Bali (Indonesia). In the East, Taoism originated in China and spread across the Korean peninsula to Japan, and the

Figure 1.2. The world's religions originated in Eurasia (mn adherents).

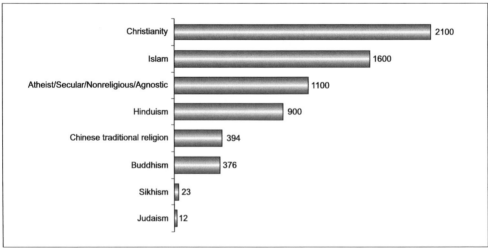

Source: www.adherents.com.

---

5. Source: www.adherents.com.
6. It is difficult to set an exact date for the origin of Hinduism given its evolution over the ages.

sociophilosophical movement of Confucianism proliferated throughout China. In Japan both of these, together with Buddhism and the official religion of Shintoism, became an important blend of everyday life there.

These religions imbibed each other and spread along Eurasia's far-flung trade routes, together with staples, luxury goods, and knowledge. Christianity, Islam, and Judaism share the same center of origin, and cross references to each other are found in their scriptures. Moreover, recent historical and comparative religious studies have highlighted similarities between Christianity and Eastern religions carried by the Greeks who came to India with Alexander the Great (see table 1.1).

Despite the similarities, there can be significant differences in perception of life between Western and Asian beliefs. Obviously, comparisons bear the danger that a person does not understand enough about the religion which he is judging as it may propose a different approach from his own. Businesspeople tend to misinterpret religious attitudes of counterparts belonging to different cultural contexts, which leads to biased decisions derived from subjective perceptions. It is worth highlighting some of the most striking differences:

- For Western religions, there is a natural hierarchy with man at its very center. Western thinking distinguishes clearly between religion and philosophy, or belief and knowledge. Asian believers think that man is only part of a harmonious but complex cosmos, with which man will merge after death. Eastern thought resolutely believes in the reality of the unseen world, in interdependence and interconnectedness of all (including invisible) things, and in the need to escape from the limits of individualism, which is connected with bodily pleasures and the illusion of separateness.
- While Western religions believe in one life, Asians are convinced that living beings go through numerous rebirths, a cycle that can be broken only after a being has found the right path and has been liberated. In this case, the being can attain liberation by strictly following

Table 1.1. Christianity and Asian religions.

Christianity	Asian religions
Existence of a single source or one truth represented by one Single Creator, God	Existence of a Transcendent Being (Brahman for the Hindus) that created and preserves the universe and mankind
Trinity: Father, Son, and the Holy Spirit	Hindu Trinity: Brahma, Vishnu, Shiva
Life of Christ: son of God divinely conceived, birth foretold, birth in manger at Nazareth, depicted as shepherd, appeared at a critical time for country, preached love and peace	Life of Krishna: incarnation of God, birth foretold, birth in prison at Dwarka, depicted as cowherd, appeared at critical time of country, teaching of devotion to the Supreme and duty (*dharma*)
Structure of the Catholic/Protestant Church	Structure of the Buddhist Chaitya
Rigorous asceticism of certain early Christian sects	Asceticism of Jain and Buddhist saints
Christians believe in sin and redemption through refuge in Christ.	Hindus believe in karma and suffering and redemption through one's own actions and surrender to God.
Christianity advocates surrender, unconditional love, forgiveness, harmlessness, and inner purity.	Hinduism advocates egolessness, compassion, nonviolence (*ahimsa*), and inner purity.
Christians believe that those who do good are rewarded after death with a place in heaven, while evildoers are condemned to hell.	According to Theravada Buddhism, evildoers go to hell, righteous people go to heaven, and some people are born again.

the "path of deliverance," a sublime state of spirituality that Buddhists[7] call *nirvana* or the inner freedom from worldly desires, which are the root cause of personal suffering.

- Asians believe in the law of *karma*, pushing humans upward toward God in cases of good deeds in their lives or entering a downward spiral toward renewed material existence. Karma may be defined as a kind of cosmic justice, a moral law of cause and effect where every act bears inevitable consequences.
- Asian religions are more abstract, holistic, and philosophical than their Western counterparts; they do not share the view that personal immortality is possible. For them, human beings are not in a position to resurrect with the same features and physiognomy, as Christianity claims. Hindu pantheism defines liberation as the fusion of *atman* (soul) with *Brahman* (God) in a non-figurative manner.
- Asian religions encourage worshippers to look inward for the essential answers and search the truth within their souls through lifelong cycles of inner contemplation and meditation rather than looking for external ideas, advice, and support via, for example, an institutionalized church. Buddha did not resort to any priest or outer revelation to discover the absolute truth; neither did he accept a self involved in attaining true knowledge. Buddha's very quest for truth started with the observation that truth must be higher than physical reality and the current speculation at that time.
- Asian religions have a high philosophy content; they teach ways and practices oriented toward reducing suffering by improving a person's spirituality and behavior (through yoga, meditation, contemplation, etc.); Western religions pursue a different path by establishing a strict code of conduct for human beings to follow (e.g., via the Ten Commandments).
- Animals as "alternative beings" have a much higher standing in Asian religions than with Christians or Jews because the reincarnation rule works backward in case a human being has not fulfilled his/her duties in life. Buddhist and Jain compassion, for example, extends to all beings, including animals, as all have a divine nature and are seeking liberation.

Religion and faith form the identity of a people and their values; they pervade all aspects of their lives, including business attitudes and patterns of interpersonal relations. For European managers habituated to secularism, rationalism, and clarity in behavior, the high visibility and dominance of religion in the rest of Eurasia (except for China) can seem archaic or exotic. An effective approach is to acknowledge the commonalities to overcome prejudices and respect religious sentiments of interlocutors. Prejudice can derive from a feeling of superiority that one's own belief is better than that of others or from mere ignorance of the concept underlying the faith of others. It can have its origin in the visitor's (investor) and host's (recipient) thinking and degree of open-mindedness, no matter where the partnership or transaction takes place.

1.1.2. The world's languages have their roots in Eurasia

Almost all the world—90%—speaks one or other Indo-European or Sino-Tibetan language as a primary or secondary language. Regardless of certain variations in language classifications, the Indo-European family is the largest—3 billion users according to certain statistics—

---

7. Buddha means "the Enlightened One," the one who freed himself from suffering and despair by ridding himself of illusory worldly attachments and desires.

and the second largest is the Sino-Tibetan family (2.5 billion users). Both families stem from Eurasia. The Indo-European languages rose from a common ancestral (reconstructed) language called Proto-Indo-European (4000 BC), whose original homeland is possibly the steppes of the Black and Caspian seas or Anatolia. From these centers, the languages spread (see figure 1.3) and branched off into local variants right from the third millennium BC through the agricultural revolution, which created the food surplus that impelled the

Figure 1.3. Origin and spread of the Indo-European language family.

a. Origin of Indo-European languages

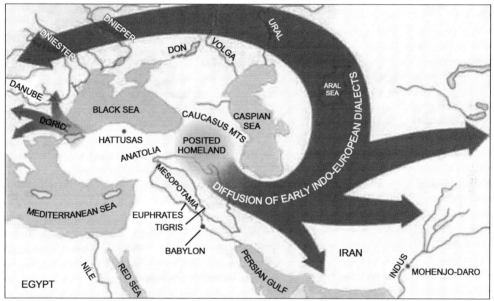

Source: T. V. Gamkrelidze and V. V. Ivanov, Scientific American, March 1990, p.110.

b. Spread of the Indo-European language family

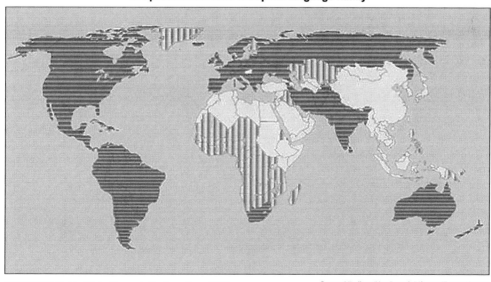

Horizontal lines: countries with a majority of speakers of IE languages.
Vertical lines: countries with an IE minority language with official status.

Source: http://en.wikipedia.org/wiki/Image:IE_countries.png.

Indo-Europeans to found villages and city-states. From here they branched off under the impulse of trade, conquest (e.g., Roman Empire, Islamic conquests), colonization (e.g., the British and other European empires), settlement (e.g., North America, Australia), or the spread of religion (e.g., Buddhism). The ancestral language of the other Eurasian language family, Sino-Tibetan, is thought to have originated in the region of the Himalayan plateau where the rivers of East and Southeast Asia spring from. It split into Proto-Chinese and Proto-Tibeto-Burman sometime around 4000 BC. Chinese and East Asian languages have spread in the eastern part of the continent. The Chinese part comprises exclusively Chinese languages and dialects, which are linked by a common writing system. The Tibeto-Burman languages branched off from the source language when these peoples migrated southwards. The Sino-Tibetan family consists of around 390 languages, but apart from Chinese (the language with the largest number of speakers), Tibetan, and Burmese, the other languages have few users, making research difficult.

The Indo-European family has been the subject of intense research, including the reconstruction of Proto-Indo-European, as it sheds light on human movements, which have defined the culture and identities of the Indo-Europeans over the ages. About 443 languages belong to this family, including major living languages (see table 1.2)—Bengali, English, French, German, Hindi, Portuguese, Russian, and Spanish (each with more than 100 million native speakers).

The influence of a language does not derive from its numbers. The most influential languages[8]—based on number of primary speakers, number of secondary speakers, number and population of countries where used, number of major disciplines using the language internationally, economic power of countries applying the languages, and socioliterary prestige—are not necessarily those that have the largest number of speakers. Apart from Arabic and Japanese, all the languages are Eurasian. The most influential language today is clearly English. Its flexibility and spread via the Internet (see figure 1.4) and other mass

Table 1.2. Ranking of world languages.						
Rank	Language	Family	Number of speakers (mn)			Number of countries
			First language	Second language	Total	
1	Chinese[a]	Sino-Tibetan	938	20	958	5
2	English	Indo-European	322	150	472	115
3	Spanish	Indo-European	332	20	352	20
4	Russian	Indo-European	170	125	295	16
5	French	Indo-European	80	190	270	35
6	Portuguese	Indo-European	170	28	198	5
7	Arabic[b]	Afro-Asiatic	175	21	196	24
8	Bengali	Indo-European	189	–	189	1
9	Hindi/Urdu	Indo-European	**182**	–	**182**	2
10	Japanese	Altaic	125	8	133	1
11	German	Indo-European	98	9	107	9

a. Chinese: Mandarin, Xiang, Hakka, Gan, Minbei. French: French, Haitian Creole.
b. Arabic: Egyptian, Moroccan, Saidi, North Levantine, Mesopotamian, Najdi, Tunisian, Sanaami.
Source: Summer Institute for Linguistics (SIL), Ethnologue Survey (1999). (http://www2.ignatius.edu/faculty/turner/languages.htm).

8. See also George Weber, "Top Languages," Language Monthly 3 (1997): 12–18.

Figure 1.4. Top Internet languages, 2007 (mn users).

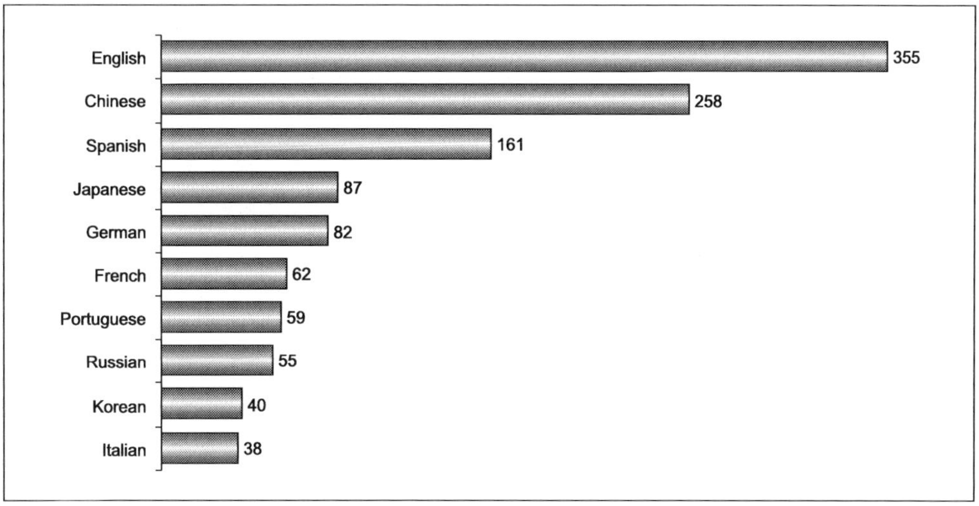

Language	Users (mn)
English	355
Chinese	258
Spanish	161
Japanese	87
German	82
French	62
Portuguese	59
Russian	55
Korean	40
Italian	38

Source: www.internetworldstats.com.

media almost make it a *lingua franca* for international business although vast differences prevail in pronunciation and the use of words and idioms, including in English-speaking countries (USA, UK, Australia, India, Malaysia).

1.1.3. Culture and mentality: The other two soft factors

Language is derived from and also impacts greatly on culture, which influences business behavior and mentality. Cultural attitudes and beliefs determine a people's way of life and thinking, in relation to time, change, authority, family, decision-making, risk, and nature. Cultural subconsciousness impacts strongly on business attitudes and reactions vis-à-vis foreign partners and investors. Chinese business etiquette, for example, which in many ways molded social norms across East Asia (e.g., Japan, Korea), is very different from Indo-European thinking although some of the traits of social behavior can be found in Indian, Middle Eastern, and Southern European thinking (see box 1.1). Culture also shapes a people's overall approach to more tangible daily situations and socioeconomic

---

Box 1.1. Chinese cultural characteristics. Group orientation (company as enlarged family)

- Family replaces state protection
- Hierarchy, respect of elders
- Importance of soft factors
- Work not separated from private life
- Conflict prevention and harmony (face)
- Emphasis on process rather than final result
- Patience as valuable as performance (time factor not so relevant)
- Flexibility vs. contractual formalism
- Importance of networking

relations: industrial organization, social cohesion, health and old age insurance, taxation, and general policymaking with respect to administrative practices and subordination at central and regional levels. A society's value system, which represents the basic element of its culture, determines its attitude toward innovation and entrepreneurship and can be considered a determining factor of a country's competitiveness.[9]

Outside central and northern Europe (e.g., Germany, Netherlands, Scandinavian countries) where quite formal relations prevail, great emphasis is put on friendly human relations as a prerequisite for developing lasting business partnerships. This also applies to southern Europe, which in many ways has a "high-context" culture similar to Asian countries and Russia. As a rule, Asian (and also Russian) businesspeople strive to have good personal relations with their foreign counterparts before they are ready to engage in joint projects. Great importance is attached to building friendship; formalities such as signing letters of intent or contracts are secondary. In such cultural contexts, it is important to invest time in cementing a relationship rather than concentrate everything on drafting perfectly formulated agreements supposed to protect the signatory from unexpected occurrences. Especially at the beginning of a relationship, business partners are expected to communicate and meet regularly instead of focusing exclusively on written communication, which commits the writer and might be interpreted wrongly by the receiver.

Cultures in the contemporary world can be seen as combinations or variations of two types: individualism and communitarianism or collectivism.[10] Individualism suggests an atomistic conception of society, emphasizing individual initiative, decision-making, and achievement at both personal and corporate levels. Communitarianism, by contrast, takes a more organic view, stressing the value of belonging to groups, networks, and organizations that make decisions and protect people in exchange for their loyalty.[11] Communitarian value systems, typical of Asian societies, can differ significantly depending on whether they are conditioned by underlying Muslim (Pakistan, Indonesia), Hindu (India), Buddhist and Shinto (Japan, Southeast Asia), or Confucian (China, Taiwan) religious practice and beliefs. Similarly, the individualistic value system of the Scandinavian, Anglo-Saxon, Germanic, and Latin (e.g., Greek, Italian, Portuguese, Spanish) countries has led to distinct governance models and industrial performance.

With increasing globalization and access to media and communications, cultural attitudes and their impact on business behavior and performance are converging. At the same time, cultural patterns are extremely complex and diverse, and they must be understood. Even in a world of fast communication and transport where nationalities meet and relate to each other every day, managers tend to overlook the powerful impact of culture as the decisive soft skill for success or failure in international markets. A better way than to group societies under the two broad categories "Western" and "Eastern," as is commonly done,

---

9. R. Franke et al., "Cultural Roots of Economic Performance: A Research Note," *Strategic Management Journal* 12 (1991): 165–173.
10. D. Hickson and D. Pugh, *Management Worldwide* (Penguin Business, 1995), 25.
11. G. Lodge et al., *Ideology and National Competitiveness: An Analysis of Nine Countries* (Harvard University Press, 1987), 9–10.

is to use more specific subcategories (see figure 1.5).[12] All of these subcultures, except the African one, can be found in Eurasia.

Interpreting correctly the "unknowns of timekeeping, symbolism, negotiating, and decision-making" can provide valuable insight into how foreign cultures tick.[13] Eurasian business cultures may be placed in eight groups along or between opposed attributes (see figure 1.6). Some countries (e.g., Germany/UK; China/India) have quite similar behavior profiles, and differences are a matter of degree rather than opposition.

Figure 1.5. The world's cultural families (examples of countries).

EAST/CENTRAL EUROPEANS	ARABS	AFRICANS	SOUTH ASIANS
Russia Poland Ukraine Czech Rep. Bulgaria	Saudi Arabia Syria Egypt Bahrein	Nigeria South Africa	India Pakistan

EAST/ SOUTHEAST ASIANS	ANGLO - SAXONS	LATINS	NORTH/ CENTRAL EUROPEANS
Japan China Taiwan Indonesia Malaysia	UK USA Canada Australia New Zealand	France Italy Spain Portugal Brazil Mexico Argentina Peru	Germany Austria Sweden Finland Switzerland

Figure 1.6. Attributes of business culture.

Deal - focused The result of the work is the prime objective **Germany, USA**	Intermediary position France Italy Russia UK	Relationship - focused Transactions depend on building good personal relationships **India, China, Japan**
Formal Business relations are formal and respectful Top - down business style Strict reporting lines **China, India, Russia, France**	Germany UK	Informal Business relations are informal and casual Egalitarian business style Flexible, multi - channel reporting **Italy, USA**
Monochronic Strict timekeeping Tight scheduling Long-term planning **Germany, USA**	China France	Polychronic Stretchable time Flexibility Rapid response **India, Italy, Russia**
Restrained Controlled emotions **China, Germany, Japan, UK**	India USA	Expressive Expressed emotions **France, Italy, Russia**

Source: Adapted from B. Tomalin and M. Nicks, The World's Business Cultures and How to Unlock Them (2007): 44-50.

12. Hickson and Pugh, *Management Worldwide*.
13. R. Gesteland, *Cross-Cultural Business Behaviour* (Handelshøjskolen, 1997).

It is noteworthy that with time, cultural fundamentals can change, leading to many variations and combinations, as reflected by the individualistic behavior of a growing number of Chinese managers in private enterprises, especially when they operate outside China. Conversely, some Russian oligarchs who have been accused of accumulating wealth without respecting shareholders and stakeholders have been adopting a fairly social attitude oriented toward the advancement of their communities and employees. New challenges and situations make cultures dynamic; exposed to global influences, cultural values are pressured to change, reorganize, and adjust.[14]

In a fast-changing global setting, managerial leaders must help forge new visions based on attainable goals. Cultural adaptability and getting the chemistry right—i.e., understanding the "software of the mind" of the foreign counterpart—will greatly decide business success in the megamarkets and elsewhere. Leadership, strategy, structure, and culture are interlinked. When studying why certain investment projects succeed while others fail, it becomes clear that much depends on the ability of top leaders to transform biased cultural attitudes and adapt them to new challenges related to entrepreneurship, foreign competition, multicultural staff, opportunity-led thinking, and employee participation in results. New compromises and syntheses of the prevailing cultural mix in a company can prove extraordinarily effective when penetrating new markets. A corporate strategy that is insensitive or runs counter to cultural patterns either at the corporate or country level is bound to fail. A high degree of intercultural awareness, openness, and empathy is required when dealing with foreign stakeholders from other sociocultural contexts.

Strong intercultural understanding needs to be fostered first at schools and universities, and further right from the first years in a company, also during post-merger integration after an acquisition, through internal training and education programs with a strong focus on foreign languages and teaching about other civilizations, religions, and cultures. A new approach to culture includes flexibility and a speedy reaction to opportunities, especially in fast-moving environments, where old thinking (e.g., reactive planning) would only cause a company to become a latecomer instead of a pioneer in conquering new markets.

1.2. Reviving Eurasia's old trade routes

Eurasia is the most extended stretch of land in the world, uninterrupted by large seas or oceans. The movement of people across it was easier than venturing across the ocean to other continents. Whether through invasions or migrations, such movements only led to greater assimilation among races, religions, and language groups across the continent. Along major trade routes checkered with caravans, chains of monasteries, and rest houses, royal courts in medieval Europe and caliphs in Asia shared similar forms of diplomatic address and codes of honor when receiving travelers and scholars from other lands.[15] Along the way, newcomers generally found hosts ready to provide food and shelter, but they were also eager to engage in intellectual debates and philosophical discussions to exchange ideas and experiences. This commonality linking the continent's great civilizations throughout

---

14. M. Porter, *The Competitive Advantage of Nations* (London: Macmillan, 1990).
15. Stewart Gordon, *When Asia Was the World* (Da Capo Press, 2008).

Europe, the Middle East, Central Asia, India, Southeast Asia, and China made it possible to share knowledge, gifts, merchandise, and traditions in a borderless world.

Eurasia has dominated world history for almost three millennia starting from the early civilizations in Asia Minor (Mesopotamia, Egypt), the Indus Valley (Harappa and Mohenjodaro), and the Yellow River region (Shang China). As the cradle of mankind and epicenter of commerce and diplomacy, it inspired all the other continents with whom it established trade and other links to launch a process of ever-growing interconnectedness and interdependence, termed today as "globalization."[16] The long vegetation and climate belts that roughly stretch in the east–west direction benefited early doctors, philosophers, scientists, agriculturalists, and settlers, allowing people to disseminate knowledge and bring in new techniques from other regions. In this way, technology diffused faster and farther. Specialization based on local resources gave rise to active trade across the entire space.

Alexander's march across Persia; the Moghul invasion of northern India; the spread of Buddhism throughout East and Southeast Asia from India; the Central Asian hordes that colonized large parts of the continent; the spread of Islamic law and customs on the Arabian peninsula, in North Africa, and throughout Central Asia up to Southern Russia; and the Cossacks and Tartars who brought grain and timber down the Volga to Central and South Asia—these are only a few examples of borderless exchange. Adjacent regions prospered thanks to the geographical advantages they shared.

Interestingly, the two giants, India and China, had traded with each other as early as in 680 BC, first by establishing a sea route and then a land route across the Himalayas. China absorbed Indian ideas and concepts for many centuries, inspired by Xuenzhang's travels to India under the Tang dynasty in the seventh century. Confucianism and Taoism both were stimulated by Buddhist religious thought and Hindu scriptures and mythology (e.g., Rig Veda, Upanishads). During the three or four centuries preceding the Christian era, Hindu dynasties established their rule over most territories stretching from northern India, Burma, Siam, Laos, and reaching to southeastern China. The ancient Hindu Sanskrit and Pali languages were used in official documents and inscriptions. Temples and other monuments were built after the Hindu style, while Brahmana priests were employed for propitiatory ceremonies. The introduction of Buddhism is considered as one of the most important events in Chinese history and since its inception a major factor shaping Chinese civilization, including art, philosophy, literature, and medicine. Many precious goods such as gems, pearls, diamonds, cloth, spices, and tea also came from India, while China sent back silk, porcelain, furs, and other luxury articles. In addition to several land routes, there were two sea routes functioning regularly between India and China. Whereas India continued to adopt policies of free trade along major sea routes, edicts in China reversed the policy of imperial fleets.[17]

The steppe regions in the midst of the continent long remained inhabited by mounted nomads, who from the central steppes could reach all areas of the Asian continent. The

---

16. Nayan Chanda, *Bound Together: How Traders, Preachers, Adventurers and Warriors Shaped Globalization* (Caravan, 2007).
17. Zeng He's and Ma Huan's naval expeditions from Malacca to Malabar on imperial fleets were abruptly ended in the AD 1440s. See Gordon, *When Asia Was the World*, 117–135.

earliest known such expansion out of the steppes is that of the Indo-Europeans toward 2000 BC who spread their languages and customs into the Indus valley, Middle East, Europe, and to the borders of China. Asia's three coastal regions (East and Southeast Asia, South Asia, Middle East) evolved in a similar manner as the interior regions, with each of them developing early civilizations around fertile river valleys. The civilizations of Mesopotamia, the Indus Valley, and the Yellow and Yangtze rivers in China shared many similarities and very likely exchanged technologies and ideas such as mathematics, the compass, and the wheel. Ancient Egypt also shared this model.

Compared with Europe, the small western appendix of the continent, Asia's mega regions have few obstructions internally, even though they are ringed by mountains and deserts. This meant that it was far easier to establish unified control over huge territories, and this did occur with massive empires permanently dominating Russia, the Middle East, China, and much of India. Conversely, Europe has always been riddled with internal mountain ranges—the Carpathians, the Alps, the Pyrenees, and many others—which favored the survival of local dialects and customs. Throughout its history, Europe was divided into many smaller states with their own cultural peculiarities, food habits, and languages. This very specific trait has impacted social organization and business behavior until modern days, even though political efforts continue to be made to push forward economic integration by establishing a unified market backed by a common currency. Thus, Europe (especially its core region comprising today's Germany, Central Europe, and Scandinavia) remained isolated and comparatively undeveloped, with only its southern tips, namely Greece and Italy, being able to borrow technologies and ideas from the Eurasian continent via Middle Eastern and North African trade routes.

Europe caught up on Eurasian developments and inventions during the Iron Age, which made large stands of timber essential to a nation's success because smelting iron required much fuel, and the centers of human civilizations gradually moved as forests were destroyed. The Mediterranean region, the apex of European civilization until the eighth century, was gradually supplanted by the German and Frankish lands, which became dominant. In the Middle East, the main power center became Anatolia with the once dominant Mesopotamia its vassal. In China, the economical, agricultural, and industrial center moved from the northern Yellow River to the southern Yangtze, though the political center remained in the north. In part, this is linked to technological developments, such as the moldboard plow, that opened up once marginal areas for food production.

Eurasian civilizations developed in parallel, always receiving inspiration from one another. Religion and culture played a fundamental role in determining in many ways economic and technological advancement, but also in the intensity of exchange between regions. Religious and ethnic *diasporas* formed important minorities, which could be used by countries as cultural bridges to promote trade and technological exchange. Whenever a civilization attempted to oppress its minorities, which acted as "door openers" to the other culture, and isolated itself from the others, it fell behind in terms of technological progress. China, which was the origin of many inventions such as the compass, gunpowder, and ink, could not reap immediate benefits. Following Emperor Xuande's (Ming dynasty) decision in the early fifteenth century to stop funding shipbuilding for exploratory missions, the country decided to pursue an isolationist course for fear of being infected by developments in other parts of the world that were considered less civilized. By cutting its trade links with other Eurasian powers for many centuries, China fell technologically behind rival economies. It took China six centuries to recover from economic stagnation and foreign domination, both consequences of self-centered policies.

Like other civilizations on the Eurasian continent, China succumbed to the rule of conquests with the concomitant intermingling of races, which also had a stabilizing effect as it led to cultural revival. When the Qing (Manchu warriors from the north) wrested power from the Ming government in 1644, the country was in a state of economic decline and social decadence. To reinforce control of their newly minted, multi-ethnic realm, the Qing rulers commissioned spectacular and highly diverse art, inviting sculptors, painters, and poets to produce wonderful treasures which can still be admired today. Instead of destroying the Chinese culture, they embraced it, learning Chinese, moving into the Forbidden City, maintaining its Confucian bureaucracy, and accepting the various Buddhist denominations throughout the empire. China reached its widest geographic spread under Qing rule, which however resisted foreign influence and exchange albeit increasingly unsuccessfully.

A fateful turning point for China was the Opium War (1839–1842), caused by the Qing government's attempt to suppress the long-established but locally illegal importation of Indian-grown opium organized by the British East India Company. China's eventual defeat enabled consolidation of the British presence in Hong Kong and in time the forced opening of more and more Chinese ports to foreign trade and military presence. A disastrous series of foreign wars and internal rebellions lasting for more than a century led to the fall of the dynasty in 1912, Japan's annexation of Manchuria in 1932, and the proclamation of the People's Republic in 1949. Only after political messianism had burnt itself out in the cultural revolution of the late 1960s was it possible for China to start normalizing its relations with the rest of the world. Deng Xiaoping's announcement of the "Four Modernizations" in 1978 subsequently opened the door to foreign involvement on more equitable terms in the Chinese economy, which has since been propelled to the highest levels in the country's modern history.

Incidentally, the Opium War had a no less profound effect on India, the source of the opium. The opium trade in fact accounted for 11% of the Indian balance of payments in 1858–1859, when the British government abolished the East India Company and assumed direct rule of the subcontinent. The trade remained important well into the twentieth century and was a key factor in maintaining the British Raj. A further indirect consequence was that the energies of native-born elites were substantially diverted from entrepreneurship to the struggle for independence and freedom from British capitalism. After independence was achieved in 1947, ideas of national self-sufficiency and socialist planning influenced economic policy for a long time. Only in the last two decades has there been movement away from the "permit raj" and a genuine opening-up to all comers, again as in China with dramatic effects on economic growth.

Japan had equally long remained in isolation during the period of the Tokugawa shoguns (1603–1867). Ocean-going shipping had been prohibited, and foreign contact was limited to modest activity by Chinese traders and annual visits by the Dutch to an island off

Nagasaki. This maritime embargo was finally broken by the Americans, and Commodore Perry's arrival in 1853 provided the catalyst for the political revolution, social modernization, and economic transformation known as the Meiji Restoration (1868–1912).

Russia represents yet another variation on the theme of isolation versus openness. From earliest times, three great rivers—the Dnepr, the Don, and the Volga—helped shape the Slavic heartland of what became Russia. Cultural and economic diffusion initially spread northwards from the ancient Greek colonies on the Black Sea and later from Byzantium. Eventually, however, a powerful drive came down from the far north in Scandinavia with the arrival of warriors who founded the first Russian principalities. A sharp discontinuity in the political and economic development of these early states occurred in the thirteenth century with successive invasions by Mongols and Tatars, to whom Russian rulers were obliged to pay tribute for more than three hundred years. A further shock was the fall of Byzantium to the Turks in 1453. This broke the land link that Russia had provided between the Orient and Western Europe.

The chief items in Russia's trade with Western Europe had traditionally been oriental luxury goods shipped along the great rivers and furs and forest products from Russia itself. By the sixteenth century, the oriental trade became mostly seaborne in Portuguese, Dutch, and British vessels, so avoiding the problematic land routes. By that time, a Russian state ruled by a tsar in Moscow had overcome the remnants of the Golden Horde and was dealing extensively with the West in furs and primary products. The Russian economy was, however, quite unlike its Western counterparts. One legacy of Mongol overlordship was the persistence, indeed intensification, of serfdom, which was not to be dismantled (partially) until 1861. Another legacy was an abiding suspicion of foreigners. The comparative absence from trade of even simple manufactured products was likewise no accident. Although European, Russia, defined to the east by the Ural Mountains, did not lack mineral resources, though these were poorly distributed—e.g., coal was seldom close to iron ore. Efforts at exploitation, sometimes with foreign help as in the reign of Peter the Great (1672–1725), were only modestly successful. Russia's first industrial revolution had in fact to wait until late in the nineteenth century when after the shock of defeat in the Crimean War and with pressure from a rapidly rising population—doubling in fifty years to more than 160 million in 1910—economic modernization was urgently necessary. Fears of revolution at home and military humiliation abroad were even strong enough to allow substantial foreign participation in this development.

At its peak when Witte, a German called to the court, was imperial finance minister (1893–1903), industrial output was increasing by an average of 8% a year, compared to 3% a year in earlier periods. By 1900, there were 269 foreign-owned joint-stock companies in Russia, accounting for about half of all joint-stock company investment in the country. Whether or not such dramatic changes in the size and ownership of the Russian economy were ultimately sustainable, war and revolution actually put an abrupt end to them. When large-scale economic development re-started in the late 1920s, it was under the very different circumstances of "socialism in one country." Only after the momentum of the Soviet economy began to falter in the 1970s, and lasting economic reform proved impossible to achieve within a collectivist framework in the 1980s, would the opportunity return, in the 1990s, for foreign trade, inward investment, and intercontinental transport to resume in a genuinely open way.

Corporate executives need to keep this historic perspective in mind to be able to transcend cultural and ethnic divides imposed by today's nation-states. Kyrgyzstani author Tschingis Aitmatow[18] commented, "Nowadays there is so much talk of globalization, but it is not a new idea. The Silk Road linked countries and cultures many hundreds of years ago. The revived Eurasia, connecting Europe and Asia, existed back then; now it is a case of putting a whole region back on the map. The Silk Road is returning to the consciousness of tourists, traders, and investors; it must and will again become a bridge between people."[19]

The recent North–South Corridor Agreement signed between India, Iran, and Russia for establishing a transport link is yet another instance of how a new corridor follows an ancient route. Only the merchandise has changed as grain and furs have given way to oil, machinery, and consumer goods. It took four centuries to rediscover that this old trade route reduced the distance from 16,000 kilometers via the Suez Canal and the Mediterranean Sea to 6,250 kilometers. It will cut transport time by at least ten to twelve days and cut transport costs by about 15%–20%. Several other projects are under way to create large free trade corridors along ancient routes between the eastern and western parts of Eurasia.[20]

In the very north, the expansion of the Trans-Siberian and Yamal railways—along the routes used by the Cossacks—will eventually lead to improvement of logistics across the continent and cut container handling and transport time. Further south, but still north of the Silk Road, China and Kazakhstan decided to establish a pipeline corridor that will connect the oil and gas fields of Central Asia with the boomtowns of China's east coast. Energy pipelines will also connect Siberia with Japan, the Koreas, and Northern China from Russia. Germany's then-chancellor Schroeder signed an agreement with Russia's then-president Putin in October 2005 to build a direct gas pipeline across the Baltic Sea, which will make both countries less dependent on transit countries (the Baltic states, Poland, Belarus, Ukraine). Further west, India will expand its communication and energy links with Middle Eastern economies, from which it gets most of its fossil fuels.

Horse-track caravans, the main means of overland transport in earlier days, have been replaced by cars, trains, and planes, enabling businesspeople to cover distances much faster and with less effort. Infrastructure will see huge improvements, enabling the megamarkets to extend cooperation between them and other nations. Transcontinental fast-speed trains and modern motorways are going to connect China, India, and Russia to the EU, which in the last ten years has extended to the western borders of Russian territory through the accessions of Finland and the three Baltic states of Estonia, Latvia, and Lithuania. As in former days, when the Silk Road and other trade routes represented vital arteries for

---

18. Interview with ZDF television, Germany, February 2007.
19. The TRACECA (Transport Corridor Europe Caucasus Asia) project of the EU aims to assist countries in the region in developing a transport corridor on a west–east axis from Europe, across the Black Sea, and through the Caucasus and the Caspian Sea to Central Asia.
20. See 4.1 (energy) and 4.3 (infrastructure) for examples of projects linking the countries of Eurasia.

Figure 1.7. Silk Road and major Eurasian trade links (200 BC to AD 1600).

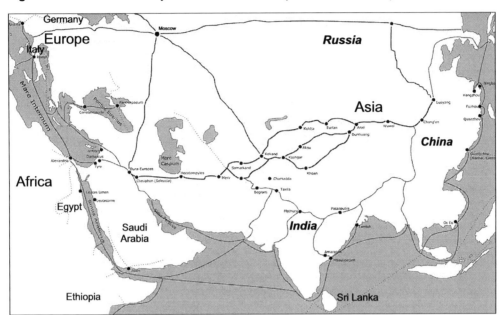

connecting foreign lands (see figure 1.7), today's opening of borders between nations bears the unique opportunity to launch a new era of international relations based on cooperation, mutual respect, understanding, and trust, not on misrepresentation and confrontation.

1.3. Eurasia's regional groupings

Over the centuries, civilizations on the Eurasian continent have grown more interdependent. The twentieth century has seen countries coming closer in collaborative arrangements, putting behind them the conflicts that shaped their identities. Trade—movement of goods—continued despite these upheavals. There had always been movement of people, from even before the westward and southward spread of the Indo-Europeans from Central Eurasia in 4000 BC. In the last century, it was manifested in colonization and immigration. Movement of capital is more recent, the vehicle being investments by transnationals and financial institutions away from their home markets.

Today, nation-states across Eurasia are coming together to form or intensify regional groupings (EU, ASEAN, SAARC, GCC, and others), to which those outside the group are often invited as observers (see table 1.3). These groupings are usually constituted for economic reasons to reduce trade barriers and ease investment; in most cases, they strive for political cooperation and may promote interregional projects of cultural and technological exchange. Ultimate political integration is the highest aim, whereas simple free trade areas and customs unions represent the lowest degree of integration.

Europe has gone farthest and deepest in economic integration by uniting almost all the economies of Western, Southern, and Eastern Europe. Other countries further south, including Turkey, are seeking membership. What started as the European Coal and

Table 1.3. Eurasia's regional groupings, 2008.

Geographic dimension	Economic, political grouping	Member countries
Western, Southern, Eastern Europe	European Union	Austria, Belgium, Bulgaria, Cyprus, Czech Republic, Denmark, Estonia, Finland, France, Germany, Greece, Hungary, Ireland, Italy, Latvia, Lithuania, Luxembourg, Malta, The Netherlands, Poland, Portugal, Romania, Slovakia, Slovenia, Spain, Sweden, UK
Southeastern Europe (Balkans)	Application for EU membership	Croatia, Macedonia (ex-Yugoslavia), Turkey
South Asia	South Asian Association for Regional Cooperation (SAARC)	Bangladesh, Bhutan, India, Maldives, Nepal, Pakistan, Sri Lanka
Indian Ocean	Indian Ocean Rim Association for Regional Cooperation (IOR-ARC)	Australia, Bangladesh, India, Indonesia, Iran, Kenya, Madagascar, Malaysia, Mauritius, Mozambique, Oman, Singapore, South Africa, Sri Lanka, Tanzania, Thailand, UAE, Yemen Dialogue partners: China, Egypt, France, Japan, UK
West Asia, North Africa	Organization of Arab Petroleum Exporting Countries (OAPEC)	Algeria, Bahrain, Egypt, Iraq, Kuwait, Libya, Qatar, Saudi Arabia, Syria, Tunisia, UAE
	Gulf Cooperation Council (GCC)	Bahrain, Kuwait, Oman, Qatar, Saudi Arabia, UAE
Central Asia	Commonwealth of Independent States (CIS)	Armenia, Azerbaijan, Belarus, Georgia, Kazakhstan, Kyrgyzstan, Moldova, Russia, Tajikistan, Turkmenistan, Ukraine, Uzbekistan
Central Asia	Economic Cooperation Organization	Afghanistan, Azerbaijan, Iran, Kazakhstan, Kyrgyzstan, Pakistan, Tajikistan, Turkey, Turkmenistan, Uzbekistan
East and Central Asia	Shanghai Cooperation Council (SOC)	Founding members: China, Kazakhstan, Kirghizstan, Russia, Tajikistan, Uzbekistan Observers: India, Iran, Pakistan
Southeast Asia	Association of Southeast Asian Nations (ASEAN)	Founding members: Indonesia, Malaysia, Philippines, Singapore, Thailand Subsequent members: Brunei Darussalam, Cambodia, Laos, Myanmar, Viet Nam
Asia Pacific	Asia Pacific Economic Cooperation (APEC)	Australia, Brunei Darussalam, Canada, Chile, China, Indonesia, Japan, Korea, Malaysia, Mexico, New Zealand, Papua New Guinea, Peru, Philippines, Russia, Singapore, Chinese Taipei, Thailand, USA, Viet Nam

Steel Community of six nations in 1951 has become a union of twenty-seven nations in 2007, with coalescing economic, foreign, and defense policies, a parliament and other institutions, and a common currency for a growing number of member states. The EU represents a model of genuine regional integration that is still focused on Europe but already being emulated by others. To reduce the gap in wealth, institutions, and good governance, North African nations, for example, pushed for a "Mediterranean Union" with the EU and found France, Portugal, and Spain as active promoters of the project.[21]

Asia is following a similar path, but its geographic immensity and different cultures, peoples, and political systems have so far not allowed it to go beyond the creation of regional free-trade zones to be followed by customs unions in a few years (ASEAN, GCC). Gulf countries are front-runners and have so far got closest to the EU's integration efforts.

---

21. See www.ec.europa.eu/external_relations/euromed and José Ignacio Torreblanca, "Barcelona Process. Mediterranean Union: Rhetoric vs. Reality," *El País,* July 15, 2008.

Rising oil prices allow them to invest in energy, railway, and water linkages. In June 2008, the central bank governors from the five Gulf nations approved a draft monetary union treaty aimed at introducing a common currency by 2010 and creating a single central bank, which will set monetary policy such as interest or foreign exchange rates.[22] To strengthen unity, the Gulf Cooperation Council (GCC) will introduce a unified identity card for its 40 million Gulf nationals and extend social security for GCC citizens working outside their countries.

Discussions about EU enlargement toward the east (e.g., Ukraine) and southeast (e.g., Croatia, Montenegro, Serbia), and greater cooperation within and between regional groupings (e.g., EU–ASEAN, EU–CIS), is a signal that the Eurasian continent is moving toward closer integration. Not only will the regional groupings benefit from this trend, but also individual nation-states. Significantly, political tensions and military conflicts on the Eurasian continent are concentrated in those countries that are disconnected from economic and political groupings (e.g., Iran, Iraq, Afghanistan, North Korea) and are thus deprived of a support network. Thus, smaller countries gravitate around the three large ones (China, India, and Russia)—just as in the EU—which enables them to better voice their concerns and negotiate trade, investment, and financial deals.

By forming regional groupings, the major economies of Eurasia are growing into a true multilateral entity, which, even if not formally united, already forms a political counterweight to the United States in international forums and organizations. Western Europe will need the support of its Eurasian neighbors, whether as individual countries or through regional groupings, to secure raw materials and energy supplies (highlighted by the regularly occurring disputes between Ukraine and Russia over gas prices). It will also need them as outlets for European technologies, products, and services and as a main driver of breakthrough environmental practices as envisaged by the Kyoto protocol, to which all Eurasian powers adhered, whereas the US government led by then-President Bush rejected this concept of reduction of carbon dioxide emissions because of concerns with declining competitiveness of US TNCs. The driving force behind the search for new partnerships is the need for higher returns by EU companies.

The need for cooperation has never been so great on the Eurasian continent. Eurasia's emerging economies offer new markets and competitive companies, while Europe has the required skills and process know-how to help these economies reach higher levels of development even faster. This win-win situation triggered by business will have repercussions across the whole continent as well as in other world regions (e.g., Latin America,[23] Africa), and will eventually benefit the same enterprises as harbingers of new ideas. Eurasia's diverse civilizations and cultures should be viewed as enrichment and a strength rather than a risk or barrier. The European Union is a fine example of how different nations can unite to form a stronger and larger entity. Just as European companies

---

22. "Five Gulf Nations Move Closer to Common Currency," *The Wall Street Journal,* June 12, 2008.
23. Latin American countries are intensifying their efforts to gain more autonomy from the "Washington Twins"—World Bank and IMF—which are held responsible for current economic ills on the continent. The proposal of Venezuela's President Chavez to launch the Banco del Sur, a development bank for important Latin American projects, was hailed across the whole region. See "Can the Banco del Sur Fulfil Chavez's Dream," *The Hindu Business Line,* December 15, 2007.

learned to move from their home country to a wider European space, they now stand to gain in an enlarged Eurasian context.

The challenge for enterprises lies in spotting chances so that the increased interdependence of Eurasian nations through greater movement of goods, capital, and people can be turned to their competitive advantage. To achieve this, owners and managers must find answers to four important questions:

1. What are the main drivers of industrial growth and technological progress in the rising star economies of Eurasia, and how can Western companies benefit?
2. What does an overt Eurasia as a new geoeconomic reality imply in terms of corporate strategy?
3. What are the specific intelligence and operational dimensions that Western enterprises must master in Eurasia as opposed to the Americas, Europe, Japan, or Australia, where strategies can be based on fairly stable environments and developed information sources?
4. Why can export-led strategies in the long term not be a substitute to consistent FDI-led moves starting with the megamarkets and implying strong local performance for later positioning of products, brands, and services also in surrounding emerging economies?

These issues will be discussed in detail in the following chapters.

CHAPTER 2
Eurasia's megamarkets as wealth generators

Since the early 1990s, Eurasia's three megamarkets have continued to report improved macro indicators despite initial skepticism and criticism about their chosen path in Western capitals. With hindsight, these countries have not only lived up to their role as regional stability anchors, but they have exceeded all expectations, making them undisputed candidates as future economic powers.

This chapter gives a bird's-eye view of megamarket achievements in three focal areas:
- macro economics: growth of national product, employment, tax revenue, and foreign reserves;
- spending power: expansion of middle class, rise in the number of high-net-worth individuals, wealth spillover from cities to the countryside;
- global integration via foreign trade, FDI, and capital markets.

2.1. Economic performance

2.1.1. GDP and growth prospects

The list of the world's largest economies already shows a reshuffling in the rankings, which will be accentuated by the contraction in advanced economies during 2008–2010 as a result of the global financial crisis. For GDP in purchasing power parity (PPP), China will overtake the United States to take the first position;[1] India will overtake Japan; and Russia will overtake Italy, France, and the United Kingdom (see table 2.1). It is estimated that the combined share of the three megamarkets in GDP of the world's top fourteen economies will reach 42% in 2020, up from 24% in 2005. The figures do not include the unrecorded informal or "black" economy, which can add anywhere between 10% and 40% to total personal expenditure and GDP, depending on the business environment and tax laws in each country.

Although China and India will move up the ranking in absolute GDP,[2] their per capita GDP will remain significantly lower than in the advanced economies,[3] given their large

---

1. In the US-dollar-dominated market exchange rate, the United States retains its first position.
2. China became the world's third largest economy in 2007; its GDP was US$3.5 billion surpassing that of Germany (US$3.3 billion) at 2007 exchange rates. At this speed, it will take another three to four years for China to overtake Japan as the second largest economy.
3. As an example, Germany's per capita GDP (nominal), at US$44,660 (2008), is still far ahead of China's (US$3,315).

Table 2.1. The world's largest economies by 2020.

GDP in PPP (US$ trillions)			Country	GDP at market exchange rates (US$ trillions)		
Rank 2020 (rank 2008)	2020[a]	2008[b]		2008[a]	2020[b]	Rank 2020 (rank 2008)
1 (2)	29.5	7.9	China	4.4	10.1	2 (3)
2 (1)	28.8	14.3	USA	14.3	28.8	1 (1)
3 (4)	13.3	3.3	India	1.2	3.2	7 (12)
4 (3)	6.7	4.4	Japan	4.9	6.9	3 (2)
5 (5)	4.8	2.9	Germany	3.7	5.0	4 (4)
6 (6)	4.1	2.3	Russia	1.7	2.7	8 (8)
7 (8)	3.8	2.1	France	2.9	3.5	6 (5)
8 (9)	3.8	2.0	Brazil	1.6	1.6	13 (10)
9 (7)	3.7	2.2	UK	2.7	4.2	5 (6)
10 (10)	2.8	1.8	Italy	2.3	2.5	10 (7)
11 (13)	2.8	1.3	S Korea	1.0	2.6	9 (14)
12 (11)	2.5	1.5	Mexico	1.1	1.5	14 (13)
13 (12)	2.4	1.4	Spain	1.6	2.1	12 (9)
14 (14)	2.4	1.3	Canada	1.5	2.2	11 (11)
	111.4	69.0	Total	60.7	76.9	

Sources: Based on (a) Economist Intelligence Unit. Foresight 2020: Economic, Industry and Corporate Trends; (b) International Monetary Fund. World Economic Outlook, April 2009.

populations which together account for one-third of the world's total. At the same time, both GDP and per capita GDP will grow fastest in the three Eurasian megamarkets as well as in Brazil and Mexico (see table 2.2), signifying extended opportunities for expansion for EU companies. Growth in the megamarkets will be driven by rising incomes, mass consumption, demographic dividends, and investment-friendly policies of central and regional governments.

Table 2.2. Emerging megamarkets continue to grow, 2006–2020.

Country	Expected annual GDP growth (%)	
	2006–2010	2011–2020
China	7.8	6.1
India	6.6	6.5
Russia	5.7	5.6
Brazil	3.9	3.2
Mexico	2.8	3.0
USA	2.5	2.8
Japan	1.1	0.5
Germany	1.8	1.9
UK	2.1	2.2
France	2.0	1.8
Italy	1.5	0.8

Sources: Based on Economist Intelligence Unit. Foresight 2020.

It is interesting to see the differences in distribution of GDP in the macro sectors of the major economies (see table 2.3). Elsewhere than in the billion-population countries of China and India, agriculture contributes little to GDP. The transition from industry to services is most pronounced for the advanced economies and to a lesser extent in Brazil and Russia. China and South Korea are the only two among the major economies where industry still accounts for more than 45% of GDP. The advanced economies are characterized by a high services component, which contributes 65%–75% to GDP. India is the only emerging market that has bucked the trend as it has leapfrogged to services; its already self-sufficient industry is now viewed as an alternative FDI destination to China. Rising local demand in the megamarkets will continue to support industry well beyond 2020, and companies from advanced markets will continue to relocate production in search of new markets, lower costs, and raw materials. These trends are supported by government policies to create jobs in the industrial and satellite service sectors. Eventually, a strong industrial base coupled with entrepreneurship will make megamarket companies important partners for the rest of the world.

2.1.2. Tax revenue and foreign reserves

Table 2.3. Share of macro sectors in GDP, 2007 (%).

Country	Agriculture	Industry	Services
Brazil	8	38	54
Canada	3	29	68
China	12	48	40
France	3	20	77
Germany	1	29	70
India	19	21	60
Italy	2	29	69
Japan	1	26	73
South Korea	3	45	52
Mexico	5	25	70
Russia	5	37	58
Spain	3	28	69
UK	1	25	74
USA	1	20	78

Sources: Based on national accounts, OECD, and CIA World Factbook.

Since the early 2000s, farsighted policies emphasizing export growth, FDI promotion, and fiscal restraint have enabled megamarket governments to improve public finances and accumulate record levels of foreign reserves. At the beginning of 2007, China became the first country ever with reserves reaching US$1 trillion (US$1,000 billion), making it the largest foreign currency reserve holder in the world. In 2008, China's reserves have swollen to a staggering level of US$1.5 trillion. Russia's reserves surpassed the US$600 billion mark and India's the US$350 billion mark (see figure 2.1). Russia used part of its reserves to pay back its foreign loans, which it inherited from the Soviet Union, through a deal hammered out between former president Boris Yeltsin and the G7 nations. These loans, which still stood at US$120 billion in 2005, were entirely reimbursed to the Paris (governments) and London (banks) Clubs in 2006. The foreign reserves of Eurasia's new megamarkets, including both foreign currency and gold holdings, will continue to rise

Figure 2.1. Countries with the largest foreign reserves, 2009 (US$ bn).

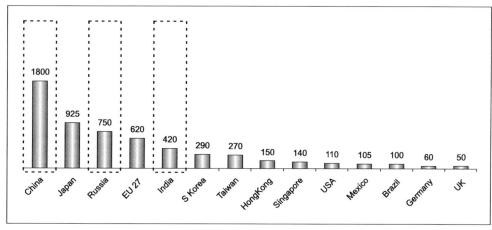

Source: Based on BIS, Bank of International Settlements Economic press

during the next decade, thus radically improving these countries' economic and political bargaining power vis-à-vis advanced and other world economies.

Economists know that future exchange rates of the world's leading currencies will not only reflect economic realities but also the monetary policies of the central banks of Eurasia's megaeconomies, which will try to focus more than ever before on removing imbalances in the global financial system by reducing their dollar assets and strengthening their own currencies as regional anchors. Assuming that market forces are allowed to prevail, such exceptionally high growth rates and rising foreign reserves will cause the megamarkets' national currencies (ruble[4], renminbi, rupee) to appreciate significantly, making it easier for companies from the megamarkets to acquire assets abroad while at the same time increasing the costs of inward FDI for foreign companies. Megamarket governments are inclined to encourage the use of their national currencies in international transactions within their respective regional blocs (e.g., Russia-CIS, India-SAARC, China-ASEAN). They also favor a mix of open capital markets and regulations to avoid speculative runs on currencies, withdrawals, or financial turmoil like the one experienced by Wall Street in September 2008.

Thanks to judicious economic management, tax revenues increased in all categories (income, corporate, value-added tax, customs, and excise) in the three countries. China's and India's tax revenues have grown 20%–30% annually since 2000 mainly because of continued economic growth and better tax collection (e.g., stricter control on tax evasion and easier collection measures). In the first half of 2008, China's tax authorities collected a record US$480 billion (+30.5% year-on-year). Such fast growth of tax revenues will give the Chinese government ample room to maneuver if a US-led global slowdown poses threats of derailing China's economic growth. Fiscal stimuli in the form of infrastructure investment, social measures, and agricultural subsidies could effectively keep long-term growth at around 10%.[5] When Russia introduced its flat tax rate of 13% on personal income in 2001,[6] tax revenue increased 28% in the first year and on average 20% annually thereafter. This model has inspired other eastern European countries such as Estonia, Slovakia, and Romania, where tax rates below 20% have also yielded high tax revenue. Inspired by Russia's success stories, several delegations of German tax experts have been touring the country during 2007–2008.

The surge in tax revenue helps to keep fiscal deficits under control: Russia recorded an average annual budget surplus of 4.5% during 2003–2008. In 2007 and 2008, high oil revenues pushed Russia's surplus above 6% of GDP[7], while India and China neared the deficit target of 3%, which is the benchmark imposed by the European Central

---

4. At first sight, Russia looks like an exception. In late 2008, Russia's Central Bank allowed the ruble to depreciate as declining oil prices started eroding the country's current account. In the long term, higher energy prices will bolster the ruble, which will benefit additionally from the government's push toward a modern and diversified economy in order to reduce energy dependence.
5. "Buoyant Tax Growth," *China Daily*, July 25, 2008.
6. Corporate tax in Russia now stands at 20% following the most recent amanedment to the tax code which was introduced on 26 November 2008.
7. Record low oil prices of US$ 40–45 a barrel at the end of 2008 put a damper on Russia's plans to maintain a high budget surplus, which will probably decrease by 2–3 percentage points until the end of 2009 when oil prices are expected to rise again.

Bank (ECB) on EU member states (see figure 2.2). If profits of state-owned enterprises were added in, China's finances would look even healthier—the country would report a surplus of around 3% of GDP.[8] This performance is better than in most of the twenty-seven EU member states, which report deficits hovering around 4%–5% or higher (including France, Germany, and Italy). In 2008, the US deficit attained a staggering record of almost half a trillion US dollars (US$490 billion), putting the country's indebtedness above 4%. By 2010, the US budget deficit could easily exceed 6% following the US$700–900 billion financial bailout package initiated by the US government in October 2008.

Apart from its constant surpluses, Russia disposes of growing reserves in its stabilization fund (US$185 billion by mid-2008), which is fed by extra tax revenues derived

Figure 2.2. State budget in major economies, 2005–2008.

	2005	2006	2007	2008
China	-5.0%	-4.5%	-2.5%	-1.0%
India	-7.0%	-4.6%	-4.0%	-3.5%
Russia	+8.0%	+6.4%	+4.8%	+5.5%
Canada	+2.0%	+1.5%	+1.0%	+0.5%
USA	-4.0%	-3.5%	-3.5%	-4.0%
Japan	-5.0%	-4.0%	-3.8%	-3.5%
Germany	-4.0%	-3.5%	-2.0%	-2.0%
France	-3.0%	-3.0%	-2.5%	-2.3%
UK	-3.0%	-2.8%	-3.0%	-3.5%
Italy	-4.0%	-3.5%	-1.8%	-2.0%

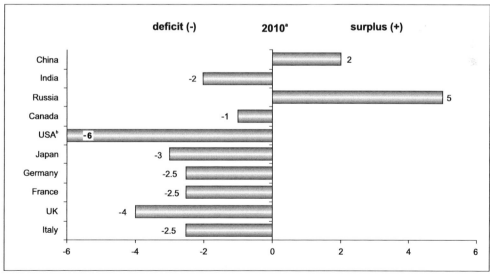

2010[a] deficit (-) / surplus (+)

- China: 2
- India: -2
- Russia: 5
- Canada: -1
- USA[b]: -6
- Japan: -3
- Germany: -2.5
- France: -2.5
- UK: -4
- Italy: -2.5

a. Estimate.
b. Following financial bailout decided by US Government end 2008.

Source: OECD, based on national statistics.

---

8. "Asian Budget Finances," *The Economist*, February 16, 2008, 72.

Figure 2.3. Tax revenue of major economies as share of GDP, 2007.

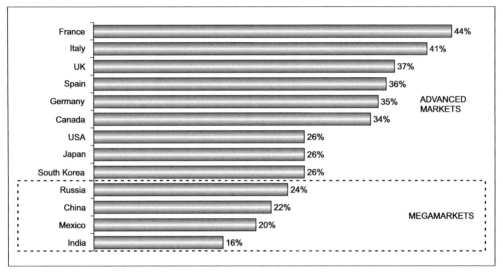

Source: Based on data derived from OECD and national statistical offices.

from energy exports.[9] The proportion of tax revenue with respect to GDP is highest in European countries but similarly structured in the United States and the three emerging megamarkets. While fiscal policy in the United States traditionally favors entrepreneurship (tax/GDP ratio of 25%), the low ratio in the megamarkets (15%–20%) reflects the political choice not to overtax businesses (which have become the new symbol of national pride) but probably also an inherent weakness in the national collection system (see figure 2.3), which means that tax revenue could be still higher. At the other extreme, the EU welfare system (tax/GDP ratio of 35%–44%) with its rigid compliance mechanisms for business is definitely not considered a sustainable model for growth by megamarket governments.

Table 2.4. New job creations by world region, 2007–2020.

	Number (mn)	Percent of world net increase
Asia (excluding Japan and South Korea), of which:	315.5	67.0
– China	**65.0**	**13.8**
– India	**132.4**	**30.2**
Latin America	45.0	9.5
USA	12.5	2.6
EU	8.4	1.8
Others	89.9	19.1
Total	471.3	100.0

Sources: EIU, Foresight 2020.

2.1.3. Employment and labor costs

The transfer of jobs from advanced economies to the emerging markets will continue in both industry and services. Asia will account for two-thirds of job creation in the world over the next fifteen years. With 130 million new jobs, India will be the biggest beneficiary with 30% of the net increase in global employment. By 2020, the EU will have absorbed only 8.5 million new jobs—i.e., 1.8% of the world total (see table 2.4).

---

9. This "reserve cushion" proves to be very valuable as it enables the Russian government to intervene effectively in case of an economic slowdown, for example, when in late 2008 the first shockwaves of the financial crisis were being felt. The stabilization fund today represents about 15% of GDP; the government's medium-term target is to raise this level to 50% of GDP.

The entry of the emerging economies into the global arena will put additional pressure on wages across the EU despite concessions by trade unions on salary freezes, longer working hours, and later retirement. Already, a decreasing workforce has to bear much higher social costs and finance the growing number of aged people and jobless who will together represent 35%–40% of the adult population in the EU. Conversely, each year China adds around 25 million and India another 20 million young professionals to its existing workforce, which taken together is almost equivalent to the existing workforce of a country like Germany. The rising number of people joining the workforce compels megamarket governments to adopt business-friendly investment and labor laws to keep unemployment below the 5% ceiling, which is half the EU average (see figure 2.4).

Although the demand for professionals has raised wages in the three megamarkets, they still lag behind those in the advanced markets (see table 2.5). At the top end, however,

Figure 2.4. Unemployment in major economies, 2007.

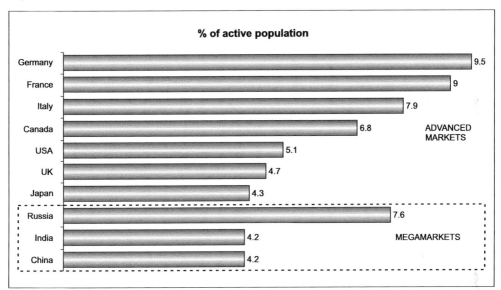

Source: CIA World Fact Book, ILO.

Table 2.5. Wages by specialization in selected AMs and EMs, 2007 (US$/hour).

Country	Worker	Engineer	Accountant	Middle manager	Top manager
Bulgaria	0.7	1.4	0.8	2.8	9
China	0.5	1.2	1.2	2.5	7
Czech Rep.	2.8	5.4	4.1	6.8	10
Germany	18.8	38.9	26.4	40.4	75
Hungary	2.0	5.1	4.6	7.4	10
India	0.3	0.9	0.7	2.1	8
Poland	3.0	4.3	4.0	6.7	10
Romania	1.4	2.6	1.2	3.2	6
Russia	1.2	1.4	1.5	2.9	13
USA	10.0	18.0	22.0	27.0	86

Source: Business Week. December 19, 2007.

CEO salaries in the megamarkets have been accelerating due to rising profits in the private sector. CEOs of top Indian companies take home 0.027% of overall managerial revenues compared with 0.007% by the top twenty global company heads. Chinese, Indian, and Russian executives of large corporations have joined the ranks of the world's highest paid managers. After long spells of high earnings, some megamarket companies can now afford to employ expatriates, which was unimaginable a decade ago.

2.2. A rising consumer class

2.2.1. Income groups and spending power

A major achievement of India and China is that these once developing countries have succeeded in reigning in and reducing absolute poverty. Between 1985 and 2005, over 103 million people in India and 162 million in China moved above the poverty line (US$1 per inhabitant per day). Poverty alleviation is not a significant issue any longer in Russia, where less than 10% of the population falls into this category. Household incomes have risen dramatically, giving rise to the widely reported, increasingly noticeable "middle class." Total urban household income in China has increased almost tenfold from RMB525 billion in 1985 to above RMB6500 billion in 2007. In India, total aggregate household disposable income has risen threefold from INR7,500 billion to INR28,500 billion during the same period. In Russia, disposable income increased almost threefold between 2001 and 2007 to reach US$700 billion in 2007. At 87%, Russia has the highest ratio of absolute and per capita disposable income to GDP among emerging economies.

The lure of the growing middle class is changing the perception of foreign traders and investors, who originally viewed the three countries merely as sales outlets for spare capacities or at the most low-cost production sites when considering an investment. In the long run, the consumers in these markets will yield more value to Western companies than their, at present, low-cost labor. Foreign companies should therefore invest in capturing these markets through local presence. By 2025, both the Chinese and Indian middle classes will exceed 600 million people, or a third of their total population (up from a seventh today). Russia's middle class will encompass 75% of the population (about 100 million people); in absolute terms, this will be much smaller compared with India and China, but the figure will exceed that of Germany, making Russia Europe's largest consumer market. Moreover, spending patterns of Russians are similar to those of their Western counterparts, raising consumer awareness and acceptance of Western brands. Middle-class consumers have annual incomes in the range of US$6,000–10,000, enabling them to acquire cars, home durables, and individual housing. These persons are favored targets of financial institutions offering mortgages and other sorts of consumer loans. Well-to-do families with assets valued at US$18,000–36,000 accounted for 15% of urban households in China in 2006. This figure will rise to 25% by 2010 and 40% in 2020. As the proportion of middle-class households expands each year, the number of families with incomes below subsistence level will drop across the three megamarkets. In Russia, there will be 7 million poor people (or 5% of the population) by 2015, down from 25 million (17%) in 2004. Rural Russia will by then be almost fully integrated in the consumption boom that is a common feature of Moscow, St. Petersburg, and other large cities.

Table 2.6. Household income groups in China and India, 2005–2025.

a. China

Income groups	Household income/year (RMB)[a]	Characteristics	Aggregate disposable income, RMB bn (share, %)		
			2005	2015	2025
Poor	<25,000	Low-paid laborers	1,371 (55%)	979 (27%)	838 (16%)
Lower aspirants	25,000–40,000	Factory workers, low-ranking government officials	1,672 (38%)	2,100 (28%)	1,678 (15%)
Upper aspirants	40,000–100,000	Well-paid migrant employees, high-ranking government officials	370 (5%)	4,877 (41%)	12,235 (61%)
Affluent	100,000–200,000	Private sector employees	148 (1%)	583 (2%)	2,079 (5%)
Elite	>200,000	Well-educated, English-speaking senior executives, party top officials	143 (1%)	790 (2%)	2,371 (3%)

a. RMB = Renminbi, US$1 = RMB 7.
Source: Adapted from McKinsey report.

b. India

Income groups	Household income/year (US$)	Characteristics	Aggregate disposable income, INR[a] trillion (share, %)		
			2005	2015	2025
Deprived	<1,969	Unskilled, low-skilled labor	5.4 (54.0%)	3.8 (35.0%)	2.6 (19.0%)
Aspirers	1,969–4,376	Small shopkeepers, small farmers, low-skilled industrial labor	11.4 (40.5%)	14.6 (43.0%)	13.7 (36.0%)
Seekers	4,376–10,941	Most varied: entry-level employees, petty officials, medium-scale traders, and businesspeople	3.1 (4.0%)	15.2 (19.0%)	30.6 (32.0%)
Strivers	10,941–21,882	Professionals, senior government officials, medium-scale industrialists, rich farmers and traders	1.6 (1.0%)	3.8 (1.0%)	20.9 (9.0%)
Elite	>21,882	Senior executives, top professionals, large business and land owners, politicians	2.0 (0.5%)	6.3 (2.0%)	21.7 (4.0%)

a. INR = Indian Rupee, US$1 = INR 47.
Source: Adapted from McKinsey Report.

Sizing and profiling the middle class is a challenge, more so because of the rapid upward mobility. The most commonly used model segments consumers according to their income and behavior characteristics (see table 2.6).

At 62% of GDP, private consumption is the main driver of growth in India. Its service model has allowed it to achieve high growth with lower fixed investments coupled with higher consumption and high savings (see table 2.7), moving in a virtuous circle of high income and consumption, more businesses, new jobs, and more income. China's investment- and export-led growth that brought prosperity to its workers and employees will rebalance and gradually also shift to a consumption-led virtuous circle; share of private consumption is expected to increase to 55% by 2025.

Table 2.7. Private consumption in major economies, 2007 (% of GDP).

	India	China	Russia	Japan	USA	EU
Private consumption	62	39	49	57	70	54
Government consumption	12	14	10	18	16	25
Investment	28	44	33	23	20	19
Net trade	–2	3	8	1	–6	2

Source: Based on national accounts.

Table 2.8. Monthly disposable income of a household, Moscow vs. Munich.

	Gross (€)	Net of tax^a (€)	Rent^b (€)	Net available for consumption (€)
Moscow	2,800	2,435	150	2,285
Munich	2,800	2,016	900	1,116

a. In Germany, tax rate of 22%, plus 6% deductions for social security (excluding contributions for pension and health); in Russia, 13% flat income tax rate.
b. Russia: monthly charges for water and heating (90 m² flat); 80% of Muscovites have paid off their flats. Germany: monthly rent or loan reimbursement including charges (90 m² flat); 70%–80% of Munich residents pay rent or pay back bank loans on their flats.
Source: Own calculations.

Consumption in Russia is fueled by the high rate of disposable income as a result of low personal debt (60% of Russians already own a flat or house), still subsidized utilities like energy and water, low flat income taxes (13% during 2000–2007), non-declared supplemental income, appreciation of the ruble, and high earnings of the energy sector[10]. A comparison of disposable income of a typical middle-class Muscovite with that of an average German city dweller (whose real wages have stalled since the late 1990s) shows that the Russian's take-home salary is practically twice as high if taxes and cost of rent are factored in (see table 2.8).

In 2007–2012, private consumption in Russia will increase by 13%–15% annually. The new megamarket middle-class consumers residing in the larger cities have become a major target for Western consumer goods companies and service providers operating in financial services, retailing, and tourism. Middle-class Chinese, Indians, and Russians purchase more branded goods and services (insurance, banking) than ever before, both at home and when they travel to foreign destinations. At the same time, consumption patterns of Europeans are changing with a general drop in disposable incomes (mainly because of high taxation, unemployment, and price hikes triggered by rising energy costs), which leaves little budget for luxury items, travel, and the usual amenities. A confident consumer market is a sure sign of the economic potential of a country. The AC Nielsen Consumer Confidence Survey across forty-one countries reveals that Indians led the world followed by Norwegians and Danes. For the third year in a row, Indians remain extremely optimistic about their economy and upbeat about the future.

2.2.2. Eurasia's new millionaires

Dynamic (although volatile) stock markets and rising real estate values and commodity prices have been instrumental in creating more wealth. Forbes's March 2008 list of

---

10. In a reverse trend, the intermittent drop in oil prices in the second half of 2008 and the subsequent devaluation of the ruble led to a contraction of national consumption and a cutback of major imports.

dollar billionaires, long dominated by the United States, has recently seen the entry and growth of billionaires from the megamarkets (see table 2.9a). In Europe, Russia's mostly young, self-made tycoons have overtaken Germany's richest; they now number eighty-seven, up from fifty-three in 2006 (when Russia was still two short of Germany's total) and are worth US$470 billion, up from US$282 billion in 2006. With nineteen of the global top one hundred, Russia now boasts more billionaires than any other country apart from the United States. In 2007, there were more billionaires living in Moscow than in New York. Russia's billionaires are also the youngest from any major economy, with an average age of forty-six, compared with a global average of sixty-one. In Asia, India, which now has fifty-three billionaires (2006: thirty-six) with a total net worth of US$341 billion (2006: US$191 billion), overtook first-ranking Japan. There are four Indians among the world's ten richest people, more than any other country (USA has only two). China has forty-two billionaires, twenty-two more than in 2006, with another twenty-six residing in Hong Kong. China saw the highest number of newcomers in 2007. Japan now only ranks fourth in Asia with a total of twenty-four billionaires. Asia's billionaires recorded a combined total net worth of US$804 billion as of March 2008. Each year, more megamarket billionaires entered the ranking, while the number of billionaires in Western economies (apart from USA) was more or less stagnant.

Table 2.9. The world's rich, 2006, 2007.

a. Billionaires by country	2006	2007
USA	419	469
Russia	53	87
China[a]	44	68
Germany	55	55
India	36	53
UK	29	29
Japan	24	24
Canada	23	23
Brazil	20	24
Spain	20	20
France	15	15
Italy	13	13
Mexico	10	13
South Korea	10	12
b. Millionaires by country	2006	2007
USA	2,498,000	2,669,000
Germany	760,000	767,000
China	300,000	320,000
Russia	88,000	103,000
India	70,000	83,000

a. Mainland China: 42 (20), Hong Kong: 26 (24).
HNWI = high net worth individuals with net fixed assets exceeding US$1 million.
Source: www.forbes.com. 2008.

Worldwide, the number of millionaires—i.e., high-net-worth individuals (HNWI) with more than US$1 million in net financial assets (excluding residence and consumables)—swelled to 8.7 million in March 2007[11] and their wealth to US$35 trillion thanks to continued growth in GDP and market capitalization of companies. The upper part of this league is comprised of 85,400 "ultra-high-net-worth individuals" with financial assets of more than US$30 million each. The United States tops the list with 2.7 million rich, about one-third of the global millionaire population (see table 2.9b). China comes second with 320,000 high-net-worth individuals. Germany, the UK, China, Canada, Australia, Brazil, and Russia each have more than 100,000 millionaires, while India has 83,000 such persons. Indians are also the most prosperous foreign community in

---

11. *The World Wealth Report*, released by Merrill Lynch and Cap Gemini.

the United States, where 200,000 millionaires are of Indian origin. The number of millionaires keeps growing in the megamarkets, where wealth creation is lauded.[12]

As the world's worst ever financial crisis unfolded in the second half of 2008, billions of dollars were wiped off the biggest fortunes, thus reducing the overall number of billionaires and millionaires across the globe. Many megamarket "oligarchs" lost part of their fortunes, especially those who pursued aggressive asset accumulation by relying on external debt finance. Nonetheless, once the dust settles wealth accumulation in the megamarkets will regain momentum as these economies will outperform their Western rivals and increase their clout in the global economy.

2.2.3. Cities and regional markets

Spending power is spreading beyond megapolises in all three megamarkets (see table 2.10). In China, where the consumer is mainly an urban dweller, consumption is spilling beyond the Big Four/Tier 1 to its lower-tier cities not only within the coastal crescent, but increasingly in the interior with support from the government's development policies. Total income of the Tier 2 cities is higher than that of the Big Four, and that of the Tier 3 cities is higher than the combined income of the Tier 1 and Tier 2 cities. In India, rising incomes will benefit both urban and rural populations; the much higher growth in urban areas has a pull effect on the rural areas through the higher demand for farm produce and labor. Daimler is already setting up a service network in Tier 2 Indian cities, where its sales have risen among the rich agricultural landowners. In Russia, too, consumption is rising in the next tier of cities with a population above 500,000.

Their vast populations and geographic spread make China, India, and Russia more a combination of diverse regional consumer markets than single markets. Moreover, internal income disparities are such that both "first" and "third" world types of consumers coexist. The megapolises with their concentration of many million consumers are good entry points. Moscow, Beijing, and New Delhi are larger markets than Belgium, Portugal, or Greece. Similarly, Greater Shanghai and Mumbai, the respective financial capitals of China and India, are each as populated as Romania and Hungary put together. The saturation and high real estate costs in the Tier 1 cities are prompting businesses to move to Tier 2 cities, which have populations ranging from 3 to 6 million. The new boomtowns have attracted companies in high-tech industries and services and already offer a higher quality of life than the megacities. High-rise buildings, office and residential complexes, malls, and luxury hotels shape the landscape of cities like Ningbo, Dalian, and Qingdao in China; Bangalore, Hyderabad, and Pune in India; and Yekaterinburg, Rostov, and Kazan in Russia. In India, some of the smaller cities with less than 1.5 million inhabitants, such as Chandigarh, Ludhiana, and Panaji, are among those with the highest purchasing power. Proactive government policies are now directing businesses to the smaller cities and towns in Tier 3 (1–2 million inhabitants) with incentives of tax holidays and concessions for land and utilities.

China has around seventy cities with a population above 1 million. India counts fifty such cities, but there are many more joining the league as urbanization increases. Russia's

---

12. Whereas, money is an almost taboo subject among Christian communities.

Table 2.10. Main cities and urban areas in megamarkets, 2008.

	China		India		Russia	
Urbanization rate	43% (2005) 59% (2025)		29% (2005) 47% (2025)		75% (2005) 80% (2025)	
Tier 1 cities (mn inhabitants)	Chongqing	31.5	Mumbai	21.0	Moscow	11.0
	Shanghai	18.0	Delhi	18.0	St. Petersburg	4.8
	Beijing	15.0	Kolkata	15.0		
	Guangzhou	13.0				
	Shenzen	12.0				
	Tianjin	11.0				
	Chengdu	11.0				
	Harbin	9.5				
	Wuhan	9.1				
	Shijiazhuang	9.0				
Tier 2 cities (mn inhabitants)	Handan	8.5	Chennai	7.5	Novosibirsk	2.0
	Xian	8.0	Hyderabad	6.8	Nizhny Novgorod	2.0
	Nantong	7.6	Bangalore	6.5	Yekaterinburg	2.0
	Qingdao	7.3	Ahmedabad	5.5	Samara	1.8
	Shenyang	7.2	Pune	5.0	Kazan	1.7
	Changchun	7.2	Kanpur	3.5	Omsk	1.6
	Zhengzhou	7.1	Surat	3.1	Cheljabinsk	1.5
	Tangshan	7.0	Jaipur	3.0	Rostov	1.5
	Fuzhou	6.6	Lucknow	2.9	Ufa	1.4
	Nanjing	6.4	Nagpur	2.5	Volgograd	1.3
	Hangzhou	6.4	Patna	2.4	Perm	1.2
	Luoyang	6.4	Indore	2.0	Krasnoyarsk	1.1
	Dalian	6.2			Saratov	1.0
	Suzhou	6.1				
	Changsha	6.1				
Tier 3 cities (mn inhabitants)	Jinan	5.9	Meerut	1.9	Voronesh	0.9
	Shantou	4.7	Bhopal	1.8	Togliatti	0.8
	Lyanungang	4.6	Vadodara	1.7	Krasnodar	0.7
	Wuxi	4.5	Ludhiana	1.6	Ulyanovsk	0.7
	Nanchang	4.5	Bhubaneshwar	1.6	Izhevsk	0.7
	Jilin	4.4	Coimbatore	1.6	Yaroslavl	0.6
	Kunming	3.8	Agra	1.6		
	Liuzhou	3.5	Nashik	1.6		
	Lanzhou	3.2	Kochi	1.5		
	Taiyuan	3.0				
	Fushun	2.3				
	30 more cities with population > 1 mn		25 more cities with population > 1 mn		10 more cities with population > 1 mn	

Source: Own research based on data from national statistical offices.

figure is smaller but still higher than any other EU country (fifteen cities with more than 1 million). As a matter of fact, cities in the megamarkets needed much shorter life spans to develop into megapolises. It took two centuries for London and more than a century for New York to grow from 1 million to 8 million inhabitants. In Shenzen, a "rising star" metropolis close to Hong Kong, the population surged from 100,000 to 12 million in just twenty-five years. Bangalore, a boomtown in Southern India, grew from 1 million inhabitants in the mid-1980s to 6.5 million in 2007, and it may well reach the 10 million mark by 2012 as a result of the rural exodus from nearby regions. More megamarket citizens will move to cities. Russians look for job opportunities in Moscow, St. Petersburg, Kazan, Nizhni Novgorod, and other agglomerations. China and India are experiencing the fastest urbanization in world history. By 2025, another 250 million Chinese and

200 million more Indians will settle down in cities, some of which have grown from farmland into bustling urban centers in less than three decades. However, farmland cannot be easily converted around urban centers (owing to stricter regulations) and urban infrastructure cannot always cope with the dramatic population growth. Mumbai, for example, will need US$40 billion to modernize its economic, social, and environmental infrastructure by 2015. Mumbai already generates one-third of national tax income and 40% of India's foreign trade (see figure 2.5), but only part of the money is channeled back to Mumbai by the central government, which feels the urgency to ensure balanced development across the country. Similarly, Moscow is by far the main tax income generator for the Russian government. Although China's revenue distribution appears to be more balanced at first sight, even here Beijing and the largest metros (e.g., Shanghai, Chongqing, Guangzhou) account for the lion's share of the federal and regional budgets.

Urbanization has certainly been a major factor of economic growth, but it also brought problems that must henceforth be tackled sensibly: traffic congestion, air pollution, utility bottlenecks, farmland reduction, and disease prevention. According to the Asian Development Bank (ADB), megamarket cities in Asia will need several hundred billion US dollars annually over the next twenty-five years to meet their financial requirements.

In recent years, the business community has been looking at investment locations outside the mainstream. Growing numbers of rural consumers represent a stability anchor especially at times of reduced activity in major agglomerations.[13] Due to the economic slowdown triggered by the international liquidity crisis, which set in at the end of 2008, rural areas of large emerging economies for the first time experience a return of temporary workers and skilled manpower that had migrated to the cities. This reverse exodus along with multi-billion government spending packages directed at infrastructure and social projects in previously neglected regions will create a spate of new opportunities for companies ready to tap the rising demand for goods and services in rural areas.

Figure 2.5. Mumbai's importance for the Indian economy, 2007.

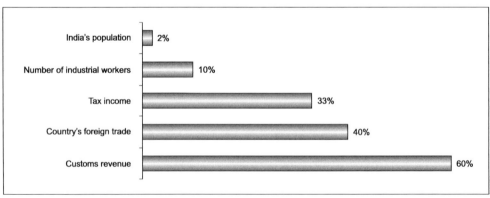

Source: Bombay First, McKinsey report.

---

13. Growth in both Guangdong and Shanghai was reported down by several percentage points in 2008 compared to 2007 due to the crisis effect. Exports from Guangdong, for example, grew by just 5.6% in 2008, down from 22.3% from the previous year. According to experts this is a natural evolution from excessive to more stable growth. See "Economic hubs face tough times," *China Daily*, January 9, 2009.

Positioning in the smaller cities and rural market, which are home to the "bottom of the social pyramid,"[14] will become a decisive factor in sustaining market leadership, particularly in China and India. The Indian carmaker Tata, for example, has developed a special car in the price range of US$2,000–3,000 that will be marketed in rural India, Africa, and Southeast Asia. In India, the larger rural population accounts for 57% of total consumption, and it is growing at a compounding annual rate of 3.9%. Over the next two decades, it will triple to reach the size of the Canadian or South Korean markets today. Rural India will mostly benefit from the demand in growing cities for agricultural and consumer products. At the same time, industry and services are penetrating the rural areas where purchasing power is growing faster than in the cities. In China, the rural population purchases 39% of goods, and its savings account for 25% of all individual bank savings. The challenge for governments will be to create jobs in rural areas and raise purchasing power. This will help to stem the rural exodus and engage in more balanced growth. Local carmakers design consumer goods, including cheap cars, geared to both their rural and suburban consumers. Western companies should not neglect the rural potential of the megamarkets as this will itself constitute a huge market in the years to come.

2.3. Integration in the global economy

2.3.1. Foreign trade scenario

The value of world merchandise exports rose by 13% in 2007 (compared with +21% in 2006) and crossed the US$13 trillion mark. Commercial services exports increased by 11% to US$3.4 trillion (compared with +19% in 2006). In 2007, Germany maintained its first position as leading exporter (see table 2.11) by establishing yet another record with foreign shipments of US$1,361 billion (+20% over 2006). With exports amounting to US$1,220 billion (+26% over 2006), China moved to second place in 2007, replacing the United States (US$1,140 billion). China will draw even with or overtake Germany by 2009 given its current expansion rates.

World trade grew less strongly during 2008–2009 as a result of economic contraction, with the three Eurasian megamarkets strengthening their positions as global traders. In 2008, their combined share in world exports exceeded 12%, twice their level in the mid-1990s. Together, the three economies already account for higher export volumes than either Germany or the United States, the world's two leading exporters. During 2000–2008, China's merchandise exports grew by 45%, Russia's by 28%, and India's by 22%—all three faster than any advanced economy. Imports of the three megamarkets grew even faster during that period, by 21%–24%. Their combined share in world merchandise imports now stands at almost 11%. China and Russia have been generating ever-growing surpluses in their trade balance since the early 2000s, while India has managed to control its trade deficit. By the end of 2007, China's trade surplus soared to US$262 billion (an unprecedented level for any major economy), up 48% from a year earlier, putting the Chinese government under increased pressure to let the renminbi appreciate further and abolish all export tax rebates to enterprises. China has become a major buyer of foreign goods, equipment, and services,

---

14. See 9.2.2.

Exports rank	Country	Exports value (US$ bn)	Imports rank	Country	Imports value (US$ bn)
1	Germany	1,361	1	USA	1,987
2	China	1,228	2	Germany	1,121
3	USA	1,140	3	China	996
4	Japan	666	4	France	601
5	France	559	5	UK	596
6	Italy	475	6	Japan	571
7	Netherlands	465	7	Italy	484
8	Canada	440	8	Netherlands	402
9	UK	416	9	Canada	394
10	South Korea	387	10	Hong Kong	371
11	Russia[a]	365	11	South Korea	360
12	Hong Kong	353	12	Spain	359
13	Belgium	328	13	Belgium	321
14	Singapore	318	14	Mexico	279
15	Mexico	268	15	Singapore	273

Table 2.11. Merchandise trade of leading economies, 2007.

a. Russia ranks 16th in imports with US$260 billion.
Source: Based on CIA, The World Factbook 2008. WTO, 2008.

Figure 2.6. Trilateral trade between Eurasia's megamarkets by 2010.

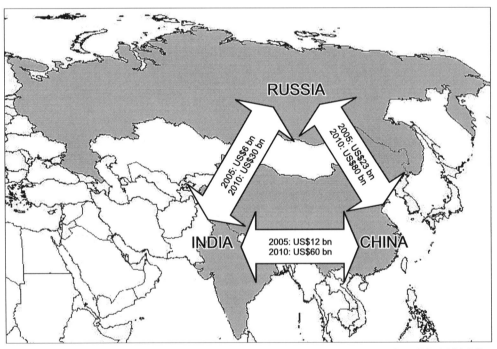

Source: National statistical offices.

thus constituting a "stability anchor" for world trade beside the EU and the United States. In 2007, its imports rose to a staggering US$966 billion (+21% over 2006). India's import levels also soared to never-before-seen levels (US$175 billion in 2007).

The megamarkets have become significant providers of services to other economies. Together, they accounted for 7% of world exports of commercial services in 2007 with an upward trend given their growing contribution to business and IT services as well as transport/logistics, financial, and travel-related services. The three megamarkets are increasingly involved in bilateral and trilateral trade with each other and form an increasingly noticeable geostrategic triangle on the Eurasian landmass. By 2010–2012, bilateral trade is expected to multiply and reach US$60 billion between India and China,[15] US$80 billion between China and Russia, and US$30 billion between Russia and India (see figure 2.6). All three countries increasingly trade with other Asian neighbors. Already in 2004, the value of India's trade with Asian nations had surpassed that of the exchange with the United States and Western Europe put together. China trades intensively with the United States, but exchanges of goods with the rest of Asia and Russia enjoy the highest growth rates. Similarly, Russia looks east to its Asian neighbors to expand its contacts and trade relations. By 2012, Asian nations will replace the EU as major customers for energy supplies from Russia.

2.3.2. FDI scenario

After decades as second-class investment destinations, the new megamarkets figure now among the most attractive locations and also new sources of FDI. Their growing importance in attracting and triggering global FDI flows will modify the world investment scenario in the years to come.

Global FDI inflows grew in 2007 for the fourth consecutive year to reach US$1.5 trillion, which represents a 25% increase over 2006 and for the first time more than the former record of US$1.4 trillion set in 2000 (see figure 2.7a). The continued rise in FDI[16] reflects strong economic performance and healthy integration between advanced and emerging economies. Increased corporate profits have boosted cross-border mergers and acquisitions (M&As), which today constitute a large share of FDI operations. Continued economic liberalization of flexible investment policies and trade regimes added further stimulus, although in asset-rich countries (e.g., Russia, Brazil, Indonesia, Nigeria) there have been notable changes in economic policy toward a greater role of the state and more restrictive regimes for foreign investors, in particular in natural resources industries.

The large emerging markets will attract growing volumes of FDI in the years to come (see table 2.12). China's accumulated FDI stock will be worth more than US$500 billion by 2008, which is twice as high as Italy's and four times Japan's figure. Over the past decade, megamarket governments have astutely channeled FDI into selected industries and regions through a combination of tax incentives, targeted promotional campaigns, and project support. More foreign investment has led to economic stability and a boost in foreign reserves, enabling governments to pursue their path of liberalization. Foreign investors are allowed to acquire majority stakes and establish wholly owned subsidiaries in most industries. Compared with smaller emerging economies with limited domestic

---

15. The bilateral trade targets between China and India have been constantly revised upwards many times after significant growth of trading activities between the two countries. The same applies to India–Russia and China–Russia figures.
16. FDI growth will temporarily slow down in 2008–2009 as a consequence of the worldwide credit slump, but will pick up again as world economies become more interdependent.

Figure 2.7. FDI inflows, 1998–2008.

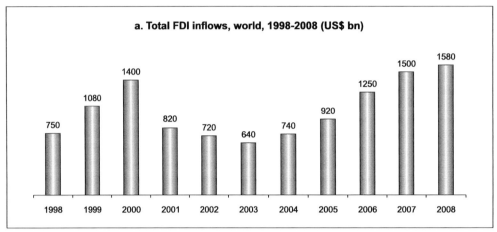

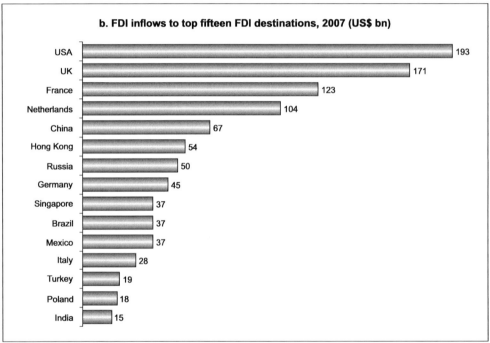

Source: UNCTAD. World Investment Report 2007.

Table 2.12. FDI inflows and stock in large emerging economies, 2006–2010.				
	2006 (US$ bn)	2007 (US$ bn)	2008–2010[a] (US$ bn)	Stock by 2010 (US$ bn)
China	70	67	75	680
Russia	29	50	55	340
Brazil	19	37	40	380
Mexico	19	37	40	390
India	17	15	25	165

a. Annual average.
Source: Based on UNCTAD, World Investment Reports.

markets and natural resources, the three megamarkets are in a favorable position to attract any type of FDI in small or large volumes: market-seeking, cost-driven, raw-materials-seeking, export-oriented, or strategic investments meant to contain competition.

2.3.3. Portfolio investments and capital markets

Portfolio investments (PI) include the purchase of treasury/enterprise bonds as well as corporate stock without acquisition of a controlling interest in a company by the investor; these transactions are carried out on national or international stock exchanges. During the past decade, there has been a dramatic increase in PI from industrialized countries to the emerging economies and vice versa. Back in 1981, the value of all shares listed on emerging markets stock exchanges was US$80 billion, which was equivalent to the market capitalization of a medium-sized multinational by today's measure (e.g., Barclays or Fiat, which ranked number 70–71 in the 2008 Fortune 500 list). By 2006, that figure had swollen to US$5.5 trillion (US$5,500 billion)—i.e., seventy times higher than twenty-five years earlier. In 1981, portfolio investors had invested less than a hundred million in emerging markets firms, nothing compared to today's levels (US$70 billion in 2006[17]) (see table 2.13). Total net private capital flows to emerging markets in 2007 totaled almost US$550 billion, thus increasing reserves and replenishing state coffers. All major categories of flows including bank/non-bank lending and direct equity investments[18] have experienced significant increases during 2004–2007. Continued buyback of outstanding

Table 2.13. Portfolio investments in emerging economies, 2004–2007 (US$ bn).

	2004	2005	2006	2007
Current account balance	150.2	257.8	317.0	361.5
External financing, net:				
Private flows, net	348.8	509.3	501.8	548.7
Equity investment	195.1	254.5	255.0	294.5
Direct equity	156.0	198.7	185.3	211.0
Portfolio equity	39.1	55.8	69.7	63.5
Private creditors	153.7	254.7	246.7	254.2
Commercial banks	60.8	141.8	143.3	161.3
Nonbanks	92.9	112.9	103.4	93.0
Official flows, net	−17.2	−58.5	−48.2	−1.9
IFIs	−15.0	−40.4	−25.7	−3.2
Bilateral creditors	−2.2	−18.1	−22.5	1.3
Resident lending/other, net[a]	−83.4	−268.8	−234.5	−242.8
Reserves (− = increase)	−398.2	−439.8	−536.1	−665.6

a. Including net lending, monetary gold, and errors and omissions.
Source: Based on Institute of International Finance (IIF), 2007.

---

17. See Institute for International Finance (IIF), the global association of financial institutions with more than 360 members in over 60 countries. The IIF publishes its annual report, *Capital Flows to Emerging Market Economies*, reflecting portfolio inflows into thirty emerging economies.
18. Private equity has become a large contributor for financing SME expansion in the megamarkets. In 2008, India counts approximately US$10 billion worth of private equity finance (2007: US$8.5 billion). This vehicle is expected to grow in importance as local businesses encounter difficulties in obtaining bank loans or raising money through IPOs (when the financial markets are down) even if they can show a plausible business plan.

bonds by institutions and governments reflects the strong current account positions in some emerging countries.

Portfolio holdings of equity and long-term debt securities reached nearly US$25.7 trillion at the end of 2006. The United States, United Kingdom, and Japan were the largest investing countries, accounting for almost 68% of such holdings. The shares of Germany, the Netherlands, Italy, and France were each within 4% to 6% of the total. US and EU portfolio investors were first drawn to emerging economies following stock market instabilities in 2001 and the almost concomitant reduction in interest rates in home markets. New investment instruments and reduced controls on capital inflows and outflows provided further stimulus.

Rising capital flows to emerging markets reflect the strong economic fundamentals (low inflation, export strength, high growth) in numerous EMs triggered by developments in the three megamarkets, which act as locomotives, as well as high levels of global liquidity in general. The integration of the megamarkets and surrounding EMs into the world economy will continue at a fast pace. Growing numbers of institutional investors, including hedge funds and pension funds, have joined the ranks of traditional investors helping to support flows and asset prices. The emergence and development of local markets, the introduction of new types of securities (particularly derivatives), asset securitization into country financing programs, and an extension of maturities has left emerging markets' debt more manageable than at any other previous point in history.

Many Western banks have launched special emerging markets funds covering either the BRICs or emerging markets in general. These funds are extremely liquid (therefore volatile and prone to risk) but have gained significantly in value since the early 2000s. Volatility is currently due rather to liquidity issues than wrong fundamentals (savings rates remain high, and megamarket companies are on their way to becoming world class). Value corrections, which took place intermittently during 2004–2008 and will continue to occur as economies expand and contract, cannot change the upward trajectory of emerging economies as magnets for private and institutional capital well into the 2020s as they decouple from trends in Western economies.

Obviously, with record levels of portfolio investment flows, the authorities of emerging economies will need to recognize that sustainability and investor confidence require strengthening of stock market regulatory frameworks and the promotion of high corporate governance standards. Numerous economists claim that PI induces an efficient flow of finance to economies facing capital shortages. But in some cases, PI is associated more with structural problems, including deficiencies in investment in the real sector of the economy (industry) and increased risk of a financial crisis following a sudden erosion of investor confidence. Of all the types of capital to enter emerging economies, PI as "hot money" has the greatest potential to destabilize the recipient economy because of its excessive liquidity and the short time horizon associated with such investments. The Mexican (1994), Southeast Asian (1997–98), Russian (1998), and Argentinean (2001) crises illustrate the vulnerability of emerging markets in case of failure by governments to control large-scale and rapid PI outflows due to fickle investor sentiments. The monetary authorities of China, India, and Russia have drawn valuable lessons from these unpleasant experiences. They have introduced control instruments and regulatory bodies that are allowed to supervise (in the case of China and India, limit) the free movement of capital[19] and ever since have pursued a policy of gradual foreign reserves build-up to counter speculative runs on their currencies and the negative effects of economic recessions.

PI need to be carefully managed to maximize benefits and minimize drawbacks through control of capital and foreign currency transactions. So far, among the megamarkets only Russia allows full convertibility of its currency, but China and India will also have to move in that direction as their economies become globally more integrated. Well-applied capital controls will probably remain in place as they reduce the ability of speculators to play on foreign exchange differentials and withdraw funds based on short-term gains; they are also meant to restrict illegal transactions linked to money laundering. Moderate capital controls augment policy autonomy and state capacity. An example, which is making the headlines, is that of Chile, where foreign portfolio investors must keep capital in the country for one year or more. So far, megamarket governments have not resorted to similar measures, but in China, for example, foreign passport holders are not allowed to buy all listed shares. At the same time, overseas investing in mutual funds and other international assets by megamarket citizens has been relaxed. Indian, Chinese, and Russian investors now have a wide choice of investment possibilities across many countries, industries, and asset classes. Some of these funds, such as Franklin Templeton, Fidelity International, or Merrill Lynch, have global fund management teams catering to this new clientele.

Large and growing stock exchanges are generally less vulnerable to external shocks because of high transaction volumes and liquidity. As a rule of thumb, a stock exchange should have a market capitalization of US$50 billion and traded volumes of at least US$10 billion annually to attract interest from global emerging market funds. The initial trigger for building up internal stock markets usually comes from large, homegrown companies that go public and list their shares to raise capital. These companies attract mutual fund managers. During 2005–2008, megamarket companies launched record numbers of initial public offerings (IPOs), which improved the prospects for more international funds to be channeled to their financial markets.

Stock exchanges in the megamarkets have played an important role in the capitalization of their enterprises. In July 2009, the Shanghai Stock Exchange overtook the London Stock Exchange to become the fourth largest bourse (US$2.3 trillion compared with US$9.8 trillion of the New York Stock Exchange) in terms of market capitalization, according to the World Federation of Stock Exchanges. The 133-year-old Bombay Stock Exchange is the oldest in Asia and the largest in the world in terms of the number of listed companies (4925 companies compared with 3232 companies on the NYSE). The Indian capital market has a fully automated trading system on all its 19 corporatized and demutualized stock exchanges and a wide range of modern products. The real strength of the Indian securities market lies in the quality of independent regulation by the Securities and Exchange Board of India (SEBI). In Russia, although the RTS Stock Exchange was

---

19. Russia, which favours a more liberal course, suffered from much higher capital outflows than China and India when the 2008 world financial crisis forced a large number of foreign investors to sell their assets and repatriate money.

established only in 1995 as the country's first regulated stock market, it now trades the full range of financial instruments from equities and options to commodity futures.

Money is also flowing in through remittances. According to a World Bank study, immigrants from EMs/DEs sent more than US$180 billion back home in 2006–2007, with rising tendency. This total is on par with FDI inflows and more than three to four times the value of foreign aid. What is more, the report reckons that money sent through informal channels could add 50% to this estimate. Again, it is the megamarkets that dominate because of their large foreign diaspora. India (US$22 billion, +3%), China (US$20 billion, +1%), Mexico (US$18 billion, +3%), and the Philippines (US$13 billion, +13%) accounted for 44% of all foreign remittances in 2007.

CHAPTER 3
Eurasia's megamarkets as a resource base

Today's emerging and developing economies have been major suppliers of natural resources from the days of the great discoveries in the fifteenth century and throughout the colonial era until today. South America was a source of gold, silver, and other precious metals for Spain and Portugal, while Asian and African colonies were used to ship jute, cotton, silk, tea, spices, and minerals to England, France, and the rest of Europe. Then oil became the most important source of primary energy to fuel Europe's industrialization. In the late nineteenth and early twentieth century, Middle Eastern, African, and Asian countries fell prey to the "militarization" of the major European powers, England, France, Italy, and Germany. Presumed energy reserves were major drivers for extending colonial rule until well into the 1960s when most colonies managed to gain their independence.

Industrialized nations remain very dependent on imports of raw materials, food, commodities, and energy from emerging economies. Raw materials TNCs have progressively expanded into EMs. Their aim is to be close to the source to ensure supplies and reduce intermediary costs. Since the fall of the iron curtain, which has defused the East–West conflict, EM governments have used their regained confidence to impose stricter rules on raw-materials-oriented investments. Western companies are prevented from acquiring controlling stakes in large domestic players or extraction sites that are considered of strategic importance for future economic development. In 2007, the Russian government reexamined production sharing agreements (PSAs) previously negotiated with international oil majors and tightened its grip on new exploration sites and distribution. The other two mega-economies, China and India, have also stepped up efforts to regulate foreign investments in mining and geological exploration of strategic oil and natural gas deposits.

With 2.6 billion consumers and continuing growth of industrial production, the thirst for raw materials and energy by the megamarkets will persist, affecting industries and enterprises worldwide. China has absorbed record volumes of iron ore and metal scrap for its expanding steel plants, resulting in worldwide shortages and price hikes across all raw materials categories. Other industries have also been consuming record volumes of minerals and agricultural inputs. To secure its energy supply, India, whose oil import dependence is projected to reach 90% by 2020, has intensified its oil diplomacy for acquiring stakes in overseas oilfields and companies. Chinese national champions are encouraged to invest in Africa (e.g., Sudan, Angola, Nigeria), Central Asia, and Latin America. Russia is a leading oil exporter but needs large quantities of equipment and components from other countries. Its oil and gas majors face increased protectionism as they try to invest downstream in Europe.

The megamarkets are not endowed with all the raw materials and energy reserves required for rapid economic expansion. Their consumption by far exceeds domestic production (especially in the case of China and India), prompting EMM governments to establish lasting economic relations with smaller EMs/DEs. Recent examples of deeper diplomatic ties are:

- China imports natural rubber and plenty of commodities from Southeast Asia; it negotiated several raw materials and energy deals on a wide front with many African and South American countries.[1]
- India and China source huge quantities of oil and gas from the Middle East, Central Asia, and Latin America (e.g., Venezuela, Brazil).
- Russia buys cotton from the former Soviet republics of Uzbekistan and Turkmenistan to revive its textile and apparel industry.

In agriculture, India and China have become almost self-reliant. Governments have adopted food security measures, which include strategic stocks of cereals and other commodities. After tumultuous years preceding its financial crisis, Russia is finally back at center stage, emerging as the leading granary in Europe and provider of rural produce for its CIS and European neighbors. Russia is widening its fish catch areas to consolidate its position as the major supplier of marine products on the Eurasian continent. Russia also boasts the world's largest forestry reserves, enabling its companies to position themselves as leading suppliers of wood-based products (e.g., building materials, furniture).

World statistics of human, natural, and energy resources reflect the growing importance of the megamarkets, which for many Western companies are poised to become an integral part of their global supply chains.

3.1. Human resources

3.1.1. Population trends

China and India have the largest populations in the world; together they account for roughly one-third of the total (see table 3.1). India has the largest young population of the world: 54% of India's population (600 million) is under twenty-five years old. Its annual spending is growing by 12%. Information technology has given these young people job opportunities and incomes their parents could only dream of. China's population is aging faster than India's, and the one-child policy, which was necessary to stem population growth, is showing its negative side effects by causing social distortions: preference for males, shortage of females, not enough children to look after parents, comfortable upbringing, and selfish behavior. Russia's population is not as young as that of China and

---

1. China's president, Hu Jintao, toured Africa and South America several times during 2004–2008 to sign agreements for securing the energy and raw materials supplies required for China's expanding industries.

Table 3.1. Markets are where people are: Population projections to 2020 (in mn).					
Rank	Country	2006	2010	2015	2020
	World	6,520	7,900	8,900	10,500
1	China	1,310	1,364	1,402	1,429
2	India	1,090	1,173	1,246	1,312
3	EU	460	490	510	540
4	USA	290	314	329	344
5	Indonesia	215	238	255	281
6	Brazil	180	203	215	245
7	Pakistan	155	175	210	230
8	Bangladesh	150	170	185	210
9	Russia	143	138	123	119
10	Mexico	105	118	139	155

Source: CIA Factbook. UN World Development Indicators.

Table 3.2. Youth bulge in emerging economies, 2006.			
Country	Children aged under 15		Population ranking
	Total (mn)	Share of population (%)	
India	363	33	2 (1,100 mn)
China	312	24	1 (1,300 mn)
Indonesia	68	31	4 (220 mn)
Pakistan	62	40	6 (155 mn)
USA	61	21	3 (290 mn)
Brazil	49	28	5 (176 mn)
Nigeria	48	44	9 (110 mn)
Bangladesh	46	34	8 (134 mn)
Mexico	34	33	11 (104 mn)
Russia[a]	23	16	7 (144 mn)

a. Rank 15.
Source: G. Heinsohn. Soehne und Weltmacht.

India, but the government has introduced many incentives to encourage births (already showing its effect), and it has a policy of controlled immigration.

EMMs dispose of an almost unlimited reservoir of young people who are an invaluable asset as workforce and consumers. The "youth bulge" is a true phenomenon of EMs, whereas AMs are characterized by aging populations (see table 3.2). India and China have the largest absolute population of young people aged under fifteen, although in many smaller EMs their share can be even higher.

3.1.2. Education and literacy

Education and literacy, coupled with large populations and job opportunities, are decisive factors for transforming a country into a mega-economy. A large population per se does not represent an asset if it is not endowed with education and purchasing power. If appropriate policy mechanisms are put in place, education and purchasing power

Table 3.3. Literacy rates in major economies, 2005, 2015 (% of population).

Country	2005	2015
Germany	96	93
Russia	95	97
China	91	98
USA	87	88
India	61	85

Source: Based on UNESCO.

generally go hand in hand as educated people acquire the necessary skills to earn a respectable income in a highly competitive job market. Education is the prerequisite for environmentally conscious behavior and the respect for nature and its resources. When Russia had achieved almost full literacy in the beginning of the 1960s, literacy levels were still low in China and India. But since the 1990s, overall literacy has gone up as a result of ambitious schooling programs and government policies to spread knowledge from the cities to the countryside (see table 3.3). Whereas 60% of India's population was reported illiterate in the 1960s, this figure was reduced to below 40% by 2005. China's progress has been even more spectacular. The country managed to raise literacy levels to 90% by the turn of the century. India's literacy rate is expected to reach 85% by 2015.

Literacy directly correlates with increased schooling at all levels: elementary, high school, and college and university. School and university enrollments have reached record levels in China and India. This is reflected in the increasing number of universities outside the capitals in Tier 2–4 cities available to students across these large continental countries. Each year, several million students graduate in China and India, of which roughly one million are engineers. Together, these numbers represent more than four times the number of engineers graduating from EU universities. Very important, female enrollment has risen to levels never seen before, giving them the same preparation for the future job market as their male counterparts. The megamarkets are attracting growing numbers of foreign students as well.

Worldwide, UNESCO projects the number of students to increase from 97 million today to 260 million in 2025. The number of foreign students studying in other countries will be around 7 million. The United States alone selects around 300,000 foreign students each year to study in its universities. The largest numbers come from China,[2] India, and other Asian countries.[3] They are usually those with the best grades in sciences and engineering-related subjects. Sixty-six percent of foreign PhD students in the United States are Asians, revealing the importance of Asia as a source of talent. Many educational institutions in the United States, United Kingdom, Australia, and New Zealand have geared up their marketing efforts to attract emerging market students, who represent an important source of knowledge (which could stay in the country) and a non-negligible part of annual university budgets.

India has pledged to join the race as a student destination by exploiting its cost advantages, English language facilities, and UK-based university traditions. Interestingly, China and Russia are also attracting growing numbers of foreign students despite the linguistic barrier. The Russian Ministry of Education calculated that the potential revenues of the national educational system from foreign students could reach US$4 billion (2007).[4] China

---

2. In 2008, 200,000 Chinese students went abroad for their college studies. The government expects a 30% rise each year until 2015. See "Record Number of Students to Travel Abroad," *China Daily,* January 17, 2008.
3. In 2007, 66% of foreign PhD students studying in US universities were from Asia compared with 19% from Europe and 15% from Latin America.
4. "Export obrazovanjia" [Export of education], *Expert,* July 26–August 15, 2004, 28–35.

attracts record numbers of foreign students from AMs and EMs because of its economic and technological achievements. As these economies gain importance, foreign students are willing to study the local languages in view of future job prospects. Degrees can be obtained at a lower cost in these countries than in North America or Western Europe. The experience gained in educational establishments belonging to high-growth environments is increasingly considered an asset, which raises opportunities for job seekers.

As these trends accentuate, European and US companies will face serious shortages of engineers. The European Commission had already reported a deficit of 15,000 engineers in the EU in 2006. Some high-tech companies, such as EADS, Siemens, and SAP, cannot fill important positions, resort to in-house training, and are compelled to transfer part of their R&D activities to EMMs.[5] A highly educated local workforce at affordable salaries incites Western multinationals to relocate service functions such as business process outsourcing (BPO)/call centers, medical research, and computer programming. EMM students are incited to study in their home countries or return to base after short spells abroad. In 2007, 10 million Indians were studying in India's 12,000 colleges, 200 universities, and elite colleges (seven IITs, six IIMs). New establishments are continually being created; some of them are at the vanguard of science and engineering. The Indian Institute of Science (IISc) in Bangalore, whose creation took inspiration from Germany's Max Planck, operates very close to industry, although it is geared to fundamental research. The government plans to open more elite universities offering courses in software, IT, biotechnology, and auto engineering. Growing numbers of EMM degree holders stay back instead of enrolling for post-graduate studies in AMs. During 2008–2010, technical universities in both China and India will grant degrees to around 300,000–350,000 engineers annually, which for each of the two countries is about twice as many as in the United States, three times the figure of Japan, and seven times that of Germany (see figure 3.1).

The world's famous business schools now consider EMMs as a fundamental element of their global strategy. Harvard Business School (HBS) researches new cases together with Indian companies. In 2005, it created the India Research Centre (HBS IRC) in Mumbai to develop knowledge on the critical challenges facing the country's business environment and key industries. HBS IRC offers an executive education program that incorporates the latest thinking on new management ideas being embraced by India's fastest-growing companies. In China, Shanghai's China Europe International Business School (CEIBS) has linked up with HBS and Barcelona-based IESE Business School to offer a global executive MBA program. The high cost (US$25,000–30,000 per year) is no deterrent, and applications keep exceeding the number of places. The demand for high-class managerial talent is equally high in Russia, a problem that is being addressed by recognized establishments such as the School of Management in the town of Skolkovo, near Moscow.

More foreign educational establishments and companies are entering into collaborative deals with megamarket universities to face shortages of qualified staff. The foreign business community is competing with rising "national champions" for the best talents, whose salaries keep rising.

---

5. News report by German First National Television ARD, January 8, 2006.

Figure 3.1. Engineering graduates in major economies, 2007–2010 (in thousands).

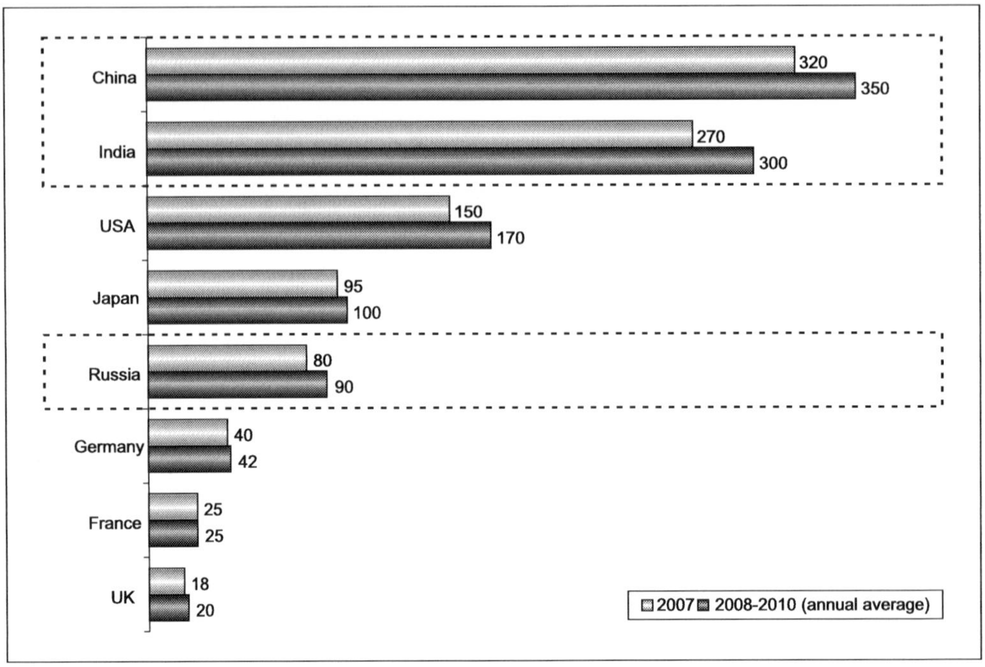

Country	2007	2008–2010 (annual average)
China	320	350
India	270	300
USA	150	170
Japan	95	100
Russia	80	90
Germany	40	42
France	25	25
UK	18	20

Source: UNESCO. National statistics.

3.1.3. R&D activity and intellectual property

The success story of the three megamarkets is linked to their emphasis on education and scientific research, which have long traditions. R&D expenses have been allocated progressively by the private and public sectors. R&D funding intensifies as high-tech industries are targeted by policymakers to prepare the workforce for the global economy. The three megamarkets are emerging as true challengers to mature economies in many of these areas (see box 3.1). Young scientists and engineers are in direct competition with their Western rivals. With rising economic wealth, these countries will host an immense pool of local scientists and firms that are constantly expanding their know-how and capital base, and are thus in a favorable position to acquire technologies, if needed by forging strategic alliances with Western partners. With size it has become easier for megamarket companies to apply for loans from domestic banks and venture capitalists who are flush with money generated by high savings and corporate profits. It is estimated that 70% of China's inward FDI enters via Hong Kong through companies, private funds, and banks controlled by overseas Chinese. India and Russia are also benefiting from a well-connected foreign diaspora consisting of high-net-worth individuals actively looking for investment opportunities in start-ups at home. State-owned development banks and agencies provide additional funding; their focus is on infrastructure, transport, health care, and education, all of which are of major public concern.

China provides a good illustration of what could happen in the future. For centuries, Chinese craftsmen had been leaders in innovations, from mathematics and printing to gunpowder and shipbuilding. Now the country is regaining its lost status. The Chinese government has given R&D top priority in two consecutive five-year plans and is

> **Box 3.1. Megamarket scientists focus on high-tech.**
> - Nanotechnology
> - Biotechnology
> - Pharmaceutical and medical research
> - New materials
> - Aerospace
> - Supercomputers
> - High-tech chemicals
> - Renewable energies
> - Energy efficiency in homes and vehicles

determined to close the gap on the leading Western economies. According to the EU Commission, China's R&D budget will exceed that of the EU by 2010. While expenditure growth is 0.2% in the EU, China's R&D expenses are expanding at 20% annually. China's state investments in R&D have trebled since 1998. Within a few years, R&D's share in GDP has expanded from almost zero to 1.2%. It took Germany more than five decades to reach a ratio of 2.6%.[6] The EU is very distant from its 3% average target and goal of becoming "the world's technologically most advanced place by 2010," a policy strongly supported by the EU Commission since 2004. China's leadership has understood the positive implications of an innovation-driven society, which will enable the country to shift from an economic model based on inward FDI and exports to one based on outward FDI and higher domestic consumption as main drivers of growth. R&D spending in China went up from 0.9% of GDP in 2000 to 1.4% in 2007.

In 2008, China counted more than seven hundred foreign-invested R&D centers, demonstrating the country's growing importance not only as a sales outlet and manufacturing platform, but equally as a center of design and innovation. The policy of inciting foreign players to transfer their know-how and technology in return for market access (e.g., tenders) is showing results. Shanghai, Shenzen, Suzhou, Dalian, and many other cities have attracted thousands of foreign high-tech players as investors. China boasts a total of twenty-five high-tech parks around first- and second-tier cities. Their numbers and specialization are increasing. There are new parks geared to renewable energies, environmental technologies, and bio sciences (molecular technologies, pharmaceuticals, veterinary sciences). India reports similar success stories in software, pharmaceuticals, new materials, and aeronautics. Since 2006, Russia has embarked on a similar path by strongly encouraging national electronics, IT, pharmaceutical, and aerospace clusters.

The three megamarkets are investing in knowledge and innovation as R&D budgets grow with economic wealth. What reinforces this trend is the strong desire of highly educated overseas Chinese, Indians, and Russians to return home and seize new opportunities. The original "brain drain" is being transformed into a new phenomenon, a visible "brain

---

6. "Forschung: Dramatische aufholjagd" [Research: Dramatic catching up], *Wirtschaftswoche Sonderausgabe* 1 (October 27, 2005): 10.

Figure 3.2. R&D spending in major economies, 2006 (% of GDP).

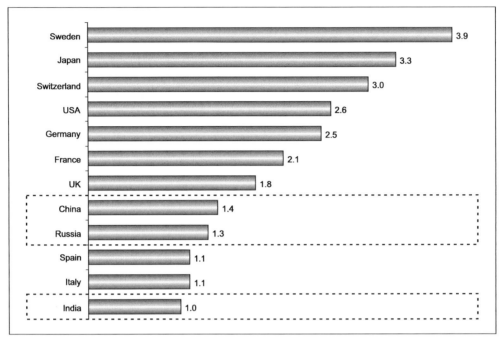

Source: OECD, The Economist. November 17, 2007.

gain" with powerful effects for the national economies. Megamarket governments are committed to maintain the high momentum. Article 20 of the Double Taxation Treaty between Germany and China stipulates that scientists from both countries are exempt from personal income tax if they conduct state-of-the-art research. Many Germans are using this loophole to gain experience and top up their net income.

The leading EU countries suffer from receding tax income, which does not leave much room for maneuvers to raise R&D spending. China and Russia spend about 1.3%–1.4% of their GDP on R&D (see figure 3.2), which is more than the ratios of Italy and Spain (both 1.1%). The EU Commission's annual R&D budget was lifted from €5 billion to €8.8 billion during 2006–2013, but it is much less than funds allocated to the EU's agricultural policy, stabilization, and regional (cohesion) funds. China's research spending is still lower than that of the United States or the EU, but it has grown faster, at a rate of 18% annually since 2000 (EU: 2.9%).

The EU remains a large R&D spender if all sources are taken into account: EU Commission, public expenditure by member states, and industrial outlays. In 2007, the EU's overall R&D expenditure amounted to US$221 billion, which was almost three times China's level (see table 3.4). The UK government's push for higher expenditures in science and technology (instead of subsidies for agriculture) had some positive effect but could not remove inherent imbalances, which during the last budgetary negotiations were perpetuated until 2013 by the other member states. What compounds the problem is that R&D expenses of private companies in Europe are also falling as many of them have run into financial difficulties. Aside from cost reasons, other companies have begun relocating their R&D function to the three EMMs, thus severely reducing job opportunities for

Table 3.4. Structure of R&D expenditure by mega region, 2007.				
Country	Public/Institutional (%)	Industry (%)	Total (US$ bn)	Share in GDP (%)
USA	36.9	63.1	284.6	2.6
EU	45.5	54.5	221.1	1.7
Japan	25.5	74.5	114.0	3.3
China	39.9	60.1	84.6	1.4
Source: EU Commission. 2008.				

scientists, researchers, and engineers in the EU. Europe's declining role as a leading R&D center has many related causes:

- Overregulated environments (for example, in biotechnology) incite many scientists and researchers to emigrate.
- Many inventions cannot be converted into marketable products due to small or stagnant domestic markets.
- Many organizations emphasize fundamental research rather than pragmatic "applied" research, which would be closer to the market.
- Europeans create fewer innovative companies as their entrepreneurial spirit is blocked by comfortable social welfare systems.
- Technologies and processes are imitated by Asian competitors who are swift at catching up and improving further.

For the moment, megamarket companies still carry the stigma of "inferior quality producers ready to copy without respecting intellectual property." Absorbing someone else's knowledge is not a new strategy. Immediately after America's independence in 1776, its government made it the official policy to steal inventions from Europe, thus expediting the country's rise as an industrial power in the nineteenth century. After World War II, Japan, South Korea, and Taiwan started off mainly as suppliers of cheap products and components, but they eventually ended up in the top league, challenging the West's leading technology companies. Taiwan has become the world's biggest supplier of computers and hardware components. South Korea's Samsung became one of the top ten recipients of patents granted by the US and EU patent offices in the 2000s. Japan's Toyota is the world's most profitable and innovative carmaker. Chinese, Indian, and Russian companies will embark on a similar path by allocating higher and higher R&D budgets.

In China and India, the biggest pressure for respecting intellectual property right now comes from domestic companies keen on protecting their know-how in an effort to reduce royalty payments to foreign technology providers. US TNCs report their Indian subsidiaries as being most active in filing international patents (see figure 3.3).

The research skills of engineers and scientists in megamarkets cannot be overstated. Many of them, especially in industries like metallurgy, automotive, construction, and IT, have been trained in the best US, European, and Japanese universities. Companies from China and India can deploy huge numbers of people to work on a project, which helps speed up development cycles, and explore new areas and alternative approaches, which would

Figure 3.3. Patents filed by Indian entities, 2006.

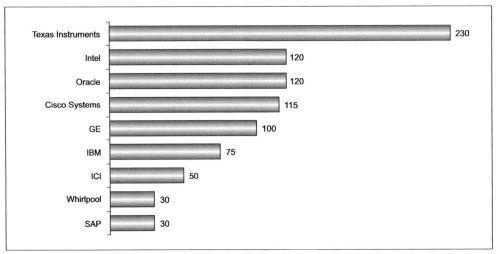

Source: Nasscom, India. 2007.

Table 3.5. Patents granted and IPR litigation cases in China, 2003–2008.

Year	Patents granted	Litigation cases
2003	185,000	7,500
2004	195,000	9,000
2005	205,000	14,000
2006	280,000	14,500
2007	350,000	18,000
2008	440,000	22,000

Source: The Economist. State Intellectual Property Office. Jones Day.

be difficult with a small and expensive personnel count. Today, megamarket players share the ambition to design and develop new products; they register a growing number of patents. As these companies establish brands and develop products, their incentive to sue will grow. They can rely on a better performing system of national courts and legal counselors ready to defend their cases, as evidenced by China's rising numbers of filings and litigations (see table 3.5).[7] In addition, they are determined to acquire stakes in Western technology companies, which will further enhance their technological edge.

3.2. Agro-resources

Agro-resources can be categorized as follows:
- Commodities (grains, cereals, fruit, vegetables, dry fruit, additives, oils, cotton, wool, forest products, rubber, animal feed, fertilizer), livestock (cattle, pigs, sheep, poultry), and animal products (milk, meat, eggs, butter).
- Semi-processed and processed food items (agribusiness-related), derived directly or indirectly from these commodities: sausages, dairy products, bakery and confectionery products, beverages, baby food, pet food, canned and frozen foods, snacks, tobacco products.
- Horticulture: flowers, plants, spices, seeds.
- Fisheries and aquaculture.

---

7. "Doing Business in China: 800,000 Lawsuits in the Making," *The Economist*, April 12, 2008, 70.

The megamarkets are undergoing revolutionary changes in their household consumption basket, which will put additional pressure on the availability of agro-resources across the globe. Across all income groups, staples such as cereals, potatoes, and pulses are being replaced by more sophisticated and expensive products: fruits and nuts, vegetables, milk and dairy products, eggs, poultry, and fish. While the percentage of food in total household expenditure has been declining sharply, the share of these high value-added items is constantly rising. In India, for example, expenditure related to cereals and pulses dropped by more than sixteen percentage points in the countryside and almost ten points in the cities compared with twenty years ago (see table 3.6).

As a result of sector modernization driven by higher domestic and foreign demand, India has become the world's biggest producer of mangoes, bananas, litchis, papayas, pomegranates, and sapotas. It has one of the highest productivities in grapes, strawberries, and other horticulture crops. China has developed its agriculture, livestock, and agribusiness along the same lines. Since 2005, Russia has adopted several measures that are showing positive effects in view of a broad-based agricultural renewal; it is in the process of setting up a complete agro-chain, which incorporates farming, fishing, transportation, warehousing, agro-processing, and retailing (see figure 3.4).

Table 3.6. Changes in India's food basket, 1983, 2007 (expenditure as % of total food).

	Rural		Urban	
Items	1983	2007	1983	2007
Cereals and pulses	55.3	38.7	38.6	29.0
Milk and dairy products	11.5	15.4	15.7	18.6
Eggs, fish, and meat	4.6	6.0	6.1	6.4
Vegetables	7.2	11.1	8.4	10.5
Fruits and nuts	2.1	34.0	3.6	5.3
Other food items	19.3	25.4	27.6	30.2
Share in total household expenses	65.6	55.0	59.1	42.5

Source: Government of India. Level and Pattern of Consumer Expenditure. 2008.

Figure 3.4. Dynamics of modern agri-chains in megamarkets.

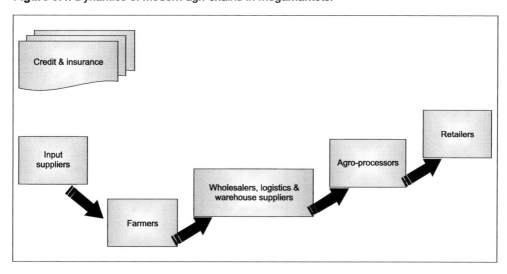

The Green Revolution and skyrocketing demand from the cities contributed immensely to the development of agriculture in the megamarkets, particularly India and China. EMMs rank among the world's leading agricultural producers for grains, pulses, sunflowers, sugar beets, potatoes, vegetables, fruits, meat, and eggs. Their meat and milk output has gone up significantly[8] as they have large quantities of livestock.

Megamarket governments pursue a strategy of making their national agro-industrial complexes (AIC) more efficient; their policies are oriented toward:

- achieving "food security";
- ensuring the "greening" of all important stages of production through new technologies;
- raising the megamarkets' profiles as exporters of agricultural produce; and
- social change in the countryside so that living standards of the rural population match those of city dwellers.

These goals are to be achieved by:

- encouraging scientific and technical developments;
- improving access to markets;
- developing social infrastructure in rural areas;
- upgrading the financial system (loans, micro finance);
- increasing investment in the AIC from banks, government, and foreign investors;
- using a differentiated approach to tailor policies to individual regions; and
- assessing the success and correcting the effects of policy implementation.

Especially in China and India, the majority of people reside in rural areas where they must find employment. In India, the agricultural sector accounts for 35% of GDP and employs around 65% of the population; output levels are going to double during 2006–2015. The agribusiness complex represents a US$70 billion industry, of which 50% is in value-added food products. Chinese and Russian authorities have proposed agriculture as a key sector to improve inequality problems, facilitate employment transformation, maintain high growth, and act as a bridge connecting them with modern industries and services. Agro-industry is encouraged so that processing gets closer to essential agricultural inputs; workers can be shifted from primary agriculture; real wages of farmers are improved; and urban migration is reduced. Agro-industry is attracting foreign companies in most of its segments: dairy products;[9] confectionery and bakery items; meat and poultry; aquaculture; frozen, tinned, and convenience foods; and beverages. Competitive pricing and higher quality standards of agricultural products have created excellent trade opportunities for EU and US companies. This includes areas such as food processing equipment and logistics that ensure a well-functioning cold chain across the entire value chain. The food industry is strictly regulated. To avoid protectionism, for example in the form of import bans or embargoes, and to avail of incentives (tax breaks), foreign investors need to switch from trading to FDI, enabling them to acquire the status of national players. They can thus get closer to the market while indigenizing or regionalizing their products to take advantage of geographic and ethnic diversity.

---

8. See 3.2.3.
9. FDI in food and beverages in China rose after the contaminated milk scandal in September 2008 that significantly reduced the prices of company assets.

3.2.1. Food commodities

CEREALS AND POTATOES

According to the Food and Agriculture Organization (FAO), world annual cereal (grain) production during 2003–2006 averaged two billion metric tons (see figure 3.5). Output is very dependent on weather conditions (drought versus abundant rains), extension or reduction of arable land, and modernization of agricultural equipment. The most important crops were maize (600 million t), rice (590 million t), and wheat (585 million t). Yields (output/area) can differ considerably depending on the region and climatic conditions. Average yields are about 3,050 kilograms per hectare for cereals, 4,295 kilograms per

Figure 3.5. Cereal[a] and potato production in major economies, 2006.

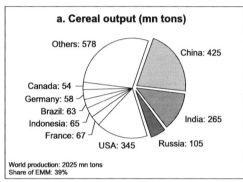
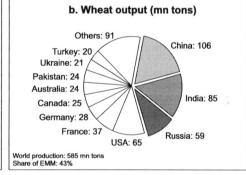
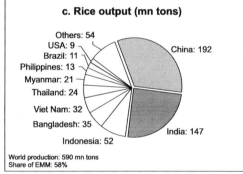
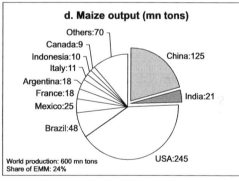
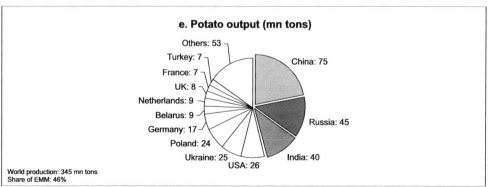

a. Includes wheat, rice, maize, rye, barley, and millet.

Source: FAO Bulletin of Statistics, FAO Production Yearbook.

hectare for maize, 3,850 kilograms per hectare for rice, and 2,690 kilograms per hectare for wheat. There is a wide gap, however, between productivity in advanced and emerging/developing economies. German farmers, for example, manage to generate output levels of 7,800 kilograms per hectare for wheat and 7,100 kilograms per hectare for cereals in general. In absolute figures, however, the three megamarkets have attained a dominant position. In potatoes, an important staple, their share in world production is a staggering 46%.

3.2.2. Non-food commodities

COTTON AND WOOL

Cotton and wool are important agricultural resources with strong impacts on downstream textiles, clothing, and industrial fibers/textiles industries (see figure 3.6). China and India have both built strong domestic textile and apparel industries, which absorb a large portion of domestic demand but are also exported worldwide. In 2008, China's global market share in textiles was 47%, India's 18%. Major exporters of cotton are the United States (about 30% of world exports), China, Pakistan, and the Central Asian (CIS) economies. East Asian OECD members (Japan, South Korea) and emerging economies are the biggest importers. World cotton prices have come under pressure as producers are running at full capacity and users switch to substitutes such as chemical fibers owing to their versatility and lower cost.

The largest producers of wool—Australia and New Zealand—are also the biggest exporters. Japan and EU economies are important importers and consumers. Sheep wool accounts for 20% of overall inputs of the world's textile industry compared with 30% for cotton and over 50% for chemical fibers. It is mainly high-grade clothing that has high wool/cotton content. Famous Italian, German, and Japanese fashion houses try to optimize their supplier and distribution networks in EMs. The megamarkets are particularly attractive for their procurement potential and as growing markets for luxury clothing.

Figure 3.6. Cotton and wool production in major economies, 2006.

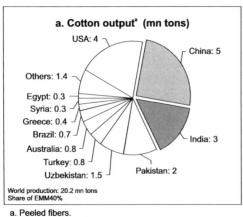
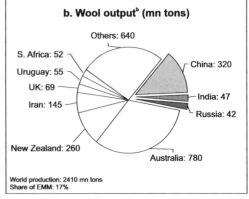

a. Peeled fibers.
b. Raw wool (sheep).

Source: FAO Bulletin of Statistics, FAO Production Yearbook.

Forestry resources

The world's forest cover is about 3.9 billion hectares. Russia leads the ranking, followed by Brazil, Canada, the United States, and China (see figure 3.7a). Total wood felling amounted to 3,350 million cubic meters in 2000 (the latest available data), of which 1,535 million cubic meters was industrial wood and 1,750 million cubic meters firewood. In many developing economies, wood is used primarily for private purposes (e.g., firewood) and industrial energy generation. About two-thirds of the trees felled are leaf-bearing types. A severe problem facing most countries is deforestation, which at the global level, according to FAO,[10] is estimated to be in the range of 13 million hectares per annum. Industrial logging, clearing, and forest conversion for agriculture, fuel wood collection by rural poor, and forest fires are considered the main causes of deforestation. Wide-ranging reforestation efforts have mitigated net deforestation and entailed an increase of forestry

Figure 3.7. Countries with largest forest cover and plantation areas, 2005.

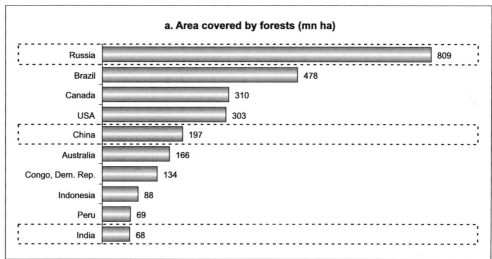

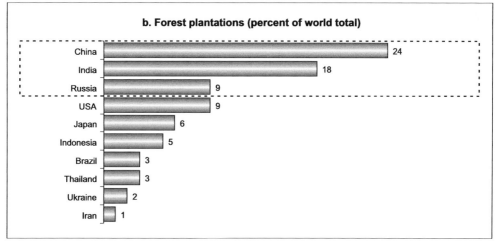

Source: FAO, Global Forest Resources Assessment (FRA). 2005.

---

10. Food and Agriculture Organization, *Global Forest Resources Assessment* (2005).

reserves in many countries. Worldwide, reforestation and afforestation affect an area of 3–4 million hectares per annum. The top ten countries account for almost 80% of the total forest plantation (see figure 3.7b). The three megamarkets lead the world ranking in new tree plantations; they have launched policies making wood their most important "regenerating" raw material. About 10% of the world's forests are under legal protection, such as parks and reserves that help to promote and organize preservation.

Price liberalization and institutional reforms have strengthened Russia's role as a major exporter of round and sawn wood. Russia is a major supplier to Germany (largest in sawn wood), Finland, and Sweden (25% of round wood imports for industrial use in both countries). Russia attracts investments in its forestry sector as rapid economic growth increases the demand for forestry products. Russia has become particularly interesting for European TNCs involved in wood processing, furniture, cellulose, paper and cardboard production, and wood constructions. Prices for wood-related raw materials, semi-manufactures, and processed products have risen and almost reached international standards in Russia due to a considerable increase in domestic and foreign demand. China has become the largest consumer of logs from tropical developing countries; they are converted into furniture, plywood, and other processed products for domestic use and export to the United States, Japan, and Europe. Timber demand in EMMs is driven by paper making, which is expected to grow exponentially in the coming years because of a boost in packaging and printing. According to Russian media reports published in 2007, "China's businessmen intend to lease one million hectares of forests in Siberia as a first step toward closer friendship and interdependence."

India's forests—mainly in the picturesque foothills of the Himalayas stretching from Kashmir to Assam, the northern highlands of the Deccan, the Western Ghats, and the Andaman Islands—have historically suffered tremendous compression from large human and animal populations looking to expand sources of fuel wood, timber, fodder, and grazing as well as faulty agricultural and irrigation practices, environmentally questionable mining, urbanization, and industrialization activities. In 2005, India had a surface of only around 68 million hectares of forestland, 13% less than ten years earlier (1995: 78 million ha). The country's forest cover has been dwindling at a fast rate of 1.3 million hectares per year during 1970–2000, corresponding to a 2.3% annual reduction. Afforestation programs (138,000 ha were planted each year in the 1980s, 38,000 ha in the 1990s) were insufficient to compensate for the loss. According to the government's national forest policy, 33% of the land area should be covered by forest, but actual forest coverage is just 21%. Degradation was slowed down, although not totally halted, by a series of measures:

- legal and policy mechanisms aimed at protecting forests and wildlife (bird sanctuaries, biosphere reserves);
- improved forestry research and education through the Indian Council of Forestry Research and Education (ICFRE);
- technological advancement in forest inventory and management;
- participatory management.

Most forests (98%) in India are administered by forest departments at the state level; they are reserved or protected for permanent timber and water supplies. Only a small percentage belongs to townships and village communes. The government has prohibited commercial harvesting of trees, except for mature, fallen, or sick trees, but this policy is widely violated. About 93% of the total timber cut in 2000 (320 million cubic meters) was burned as fuel. India therefore needs to import large quantities of timber for processing but also final products, including newsprint, printing and writing paper, and recovered paper products. Similar violations are reported from Russia's and China's remote regions (e.g., Siberia, Xinjiang/Tibet).

3.2.3. Animal husbandry and fisheries

Animal livestock determines national production capacity of meat, milk, and other dairy cultures. The world meat market has more or less recovered from the BSE[11] crisis in 2000–2001, but a certain scare remains, leading to sometimes irrational measures (e.g., sporadic Chinese and Indian embargoes on US/EU meat in 2005–2007). In 2006, world meat production stood at 255 million metric tons (see figure 3.8a). The biggest exporters of beef were Australia, the United States, and Canada; in pork, Denmark, Netherlands, Canada, and China; and in poultry, the United States, France, the Netherlands, and Brazil. For two large emerging markets—China and Brazil—meat is a major export item, with local companies investing in foreign farms to optimize the value chain. Further increases in meat trade are impeded by protectionist tariff and non-tariff barriers. Meat remains a highly sensitive area, where any country can obstruct imports if the slightest scandal occurs or retaliatory countermeasures need to be implemented.

China has the world's largest pig population, and India is leading in cattle (see figure 3.9). Both countries have very large sheep populations. Russia is recovering from a severe livestock crisis in the 1990s and is steadily increasing its animal head counts, although it still imports well over half of its meat requirement. The three countries are significant producers of meat, although the composition varies according to climatic conditions, customs, and traditions. Pork and beef are hardly consumed in India (although it holds a large cattle population for milk), which has a large Muslim population. India is the only large-scale producer of mutton. In Russia, a large amount of the meat is processed into sausages and other meat products. China is also moving in that direction, but the quality of such meat products has yet to improve to satisfy consumer expectations.

The megamarkets have developed strong milk industries. Since 2001, India has maintained the top position for overall (cow, buffalo) production after overtaking the United States. For cow milk, India and Russia hold the second and third positions (see figure 3.8b) and by 2010, they will account for 20% of world production. In China, the dairy cluster is still relatively small but is one of the fastest growing industries within the agribusiness complex. However, in September 2008, China's dairy industry was shaken by the contaminated milk incident that caused many neonatal deaths. Sector consolidation is led by the three top players Yili, Mengniu, Guangming, and Sanyuan, which control 50% of the assets, but also a growing number of well-managed regional dairies with innovative products and good distribution networks.

---

11. Bovine Spongiforme Encephalopathie (mad cow disease).

Figure 3.8. Meat and milk output of major economies, 2006.

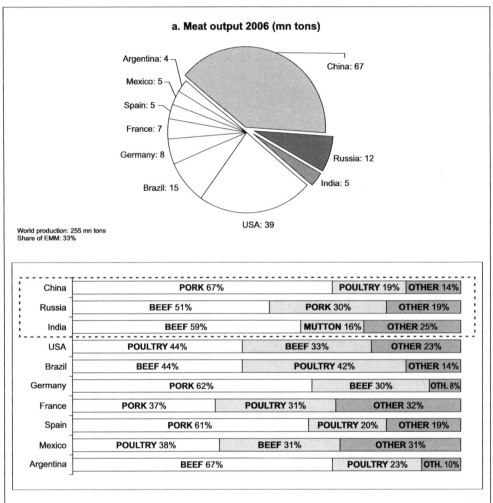

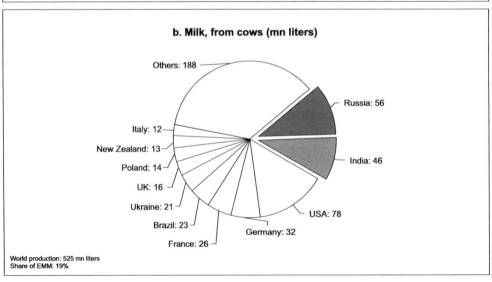

Source: FAO Bulletin of Statistics.

Figure 3.9. Livestock in major economies, 2006.

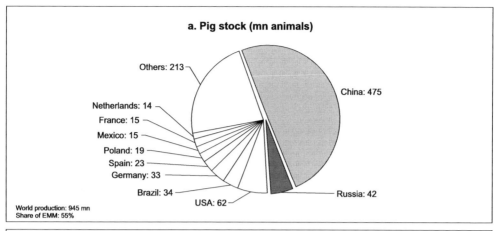

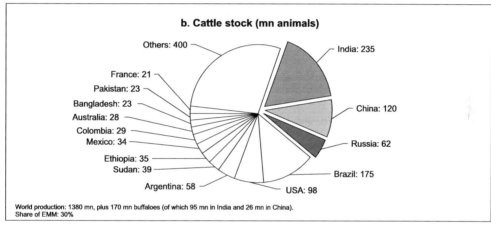

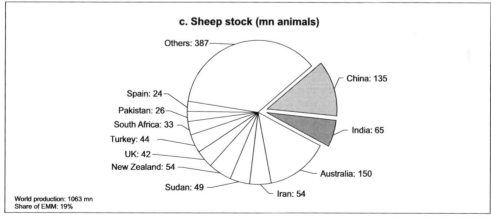

Source: FAO Bulletin of Statistics.

India's dairy cluster has benefited strongly from more stable production, which has become possible as a result of the introduction of innovative technologies and the mechanization of processes. These technical advances are creating new economic opportunities for higher income for a range of agribusiness enterprises. These developments have triggered a revolution that is transforming the socioeconomic life of millions of farmers, which could herald the beginning of the second phase of the "White Revolution." India's ethnic dairy specialties have become extremely popular, and brands such as Amul, Nestlé, Mother Dairy, and Britannia are familiar household names. They are also expanding overseas, largely among the 20 million Indians living abroad. In North America (USA, Canada) alone, the value of exported dairy-based products from India directed at the South Asian community is estimated at US$600–700 million. Many milk cooperatives operate at the state level, the leading one being TNCMPF (Tamil Nadu Cooperative Milk Producers' Federation). The second-largest cooperative is GCMMF (Gujarat Cooperative Milk Marketing Federation Ltd.), with MPDMSM (Madhya Pradesh Dugdha Mahasangh [Sahakari] Maryadit) in third place.

Dairy products can be grouped under five major headings:
- desiccated semisolid milk products
- coagulated cheese-like products
- fermented/cultured yogurt-like products
- fat-rich butter- and oil-like products
- milk rice, pudding-like desserts, and puddings

World fish production amounted to about 135 million metric tons in 2002 (the latest available figure published by FAO). Over the past decade, most of the increase has been generated by aqua- and pisciculture (in seas, rivers, and lakes), which is not included in the figures shown below. The fish catch in oceans contracted, dropping below the 90 million metric tons mark (see figure 3.10). The main reasons are increased sea pollution and reduced yields because of previous overfishing. The subdivision of oceans into national fishing zones extending two hundred miles offshore from a country's coastline led to a reduction of fleets in many countries. EU fishing boats used to go far out into the Atlantic and fish up to Iceland and Greenland, which are now protecting their territories. The catching quota for EU countries has been regulated annually since 1983, leading

Figure 3.10. Fish catch[a] in major economies, 2006 (mn tons).

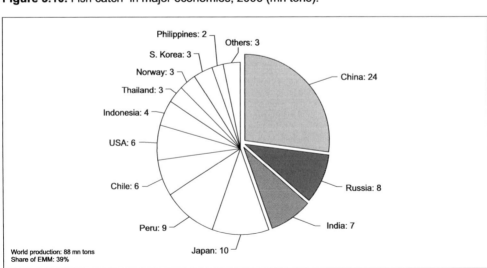

a. Excluding aquaculture and pisciculture.

Source: FAO Bulletin of Statistics.

to new partitions for the Baltic, Atlantic, and Mediterranean. Larger countries benefit most from the internationally agreed two-hundred-mile zones for fishing. Whereas the three megamarkets managed to increase their catch, most EMs, EU countries, Japan, and the United States had to switch to more sophisticated systems of aquaculture to increase output and reduce import dependence.

3.3. Raw materials, mining, and energy resources

The megamarkets are very rich in metals and minerals, which are indispensable for ensuring industrial modernization and advancing construction activities: bauxite, lead, iron ore, zinc, tin, and copper (industrial metals), as well as silver, gold (precious metals) and diamonds. These raw materials are processed and consumed domestically or exported. A brief synopsis illustrates the importance of the megamarkets as suppliers and the trends and opportunities for foreign investors who plan to set up processing units to get closer to the source of these essential inputs. Most raw materials are traded on special exchanges like the London Metal Exchange (industrial metals, including steel) or the New York Mercantile Exchange (industrial metals, precious metals), where traders fix spot prices, forwards, futures, and options to hedge against price fluctuations. The *London Metal Bulletin*[12] publishes prices based on information from producers, consumers, and traders. The spot prices for practically all metal and mineral resources have shot up since the mid-2000s, ironically because of explosive demand from the megamarkets. Whenever possible, megamarket governments strive for high self-sufficiency in strategic raw materials. The objective is to secure essential inputs for national producers and to maintain enough reserves to counter sudden supply shortages or price jumps in world markets. Their competition is increasingly being felt by advanced markets that need to pay higher and higher prices for energy and raw material inputs for their households and industrial users.[13] Russia, the world's leading raw materials and energy supplier, is pondering over the possibility to establish commodity exchanges in St. Petersburg to promote price denominations in national currency and reduce dependence on US dollar fluctuations.

3.3.1. Industrial metals

The following captions are far from complete but offer an insight into the growing importance of megamarkets for world metal production in the various categories of industrial metals (see figure 3.11):

- bauxite
- lead
- iron ore
- copper
- zinc
- tin

---

12. See www.metalbulletin.com.
13. In Germany, prices for oil, gas, and other raw materials shot up 50% during January–June 2008; in value terms, these inputs account for one-third of Germany's imports, with growing tendency. See "Energieimport 50 prozent teurer" [Energy prices up by 50 percent], *Financial Times Deutschland*, September 25, 2008.

Figure 3.11. Production of industrial metals by country, 2006.

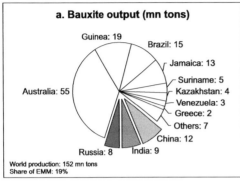

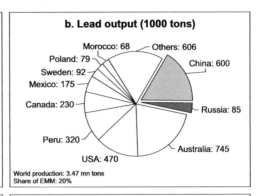

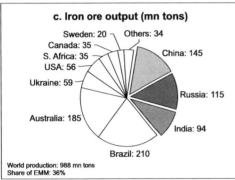

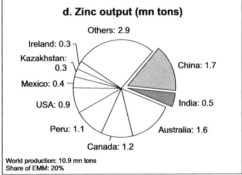

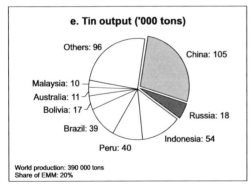

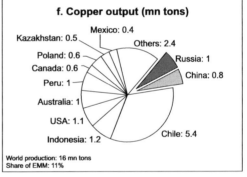

Source: World Mining Data, Vienna, World Bureau of Metal Statistics, ABARE.

BAUXITE

Bauxite is an indispensable input for the aluminum industry. Three-quarters of its production are exported by emerging and developing economies. The world's largest producers are Australia, the United States, Russia, and Jamaica. For some EMs/DEs (e.g., Jamaica, Guinea, Suriname), exports of bauxite or aluminum by-products generate most foreign currency earnings. The main producing countries are grouped in the International Bauxite Association. Russia, China, India, and Brazil have set up sophisticated aluminum processing facilities to cater to domestic and export demands. After the breakup of the Soviet Union, Russia has transformed itself into a leading supplier of aluminum semi-manufactures and is in a position to influence the world aluminum price (similar to OPEC in oil).

Lead

The biggest lead consumers are the United States, Japan, Germany, and China. Consumption heavily depends on the health of the automobile industry as around 60% of world lead output goes into the manufacturing of starter batteries; another 20% is used in the chemical industry. Lead additions to gasoline have become irrelevant since new rules have been introduced worldwide for promoting lead-free gasoline. Total lead reserves in the world are estimated at over 200 million metric tons.

Iron ore

Iron ore is the main raw material in iron and steel manufacturing.[14] Both extraction and prices for iron ore depend on the demand for iron and steel products in construction, the transport sector (automobiles, trains, ships, aviation), machine tools, and household appliances. Since the end of 2003, the world steel market has been experiencing an unprecedented boom, which strongly benefited iron ore suppliers. Most of the iron ore comes from the three megamarkets, the only exception being Australia, which has become a major exporter to China and India as these two economies continue to modernize and expand. The EU has practically become totally dependent on iron ore imports. To get closer to the source, major EU steel companies (MittalArcelor, ThyssenKrupp) are putting up new production facilities in the megamarkets. Downstream suppliers of spares, rolls, and other equipment to the steel industry are compelled to follow the steel companies to the megamarkets.

Copper

Copper is supple, malleable, and a good conductor of heat and electricity. World copper reserves are estimated at over 600 million tons—120 million in Chile, 100 million in the United States, 60–70 million in CIS countries, and 40 million each in Canada and Zambia. The biggest producer is Chile, followed by Indonesia, the United States, Russia, Australia, and Peru. The leading exporting nations meet regularly to coordinate their policies. Over the past few years, copper prices sank due to high stocks, overextraction, and increased recycling, but then demand picked up again in the mid-2000s. Opinions differ as to possible future trends. Higher demand is expected from fast-growing industries such as electronics and telecommunications (25% of sales), but copper is at the same time being replaced by other materials (fiberglass, aluminum, plastics) in consumer goods (9% of demand), equipment (11%), and construction (43%). The biggest importers of copper are Germany, the United States, and Japan.

Zinc

Half of the world's zinc output goes into the automotive and steel sectors, mainly for manufacturing galvanized steel products. Major consumers of zinc are both AMs and EMMs where large infrastructure and construction projects are underway (India's Golden Quadrilateral, China's 2008 Olympics) and a strong automotive sector is emerging.

---

14. Ninety-eight percent of iron ore is used in crude steel and iron production; 2% of output is processed in the cement industry.

Tin

The biggest users of tin are the United States, Japan, and Germany, where the metal is used for manufacturing beverage cans and other packaging items. Recycling represents 50% of tin consumption in AMs, thus putting further pressure on world prices and causing difficulties for Asian and South American exporters.

3.3.2. Precious metals and diamonds

Although traded freely, precious metals (see figure 3.12) and diamonds have a "symbolic" meaning when evaluating the level of self-sufficiency of an economy:
- silver
- gold[15]
- diamonds

Silver

Total silver production was about 19,300 metric tons in 2006. The biggest consumer countries are the United States, Japan, and Germany. Silver is used for photo-chemicals (two-thirds of world consumption), electrical and electronic industries, jewelry, and cutlery as well as medals and coins. Recycling reached a level of 60% (especially from used films). If the melting of coins, jewelry, and so forth, is taken into account, the total recycling value exceeds two-thirds of the world's silver supply. World prices for silver could therefore not follow the upward trend of gold and platinum, and investors increasingly consider it as an industrial (instead of a precious) metal. The price of silver has dropped more than five times from US$35 in 1980. The main reason for these developments is overextraction coupled with lower demand from major buyer segments (chemicals, electronics) owing to increased recycling activities.

Gold

Today's gold extraction amounts to around 2,600 metric tons. Additionally, the market is supplied with 500–600 metric tons that come from old stocks. Main applications are jewelry production (73%), dentistry and general medicine (18%), and the electronics industry (7%). South Africa is the largest producer, although its output has decreased by 35% since 1990. New sites have been discovered in Peru, the United States, Argentina, and CIS countries, leading to increased gold supplies for the world market and a reduction of the importance of South Africa, which used to cover 75% of world demand in the 1970s (its share today is 15%). The world's gold reserves of 56,000 metric tons are located mostly in southern Africa, but in deep deposits (up to 3 km below the surface), which raises the cost of extraction. In most other world sites (Russia, China, Australia), gold can be extracted by surface mining under much better conditions. The prices for gold started going up significantly in 2001 and reached record levels touching US$1,000 per ounce in early 2008.

---

15. Gold reserves, for example, can help governments make up for shortages of foreign exchange reserves.

Figure 3.12. Production of precious metals and diamonds by country, 2006.

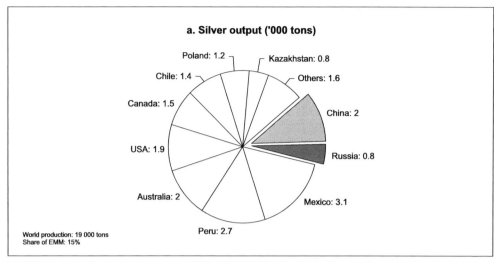

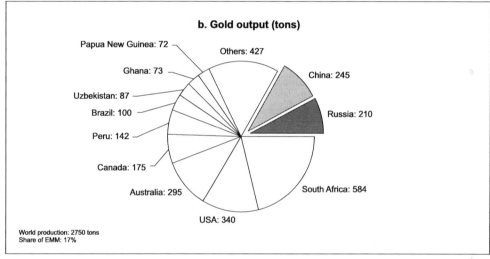

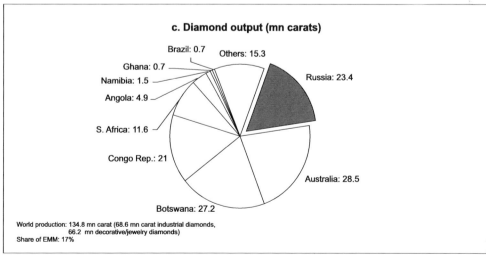

Source: World Mining Data, Vienna, World Bureau of Metal Statistics, ABARE.

Diamonds

Jewelry diamonds account for 80% of extraction. More than three-quarters of industrial diamonds are already produced synthetically.

3.3.3. Energy reserves

Economic growth depends on the timely supply of primary energy resources: oil, gas, coal,[16] hydroelectricity, and renewables (wind, sun). China, India, and Russia have introduced the latest technologies and enhanced public funding and support to encourage exploration and raise productivity and self-sufficiency. In the three countries, proven reserves of oil, natural gas, and coal have gone up. In China and India, however, the speed at which import dependence can be technically reduced is slow given that domestic needs by far exceed supplies. The two mega-economies hardly make it into the league of top fifteen to twenty countries with the largest reserves of oil and natural gas[17] (see figure 3.13). This is in stark contrast with their wealth in agricultural and mineral resources, where China and India hold leading positions in world rankings (see previous sections). Coal is an exception. With proven coal reserves of 114.5 and 92.5 billion tons, respectively, China and India are in third and fourth positions, just behind the United States (246.6 billion t) and Russia (157 million t). The governments of the two countries hope that for the other fossil/nonrenewable fuels (oil, natural gas) exploration efforts will help transform large proportions of presumed reserves into actual (proven) resources in the coming years.

At present, proven oil reserves in China (16 billion t) are a fraction of presumed reserves of 102 billion metric tons. The same applies to gas, where proven reserves are 5% of estimated reserves (2.5 trillion against 47 trillion cubic meters). According to China's ministry of land and resources, there is huge potential for further development[18] as capital investment is going to be enhanced and technology levels improved. Many foreign companies have been invited for oil and gas exploration activities. According to Chinese law, the three national oil giants, PetroChina, Sinopec, and CNOOC, are entitled to take 51% of any commercial discovery project, but they can choose to take a minority stake depending on the circumstances. They can, for example, decide to take over field operations once the contracted firm has recovered its development costs. The Chinese government typically mandates a royalty fee of 12.5% for foreign companies involved in the oil and gas sector. Discounts—i.e., lower fees—are offered for development and exploration in more remote, less accessible areas. Recent exploration efforts have centered on developing onshore oil and natural gas fields in the western provinces of Xinjiang (Tarim basin), Sichuan, Gansu, and Inner Mongolia as well as offshore fields in the Bohai Bay, Pearl River Delta, and South China Sea. Given faster depreciation and break-even cycles, offshore oil exploration has been the greater focus of Western oil majors who participate in several production sharing contracts (PSCs) with national companies.

---

16. Trends in the major energy markets, including enterprises, are described in 4.1.
17. Proven reserves account for only 20%–30% of actual reserves in China and India.
18. *China Daily* (September 2007).

Figure 3.13. Countries with the largest oil and gas reserves, 2006.

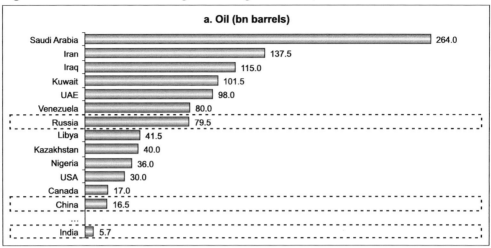

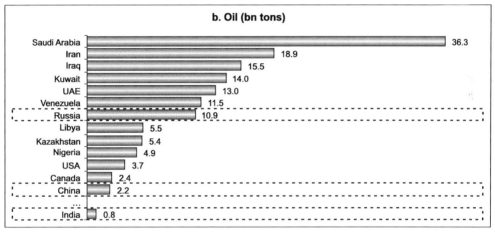

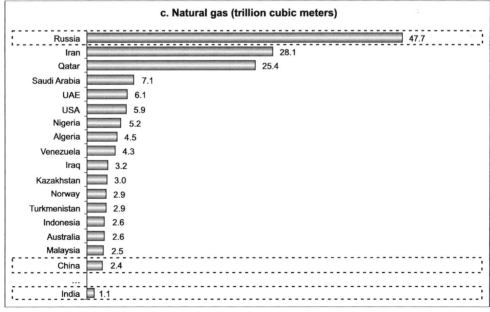

Source: British Petroleum. Statistical Review of World Energy 2007.

Roughly 85% of Chinese oil production capacity is located onshore. China's largest oil producing site, Daqing field in northeastern China, accounts for one-quarter of China's total crude oil production. Daqing is a mature oil field, and output levels have fallen despite efforts to extend its lifetime. New oil fields have been discovered in Shengli, the country's second-largest oil producing field, as well as in Liaohe and Xinjiang. The most promising offshore oil fields are in Bohai Bay and South China Sea. Recent discoveries of natural gas, if successfully developed, promise to significantly increase China's national production. The largest reserves of natural gas are located in western and north-central China. The largest find to date is the Sulige field in the Ordos basin in Inner Mongolia Autonomous Region. Another promising project is the Kela-2 field in the Tarim basin, which by 2010 will feed into the west–east natural gas pipeline connecting it with the cities of Beijing and Shanghai. In July 2006, Sinopec confirmed the existence of a gas site in Puguang, Sichuan province. Almost at the same time, CNOOC announced a new discovery in the South China Sea, the country's first deepwater natural gas field.

India had 5.7 billion barrels of proven oil reserves as of January 2007, the second-largest amount in the Asia-Pacific region behind China. Much of India's crude oil reserves are located off the western coast (Mumbai High basin) and in the northeast of the country (Assam), although substantial undeveloped reserves have been spotted in the offshore Bay of Bengal and in Rajasthan state. To help meet growing oil demand and boost output, India has promoted various exploratory and production (E&P) projects over the last several years. The Ministry of Petroleum and Natural Gas crafted the New Exploration License Policy (NELP) in 2000, which permits foreign companies to hold 100% equity in oil and natural gas projects. To date, a handful of oil fields are operated by foreign firms. During 2000–2007, the government awarded 130 oil and natural gas concessions in six licensing rounds. State-owned Oil and Natural Gas Corporation (ONGC), often in consortia with other national oil companies (NOCs), has secured most exploration blocks. Reliance, India's largest private company in this sector, is working on seven deepwater blocks in the Krishna-Godavari (Andhra Pradesh) and Mahanadi (Orissa) basins, which are poised to become India's most promising offshore hydrocarbon basins. The Indian government pledged to sign more production sharing contracts (PSCs) with international oil TNCs in order to use their deepwater experience and technical expertise.

As of January 2007, India had 38 trillion cubic feet (Tcf)—1.1 trillion cubic meters (Tcm)—of proven natural gas reserves. At present, the bulk of India's natural gas comes, similar to oil, from the western offshore regions, especially the Mumbai High complex. The onshore fields in Assam, Andhra Pradesh, and Gujarat states are also major producers of natural gas. India imports small amounts of natural gas, mainly in liquefied form (LNG) from Qatar. There have been several large natural gas finds in India since 2001, predominantly in the offshore Bay of Bengal. In December 2006, ONGC announced that it had identified natural gas off the coast of Andhra Pradesh in the Krishna Godavari basin. On the same day, ONGC announced another find in the Mahanadi basin off the coast of Orissa state. These finds could significantly lift India's natural gas reserve levels. Nonetheless, most analysts expect demand for natural gas—the major fuel in the country's energy mix—to outstrip new supply in the two decades ahead. ONGC and Reliance have therefore worked to maximize the recovery rates at the Mumbai High basin (Tapti, Panna, and Mukti fields).

In recent years, Indian NOCs have looked to acquire equity stakes in E&P projects overseas. The most active company is ONGC Videsh Ltd., the overseas investment arm of ONGC. As of 2007, ONGC Videsh holds interests in twenty-five oil and natural gas projects in fifteen countries, spanning Africa, Asia, Latin America, and the Middle East. ONGC Videsh also has a 20% stake in the ExxonMobil-led consortium that operates the Sakhalin-I project in Russia.

In terms of hydrocarbons, Russia is in a much more comfortable position than either China or India. It has plenty of reserves on its vast territory stretching across the northern part of the Eurasian continent. Its estimated reserves are five to six times higher than proven reserves, which secures it a place as one of the world's leading energy suppliers in the future, together with other countries from the Middle East, CIS, North Africa, and Latin America. Energy consumption in Russia is much lower than in China and India, which both have populations exceeding 1 billion. The challenge will consist of identifying new deposits in Eastern Siberia, which has remained largely unexplored. In the North Pole region and Barents Sea, of which Russia claims a large part, new offshore sites have become accessible with the progressive melting of the ice caused by climatic changes (global warming owing to increased CO_2 emissions). A large proportion of Russia's oil and gas production still comes from fields that have exhausted most of their recoverable reserves. Achieving continued growth at "post-peak" fields will become a major concern as oil companies run out of easy and cost-effective options to manage the rate of decline. It is expected that newer sites ("pre-peak" fields) in Western/Eastern Siberia, Yamal peninsula, and Sakhalin will account for the bulk of Russia's annual oil output in 2010–2015; they are likely to produce more than 50% of the country's oil by 2020, thus compensating losses in older fields (Volga/Ural, Western Siberia).

Megamarket governments encourage energy savings as a means to cut costs, foreign dependence, and emission levels (the three countries are signatories to the Kyoto protocol). Energy savings lead to higher efficiency, which is closely linked to energy security[19] and often covered by the same legislation. Energy security has a political dimension. In China, a draft energy law to be put into operation in 2008–2009 will instruct domestic oil companies to build their own oil reserves, which will be subject to state supervision and management. These measures would supplement government-owned inventories as buffers for supply crunches (imports account for half of China's total energy demand). In August 2006, China began filling a series of national reserve tanks to build an initial estimated oil reserve capacity of about 15 million tons.[20] The new law proposes free determination of energy prices by the market, but the government intends to retain a control over prices to lower the socioeconomic impact of sudden price hikes. With China's expectation of growing dependence on oil and gas imports in the future, the country is keen to acquire more stakes in exploration and production sites abroad (e.g., Sudan, Venezuela, Kazakhstan, Russia).

India is following a similar trajectory with respect to energy security and outward investments. Indian officials have declared that the country intends to develop a strategic petroleum reserve (SPR). To date, plans have been approved for the construction of

---

19. Reuters, *China Drafts Energy Policy Requiring New Oil Reserves,* December 3, 2007.
20. By the end of 2007, China's strategic tanks contained only about 3 million tons (22 million barrels).

storage tanks with a storage capacity of 5 million metric tons of crude oil at sites near Visakhapatnam, Mangalore, and Padur. Work at the planned storage sites began in early 2007 and is expected to be completed by 2011. The SPR project is being led by the Indian Strategic Petroleum Reserves Limited, which is part of the Oil Industry Development Board, a state-controlled organization that manages loans and grants to the oil industry.

CHAPTER 4
Eurasia's megamarkets as business platforms for pillar industries

The economic progress of Eurasia's megamarkets, especially China and its surrounding Asian EMs, has led to an expansion of capacity in the region, mostly at the expense of advanced economies, where industrial employment has decreased. The pressure for companies to move to the megamarkets will grow as a consequence of the 2008 financial crisis that most severely hit traditional industries (less so high-tech industries and service sectors) in the developed Western economies, but also as a response to policies initiated by megamarket governments to foster domestic consumption which will compensate losses incurred by plummeting exports to the West.

The decline of many industries in the West is seen by several business scholars as a sign of natural selection that will force competitive enterprises to innovate, although it is alarming politicians whose immediate concern is to preserve jobs and keep electoral promises. In the past, it was mainly low-paying jobs in textiles, furniture, and light consumer goods that went to emerging economies. Today, they aspire at leadership in value-added industries and services as well.

State-led industrial policies and a revived entrepreneurial spirit have given rise to strong megamarket companies, some of which became aggressive exporters and investors in the very countries from which they used to import technology. The three new mega-economies of Eurasia today host a broad spectrum of enterprises in traditional (pillar), high-tech, and service industries, which benefit from huge internal markets and opportunities in surrounding economies. Whether privately run or state-owned, domestic players are sharpening their competitive edge vis-à-vis their Western competitors. All along the 1990s and 2000s their market value has risen along with economic success and future market expectations. They offer foreign companies an excellent platform for expansion as customers, partners, and investors. The overall trajectory of value creation will continue despite the 2008 financial crisis which has led to a fall in sales and staff cuts, in particular among companies highly dependent on exports to North America and Europe.

The following three chapters will review trends in key sectors until 2015–2020:
- pillar industries: energy, steel, construction, vehicles, machine building, chemicals, and consumer goods
- high-tech industries: pharmaceuticals, telecommunications, aerospace, and environmental technologies
- services: IT, banking, insurance, retailing, logistics, tourism, and hospitality

The rapid progress of megamarket companies in these partly interwoven industries is a positive signal for dynamic AM companies that are ready to take on the challenge and grasp the opportunity. Before devising effective counterstrategies, Western managers must gain an understanding of underlying trends and what is at stake if they don't get their act together.

4.1. Energy

4.1.1. Global energy sector trends

The China National Offshore Oil Corporation's (CNOOC)[1] bid for the US oil and gas company Unocal in October 2005 awakened the global energy sector to the arrival of new, aggressive players from the megamarkets on the international scene. Major Western energy companies have recognized that to develop further, they can no longer ignore energy competitors from the megamarkets, where energy requirements will increase exponentially to cover electrification, industrialization, and transportation services, which have yet to reach a sizeable part of the population. Some of the megamarket energy majors have joined the ranks of the world's leading companies in terms of revenues and profits (see table 4.1). They represent attractive customers for suppliers of energy-related equipment and components. The world's two largest suppliers—Halliburton (US$24.6 billion in 2007) and Schlumberger (US$23.3 billion), both from the United States—have appointed special key account managers to cater to the requirements of megamarket energy majors.

Table 4.1. The world's top fifteen energy players, 1/1/2008.

	Revenues (US$ bn)	Profits (US$ bn)
ExxonMobil, USA	372.8	40.6
Royal Dutch Shell, Netherlands	355.8	31.3
British Petroleum, UK	291.4	20.9
Chevron, USA	210.8	18.7
Total, France	187.3	18.0
ConocoPhillips, USA	178.6	11.9
Sinopec, China	159.3	4.2
PetroChina, China	129.8	14.9
ENI, Italy	120.6	13.7
PEMEX, Mexico	104.0	3.1
Gazprom, Russia	98.6	19.3
Valero Energy, USA	96.8	5.3
E.ON, Germany	94.4	9.9
Statoil Hydro, Norway	89.2	7.5
Petrobras, Brazil	87.7	13.1

Source: Fortune Global 500, 2008.

As more countries across all continents have embarked on a high-growth path, the current trend of rising energy demand is expected to persist right up to the 2020s (see table 4.2). According to the International Energy Agency in Vienna, emerging markets will account for two-thirds of the 57% increase in world consumption of marketed energy between 2005 and 2025. In 2025, the combined consumption in these markets will exceed that of advanced markets by 9%.

The 2008–2009 financial crisis has bent down the world's energy demand curve. The price of oil and other energy sources dropped to record low levels (oil, for example, from US$140/barrel in July 2008 to under US$40/barrel in November 2008[2]), but experts predict a resumption of the nor-

---

1. In 2007, CNOOC reported sales of US$18 billion and profits of US$3.5 billion.
2. At an extraordinary meeting in Algeria on 17 December 2008, OPEC decided to cut oil production by 2.2 million barrels/day (3% of current world production) starting from 1 January 2009. Bloc outsiders Russia and Azerbaijan announced their own cutbacks by several hundreds of thousands of barrels in an effort to stabilize prices.

Table 4.2. Primary energy demand in major economies, 2005–2025.

Country/region	2025 (quadrillion BTU[a])	2005 (quadrillion BTU)	Average annual growth (%)
USA	132.4	102.0	1.3
China	109.2	47.2	4.1
EU	76.1	69.4	0.5
Russia	37.9	29.5	1.4
India	29.3	17.0	3.3
Japan	24.7	22.5	0.5
Brazil	15.1	10.6	2.5
Mexico	10.9	7.6	2.2

a. BTU = British Thermal Unit (unit of energy used in USA for power and steam generation, heating and air conditioners; it is gradually being replaced by Joules).
Sources: EIA, Annual Energy Outlook, www.eia.doe.gov.

mal trajectory once the world economy recovers, accentuating the depletion of traditional energy reserves that was already raising concerns before the crisis. First signs of a recovery with subsequent oil price hikes were observed in mid-2009 (US$65–70/barrel).

Oil which fuels transportation and industry will remain the dominant form of energy despite efforts to develop alternative sources. While OPEC countries and Russia will remain major energy producers and exporters thanks to an abundant surplus in their energy balance, all other economic regions will continue importing far more energy than they are capable of generating (see figure 4.1).[3] The concentration of this strategic resource in a few countries will stoke fears of geopolitical risk and overdependence on powerful suppliers (e.g., EU vs. Russia), driving energy-deficient countries to seek diverse sources of supply. Consequently, India and China will compete and at the same time cooperate for stakes in overseas oil fields along with traditional US and EU oil majors. Securing energy sources against disruption of supplies will be the main objective of this race.

Meanwhile, as the "after fossil fuels" scenario comes closer to reality, governments and companies are investigating renewable forms of energy (wind, solar, biomass, hydropower) and developing technologies to harness them for commercial use. Renewable sources like wind and solar power currently provide 13% of the world's energy needs (see figure 4.2); they already play an important role in progressive countries like Germany and Denmark. According to the US Department of Energy, the United States could supply its entire energy needs by covering a mere 1.6% of its land area with solar cells.[4] EU companies, which lead in R&D and equipment for this promising energy segment, participate in several profitable projects in the megamarkets. German companies are front-runners in renewable energy technology. Between 2007 and 2010, German exports in this segment will double to €15.7 billion;[5] by 2020, this figure is projected to attain €80 billion, given the soaring international demand.

---

3. In 2007, the United States imported 1.2 billion metric tons of crude oil. China came second with one-third of this volume, followed by Japan, Russia, and Germany.
4. "Cleaning Up: A Special Report on Business and Climate Change," *The Economist*, June 2, 2007, 20–21.
5. "Alternative energien übertreffen alle prognosen" [Alternative energy sources surpass expectations], *Handelsblatt*, June 18, 2008.

Figure 4.1. The world's leading ten oil and gas producing countries, 2007.

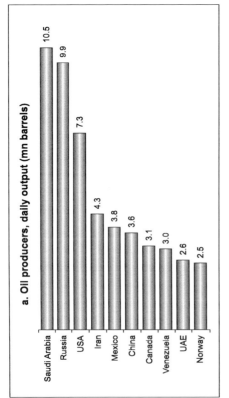

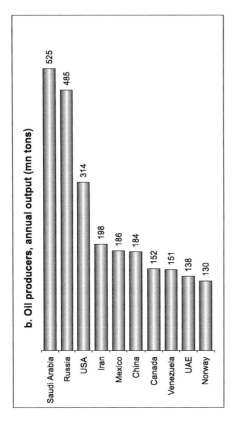

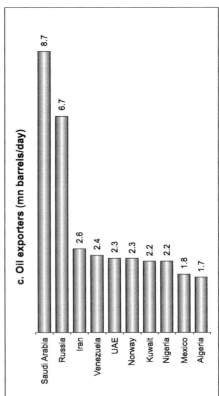

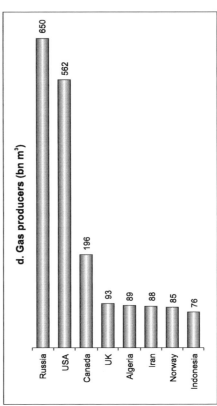

Source: *International Energy Agency.*

Figure 4.2. Share of world primary energy sources, 2006, 2020.

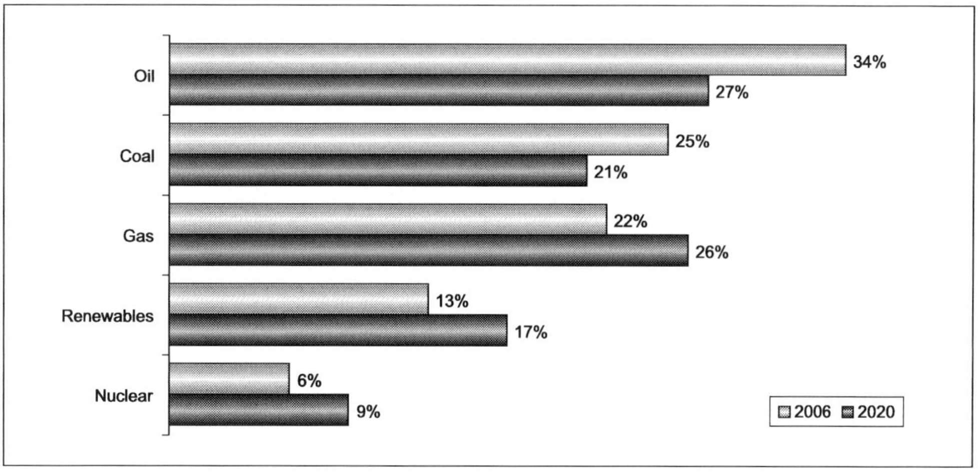

	2006	2020
Oil	34%	27%
Coal	25%	21%
Gas	22%	26%
Renewables	13%	17%
Nuclear	6%	9%

Source: International Atomic Energy Agency (IAEA)

Nuclear power, another non-fossil source, provides about 6% of the world's energy and 15% of its electricity, with the United States, France, and Japan together accounting for 56% of overall nuclear-generated electricity.[6] As of 2007, the International Atomic Energy Agency (IAEA) reported there were 439 nuclear power reactors in operation in thirty-one countries. The United States produces the most nuclear power, which provides 19% of the electricity it consumes, while France produces the highest proportion of its electrical energy from nuclear reactors—78%. The 1973 oil crisis had a significant impact on countries such as France and Japan, which had earlier relied heavily on oil for electricity generation (39% and 73%, respectively). The 1979 accident at Three Mile Island and the 1986 Chernobyl disaster raised awareness of potential risks on citizens' health and safety. New plant constructions were stopped in countries like Germany where the anti-nuclear movement fed on the fear of accidents, radiation, and strong opposition to nuclear waste transport and storage. But spiraling oil prices in the mid-2000s prompted many governments, including those from the megamarkets (see below), to bet on nuclear power again. Today, the industry faces two challenges. One is related to the limited reserves of uranium-235, which will last thirty to fifty years at the current rate of consumption. New technologies and better reactor designs (e.g., fast breeders using widely found uranium-238[7] as opposed to light water reactors dependent on the rare uranium-235 isotope) should bring relief. Safe storage and nuclear waste disposal represent the other important challenge, for which technicians have not yet found a clear response, particularly to the problem of long-term radioactive fallout.

4.1.2. Energy sector trends in the megamarkets

Russia

Russia is the world's new energy superpower. It is the world's second-largest oil producer (9.9 million barrels per day in 2007 compared with 10.5 million barrels per day for Saudi

---

6. International Energy Agency (IEA), *Key World Energy Statistics* (2007).
7. Uranium-238 represents 99.3% of natural uranium reserves, which could last several thousand years. See "Nucléaire: Le bon et le moins bon" [Nuclear power: The good and the less good], *Le Point*, July 3, 2008, 48.

Arabia) and the largest producer of gas (650 billion m³ compared with 562 billion m³ for second-place USA). Europe will continue to source energy mainly from Russia, but it will have to compete with the United States and Asian countries (especially China) for Russian energy resources. For the United States, Russia offers a strategic alternative to Middle Eastern and Latin American suppliers.[8]

The continuous hikes in oil prices from September 2007[9] have allowed Russia to surmount its financial crisis, to pay back its foreign debt, and to leverage these resources to regain geopolitical power not only in the surrounding regions but also worldwide. In 2006–2007, the oil and gas sector accounted for 61% of Russia's overall exports (US$150 billion)[10]—an extremely high dependence that will take time to reduce. Oil revenues feed directly into the state coffers through corporate profit and export taxes. The Russian government has plans to use these windfall profits for developing downstream (e.g., chemicals, pharmaceuticals, packaging films) and high–tech sectors (e.g., nano and IT technologies, electronics) to push for an industrial diversification, but has done this so far with mixed results. National politicians are in favor of modernizing the oil and gas complex itself, mainly with the help of foreign technologies. According to the government, it is not sufficient that Russia remains a major energy producer and exporter, but the country must also become a supplier of high value-added energy products (e.g., high-octane gasoline, motor oils, aviation fuel, special additives) and an innovator in new technologies for energy conservation and geological exploration, enabling a shift from extensive to intensive extraction. The task ahead is huge and challenging. Oil and gas are so essential for the Russian economy, and seven of the country's top ten companies are in the energy sector (see table 4.3). The top crude extracting companies in 2007 were: Rosneft (103 million tons), Lukoil (96 million

Table 4.3. Russia's top ten companies, 2007.			
Company	Sector	Sales (US$ bn)	Change 2007/2006 (%)
Gazprom	Gas, oil	99	+27
Lukoil	Oil	82	+41
Rosneft	Oil	49	+33
Russian Railways	Railways	41	+15
TNK-BP	Oil	39	+26
RAO UES	Electricity	28	+18
Surgutneftegaz	Oil	27	+17
Sberbank	Banking	21	+ 9
Tatneft	Oil	17	+35
Norilsk Nickel	Metals	11	+64
Source: Fortune 500. 2008. Expert.			

8. While imports covered 25% of the United States' national oil demand in 1970, the country's import dependence rose to 65% in 2007. This share is expected to rise further if adequate measures toward new sources of energy (nuclear, renewables) are not taken. See "Nuclear After Oil," *Expert*, June 12, 2006, 70.

9. In February 2008, the price of crude for the first time climbed above the psychological mark of US$100 per barrel. It reached the price of US$140 per barrel in mid-2008 before it dropped again as a result of the financial crisis in September 2008.

10. Even in the days of the Soviet Union, fossil energy represented a high percentage (58%) of all exports to industrialized countries. "Ne pererabotali" [They did not process it], *Vesti*, 2 (2006): 54–56.

tons), TNK-BP (72.4 million tons), Surgutneftegaz (64.5 million tons), Gazprom-Neft (33 million tons), Tatneft (25.4 million tons) and Bashneft (11.5 million tons). Each of these seven players has its own processing facilities and represents an important key account for foreign suppliers.

Russia's generation of 970 billion kilowatt-hours of electricity (in 2007) makes it the fourth-largest producer after the United States, Japan, and China. Distribution is dominated by joint-stock company RAO UES—the world's largest utility—which accounted for almost 70%[11] of national output; the company oversees seventy-five regional electricity companies (*energos*). The government has launched ambitious reforms to unbundle the monopolies along the value chain and convert them into joint-stock or partly privatized companies, thus creating a competitive environment and making the sector attractive for urgently required investments. The state will maintain its grip on the grid (distribution) while privatizing power generation, which represents two-thirds of the chain value. EU energy companies (e.g., Germany's E.ON and Italy's ENEL) have begun to acquire stakes in the *energos*. The demand for electricity is rising each year. In Moscow, it rose from 16,200 megawatts in 2005 to 18,200 megawatts in 2006. Demand is going to rise by 5%–7% annually and reach 25,000 megawatts by 2010–2012. In 2007, Russia's thirty-two nuclear power plants supplied 150 billion kilowatt-hours or 15% of total generation; by 2020, this output will rise to 230 billion kilowatt-hours (25% of total). The increase will come from lifetime extensions of first-generation units, their upgrading, and the building of new plants (forty new nuclear reactors by 2015 at the rate of three to four plants each year). In addition, Russia intends to develop its vast Siberian territory as an international center for storage and reprocessing of nuclear waste.

Alternative forms of energy are also drawing the attention of authorities. Russia's Ministry of Energy and Industry (Minpromenergo) has initiated projects to study the feasibility of introducing new technologies. Several cities and regions are supporting these initiatives, which they hope will enable them to reduce energy expenditure and raise energy efficiency. Examples are Krasnodar for wind energy, Astrachan for solar and wind energy, and Moscow for residential solar energy. Each year, 7 million metric tons of oil products and 23 million metric tons of coal are shipped to Russia's northern territories at extremely high costs to satisfy the energy needs of local populations. Smaller, decentralized units based on renewable energies could bring significant relief.[12]

China

China's energy shortfall seriously threatens its booming economy. Many factories in the outskirts of Beijing and Shanghai can operate only at night in summer as electricity is diverted for air-conditioning in the cities. Power cuts affected twenty provinces in 2007. Shortfall in capacity rose to 39 gigawatts in this period. By 2020, China will need to add 1,330 gigawatts of electricity generation or 48 gigawatts of new capacity each year. Although pollution concerns are checking the use of coal in AMs, China continues to be the largest

---

11. The remaining 30% are generated by nuclear power plants controlled by Russia's Atomic Energy Ministry (Minatom).
12. "Russland erwärmt sich für sonne und wind" [Russia gets warmed up by sun and wind power], *Moskauer Deutsche Zeitung* 23 (2007).

producer (1,200 mn t oil equivalent in 2006) and consumer (1,100 mn t oil equivalent in 2006). China generates 80% of its electricity through coal-fired power plants, which need to be modernized. However, in the long term, it plans to reduce its dependence on coal by gradually moving to hydroelectricity, oil and gas, nuclear energy, and renewables. The ambitious Three Gorges Dam is an attempt to ramp up hydroelectricity, which currently contributes only 15%–18% of electricity. Following the power market reforms launched in late 2002, China now has:

- five nationally competitive state-owned generators hived off from the State Power Corporation (SPC) having a combined generating capacity of 50% of the country's total;
- provincial and local government-owned generators, previously outside the SPC system;
- some independent power producers operating as partners of state-owned companies;
- two regional grid companies; and
- a proven system in place to attract foreign companies as investors and absorb foreign technologies (tenders, alliance schemes, R&D centers, etc.).

During 2007–2010, the Chinese government plans to invest around US$80 billion in electricity projects, opening valuable opportunities for Western technology suppliers. Foreign companies are increasingly keen to participate in projects geared to upgrading coal-fired power plants. China plans to rely more on modern nuclear power plants in the future. At present, nuclear energy accounts for only 2.5% of domestic energy consumption (6.6 mn t oil equivalent). By 2010, it is expected to rise to 4% with the help of technologies provided by France, Russia, and the United States.

For oil and gas, Chinese oil corporations—state-owned and funded by low-interest borrowings from public banks—are aggressively buying up foreign assets to ensure their access to oil and natural gas in Brazil (pipeline), Iran (Yadavaran oil field), Kazakhstan (stake in local companies, pipelines), and Sudan. China's oil and gas sector is controlled by three state-owned enterprises (SOEs): PetroChina (northern China), Sinopec (southern China up to the Yangtse river), and CNOOC (offshore activities). PetroChina and Sinopec control oil and gas distribution and processing as well as drilling and exploration. The two companies are major investors in processing plants (including downstream chemicals) and pipelines. The 4,200-kilometer-long east–west pipeline connecting the oil fields of Kazakhstan with the eastern Chinese agglomerations is being financed and built by PetroChina. In 2007, PetroChina generated record profits of US$14.9 billion, almost four times that of its rival Sinopec.

The hub of the oil industry is moving from the depleting fields in the northeast (Daqing) to the west (Xinjiang) and center (Liaoning, Shandong). Intensive exploration has raised the country's own proven reserves from 16.3 billion barrels in 1984 to 22.1 billion barrels in 2007; production has increased from 2.9 million barrels per day in 1984 to 3.8 million barrels per day in 2007.[13] Similarly, proven reserves of natural gas rose by almost 300% from 0.89 trillion cubic meters to 2.35 trillion cubic meters in 2006. The main finds are

---

13. *BP Statistical Review of World Energy*, June 2007.

in the west and north, but new offshore fields are also being discovered along the coastline stretching from the far south (South China Sea) to the northeast (Bohai Bay).

Renewables are another area of interest for Western investors. China currently operates forty-five wind farms across the country's northern and eastern areas. Their capacity is 760 megawatts, which is modest compared with the country's total generation capacity of 440 gigawatts. The potential for solar technologies is also far greater than what is actually in use. In Rizhao, Shandong province, the government is implementing renewable energy schemes (e.g., solar-powered street lamps; solar-fueled hot water, heating, and air-conditioning systems) that have transformed the coastal city into a model for green development throughout China. Many Chinese companies have settled down in the city's industrial park; some of them provide the solar technologies for buildings used in the 2008 Olympics.[14] The demand for biofuels is also expected to grow. Biodiesel output will be increased in two phases, to 200,000 metric tons by 2010 and then to 2 million metric tons by 2020. US and Indian companies[15] have invested in crop-rich agricultural land (e.g., Inner Mongolia) together with local joint-venture partners. The Chinese government will allocate more funds for research and support to investors through low-interest loans and tax rebates; it thus hopes to lift the share of renewable energy in the country's energy mix from 7% in 2007 to 12% by 2012. The energy policies of Germany and India serve as examples.

INDIA

India's economic growth since the mid-1990s has placed energy supply high on its political agenda and has accentuated energy security in its foreign policy. To maintain the current growth momentum, it needs to increase its primary energy supply by 6% annually. Already, consumption increased by 7% annually during 2005–2008. India's strategy to achieve this hinges on:

- creation of emergency reserves on eastern and western coasts;
- reduction of dependence on oil and shift toward liquid natural gas (construction of LNG terminals and pipelines);
- increasing domestic production of oil and gas through exploration (New Exploration Licensing Policy);
- diversification of oil and gas suppliers;
- energy security through participating interest in overseas oil and gas fields;
- privatization of oil corporations;
- adoption of clean coal technologies to reduce pollution from thermal power plants and to increase their efficiency;
- improvement of end-user fuel efficiency;
- reduction of subsidies;
- promotion of next-generation renewable energies (solar, wind, tides, biomass); and
- stricter pollution control on industry and transportation.

---

14. "Solar City: Growing Pains of a Superpower," *New Scientist,* November 10, 2007, 54.
15. Examples are Seattle-based General Biodiesel and Delhi-based Uniflex.

Table 4.4. India's primary energy mix, 2007.		
Source	Mn t oil equivalent	Share (%)
Coal	204.8	54.5
Oil	119.3	31.7
Natural gas	28.9	7.6
Hydroelectricity	19.0	5.1
Nuclear	3.8	1.1
Total	375.8	100
Source: BP Statistical Review of World Energy. 2 008.		

Table 4.5. India's leading oil and gas companies, 1/1/2008.			
	Ownership	Sales (US$ bn)	Profits (US$ bn)
Indian Oil	State	57.4	2.0
Reliance Industries	Private	35.9	4.8
Bharat Petroleum	State	27.9	0.5
Hindustan Petroleum	State	27.7	0.4
Oil & Natural Gas	State	24.1	4.9
Source: Fortune 500. 2008.			

India is the fourth-largest energy consumer after the United States, China, and Japan. Its energy mix comprises all forms of primary energy (see table 4.4). These marketed energy sources represent around 65% of total consumption, the remaining demand being met by non-marketed biomass sources mainly in the rural areas, which, however, are being rapidly replaced by conventional marketed fuels. Coal will remain the dominant form of energy in India for the coming decades because of adequate available proven reserves of 92.4 billion metric tons (more than 10% of the world's total). To mitigate pollution, India will adopt clean coal technologies (gasification combined cycle). The government plans to raise the shares of natural gas and nuclear power in the energy mix to 11% and 4%, respectively, by 2015.

India's hydrocarbons sector is dominated by state-owned enterprises, although the government has taken steps in recent years to deregulate the industry and encourage greater foreign involvement (see table 4.5). India's state-owned Oil and Natural Gas Corporation (ONGC) is the dominant player, accounting for roughly three-fourths of the country's oil output during 2006–2008. India's downstream sector is also dominated by state-owned entities, although private companies have become more important in recent years. The Indian Oil Corporation (IOC) is the largest state-owned company in the downstream sector, operating ten of India's seventeen refineries and controlling about three-quarters of the domestic oil transportation network and many of the country's filling stations. Reliance Industries launched India's first privately owned refinery in 1999 and has ever since been increasing its market share in India's oil sector.

India's dependence on oil imports (70% of requirement) is a cause of concern as it erodes export earnings and makes the country vulnerable to supply disruption. The country's largest companies—ONGC, Hindustan Petroleum, Bharat Petroleum, Indian Oil Corporation, Reliance Industries, Essar Oil—which are mostly state-owned (except for Reliance and Essar), are encouraged to engage in outward FDI to secure the country's energy supplies. The New Exploration Licensing Policy has resulted in twenty-one oil and gas discoveries of 800 million metric tons up to 2007 through private and joint ventures mainly in Rajasthan and off the coasts of Andhra Pradesh, Gujarat, and Maharashtra. India is also negotiating its participation in the Turkmenistan–Afghanistan–Pakistan and Iran–Pakistan–India natural gas pipelines. The Gas Authority of India Ltd. (GAIL) holds a 10% stake in China Gas Holdings. The natural gas sector will require large-scale investments in infrastructure such as port terminals, LNG conversion plants, and pipelines. Coal bed methane and gas hydrates are other options that are being explored. A presence in India is of strategic importance for the leading Western players as it opens opportunities to participate in profitable cross-border projects involving surrounding countries. The Indian government is further deregulating the sector, by gradually liberalizing tariffs and prices, in order to attract investments. Strategic alliances between Indian and foreign players will therefore increase in the future.

In 2007, India's installed capacity for electricity was 115,500 megawatts (70% thermal, 25% hydropower). The government plans to install an additional 100,000 megawatts by 2012, requiring an estimated US$180 billion in investments. The electricity sector has been opened up to private and foreign players, and reforms have been undertaken to restructure the state electricity boards (unbundling of generation, transmission, and distribution) and restore their financial health. Pre-feasibility reports have been prepared for more than sixty hydropower projects to attain the target of adding 50,000 megawatts; these projects are also open to joint ventures between state electricity boards and private players. Five thermal power megaplants of 4,000 megawatts each will be installed in the states of Rajasthan (Mundra), Madhya Pradesh (Sasan), Maharashtra (Konkan), Karnataka (Karwar), and Chattisgarh (Akaltara).

Nuclear power generation in India is controlled by the Department of Atomic Energy. Fifteen nuclear power plants (3,310 MW) are in operation, and seven are being constructed (3,420 MW). They are operated by the Nuclear Power Corporation of India. The country will need twenty to thirty nuclear power plants by 2015 to meet its electricity requirements. In a landmark decision, the US government in 2008 pushed through a nuclear deal with India, allowing it access to foreign nuclear technology for civilian use (the country had been shut out after refusing to sign the Non-Proliferation Treaty [NPT]). The forty-five nations' Nuclear Suppliers Group (NSG) approved the deal on September 6, 2008, paving the way for final endorsement by the US Congress.[16] Energy companies from countries such as France, Germany, Japan, Russia, and the United States stand to reap huge profits from building reactors and other nuclear infrastructure for India.

In keeping with its strategy to diversify energy sources, India is strongly promoting the exploitation of renewable energies (solar, wind, small hydro projects, waste-to-energy, biomass), with which it is generously endowed (see table 4.6). It is perhaps the only country with a special government department for them, the Ministry of New and Renewable Energy. The ministry hopes to add about 100,000-megawatt capacity from renewable sources by 2050. So far, 7,500 megawatts have been harnessed, constituting 6% of the entire power-generating installed capacity in the country. India ranks fourth worldwide in both solar (after Germany, USA, and Japan) and wind energy (after Germany, Spain, and USA). The renewable energy market in India is estimated at US$1.5 billion and is growing by 15% each year. The government has set a medium-term goal of electrifying 25,000 remote villages and meeting 10% of the country's energy supply through renewable sources by 2012.

---

16. "45-Nation Group OKs Landmark US-India Nuke Deal," *International Herald Tribune,* September 6, 2008. The deal is seen as a strategic move on the part of the United States to cement relations with its booming democratic partner in Asia and counterbalance China's rise.

Table 4.6. India's renewable energy potential until 2012.		
Source	Potential (2012)	Exploited capacity (2006)
Biogas plants	12 million	3.7 million
Biomass-based power	19,500 MW	727 MW
Efficient woodstoves	120 million	20 million
Solar heating	10 million m² collector area	1 million m² collector area 580,000 solar cookers
Solar photovoltaic	5 x 10¹⁵ Wh/yr	44 MW
Small hydro	15,000 MW	2,180 MW
Wind energy	13,000 MW	4,300 MW
Waste-to-energy	2,100 MW	46.5 MW
Ocean thermal	50,000 MW	Nil
Sea wave power	20,000 MW	Nil
Tidal power	9,000 MW	Nil

Source: Ministry of Non-conventional Energy Sources, Planning Commission, India. 2008.

4.1.3. Challenges for foreign energy companies

Further opening of energy markets and attempts to reach outward by megamarket companies will increase both the need and chances for foreign players to participate in joint projects and engage in asset and share deals. The creation of integrated energy champions in the EU[17] gives them sufficient financial clout to succeed internationally and eventually also in the megamarkets.

Practically all the leading energy companies in the megamarkets are listed on the national stock exchanges, which makes their management results-oriented and accountable to shareholders. Some of the companies are more open than before to collaboration proposals or reciprocal investments depending on the nature of the project. But overall, government approvals are required for strategic projects with implications for the country's energy supply, especially if they are close to the upstream source of energy (e.g., acquisition of a 50% stake or more in an oil or gas company). Russia, for example, does not allow majority participations in its state oil majors or important projects (e.g., main gas and oil fields). Control lies with domestic, mostly state-owned organizations. TNK-BP, a fifty-fifty joint venture with British Petroleum, is the big exception, but tensions rose in 2008 over the future strategy between the UK group and TNK's Russian shareholders (private oligarchs). It would be equally unthinkable for the Chinese government to allow a Western major to acquire a controlling stake in one of the country's big three oil companies (PetroChina, Sinopec, CNOOC). Moreover, China has not yet opened oil distribution (wholesale, filling stations) to foreign investors. India, equally restrictive in former days, has become far more liberal with foreign investors. In 2006, the Indian government opened the market in many energy segments:

- 100% FDI is allowed in power generation, distribution, and transmission.
- 100% FDI is allowed for both LNG projects and natural gas pipeline projects, with prior approval from the Foreign Investment Promotion Board.

---

17. Examples are Electricité de France and Gaz de France, E.ON and Ruhrgas in Germany, Electrabel and Distrigaz in Belgium, Enel and Camuzzi in Italy, and Endesa and Gas Natural in Spain.

Foreign equipment suppliers can benefit most as they can secure long-term contracts for supplies and services (consulting, maintenance, operations). However, it may take years of lobbying, intensive marketing, and test projects to prove one's competence and acquire the status of privileged supplier of a megamarket oil and gas giant. Certain strategic projects may remain subject to lengthy bidding processes, which are not transparent to foreign enterprises without access to insider information from within the ministry in charge or the partner company in question. It remains difficult for foreign equipment suppliers to acquire majority stakes in local companies if these belong to integrated energy firms that prefer to maintain control over their "strategic subsidiaries" (e.g., supplier of drilling rigs) rather than outsource this task to third parties. Nevertheless, given the high depreciation levels over the past few years (e.g., oil refining plants in Russia), demand for equipment for plant modernization will rise. The 2008 financial crisis has pushed many oil and gas majors into wide-scale cost-saving programs, which will benefit Western suppliers of value-added inputs aimed at raising efficiency levels and reducing environmental damage (e.g., chemical additives, seals).

Foreign investors dependent on oil by-products as input materials for their final products may consider a production site in Russia from which to supply their Chinese and Indian subsidiaries. Importing value-added items instead of relying on energy inputs from foreign sources (Russia, Middle East) or nationally controlled refining capacities in China or India can make the company less dependent on supply shortages or sudden price peaks. Many plastic products including polypropylene-based packaging materials, for example, depend on deliveries of semi-processed materials from oil refineries. A strategic partnership between packaging companies located in Russia and India could thus help establish a competitive value chain, which would give both sides an edge over competitors.

4.2. Steel

4.2.1. Global steel sector trends

During the industrial recovery after World War II, European countries and the United States dominated steel making until suddenly, in the early 1970s, Japan and shortly afterwards South Korea emerged as more cost-effective producers in a world reeling from the first oil shock. The two countries are now being challenged by the three megamarkets. China already overtook Japan and the United States in 1996 to become the world's largest steel producer. Since 2002, China's production has continuously exceeded that of all EU countries combined. India and Russia will be challenging the United States and Japan by 2015 with annual production volumes exceeding 100 million metric tons.

In 2009, China will account for almost one-third (450 million t) of world steel output (see table 4.7); by 2010–2012 its share will be almost 40%. In 2007, it exported 65 million metric tons of steel products. Chinese steel majors are competing in the EU and US markets[18] with a wide variety of standard and sophisticated products, thus threatening established players and prompting governments to raise protectionist barriers.

---

18. In 2006, the shares of China's steel exports were: Asia: 53%; EU: 15%; US: 10%; others: 22%.

Table 4.7. World steel production by country, 1995–2010 (million t).

	1995	2000	2002	2004	2006	2008	2010
China	95	127	183	272	333	450	580
EU 25	181	187	181	194	186	200	210
Japan	102	106	108	113	113	120	115
USA	95	102	92	100	92	90	100
Russia	52	59	60	66	64	75	100
India	22	27	29	33	34	55	85
South Korea	37	43	45	48	49	54	60
World	752	848	904	1,070	1,240	1,400	1,600

Source: International Iron and Steel Institute (IISI). 2007–2008.

Table 4.8. World steel demand by country, 1995–2010 (mn tons).

	1995	2000	2002	2004	2006	2008	2010
China	101	138	207	302	350	420	490
EU 25	163	178	172	182	185	190	190
USA	113	133	118	124	126	135	125
Japan	84	80	74	81	82	85	95
South Korea	37	40	45	48	50	55	55
India	26	30	33	38	42	70	75
Russia	26	33	32	37	40	65	80
World	743	849	917	1,084	1,240	1,450	1,620

Source: International Iron and Steel Institute (IISI). 2007–2008.

Globally, steelmaking capacity will exceed 1.6 billion metric tons by 2010 (2007: 1.3 billion t); more than half of this expansion is planned in Asia. New capacity in the AMs will be limited because of high production costs and stagnating user markets. According to the International Iron and Steel Institute (IISI), demand for steel products will exceed 1.4 billion tons (+5%) by 2008 (see table 4.8). Future growth will be concentrated in Brazil, China, India, and Russia (BRICs), where demand will rise by 11% annually during 2007–2010. Today, BRICs account for 40% of world steel demand. Conversely, demand will stagnate or even shrink in the AMs because of substitution by lighter materials such as plastics and composites in transport, construction, consumer durables, and other applications.

The steel industry has been affected by price fluctuations owing to changes in input costs. Supplies of the most important raw material, iron ore, are dictated by the price policies of three large suppliers that together control 45% of world output: Vale do Rio Doce, Rio Tinto (both Brazilian), and BHP (Australian). The response to this oligopoly has been further consolidations in the steel industry (see table 4.9). Mittal's acquisition of Luxembourg-based Arcelor for US$32 billion (2006), Tata's takeover of Corus in the UK for US$12 billion (2007), and Gerdau's (Brazil) acquisition of US steelmaker Chapparal for US$4 billion (2007) are recent examples. These acquisitions are a first warning signal to EU, US, and Japanese steelmakers to react to major players from the megamarkets. Today, the world's top fifteen steelmakers control 80% of the world's steel output. It is expected that in ten years these will be reduced to four to six mega steel players, each with a production capacity of 100 million metric tons or more. In 2007, ArcelorMittal reported output levels in excess of 115 million tons, three times more than second-placed Nippon Steel.

In 2008–2009, in a reverse trend most leading producers announced output cuts of up to 20% due to drops in prices in the aftermath of a widespread financial crisis and credit crunch that adversely impacted demand from automakers, equipment manufacturers and building companies. Consolidation trends will put pressure on steelmakers in Japan, India, Russia, and China, where the industry is still fragmented. The Chinese government has revealed plans of merging steelmakers into larger national champions. Such companies will have the bargaining power and financial clout to acquire smaller players and also to buy into raw materials providers to secure supplies.[19]

Table 4.9. The world's top twelve steel companies, 1/1/2008.

	Output (mn tons)	Sales (US$ bn)
Mittal-Arcelor, UK	115	105
Nippon Steel, Japan	47	42
Posco, South Korea	33	34
JFE, Japan	32	31
Thyssen-Krupp, Germany	26	69
Baosteel, China	24	30
Tata–Corus, UK	24	26
Severstal, Russia	22	17
US Steel, USA	20	15
Nucor, USA	18	13
Evraz Holding, Russia	18	10
Riva, Italy	18	11

Source: International Iron and Steel Institute. Fortune 500, 2008.

Like other traditional industries, steel is feeling the impact of the 2008 credit crisis, which left numerous users (auto companies, machine-tool makers, construction companies) reeling under the sluggish demand from end consumers and users. For 2009, steel makers in Germany reckon with an 8% contraction, whereas output in China could drop by 17%.[20] Companies are cutting costs and restructuring to reduce the adverse effect of the crisis. Starting from 2010–2011, steel prices are expected to pick up again as western economies recover and additional demand is generated by a growing number of emerging economies.

As a pillar industry for economic transformation and industrialization, the steel industry is subject to various degrees of government control in the megamarkets. China's larger steel plants have been reorganized into joint-stock companies run by professional managers, but the state still holds a majority share in most of them. In Russia, private steel companies emerged after political transformation in the 1990s, but their moves are monitored closely by the government. Indian authorities allowed private companies to set up new plants right after independence in 1947, many of which were built with Russian and German technology (e.g., Tata Steel, Essar, Jindal). But in India, too, a state-owned company (SAIL) ranks second among the leading domestic players in the industry. Megamarkets are reacting to AM protectionist measures intended to prevent market-distorting investments initiated by foreign players; for example, US and EU authorities have tried to restrict

---

19. China Investment Corporation, a US$220 billion sovereign wealth fund fed by foreign reserve assets accumulated by China, already bought stakes in BHP and other iron ore suppliers. These minority investments are part of a strategy to influence price levels or even benefit from possible mergers, like the one between BHP and Rio Tinto, which would create the world's largest mining group (sales of US$100 billion and more than 100,000 staff in 2008).
20. "Stahlkonzerne senken ihre Kosten massiv" [Steel majors massively cut their costs]. *Handelsblatt*, November 25, 2008.

investments by Russian steelmakers, which has immediately stirred counter-reactions and then led to sporadic takeovers (e.g., Severstal in Italy, Evraz in USA).

4.2.2 Steel sector trends in the megamarkets

CHINA

China is in the midst of prolonged industrialization and modernization. Output of automobiles, machinery, ships, and white goods continues to grow, although at a lower pace following the global downturn of 2009. Development of the western and northern regions, infrastructure expansion, construction projects for the 2008 Olympics, and the implementation of the eleventh five-year plan have contributed to further boosts of steel demand, which will not peak before 2012–2015. Against this positive background are serious concerns about overcapacity and inefficiency, which would adversely affect the industry in case of an economic slowdown.[21] The government had initially supported intensive capacity expansion through investments and raw material subsidies in line with its import substitution strategy. But in many companies per person productivity is still very low by international standards (37 t per year compared with 200 t per year in the AMs).

The local industry cannot meet the requirements for high-grade steel and specialty products, which have to be imported. China's iron ore mines have not kept pace with the surge in demand of local steelmakers, who have to purchase increasing volumes of raw materials abroad. Top steelmakers have grown very fast in the past few years, and there is a tendency toward creating larger units through mergers and acquisitions. The ten largest companies account for only 35% of steel output in a still patchy industry (see table 4.10). Foreign steelmakers (e.g., Mittal, Evraz) try to capture a slice of the domestic market by buying stakes in local firms or by setting up greenfield joint ventures (e.g., ThyssenKrupp and Angang Steel). China's fragmented industry of two hundred companies will be the scene of many consolidations and restructurings, mainly through mergers and acquisitions, in the years to come. Larger domestic companies will try to prevent foreign rivals from garnering market share in China and at the same time attempt to improve their global positions.

Table 4.10. China's top ten steel companies, 2007 (mn tons).

Baosteel	24.4
Anshan	15.3
Wuhan	12.3
Shougang	9.5
Maashan	8.5
Tangshan	8.3
Shagang Jiangsu	7.9
Hua Lin	7.6
Jinan	7.4
Handan	6.8
Total top ten	108.0
Share in national production	35%

Source: Annual reports.

---

21. As a result of the 2008 financial crisis, many Chinese players had to revise their expansion plans for 2009–2010. Export of steel products from China dropped by 50% during the fourth quarter of 2008 and the first quarter of 2009. Large companies like Baosteel are therefore preparing to diversify into high-margin segments (shipbuilding, defense, aerospace) and to acquire smaller rivals (who were hit by a drop in prices) while benefiting from the government's economic stimulus package aimed at financing massive infrastructure and construction projects during 2009–2012. "Nine to watch in 2009: Baosteel", *China International Business*. January 2009, 29.

INDIA

India's high growth (>7% in 2008) bodes well for its steelmakers as the industry's growth rate is usually 1.5%–2% above GDP. Demand has outstripped supply since the mid-1990s and particularly from late 2002 when user industries like construction, automotive, machinery, and consumer durables began to grow rapidly. Capacity expansion has become imperative, and the target is to reach 110 million metric tons by 2015 (+55 million t compared with 2008). Local fuel supply shortages compel Indian steelmakers to import 15 million metric tons of coal and 3 million metric tons of metcoke annually. To secure the coking oil supply, the government encourages joint ventures and equity participations by both steel and coal companies in foreign mines.

Table 4.11. India's top five steel companies, 2007.

	Ownership	Sales (US$ bn)	Capacity (mn t)
Tata-Corus	Private	26.0	24.0
Steel Authority of India (SAIL)	State	10.0	15.0
Essar	Private	2.8	6.0
Ispat	Private	2.1	4.0
Jindal[a]	Private	0.9	2.9[b]

a. Including stainless steel.
b. By 2011–2012, capacity will rise to 12 mn t by adding two production sites.
Source: Annual reports.

The country's mostly private steelmakers (see table 4.11) have clearly taken the path of efficiency through cost control; selective introduction of state-of-the-art technology for improving productivity, quality, and value; international trading; and investment. Along with organic growth, the steel majors are looking for acquisitions with synergies in terms of supply management, forward integration, and market access rather than mere capacity increases. This contrasts with the many Chinese steel players who are still burdened with overcapacities and process- and management-related inefficiencies. India will remain one of the world's lowest-cost steelmaking locations; it has burgeoning construction and automotive industries to fuel demand, and its proximity to other steel-hungry markets in East and Southeast Asia attracts foreign investors (e.g., ArcelorMittal, POSCO). India, which is still adding capacity, will see more greenfield investments controlled by local players.

RUSSIA

Russia accounts for around 7% of world crude steel output, and it is a large exporter. The devaluation of the ruble in 1998 in addition to low energy, labor, and raw material costs gave Russian steel a trade advantage. The industry survived the implosion of the old Soviet economy by focusing on exports (almost 46% of output). But anti-dumping tariffs imposed by the United States and the EU, impending WTO membership, shrinking exports to China where more local capacity goes onstream, and higher input costs are bringing about changes in the industry. Better technology (e.g., continuous casting), quality management, and higher productivity are being adopted to achieve the high product standards required to maintain the competitiveness of Russian steel in the face of better offerings from foreign producers.

New investments address environmental concerns, and non-core assets have been hived off. Meanwhile, economic growth has spurred domestic demand. Infrastructure development (e.g., highways, railways, ports, gas pipelines), construction, and manufacturing

Table 4.12. Russia's top five steel companies, 2007.				
	Output (mn t)	Sales (US$ bn)	EBIT (US$ mn)	Market capitalization (US$ bn)
Severstal	19.0	17.0	1,300	9
Evraz Holding[a]	17.5	9.5	905	8
Magnitogorsk MMK	12.0	6.0	960	7
Novolipetsk NLMK	8.5	5.5	1,385	14
Mechel[b]	5.9	4.7[c]	380	3

a. Following acquisition of Oregon Steel in the United States and 51% of Delong in Singapore.
b. Diversified group including interests in mining, iron ore, and metals.
c. Of which steel (US$3.3 billion).
Source: Troika Dialog, Expert. Annual reports.

(e.g., automobiles, machine tools) absorb an increasing percentage of output. The improved quality of Russian steel allows user industries to substitute imports with local products.

The industry structure is changing from the vertical integration prevalent during the Soviet era to horizontal integration. Three companies (Severstal, Evraz Holding, and Magnitogorsk Metal Plant) account for 70% of supplies. Russian steel companies (see table 4.12) have lined up investments in plant refurbishment and capacity expansion for the next five to ten years. They have started investing abroad by forging alliances (e.g., Severstal with Usinor) and making acquisitions (e.g., Evraz's acquisition of US steelmakers). They are also looking at expansion options in other emerging markets (e.g., Evraz's purchase of a majority stake in a South African mining company in 2007; acquisition of 51% of Singapore's Delong Steel for US$1.5 billion to conquer the Chinese market). Russian government policy is supportive of these moves as it intends to strengthen this strategic industry so that it can face international competition.

Russia will invest huge sums in the replacement and modernization of its steel facilities. Steel majors aim at higher productivity by improving quality and widening the product range to include more value-added products (e.g., cold-rolled, galvanized, and coated products). Higher security standards and better control of the environmental impact are high on the agenda. Russian steelmakers will expand abroad and forge alliances to share management practice, marketing expertise, and contacts. They know that outward investments are vital to increase thrust, bypass anti-dumping, and secure supplies such as iron ore and coking coal.

4.2.3. Challenges for foreign steel companies

Growth in the steel industry has shifted from AMs to the megamarkets, but EU steelmakers are not adequately represented there. Some of them managed to expand their presence by investing in existing (mostly smaller) structures and turning them around (e.g., MittalArcelor). Others have launched greenfield projects with local partners, which led to the transfer of knowledge about production processes and technologies (e.g., ThyssenKrupp). While the megamarkets have raised quality standards, certain types of specialty and stainless steel required by the aerospace, automobile, shipping, and construction industries still need to be imported.[22] However, successful expansion is not feasible through exports only; in the long run, foreign companies must turn into local players via FDI in forward integration, production, and service platforms.

National steel champions from the megamarkets will increasingly inject capital in turnaround candidates in other emerging and developing economies (e.g., Tata Steel in South Africa, Baosteel in Pakistan) as Mittal did successfully across the planet in the 1990s (but strangely enough, not sufficiently in Eurasia's three megamarkets). Alliances with megamarket players may open sales and supply channels for EU steelmakers eager to enter the new growth economies in Central and South Asia, Africa, and Latin America, where megamarket companies are well established.

Table 4.13. Steel capacity expansion plans in the megamarkets by 2010.

Country	Number of projects announced	Total capacity (mn t)
China	98	120
India	64	55
Russia	8	12

Source: OECD. 2008. Capacity Expansion in the Global Steel Industry.

EU equipment suppliers specializing in steel plant machinery, conveyor lines, working and support rolls, and so forth (e.g., SMS Demag, Danieli, Akers), have extended their client base to the megamarkets, where they have set up special sales offices, service centers, and assembly sites. They participate in tenders but equally in restructuring and greenfield projects. According to the OECD, almost two hundred projects have been announced for the three megamarkets, which bodes well for EU suppliers (see table 4.13).

4.3. Infrastructure and construction

4.3.1. Global construction and infrastructure trends

Construction activity has slowed down considerably in Western Europe. New investments are made mostly in renovation, replacement, or refurbishing. Germany experienced its last construction boom after reunification when former East Germany's infrastructure (motorways, railways, bridges) was completely rebuilt during 1990–1995. Spain, one of the most dynamic construction markets in the EU in the 2000s, has now approached saturation point. The slowdown is affecting also Japan and particularly the United States, where the subprime mortgage crisis has a damping effect on residential construction.

On another front, Morgan Stanley predicts that emerging markets will spend US$22 trillion on infrastructure (roads, railways, electricity, telecommunications) during 2008–2017.[23] China will account for 43% of this figure, followed by India at 13%, and Russia at 10% (see figure 4.3). For 2007, the World Bank reports investments to the order of US$1.2 trillion on roads, railways, electricity, telecommunications, and other projects in emerging economies, equivalent to 6% of their combined GDPs—twice the average infrastructure-investment ratio in industrialized countries. State-led infrastructure projects cofinanced by international agencies such as the World Bank

---

22. Examples of specialty steel SMEs exporting from the EU are Breitenfeld (Austria) and Riva (Italy).
23. "Building BRICs of Growth," *The Economist,* June 7, 2008, 80.

Figure 4.3. Infrastructure investment in emerging markets, 2008–2017.

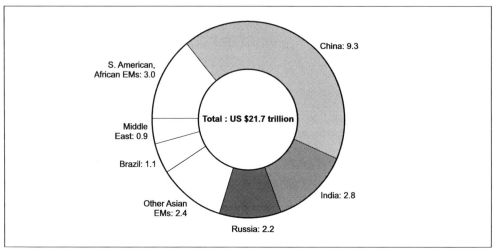

Source: Morgan Stanley. The Economist. 2008.

have been a pivotal element in the development strategies of China and India. Since the turn of the century, a growing number of private funds have invested in infrastructure projects in EMs. The projects usually involve the participation of Western private banks and development agencies that enjoy AAA ratings and thereby much lower refinancing rates than local financial institutions. State and private entities are working together in many countries through public–private partnerships and build, operate, and transfer (BOT) schemes to fund urgently needed work, which otherwise would be beyond the financial possibilities of either.

Table 4.14. Transport infrastructure in major economies, 2005, 2010.

	Railway network ('000 km)		Road network ('000 km)	
	2005	2010	2005	2010
USA	157	162	6,400	6,700
Russia	86	92	600	750
China	61	95	3,320	3,600
Canada	72	76	900	950
India	63	82	1,750	2,100
Australia	40	45	810	940
Argentina	37	42	230	260
Germany	36	37	235	245
Mexico	27	35	340	375
Brazil	30	34	1,725	1,950
France	31	33	900	950
Japan	20	22	1,170	1,250

Source: CIA Factbook. 2007.

Now that the long boom that started in the early 1990s in Western Europe and the United States appears to be tapering, the EU's leading construction multinationals—e.g., Bouygues (France), Hochtief (Germany), Impregilo (Italy), Laing O'Rourke (UK), Skanska (Sweden), and Strabag (Austria)—are stepping up efforts to win contracts and acquire assets in the megamarkets. They have the technology and expertise to participate in ambitious infrastructure projects, including road and railway maintenance and expansion (see table 4.14), but also ports, airports, utilities and energy-related projects (e.g., power plants), and most areas of residential, commercial, and industrial construction (see box 4.1). While integrated construction companies have a large footprint, medium-sized players specialize in specific domains. The concomitant boost in demand for ce-

Box 4.1. Opportunities for construction-related activities in the megamarkets.

- Physical infrastructure: bridges, dams, waterways, tunnels
- Transport infrastructure: roads, ports, railways, airports
- Telecommunications: networks, mobile infrastructure, satellite systems
- Utilities infrastructure: water distribution, water treatment, waste collection systems, waste treatment (composting, incineration)
- Energy infrastructure: electricity generation, nuclear power plants, liquefied gas terminals, gas and oil pipelines, exploitation of oil and gas fields
- Residential, commercial and industrial infrastructure (factories, investment development zones)
- Cement and other construction materials

ment and other construction materials is good news for such European materials suppliers as CRH (Ireland), Heidelberger (Germany), Holcim (Switzerland), Italcementi (Italy), and Lafarge (France), who seek to compensate losses in western markets, which were further aggravated by the 2008–2009 financial crisis. The world's largest public works and infrastructure projects will be concentrated in the megamarkets.

EU firms seeking to expand in the megamarkets face increased competition from domestic rivals that have the advantage of knowledge of local rules, the intricacies, as well as contact networks. According to the World Bank, local companies have bid successfully for over 50% of international tenders issued by governments of emerging economies for energy and telecommunications projects during 2003–2008. For concessions in the field of energy, raw materials, and roads, local governments tend to favor projects involving national players who are encouraged to control the majority share as lead contractors in the consortium. Megamarket infrastructure companies are growing fast thanks to their successful participation in domestic infrastructure projects. For international transport-related tenders (railways, roads, airports), they tap the expertise of Europe's infrastructure multinationals, which post higher revenues and profits (see table 4.15).

Table 4.15. The world's top infrastructure and construction companies, 1/1/2008.

AM players	Sales (US$ bn)
Vinci, France	42.0
Bouygues, France	40.7
Hochtief, Germany	22.5
Skanska, Sweden	20.5
Strabag, Austria	15.0
Impregilo, Italy	8.0
Megamarket players	**Sales (US$ bn)**
China Railway Construction Co.	23.3
China State Construction, CSCEC	22.1
China Communications Construction, CCC	20.0
China Harbor Engineering Company	8.2
Transstroi, Russia	1.2
Sistema-Hals, Russia	1.1
Gammon, India	0.9
Larsen & Toubro, India	0.9
GMR, India	0.8
Mirax, Russia	0.5
GVK, India	0.1

Source: Annual reports. Fortune 500. 2008.

4.3.2. Infrastructure development in the megamarkets

CHINA

China's achievements in infrastructure are impressive (see figure 4.4). In eight years (2000–2008), the country built more than 30,000 kilometers of new highways, which has thrust the country to third position in the world. In 2006 alone, China built 8,500 kilometers of modern expressways, and 100,000 kilometers of new roads were tarred in rural areas. For 2007–2010, Chinese authorities have earmarked a budget of US$90 billion to modernize 200,000 kilometers of roads, including expressways and main arterial roads (as a comparison, Germany will invest US$6 billion in road development during this period). As a response to the financial crisis, these plans were again enhanced after the announcement of a record stimulus package worth US$586 by the Chinese government on 10 November 2008. The money will be spent on new infrastructure projects to boost national demand during 2009–2012. According to a CIA report released on 21 November 2008, the United States may by 2012-2015 (i.e. ten years earlier than expected) lose its status as the world's leading power to China, which has now the potential to become the main engine of world economic growth thanks to its multibillion infrastructure projects.

Road financing is ensured through special government funds backed by multilateral donors (e.g., World Bank, ADB) and international bank consortia. In addition to government-funded projects, several BOT schemes have been launched involving private investors and specialized national financial institutions as lenders (e.g., CITIC). The biggest private equity investors in road construction are overseas Chinese business tycoons based in Hong Kong, Singapore, Taiwan, the United States, and Australia.

Figure 4.4. China's infrastructure projects until 2015.

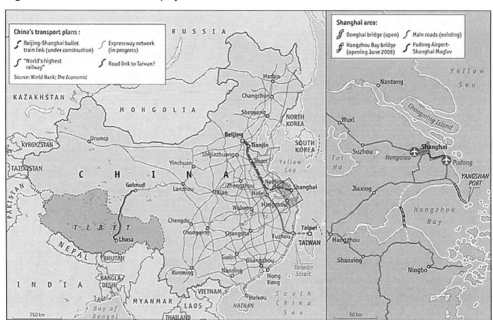

A total of 17,000 kilometers of new railway tracks will be laid linking coastal areas to the interior regions; this will expand the existing national network of 72,000 kilometers by another 25%, placing China in second place in the world, ahead of Russia. A few strategic railway projects have been completed or are at their final stages (see box 4.2). According to the World Bank, China's railways carry 25% of the world's railway traffic on just 6% of its track length.[24] According to revised figures, the track length will grow by 60% between 2007 and 2015 to 120,000 kilometers, which is the biggest railway expansion undertaken by any country since the nineteenth century. Railway expansion is expected to bring down logistics costs,[25] which amount to 18% of GDP (compared with 10% in USA).

The boom years will continue beyond the 2008 Olympics and affect all infrastructure and building segments. New residential and office buildings, shopping malls, roads, railways, subways, and airports were developed specially for the Olympic Games. The government's allocations amounted to US$40 billion; the main beneficiaries were the larger cities that hosted the sports events: Beijing, Shanghai, Shenzen, Tianjin, and Qingdao. As part of the program, Beijing upgraded its subway and commuter train system. The eleventh plan (2006–2010) highlights major infrastructure projects, which include port-related construction, road and transport infrastructure, oil utilities, and development of water infrastructure. Special emphasis is laid on regional airport development and upgrading work. Sector insiders expect the construction industry, which ranks second in Asia after Japan, to grow at an average rate of 7.5% during 2007–2011.[26] The industry is expected to be worth about US$325 billion by 2011, contributing about 5.8% to China's GDP.

During 2006–2010, China will build forty new airport terminals, mostly with extended runways, and modernize its air traffic management and control system (estimated investment: US$7 billion). The capital's new three-kilometer airport terminal, which was completed in 2008 within four years by an army of 50,000 workers, is the world's largest of its kind (17% bigger than all the five terminals at London's Heathrow put together). The extension of Shanghai Pudong airport, whose handling capacity will be

---

Box 4.2. Railway projects in China, 2005–2008.

- Tibet Railway—1,120 km new link on the Tibetan Plateau at 4,000 m average altitude; this project, which was finalized in 2006, is the most expensive and highest railway link in Asia (total investment of US$4 billion)
- Beijing–Shanghai high-speed train line of 1,500 km (US$30 billion, the most expensive project in China's railway history)
- Hangzhou–Shanghai fast-train link
- Beijing–Tianjin bullet-train link
- Southwest and northwest railways, which will connect China with its neighbors Myanmar, Thailand, Viet Nam in the South, and Russia in the North

---

24. "China's Infrastructure Splurge," *The Economist*, February 16, 2008, 28–30.
25. See 6.4.
26. BMI's *China Infrastructure Report*.

more than trebled to 70 million passengers by 2008, will cost US$2.5 billion. A total of US$10 billion will be invested in maritime port construction projects across the country to improve container throughput, bulk materials handling, and port navigation. By 2008, the Shanghai International Shipping Centre will be finalized as well as 160 new deep seawater berths in the country's major port cities. Dalian, Tianjin, and Shanghai, which were granted free port status in 2006, are attracting investors who participate in infrastructure and logistics projects in specially dedicated tax-exempt and bonded areas. A recent superlative is the thirty-six-kilometer six-lane highway across Hangzhou Bay, the world's longest sea-crossing bridge, which was opened for traffic in June 2008. It will halve travel time between two of China's busiest ports, Ningbo and Shanghai, to about two hours.

The biggest national infrastructure companies are state-owned and specialize in specific construction segments and/or regional projects: China State Construction Engineering Corporation (CSCEC), China Railway Engineering Corporation (CREC), China Railway Construction Corporation (CRCC), China Harbor Engineering Company, Road and Bridge Construction Company, China Communications Construction Company, Zhejiang Expressway Construction Company, and Jiangsu Expressway Construction Company. Some of these companies have made it into the world's top rankings. It is difficult for foreign companies to act independently as most important tenders are won by consortia led by these players.

INDIA

Starting from the early 2000s, India's authorities began allocating the highest resources ever for modernizing the country's infrastructure in an effort to support and accelerate inclusive growth. The eleventh five-year plan (2007–2012) will increase the investment in infrastructure (electric power, roads, railways, ports, airports, telecommunications, irrigation, drinking water, sanitation, storage, and warehousing) from 5% of GDP in 2002 to 9% of GDP during the plan period. The strategy for infrastructure development will rely on public–private partnerships in variable degrees depending on the segment. The Indian government has earmarked more than US$500 billion (including power and telecommunications, representing almost 50% of the total) for infrastructure projects during 2007–2012 (see table 4.16). Infrastructure is also seen by the government as a stimulator of growth post the 2008 financial crisis and will thus be given added attention.

The country's railway network is the world's second largest with a track length of 108,706 kilometers (63,028 km of route length). Indian Railways runs around 11,000 trains every day (of which 7,000 are

Table 4.16. Projected infrastructure investment in India's eleventh five-year plan, 2007–2012.

Segment	Investment (US$ bn)	Private sector share (%)
Electricity	163.6	28
Roads and bridges	78.5	34
Telecommunications	64.6	69
Railways	65.5	19
Irrigation	63.3	-
Water supply and sanitation	35.9	4
Ports	22.0	62
Airports	7.7	70
Warehouses	5.6	50
Gas	4.2	39
Total	510.9	-

Source: Indian Government. 2007.

passenger trains), transports 13 million passengers daily, and employs 1.4 million persons. In 2007, freight transport totaled 790 million metric tons. Railways are an important economic factor linking smaller remote towns and rural areas to major agglomerations. The government's new expansion plan will allocate US$65.5 billion for an additional 8,130 kilometers of railway lines (including two dedicated freight corridors: Mumbai–Delhi, Kolkata–Delhi), privatization of container movement, redevelopment and modernization of twenty-two railway stations, improved rolling stock, modernization of signaling and telecommunication systems, electrification, new metropolitan transport projects, and rehabilitation of up to 56,000 rail bridges. Over the past few years, Indian Railways has been turned around into a profitable enterprise; in 2007, it had a cash surplus before dividend of US$5 billion.

India's inadequate road network of 3.3 million kilometers has become the major bottleneck for maintaining a high growth momentum of 7%–8%. Many of India's roads are still not surfaced, and the better roads are permanently used causing heavy congestion and fast wear. Although national highways constitute 2% of the total network, they carry 40% of total road traffic. Secondary roads (state highways, district roads) constitute 13% of the total and carry an additional 40% of road traffic. Rural roads, on the other hand, carry only 20% of traffic but are vital for rural connectivity and agricultural growth and rural prosperity. About 65% of freight and 87% of passengers are transported by road.

The National Highway Development Plan (NHDP)—US$56.8 billion—was launched in 1998 for construction of the four- to six-lane Golden Quadrilateral (5,846 km) linking New Delhi, Mumbai, Chennai, and Kolkata, and the North–South (Kashmir to Kanyakumari) and East–West (Silchar to Porbundar) Corridors, totaling 7,300 kilometers, as well as connection of ports to the highways (1,000 km) (see figure 4.5). Some expressways are already world standard. By 2009, the main trunk lines of the quadrilateral highway system project will be laid, shortening driving time from Delhi to Mumbai from one week to 1.5 days. The PMGSY[27] is another massive program, started in 2000, for expanding rural road connectivity to all communities of greater than 1,000 inhabitants, and later to communities of greater than 500 inhabitants. About 368,000 kilometers of new roads will be constructed, and 370,000 kilometers of roads will be upgraded at a cost of about US$26 billion. In addition to the completion of the NHDP, high priority will be given to improving riding quality of the roads so that they can handle the high traffic density and high speed. These projects offer good prospects to foreign companies involved in civil engineering work (road paving, bridges, canals, tunnels, etc.).

India has a coastline of around 7,517 kilometers with twelve major ports and 187 notified non-major (minor/intermediate) ports along the coastline and sea islands. Almost 95% by volume and 70% by value of India's global merchandise trade is shipped by the sea routes. As of March 2008, these ports handled 624 million metric tons of cargo. By 2012, Visakhapatnam (82 million t) will be the biggest throughput port followed by Kandla (71 million t), and the country's port capacity will be doubled to 1,018 million metric tons. Containerized cargo represents 30% by value and 55% by volume of India's

---

27. The Pradhan Mantri Gram Sadak Yojana (PMGSY) was launched by the government of India to provide connectivity to unconnected rural habitations as part of a poverty-reduction strategy.

Figure 4.5. India's Golden Quadrilateral project and main highway corridors, 2005–2010.

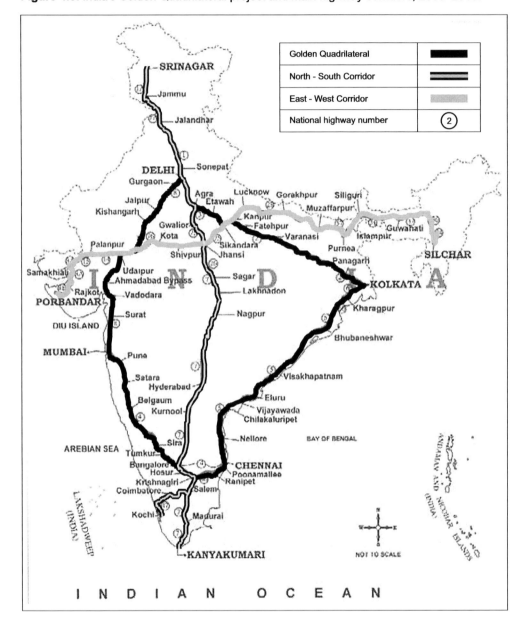

external trade; it will rise to 21 million TEU[28] by 2016 from 7.4 million TEU in 2007. India's largest container port is Jawaharlal Nehru Port Trust (JNPT) in Mumbai; it has a handling capacity of around 4 million TEU, which is five times less than Hong Kong's. India's southern ports (Chennai, Tuticorin, Vallarpadam, Colachel) will be converted into major transshipment hubs for international container traffic, competing with Colombo port in Sri Lanka with a projected capacity of 10 million TEUs by 2010. Specialized ports like Mangalore will be equipped with modern terminals for bulk cargo and cruise vessels.

---

28. Twenty-foot equivalent standard containers.

To meet the 10% growth in traffic, the feasibility of developing new deep-draught ports along the east coast is being studied. Improvement in labor productivity, procurement of multitasking equipment, privatization of certain operations, higher IT penetration, private sector participation for construction of new berths, and hinterland connectivity are all high priorities. Policy changes will also be made for the corporatization of ports (i.e., conversion into "port authorities" run like private companies) and development of new container terminals (Ennore, Vallarpadam, Mumbai). The total project outlay for Indian ports is US$22 billion.

India's airports, another area of strategic focus in the country's infrastructure development plan, will handle 205 million passengers and 2,683 thousand metric tons (TMT) of cargo by 2012. This will require the development of forty-five major airports. Delhi and Mumbai airports are being modernized and restructured by consortia of private companies, Chennai and Kolkata by the Airports Authority of India. The international airports at Bangalore and Hyderabad have been completed by private consortia, which also operate them. Those of thirty-five other metro cities will be improved in phases by both private and public agencies. Lead agencies and consortia for these projects are selected through international tenders. One hundred percent FDI is allowed in airport infrastructure including greenfield airports (compared with 49% in civil aviation). Another priority is to use the availability of skilled manpower to make India an important hub for aircraft maintenance, repair, and overhaul in the Asia-Pacific region.

The Indian polity and government recognize the importance of infrastructure for sustainable economic development. Policies are amended to encourage investment from the private sector, including the liberalization of FDI norms to attract foreign companies. Master plans and programs have been launched to cover all the segments, and financial resources have been mobilized from domestic funds (including special purpose vehicles), international donors, and financial institutions. The latter are often involved in project design and in ensuring a transparent tendering process. In the example of road infrastructure, on certain stretches, the government allows private sector funding with a debt–equity ratio of 4:1 and FDI of up to 100% in equity. Concession periods are of thirty-year duration before the roads are transferred back to the state. Revenue is generated from tolls. The BOT concept is now being tested for airport terminals, which private investors can operate on a lease-and-buy-back basis. India has privatized many of its expressways, ports, and airport terminals under BOT schemes. Numerous foreign companies interested in benefiting from this market have tied up with Indian companies to bid for special projects such as the US$400 million Bandra–Worli Sea Link in Mumbai—the world's second-largest sea link project—to connect the western suburbs to the central district by an eight-lane, cable-stayed bridge with prestressed concrete viaduct approaches. Domestic players such as Hindustan Construction Company and Larsen & Toubro have grown fast through BOT projects and, besides their vast contact network in India, now offer their expertise in the Middle East, CIS, Iran, and Africa.

Russia

Inspired by the success of infrastructure development in China and India, Russia is positioning itself to become "Eurasia's land bridge" owing to its geography at the very center of the Eurasian continent. At a conference of Asian leaders in Japan in October

Figure 4.6. Main routes on the Eurasian Land Bridge.

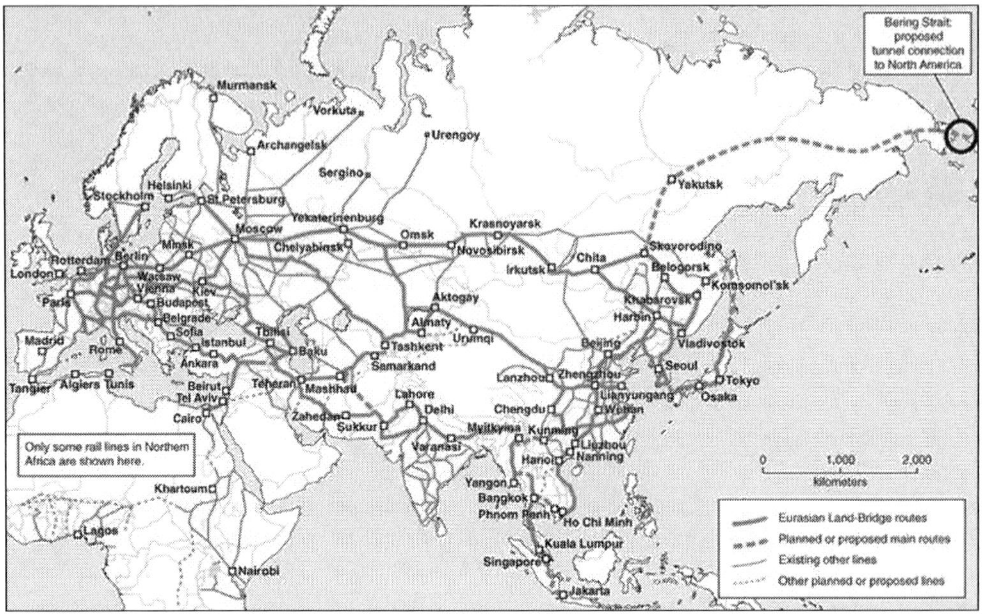

Source: http://www.schillerinstitute.org/economy/maps/maps.html.

2005, former President Putin declared the building of new roads, ports, airports, railways, and pipelines a top national priority (see figure 4.6). Russia's Stabilization Fund, which accumulated US$120 billion by the end of 2008, was originally set up to channel windfall oil revenues into national priority projects, including infrastructure. The federal authorities have earmarked US$570 billion worth of funding for infrastructure expansion and upgrading until 2015. The spending plan announced in May 2008 by Prime Minister[29] Putin calls for building a total of 17,000 kilometers of roads, 3,000 kilometers of railroads, and more than 100 airport runways. It will also boost annual port capacity to 400 million metric tons of cargo.[30]

Infrastructure specialists have calculated that US$90–130 billion is required over the next ten years just for overhauling the existing east–west road network (excluding motorways), which connects Russia's regional capitals. A new trunk line from St. Petersburg passes through Yekaterinburg and Irkutsk to Chita and into northern China (Harbin, Changchun). Construction of first-class expressways (three to four lanes in each direction), the cost of which can rise to US$40 million per kilometer depending on the type of soil, will be funded by issuing special infrastructure bonds and through private–public partnerships, including BOT projects.

The establishment of a uniform transport corridor across the whole country, where logistics operators can reach any important location by truck and fast-speed trains can drive at a speed of up to 450 kilometers per hour, is becoming a realistic vision against the backdrop

---

29. In March 2008, Dmitry Medvedev succeeded President Putin, who became prime minister. The overall policy direction stayed intact, with the two men favoring power-sharing as a more reliable option to solve complex global issues of climate change, energy, foreign policy, economy, and finance.

30. "$570 Billion for Transport Overhaul," *The Moscow Times,* May 21, 2008, 5.

of high foreign currency reserves, well-filled state coffers, and a political will to promote industrial diversification across the country by reducing energy/commodity dependence. Siberia will play a crucial role in the government's strategy to improve links between Europe and Asia. During 2007–2010, US$4.3 billion will be invested for overhauling the Trans-Siberian railway. The new Siberian Yamal railway line, which will run parallel north of the Trans-Siberian route and link western Siberian towns to the eastern port cities, will accelerate the transport of people, goods, and natural resources between Russia, China, Korea, and Japan. Other milestone projects are under consideration. A sixty-eight-mile undersea tunnel across the Bering Strait, the longest of its kind, will link eastern Siberia and western Alaska, two unexplored regions where winter temperatures fall to –60° Celsius. Both Russian and American companies pitched for this ambitious project in Moscow on April 24, 2007, stating that it would unlock hitherto untapped resources and bolster regional economies and trade between both countries.[31] The railway tunnel will trigger the construction of new oil and gas connections and the extension of electricity lines and fiber-optic cables for telecommunication. Another important project, the new Siberia–Pacific Ocean oil pipeline, will help channel energy resources from Russia to Japan and China. These projects are observed with suspicion by Europe's political leaders who fear that Russia could divert more of its raw materials and energy supplies to Asia.

Russia pursues obvious strategic aims with its infrastructure expansion plan. The volume of trade between Europe and Asia amounts to US$600 billion, of which only 1% uses Russia's transport infrastructure. Sea deliveries account for 98% of cargo turnover between Europe and the booming Asian economies. The extension of Russia's transport infrastructure will increase transit shipments by 25–30 million metric tons by 2010–2012, which will enhance the country's role as a central logistics hub on the Eurasian continent. Newly generated activities will bring otherwise remote cities into the mainstream and attract investments required for trade, industry, and finance along the main transport lines. Russia will need to act quickly as it already competes with similar efforts undertaken by China and Central Asian countries (Kazakhstan, Kyrgistan, Uzbekistan, Turkmenistan) to revive transport links along the former Silk Road. Russia's advantage is that the northern route is much shorter and goes through only one country up to the port of St. Petersburg, which is connected by feeder networks to the main EU ports (Hamburg, Bremen, Rotterdam, Le Havre). The Silk Road crosses eleven countries, which have not signed free trade or customs union agreements.

If Russia succeeds in establishing a workable multimodal transport network—as an alternative to the sea route used by shipping lines around the continent to the south—it can add true value to Eurasian logistics operators.[32] Logistics companies constantly seek to reduce costs by shortening geographic distance and time difference—both decisive factors in satisfying a clientele demanding just-in-time solutions. In theory, it takes eleven to twelve days to forward a container overland compared with four to five weeks by sea. Europe's leading carmakers, particularly Volkswagen, are testing the overland route to move components between production units and dealerships across Eurasia's landmass. Success will depend on whether Russia's state organs (e.g., railway ministries, customs

---

31. A. Nicholson, "Russian and US Backers Push Bering Tunnel" *The Associated Press,* April 25, 2007.
32. See 6.4.2.

authorities, taxation bureaus, etc.) manage to coordinate well with their counterparts in neighboring countries.

The Russian government has issued a record number of tenders since the mid-2000s for important infrastructure projects including motorway construction, road refurbishing, and the expansion of strategic railway and pipeline links across the European and Asian parts of the country. It has additionally designated areas for special economic zones, including knowledge and techno parks, to attract foreign and domestic investors. Such cost-intensive projects would not be of interest to investors without the state's active involvement in setting up the necessary facilities such as staff housing, offices, shopping areas, social facilities (schools, hospitals), and access to roads, train links, port facilities, and terminals.

EU construction companies are stepping up their presence in Russia. Some of them have sold stakes to Russian partners (e.g., Strabag to Basic Element), which they hope will facilitate access to this fast-growing market. Turkish, Chinese, and Indian construction firms have become extremely active as well and compete on a number of important projects such as the new St. Petersburg–Moscow expressway and the fourth ring motorway around Moscow.

4.3.3. Trends in housing and building materials

The building segment of the construction industry is also witnessing high growth thanks to the national social housing programs and the mushrooming of private residential, institutional, and commercial building projects across major cities. After decades of stagnation and deterioration, the urban landscape is being completely transformed to overcome the shortage of living and office space. In response to the surge in consumption, promoters are building large malls and entertainment complexes. The potential for investors and operators in the non-infrastructure segment is therefore considerable.

In Russia, about 40% of residential buildings are totally depreciated, and most of them are on the replacement list of public authorities. Although the number of housing projects has been increasing annually (market value in 2007: US$60 billion), demand still cannot be satisfied. The target is to double the volume of available living space from 40 million square meters in 2006 to 80 million square meters by 2010. Thanks to their direct access to information and contacts with decision-makers in municipalities, Russian building companies are better positioned to corner the lion's share of this huge and still expanding market. Some of them take on projects as general contractors and then outsource construction to Western building multinationals, from which they gain valuable expertise. Russian players have grown financially to become powerful, vertically integrated holdings comprising construction firms, cement factories, building materials units, engineering companies, and investment banks. For Western companies, the only way forward is to buy stakes in local companies, which have become five to six times more expensive than at the start of the boom in the early 2000s. In a reverse trend, Russian construction companies are very keen on acquiring stakes in "specialty" companies (e.g., construction scaffoldings, high-performance building materials, facades, architectural design bureaus) in the West, particularly Europe.

China and India are in an equally favorable position. In both countries, demand for housing outstrips supply, giving rise to a construction boom in all major cities. Private speculators further fuel this boom by buying flats, offices, and commercial sites to later resell them at a profit or to lease them out. Authorities in China have tightened bank lending by raising the discount rate and introducing a speculation tax on short-term deals. Prices even in second- and third-tier cities have climbed by as much as 20%–30% annually since 2002. In Shanghai, lease rates for offices went up more than 120% during 2005 and 2008, making it one of the world's hot spots for real estate investors. Similarly, demand for office space in India rose from 11 million square meters to 90 million square meters during 2004–2008, which resulted in soaring prices as demand could not be met by supply. As the premium property market slowed down after the 2008 financial crisis, Indian construction companies focus on innovative and efficient technologies for construction of medium- and low-cost housing, a large and truly promising segment for the years to come.

The building boom in the megamarkets led to price hikes for cement (see table 4.17) and building materials, which subsided with the financial crisis in end 2008. The general outlook for vendors of cement, asphalt, paving, floorings, paints, and fittings looks excellent on the back of high demand from housing development projects. Their plants are running at high capacity because of the "internal" housing and infrastructure boom, and they have hardly any possibility of responding to rising demand also in neighboring countries (e.g., Dubai and other Middle Eastern economies for India).

The world's leading cement and building materials players (see table 4.18) have been trying to raise their stakes in the emerging megamarkets, with mixed success. Some of them have reoriented their strategies that were geared to the EU and US markets (e.g., Lafarge); others are relative newcomers (e.g., CRH, CEMEX). These companies prefer wholly owned operations (greenfield projects, outright takeovers, or chains of majority participations) over joint ventures (especially with state-owned enterprises). But legal control is not a guarantee of success either, especially if competitors possess already the requisite capacities and use price dumping to defend their market positions. In India, which is the world's second-largest producer of cement (160 million t annually) after China, domestic

Table 4.17. Cement production in major economies, 2005, 2010 (mn t).

	2005	2010
China	750	1,350
India	110	280
USA	90	110
Japan	75	82
Russia	40	70
Brazil	45	70
South Korea	57	70
Mexico	35	60
Spain	42	47
Italy	42	45
France	20	25
Germany	28	29

Source: Based on information released by Heidelberger Zement.

Table 4.18. The world's top building materials companies, 1/1/2008.

	Sales (US$ bn)	Cement capacities (mn t)
CRH, Ireland	28.7	125
Lafarge, France	24.1	175
Cemex/Rinker, Mexico	21.7	96
Holcim, Switzerland	22.5	198
Heidelberger Zement, Germany	16.3	97
Italcementi, Italy	7.4	71
Anhui Conch, China	6.7	70
Taiheiyo, Japan	5.6	70
Vulcan/Florida Rock, USA	4.5	58
Buzzi, Italy	3.9	55
Eurocement, Russia	1.8	24

Source: Annual reports. Fortune 500. 2008.

enterprises have grown sufficiently to be serious contenders for tenders and often secure contracts because of better connections with local builders and the authorities. The same applies to China and Russia, where domestic cement producers hold the largest market shares. In Russia, Eurocement[33] dominates the domestic (40% market share) and CIS markets and can thus dictate price levels. Siberian Cement, Russia's second largest player with a capacity nearing 10 million t, is a major participant in construction projects, including state-backed infrastructure tenders, east of the Urals; in 2009–2010 the company has ambitious expansion plans for Africa, India and Turkey. In China, Western players are bedeviled by domestic units which engage in dumping owing to excess capacities. Lafarge (France) and Holcim (Switzerland) have invested massively in local operations but with mixed results as to profitability and market share. Their biggest challenge is to convince megamarket key accounts of the advantage of their business model. India seems to be the first megamarket where selected foreign cement majors have realized successful acquisitions enabling them to secure market share (e.g., Holcim-ACC).

4.3.4. Challenges for foreign construction companies

Many of the world's new mega projects will be located in the megamarkets: Beijing 2008 Summer Olympics, Shanghai's 2010 World Expo, India's Golden Quadrilateral, Tibet railway, Three Gorges Dam, Trans-Siberian railway, Sochi's 2014 Winter Olympics, Middle East–India pipelines and communication links, just to name a few. Unlike the AMs, infrastructure is still being developed in these countries. For example, 70% of the world's new airport projects and 50% of new port facilities will be constructed in the megamarkets and surrounding economies.

EU construction companies need to foray into the megamarkets before local rivals reach critical mass and become serious competitors in global markets. These competitors already have the advantages of low labor costs and financial strength to act as investor-developers, to which they are adding improved planning and engineering capabilities. EU companies have so far managed to reach Russia (Strabag, Hochtief, Bouygues) but have yet to penetrate China and India, where they should proactively bid aggressively for tenders and, in the long term, establish a local presence either on their own or through an alliance with a local company, depending on the FDI limit imposed by the government for different sectors.

State-owned monopolies still have a stranglehold on road, bridge, and tunnel construction projects in China and Russia. Local private enterprises have, however, managed to loosen it to a certain extent. Investments in utility companies in energy, water, and waste segments are more or less controlled by the respective authorities, whereas telecommunications has been opened to foreign influence. Large projects in India rely more heavily on private enterprises, which have contributed to the growth of local infrastructure and construction companies. Competition among these companies is fierce, and each has built privileged relations with the various authorities.

EU companies should focus on projects that are structured transparently as this reduces extra-commercial costs and user charges (e.g., BOT schemes). Some of the projects are

---

33. In September 2008, Eurocement acquired a 6.5%-stake in Holcim (Switzerland).

co-funded by multilateral agencies (World Bank, Asian Development Bank) or through bilateral cooperation (Japan, Germany's KfW), which have more accessible bidding processes. The megamarkets are tough markets also for European engineering companies and suppliers of construction materials, including cement, who face competition from strongly established local firms nurtured by buoyant home markets and close connections with key accounts (builders, developers, state organs).

Despite their size, EU players face difficulties in winning tenders and creating true megamarket profit centers. Personal relations play an overlarge role in public projects; to build these, there are few alternatives to a local presence. EU companies need to overcome their reticence to lobbying for large projects and take the assistance of local teams of qualified lobbyists, engineers, and marketing specialists who can help them outmaneuver the existing politician–contractor nexus, introduce frugal engineering, and contain cost overruns. They can also acquire majority stakes in local infrastructure and construction companies, developers, and contractors to shorten lead time.

4.4. Vehicles and transport equipment

4.4.1. Global vehicles and auto components trends

World vehicle[34] output stood at 70.5 million units in 2008. The industry's global turnover was €2.2 trillion, which is equivalent to the sixth-biggest economy in the world, and it employed 9 million persons. The vehicle industry is an established pillar sector in the leading AMs, contributing up to 10% of GDP in countries like Germany and Japan. But growth has been sluggish (EU: +0.2%; negative in USA). EU producers were helped by a 14% growth in registrations in Eastern European and Asian countries in 2007–2008, which were spurred by rising incomes and low taxes, according to the Brussels-based automotive industry association (ACEA). In September–December 2008, the leading carmakers were forced to cut output as sales dropped by 25–30% in the wake of a worldwide liquidity crunch and sluggish consumer demand. At the time of writing, experts predicted a recovery toward mid-end 2010, but with a focus of demand in emerging economies.

All top ten car manufacturers are currently located in AMs (see table 4.19), but they are hindered by rising costs, stagnant home

Table 4.19. The world's top fourteen car companies, 1/1/2008.

	Sales (US$ bn)	Profits (US$ bn)
Toyota, Japan	230.2	15.0
General Motors, USA	207.3	–2.0
Daimler, Germany[a]	177.2	5.4
Ford, USA	172.5	–2.7
Renault Nissan, France	150.5	7.8
Volkswagen, Germany	149.3	5.6
Honda, Japan	105.1	5.3
Peugeot Citroen, France	83.0	1.2
FIAT, Italy	80.1	2.7
BMW, Germany	76.7	4.3
Hyundai, Japan	74.9	1.7
Volvo, Germany	42.3	2.2
Suzuki, Japan	30.7	0.7
Mazda, Japan	30.4	0.8

a. Following divestment from Chrysler.
Source: Fortune 500. 2008.

---

34. Cars and commercial vehicles. Source: International Organization of Motor Vehicle Manufacturers (OICA).

demand, and declining market shares worldwide. Experts predict that in eight to ten years, world car production will be controlled by no more than five to six mega manufacturers, which could include one to two megamarket companies. The first signs of an imminent consolidation to reduce overcapacity in the struggling automobile industry became visible in November 2008–January 2009, when the three big US car makers sought a US$25 billion bailout from Congress to bridge a liquidity crunch caused by plummeting sales in the domestic market. Some Congressmen blame the industry's predicament not so much on the deepening global financial crisis, but primarily on the failure of management to accelerate process streamlining and to respond to the urgent need to develop fuel-efficient models.

For many years, newcomer economies have tried to establish a strong vehicle industry. While some of them have succeeded (Brazil, China, India, Iran, Mexico, Russia, South Korea), others have failed in spite of government subsidies (Indonesia, Malaysia, Pakistan, Thailand, Turkey). The Triad regions of Europe, the United States, and Japan continue to account for 50% of production and 80% of sales.

Despite problems related to traffic congestion and pollution worldwide and consumer saturation in the AMs, optimists predict that the next twenty years will see more cars produced than in all of the past 120 years. The megamarkets will account for most of tomorrow's extra demand and capacity, which may reach 100–110 million units by 2015–2020 (see table 4.20). The world's leading car multinationals are all growing much faster in the megamarkets than in their established home markets.

Growth potential is highest in China and India, where car ownership grew by 70% and 60%, respectively, during 1997–2007, but in absolute figures, it is still much lower than in the AMs (see table 4.21). Fifty percent of the world's new vehicle capacity planned up to 2015 will be added in Asia and Russia. Domestic manufacturers in these countries will develop more new products geared to local and international

Table 4.20. Vehicle production in major economies, 2007, 2015.

	2007 (mn units)	2015[a] (mn units)
USA	12.0	15.0
Japan	10.5	14.0
Subtotal	22.5	29.0
Germany	5.5	6.0
France	3.7	4.0
South Korea	3.5	5.0
Spain	3.0	4.0
Canada	2.7	3.0
UK	1.9	2.5
Italy	1.2	1.5
Subtotal	21.5	26.0
China	5.1	15.0
Brazil	2.2	5.0
India	1.5	9.0
Russia	1.5	7.0
BRIC subtotal	10.3	36.0
World total	65.0	110.0

a. Forecast published before 2008 financial crisis.
Source: EU Automotive Association. 2007.

Table 4.21. Passenger car penetration in major economies, 2007, 2010 (cars/1000 inhabitants).

	2007	2010
Germany	550	570
USA	500	520
UK	480	490
France	470	490
Japan	440	450
South Korea	180	200
Russia	160	220
Mexico	130	150
Brazil	90	110
China	18	45
India	9	25

Source: World Automotive, World Bank. Smith Barney. 2008.

consumers (e.g., Nano car from Tata, light vehicles from FAW, jeeps and trucks from Mahindra & Mahindra). Some of them will expand their portfolios with premium brands from the AMs to gain access to state-of-the-art technologies (e.g., Tata's acquisition of Jaguar and the Land Rover from loss-making Ford). The demand for small cars produced in the megamarkets (Nano, QQ), based on green technologies such as biofuels and hybrid propulsion to reduce emissions and fuel consumption, could rise significantly in Europe due to decreasing disposable incomes and increasing fuel and maintenance costs.

Component suppliers, whose fortunes depend on their customers, will follow them to the megamarkets. The components segment is dominated by a few global players and several medium-sized companies; both face pressure from lower-cost producers in the megamarkets and in some cases are acquired by them following lower valuations due to market constraints in AMs in 2008–2009. Outsourcing of car parts will grow almost sixfold from US$65 billion in 2005 to US$375 billion in 2015. More than one-quarter of this growth will be generated in China (US$60–70 billion), India (US$25 billion), and Russia (US$8 billion).

4.4.2. Vehicles and auto components trends in the megamarkets

Car manufacturing has become the symbol of international prestige and technological prowess for megamarket governments. China has announced its political intention to create national car and auto components champions that are large enough to compete on a global scale. The Indian government's auto policy recognizes that the industry brings in a high degree of value addition to the country and aims to make India an international hub for small, affordable passenger cars. The Russian government has declared the national car industry a major determinant of the country's status as a true industrial power.

CHINA

By 2012, China is expected to replace Japan as the second-largest car market. In March 2008, vehicle sales including cars, trucks, and buses in China touched 9 million units[35] (see figure 4.7), after expanding by 25% in 2007 and 20% in 2006. This represents a market of roughly US$90–95 billion (2.8% of GDP) with prospects to treble by 2015–2020,

Figure 4.7. Vehicle sales in China, 2000–2010 (mn units).

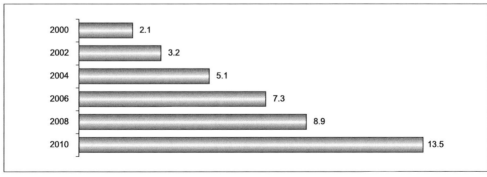

Source: Chinese Automotive Manufacturers Association. 2007.

---

35. According to the China Association of Automobile Manufacturers, June 2008.

which allures the world's leading manufacturers.[36] Passenger vehicles represent the largest segment, with 6.2 million cars sold in 2007, around 20% more than in 2006. Given that only 4% of the population owns a car, compared with 60% in Europe and 80% in North America,[37] the market will continue to grow for decades to come. It is expected to overtake America's within a decade.

Since it started promoting the industry in the late 1980s, the Chinese government has been regulating FDI by limiting foreign participation in equity to 50%. Even today, foreign companies must enter into a joint venture with a local partner, very often a state-owned enterprise connected to the federal and regional governments. The top ten vehicle companies are all joint ventures; they hold 80% of the domestic automobile market. The three leading players are First Automotive Works, or FAW (993,000 units, US$26.4 billion turnover in 2007); Shanghai Automotive Industries Corporation, or SAIC (919,500 units, US$22.6 billion turnover in 2007); and Dongfeng Motor Corporation (739,000 units, US$15.5 billion turnover in 2007). The first two are partners of Volkswagen, GM, and Toyota, and Dongfeng is the partner of Citroen. Chinese players often cooperate simultaneously with several foreign partners and have begun to compete directly with them in overseas markets, thus causing mistrust. The first two producers—FAW and SAIC—aim at sales of US$30 billion each by 2010. In December 2007, SAIC grew bigger after merging with Nanjing Auto (NAC) to rival Western and Japanese car companies.

Chinese consumers today have a wide choice of brands and models in all price categories. Luxury limousines, sports cars, and vans are popular; they are mostly imported. Low fuel consumption and easy maneuverability in congested cities makes small cars popular among consumers. Middle-class households prefer the spacious family sedans in the limousine segment. In the premium segment, newcomers BMW, Mercedes-Benz, Toyota, Lexus, and Nissan aggressively promote new models to challenge Audi's dominance. This segment (10% of total demand) is reporting the highest growth rates. Reduced customs tariffs as a result of WTO accession combined with high purchasing power have boosted car imports, which represent about 7% of the total market (2007), but their share could reach 13%–15% by 2012.

Competition has become fiercer owing to overcapacities, shrinking profits, and deflating prices. Car prices are falling by 8%–12% a year.[38] Yet, it costs more to build middle-class sedans and premium cars in China because essential components have to be imported. Price erosion has halved the margins of Volkswagen, Citroen, Toyota, BMW, and many others during 2004–2007.

Chinese carmakers in the lower segments are more price competitive than foreign players; they are encouraged by the government to improve their designs and to venture into foreign markets. For this, they have access to preferential loans and can acquire land at special rates, which gives them a competitive advantage. Geely, founded in 1986, plans to

---

36. The world's six largest carmakers pledged US$17 billion to build new factories in China, corresponding to an additional capacity of 4 million vehicles until 2010.
37. "Carmaking in China," *The Economist*, April 26, 2008, 73.
38. According to the China Association of Automobile Manufacturers, domestic car prices will ultimately be 40%–50% lower than in developed markets.

sell 25,000 vehicles in 2009 and 100,000 by 2012–2015. Its rival Chery targets 2 million units within the next five to eight years (2007: 490,000), 50% of which will be exported. Brilliance, BMW's joint-venture partner, started exporting its first batch of family sedans to Europe from Dalian port in February 2007. In only four years, the company increased its sales by 1,000%; it plans to sell 150,000 cars by 2010. In 2008, a four-door Brilliance sedan costs six to eight times less than the corresponding model of Audi or BMW. Despite quality defects, the company appeals to a large clientele of middle-income consumers.

Table 4.22. Country of origin of cars sold in China, 2007, 2010.

	2007 (%)	2010 (%)
Japan	36	34
EU	20	17
China	19	23
USA	13	11
South Korea	12	15
Total	100	100

Source: Chinese Automotive Manufacturers Association. 2008.

Chinese brands account for 19% of all vehicles sold in China, and their share is rising (see table 4.22). Conversely, EU brands slipped in importance, from 50% in 2000 to 20% in 2007. In 2007, exports of China-made cars surged 100% to 343,000 vehicles and will exceed 500,000 by 2010, about 10% of Japan's export volume. Chinese cars sell well in Africa, Latin America, the Middle East, and Russia.[39] In the budget segment, Chinese sedans and vans, at prices between US$9,000 and US$12,000, are perceived as value for money by Russian and other emerging markets consumers. It will be more difficult for Chinese producers to establish equivalent distribution and after-sales networks in Western economies, where brand awareness, safety rules, and emission standards are much higher.

China's car component market is valued at US$12 billion (2007). Its growth rate accelerated after the government imposed higher local content for domestic car manufacturers. Cars manufactured in China but with imported key parts are considered "imported" and therefore subject to higher duties. This policy is meant to improve prospects for local parts makers. Foreign OEM manufacturers that follow the car multinationals to China have intensified their presence. Half of the components produced in China are exported (value: US$6 billion in 2007). About one-fourth of the 1,700 components makers in China are foreign-controlled.

INDIA

India has lately emerged as a very promising FDI destination for foreign carmakers and auto component manufacturers. With combined sales of US$34 billion and total investments reaching US$14 billion (2007), the automotive industry has turned into a pillar industry, contributing 4% to GDP and providing employment to 450,000 people. India is expected to move ahead of the United Kingdom and Canada when its car production surpasses 2 million units by 2009 (see table 4.23). Passenger cars and commercial vehicle sales doubled in just five years, from 0.8 million units in 2001 to 1.8 million units in 2008. Sales crossed the 1 million mark in 2004, when India's 24% growth in demand even outstripped that of China (14%). Today, India is one of the world's

---

39. In Russia, sales of China-made cars tripled in 2007 to 22,000 units; by 2010–2012, experts predict a twentyfold increase to 450,000 units.

Table 4.23. Vehicle production in India, 2002–2010.

	2002	2004	2006	2008	2010
Passenger cars	500,500	783,000	1,046,000	1,660,000	2,290,000
Utility vehicles	106,000	146,000	196,500	260,000	390,000
MPVs[a]	64,000	67,000	69,500	85,000	120,000
Total	670,500	996,000	1,312,000	2,005,000	2,800,000

a. Multi-purpose vehicles.
Source: Indian Automotive Association.

fastest growing auto markets. During 2006–2008, sales of vehicles climbed 38%, those of two-wheelers 27%. Demand for vehicles (excluding two-wheelers) is expected to double to about 3–3.2 million units by 2010 as more people move upwards in the midst of high optimism and business confidence. By 2012, India will close the gap with Germany and then, toward 2015, overtake Russia as the world's third-largest car market.

Car ownership in India stands at eight cars per thousand people, leaving even more room for expansion than in China. The biggest guarantor is India's young population; 45% is below nineteen years of age, and most of them will join the labor market by 2012–2015. Easy availability of car loans contributes significantly to this demand. Indian car owners have become brand conscious. At the same time, they look for value-for-money such as fuel efficiency and low costs of repair and spare parts. Most of the growth will come from the replacement of older vehicles, upgrading from two-wheelers to cars—particularly to ultra-cheap vehicles like the Maruti, Hyundai, or the newly introduced Nano—and the purchase of a second and third car in the same family. Product life cycles shrink as producers accelerate launches of new models. The period 2005–2008 saw the introduction of forty-five models, including fourteen super luxury models. Premium brands like Audi, Lexus, Infiniti, BMW, and Daimler are visible in ultra-posh showrooms that luxury car dealers have opened in the larger cities to cater to big-ticket customers. Some of these new dealerships are part of an international network that also owns showrooms in Russia and China.

So far, EU brands, apart from Mercedes, are underrepresented. The dominant positions were taken by Indian (Maruti, Tata), Japanese (Honda, Toyota), South Korean (Hyundai), and lately US (General Motors, Ford) brands, which cover the low- and medium-price segments (see figure 4.8). Volkswagen intends to redress the situation by investing €580 million during 2009–2011 in its new plant in Pune where it will produce the Fabia (Skoda brand) and Polo. The company also plans to introduce the "Up," a small car geared to the requirements of emerging and developing economies.[40] India is Asia's third-largest producer of small cars and is poised to become a global production and R&D hub for this segment. Tata's ultra cheap Nano, launched in March 2009, is expected to have a sales potential of 1 million units in India and an additional 1–1.5 million abroad.

In 2002, the Indian government removed limits to FDI in the automotive sector as part of its new auto policy, which encourages know-how transfer and innovation through open competition. Foreign companies can set up wholly owned subsidiaries without depending on a local partner. Import duties on components and CKDs (completely knocked down

---

40. "VW will indischen markt erobern" [Volkswagen plans to conquer the Indian market], *Handelsblatt*, August 4, 2008.

Figure 4.8. Market share of India's leading automakers, 2008 (%).

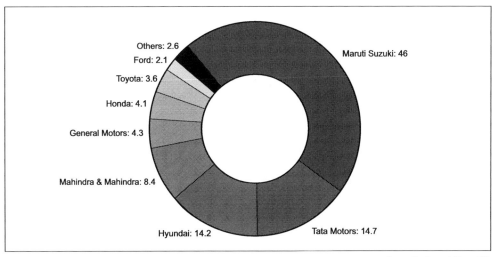

Source: The Economic Times. 2008.

units, i.e., in kit form) were halved to 15% in 2006 compared with 2002. India's car industry was compelled to restructure, absorb technologies, and link up to global supply and distribution networks. The industry is already known for its "frugal engineering." Multinationals like Daimler, GM, Honda, and Toyota have opened technology and knowledge centers in India to capitalize on its highly qualified specialists.

Along with these developments in the national car industry, India's auto component sector has become highly competitive and set out for further global reach. It has grown from US$2.4 billion in 1997 to US$18 billion in 2008, most of the growth having been generated over the past five years. Exports already represent 20% of the segment's overall turnover (+30% over 2006–2007) as more multinationals join Ford, General Motors,[41] Fiat, and Daimler in sourcing components from India. A growing number of multinational OEMs (Delphi, Bosch, Plastic Omnium) have established or plan to launch new operations owing to India's cost advantage of 20%–25% coupled with skilled engineering capability available locally. The component segment aims at export levels of US$25–30 billion by 2015 and a global market share of 5%–6%. Toward this end, around US$1 billion will be invested in the coming decade to increase capacity and acquire new technologies.

India hosts many world-class parts suppliers that expand abroad by acquiring competitors. In 2006, Bharat Forge (BFL) acquired Germany's Carl Dan Peddinghaus, enabling it to become a design- and innovation-driven company. It plans to establish itself as a system provider for Western car multinationals. According to BFL's CEO, Mr. Baba Kalyani, the aim is to "combine the advantages of Germany's and India's family businesses to fight international competition."[42] Additionally, BFL positioned itself in China through a majority joint venture with FAW to counter competition in mass-produced forged parts. TVS Group, India's largest auto components firm, exports around a third of its output

---

41. Example: General Motors will ship parts worth US$1 billion from India to its global production units by 2010.
42. "Bharat Forge fordert Thyssen-Krupp heraus" [Bharat Forge challenges Thyssen-Krupp], *Handelsblatt*, August 9, 2005.

and has invested in facilities in the United States. One of the TVS companies, Sundaram Fastener, has won the General Motors "Supplier of the Year" award five times; it supplies 100% of GM's radiator caps worldwide.[43] Rane Group, another leading player, succeeded in reducing defects from 10,000 parts per million to 250. It exports 28% of its engine valves. India's auto component industry today consists of 420 firms in the organized sector, which represents 85% of the industry's output. Another 10,000 firms belong to the small, unorganized sector.

RUSSIA

Russia's automotive sector offers different but equally interesting features; it is a high-value market with a strong representation of medium and premium brands. The number of cars in use is growing much faster than in the rest of Europe—it trebled from 10 million in 1992 to 30 million in 2007. About half of Russia's existing fleet is over ten years old and needs replacement. In 2006, for the first time, more than 2 million vehicles were sold, of which 51% were foreign brands (mostly produced[44] in local factories). Until 2015, sales are expected to grow by 300,000–350,000 units each year (+ 7%–8% p.a.), with a dip in 2009. By then, Russians will be buying more than 5 million cars in a year,[45] making it by far the largest market in Europe. Russia's car market already outstripped Germany's in 2008 (3.4 vs. 3.2 million units sold, respectively). In value terms, Russia's car market will be worth US$75–80 billion by 2010, which will be just 30% below China's market value (although half its size in volume), mainly because of the higher proportion of premium and luxury brands. Between 2004 and 2008, practically all major luxury brands, including Lamborghini, Ferrari, Maserati, Porsche, Hummer, Rolls-Royce, Bentley, and Maybach, decided to keep bigger stocks with their local dealers in response to record sales that beat all expectations. This growth will be sustained as more urban dwellers join the ranks of the upper middle class.

Domestic car production (Russian and foreign brands) reached 1.7 million units in 2007 and will increase by 60%–80% until 2010–2012. The share of Russian brands (60% today) will decline further to about one-third of total production (see table 4.24) as foreign competitors penetrate the market with lower-priced models of fairly good quality. Domestic producers have found it hard to compete, first with imported secondhand cars and more recently with imported new cars and foreign brands made in Russia. By 2015, one-quarter of all foreign-branded cars will probably come from China as replacements of the older Russian models (Lada, Moskvich).

The biggest asset for foreign investors in Russia is the combination of market size, relatively low input costs (energy, labor[46]), and availability of raw materials. Ford, Renault, and Kia assemble cars in Russia, while Volkswagen, GM, Toyota, and Nissan announced investments in new plants (see table 4.25). Foreign carmakers will invest altogether US$2.2 billion to produce more than 700,000 vehicles by 2010. Producers from South Korea

---

43. "Outsourcing Acquires Wheels in Chennai," *The Indian Express,* December 7, 2005.
44. In 2007, the number of foreign car brands manufactured in Russia reached 450,000 units.
45. "Cars in Russia. Crisis? What Oil Crisis?" *The Economist,* June 7, 2008, 65–66.
46. Out of a total cost advantage of 25% for Russian manufacturing, labor accounts for only 5%.

Table 4.24. Russia's leading automakers, 2007, 2010.		
	2007	2010
Avtovaz	717,000	660,000
HIS-Auto	82,000	75,000
GAZ	66,000	60,000
GM-Avtovaz	58,000	50,000
Kamas	41,000	48,000
UAS	31,000	28,000
Tagas	30,000	25,000
Russian brands	1,025,000	946,000
National production[a]	1,700,000	2,850,000
Russian brands (%)	60	33

a. Including foreign brands produced in Russia.
Source: Russian Automobile Manufacturers Association. 2008.

Table 4.25. Greenfield projects by foreign carmakers in Russia, 2007–2010.			
Factory	Employees	Investment (US$ mn)	Cars produced
Volkswagen	3,500	425	115,000
Renault	2,300	230	60,000
Ford	2,100	260	70,000
Volvo	1,000	100	15,000
Nissan	750	200	50,000
General Motors	720	115[a]	25,000[a]
Toyota	600	100[a]	20,000[a]
Suzuki	500	115	30,000

a. Company plans to double investment and capacity.
Source: Smart Money, June 25, 2007.

(Daewoo, Hyundai, Kia) and Japan (Mitsubishi, Toyota, Nissan, Mazda) dominate the rankings and have become the most favored brands among Russians. South Korean carmakers have understood the importance of the Russian market, which has become a high-priority destination for their investments. European brands dominate the premium and luxury segments mainly through imports. It took Volkswagen ten years to decide to invest in local production. The new plant in the city of Kaluga with an initial capacity of 60,000 vehicles was inaugurated in 2007. But Volkswagen, the dominant player in Europe, has a long way to go; its market share in Russia is hardly 1%. Competition is expected to become fierce in the low-price segment as Chinese brands start penetrating from the eastern regional markets. To gain the trust of Russian owners, Chinese carmakers offer guarantee periods of up to three years or 100,000 kilometers.[47]

The government sees the automotive industry as a key driver of industrial diversification in an economy still dominated by raw materials and energy resources. It encourages FDI in local car companies, such as Renault's acquisition in 2008 of a 25% stake in Avtovaz for US$1.3 billion. More favorable tax rules apply to investors that open plants in designated areas (SEZs) surrounding the larger cities. The government has set a target of 75% of sales for domestically assembled cars by 2010. Its priority is to bring more value-addition to the country. To enjoy reduced duties, companies need to increase local content from 10% to 30% within three years of operation. Attracting foreign car components makers as investors and know-how providers is another challenge in the coming years. In late 2005, the Russian government lifted duties for key parts in an attempt to attract FDI in the industry. Foreign companies are not compelled to establish partnerships with local producers as in China. While new cars are subject to a 25% import levy, the duty for parts can vary from 12%–15% to 3%–5% depending on whether they are used for local assembly or production.

Russia's automotive component sector is technologically weak and fragmented but making visible progress. Some 95% of the more than two hundred suppliers sell to Russian carmakers that did not have high quality expectations in the past. As more foreign carmakers increase

---

47. "Kitaiskie zeremonii" [Chinese ceremonies], *Expert*, December 2005, 98–101.

their investments, sales of locally manufactured components will rise. More stringent safety and environment standards will demand regular replacements of specific parts. Foreign suppliers established in Russia currently limit themselves to low value-added components. As car production expands, more sophisticated components will be produced in Russia. Local car producers, who have a long tradition of vertical integration and in-house part manufacturing, will outsource more work. The share of high-quality parts according to international standards in Russian cars is expected to increase to 40% by 2010–2012. At the same time, the local content of foreign cars produced in Russia will rise to 50%, generating a market for OEM components worth €5.1 billion by 2014 (+20%).

4.4.3. Trends in other transport equipment segments

Trucks, buses, and two-wheelers are other fast-growing vehicle categories within the automotive industry. In China, the demand for heavy-duty trucks with a capacity of over 15 metric tons, equipped with electronics, satellite tracking systems, and other advanced technologies, will rise steeply as the demand for logistics and transport services grows thanks also to the concomitant expansion of six- and eight-lane motorways. National capacities already exist for light trucks with low technology content (e.g., FAW, Dongfeng). Many heavy-duty trucks for special use (e.g., raw materials transport, mining, waste collection) still need to be imported, but there is government pressure to launch local production of special-application vehicles. The demand for buses, including airport coaches, city buses, and luxury coaches for long-distance travel, has gone up steeply. However, while names like King Long, Foton, JMC, and DFAC are seen on the roads, the big European brands like MAN, Iveco, and Scania are absent. What went wrong? A combination of factors has led to a strategic disadvantage for heavy vehicle and bus makers from the EU/United States in China:

- wrong managerial assessment of local partners and market trends;
- lack of creativity to find localized solutions and to promote winning concepts at the highest levels of government and industry (e.g., industry association);
- mutually annihilating competition between Western players, which raises the bargaining power of Chinese producers and local authorities;
- insufficient political support at EU or national levels (member states), while local players are strongly backed by their federal and provincial governments.

India is the world's fifth-largest commercial vehicle (CV) market. Almost 70% of goods and more than 80% of passengers are transported by road. The upward trend in demand for CVs is attributed to the improved highway network and the evolving hub-and-spoke model. The ban on the overloading of trucks and containerization has shifted preference to multi-axle trucks even though medium-sized CVs continue to dominate the market (65%). Specialization (cement mixers, LPG carriers, mobile cranes, etc.) is also increasing in the truck segment. The bus segment will be driven by the rapid growth of inter-city passenger traffic and rising demand for luxury coaches for long-distance travel.

Tata[48] entered the CV segment in collaboration (1954–1969) with Mercedes-Benz and established its leadership; it now covers all CV categories including tractors and has a

---

48. Tata is among the top ten producers worldwide for commercial vehicles in the 5–15 metric ton range.

market share of 60%. It is followed by Ashok Leyland, Mahindra & Mahindra, Eicher Motors, and Swaraj Mazda. With the arrival of MAN (joint venture with Force), Renault, and Volvo, competition will intensify for large trucks and coaches. Hyundai, Scania, Stokota, and Ural (both from Russia) are some other international players who have plans to enter the Indian CV market. EU companies can set up their own units in India (e.g., Volvo) as there is no restriction to FDI; companies like MAN, however, prefer to work with a local partner (Force). The key factor of success will be the ability to offer high technology products with a wide range covering all the evolving market segments.

Russia is the only megamarket with a high visibility of imported EU trucks and buses. Many of these are imported used vehicles. Companies like MAN, Volvo, Daimler, and Iveco have set up dealerships, but the price differential is high compared with local offers from MAZ (Belarus) and KAMAZ, for example; these have taken the lead in the truck segment. MAN (out of its joint assembly operation with MAZ in Belarus) and Scania (assembly unit near Moscow) sell trucks to profitable private transport firms as well as large companies in energy and raw materials extraction where price is not the main selection criterion. Volvo has set up an assembly unit for buses north of Moscow to better serve the market. Daimler envisages acquiring a 42% stake in the country's leading truck maker KAMAZ to participate in a fast expanding market[49] (see figure 4.9).

Russia is a growing market also for light commercial vehicles (LCV), including vans and minibuses, especially in the larger cities where they supplement public transport by introducing flexibility, cost advantage, and convenience. The LCV market is forecast to increase from 240,000 vehicles in 2007 to 400,000 by 2012. Russian producers, especially GAZ, have maintained a strong position in LCV with an overall market share of 80%. Foreign vehicle manufacturers recognizing the potential—Ford, Volkswagen, Renault, Fiat, Citroen, and FAW (China)—have come up with innovative solutions for this promising segment.

The world's two-wheeler market (scooters, motorcycles) is dominated by Indian, Chinese, Japanese, and to a lesser extent Italian and British producers. In India, the world's largest two-wheeler market, motorcycle sales average 350,000–400,000 units a month; the market is valued at €16 billion. However, at thirty-five units per thousand inhabitants, two-wheeler penetration is still low, leaving immense potential for growth. The main Indian players are Hero Honda, Bajaj, and TVS Motor. All leading Indian players started as joint ventures with world leaders: Bajaj-Kawasaki, Hero-Honda, TVS-Suzuki, LML-Daemlin, and Kinetic-Hyosung. Indian manufacturers have bought out their original licensors (e.g., Bajaj from Italy, Royal Enfield from the UK).

India also ranks first in three-wheelers (auto rickshaws). This category has long been dominated by India's Bajaj Auto, the world leader, who must now accommodate a resurgent Piaggio, TVS (India), and Honda India. In 2007, around 450,000 three-wheelers were produced in India, of which 20% were exported.

---

49. Daimler acquired the first stake of 10% from "Troika Dialog" for US$ 300 million in December 2008. Despite the financial crisis, which reduced Kamaz's market capitalization by 60% (from US$ 2 billion before the crisis), Daimler was compelled to pay four times the market price as the deal had been concluded in mid 2008. "Kamazovskaja desjatina" [Kamaz's 10th stake], *Expert*, December 15, 2008, 10.

Figure 4.9. Russia's truck market and major players, 2002–2008.

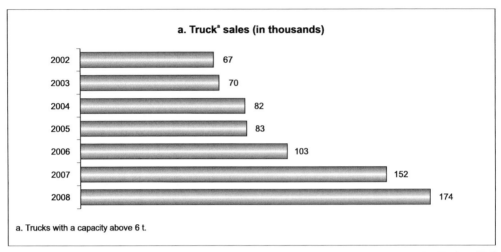

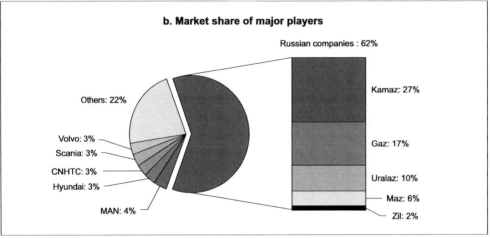

Source: VDA. 2008.

The future is likely to see a fragmentation of market share and higher segmentation of the two-wheeler markets in both China and India. The premium segment constitutes more than 50% of the market, which is moving toward more powerful bikes with engines larger than 250 cubic centimeters. Intense competition puts pressure on prices but also fosters innovation. It is interesting to note that Chinese scooters found a huge market in war-trodden Iraq as these rapid two-wheelers allow drivers to navigate quickly through checkpoints and avoid traffic jams.[50] Indian two-wheelers are exported to Africa, Iran, and across South and Southeast Asia (especially Indonesia).

Tractors represent a further segment where megamarket companies strive for world leadership. With around 290,000 tractors sold in 2008, the Indian tractor market is the largest in the world, followed by the United States, China, and Russia. Mahindra & Mahindra, India's major player, enjoys a 50% market share at home and already sets its sights on becoming the largest tractor company in the world, following acquisitions in

---

50. "Iraqis Take to Chinese Scooters to Avoid Road Chaos, Checkpoints," *The Indian Express*, December 26, 2006.

Table 4.26. Investment in rolling stock by Russian Railways, 2005–2030 (in units).				
	2005	2006	2007	2008–2030
Cargo wagons	8,000	8,500	11,400	996,000
Passenger wagons	653	738	895	29,600
Locomotives	182	278	306	23,400
Source: Russian Railways. RBK Daily. November 29, 2007.				

China (Jiangling Tractors) and Romania (Tractorul, for expansion into the EU). Russia is experiencing a revival of farms and cooperatives, which has led to a boost in demand for tractors and other farm equipment (+20% annually during 2005–2008). Vladimir, Cheljabinsk, Lipetsk, and Minsk Tractor Works (MTZ, Belarus) as well as Claas from Germany (combines) have been major beneficiaries of these developments. Renault (tractors) and John Deere (USA) also plan to raise their stakes in Russia.

There are two other transport categories that enjoy wide-ranging government support: trains and ships. Investments will be significant for both categories in the coming decades in all three megamarkets. Russia's National Railways, for example, plans to purchase 350–450 new locomotives, mostly fast-speed trains, and other rolling stock every year up to 2030 (see table 4.26). Foreign companies like Siemens, Bombardier, Alstom, Finmeccanica, Hitachi, Kawasaki, and Mitsubishi are invited to enter into partnerships with domestic companies. China and Indian Railways also plan to invest in the coming decade given the massive infrastructure modernization and replacement requirements in both countries.

Russia will push forward a huge construction program for advanced ships during 2009–2015. It strives to become a major world supplier of special-application vessels: ice-breakers, skegged vessels, airfoil craft, and twin-hulled hovercraft for passengers and cargo. For certain categories, it will partly compete with leading EU countries such as Germany, Italy, and Sweden. Pulled by growing demands at home, India and China will also expand their shipbuilding capacities and domestic fleets. In China, two state-owned conglomerates control the country's shipyards: CSIC north of the Yangtse River and CSSC to the south. They plan to treble their capacities by 2015 to 24 million deadweight tons. The world's largest shipyard is being built on the Yangtse island of Changxing off the city of Shanghai on an area of 1.8 million square meters with an investment of US$3 billion. China is challenging the dominant positions of South Korea and Japan as the world's leading producers of oil tankers, bulk cargo, and container ships.

The Indian government has developed a National Maritime Development program with a vision to make India a leading player by the year 2025. India's shipbuilding industry, which was hampered by restrictive laws, has revived after liberalization. Several private companies (ABG Shipyard; Bharati Shipyard, which acquired the British Swan Hunter; Tata Steel; L&T; Reliance) are setting up shipbuilding yards mainly off the coasts of Gujarat, Goa, and Orissa. A major new development is the decision of the Ministry of Defense to source the bulk of its annual spending from the private sector, which has spurred construction of warships and submarines by private companies like L&T, Tata, and Mahindra. Presently, India's strength lies in the construction of small and medium-sized ships. With its intellectual capital, it should become a center of excellence for design and R&D for the world shipbuilding industry in the region.

4.4.4. Challenges for foreign vehicle companies

Table 4.27. Car demand in the megamarkets, 2007, 2015.

	Units sold (mn)		Market size (US$ bn)	
	2007	2015	2007	2015
China	6.0	15	85	220
Russia	2.5	7	45	120
India	2.0	9	30	90

Source: National statistics. Business journals.

Since the early 2000s, EU vehicle makers have been under pressure to expand their businesses in the megamarkets as they have come under increased threat by local players in all vehicle categories. But despite their increased focus on the megamarkets, EU manufacturers have not really found a way to establish leadership, neither as independent players nor through joint ventures. To garner higher shares of these fast-expanding markets (see table 4.27), they need to adjust their offers to local preferences and climatic conditions. The Chinese, for example, prefer comfort and fuel economy to speed and sporty driving. Cars can hardly be sold without automatic gear boxes, four doors, and leather seats. Security (e.g., air bags, reinforced doors) and status features (e.g., double exhaust, shaded windows) are prime considerations in Russia. Indian consumers look at value for money and fuel consumption (diesel cars), for which they are willing to compromise on comfort (e.g., stick instead of automatic gear). The sale of heavy-duty vehicles (trucks, buses) underlies similar rules: flexible business model and unique selling proposition combined with a superior strategy to reach main megamarket buyers (e.g., transport companies, industrial clients).

As multimillion-dollar projects in the vehicle segment shift from drawing board to reality in the megamarkets, EU component producers will be compelled to follow their car company customers to these foreign markets. Some car multinationals, like Volkswagen in Russia, have planned larger facilities to accommodate their priority suppliers. The megamarkets will thus be of high strategic value to components makers as well.

Companies belonging to the vehicle cluster have four basic options when expanding in the megamarkets:
- stand-alone (most frequent variant);
- alliance with local or international partners (often lobbied or imposed by governments like the Maruti-Suzuki venture in India or the SAIC-Volkswagen alliance in China);
- acquisition of a stake in a local company (e.g., Renault's 25% stake in Russia's Avtovaz for US$1 billion);
- piggyback with selected mega customers (mainly for components makers).

In the coming years, M&As including cross-shareholdings will probably rise given that greenfield investments have proved to take a long time to become fully operational.

4.5. Machinery and equipment

4.5.1. Global machinery trends

Machine building includes the production of machine-tools and mechanical equipment used for various types of manufacturing applications. This industry forms the backbone of industrialized countries and is one of the last bastions where AM companies indisputably dominate the global economy. The world's famous machinery companies are headquartered in Germany, Italy, Switzerland, Austria, Sweden, Japan, and Taiwan. Machinery producers from Europe—mostly medium-sized and family-owned enterprises—have reported good financial results and high export ratios of up to 60%. German companies, for example, have benefited greatly from globalization and succeeded in multiplying their sales several times in both advanced and emerging markets since the early 2000s. Some of them have set up global networks of sales offices, service and spares centers, and assembly outlets to better serve their worldwide customers.

All user industries from automotive, steel, telecommunications to food processing require machinery and equipment to raise productivity and performance levels. Buying patterns of users vary with general investment conditions and the capacity building cycle, characterized by growth periods of three to four years, followed by sometimes equally long slowdowns. The creation of new capacity in the emerging markets has lengthened the upward cycle and compensated for the shortfall due to saturation in the AMs. Germany's positive balance of trade derives from the surplus due mainly to exports of machinery to these markets. EU machinery manufacturers have, however, to contend with high costs in their home markets. Many therefore are investing in the new markets where their new customer base lies. In a recent survey, 43% of German machine builders declared that they envisage investments in foreign countries to avoid high taxation and labor costs in Germany. China and India, but also Russia, are the favored destinations. Germany's leading brewery and bottling equipment suppliers (e.g., Ziemann, Krones, KHS), for example, already realize up to 50% of their sales in emerging economies. They now plan to establish local manufacturing and assembly facilities closer to their megamarket customers. Similar trends are noticeable in packaging, printing, and other areas as industrial modernization speeds up in the three countries and surrounding economies. During 2000–2008, the number of German machine-tool makers with foreign sales and assembly subsidiaries rose from 27% to 45%. The leading companies (e.g., Deckel Maho Gildemeister-DMG, Trumpf, Index) are present in the megamarkets (see table 4.28).

In 2007, world machinery production rose by 6% to €1.31 trillion (€1,310 billion). The United States, Japan, and Germany remain the top three suppliers, but growth in these countries has been modest. Sales of the world's leading manufacturers are increasingly oriented to the megamarkets, where practically all industries are experiencing a protracted boom. For German textile machinery suppliers, for example, China has become the largest export market, followed by India, which has displaced the United States and Turkey to third and fourth positions. Russia is a major customer of German and Italian equipment companies, which supply shop floor machinery, construction, earth-moving equipment, and heavy-duty machines used in the energy and raw mate-

Table 4.28. The world's top seven machine-tool companies, 2007.

Company	Sales (US$ bn)
Trumpf, Germany	2.5
Gildemeister, Germany	2.1
Yamazaki-Mazak, Japan	2.0
MAG IAS, USA[a]	1.7
Amada, Japan	1.6
Okuma, Japan	1.6
Mori Seiki, Japan	1.5

a. Acquired German SMEs: Witzig & Frank, Hueller Hille, Cross Hueller, Ex-Cell-O.
Source: German Machine Builders Association-VDMA. 2008.

rials extraction sectors. The shortfall in domestic machinery production in the megamarkets is compensated by imports including high-end and secondhand machinery; sometimes whole plants of companies acquired in the AMs are relocated.

But the boom in the megamarkets has also benefited local companies who now challenge their Western rivals. China's machine builders managed to treble turnover in six years and have reached sales volumes of more than €130 billion in 2007 (+20% over 2006). Russia's machine-building sector is growing equally fast, by 15% in 2006 and 18% in 2007. Russia has made it into the league of top ten equipment-producing countries, replacing Switzerland. Growing at around 16%, India's machinery industry is a major exporter of heavy and light engineering goods for the energy, fertilizer, cement, steel, petrochemical, mining, and construction industries.

A closer look at the international ranking shows that Asian producers hold an increasing share in world markets that were formerly dominated by EU and US players (see table 4.29). In machine-tools and general machinery, China ranks fourth. According to the German Machine Builders' Association (VDMA), while China and India represent no immediate danger to the German machine-tool industry, the two countries will, within ten years, cover one-third of the world's standard machine market, which is now served by Taiwan, South Korea, Spain, and Italy. This trend can already be observed in selected segments such as food processing, packaging, and textile machines. German and Japanese producers operating in the high-tech segment, including CNC-guided machine-tools, will experience more competition once Chinese and Indian suppliers start offering state-of-the-art solutions for these categories.

Although the threat is not imminent, it should not be taken lightly. Chinese, Indian, and Russian engineers can do exactly what Japanese, South Korean, and Taiwanese companies did throughout the 1980s and 1990s when they meticulously copied and improved on existing technologies by means of patent screening, reverse engineering, and shop-floor optimizations. They are learning from local users who, to save costs, purchase secondhand machinery and relocate entire plants from defunct companies in Europe. Megamarket companies may not be as innovative as Western competitors (e.g., high-quality

Table 4.29. The world's leading machinery markets, 2007, 2010.

a. General machinery	Sales 2007 (€ bn)	Sales 2010 (€ bn)	Growth (%)
USA	250	270	2.0
Japan	187	198	3.0
Germany	185	205	3.5
China	130	184	10.0
Italy	90	101	3.0
France	50	52	0.1
UK	35	28	–1.5
Russia	30	36	5.0
Total	1310	1520	3.0

b. Machine-tools	Sales 2007 (US$ bn)	Change 2007/2006 (%)	World share (%)
Japan	8.7	+8	17.9
Germany	8.6	+6	17.8
Italy	4.7	–4	8.7
China	3.5	+6	7.2
USA	2.6	–20	5.4
South Korea	2.5	+8	5.2
Taiwan	2.5	–3	5.2
Switzerland	1.9	–21	3.9
Spain	1.0	–9	2.1
France	0.8	–10	1.7
Others	11.7	+1	24.1
World	48.5	+2.5	100

Source: Adapted from VDMA, Statistical Yearbook Machine Building, 2007.

color printing), but things will change as more mechanical engineers are being trained and decide to return home after receiving foreign education. The leading equipment producers in China and India have started to recruit Western specialists to close the technological gap.

4.5.2. Machinery trends in the megamarkets

As the megamarkets rise to industrial might, there is an insatiable demand for top-class and standard machinery in practically all industries. For basic equipment needed in steel, automobile, chemicals, electronics, and consumer goods industries as well as the machinery sector itself, megamarket producers are closing the gap with AM suppliers. Local demand for general purpose machinery in manufacturing, construction, and agriculture in the three megamarkets is already being satisfied by low-cost local suppliers. However, most customized, high-tech equipment—a segment dominated by Western players—needs to be imported. But Chinese, Indian, and Russian machine-tool makers are attracted to the medium- and higher-quality markets where demand is growing proportionately faster than in traditional segments. It emanates from companies that have to upgrade their process technologies and restructure to become more competitive. This opens opportunities also for EU suppliers providing customized solutions and 24/7 after-sales services.

CHINA

China's State Council, the country's top political body, has designated the machinery industry as a pillar industry for the coming two decades. China's leaders understood that equipment quality would ensure the success of their industrial modernization policies. As a result, some Chinese producers have become profitable and started exporting standard machinery to both emerging and advanced markets. China became a net exporter of machinery in 2005 following a 50% rise of foreign sales to RMB104 billion (€10 billion). The industry year-on-year average growth is forecast to be 15% until 2012. China is also securing market access by acquiring EU companies. Two well-known German machine-tool makers—Adolf Waldrich Coburg (acquired in 2005 by Jingcheng Machinery) and Schiess (acquired in 2006 by Shenyang Machine Tools)—reported growing employment and sales figures during 2006–2007 as a result of their alliances.[51] The success of such Sino-German alliances is attributed to the relative autonomy granted by the Chinese owners to the German management and the division of work between the Germans (high-tech machines) and Chinese (standard machines). More acquisitions by Chinese machine builders in Europe and the United States will certainly follow.

In the coming years, the Chinese industry will have to overcome certain weaknesses if it wants to join the big league. It is fragmented, and many small companies suffer from lack of funds and economies of scale. Chinese managers need to develop service awareness, innovative capabilities, and better-quality human resources by switching from rote learning to innovation based on its own initiatives.

---

51. "Chinesisch-Fränkische symbiose" [Chinese-Franconian symbiosis], *Handelsblatt,* October 29, 2007.

India

India's machinery industry (growth: +16%) is characterized by a large range of products (almost all major capital goods are domestically manufactured)—a legacy of the earlier import-substitution policy of the pre-1990s era. Its product portfolio has therefore been developed partially out of its own innovations and R&D efforts. India's machinery producers have come a long way since liberalization, delicensing, and economic reforms were pushed through in the late 1990s. The industry has shown its capacity to manufacture large-sized plants and equipment for various sectors, including innovative air pollution control systems. The heavy electrical industry meets the entire domestic demand. The Indian market, although growing, is still too small to ensure volumes and economies of scale. Exports are of relevance to about four hundred companies in the industry. In addition to building volume, some of these family-controlled SMEs will have to upgrade their products (they lack finish) and enhance productivity, and although customer service is more responsive than that of foreign counterparts, the quality of the service call needs to be improved. Any long-term success must be driven by exports and alliances with foreign technology leaders.

Some Indian equipment producers have cooperated with their customers in buying out major units in the United States and the EU with the aim to relocate the entire machine park to India. In the case of Gujarat Heavy Chemicals and Dalmia Group, for example, secondhand textile machinery was combined with locally made equipment and integrated into new capital goods.[52] Similarly, large-scale Indian printing companies have imported large quantities of secondhand offset printing, engraving, and gluing equipment, which was combined into new systems.

Russia

In Russia, investment in new industrial plants increased by over 40% during 2004–2007. This trend will persist until 2015 as 65%–70% of the equipment is depreciated after more than twenty years of use. There is a strong demand for new machines in practically every industry as companies replace assets and equipment for manufacturing, warehousing, and R&D centers. Russia's machine builders have devised strategies to fend off foreign competition and to improve their position, especially in Russia and CIS. Enterprises producing equipment for the energy, defense, construction, manufacturing, and agro industries will be at the center of this growth. Suppliers of machinery to the auto segment will gain from increased investments by foreign carmakers and the expected plant modernizations. Large agricultural machinery companies like Rostselmash and Agromashholding were able to expand into other CIS countries by acquiring local players. The largest producer of energy-related equipment, Power Machines (Silovye Mashiny), increased its earnings by 30% annually during 2004–2007. A takeover attempt by Siemens was thwarted by the Russian government on grounds of national interest. Russia's energy monopoly, UES Rossiya, plans to invest about US$1 billion in new facilities during 2007–2009. Railway equipment is another promising segment: Russian Railways plans to increase capital spending as part of a US$16 billion investment plan during 2007–2010.

---

52. "Textile Companies Scan EU, US Markets for Second-hand Machinery." *The Hindu Business Line,* December 4, 2005.

4.5.3. Challenges for foreign machinery companies

EU equipment manufacturers are cautious and protect essential trade secrets by keeping core activities at headquarters. They hesitate to make major investments in geographically distant economies, especially when they are not familiar with the local culture and mentality. Machinery suppliers are usually conservative and deeply entrenched in regional communities (e.g., Germany's Baden-Wuerttemberg and Westfalia, Italy's Lombardy) where local customs and family ties prevail. But with increased international competition, especially the emergence of potent machine builders in Asia and the megamarkets, Western CEOs realize that moving into the new markets with local facilities will reduce costs, improve customer relations, and allow them to expand further into adjacent markets. Famous machine builders and printing equipment makers from Germany and Switzerland are expanding their network of service and training centers to major megamarket cities to be more accessible for customers; others have launched small-scale assembly and manufacturing operations (e.g., Index in Northeast China). Internationalization efforts of EU machine builders are thus no longer limited to foreign trade but will henceforth include FDI in the form of strategic alliances, acquisitions of local companies, or brownfield/greenfield projects.

EU producers understand that they must keep innovating and investing in breakthrough technologies if they want to stay ahead and shape key developments (see table 4.30). Capital goods developed for the future will have to respond to new applications and new materials, faster product cycles, high precision, and a high degree of singularity and customization. Safety, cost savings, and environmental aspects, which distinguish EU machine builders from their competitors, must be promoted aggressively as they will help them maintain their leadership.

The competitiveness of EU companies will depend on whether they can master six megatrends that will have a decisive impact on the industry's future:

- more complex work-piece characteristics (geometry, surface, etc.), which will influence milling technologies, processing of work-pieces, and retooling
- new work-pieces, which stimulate the discovery and use of new materials and alloys
- more demanding and diverse user expectations, which must be satisfied by means of reduced batch numbers but wider product variations
- faster product changes, which will lead to short manufacturing cycles with complex tooling
- environmental protection, which has become a high priority with users, end consumers, and state regulators
- new business models, particularly product–service combinations, which influence the design and functionality of the machine-tool, equipment, and their main elements

Producing high-tech machines in the megamarkets is not necessarily cheaper than in AMs. Problems related to relocation of production are often underestimated. High-precision parts that are not available must be imported at high costs because local vendors deliver inconsistent quality. Specialists need to be flown in to solve problems and check main vendors to set up a well-functioning supply chain for local content. Shop-floor productivity is usually lower than in AMs because local technicians and workers lack requisite training.

Table 4.30. Technology trends in machining, 2010–2015.

Technology	Trends
High-speed machining	Reduction of machining time by increase of cutting speed through new machine concepts and higher performance potential of cutting materials
Dry machining/ Minimum quantity lubrication	Reduction or elimination of coolants in machining in order to reduce environmental and cost burdens
Hard machining	Cutting and special finish machining of hardened materials by means of a defined cutting edge (turning, milling, drilling)
Complete or integrated machining	Integration of various machining processes such as turning, milling, gear cutting, and grinding in a single machine to finish the workpiece in one set-up
Micro processing	Metal and non-metal cutting processes for generating miniaturized components with geometric dimensions in the micron range
Linear direct drives	New highly dynamic drive elements of simple construction for direct generation of linear movements
Rapid prototyping	Rapid realization of prototypes and pre-production series of new products for geometrical and functional testing
Internal high-pressure forming	Generation of complex geometries from a single workpiece by using high hydraulic pressure
Near net shape forming	Generation of the final contour of a workpiece as to shape, dimensional accuracy, and surface quality, in a single forming process
Lasers in material processing	Laser beam sources: distinctly higher output, miniaturization, increased flexibility by means of new beam control; integration of semi-conductor components (diode lasers) Laser systems: cutting systems with extremely high process dynamics, particularly compact and easy-to-integrate marking and inscribing systems, innovative solutions for welding; micro-processing
Control systems	Innovative control systems must keep up with growing requirements; decentralization, remote diagnostics via Internet, and error detection up to the level of field equipment (sensors, actuators)
Simulation	Efficient tools and computer-aided systems are helping designers and developers in creating precise and economic production systems for the future
Responsible resource management	Ecological and energy-saving treatment of natural resources must increasingly characterize concept and structure of machine-tools

Source: Adapted from VDW. The German Machine Tool Industry 2001. Frankfurt. 2002.

Rather than transfer the entire production process, EU companies should carefully decide on the know-how areas (e.g., service) that should be transferred and those that should remain at headquarters (e.g., sophisticated engineering). Key pointers for containing the effects of supply- and quality-related problems include:

- limiting joint ventures to sales, making optimum use of local distribution networks (e.g., those of large Chinese machine-tool makers);
- not seeking low costs only, but putting energy into building lasting partnerships with producers and suppliers sharing the same objectives;
- avoiding size mismatches (e.g., a joint venture between a giant, state-owned company from China or Russia and a family-owned company in the EU); India offers EU players many equivalent SMEs, but here too cultural and philosophy aspects of how the partners see quality or view joint business development may lead to divergent opinions; and
- expanding the application scope from components to integrated systems or turnkey solutions, as many leading companies (e.g., Heidelberger, Fobro) have successfully done.

4.6. Chemicals

4.6.1. Global chemical sector trends

The chemical industry covers a broad spectrum of segments for organic and inorganic substances: petrochemicals, fertilizers, dyestuffs, pesticides, coatings, and high-value specialty chemicals. Most of these segments will record high and rapid growth in the megamarkets in the coming years.

Globally, chemicals represent a US$1.9 trillion (US$1,900 billion) industry. The world's four largest markets (USA, Japan, China, and Germany) absorb around half of the world's demand for chemicals. China overtook Germany in 2005 to become the world's third-largest market for chemical products after the United States and Japan (see table 4.31). Accounting for a total volume of US$530 billion, Asia is now bigger than North America (US$490 billion) and will overtake Europe (US$590 billion) toward 2010 as the world's most important region for chemical products. Within Asia-Pacific, Japan still represents the biggest market for basic and fine chemicals, but China and India are closing the gap as they continue growing much faster. Analysts predict growth rates of 10%–12% annually for the next six to eight years for both countries, which is three times higher than the average growth in the United States, Germany, and Japan. By 2015, China's share in the Asia-Pacific market will be 37% against 22% for Japan and 16% for India (see figure 4.10).

Table 4.31. The world's leading chemical markets, 2004–2010 (€ bn).

	2004	2005	2010
USA	415	430	510
Japan	186	190	195
China	137	151	260
Germany	142	149	170
Total, top four	880	920	1,135
Other markets	920	935	975
Total, world	1,800	1,855	2,110
Share, top four (%)	48.9	49.6	53.8

Source: Verband der Chemischen Industrie (VDI), Germany. 2008.

Figure 4.10. Share of chemical markets in Asia-Pacific, 2005, 2015.

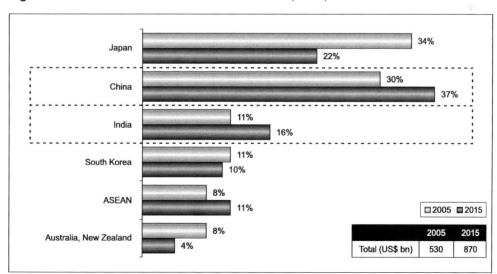

Source: Chemical & Engineering News. 2007.

Table 4.32. The world's top fourteen chemical companies, 1/1/2008.

Company	Sales (US$ bn)
BASF, Germany	79
Dow Chemicals, USA	54
Bayer, Germany	45
Royal Dutch Shell, UK[a]	42
ExxonMobil, USA[a]	37
SABIC, Saudi Arabia	34
Total, France[a]	31
Du Pont, USA	31
Mitsubishi Chemicals, Japan	26
Sinopec, China[a]	26
Formosa Plastics, Taiwan	19
Lyondell, USA	19
AKZO, Netherlands	18
Linde, Germany	17

a. Chemicals division.
Source: Chemical and Engineering News. Fortune 500. 2008.

EU and US chemicals players are world leaders. For five consecutive years, BASF, Dow Chemical, Bayer, and DuPont have maintained their leading positions (see table 4.32). Three oil giants—Royal Dutch/Shell, Exxon Mobil, and Total—have also made it into the top ten owing to their strong chemicals units. Other oil giants such as China Petroleum & Chemical (Sinopec), British Petroleum, Saudi Basic Industries Corp. (SABIC), and Germany's Bayer fell in the ranking after divesting their chemical businesses. In 2006, the world's top fifty chemical companies reported combined sales of US$706 billion (+15% compared with 2005). The sales cutoff for the top fifty increased 4% in 2006 to US$5.9 billion.

Capital and R&D spending are high in the profitable chemical industry (see figure 4.11). The aggregate operating profit margin of the top fifty players was 9% in 2006, up from 6% in 2003. This positive trend is expected to last well into the next decade due to strong demand in both advanced and emerging economies. Europe has the highest number of large players. In 2006, there were twenty-two EU companies among the top fifty with combined sales of US$310.5 billion. European companies' share of total world sales was 45%. Japan had eight companies in the ranking, with combined sales of US$89 billion in 2006 and a share of 13%.

4.6.2. Chemical sector trends in the megamarkets

CHINA

China is an attractive location for producing base chemicals, in which the country posts a comfortable trade surplus. The country remains, however, a net importer of high-performance and fine chemicals, although it strives to reduce this dependence. Chinese chemical companies are developing value-added products in the specialty segment, such as:

- chemical by-products for medicines (competing with Swiss, UK, and US players);
- food additives (competing with Japanese, US, and European players);
- fine chemicals for animal fodder such as lysine (in direct competition with market leaders BASF and Degussa);
- new-generation pesticides and insecticides;
- vitamin C products;
- antibiotics (competing with the Dutch DSM-Group's range, which is nowadays mostly produced in China);

Figure 4.11. Performance of the world's top fifty chemical companies, 2003–2009.

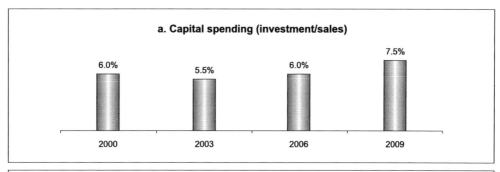

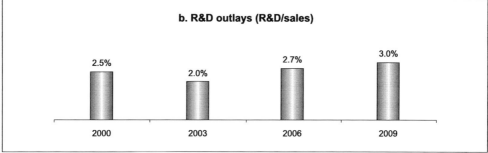

Source: Chemical and Engineering News. 2007.

- high-performance chemicals (compelling Rhodia and Degussa to relocate production and R&D to China);
- plastics (China raised its output of high-performance plastics and polymers, for which it buys increasing volumes of plastic waste, thus depriving plastic waste treatment plants in Germany of vital feedstock).

Explosive growth in the main user segments (e.g., vehicles, electronics, construction, agribusiness, paper, textiles) has led to investments in high value-added areas. The bulk chemicals segment faces a problem of oversupply as hundreds of smaller players expand their capacities. They accept far lower margins than multinationals, which have to balance global investments. At the same time, stricter standards in Europe compel companies to relocate to countries like China, which represent huge future markets. EU plastics processors, for example, have begun to transfer innovative technologies in order to bypass EU legislation that imposes extremely high recycling rates. Investments in polluting plants for basic chemicals are directed to the production of specialty chemicals such as technical polymers, special pigments, and high-tech plastics. These investments have become necessary as the demand for sophisticated products grows; this is a segment where Western companies must increasingly defend their positions vis-à-vis emerging Asian rivals.

China has about 12,500 small and medium-sized chemicals firms. But the market is dominated by a handful of large corporations that pursue an aggressive strategy of consolidation by acquiring other players. In the face of mounting international competition, some companies have merged into larger structures such as China United Chemical Industrial Corporation, Jilin Chemicals, Shanghai Chemicals, and Zheijang Nice Chemicals. Sinopec, a petrochemical company, is also expanding its chemicals unit.

Western chemicals giants have launched megaprojects in China to boost their turnover in Asia, particularly China. The Chinese market accounts for only 4%–5% of overall sales for the top three chemicals multinationals (Bayer, BASF, DuPont), which is hardly commensurate with the country's future potential. In September 2005, BASF inaugurated its new chemical plant in Nanjing, a cooperation project with its Chinese partner Sinopec. The plant, BASF's highest investment in Asia totaling €2.4 billion over four years, produces special pigments for paints, textiles, and building materials. The China operation will be the group's sixth integrated site where final products of one unit become direct inputs for downstream units and processes. By 2020, BASF plans to generate at least one-third of its worldwide revenue in Asia; by then China will account for 10% of the group's total sales. Similarly, Germany's Bayer will raise its plastics production and, like BASF, intends to more than double its China share in the group's turnover from 4.5% to around 10%. Degussa, which ranks third in Germany, expects to treble its sales to €1 billion by 2010 and to double the share of China sales (currently 3%). DuPont, Dow Chemical, ICI, and Lanxess (a spin-off from Bayer) are expanding their China operations as well. Akzo, the biggest chemicals company in the Netherlands, plans to increase its paint output in China by investing in new plants.

In 2007, fifty chemicals investment projects were under way totaling at least US$3 billion in capital outlays—compared with only one such project in the United States today. Seven "crackers" (including the BASF-led project) built by Sinopec and other chemicals companies are expected to come onstream by 2010—an expansion that would push up China's ethylene capacity by 25% annually. China will then be able to cover half of its needs, compared with one-third today. Four chemicals giants plan to allocate multibillion-dollar funds for their China operations during 2007–2010: DuPont (US$7.7. billion), BASF (US$6.5 billion), Bayer (US$3.5 billion), and Dow Chemicals (US$1.2 billion). The Chinese government has demarcated special areas, such as Changxing island industrial zone in Liaoning province, for attracting more investors in basic and advanced chemicals.

INDIA

The chemical industry ranks fourth in India's economy after iron and steel, machine building, and textiles, and it generates 13% of India's manufacturing output. It contributes 7% of GDP and 14% of exports. The industry is made up of around 14,000 units with a total invested capital of Rs5800 trillion (US$115 billion). India is the second-largest producer of agrochemicals in Asia. According to Chemtech Foundation, the Indian chemical market has the potential to reach between US$60 and US$70 billion by 2010 (up from US$35 billion in 2006) given its double-digit annual growth since 2000. This will position India as a global supplier of specialty and knowledge chemicals, and as an investment destination for these promising segments. By 2010, the balance will shift from basic segments to the knowledge segments, which will account for 35%–40% of the total market (up from 20% today). Basic chemicals produced in India today include synthetic rubber, chemicals for leather processing, paints, additives, insecticides, lubricants, resins, and fertilizers. The main factors driving the Indian chemical industry's growth are higher domestic demand and realization of the export potential. All end-user industries from food packaging, textiles, and paper to vehicles and pharmaceuticals are recording high growth. The industry's main strengths lie in the quality of its production processes, the availability of technical manpower, and its abundant raw materials.

The main impediment to growth is the legacy of the old economy resulting in unsupportive regulations, inconsistent tariffs, and fragmentation of the industry. India's chemical industry, which operated under a protected regime behind high import barriers, has been thrown open to foreign competition since tariffs were slashed and markets liberalized starting from the early 2000s. Indian companies are now under pressure to streamline their operations in order to cut costs and improve product and process quality. A few dynamic players managed to strengthen their positions in the global arena by stepping up marketing, management processes, and in-house research. Indian firms are gaining ground in specialty segments such as agrochemicals (pesticides, insecticides, herbicides) and biotechnology applications (e.g., bio-engineered seeds for resistant cotton and food crops, genetically modified plants). They are supported by the large English-speaking, educated human capital base comprising 3 million graduates, 700,000 postgraduates, and 2,000 PhD students who qualify in biosciences and chemical engineering each year. It is estimated that 10% of researchers and 15% of scientists in biotechnology-related R&D in the United States are of Indian origin, and growing numbers are potential returnees. Consolidation is an imperative to achieve global scale. With growing exports, Indian companies are also establishing a brand name in international markets. The Indian government is committed to removing regulatory and tariff obstacles to growth; it thus hopes to attract more FDI to the industry.

Russia

Russia's chemical industry has experienced an unprecedented revival since 2000. Most leading chemical players report double-digit growth rates (see table 4.33). They benefit from linkages with upstream oil enterprises, which feel the positive repercussions of high energy prices. Russian chemical plants have increased their capacities to keep pace with the fast-growing economy. By 2015, the share of chemicals in national GDP will rise to 3%, from 1.7% today. They have stepped up their exports, particularly to nearby CIS and Eastern European countries, where the Russians compete seriously with AM producers.

Table 4.33. Russia's top six chemical companies, 1/1/2007.

Company	Sales (US$ bn)	Profits/sales (%)
Sibur	3.9	19.4
Nizhnekamskneftechin	1.6	9.8
Salavatnefteorgsintes	1.5	19.5
Amtel	0.9	13.3
Kazanorgsintes	0.7	16.8
Nizhnekamskshina	0.6	1.7

Source: Expert, October 3–9, 2007.

Russia has developed strong agrochemical (mineral, nitrate-, calcium-, and phosphor-based fertilizers) and petrochemical clusters. Fertilizer companies enjoy high demand from financially strong agroholdings, some of which invest in backward integration to ensure supplies. Plastics and synthetic rubber companies also draw advantages from a growing domestic market. The demand for these products is keeping pace with overall growth in manufacturing and sometimes even outpacing it. During 2003–2007, the demand for various types of polymers grew by 20%. The profits of the leading companies in this segment increased accordingly. Financial figures would look even better if more Russian companies were in a position to expand and upgrade their plants, which for many years have run at 90%–95% capacity, causing high operational costs due to depreciated equipment.

Six new large chemical plants will be installed by 2015 in an effort to cut imports of value-added products, including plastics, for booming industries such as the car sector. Nizhnekamskneftekhim, Russia's second-largest chemicals producer, opened a large new polystyrol production facility outside the city of Kazan. It will benefit Russian user industries, which had to import most of their requirements of this polymer earlier. In another case, Kazanorgsintez signed a license agreement with the Japanese company Asahi Kasei Chemicals for producing polycarbonates. This product was previously not produced in any significant quantity in Russia. Sibur and Amtel, two other leading players, have come up with ambitious investments in plants for tires and polymers to withstand the expansion of two foreign rivals: France's Michelin, which by 2009 plans to invest US$60 million, and Finland's Nokian, which will invest US$57 million in Russia. EU's chemicals giants BASF and Bayer are also trying to establish a firm market presence by setting up regional sales offices, production facilities, and laboratories. For EU chemicals and equipment suppliers, Russia represents a useful platform for sales to other CIS countries that have maintained historical links with Russia. Belgium's Solvay is engaged in the largest project by a Western chemical TNC in Russia so far. During 2005–2008, the company will allocate €500 million for a polyvinylchloride (PVC) plant in Volgograd with a total capacity of 200,000 metric tons. Russia has a deficit of about 55,000 metric tons in this plastic, and the demand is growing at 30% annually owing to the resurgent construction sector.

4.6.3. Challenges for foreign chemical companies

The chemical industry in the megamarkets is characterized by exploding demand, especially for specialty chemicals. The growing population of megamarket players in value-added segments will lead to intense competition, which individual companies will try to avert through consolidation, specialization, divestment, and cost optimization via economies of scale in manufacturing, distribution, and logistics. Megamarket players are expected to invest more in R&D for new products and processes and in IT to improve supply chain efficiency, which will pose additional threats for established AM players. On the other hand, a stronger local industry offers better partnership options for EU/US companies and new opportunities for AM suppliers of equipment, precision instruments, and services.

Applicable key factors of success for EU/US chemicals companies are:
- feasible balance between proximity to key accounts and raw materials;

- extension and adaptation of the product range and process capabilities to local conditions;
- market development for not-yet-available specialty chemicals: technical polymers, tensides, fine chemicals, additives, special paints, etc.;
- better key accounts management to nurture personal relations for steady order flows;
- ceaseless innovation and protection of know-how to fend off competitors;
- retaining of core competencies and outsourcing of only what is less relevant; and
- precautions against product imitations, patent infringements, connivance between local governments and business, overcapacity, and price falls.

4.7. Consumer and luxury goods

4.7.1. Global trends in consumer goods

Until the mid-1970s, European and US producers were uncontested leaders in practically all consumer goods categories (see box 4.3). Then, in the 1980s and 1990s, Japanese, South Korean, and Taiwanese companies began to chip away market shares in textiles, fast-moving consumer goods (FMCG), and selected consumer durables. Things started deteriorating for Europe when toward the early 1990s China emerged as a major supplier. India and other emerging economies from Asia (Bangladesh, Pakistan, Philippines, Viet Nam) followed. AM companies were compelled to close down or shift production to Asia to match the low costs. Fashion and luxury goods will be the last bastions of dominance by EU and US players at the end of the 2000s. The EU and US textile and apparel industries were severely hit by the removal of textile quotas negotiated in a WTO deal with China in 2001, which took effect on January 1, 2005. Overnight, China increased its global share in textiles and apparel from 30% to 52%, India from 15% to 24%. This market is estimated at US$470 billion worldwide.

China

Trade liberalization and government support helped Chinese companies expand into all consumer goods segments. China is today the largest exporter of toys, sports goods, watches, bicycles, and household items. China's nine thousand toy plants are spread across

---

Box 4.3. Light industry categories: consumer and luxury goods.

- Basic consumer goods: textiles, apparel, leather wear, and related products
- Fast-moving consumer goods (FMCG): toys, personal care, cosmetics, kitchen utensils, detergents
- Consumer durables: white goods, consumer electronics, PCs
- Luxury goods: fashion clothing, design accessories, cosmetics, jewelry
- Packaging: flexible packaging (polyester films, PET, BOPP, holograms, laminates, "green" polymers based on pollution-free feed stocks such as grain), special packaging (folding boxes for cosmetics, pharmaceuticals, glass)

Figure 4.12. China's global dominance in consumer goods, 2008.

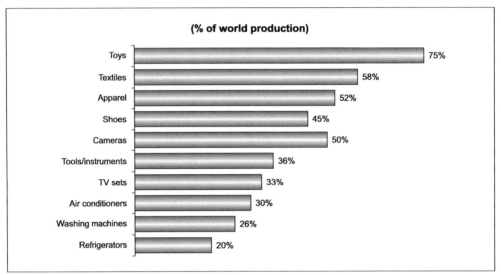

Source: German Federal Statistical Office. 2008.

the country; they produce 75% of the world's output, export to more than a hundred countries, and employ about 3.5 million people. China itself has become a huge market of 300 million children aged one through fourteen (25% of the total population).

Despite recurring problems related to quality[53] or copyright infringements, no other country in the world has built such a powerful industrial base or commands such high global market shares in so many product categories (see figure 4.12): apparel, bags, accessories, toys, home appliances, personal care and cosmetics, white goods, TVs, cameras, computers, and electrical tools. The country's trade surplus with the EU and the United States stems mostly from exports of consumer goods. In the two coastal mega regions of Guangdong/Shenzen/Fujian (Pearl River delta) and Jiangsu/Zhejiang (Jangste River delta), China has created the largest and most competitive manufacturing belts for FMCGs in the world. Guangdong province accounts for 40% of China's total exports and 50% of FMCG sales to foreign countries. About 25% of this volume is absorbed by Western retail giants (e.g., Wal-Mart, Carrefour, Quelle[54]), and another 25% by foreign multinationals with production facilities in China. Chinese brands like Haier (refrigerators) and Hisense (television sets) are gaining recognition in world markets after growing mainly at home during the past twenty years.

Furniture is a new category under attack by China's enterprises. Chinese imports into Germany increased by over 40% during 2006–2007[55] (see figure 4.13). At the same time, imports from Italy, the traditional supplier, rose by only 2%. Polish imports, which are still dominant, decreased by 22%. The figures for other EU countries like Belgium, Denmark,

---

53. In the second half of 2007, Mattel recalled more than 10 million Chinese-made toys because of lead paint and tiny magnets that could be swallowed by children.
54. See 6.3 (retailing).
55. "China startet attacke auf den möbelmarkt" [China launches attack on the furniture market], *Handelsblatt,* September 7, 2007.

Figure 4.13. Origin of furniture imports into Germany, 2006–2007 (€ mn).

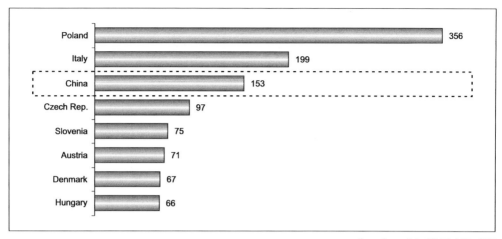

Source: German Federal Statistical Office. 2007.

France, and the Netherlands also show a significant rise in imports of Asian furniture, as reported by Eurostat, the EU's statistical office. China seems to be gradually replacing other central European countries. About 130,000 EU companies produce furniture worth €95 billion, accounting for about 43% of world production. But the balance is tilting toward China, which produces furniture worth €70 billion and accounts for 25% of furniture imports into Europe. China's success is inspiring new suppliers from India, Indonesia, Malaysia, and other Asian countries, whose furniture is increasingly visible in stores in Europe and the United States.

China has become a center for producing paper- and cardboard-based packaging: folding boxes, gift boxes, and bags. Chinese printers have diversified into these areas, linking up to a centuries-old printing tradition. The Asian Packaging Centre, located twenty kilometers away from the city of Hangzhou, is the largest industrial park of its kind in the world.

India

India has through the ages been a major supplier of textiles; today, it exports industrial yarns, dyed and printed fabrics, and garments. Another important export item is leather goods[56] (bags, belts, wallets, shoes), for which it holds the highest share of the world's market. For consumer durables, India is still a net importer, but both domestic and foreign brands see it as a reliable investment platform for exports to nearby SAARC, ASEAN, Middle East, and East and South Africa.

The situation in India's consumer durables market—estimated at US$12 billion (2008)—reflects a worldwide scenario. European and Japanese brands have a relatively small presence; the goods are high-priced (e.g., Electrolux, Míele, Siemens, Sony) whether they are imported or produced locally. The consumer durables market is dominated by South Korea's LG and Samsung and the local brand Videocon. Chinese products

---

56. India has the world's largest cattle population. See 3.2.3.

Table 4.34. Demand for big-ticket consumer goods in India, 2005–2015 (mn units).				
	2005	2010	2015	Producers[a]
Color TVs (CTV)	11.0	35.0	65	LG, Onida, Philips, Samsung, Sony, Videocon
Refrigerators	4.0	9.0	20	BPL, Electrolux, Godrej, LG, Samsung, Whirlpool
Washing machines	2.0	5.0	15	Electrolux, LG, Samsung, Siemens, Videocon, Whirlpool,
Air conditioners	1.3	4.0	8	Blue Star, Daikin, Samsung, Voltas
PCs	1.0	4.5	12	Compaq-HP, HCL, IBM, Sony, Samsung, Toshiba, Zenith

a. Indicative, not exhaustive, list.
Source: LG Annual Report. 2007.

(e.g., Haier) are still perceived as inferior in quality; they are entry-level products because of their low price ("China price") and discounts. The demand for consumer durables in India is set to grow at 12%–15% annually during 2007–2012 (see table 4.34), fueled by a growing middle class with rising incomes, changing lifestyles, and greater product awareness. Many middle-class consumers are upgrading to technologically superior products. Sales of the five main items—televisions, refrigerators, washing machines, air conditioners, microwave ovens—rose from US$4.1 billion in 2006 to US$5.1 billion in 2007. This fast-growing internal market is bound to attract additional industrial capacity, which in the coming years will also serve overseas markets.

The FMCG sector in India is valued at US$18 billion (2007); it is set to double in 2012 owing to an estimated tenfold increase in the middle-class population and threefold rise in household income and aggregate consumer spending. The sector is dominated by the multinationals Hindustan Unilever, Nestlé, Procter & Gamble, and Henkel with strong distribution networks. Hindustan Unilever has been present in India since 1933 and has merged well into the landscape. However, brands from large and even tiny Indian companies can compete strongly at local levels. This is the sector where "bottom of the pyramid" strategies[57] are paying off handsomely, particularly in the rural markets.

Packaging—an associated category (consumer goods need to be packed, promoted, and transported)—shows strong growth as well. Investors are turning their attention to India, which has suddenly emerged as the Asian hub for flexible packaging (polyester/BOPP films, laminations, metallization, holograms). Some of the world's leading polyester film producers[58] and converters (they laminate and print films into high-grade packaging materials) are based in the industrial zones surrounding Delhi and Mumbai. These companies have stepped up their foreign investments (e.g., Middle East, Mexico, ASEAN, China, USA) to get closer to their overseas customers in the food and beverages, pharmaceuticals, and FMCG sectors. Printers and packaging companies have added capacity by purchasing initially secondhand and now new equipment from Germany and Switzerland.

57. See 9.2.2.
58. India's integrated companies like Flex (sales 2007: US$500 million) or specialized film makers like Poliflex, Jindal Polyfilms, and Garware report annual growth rates of 25%–30%. They have embarked on huge expansion projects in India and other emerging markets (e.g., Flex in Mexico) while attempting to acquire knowledge-rich firms in the EU and the US.

Russia

Russia's widening trade deficit in consumer goods is financed through comfortable surpluses generated by energy and raw materials exports. But authorities are keen to support entrepreneurs in correcting this imbalance, especially in areas that were still alive in Soviet days: textiles, garments, footwear, leatherware, white goods, and televisions. EU companies are contributing to the revival by setting up production facilities for white goods (Bosch-Siemens, Candy, Indesit-Ariston). It is only a matter of time before Japanese and South Korean investments in consumer electronics will follow.

Like other European economies, Russia feels the competition of China. In 2007, only 25% of national demand for textiles and apparel could be satisfied through local production; the rest had to be imported. Russia's textile, apparel, and footwear companies were restructured to move to higher-quality segments (e.g., designer clothes, luxury goods, sports), with which they hope to conquer foreign markets. The main assets of Russian producers are talented engineers and designers, proximity to the expanding CIS markets, and aggressive branding. Average salaries of factory workers are lower in Russia than in Romania or Bulgaria, where EU players had originally relocated their production units.

The Russian textile association calls upon members to execute an action plan in order to better compete against aggressive Asian rivals:[59]

- raise technology levels by investing in modern equipment;
- optimize internal processes and coordination between departments;
- shorten time to market (i.e., the period between product development and market introduction);
- recruit creative talent to strengthen in-house design departments;
- offer fashionable products at an affordable price in visible outlets to increase brand recognition;
- open own retail outlets in major cities in Russia and CIS countries to raise location advantages vis-à-vis key accounts;
- build brand equity that appeals to brand-conscious consumers in Russia, the CIS, and the EU;
- work out winning concepts with all the partners in the value chain to strengthen the national textile and apparel cluster;
- build strategic alliances by acquiring stakes in other companies;
- attack Asian competitors in their home countries by acquiring stakes in leading Asian companies;
- invest in important markets like the EU, China, and India (assets, stakes, own stores).

Russian producers believe that strategic alliances with EU companies will help to abate the flow of Asian consumer goods imports.

---

59. "Rynok textilija" [Textile market], *Expert*, April 18, 2005, 32–39.

Russian packaging companies have benefited from high costs in Europe, which drove many EU companies out of business. As a result, secondhand and new equipment finds its way to Russia and the CIS countries, where large Western food (Nestlé, Kraft, Heinz, Pepsi) and consumer goods (Unilever, P&G) multinationals are setting up brand-new plants. The revival of consumer goods, including the FMCG segment, will lead to a mutually reinforcing situation benefiting suppliers of technical solutions and all kinds of equipment (machine-tools, bottling, robotics for manufacturing and logistics, conveyor belts, etc.).

4.7.2. Global trends in luxury goods

Fashion apparel, design accessories, cosmetics, watches, and jewelry fall under this category. The world market for luxury goods is estimated at US$150 billion; it will grow by another 30% within the next five years[60] (see table 4.35).

Italian, French, and Swiss companies dominate the luxury segment. US and Japanese companies occupy niches for watches, designer clothes, and jewelry, but they have not been able to really challenge Europe's dominance so far. The industry has undergone consolidation following a spate of mergers and acquisitions aimed at extending portfolios and removing excess capacities to secure margins. Fashion companies are stretching their brands to include watches and jewelry, which, unlike clothing, are not seasonal and lend prestige as long-lasting status symbols.[61] The trend is to shift to multi-brand holdings away from single-brand firms, which are vulnerable to downturns in their respective market niches. The sector leader, LVHM (France),[62] owns many brands including Louis Vuitton (handbags), Tag Heuer (watches), Moët & Chandon (champagne). Fashion houses like Hugo Boss (Germany), Escada (Germany), Prada (Italy), Gucci (Italy), Burberry (UK), and Loewe (Spain) also include high-end accessories in their range. Other players have diversified into luxury hotels, restaurants, and holiday resorts. Swiss watches and jewelry holding Compagnie Financière Richemont (CFR), the world's second-largest luxury conglomerate after LVMH, sells the Cartier, Lange & Soehne, and Mont Blanc brands in the megamarkets, which have become profitable propositions for most companies. Gucci decided to allocate 60% of its investment for 2009–2010 to Asia following extraordinary revenue growth (40% in 2007 compared with 19% for USA and 16% for the EU).

Table 4.35. Share of major luxury goods markets, 2007, 2012 (%).

	2007	2012
Japan	39	36
USA	16	15
EU	15	12
China	12	20
Russia	4	5
India	2	3
Others	10	9
Total, world	US$150 bn	US$195 bn

Source: LVMH. Corporate annual reports.

---

60. Luxury goods sales have decreased by 10% in the last quarter of 2008 as a result of higher cautiousness of well-to-do customers in the wake of the credit crisis. Once the economic outlook brightens up, confidence is expected to set in and sales will go up again.
61. "Luxus weckt wieder Begehrlichkeiten" [Luxury awakes lust], *Handelsblatt*, October 7, 2005.
62. LVMH owns about fifty prestigious brands in categories such as wines and spirits, perfumes and cosmetics, watches, jewelry, retail, and the media. The group's top brands include Dom Perignon champagne, Tag Heuer watches, and Christian Dior perfumes.

The megamarkets with their growing numbers of millionaires, super rich, and rich have drawn the attention of luxury goods makers around the world. The middle classes of these countries are upwardly mobile and good customers of luxury and semi-luxury goods.[63] They look for the original, less the imitation, and are therefore being intensively canvassed by Western producers. The market for fake products cannot, however, be discounted; it is also growing, but luxury brands ceaselessly take strong actions, broadcast widely by the media, against counterfeiters.

CHINA

With a share of 12% in 2006, China occupies third position after Japan (39% of world total) and the United States (16%).[64] At the present speed of development (annual growth rates of 15%–20%), the country's share in the global luxury market will rise above 20% by 2012. About 180 million consumers, or 14% of China's population, can already afford luxury brands. Italy's Armani increased sales by 35% in China each year during 2005–2007. France's luxury goods brand Louis Vuitton (part of LVMH) generates 50% of its export turnover in China. The importance of the US and EU markets will diminish as the number of wealthy people increases in the megamarkets and other emerging economies (see table 4.35).

INDIA

In January 2006, India's government offered foreign luxury goods a helping hand by allowing FDI up to 51% in single-brand stores, hence allowing the luxury brands a majority stake in joint ventures. India suddenly became an enticing growth market to brands such as Cartier, Christian Dior, Gucci, Hermès, Jimmy Choo, Louis Vuitton,[65] Moschino, Piaget, Tiffany, and others. There are now about 1.6 million Indian households that spend an average of US$9,000 a year on luxury goods. Louis Vuitton's business is expanding by 30% annually in India. To house these brands, two luxury malls are planned in Delhi, and hundreds of others are in various stages of construction and planning throughout the country. India does not have the problem of counterfeit luxury goods (although it is there for consumer goods), which makes it more attractive. But high import tariffs constrain growth; the customs duty on luxury watches, for example, is around 50%.

Indians always had a predilection for luxury goods: India is the largest consumer of gold. It is a major player in the gems and jewelry segment, exports of which exceeded US$20 billion in 2007, accounting for 55% of global exports of cut and polished diamonds in value terms. India is the world's undisputed leader in processing rough diamonds: eleven out of twelve stones set in jewelry worldwide are processed in India. The vast talent pool that has grown as a result is employed in jewelry design; India now has its own jewelry brands, which have opened outlets in the Middle East, Europe, and North America, where they cater to a wealthy clientele of young and upwardly mobile buyers of Indian and other origins. Exports of cut diamonds have fallen as entrepreneurs prefer to add value

---

63. An interesting indicator is the print run of lifestyle magazines. *Vogue*, for example, was launched in mid-2005 in China where it already sells 300,000 copies.
64. "Luxury Goods: Less Exuberant," *The Economist,* December 8, 2007, 73–74.
65. Louis Vuitton owes much to India's maharajahs, who discovered the designer and flooded his factory with orders in the late nineteenth century.

by producing jewelry that is sold in India, where demand is growing faster. The gems and jewelry industry in India works according to strict standards and strives to build trust and satisfy a demanding clientele.

Russia

Russia accounts for 4% of global luxury sales. By 2012, its share will most probably double, which would make Russia the fastest-growing emerging market. Like Chinese and Indians, Russians have a long tradition of exhibiting, presenting, producing, and consuming luxury goods. At the time of the Russian tsars, luxury goods were transported and exchanged with dignitaries from other lands across major trade arteries. Today, Russia is the world's leading producer of precious metals (e.g., gold) and diamonds.

While economic growth and wealth creation are increasing at a fast rate, Russians are on a spending spree (possibly to make up for opportunities lost during Communism) and not inclined to put much away. Merrill Lynch calls Russia "a young consumption economy unwilling to save." Russian travelers' offshore spending will remain a key driver of global luxury goods spending. In 2008, 23 million outbound tourists from Russia visited over a hundred countries and in most cases have become the biggest foreign spending community.

Italy's high fashion and luxury goods industry is well established in Russia. According to Altagamma, the association representing Italy's top design, fashion, and luxury brands, Italian firms are highly visible with all the big brands having their own outlets in Russia. A survey conducted in 2007 showed that more than 100 Italian luxury companies were present in Russia with around 340 mono-brand stores. That compares with 26 French brands and 40 mono-brand stores. It is estimated that Italian firms hold a share of about 65% of Russia's luxury market compared to 20% for French firms that come second. Italian producers have begun to invest together in multi-brand stores, particularly in Moscow and St. Petersburg. These stores are supported by regional export promotion bodies (e.g., Marche, Puglia, Tuscany). Insiders report that Moscow and St. Petersburg are close to saturation as more and more foreign firms pour into the country trying to take a slice of the pie through these two cities. Local partners, who traditionally support foreign luxury goods companies to position their brands (e.g., Mercury/TSUM, Bosco di Ciliegi/GUM, Crocus/Jamilco) have become very powerful as they are being canvassed by all sides. They control the distribution channels in major regions and neighboring CIS countries.

4.7.3. Challenges for foreign consumer and luxury goods companies

Incoming competition and relocations to lower-cost countries have decimated the EU's textile industry, once a large employer. About 40% of the remaining textile manufacturing capacity in the EU is expected to disappear by 2015–2020. Italy, which accounts for about one-third of the textile industry's workforce in the EU, lost almost 600,000 jobs during 1998–2007. Italian shoe producers cut jobs from 118,000 in 1997 to less than 80,000 in 2007. Most other consumer goods segments are equally threatened. Protectionist measures have so far had little impact in stemming the inflow, much less leading to a recovery; instead, they gave rise to gray imports and higher prices for official imports. Megamarket companies are using their newly acquired financial strength to buy up companies and gradually also penetrate the high fashion and luxury segments.

The leading companies have gained respite by shifting production to low-cost Bulgaria, China, India, Morocco, Pakistan, Romania, Tunisia, and Turkey. They focus on core strengths such as design, branding, research, and marketing. Successful Italian brands like Geoxx (shoes), Ermenegildo Zegna (men's wear), and Navigara and Champion Europe (sportswear) decided to remain trendsetters. They moved up-market by innovating and globalizing their activities (opening stores, acquiring suppliers). Some of them have local design bureaus and manufacturing units. Top consumer goods companies segment customers carefully and adapt their offers accordingly. They generate sufficient cash flow to recruit the best talents. Austria's two leading companies for special textiles, Getzner Textil AG and Linz Textil, ramped up their marketing to offer Western-quality standards to Chinese clients.[66] High performers also beat competitors by accelerating the release of new collections and shortening innovation cycles (the "fast fashion" strategy); they then work closely with retailers for implementing the strategy. Fast fashion is a huge market worth several hundred billion euros in Europe and expanding fast (see figure 4.14). Apparel chain store Zara from Spain (subsidiary of Inditex) gets in new ladies' collections every week. Most Asian suppliers cannot cope with the speed at which new collections are launched and the brand's quality requirements.

To satisfy ever-changing customer demand, EU retailers are compelled to cut transport time and mix orders from Asia and nearby regions. Most orders are placed in four geographies: the EU, Mediterranean (Morocco, Tunisia, Turkey), Eastern Europe (Ukraine, Romania, Bulgaria), and the Far East. Chinese and Indian companies are responding by putting up factories in Eastern Europe, North Africa, and Turkey to improve reactivity for the time-critical EU markets. Fast fashion enabled Spain's Zara to increase its store sales by 22% in 2007. Hennes & Mauritz (H&M) from Sweden and fashion retailers Mango and Top Shop are growing at double-digit rates as well.

EU companies, particularly lesser known brands, will have to contend with new mega-market designers, who are encouraged to create their own original collections instead

Figure 4.14. Fast fashion market in Europe, 2007 (€ bn), and change over previous year (%).

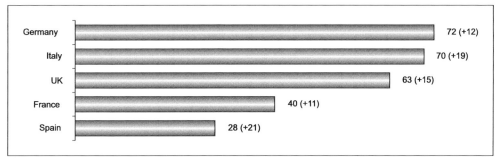

Source: Bain & Co. Expert. July 19, 2007.

---

66. "Textilindustrie macht gegen China mobil" [Textile industry mobilizes against China], *Wirtschaftsblatt*, March 20, 2004.

of limiting themselves to work subcontracted by foreign designers, fashion houses, and retailers. Local designers are gaining popularity among buyers avid for brands that cater to their tastes. Famous success stories are:

- Manish Arora, Rohit Bal, Ritu Beri, and Rina Dhaka from India;
- Bruno Basso, Carlos Miele, and Alexandre Herchcovitch from Brazil;
- Vivian Tam, Bi Li, and Han Feng from China; and
- Ms Oumou Sy from Senegal.

While some luxury makers rely on global brand promotion, others adapt their approaches and pay local celebrities (e.g., India's Bollywood stars) and sportsmen (e.g., Chinese basketball player Yao Ming) as brand ambassadors who endorse their creations.[67] To implement this strategy and cater to a growing number of affluent and educated people, EU luxury goods companies like Gucci and Dior plan to recruit young professionals with the help of business schools.

Western luxury goods brands will also have to proffer convincing arguments to prove that the high price paid for their creations is a good investment. For many wealthy Indians, for example, luxury goods are limited to valuables (jewelry) that are handed down through generations or are a form of investment when they are not a means of converting undeclared wealth. Paying a premium for design and brand will require some client education.

---

67. "Luxury, a Bagful of Style," *India Now* 2 (2005): 36–38.

CHAPTER 5
Eurasia's megamarkets as business platforms for high-tech industries

After more than ten years of uninterrupted growth, China and India are in a position to venture into high-tech industries—a field so far dominated by Western nations with their well-developed financial and institutional infrastructure (educational establishments, government allocations for R&D, venture capital). All three megamarkets are investing massively in knowledge-intensive industries such as IT, telecommunication, electronics, supercomputers, aeronautics and satellites, and new composite materials, as well as in life sciences and biotechnology. Governments understand that a competitive edge in high-tech industries makes an economy less vulnerable to economic downturns than if they relied only on low-tech goods and commodity-related activities.

Russia, flush with windfall oil profits, is reviving its former technological leadership. High prices for energy and raw materials in international markets have boosted the country's tax revenues,[1] trade surplus, and foreign reserves to unprecedented levels, providing a broad base for industrial diversification, the establishment of techno parks, and support to enterprises through special state programs (e.g., stabilization fund, industrial development banks). Similarly, China and India have promoted high-tech zones as an effective vehicle for attracting know-how and advanced management practices via FDI. In the decades to come, investments in technology- and knowledge-rich industries will be a major factor in propelling the megamarkets into the leading nations' league.

It is estimated that almost half of the R&D expenditure will come from the private sector in the form of venture capital or private equity. Additional competitiveness will stem from fast-growing financial markets as well as indigenous scientific breakthroughs in agriculture, physics, chemistry, biology, astronomy, medicine, and industrial processes. R&D costs in the megamarkets are a fraction of those in the United States or Europe. Each year, the three countries lure back thousands of elite scientists and scholars who take on jobs in cutting-edge technology companies' research organizations.[2]

According to figures released by the OECD, China surpassed the United States as the world's top high-tech exporter in 2004; a year earlier, it had overtaken the EU and Japan. In 2007, China exported US$270 billion worth of high-tech products including electronic components, computers, mobile phones, and other telecom equipment (the US figure

---

1. Russia has been reporting a budget surplus of 3%–4% annually during 2001–2006. See 2.1.2.
2. *New Scientist*, November 10, 2007.

was US$185 billion). China accounts for 30% of all IT and electronics imports into the United States (up from 10% in 2000), more than any other country including Taiwan, Japan, and South Korea. China holds about 50% of the world's electronic component market, India 5%, and Russia 2%, all three with growing tendency. It is true that a large share of China's high-tech exports are accounted for by multinationals residing there, but Chinese companies keep adding high-tech capacity, too. Today, China's electronics exports cover all the categories needed to close the loop: chips, semiconductors, wafers, integrated circuits (ICs), and other digital devices that are incorporated into end products like PCs, notebooks, office computers, car and consumer electronics, and radio and satellite technologies, which are equally coming more and more from China.

EU/US companies are still strong in high-tech, especially pharmaceuticals and aerospace, but there are areas where EU companies had to give way to stronger competitors. One such area is electronics. Apart from Siemens and Philips, there are practically no noticeable EU companies left in the computing and electronics industry (see table 5.1). Italy is a case in point. Whereas in the 1970s it hosted several large companies producing chips, office computers, and car and consumer electronics, only 7% of the country's exports can today be considered knowledge-intensive (compared with 18%–20% for China and India). Companies in France, Greece, Portugal, and Spain encounter similar problems and had to withdraw from several high-tech industries after failing to grow.

This chapter will study the trends in four high-tech sectors:

- pharmaceuticals
- telecommunications
- aviation and aerospace
- environmental technologies

Table 5.1. The world's top fourteen computing and electronics companies, 1/1/2008.

Company	Sales (US$ bn)	Profits (US$ bn)	Category
Siemens, Germany	107.3[a]	5.0	Electrical, electronics
Samsung, South Korea	106.0	8.0	Computers, office equipment
Hewlett-Packard, USA	104.3	7.2	Computers, office equipment
IBM, USA	98.8	10.4	Computers
Hitachi, Japan	98.3	–0.5	Electrical, electronics
LG, South Korea	82.0	2.9	Electrical, electronics
Matsushita Electric, Japan	79.4	2.5	Electrical, electronics
Sony, Japan	77.7	3.2	Electrical, electronics
Toshiba, Japan	67.1	1.1	Electrical, electronics
Dell, USA	61.1	2.9	Computers, office equipment
Hon Hai, Taiwan	51.8	2.4	Electrical, electronics
Fujitsu, Japan	46.7	0.4	Computers, office equipment
NEC, Japan	40.4	0.4	Computers, office equipment
Philips, Netherlands	37.0	5.7	Electrical, electronics

a. Including sales in power, telecom, and industrial engineering.
Source: Fortune 500. 2008.

5.1. Pharmaceuticals

5.1.1. Global pharmaceutical sector trends

The world pharmaceutical market doubled in value to above US$650 billion in the decade to 2007, chiefly from growth in North America and the EU. During this period, the industry grew at 8% per annum—i.e., three times faster than GDP in AMs. The next decade could see further doubling of sales and price hikes, for the following reasons:

- Populations are aging in the AMs where drug demand will increase.
- There is a growing need for natural (biotech) medicines, which draws the attention of big pharma; sales in this segment will reach US$250 billion by 2015, or 20% of the world pharmaceutical market, which by then will exceed US$1 trillion.
- There is high growth in the leading emerging economies, where markets are being deregulated and an operational health-care sector is in formation; health-care spending is currently below 4% of the GDP in the megamarkets compared with 8% in the EU and Japan and 15% in the United States.
- India and China will increase their weight in generics but also in proprietary drugs and biotechnologies to gain global market share.

The world ranking has remained quite stable with the United States, Japan, and Germany in the lead since the 1990s. But the megamarkets are catching up. China is expected to replace Germany as the third-largest pharmaceutical market by 2010, and Russia will displace Italy from seventh position just behind France (see table 5.2).

Chinese and Indian pharmaceutical companies are smaller than their Western counterparts (see table 5.3), but within one decade (1997–2007), many of them grew into multibillion-dollar businesses. They have reached critical mass for investing in R&D and M&As. They aim to multiply their annual revenue to US$5–8 billion by 2015, which would bring them closer to the world's leading pharma multinationals.

Table 5.2. The world's leading pharmaceutical markets, 2007, 2010.

Country	2007 (US$ bn)	2010 (US$ bn)
USA	185	220
Japan	65	85
China	28	65
Germany	30	42
India	12	38
France	17	22
Russia	7	15
Italy	14	15
Others	292	448
World	650	950

Source: Verband der Chemischen Industrie. 2007.

Table 5.3. The world's top thirteen pharmaceutical companies, 1/1/2008.

	Sales (US$ bn)	Profits (US$ bn)
Johnson & Johnson, USA	61.1	10.6
Pfizer, USA	48.4	8.1
GlaxoSmithKline, UK	45.5	10.4
Roche, Switzerland	40.3	8.1
Sanofi-Aventis, France	40.0	7.2
Novartis, Switzerland	39.8	11.9
AstraZeneca, UK	30.0	5.6
Abbott Laboratories, USA	25.9	3.6
Merck, USA	24.2	3.3
Bayer, Germany[a]	20.5	3.0
Bristol Myers Squibb, USA	20.0	2.2
Eli Lilly, USA	18.6	3.0
Boehringer Ing., Germany	12.5	1.2

a. Including Schering.
Source: Fortune 500. 2008.

Table 5.4. Time frame for launching a new drug.

	Molecules	Time frame
a. Upstream research	100,000	2–4 years
b. Preclinical development	100	1–2 years
c. Preclinical development, Phases I, II, III	10	6–8 years
d. Registration	1	1 year
Total R&D (a–d)		10–14 years
e. Launch, Phase IV	Patent protection for maximum another 10 years	

Source: Pfizer.

R&D expenses are astronomically high in the pharmaceutical sector. Developing a new prescription drug takes between twelve and fifteen years (see table 5.4) and costs US$0.8–1 billion in R&D.[3] Although a patent is granted for up to twenty years, the actual period for recouping the investment is only five to ten years after discounting time for testing and clinical trials. To recoup these expenses, large pharmaceutical companies have to invest heavily in marketing and advertising. In 2006, the advertising budget of US pharmaceutical companies was US$57.5 billion, almost twice as high as their overall investment in R&D (US$31.5 billion).[4]

The high cost of proprietary medicine drove the megamarkets toward production of cheaper generics for the benefit of their large low-income populations. EM governments aim to make medicines more affordable for the world's poor and accuse big pharma of doing too little for developing cheaper drugs. Western TNCs, supported by their governments, fight for strict adherence to WTO rules, which favor patent holders; they threaten that without respect of intellectual property rights (IPRs),[5] there won't be sufficient funding for R&D-based innovation. IPRs have thus become a critical issue. Patent infringements cost patent holders—mostly AM multinationals—US$20 billion every year and put patients' health at risk due to counterfeits. The World Health Organization (WHO) estimates that up to 10% of all medicines sold in the world are fakes.[6] To hedge risks for prescription drugs, large players invest in biotechnology, non-prescription drugs (generics), and diagnostics equipment.

Size is no guarantee for survival as the sector passes through the consolidation phase. Hoechst, one of the three German pharmaceutical flagship companies, closed down its operations after being merged into Rhone-Poulenc in 2004. Most research facilities near Frankfurt were shifted to France. Aventis, the group that emerged from the merger, was integrated with its brand into Sanofi in 2006. Mergers and acquisitions in Europe totaled more than US$114 billion during 2004–2007. This wave has not yet enveloped the megamarkets, where the process has just begun. Litigation also plagues the pharmaceutical sector and can accelerate consolidation. Sales of Germany's Bayer dipped sharply after

---

3. Pfizer spent US$7.9 billion on R&D (16.3% of sales) in 2007, equivalent to launching eight to ten new medicines.
4. M. Gagnon and J. Lexchin, *More Money for Advertising than for Research* (Toronto: Plos Medecine, 2007).
5. TRIPS (Trade-related intellectual property rights) protect drug patents held mainly by pharmaceutical TNCs. But megamarket companies, supported by their governments, are increasingly reluctant to comply, saying that patent holders (Western pharmaceutical MNCs) charge too much for medicines that are badly needed by local populations. They therefore try to impose on TNCs compulsory licensing of production to local generics producers before patents expire.
6. Large MNCs like Pfizer, Roche, and Novartis alert patients about counterfeit drugs through their Web sites and cooperate with customs to detect fraudulent preparations at ports of entry or other important entry points. See "Gefährliche pillen. Skrupellose deals mit falschen arzneien" [Dangerous pills. Unscrupulous deals with faked medicines], *Handelsblatt*, September 30, 2005.

withdrawal of cerivastatin (Lipobay) and a collective legal claim against it in the United States. To make up for the loss of clout, Bayer later acquired Schering in 2006, but the pharmaceutical part of the group has still to reach the level of the mid-1990s. Some of the smaller EU players managed to thrive by focusing on profitable niches (e.g., Germany's Merz and Schwarz Pharmaceutical, Austria's Ebewe and Gebro, France's Servier).

It is interesting to note that the demand for pharmaceuticals—like that for food and beverages—has hardly been affected by the 2008–2009 financial crisis that has hit most other industries.

5.1.2. Pharmaceutical sector trends in the megamarkets

Pharmaceutical sales across megamarkets have grown by 20%–25% annually since 2002, three to four times faster than in AMs. Western players face increased competition from local companies. Most successful start-ups in the megamarkets have built their success on generic and bulk drugs based on expired patents. The same companies are now venturing into proprietary drugs developed through their own R&D. They benefit from the many partnerships with Western players and can draw on the huge pool of qualified chemists, biologists, and doctors who studied abroad and worked in Western multinationals.

CHINA

China's pharmaceutical industry is expected to maintain its momentum of steady growth up to 2015, which by modest count will translate in triple output and revenues compared with today. In 2007, sales of pharmaceuticals in China reached US$28 billion. With growth rates exceeding 10% annually, China looks set to overtake Japan and become the second-largest pharmaceutical market by 2015. Record FDI inflows have led to the establishment of modern plants with sufficient capacity to supply foreign markets as well. China's foreign trade in drugs amounted to US$30 billion in 2006, and its trade surplus is widening.

Rising living standards and an aging population will result in higher expenses for medical products. Chinese citizens spend on average US$10 on prescription drugs each year or fifty times less than the average American (US$500). The world's top pharma players realize on average only 3%–5% of their global sales in China and see ample room for expansion. UK-based AstraZeneca reported a 40% rise in its China sales compared with a modest 6% in the United States and 2% in Europe.[7] The large multinationals are investing in local R&D facilities to cut costs. By 2012, US-based Bristol-Myers Squibb plans to test each new drug on Chinese patients.[8] China is attracting FDI from pharma companies from other emerging markets. India-based Orchid Chemicals & Pharmaceuticals has tied up with the North China Pharmaceutical Corporation (NCPC),[9] with whom it will expand into the Asian and European markets.

---

7. "Foreign Pharmaceutical R&D Centers Come to China," *China Today*, February 2006.
8. "Big pharma forscht in China" [Big pharma develops in China], *Handelsblatt*, January 1, 2008, 41.
9. NCPC's sales in 2007 stood at US$9,320 million and profits at US$56 million. It has pioneered fermentation-based products (penicillin, streptomycin), semi-synthetic antibiotics, vitamins, and recombinant DNA formulations.

In 2007, there were over 2,300 foreign-funded pharmaceutical and biochemical enterprises with production facilities in China. They accounted for 23% of the market against 28% for imported drugs and 50% for purely domestic players. Almost 80% of the local companies are small-scale, scattered across the country, and mostly using outdated equipment. Some of them have subcontracting arrangements with larger Chinese or foreign-invested groups. They are compelled to raise quality standards to compete and become attractive prospects for partnerships. Foreign companies can choose their entry mode freely but must select their partners carefully. They may opt for a wholly owned subsidiary or acquire a local target.

Proprietary medicine producers with integrated state-of-the-art facilities have set up operations in the provinces of Jiangsu, Zhejiang, and Guangdong. Their intention is to produce high-quality drugs to replace less affordable imports. Examples of such companies are Xian-Janssen, 999 Group, Harbin Pharmaceutical Ltd., Jilin Xiuzheng Pharmaceutical Group, Dalian Merro, and Shenyang Pharmaceuticals. In the eye of the Chinese consumer, these players have reached a standing like foreign multinationals. According to experts, China is capable of producing over 1,500 types of drugs in twenty-four segments. It is a major producer of herbal medicines, of which it exports about US$16 billion annually. Traditional (Chinese) medicine represents a vast source of knowledge for proprietary drugs. China is also turning into an important center for customized research. Wuxi Pharmatech trebled its capitalization to US$190 million after going public in August 2007. The company grew thanks to contract research for Western multinationals. Today it employs more chemists than Pfizer has working for them in China.

INDIA

The Indian pharmaceutical industry has been successful in ensuring that essential drugs are available at low cost to large strata of the population. This was the result of the 1970 legislation that abolished product patents and instituted process patents, which legalized reverse engineering. When India joined the WTO in 1995, it amended its patent laws in conformance with WTO's trade-related intellectual property rules. The pharmaceutical industry responded by stepping up exports of generic products and entered into R&D agreements and strategic alliances with Western counterparts. The outward-looking strategy paid off. Today, India's pharmaceutical industry produces almost one-quarter of the generic drugs in the world. It ranks third as a producer of active pharmaceutical ingredients (6.5% of world output[10]). The development of the contract research and clinical trials businesses, the new patent regime (product rather than process patents), acquisitions of foreign companies, and legislative reforms will contribute to further growth.

The industry has grown threefold from US$4 billion in 1996 to US$12 billion in 2007. Generics[11] account for 80% of the turnover. At annual growth rates of 30%–35%, the overall market (generics and proprietary medicines) is likely to triple to US$38 billion by 2012–2015. About 45% of India's production (US$20 billion) will be exported. The share of proprietary drugs will grow from 15% to 25%, that of biopharma from

---

10. According to the Indian Chemical Pharmaceutical Generic Association, this share will increase to 10.5% by 2010.
11. US$10 billion, which is equivalent to one-fifth of the world generics market of US$50 billion.

5% to 10%. In 2010, India's share in the global generics market will grow from today's 22% to around 35%.[12]

Indian pharmaceutical companies have developed high-standard scientific and manufacturing capabilities (see table 5.5). They have the largest number of FDA-approved facilities outside the United States (over one hundred in 2007). Although generics and active pharmaceutical ingredients (APIs) remain staple products, major companies are stepping up R&D for new drug discovery to remain in the forefront. Ranbaxy, India's largest pharma player, intends to quadruple its sales to US$5 billion by 2012.[13] The company invests 9% of its revenues in R&D with the aim of generating 40% of its turnover with new in-house products. The company's new R&D center near Delhi employs more than 1,200 scientists and researchers; a total of 350 patents were filed during 2005–2007. Dr. Reddy's and Cipla—India's number two and number three companies—work intensively with Western partners on new formulations. Dr. Reddy's hopes to bring its first proprietary drug—a diabetes medicine—to market by 2009. Cipla is best known for its low-cost AIDS drugs.

Table 5.5. India's top five pharmaceutical companies, 2007.

Company	Sales (US$ mn)	R&D (% of sales)	Disease focus
Ranbaxy	1550	9	Urology, malaria
Dr. Reddy's	1500	15	Diabetes, cancer
Cipla	905	8	AIDS, malaria
Piramal	365	8	Cardiology, diabetes
Sun Pharma	330	4	Cardiology, neurology

Source: Annual reports.

Table 5.6. Cost of drug development and manufacturing in AMs and India, 2007.

a. Cost of development (US$ mn)	AMs	India
Discovery	10–20	7–14
Preclinical in vivo/in vitro testing, animal studies	4–5	1–1.5
Phase I, 15–30 volunteers	3–6	1–2
Phase II, 50–80 volunteers	20	10–12
Phase III, 5,000 volunteers	150–200	90–130
b. Cost of production (US$ mn)	**AMs**	**India**
Tablets	30–40	10
Soft capsules	30–40	10
Injectables	25–30	7–9

Source: Ranbaxy. 2008.

Fifteen of the world's largest twenty TNCs are present in India. GlaxoSmithKline is the biggest of them, ranking fourth in the sector in terms of revenue just after India's top three players. In 2006–2008, TNCs invested more than US$250 million in R&D facilities in India. Their presence has increased since the amendment of the patent regime. Foreign companies dominate the over-the-counter market. Altana from Germany opened its own research center in Mumbai. According to the CEO, "Costs are a fraction of Germany's [see table 5.6]. Good chemical engineers can be found and recruited easily, and their willingness to work as well as professional commitment is very high. Research functions and clinical trials will therefore be increasingly relocated to India. R&D costs in India are about one-fifth of what they are in the United States or the EU. A chemist in India earns US$60,000 a year compared with US$250,000 in the EU, United States, and Japan, not counting employer's social security charges, which account for an additional 80% on top of gross salary in countries like Germany or France."[14]

---

12. The world generics market will grow by 18% annually during 2005–2010.
13. In June 2008, Japan's Daiichi Sankyo acquired a majority stake in Ranbaxy.
14. This quotation is from Altana's India boss, Volker Figala. "Pharmazeutische industrie investiert in Indien" [Pharmaceutical companies invest in India], *Handelsblatt*, September 9, 2005.

The growing number of Indo-foreign alliances—e.g., Bayer-Ranbaxy, GlaxoSmithKline-Biocon, Novartis-Piramal Healthcare—have prompted mergers elsewhere in the world, such as the one between Israel's generics major Teva and the US market leader Ivax,[15] mainly to prevent Indian competitors from engaging in similar moves. There are also numerous medium-sized Indian companies, such as Piramal, Elder, Unichem, and INTAS (all four in the US$150–250-million turnover range), that have wide distribution networks and can contribute valuable expertise in chemistry, formulations, and preclinical work to a global drug-discovery pipeline.

Indian companies have been engaged in a number of acquisitions in the AMs:
- Wockhardt bought Germany's Esparma (generics) for US$9 million and CP Pharmaceuticals in the UK for US$16.5 million.
- Ranbaxy bought Aventis's generics daughter RPG.
- Torrent bought Heumann from Pfizer.
- Zydus Cadila acquired the French daughter company of the US firm Alpharma.
- Dr. Reddy's bought US pharmaceutical company Trygenesis and German Betapharm for €420 million from a financial investor.[16]
- Sun Pharmaceuticals bought Able Laboratories in the United States.

While India's expertise in chemistry rivals that of the best labs in the world, many new drugs are developed through molecular processes. The national biotechnology development strategy sets a target of US$7 billion by 2012 for the biotechnology industry. To achieve this, the government will invest nearly US$1.6 billion by 2012 to revamp biotechnology education programs and create global centers of educational and research excellence. India's modest biotech industry has produced its first US$100-million-a-year company, Biocon. This company, with headquarters in Bangalore, makes generic versions of bioengineered, protein-based drugs. More biotechnology start-ups are mushrooming with financial support from banks and private equity investors. Contract research and manufacturing are gaining ground in India, which expects to increase its share of the global market from the current 6%–7% to 15% by 2010. The leading contract manufacturer is Piramal Healthcare. Other outsourcing activities include clinical research and trials, packaging, and labeling.

Russia

Russia is making remarkable progress toward establishing a homegrown pharmaceutical industry. Annual growth rates of 11%–13% make Russia the most dynamic pharmaceutical market in Europe. The overall market will expand from US$7 billion to US$15 billion by 2010–2012. By then, annual per capita spending on medicine will be US$105, or one-third of the level of major EU countries (e.g., Germany: US$330). Imports account for 75% of consumption, but domestic production is growing, fueled by foreign investment.

The world's top players who currently export to Russia (e.g., Bayer-Schering, Berlin Chemie, Boehriger, Gedeon-Richter, Novartis, Sanofi) are intensifying their manufactur-

---

15. "Doppelstrategie soll Ranbaxy globale groesse bringen" [Dual strategy will make Ranbaxy globally big], *Handelsblatt*, August 16, 2005.
16. India's Ranbaxy and foreign groups (e.g., Israel's Teva) had handed in competitive bids.

ing, research, and innovation capabilities there. They seek to acquire local players (see table 5.7) with established manufacturing, R&D, and distribution. Two cases stand out: Stada's takeover of both Nizhpharm for US$96 million and Makiz for US$135 million, and Hungary's Gedeon-Richer acquisition of Akrichin for US$128 million.[17] At present, Russian producers hold 8%–12% of the national market, depending on the drug. Given their weak research experience, Russian companies are obliged to focus on generics; their shares therefore trade at a considerable discount. Local companies seek alliances to enlarge their product range. Russia is a major supplier to CIS countries: US$240 million in 2006 with growing tendency.

Table 5.7. Russia's top pharmaceutical companies, 2007.

	Turnover (US$ mn)
Otechestvennie Lekarstava	130
Mictogen	120
Pharmastandard	100
Veropharm	85
Nizhpharm	70
Pharmcenter	58
Akrihin	45

Source: Annual reports.

To reduce import dependence, authorities support research and FDI promotion projects through tax incentives and low-interest finance. The Russian government will inject US$2 billion into this strategic sector to improve availability of essential drugs outside the two agglomerations of Moscow and St. Petersburg during 2008–2010. Once Russia joins the WTO, important changes are expected in drug prescription and quality control rules to safeguard the interest of patients by ensuring safety, efficacy, authenticity, and quality of drugs, as is the practice in the AMs. However, drugs vary greatly in the degree and stringency of quality control, product testing, and manufacturing practices to which they are subjected by regulators. Most of today's drugs can be found in Russia. There is a strong demand for drugs to treat gastrointestinal (19% of sales in 2007), central nervous system (14%), respiratory (12%), and cardiovascular (11%) diseases.

5.1.3. Challenges for foreign pharmaceutical companies

The pharmaceutical markets in China, India, and Russia will continue to grow at a high rate into the 2010s. Experts predict an exponential rise in R&D alliances between local and foreign companies. More compounds will be developed and tested in the megamarkets up to proof of concept and phase I trials in animals and humans. Western companies try to cut costs by shifting activities including surveying of chemical libraries and early stage trials to running of basic and applied research labs. But they also realize that the aim of their megamarket competitors is to play a bigger part in the drug-discovery league along with their AM competitors and may not accept being only part of a global pipeline controlled by others. They seem to have the local authorities on their side.

For foreign producers, megamarket investments offer many advantages across all disease categories, which will all develop fast (see box 5.1). EU companies in related healthcare and medical segments can also benefit, for example: hospital supplies, laboratory instruments, production equipment, health-care services. EU pharmaceutical distributors

---

17. "Poglotitjel dolei" [Acquirer of stake], *Expert*, November 19, 2007, 14.

Box 5.1. Reasons for investing in the megamarket pharmaceutical sector.

a. Advantages:

- Expiry of many world patents within the next 4–5 years
- Excellently trained doctors and scientists with internationally recognized degrees
- Growing number of adults who can afford health care because of own or children's high disposable incomes
- Widening insurance coverage
- Lower costs for R&D and clinical trials
- Existence of companies with far-sighted management and operating in world markets
- Existence of traditional medicine as source of ideas and knowledge for new drugs

b. Disease categories:

- Antacids
- Anti-anemic
- Anti-cancer
- Anti-diabetes
- Antibiotics
- Anti-viral (e.g., AIDS)
- Cardiovascular therapeutics
- Extension of life, longevity
- Neurology, antipsychotics
- Obesity and metabolism-related diseases (anti-smoking)
- Vaccines
- Vitamins

with strategic interests in wholesaling, retailing (pharmacies), and logistics[18] can find good business opportunities. Venture capital and private equity investors are on the lookout for opportunities.

The thinking in boardrooms of Western pharmaceutical companies is changing. In a recent reorganization, GlaxoSmithKline combined all its small divisions that deal with developing countries into one emerging markets group. Serving these markets with a unified team of professionals will allow it to enhance local intelligence and research expertise. Rather than seek a presence to cut costs, the main goal is to exploit available knowledge and satisfy local needs, for example, by coordinating research and supplier relations. The challenge lies in understanding the peculiarity of each market while trying to serve as many segments as possible (the affluent, middle class, rural poor). For this, multinationals must be adept

---

18. Germany's pharmacy retailer Celesio (ranked number one in the EU) acquired a majority stake of Protek, Russia, in November 2007. Protek is Russia's largest pharmaceutical distributor with a market share of 25% and sales of US$2.2 billion (2007).

at offering a range of products at different price points. They are challenged to accelerate the process of bringing new drugs to market that are medically effective, affordable, and differentiated from the competition. Low-cost research in the megamarkets can facilitate this process (e.g., low-cost anti-AIDS drugs from Cipla for Africa).

The patents on many of the medicines launched in the 1990s will expire over the next few years, leaving many Western companies very exposed; only four out of ten companies have enough products in their pipelines to fill the impending revenue gap. The second paper in the Price Waterhouse Coopers (PwC) Pharma 2020 series explores how pharma companies could dramatically improve their R&D productivity. It contends that by 2020 the R&D process may be shortened by two-thirds, success rates may dramatically increase, and clinical trial costs could be cut substantially. New computer-based technologies will create a greater understanding of the biology of disease and the evolution of "virtual man" to enable researchers to predict the effects of new drug candidates before they enter human beings. Along with changes underway in the regulatory and sociopolitical environment, this will enable big pharma to overcome the most fundamental issues it needs to address over the next decade.

Although tight drug price controls and poor IPR protection threaten the potential of many emerging markets, pharma multinationals are becoming increasingly active in these countries as the potential for higher health-care spending in the future is outweighing any potential setbacks. Emerging markets present new opportunities for mature drugs whose sales are declining in major Western markets, which is a highly attractive option, especially at a time when many drugs are on the verge of patent expiry. Generally speaking, enforcement of IPR will open new avenues to EU players in the megamarkets, including:

- conducting cost-effective clinical trials
- subcontracting and procurement for bulk producers
- using R&D facilities and outsourcing to contract research organizations (CROs)[19]

A significant majority of pharma and biotech companies acknowledge that as much as 25% of their revenues by 2015 will have to come from emerging markets if they want to continue playing in the big league. The biggest challenge lies in meeting business goals by adopting the right strategy, which implies overcoming obstacles related to know-how leakage, building special relationships with government agencies and the medical community, and developing local sales forces and marketing channels to deliver the products.

5.2. Telecommunications

5.2.1. Global telecommunication sector trends

During the 1980s and 1990s, starting with the United States, followed immediately by the EU, the telecom sector was gradually opened and freed from state monopolies. Wide-ranging reforms and privatization introduced competition and subsequently a wave of

---

19. Pharma production lines and medicine-related research facilities in China and India are already world-class. Both countries boast more FDA-approved labs and plants than any other country outside the United States.

mergers and acquisitions (e.g., Vodafone's takeover of Mannesmann in 2000). Enterprise performance improved, resulting in better services and lower tariffs for end users.

The telecom industry comprises four segments:
- telecom hardware: fixed line equipment, mobile handsets, telecom infrastructure
- telecom software
- telecom services: fixed line, mobile, and broadband services
- Internet-enabled services including e-commerce

Pathbreaking technologies are bringing about the convergence of telecom (fixed and mobile telephony, Internet), data processing (PCs), and broadcasting (radio and TV) technologies, which has created an infinite number of applications—and business opportunities—for conveying voice, data, and images. In this technological upheaval, fixed telephony is losing ground to mobile telephony and voice over Internet protocol (VOIP). It is against this technology background that megamarket telecom enterprises are growing, on the back of high demand from their huge populations (for China and India).

Table 5.8. The world's top telecommunication companies, 1/1/2008.

a. Operators	Sales (US$ bn)	Profits (US$ bn)
AT&T, USA	118.9	12.0
Verizon Communications, USA	93.8	5.5
Nippon Telecom, Japan	93.5	5.6
Deutsche Telekom, Germany	85.6	0.8
Telefonica, Spain	77.3	12.2
France Telecom, France	72.5	8.6
Vodafone, UK	71.2	13.4
China Mobile, China	47.1	8.4
Telecom Italia, Italy	43.4	3.4
British Telecom, UK	42.3	3.5
Sprint Nextel, USA	40.1	1.3
KODI, Japan	31.4	1.9
COMCAST, USA	30.9	2.6
Vivendi, France	29.6	3.6
America Movil, Mexico	28.5	5.4
China Telecom, China	27.9	2.2
b. Hardware, equipment	Sales (US$ bn)	Profits (US$ bn)
Nokia, Finland	69.9	9.9
Motorola, USA	36.6	-49.0
CISCO Systems, USA	34.9	7.3
L.M. Ericsson, Sweden	27.8	3.2
Alcatel-Lucent, France	24.7	-4.8

Source: Fortune 500. 2008.

Until the end of the 1990s, the world's leading telecom companies were those from the AMs. The spread of telecommunications in the megamarkets in the 2000s has brought their players to the fore; often backed by government funding, they gained strength through aggressive marketing and public offerings, which funded further growth. They are now in a position to expand domestically and internationally (see table 5.8). China Mobile, the country's leading telephony provider, posted sales nearing US$50 billion in the first quarter of 2008 and a market capitalization exceeding US$350 billion, which is one of the highest in the world in the industry. China Telecom, the country's number-two operator, is growing at the same pace. In India, where telecom is a model of the benefits of delicensing and the entry of the private sector, the reforms paved the way for the creation and rapid growth of large private enterprises like Bharti Airtel, Reliance Communications, Idea!, Tata Indicom, and many other regional players. Russian operators (mostly private) such as Sistema-MTS, Beeline, and Megafone have also significantly increased their capitalization with shares climbing fivefold during 2004–2008.

The Internet is a high-growth segment linked to telecom; its use was almost inexistent in the megamarkets in the late 1990s. According to Chinese statistics, the number of Internet users (253 million) exceeded that of the United States in July 2008. By 2010, subscriptions in China will be above 300 million users. By 2015–2018, it will be India's turn to outpace the United States (see table 5.9). China has three times as many subscribers ("netizens") as Japan and four times as many as Germany. The potential in the megamarkets is enormous given that Internet penetration is only 5% and 19% of the billion-plus populations of India and China, respectively, and 21% in Russia.[20] The average Chinese or Indian user spends fourteen to nineteen hours a week online compared with seven to ten hours in the United States. About 70% of all Chinese or Indian users are under thirty, compared with 30% in the United States, and for the time being they are mostly urban.

Table 5.9. The world's leading Internet subscriber nations, 2004–2015 (mn subscribers).

	2004	2006	2008	2010	2015
USA	187	206	220	240	260
China	103	145	260	340	520
Japan	66	73	85	100	110
Germany	45	50	55	65	70
India	25	39	80	145	230
Russia	15	25	38	55	65

Source: www.internetworldstats.com.

5.2.2. Telecommunication sector trends in the megamarkets

The governments of China, India, and Russia consider telecommunications (both hardware and services) as a top priority sector for economic growth. A modern telecommunications network is thought to play a vital role in reducing the urban–rural divide. Like energy, roads, and railways, the network is viewed as essential infrastructure for developing remote areas and checking rural exodus in addition to the other obvious economic advantages accruing from better communication in any large country. Megamarket players therefore enjoy government support, despite the sometimes complicated bargaining rounds for licenses and protracted negotiations for much-needed policy changes. In China and Russia, networks are still controlled by the state, whereas India has opted for increasing privatization of fixed and mobile telephony services and networks.

Three segments will be in the spotlight in the coming years: fixed line market (to increase national coverage and link up with international lines), mobile market (to connect with the rural poor), and Internet market (for educational purposes, business, and entertainment). According to the leading companies, megamarket buyers are attractive targets for testing new features and technologies, such as mobile Web browsing, picture messaging, video telephony, or the latest fad, mobile TV[21] (Western consumers use mobile phones mainly for voice calls and text messages). In Russia, store keepers report that consumers can choose from eighty-plus new models compared with less than forty models in a telecommunication outlet in the EU. Most Chinese and Indians spend a much higher part of their monthly income on mobile services (mainly through prepaid phone cards) than Americans or Europeans, which illustrates the perceived value of information and communication technologies (ICT) for these fast-growing populations.

---

20. "Chinese Are World's Top Netizen Group," *China Daily*, July 25, 2008. For statistics, see China Internet Network Information Center (CNNIC), www.internetworldstats.com.
21. "New Technologies for Emerging Markets," *The Economist*, September 10, 2005.

CHINA

China's achievements in telecom are impressive. In just ten years, companies like Huawei, ZTE (both telecom equipment), China Mobile, and China Unicom (telecom operators) have become famous international brands with record capitalizations on domestic and foreign stock exchanges. Today, China leads the world in terms of production, exports, and use of telecom products such as handsets and cellular phones. In mobile telephony, the country is pushing its own 3G (third generation) TD-SCDMA standard based on the EU's WCDMA. Nokia-Putian, Siemens-Huawei, Alcatel-Datang, and Ericsson-ZTE are all joint ventures designed to develop technologies under TD-SCDMA. Inadequate chips are the biggest remaining obstacle, which the Ministry of Information plans to overcome by encouraging more foreign chipmakers to come to China (e.g., Intel's US$4 billion investment in Dalian during 2008–2011).

Over the past decade, China's telecom industry has grown steadily at rates between 15% and 20% annually. The number of telephone subscribers reached 950 million (handset subscribers: 510 million; fixed telephone customers: 440 million) in mid-2008. Every month, China's mobile population is growing by 6–10 million new subscribers[22]—i.e., at a speed outdating statistics as soon as they get released. China has also become the world's largest producer of fixed and mobile sets. In 2009, 50% of all mobile sets produced worldwide will come from China. Domestically produced and assembled handsets, including those made under a foreign brand or by a foreign-invested company, hold about 60% of the market; the rest is imported (see figure 5.1).

Internet use has grown extremely fast in China since the late 1990s. Explains Dr. Charles Zhang of Sohu.com: "People log onto the Internet and Sohu.com because, in China, it is difficult and expensive to access *Forbes*, Reuters, or *The Washington Post*. People are accustomed that print media has all been state-controlled and official, and the Internet filled this void." Almost 68% of online use in China is devoted to news, more than searching and e-mailing. The most popular search engine for Chinese users is Baidu, which is able to recognize people's names within strings of Chinese characters and which currently has about 60% of the domestic market compared with Google's 20%.[23] The leading US Internet companies have stepped up efforts to grow in China through financial acquisitions and alliances with local partners, which have become a vital entry route. Recent examples are:[24]

- acquisition of 40% share of Alibaba by Yahoo! for US$1.5 billion;
- acquisition of online auction platform Eachnet by eBay for US$280 million;
- acquisition of 52% stake in online travel agency Elong by US Internet company Interactive Corp.;
- acquisition of online bookstore Joyo.com by US company Amazon.com for US$75 million; and
- investment by search engine company Google in an R&D center.

---

22. "China wird Nokias wichtigster markt" [China is becoming Nokia's main market], *Financial Times Deutschland*, February 24, 2005.
23. "Boys from the Wang Ba," *New Scientist*, November 10, 2007.
24. "Internetkonzerne buhlen um kunden aus China" [Internet companies vie for clients in China], *Financial Times Deutschland*, August 12, 2005.

Figure 5.1. Mobile brands and production in China, 2002–2008.

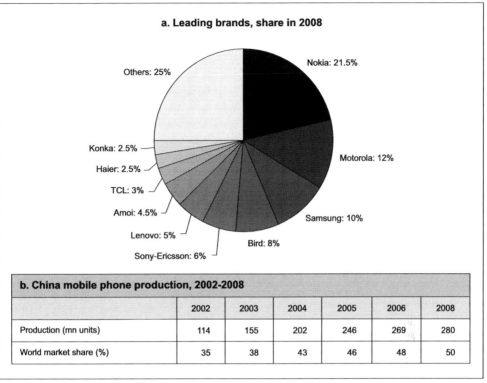

Source: Wirtschaftswoche, iSupply. 2008.

INDIA

Thanks to privatization, India is adding around 8.5–12 million new mobile subscribers to the network each month, mostly in the rural areas; its growth has now surpassed China's. In June 2008, India reached the target of 335 million telephone subscribers (fixed and mobile) to become the third-largest telecom network in the world after China and the United States. The target for 2012 is 560 million subscribers; 3G and WiMax will further augment the growth rate. By 2010, the number of mobile subscribers will reach 350 million, or 30% of total population.[25] Mobile telephony has helped to raise teledensity[26] in India to 27% (June 2008), compared with the world's average of 22% (70%–80% for AMs); the government has set the target at 40%–45% by 2010. Such figures explain why more telecom companies from the EU, Japan, Russia, South Korea, and the United States are so keen on expanding in India.

Mobile telephony received a stimulus in May 2003 when the government ruled that incoming calls should not be charged. Telecom reforms in India were launched in the 1980s. "Corporatization" of services began when Mahangar Telephone Nigam Ltd. (MTNL) for Delhi and Mumbai and Videsh Sanchar Nigam Ltd. (VSNL) for all international services were spun off from the Department of Telecommunications. VSNL was later bought

---

25. "Mobile Telecoms. Calling across the Ocean," *The Economist,* May 10, 2008, 69–70.
26. Number of adults owning a phone.

out by Tata. Telecom services were privatized in 1992. In 2005, the Indian government raised the ceiling on FDI for foreign telecom operators to 74% (from 49%); for the other related industries (e.g., equipment manufacture), foreign investors are allowed to set up 100% wholly owned subsidiaries. The Telecom Regulatory Authority of India (TRAI) has carved up the market into twenty-three different service areas or "circles."[27] Operators must have a separate license for each circle, and license fees vary with the type of circle. The circles correspond in general to India's twenty-eight states. The beneficial effect of the reforms is seen in the increased cumulative telecom[28] revenues, which grew by 21% in mid-2008 to US$30 billion (US$20 billion in 2007). Telecommunications' contribution to GDP increased from 1.7% in 1997 to 2.7% in 2007[29] and is expected to be around 3% by 2010.

Whereas state-owned BSNL and MTNL have retained control of the fixed-line market, they now also offer broadband and IPTV services to compensate for falling fixed-line subscriptions. To keep up with the surge in demand for mobile services, the thirteen private operators (see table 5.10) will invest up to US$12 billion until 2010 to expand their networks; some may enter into infrastructure-sharing arrangements to lower costs. Third-generation networks are also being built. The M&A process has already begun in the industry where size is important: Spice Telecom merger with Idea Cellular; sale of majority share by Shyam Telecom to Sistema (Russia); integration of VSNL into Tata Communications; acquisition of Tata's stake in Idea Cellular by the Aditya Birla Group.

Table 5.10. India's mobile telcos and their subscriber base, 31/1/2008.

Mobile line operators	Technology	Subscribers (millions)
Bharti Airtel	GSM	57.5
Vodafone Essar	GSM	41.0
BSNL (state-owned)	GSM	38.0
Reliance Communications	CDMA	37.0
Tata Teleservices	CDMA	22.5
IDEA Cellular	GSM	22.0
Aircel	GSM	10.0
Reliance Telecom	GSM	6.0
Spice Telecom	GSM	4.0
MTNL (state-owned)	GSM	3.3
BPL Mobile	GSM	1.3
HFCL Infotel	CDMA	0.3
Shyam Telelink	CDMA	0.1

Five new players were awarded licenses in January 2008: Datacom, Loop Telecom, S Tel, Swan Communications, and Unitech.
Source: Telecom Regulatory Authority of India (TRAI), 2008.

India's telecommunication majors also seek to strengthen their positions in foreign markets. Tata Communications increased its ownership in Neotal (South Africa) and collaborates with Etisalat (UAE). Unitech, which received its license in January 2008, seeks a partner for 25% of its stake. Bharti Airtel bid for South Africa's MTN, Africa's largest mobile phone operator, for an approximate value of US$19 billion in June 2008; it already has operations in Seychelles and Channel Islands, and plans for Sri Lanka. Reliance is investing in Uganda and Sri Lanka. MTNL has a wireless joint venture in Nepal in addition to its operation in Mauritius.

Despite low tariffs, India's large volumes ensure high profitability. Operating margins of Indian companies are on average

---

27. "Metro" circles cover the four main cities; "A" circles for regions with other large cities, "B" circles covering regions with smaller towns, and "C" circles for rural areas.
28. Fixed and mobile telephony, broadband, radio trunking, and VSAT services.
29. "Telecom's Policy Pitfalls," *Business Today,* December 16, 2007.

Table 5.11. Foreign telecommunication companies aspiring for the Indian market, 2006–2008.

Vodafone, UK	Acquired majority stake in Hutchison-Essar for US$11 billion
Sistema, Russia	Bought 51% stake of Shyam Telecom for US$500 million
Maxis, Malaysia	Bought 65% of Aircel for US$1.1 billion
Telenor, Norway	Is already in Bangladesh and Pakistan
Telefonica, Spain	Acquired O2 in the UK for US$32 billion, seeks presence in EMs
France Telecom, France	Tried to buy stake in BPL Mobile
Telecom Italia, Italy	Already entered Brazil and is keen on other megamarkets

Source: Business Today. India. December 2007.

25%–35%, which are attractive also for foreign operators (see table 5.11) such as Maxis Communications Berhad (Malaysia), AFK Sistema (Russia), and Millicom International (Luxembourg). UK's Vodafone picked up a 52% stake in Hutch-Essar, India's biggest operators for US$11.1 billion.[30] The company is the first EU operator to venture into India. AT&T sold its stake in Idea Cellular but offers ILD services while it seeks another local partner. Other European players, including those from Russia, will raise their stakes in India in the future now that FDI restrictions have been eased.

The telecom equipment industry is growing to keep pace with the telecom industry's growth. Mobile phone production will grow by 28% between 2006 and 2011 when revenues will reach US$13 billion. Presently the telecom equipment sector is dominated by international majors like Nokia (number-one ranking), Sony Ericsson, LG, Motorola, Samsung, and Alcatel-Lucent, who have set up manufacturing bases in India. Nokia launched Rs1000 (US$25) cell phones with basic features like voice and SMS only. Kyocera, which acquired the mobile equipment division of Qualcomm, set up a mobile manufacturing plant in India, from where it will export to Africa, Southeast Asia, Australia, and New Zealand. Chinese equipment vendors Huawei and ZTE have launched joint ventures to produce handsets and fixed wireless terminals. Telecom infrastructure also offers excellent opportunities. TRAI estimates that the country will need about 350,000 telecom towers by 2010; the largest producer is the Indian company Quipo. India's strength in IT makes it a natural R&D platform and engineering center for foreign telecom operators (Qualcomm, Alcatel ZTE, Nokia).

Russia

The period 2001–2007 has been one of the most remarkable in Russia's telecom history. Telecom and IT sales climbed to US$30 billion.[31] Each year, the market grew by 25%. By 2010, sales are expected to reach US$45 billion. The following trends contributed to these positive developments:

- rapid expansion of Russian operators into regional markets
- consolidation in the industry through M&As, which led to the modernization of equipment and networks as well as higher efficiency
- swift penetration of broadband technologies for providing new generation telecom services, including IP telephony, Wi-Fi, and 3G

---

30. "Vodafone Ventures into India," *Business Standard*, May 5, 2007.
31. Two-thirds in telcom, one-third in IT.

- record spread of mobile phones, whose number has surpassed fixed phones
- opening of new markets in the CIS countries (mainly served by Russian operators)

A new law on communications came into force in 2004; it outlines and reinforces the regulatory authority of the Ministry of Telecommunications and sets the legal basis for the industry. All operators, including mobile phone companies, will contribute part of their revenues (3%–4%) to a universal service fund. The money is used to provide telecom services in remote areas, which would otherwise be uneconomic to connect, even at high tariff rates. The law guarantees Russian citizens a pay phone within an hour's walk, a free public phone for emergencies in every village, and a point of access to the Internet in every town of at least five hundred people. The telecom infrastructure is still of uneven quality and accessibility across Russia. While major population centers are quite well served, there are about 54,000 rural communities with limited access. Russia reports 32 phone lines per 100 people, which is half the density of the United States or the EU (60–70 lines per 100 inhabitants). To lift the telecom network to the international standard, US$35 billion will be allocated to infrastructure over the next ten years, opening vast opportunities for AM equipment and software providers.

Telecom services are mostly offered by four holding companies (see table 5.12): Svyazinvest (state-owned), Sistema, Alfa Group, and TelecomInvest. Svyazinvest-Rostelecom is Russia's dominant provider of domestic long distance (DLD) and international services (ILD), controlling practically all regional networks. The company has stakes in thirty international cable systems and cooperates with four hundred international operators. Privatization of Svyazinvest has been kept on hold since fixed networks are considered a strategic domain that is linked to national security. Sistema, the largest private operator of fixed (MGTS in Moscow) and mobile lines (MTS, across Russia), bought back in 2006 the 10% stake held by Deutsche Telekom in MTS, thus regaining control over Russia's largest cellular operator. In a reversal of roles, Sistema then made several failed attempts to buy a stake in Deutsche Telekom, which is being objected by the German government.

Three state monopolies—Russian Railways, Gazprom, and RAO Unified Energy Systems (RAO UES)—have invested in their own telecom infrastructure. Transtelecom, established by Russian Railways, owns a 45,000-kilometer trans–Russian fiber-optic network. Gazsvyaz is the telecom subsidiary of Gazprom. Similarly, the electric utility RAO UES has created UES Telecom. These enterprises plan to expand their own nationwide telecom networks by laying more cables along their rights-of-way, to preempt competing service providers. Foreign operators have not been strongly represented in the Russian telecom market ever since Deutsche Telekom withdrew its investment in MTS. Telenor from Norway has made several attempts to purchase Vimpelcom from Alfa.

Russia's handheld phone market has grown exponentially. In 1999, when the country was in the midst of its worst financial crisis ever, only 500,000 cellular phones were

Table 5.12. Russia's top four telecommunication operators, 2000–2008 (market share, %).

	2000	2004	2008
Sistema Telecom	19	34	38
SvyazInvest	45	35	30
Alfa Group	5	18	19
TelecomInvest	7	9	11
Other	23	4	2

Source: Kominfo Consulting, ABK, Troika Dialog. 2007.

Figure 5.2. Mobile sets sold in Russia, 1999–2010 (mn units).

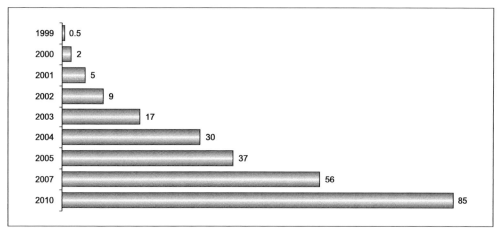

Source: Evroset, Russia.

sold. In 2007, this figure had surged to 56 million (see figure 5.2). While growth is slowing down in Moscow and St. Petersburg, a significant potential remains to be tapped in the regions. The market is ready to absorb 85 million sets by 2010; by then most Russian adults will own a mobile phone. Although handsets already outnumber fixed-line phones, cellular penetration is 38%, which is lower than that of any EU country. Penetration rates in Moscow (and its suburbs) and St. Petersburg are much higher, at 63% and 45%, respectively. MTS is the largest mobile operator with around 24 million subscribers, followed by Vimpelcom with 17 million and Megafon with 10 million (2007). These mobile operators post EBITDA[32] margins of 50%, making them more profitable than their AM competitors.

By 2007, Internet service subscribers numbered almost 30 million users. With around 350,000 .ru domains, Russia has joined the top ten of the world's most active domains. Russia's Web hosting market is growing at 30%–40% per annum. IP, or Internet protocol, telephony is developing rapidly because of its low cost. Broadband communications, especially DSL (digital subscriber line) technology, is another expanding segment, mainly in Moscow and St. Petersburg. But altogether Russia still has fewer DSL lines than Estonia.

5.2.3. Challenges for foreign telecommunication companies

China and India will gradually climb to ranks one and three for telephony hardware and software (fixed and mobile), competing with the United States. A major challenge for telephony (this also concerns Russia) will be geographic coverage. Governments are committed "to connect the remote corners of their countries, reaching out to places where bridges, roads, trains and planes have not reached yet" (Russia's Ministry of Telecommunications). Both China and India aim to connect 50% of the population by mobile or fixed telephony by 2012–2015 and to add hundreds of millions of new Internet

---

32. EBITDA: earnings before interest and tax, depreciation, and amortisation (approximate measure of operating cash flow).

Table 5.13. Telephony and Internet subscribers in megamarkets, 2000–2010 (in mn).					
	2000	2004	2006	2008	2010
India, fixed lines	10.0	50	80	140	180
India, cellular	2.0	20	60	170	340
India, Internet	0.5	25	39	80	145
China, fixed lines	-	-	270	440	490
China, cellular	-	-	277	510	750
China, Internet	25.0	103	145	230	320
Russia, fixed lines	-	60	70	80	90
Russia, cellular	0.5	-	40	55	75
Russia, Internet	-	15	25	38	55

Source: Based on UNCTAD based on ITU World Telecom Indicators Database, 2007. Specialized journals.

subscribers (see table 5.13). By 2020–2025 (Russia probably earlier), full connectivity will be attained in all urban and rural areas. The epicenter of mobile telephony growth has already started shifting from the metros to the rural areas. In India, the GSM segment, for example, witnessed a sharper rise in demand in the second-, third-, and fourth-tier cities than in the larger metros in 2007.[33] Just like Nokia in India, AM telecom companies need to focus on the emerging rural areas.

Most of the top fifteen international telecom TNCs (service providers, hardware producers) plan to increase their stakes in the megamarkets. Russia was the first to attract foreign capital. The share a foreign entity can hold is restricted in the three megamarkets to allow the growth of national telecom majors, who are now in invincible positions. Even where the market appears to be liberal (India, Russia), caution is needed. Local authorities can lobby against any foreign influence unless this involves significant transfer of know-how. To win the licensing bodies over as partners is an uphill battle for any foreign player. Many investors prefer to invest in existing companies with a good network. But this approach is fraught with obstacles owing to restrictions and protectionist measures. In China, for example, only Vodafone (UK) and Telefonica (Spain) managed to acquire shares in local companies, but in both cases, the participation is below 15%. The greenfield route is, however, even more difficult to implement given the already dominant position of domestic players. Foreign companies are counting on the government's pledge to restructure the sector and allow more competition.

Good prospects for AM companies exist in digital switching equipment, high-speed broadband Internet access technologies, multiservice and multimedia solutions, and call center equipment. But the equipment and telecom services markets are not easy to crack. All telecom equipment to be connected to the public switch telephone network must be approved and certified for product compatibility and safety. Megamarket authorities usually do not recognize foreign test data, so obtaining approvals can be a lengthy process. Clever FDI therefore seems to be the best way of penetrating the megamarkets and participating in their remarkable growth.

---

33. "Mobile Telephony," *The Hindu Survey of Indian Industry* (2008): 135.

Another area to watch carefully is triangular investments across the megamarkets, which are on the rise. AM companies should observe their non-AM competitors with whom they might even strike partnerships to share the work in large telecom projects. A stake in the most active megamarket companies enables Western players to grow with such projects. Russia's Sistema, for example, invested US$500 million during 2006–2008 in India's telecom market and acquired a telecom equipment maker in China. The tactic seems to be slightly different and more "holistic" from the approach pursued by Western TNCs in that the acquired target, besides helping to conquer the national market, is also used to strengthen the supply chain from India/China to Russia. All possible political channels have now been activated on the Russian side so that Russia's major operators gain a foothold in the Chinese telecom market. The two governments were also instrumental in a deal between Rostelecom and China Telecom for building a fiber-optic line between the two countries. EU companies should closely watch Russia's increased involvement in mega deals in the Far East on the other side of the continent. In another landmark case, on September 8, 2008, KDDI, a leading Japanese telecom company, and Rostelecom announced the commercial operation of the Russia-Japan Cable Network (RJCN), which is based on a system of high-speed submarine cables supplementing the existing Russia–Japan–Korea network. The RJCN, which took two years to build, employs state-of-the-art technology including digital dense wave division multiplexing (DWDM) equipment to enhance throughput. The new cable system has a full-ring protection ensuring that the Russian operator has the capability to reliably transmit the growing international traffic volumes of the Europe–Asia transit market alongside the primary Russia–Japan route. In an important development in August 2009, Tata Communications, India, bagged a licence for international long distance services in Russia, where it will offer the full range of voice and data services. The company is now present in 40 countries.

5.3. Aerospace

5.3.1. Global aerospace sector trends

Aerospace has been a traditional stronghold of the advanced economies where national players keep charting new paths for state-of-the-art technologies. The global aerospace market is clearly dominated by Western, mainly US, multinationals (see table 5.14) such as Boeing, EADS, Honeywell, and Lockheed Martin. They all manufacture different types of aircraft. AM companies also lead in the area of aircraft electronics, components, engines (e.g., GE Aircraft Engines, MTU, Pratt & Whitney, Rolls-Royce, Snecma), and satellite technologies (e.g., Alenia-Alcatel, Thales). Airbus and

Table 5.14. The world's top twelve aerospace companies, 1/1/2008.

	Sales (US$ bn)	Profits (US$ bn)
Boeing, USA	66.4	4.1
United Technologies, USA	54.8	4.8
EADS, Netherlands	53.6	–0.6
Lockheed Martin, USA	41.9	3.0
Honeywell International, USA	34.6	2.4
Northrop Grumman, USA	32.0	1.8
BAE Systems, UK	28.6	1.8
General Dynamics, USA	27.3	2.1
Raytheon, USA	22.4	2.6
Finmeccanica, Italy	19.9	0.7
Bombardier,[a] Canada	17.5	0.3
Thales, France	16.8	1.2

a. Including railway business.
Source: Fortune 500. 2008.

Boeing, together with Russia's Ilyushin and Tupolev, are the world's only companies making large aircraft with a seating capacity of one hundred and above. Smaller aircraft (below seventy seats) are produced by Embraer (Brazil), Bombardier (Canada), and Sukhoi (RRJ—Russian Regional Jet). The two European players Fokker and Fairchild-Dornier ceased their operations in the early 2000s, mainly because of high development costs and belated penetration of emerging markets. Numerous large and medium-sized components suppliers and software companies in the Triad (EU, Japan, USA) today belong to this profitable high-tech cluster comprising three major segments: aircraft, engines, and satellite technologies. These companies serve private customers but also benefit from state orders including the two space agencies ESA and NASA.

Boeing and Airbus expect above-average demand for aircraft throughout the 2010s and 2020s, although with intermittent contractions during 2008–2010 owing to the effects of the financial crisis. According to forecasts, 16,600 new passenger planes will be ordered during 2010–2025, or an average of 1,100 aircraft per year, representing a market of US$3 trillion (see table 5.15). Many new orders will come from emerging economies, especially China and India, where domestic and overseas air travel is fueled by large populations with growing disposable incomes. In China, domestic airlines will spend US$340 billion on 3,400 new aircraft—nearly quadrupling the current fleet of about 1,000—by 2025. Russia's national carrier Aeroflot placed orders for new aircraft worth US$19 billion during 2006–2008. Airbus estimates that India will require 400–500 new aircraft until 2019. The greatest demand for passenger planes will come from the Asia-Pacific region (31% of the total), North America (27%), and Europe (24%).[34] While traffic demand will nearly triple, airlines will more than double their fleets of passenger aircraft (with over one hundred seats) to 28,500 in 2025.

The trend toward higher fuel prices (despite the temporary fall due to the financial crisis in late 2008) is forcing airlines to rethink their aircraft designs. Older and less efficient aircraft are being phased out. Almost 43% of the new aircraft purchased will be replacements. Fleet size is also being reduced. Old passenger aircraft are being converted for transporting cargo, for which there is a backlog demand in emerging markets. Large aircraft will account for over 80% of the extra demand for aircraft. There is also a growing need for smaller regional jets with fewer than one hundred seats for short-haul domestic routes. At least 1,600–2,000 new regional jets could be purchased worldwide by national and regional airlines between 2008 and 2025, according to Canadian aircraft maker Bombardier. The market for executive jets, a field dominated by North American manufacturers, is also growing.

Table 5.15. Aircraft market forecast, 2008, 2025.

	Planes in use 2008	Planes in use 2025	New orders 2010–2025
Passenger planes	14,300	28,500	16,600
Freight planes	1,850	3,800	730

Source: Airbus, 2008.

---

34. Airbus, global market forecast, 2025.

Figure 5.3. Air passenger market forecast for 2010.

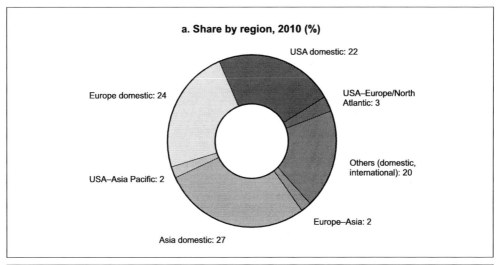

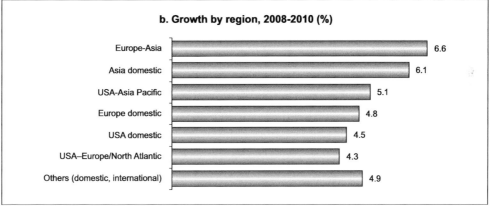

In 2007, 2.5 billion journeys were undertaken on scheduled flights worldwide, 5% more than in 2006. By 2010, another 500 million passengers are likely to take to the skies, predicts the International Air Transport Association (IATA). The association representing some 250 of the world's leading airlines believes that by then America's domestic air travel market (see figure 5.3)—at present the world's largest with 750 million passengers a year—will be overtaken by both Asia (27% of world market) and Europe (24%). The largest growth rates are expected between Europe and Asia (6.6%) and Asian domestic routes (6.1%).

5.3.2. Aerospace sector trends in the megamarkets

CHINA

With 160 million passengers transported in 2007, China has risen to second position in civil aviation, just behind the United States. To become less dependent on foreign suppliers, China plans to build its own regional aircraft named ARJ21s, with the government's financial support. Such subsidies could ultimately backfire if they usher in

WTO disputes with private manufacturers such as Bombardier or Embraer. But for now, ACAC, the company in charge of the ARJ21s, is counting on its home market, which offers a guaranteed customer base among China's state-owned airlines. The Civil Aviation Administration of China (CAAC), the sector's watchdog, announced that it will block the launch of any new Chinese airline until 2010, unless the new carrier flies China-made ARJ21s. All of the seventy-one ARJ21s sold so far have been supplied to Chinese carriers serving the fast-growing mainland travel market. The government still controls fleet purchases; that will provide a big boost to marketing efforts. ACAC hopes to build fifty jets a year. The supply chain is functional. Fuselage sections are built at factories throughout China (Chengdu, Xi'an, and Shenyang) and shipped to Shanghai for final assembly and testing. Critical components, such as advanced electronics and engines, are sourced from nineteen foreign suppliers, including Siemens, GE, and Honeywell. Meeting delivery dates will be only ACAC's first step in establishing itself as a player in the aviation industry. Potential buyers will want assurance that service and maintenance needs can be met over the long run. If the jet is sold outside China, its safety will need to be certified by international agencies including the US Federal Aviation Administration, which opened an office in Shanghai to monitor the main projects. There have been talks with Bombardier, which has decided to invest US$100 million with ACAC in designing additional versions of the ARJ21s.

The ARJ21s represent only the beginning of China's aerospace ambitions. China also has plans to revive its large-plane project, which the State Council approved in February 2007. Chinese leaders pledged to invest at least US$6 billion to produce a 150-seat jetliner by 2020 as a direct competitor of the Boeing 737 and Airbus A320. The government has included this priority project in the eleventh five-year plan (2006–2010) along with moon exploration and manned spaceflights. In May 2008, China's prime minister, Wen Jiabao, launched the Commercial Aircraft Corporation of China (CACC), which will be responsible for building the plane. Advocates of the project say that it will play a key role in promoting the nation's economy and in upgrading its industrial and technological capabilities. Large aircraft production is a highly advanced enterprise with a pull effect on other industries including electronics, machinery, chemicals, and metallurgy. The biggest test China faces is to make the program commercially viable. "The challenge is not to build the aircraft, but to sell it to international customers and support it through after-sales so that there is return on investment," said Laurence Baron, president of Airbus China.[35] The danger is that by the time the Chinese have their A320/737 rival ready, Airbus and Boeing will be selling their next-generation aircraft, which will deliver a vast improvement in operating economics. Nevertheless, Western aircraft makers should take the Chinese seriously because they are playing a long game and have proven in the past that they are capable of reshaping entire industries to their own advantage.

China is gaining experience in servicing aircraft, which represents a valuable asset for learning about critical parts (fuselage, electronics), engineering, and systems. Aerospace companies like Airbus involve Chinese partners in maintenance, repair, and overhaul (MRO) for their jets including the new A380 super jumbo. Cost-intensive operations are moving to Chinese suppliers given that labor accounts for 70% of total airframe heavy

---

35. "Race Is On to Get Plane Project off the Ground," *China Daily*, January 24, 2008.

maintenance costs against 20% for materials and 10% for outside repairs.[36] In 2007, Chinese companies generated US$1.3 billion in MRO activity, thus accounting for 4% of global MRO demand or 17% of MRO demand in Asia. According to Lufthansa, China's MRO market will double to US$2.6 billion by 2010. Ameco Beijing, a joint venture between Lufthansa and Air China, built two new hangars for maintenance, overhauls, and painting of wide-body jetliners in 2006–2007. The total investment was US$70 million and demonstrates Ameco's interest in maintenance of large planes (A380s, Boeing 747s, Boeing 777s). According to the Civil Aviation Administration of China, China has 340 MRO suppliers, employing more than 33,000 people. Chinese MRO companies overhauled more than four hundred aircraft in 2007. Major MRO companies such as GAMECO, TAECO, and STARCO are expanding their hangars and maintenance crews across all major national and regional airports. They are engaged in alliances with Western partners to improve their skills and increase efficiency.

National flight universities and academies like the Civil Aviation Flight University of China (CAFUC) are expanding their facilities to include research labs and cockpit/flight simulation centers. About 95% of Chinese commercial pilots graduate from CAFUC. In China, orders for aviation training equipment (e.g., flight recorders) will grow faster than in any other country in the world. Ideal simulators reproduce real cockpit situations exposing trainees to various weather conditions.

China has made big strides in space-related technologies and has become a serious contender since it succeeded in launching its own astronauts into orbit (third country to do so after USA and Russia). The China National Space Administration (CNSA) plans to expand its manned spaceflights. It spends a total of US$10 billion on its space program, approximately the same as the annual budget of NASA, which is three times higher than that of the European Space Agency (ESA). China's third human spaceflight (Shenzhou 7) included a successful spacewalk on September 27, 2008. *Shenzhou 8* (2009–2010) is set to showcase the ability to dock, the expertise needed for establishing the country's own space station. China signed multimillion-dollar contracts with several countries (e.g., Venezuela, Iran) to carry foreign satellites on its Shenzou flights. China will launch more of its own satellites for better environmental monitoring and disaster prevention. About 200 million people are affected each year by floods, drought, earthquakes, typhoons, and landslides; economic losses caused by such natural disasters amount to 3%–5% of GDP.[37] China's space technology–based disaster mitigation program is also intended to train specialists in developing countries.

INDIA

Air travel in India is no longer a luxury but a necessity. According to India's Civil Aviation minister, "less than 1% of India's 1.1 billion people fly, so there is tremendous room for growth. With 40 million domestic air tickets bought in 2007, India's level is about one-third that of China [130 million]."[38] Liberal agreements are a stimulus to growth

---

36. "Ground Control," *China Business Weekly,* October 17–23, 2006.
37. "China's Environmental Concerns," *China Daily,* April 28, 2004.
38. "Aviation in India. The Flying Elephant," *The Economist,* March 10, 2007.

Table 5.16. Aircraft orders by Indian carriers, 2007–2009 (number of aircraft).

	Orders placed	Investment (US$ bn)
Air India	50	5.0
Indian Airlines	43	4.0
Kingfisher	34	1.7
Air Deccan	42	1.7
Jet Airways	16	13.0
Total	230	12.6

Source: Airbus. 2007.

as they allow foreign airlines greater access to Indian skies and private domestic carriers (e.g., Jet Airways, Kingfisher) to fly on international routes whereas earlier only the state carrier Air India was allowed to fly to foreign destinations. In 2007–2008, domestic passenger traffic rose 39% and international passenger traffic 15%. New aircraft orders will exceed US$12 billion during 2007–2012. Air India,[39] which joined Star Alliance in December 2007, aims at a fleet of two hundred aircraft by 2012 to match Lufthansa, Singapore Airlines, British Airways, and Emirates. The eighty-five-aircraft fleet, mostly Boeing, of Jet Airways, India's biggest private airline, is the youngest in the world; the airline plans to expand its fleet by 40% to 117 aircraft by 2011. Kingfisher, the second-ranking private airline and one of Airbus's largest customers, currently operates forty-two aircraft; it has placed orders to more than double its fleet to meet with growing demand. Other Indian airlines have also increased and upgraded their fleets (see table 5.16).

Aviation growth will spur that of the aeronautical industry and its allied engineering and IT products. The entry of low-cost airlines will herald change as they need to keep costs low. More than 80% of the commercial aircraft and parts are imported, making India's aviation industry dependent on high-cost imported supplies. Local manufacturing of light-bodied and other aircraft, as well as components for aircraft maintenance, is a business opportunity. Satyam Computers has entered the global aerospace and defense marketplace through its alliance with the US global defense and technology company Northrop Grumman. State-owned Hindustan Aeronautics Limited (HAL) created a joint venture with Larsen and Toubro (L&T) to develop aircraft components. Techspace Aero, Belgium, supplies components for the ongoing Kaveri indigenous engine development program. To promote the industry, the Indian government plans to establish aviation hubs, which will group industries to manufacture aircraft components, engine parts, and repair and overhaul facilities. Aircraft maintenance is in great demand. It is economical to have maintenance facilities for aircrafts in India compared to other developed countries.

India plans to play a bigger role in aircraft design and production for both civil and military applications. Cooperation between India and Russia is entering a new phase. The two countries agreed in 2007 to develop the fifth-generation fighter, which will be built at the HAL and Sukhoi Military Aviation plants. The agreement, the most ambitious Russia-Indian military program, heralds a new stage in bilateral cooperation aimed at developing new-generation aviation technology. The Russia-Indian warplane will outperform any other similar aircraft with its outstanding maneuverability. It features engines with round rotating nozzles for better aerodynamics; supersonic speed will enhance its combat

---

39. Air India (international) and Indian Airlines (domestic), India's two state-owned carriers, were merged under the Air India brand in 2007.

efficiency. The aircraft will be equipped with advanced avionics, long-range weapons, and other radio-electronic equipment to hit small targets.

The Indian electronics industry is developing automated electronic countermeasures (ECM) systems, secure data-exchange networks, and fire-control systems for long-range tactical missions. India has also strengthened ties with its Western partners. EADS's subsidiary Eurocopter subcontracted airframe production for its Ecureuil-type helicopters to HAL. The first Indian-made airframe will be delivered in 2008. The Fennec, the military version of the Ecureuil series, is one of the two helicopters short-listed by India's Ministry of Defense for replacing the current Cheetah/Chetak fleet of the Indian Army in the near future. These military projects will further enhance the development of new aviation technologies.

The two civilian aircraft developed by the National Aerospace Laboratories (NAL) are undergoing test flights and international certification. NAL estimates that India will need two hundred Saras aircraft over fifteen years. Work on the first public–private partnership in aircraft design between NAL and Mahindra Plexion Technologies is at the fabrication stage, and the first prototype will be tested in 2009. HAL, a pioneer in the manufacturing of military aircraft and helicopters, will embark on the manufacturing of civil aircraft designed by NAL. Both Airbus and Boeing have development centers in India at Bangalore and Nashik, respectively. India will be a key center for the designing of Airbus's extra-wide-bodied A350 aircraft. In addition to leveraging India's R&D potential, Airbus seeks to use India for component manufacturing.[40] Six global defense majors, including US giants Lockheed Martin and Boeing, and European consortium EADS, plan to invest an estimated US$2–3 billion in India's defense and aerospace industry.

India's homegrown space program, implemented by the Indian Space Research Organisation (ISRO), achieved twelve consecutive successful launches during 1995–2007, which is equivalent to one launch per year on average. In August 2008, it broke the world record by simultaneously launching ten satellites, including nano satellites from Canada, Germany, and the Netherlands. This and the development of a third launcher (polar satellite launch vehicle, PSLV) should help India garner a larger share of the global commercial satellite launch market. Antrix, ISRO's commercial arm, is targeting sales of Rs7 billion (US$170 million) by 2010.[41] ISRO's advantage is that it is reliable and cheaper: US$8,000-per-kilogram payload compared with US$18,000 per kilogram charged by other satellite launch companies such as Lockheed Martin or EADS-Astrium. ISRO has placed foreign satellites in orbit since 1999 for German, Italian, Belgian, US (NASA), and other clients. Its own first satellite was launched in 1975; since then more than fifty have been added for remote sensing (resource monitoring and management), GIS and GPS applications, telecommunications, broadcasting, and education (distance learning) to bring the benefits of high technology closer to the average Indian. Initially, it used Russian and Europe's Ariane launchers, especially to lift big payloads into geostationary orbit. ISRO's PSLV C-11 launcher, an upgrade of the standard configuration, is designed to place heavy payloads (around 4 metric tons) in orbit. It was used to launch ISRO's lunar mission Chandrayaan 1 in late 2008. The objective is to undertake high-resolution remote sensing

---

40. More than half the doors of Airbus's A320 are produced at HAL. Infosys participated in the design of the A380. Boeing also works with HAL as well as Tata.
41. "India Goes into Space on a Shoestring," *Financial Times,* May 4, 2006.

of the moon's surface for a 3-D atlas (resolution 5–10 m) of the near and far side of the moon and to conduct chemical and mineralogical mapping. The second mission, *Chandrayaan II*, is a joint venture with Russia for landing scientists on the moon to collect samples, preparations for which are already underway. India was also entrusted to carry two US (NASA) payloads on India's first scientific lunar mission in 2008. Closer space cooperation is also expected between India and China.[42]

Underpinning these efforts are the academic institutions that offer aeronautical engineering courses for research scholars, engineers, and technicians. The most prominent are the aeronautics departments of the Indian Institutes of Technology (IITs) and Indian Institute of Science (Bangalore), which have programs up to PhD and diploma courses for aircraft maintenance engineers; education for related professions is offered by several organizations, such as the Indian Institute for Aeronautical Engineering and Information Technology (Pune). The Aeronautical Society of India (AeSI) is the main professional organization for aeronautics, aerospace, and aviation. Its primary purpose is to advance the sciences, engineering, technology, and management of these disciplines to foster professionalism of those engaged in these disciplines. AeSI conducts the associate membership examination (bachelor's degree) for aeronautical engineers.

India's space program contributes to the government's effort to overcome the rural–city divide. It allowed the launching of a series of telecom and broadcasting satellites, which already give 90% of the population access to satellite television and mobile usage. Scientific research and earth observation have become easier and more reliable. Data sent by remote-sensing satellites are widely used in agriculture, water planning, urban settlement, mineral prospecting, drought and disaster relief, and many environmental applications. Satellite-based hydrological mapping has raised the average success rate of finding clean water from 30% to 90%; villagers need this type of information to dig new wells. The program also provides valuable input for upgrading educational levels of rural people. A recent launch, Edusat, aims to support a government plan to build a nationwide distance-learning network.

Russia

Russia has a very long aerospace tradition, and the government intends to maintain a strong international standing. In April 2007, the Russian government created Unified Aircraft Corporation (UAC/OAK), a national holding merging the production, sales, procurement, and R&D activities of four national champions: Ilyushin, Sukhoi, Tupolev, and MiG. The government holds 75% of the shares of these strategic players. After the merger, OAK controls 10% of the world's aircraft market and is in a position to challenge Airbus and Boeing. OAK intends to raise production to 150–200 aircraft by 2010, which is three times the 2006 output of its members. The company will sell US$8 billion worth of aircraft, of which 30% will be exported. Local suppliers can count on more orders, which should help revive the country's aerospace cluster.

Russian engineers from Sukhoi (which also cooperates with Boeing) and Antonov are working on the development of regional jets with a capacity of seventy to one hundred

---

42. President Hu Jintao and Prime Minister Wen Jiabao visited India's satellite center in Bangalore on various occasions during 2005–2007.

seats to serve the growing demand for domestic travel. These two companies will compete with Embraer and Bombardier. To make the aircraft more competitive (15% cheaper than Western competitors), 70% of the parts will be produced locally. Thales, Liebherr Aerospace, and Snecma (joint venture with NPO Saturn) hope to supply engines and other parts. Alenia Aeronautica from Italy agreed to take a 25% + 1 stake in Sukhoi for US$250 million. Under Russian law, this stake gives Alenia the right to participate in the strategy formulation process of the state-controlled firm. Alenia will be responsible, through its specially created company Superjet International, for marketing the plane to Western airlines and ensuring after-sales and repair services. Ironically, the Superjet replaces the 738 Regional Jet from Fairchild Dornier, which in April 2002 was forced into insolvency under German law.[43]

Market forces and competition have prompted AM aerospace companies to increase their stakes in the Russian market. EADS has thus acquired a 10% stake in Irkut. The Russian company produces parts for Airbus; it projects to increase sales from US$300 million to US$1.8 billion as a result of this alliance.[44] Airbus will buy US$110 million worth of mechanical parts, including those for its helicopter subsidiary, from Russian suppliers. The cooperation with Russia will deepen after the launch of the super airliner A380. EADS's engineering center (ECAR) in Moscow already employs 150 qualified constructors whose task is to design technical parts. A fully equipped R&D center will be added to conduct fundamental research using Russia's strong scientific base. Airbus sources 55% of its titanium requirements from Russia's VSMPO-Avisma. Boeing is also planning to source more raw materials and components from Russia. The company's New Dreamliner 787 has a titanium content of 20%, which is four times more than its earlier models. Through its joint ventures with Russian suppliers, Boeing intends to reduce supply-related costs by 20%–25% compared with those through its current AM suppliers. By sourcing locally, Boeing and Airbus also hope to book more orders from the state-owned carrier Aeroflot and other domestic airlines (Pulkovo, Sibir).

Russia is one of the world's leading space powers. Under the presidency of Mr. Putin (today, prime minister), the space sector was reshuffled, testifying its relevance to the country's defense and security. The Federal Space Agency Roskosmos, which also works with ESA and NASA, was completely reshuffled. Russo-European cooperation was scaled up with the signing of an agreement in 2005 that enables the Russian Soyuz launcher to take off from the European space launch center in Kourou (French Guyana). The first launch is due in 2008–2009. For the Europeans, the launch represents an important milestone as launches of light-weight satellites on a Soyuz launcher would bring costs down by about 40% compared with ESA's Ariane 5 rocket, which is more suitable for heavy payloads. With intensifying global competition and the growing role of civil applications (telecommunication, navigation, earth observation, science), cost-cutting has become a major factor for maintaining high levels of competitiveness in the space sector.

---

43. The corporation had accumulated a debt of US$670 million. A bailout plan by the German/Bavarian governments failed on the grounds that it would violate Article 90 on state aid of the EU treaties.
44. "Aerospace Industry," *Expert*, September 12–18, 2005, 21.

Table 5.17. Satellite launches in Russia, 2001–2007.						
	2001	**2002**	**2004**	**2005**	**2006**	**2007**
Telecommunications	10	17	18	11	15	19
Scientific missions	1	4	2	9	8	9
Military missions sponsored by Ministry of Defense	3	5	0	0	2	5
Russian satellites	12	12	8	5	8	12
Foreign satellites	2	14	2	15	16	18
Source: Roskosmos, Business Week Rossija, November 21, 2006.						

At the end of 2005, the Russian cabinet approved a ten-year space exploration program. US$11 billion will be earmarked for strategic projects including those for civilian applications:

- development of the Angara family of rockets
- improvements on the Soyuz-2 launch vehicle
- deployment of several telecommunication, television broadcasting, weather, and other satellites
- modernization of the Glonass navigation system
- design of a new passenger spacecraft such as the six-seat Klipper to replace the current three-seater Soyuz-TMA
- interplanetary missions

Russia's space know-how ranges from manned spaceflights (including some by foreign millionaires) to the launching of commercial satellites for foreign and domestic customers (e.g., telecom operators, large energy companies, ESA). Two trends are worth highlighting:

- increase in the number of civilian satellite launches (see table 5.17)
- increase in the number of satellite launches on behalf of foreign customers

Russia is a major contributor of scientific and financial input to the International Space Station. After the accidents of the US *Challenger* (1986) and *Columbia* (2003) space shuttles, Soyuz was for long the only carrier to be used for replacing crews and supplying the station with provisions. Russian cosmonauts have shown high endurance in manned spaceflights, where they have broken consecutive records for length of stay in outer space. The civilian satellite program represents a market of around US$2.5–3 billion annually; it covers telecommunication, earth observation, and navigation satellites. The Glonass navigation system (comparable to GPS in USA) is used for civilian and military purposes.

5.3.3. Challenges for foreign aerospace companies

Competition from megamarkets can already be felt in the large aircraft (Russia), turboprop (China, Russia), helicopter (India, Russia), and transport plane (Russia) segments. Megamarket governments see aerospace as a priority sector for improving their standing and high-tech image and for reducing their dependence on imports. Russia managed to remain in the world's aviation club after allocating funds for restructuring and consolidating the industry following years of crisis. China and India are ambitious newcomers.

Political leaders in the megamarkets leverage growing domestic demand to pressure Western manufacturers into raising local content and transferring know-how. To ensure orders, Airbus and Boeing plan to source several million dollars' worth of components from China, India, and Russia each year, including doors, wings, electronics, and new materials. But the unions fear that know-how and jobs will be lost to megamarket scientists and engineers. They underline the risk of IPR infringement and re-engineering by megamarket joint venture partners (mostly SOEs), who will then compete with the Europeans in third markets. According to EADS, "Such worries cannot be justified in a global knowledge economy where networking with local partners is the key factor of success." More than 50% of Airbus planes currently flying already have parts made in China integrated in them.[45]

Building commercial aircraft cannot be a purely national enterprise any longer. Boeing and Airbus increasingly depend on outsourcing (Airbus has sold some of its production facilities to its suppliers), effective supply chains, and risk sharing with global partners, some of which are involved from the design stage to produce not just components but entire sections of the plane. Airbus is forced to relocate part of its production (despite union opposition) because it must reduce exposure to high production costs in Europe and also become less prone to exchange rate fluctuations. According to Airbus, a €0.10 (10 cent) rise in the €/$ parity causes US$1 billion in losses for the plane maker given that aircraft is sold in US currency outside the EU.[46]

The aircraft segment, fueled by increased air travel, also beckons AM fuselage manufacturers, who must innovate by designing noise-absorbing, fuel-efficient, and environmentally friendly engines. Companies like MTU, Pratt & Whitney, Rolls-Royce, and Snecma follow their customers and increasingly look at megamarkets as promising investment destinations to supply locally built or assembled aircraft and take an active part in replacement and maintenance orders. Their biggest challenges include a shortage of trained manpower and constant staff rotations because of high demand but also the regulatory framework in place representing a moving target in the light of the constant environmental watch of effects of sudden aviation growth by legislators.

5.4. Environmental technologies

5.4.1. Global environmental trends

There is growing awareness that resources are depleting and that the downside of economic growth is pollution and other environmental problems. Most countries are signatories to the Kyoto Protocol[47] and the Basel Convention, which they are committed to implement

---

45. "A New Pilot for Airbus," *The Economist*, October 1, 2005, 64.
46. "The Future of Airbus," *BBC Business Report*, September 9, 2008.
47. The Kyoto Protocol requires specific commitments by countries to reduce their emissions of greenhouse gases in the period of 2008–2012 by an average of 5.2% below their 1990 levels.

through legislation and enforcement. These concerns have given rise to an industry of environmental goods and services. A slew of companies in the components, equipment, consulting, engineering, and remediation segments are helping countries and companies meet their green obligations.

The world market for environmental goods and services is expected to reach US$990 billion by 2010, comparable in size to the aerospace and pharmaceutical industries. AMs, particularly the United States, Germany, and Japan, represent 85% of the market. However, low growth rates of 1%–3% show that these markets have matured, although higher growth rates are forecast for areas such as cleaner technologies and processes, renewable energy, waste management, and environmental consulting services. The industry is dominated by small and medium-sized companies except in Germany, which has several large companies.

Growth will shift to emerging markets in Asia, Eastern Europe, and Latin America, where the rates will reach 6%–10%. The main segments are water and wastewater treatment, waste management, air pollution control, and environmental monitoring and instrumentation. Above-average growth is expected to persist in this industry as companies strive to improve operational performance through better environmental compliance.

Megamarket governments are keen to show their concerns over climate change and ecological disasters in their backyards—e.g., shrinking of the permafrost zone on the Tibetan plateau; retreat of glaciers in the Himalayas; droughts, floods, typhoons, and sandstorms; air pollution due to carbon dioxide emissions. At the same time, they believe in the principle of common but differentiated responsibility. They maintain that the responsibility of curbing emissions lies with the AMs, which have accumulated emissions over a long period of time. The United States (4% of the world's population) is responsible for 23% of emissions; per capita emission levels are five times higher than China's and eighteen times those of India. The AMs, on the other hand, assert that rapid industrialization and economic growth in the megamarkets will be responsible for a growing part of future emissions (see figure 5.4). In this context, the Clean Development Mechanism (CDM)[48] and trading of carbon credits are significant instruments for reducing greenhouse gases.

Earlier, megamarkets promoted industrial investments indiscriminately because they were believed to have a positive impact on employment and technology levels and to raise a nation's competitiveness. The environmental consequences of such short-term views are now waking up megamarket governments to the need to address them. Aggressive environmental organizations and greater public awareness of the environmental damage are compelling governments to act.[49] The authorities have started taking measures to check industrial pollution, such as factory inspections, environmental audits of large projects before approval, and incentives for green projects. But enforcement not being very strict, it will take the megamarket governments many more years

---

48. The Clean Development Mechanism (CDM) allows net global greenhouse gas emissions to be reduced at a much lower global cost by financing emissions reduction projects in developing countries where costs are lower than in industrialized countries.

49. There are many environmental organizations and NGOs acting as pressure groups on megamarket governments. Russia now has a green party, too; it is expected to gain popularity although it may not have the same power base yet as in Germany, Austria, or the Netherlands.

Figure 5.4. Carbon dioxide emissions[a] in major economies, 2006.

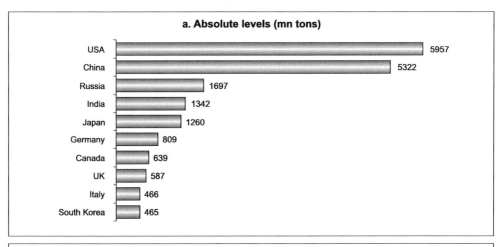

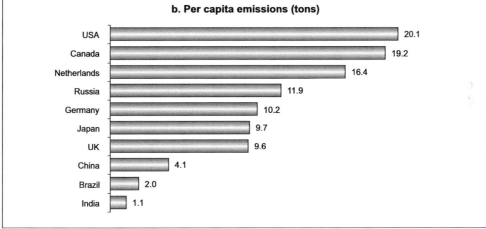

a. CO_2 emissions from burning of fuels (oil, gas, coal), not deforestation and other sources.

Source: EIA. Netherlands Environment Assessment Agency. Indian Center for Science and Environment. 2007.

to achieve AM standards. To gain international publicity, China publishes green GDP accounting data, which are calculated by subtracting from GDP economic losses incurred by pollution. Currently, the formula only considers some of the parameters for environmental pollution cost and does not include the costs of natural resources depletion and ecological damage.[50]

Megamarkets also want to demonstrate that they are eco-friendly because their companies face non-tariff barriers often linked to non-compliance with environmental norms. EU legislation, for example, expects not only end products, but also R&D, production, packaging, transportation, and re-utilization to meet strict standards. Packaging materials, for instance, must be 95% recyclable. The EU has advanced to biofilms, while megamarket units still use non-recyclable plastic films.[51]

---

50. "China Publishes Green Statistics," *China Daily*, February 13, 2007.

51. See 4.7 (consumer goods).

5.4.2. Environmental trends in the megamarkets

CHINA

Since China embarked on its fast-track industrialization program, its environmental situation has deteriorated. A growth model based on manufacturing, investment, and exports has led to serious pollution, resource shortages, and frictions with other countries. Pollution-related health damage and accidents have taken a heavy toll on the population's health, especially in rural areas. The main pollution sources range from uncontrolled landfills and smog to water contamination because of illicit discharges of industrial waste into rivers and lakes.

Controlling pollution is, together with energy conservation, a priority in the eleventh five-year plan (2006–2010) approved by China's Peoples' Congress. The government, in a State Council Resolution, has set the following ecological targets for 2010:

- energy consumption per unit of GDP to decrease by 18%
- average water-use efficiency for agricultural irrigation to be improved by 50%
- reuse rate of industrial solid waste to be raised to above 60%
- recycle and reuse rate of major renewable resources to be increased by 65%
- final industrial solid waste disposal to be limited to about 500 million metric tons
- resource productivity per ton of energy, iron, and other resources to be increased by 25%

Cities suffer from the negative consequences of rapid urbanization. By 2010, 47% of the people will live in the cities (21% in 2001), representing an unprecedented rural exodus. The construction of urban environmental infrastructure (sewage and waste treatment facilities) cannot cope with the influx of migrant laborers from the rural areas. According to the State Environmental Protection Agency (SEPA), environmental pollution causes US$80 billion in economic losses (2007), or 3% of GDP. The country failed to meet international emission-reduction targets. The goal was to reduce chemical oxygen demand (COD), a water pollution index, and sulfur dioxide (SO_2) emissions by 2% in 2006 as part of an ambitious plan to reduce them by 10% by 2010. Instead, SO_2 emissions increased by 1.8% and COD by 1.2%. Emission cuts are difficult to obtain because of fast growth, which for China means more coal burning by smokestack units. Consumption of coal grew by 230 million metric tons during 2004–2007, resulting in the release of 2.8 million metric tons of sulfur dioxide from coal burning alone. A law stipulates that all coal-fired power plants must be equipped with desulphurization devices by 2010 or they will be closed down. Meanwhile, the output of paper products, one of the major sources of COD, reached more than 67 million metric tons, an increase of 30% during 2004–2007. The government plans to cut energy consumption per unit of GDP by 20% by 2010, but it is struggling to stay within these limits. China will spend US$50 billion, or 2% of its GDP, on environmental protection until 2012. About half of this expenditure will come jointly from the central (12%), provincial, and local governments (38%). The remaining half will have to be invested by enterprises under strict enforcement of regulations.

Chinese authorities want to see considerable improvements in three areas: water, air, and solid waste. While provinces are called to improve the water quality of rivers and lakes, the

Figure 5.5. Environmental infrastructure expenses in key Chinese cities, 2007.

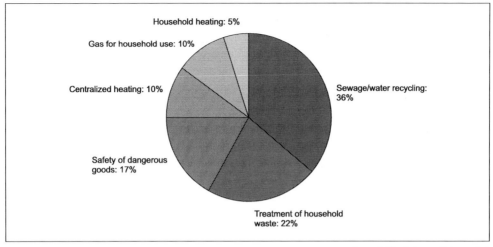

Source: All-China Environment Federation. 2008.

large cities (see figure 5.5) will invest in sewage and wastewater treatment facilities, often funded through water tariffs (on residents) and wastewater surcharges (on companies). Groundwater contamination is a serious problem, and local environmental protection agencies cannot cope with the inspection work. If caught, polluters are heavily fined. Solid waste treatment, predominately by means of incineration and landfills, is expanding as a result of enforcement (solid/hazardous waste law). Major cities and provinces have set up hazardous and medical waste treatment centers and warehouses for radioactive waste (at provincial level). The City of Beijing spent US$6 billion on environmental clean-up including waste disposal ahead of the 2008 Olympics.

The central government pursues ambitious plans to build ecologically clean cities as resource-conserving models where:

- citizens enjoy grade II air quality on 80% of the days in a year;
- city sewage treatment rates are higher than 70%;
- the rate of non-harmful disposal of household refuse is higher than 80%; and
- more than 35% of the urban areas have a green canopy.

Industrial waste is the biggest cause of water pollution, the other being sewage and agricultural pollutants. Illegal discharges from industrial enterprises and air pollution caused by vehicle and factory emissions are major concerns of authorities. Pollutants discharged by automobiles account for 80% of air pollution in the big cities. This tendency can theoretically be halted by actively promoting the use of low-pollution electric cars, hybrid (electric-cum-petrol) traction, and small-engine vehicles and by limiting large vans and jeeps in downtown areas. Authorities aim to curb SO_2 and acid rain caused by vehicle emissions. Europe-3 emission norms compel refineries to produce cleaner fuels. Since 2000, leaded petrol has been prohibited across the country.

The government also engages in eco-agriculture and ecological demonstration zones, including dry farming, water-saving agriculture, reforestation, sandstorm prevention, and the protection of pastures. Special measures concern the protection of cultivated land, water, and soil by limiting areas used for industry and construction. In 2007, total farmland used for construction and industrial purposes decreased by 37% over 2006. To relieve the burden, the government has built a number of eco-industrial parks promoting ecological value chains (clusters) with businesses sharing resources, information, and materials including each other's industrial waste, discharges, and by-products as sources of raw material or energy. Denmark's Kalundborg Eco-industrial Park served as an example for establishing the Binzhou Park in Shandong province.[52] In 2007, twenty ecological parks were operational in China. Authorities are committed to preserve biodiversity by promoting nature reserves and protected eco-areas. Because of their scenic beauty and history, some of these places have been included in UNESCO's World Heritage List.[53]

Since 1996, China has passed many environmental laws (see box 5.2). SEPA, the country's environmental agency, was granted ministerial status in 1998. It reports directly to the State Council, China's supreme political body. Checks and enforcement have been strengthened. During 2002–2007, three thousand industrial enterprises in the iron and steel, cement, power, iron alloy, coking, papermaking, and textile printing and dyeing industries were forced to shut down for having caused hazards and violated legislation. Over five thousand enterprises in chemicals, light industry, power generating, coal, machinery, and building materials have passed the test for clean production. About thirteen thousand enterprises received the ISO 14,000 Environmental Management System certification, and twenty thousand products were granted environmental labeling certification. The government encourages clean production that makes full use of resources throughout the production process and establishes a system based on "the polluter pays" principle. As part of its commitment to promote a recyclable economy by 2010,[54] the government is encouraging greater use of renewable energy (10% of electricity consumption compared with only 3%

Box 5.2. Environmental laws in China, 2008.
- Law on prevention and control of water pollution
- Law on marine life protection
- Law on prevention and control of air pollution
- Law on noise prevention
- Law on solid waste and radioactive pollution
- Law on evaluation of environmental impact
- Law on renewable energies
- Law on "recyclable" economy
- Special legislations on water, clean production, renewable energy, agriculture, grasslands, and animal husbandry

---

52. "Building an Eco-industrial Chain within an Industrial Park," *China Today*, February 2006.
53. See 6.5 (tourism and hospitality).
54. "Learning from Nature. China Develops a Recyclable Economy," *China Today*, February 2007.

in 2003) and significant reduction of carbon dioxide emissions, for which China ranks second after the United States.

INDIA

India's rapidly growing population, along with urbanization and industrialization, has placed considerable pressure on the country's infrastructure and natural resources. While industrial development has been instrumental to economic growth, it has harmed the environment. Deforestation, soil erosion, and land degradation continue to worsen rural areas, while booming metropolises suffer from water degradation, inadequate municipal services, and serious air pollution. Higher energy consumption in the industrial, transportation, and residential sectors continues to drive up India's emission levels.

After the 1984 Bhopal disaster, in which a toxic leak from the city's Union Carbide chemical plant killed more than three thousand people, environmental awareness and activism in India have sharpened. The Ministry of Environment and Forests (MoEF) was created in 1985, and the Environment Protection Act was passed in 1986.[55] It follows the Water (Prevention and Control of Pollution) Act (1974) and the Air (Prevention and Control of Pollution) Act (1981). The Central Pollution Control Board was constituted in 1974. Forests, wildlife, and biodiversity protection are covered by separate acts. The priority areas defined in the eleventh five-year plan (2007–2011) are:

- environmental impact assessment;
- afforestation;
- air quality improvement;
- water quality (including rivers);
- waste management;
- biodiversity;
- environmental awareness and education;
- environmental research and development;
- conservation of natural resources and ecosystems;
- impact and implications of climate change, responses to climate change; and
- disaster management.

Strict laws and judicial action as well as awareness are driving the market for environmental goods and services in India; it is valued at US$15.5 billion (2007) and is growing at 10%–12% per annum. Another important driver is the Charter on Corporate Responsibility for Environmental Protection, which is a time-bound action plan for compliance with regulations by polluting industries.

The industry is dominated by medium-sized and small companies that supply mostly end-of-pipe treatment plants so that companies can demonstrate compliance. The main

---

55. The act allows the government to set standards on environmental quality, procedures for handling materials, and rules for siting industries, and it provides for compulsory reporting of pollution and recovery of costs of cleanup from the polluter. The act allows any person to make a complaint against a polluter to the courts; it includes rules governing management of urban, hazardous, biomedical, and other wastes.

business activities therefore concern conventional air pollution equipment, wastewater management, environmental consulting, solar cells, and hydraulic turbines. The smaller companies lack capital and R&D capacity and the technology to handle complex pollutants. The technology-rich and experienced EU companies can fill this gap efficiently and profitably. Foreign companies are present in India through licensing, joint ventures, or their own subsidiaries. They are mainly from the United States, Germany, United Kingdom, and Canada, as well as France, Italy, and the Netherlands. Foreign investment with 100% foreign equity is allowed in India. Incentives are also given for promoting the environmental industry.

Waste management and recycling offers a high business potential in India. Urban India produces more than 100 million metric tons of waste annually. Almost all is dumped in landfills without any treatment. The Municipal Solid Waste (Management and Handling) Rules were enacted in 2000 to address this issue. Privatization of the different segments of the value chain is being gradually introduced by various municipalities. The first such contract was awarded to an EU company for the city of Chennai. Delhi has moved further in privatization of waste collection and treatment plants. Waste management is an industry whose potential is untapped.

Recycling in India has been a mostly non-formal industry that is market-driven; the system is a symbiosis of companies, mostly non-governmental organizations, and societal actors like ragpickers. But resource depletion and high input costs as well as the high potential are prompting large private companies to enter this business and to formalize it. The diversified conglomerate ITC, which has a packaging business, is expanding its organized wastepaper-recovery model to various cities after a successful pilot project in Chennai. The basic stipulation in the Municipal Solid Waste Rules that waste must be sorted into compostables and recyclables at source (household) will be the cornerstone of the recycling industry. E-waste is a new phenomenon in India. PC ownership grows in triple digits (604% between 1995 and 2005); around 1.4 million PCs are made obsolete each year, and the number is growing. It has spawned an as yet informal industry of dismantlers and recyclers, which has grown spontaneously from the scrap industry.

India's high pollution level is not due to the absence of environmental laws but to the lack of enforcement at the local level. In 1998, India's Supreme Court issued a ruling requiring all buses in Delhi to run on compressed natural gas (CNG) by March 31, 2001. Compliance was to be attained by converting existing diesel engines or by replacing the buses. However, out of a total fleet of twelve thousand, only two hundred CNG-fueled buses were available by the initial deadline. To ease the transition, the local government changed course and allowed for a gradual phase-out of the existing bus fleet. Today, most buses, three-wheelers, and small taxis in Delhi, Mumbai, and Kolkata run on CNG fuel. Emission norms for passenger cars and commercial vehicles were tightened again in 2000–2001 (Euro I standard for second-tier cities, more stringent Euro II standard for Delhi, Mumbai, Chennai, and Kolkata). Additionally, the sulfur content of motor fuels sold in the four mega cities was restricted to 500 parts per million in alignment with tighter vehicle emissions standards; in all other cities, it was limited to 2,500 parts per million. Efforts to improve urban air quality will have to tackle the problem of growing vehicle ownership and used exhaust systems. In Delhi, emission limits for petrol- and diesel-powered vehicles came into effect in 1991–1992, when the use of vehicles older than fifteen years was prohibited.

Air quality is constantly threatened by coal-fired power plants. Like China, India relies heavily on such units for generating electricity. India's Central Pollution Control Board has been reluctant to set stricter sulfur dioxide and nitrogen oxide emissions limits (while thermal plants running on other fossil fuels face such limits). Many of India's highly polluting coal-fired power plants will remain in operation for many years to come given the high capital cost required to replace them. In 2006, India overtook Japan to become the world's fourth-largest carbon dioxide emitter. India's 75% growth in carbon emissions during 1990–2006 was only surpassed by China's rate (136%). India's emissions will continue to rise until 2020, thus offsetting the reduction planned by the EU and other AMs eager to implement the reduction targets set by the Kyoto Protocol, to which India adhered in 2002. India's contribution to world carbon emissions is expected to grow on average by 3% annually during 2005–2025, according to the EIA (compared with 4% for China and 1.5% for USA). The absolute increase in emissions will depend on how long the country will continue to rely on coal as a major source of energy and whether coal-fired plants can be switched to more efficient technologies.

Government policies, intervention, and support are indispensable for the environmental industry. At the same time, the Indian government recognizes that the best way forward is through public–private partnerships and FDI in the sector. This approach is slowly permeating the waste and pollution control industries.

Russia

Russia is the world's largest country with some of the planet's richest natural resources. In addition to huge deposits of fossil fuels, Russia has over 20% of the world's boreal forest cover, a vast Arctic tundra, endless steppe lands (*taiga*), and Lake Baikal—the world's largest interior lake, accounting for 20% of the world's freshwater. The Arctic, the Siberian forests, and Russia's Far East regions—home to geothermal resources, indigenous peoples, and endangered wildlife—are important ecosystems that help preserve the world's biological balance. Yet, Russia has inherited a legacy of environmental problems from the Soviet Union since its demise in 1991. Blatant disregard for nature reinforced by the regime's aggressive but irresponsible industrialization has left the country grappling with numerous environmental problems, from severe air pollution to radioactive contamination. In addition, the Soviets bequeathed to Russia an economy dependent on a military–industrial complex and extractive industries that are energy-intensive.

The environment has become a more pertinent issue in today's Russia. The country's Environmental Protection Law and the Law on Ecological Expert Review prohibit the financing or implementation of any project that could have a harmful effect without prior impact assessment by the project sponsor. Current legislation does, however, permit a company to discharge hazardous substances after obtaining a permit and subject to the periodic payment of a fee based on the type and amount of the pollutant. The country is also a signatory to the United Nations Framework Convention on Climate Change (1994) and the Kyoto Protocol (1999).

Air pollution is a significant problem for major Russian cities. Russia ranks among the three countries with the highest carbon dioxide emission levels. Power plants are aging and lack modern pollution control equipment, resulting in large amounts of toxic emissions and waste. Russia's industrial sector is, together with vehicle-generated emissions, responsible for most damage. Thanks to robust economic growth, the number of cars on Russia's roads is increasing dramatically. But authorities are becoming stricter as overall environmental awareness grows. New cars have catalytic converters, and stricter rules apply for gasoline standards (Euro III norms by 2009, Euro IV norms by 2010).

Oil and gas extraction is another area of concern as it is a significant source of natural damage, apart from its contribution to air pollution. Environmental standards are weak, enforcement is poor, and accidents such as pipeline leakage and tanker spills have caused contaminations across Russia (e.g., Tyumen, Khanty-Mansiysk). Oil spills have polluted drinking water and are supposed to be the cause of increased cancer incidence in several affected areas. Planned oil and natural gas pipelines from eastern Siberia to Asian markets are being challenged by environmental groups who claim that Russian officials are ignoring the protected status of the Siberian Plateau, which covers parts of Mongolia, China, Russia, and Kazakhstan. Such road and pipeline projects would not only incur enormous costs in both construction and maintenance, but they would also have a severe impact on the environment, since they would be routed through highland marshes, tundra, permafrost areas, mountain passes, and elevated plateaus. The Natural Resources Ministry, created in 2000 from the fusion of the State Committee for Environmental Protection and the State Committee on Forestry, is stricter in penalizing oil companies for violating the ecological terms of their field license agreements.

Currently, there are ten operating nuclear power plants with thirty reactors in Russia, some of which are first-generation RBMK reactors similar to the ones that operated in Chernobyl in Ukraine. Despite safety concerns, Russia seeks to extend the operating life of several reactors that are nearing the end of their proscribed operating lifespan and to increase the country's nuclear capacity by building forty new reactors by 2030. Radioactive contamination has damaged several regions in Russia. Nuclear waste from both civilian and military nuclear power installations has become a severe threat to the country's environmental health. Adding to the problem, in 2001 the Russian parliament approved legislation to allow the storage of foreign nuclear waste on Russian soil. Atomic energy authorities claim that between 10,000 and 20,000 metric tons of nuclear waste could be imported for storage and reprocessing over the next decade, with the storage plan projected to earn the country US$20 billion in foreign revenues over the ten-year period. Now that the country has accumulated ample foreign reserves, which allow it to be less dependent on such foreign currency earnings, this plan may be shelved.

5.4.3. Challenges for foreign environmental companies

The main challenge for EU environmental companies is to find ways to effectively deploy the technologies and knowledge that were developed under a rigorous domestic regulatory regime into markets without such regimes. The second challenge is to find ways of generating income from that deployment. The environmental industry is dependent on government regulations and in most cases on procurement from government agencies. Both take time and very often aggressive lobbying.

Environmental companies use leading-edge technologies, whose mechanisms and benefits may not be understood by government officials who lack knowledge about the applications. In countries where the law requires foreign companies to tie up with a local partner, it is difficult for a company dealing in a new technology to identify business partners who are prepared to share that risk. Intellectual property rights infringement is also a prime concern. But the business prospects in the megamarkets are attractive enough to justify the effort to find appropriate solutions to these issues.

EU and AM suppliers of environmental technologies will find wide applications in industry, construction, public utilities, commerce, and agriculture. At least as far as 2015, there will be five areas of top priority for megamarket authorities:

- waste: collection, treatment, incineration, composting, and disposal; sludge treatment and disposal, landfill management
- water: water treatment and supply, wastewater treatment, reuse, sewage systems, water monitoring, drinking water purification, consultancy for river basin management and flood control
- air: purification, pollution control
- recycling: plastics, metals, glass, e-waste, nuclear waste, crop residues
- energy saving: industrial, residential, energy sector

In waste management and recycling, many large and medium-sized industrial groups from the EU, Japan, the United States, and other emerging economies have made various attempts to enter the megamarkets. Among the foreign companies that are already active are Veolia, Fanalca (Colombia), Plastic Omnium and Otto (waste containerization), and JCB (vehicles). Biomedical and hazardous waste management are other activities with high prospects; both are governed by laws that provide the necessary framework.

The market for measuring stations to monitor water and air quality is also growing. Excellent prospects exist for analytical instruments, vehicle emission particulate reduction devices, water filtration equipment (e.g., biological filtration), disinfection technologies (UV, membrane, and ozonation), mechanical waste sorting and separation, composting, incineration, and waste-to-energy technologies. Air pollution control technologies include gas desulphurization systems (energy sector), air monitoring instruments, and vehicle emissions control and inspection devices.

Despite their apparent strength, EU companies should not become complacent. A growing number of domestic, US, and Asian companies have appeared on the scene with similar technologies and attractive service-cum-advisory packages (often at a lower price) to garner a larger share of this lucrative market. In most cases, concepts are adapted to domestic requirements, which are clearly favored over imported solutions.

The outlook for foreign investors in the megamarket environment industry is generally very good. Strict legislation is steering domestic industries toward adopting efficient systems. Manufacturing companies are compelled to invest in clean technologies for effluent treatment and energy efficiency in the chemical, paper, and steel industries. The three countries offer excellent opportunities for suppliers of equipment that helps reduce emissions.

But they must face a growing number of megamarket rivals. The success of indigenous alternative energy and environmentally conscious companies will eventually push the megamarkets to become cleaner. Cases in point are China's Suntech, the world's third-largest producer of solar cells, and India's Suzlon, a world leader in wind turbines. These companies, and soon many others, have joined the international M&A race by acquiring assets in foreign companies. Their advantage is the speed and managerial determination (they are mostly run by the original founder family) with which they remove competitors and consolidate assets at home and globally.[56]

---

56. In 2007, Suzlon acquired 33.66% of Germany's REpower for US$1.6 billion; in an additional bid in September 2008, it raised the stake to 90%, outmaneuvering French rival Areva. In 2006, Suzlon had bought Hansen Transmissions International NV, a leading wind turbine gearbox manufacturer in Belgium for €465 million in an all-cash deal. In October 2008, Suzlon reported that it was planning to acquire Coimbatore-based Shanthi Gears in India.

CHAPTER 6
Eurasia's megamarkets as business platforms for service sectors

The attribute "industrialized" in fact no longer applies to a majority of the OECD economies; the more appropriate term is "service-based" economies. The sector accounts for almost 75% of GDP in the United States and United Kingdom. Its share in the economies of Germany, France, and Italy is between 60% and 65%. The megamarkets are moving in a similar direction. India is already very service-dependent; in China and Russia as well, the share of industry has receded to under 50% of GDP.

A closer look at developments in the major service industries worldwide suggests that EMMs/EMs will take away market share from AMs. Led by China and India with their ever-growing pool of educated and service-minded people, EMM companies first serve their domestic markets (e.g., inbound tourism, retailing, banking) and then gradually go global (e.g., IT, logistics). The rise of India in IT and retailing and China in international logistics and tourism are just examples of a trend bound to persist well into the first two to three decades of the twenty-first century (see table 6.1).

6.1. IT services

6.1.1. Global trends in IT services

IT and IT-enabled services (ITeS) comprise software- and business-related tasks that help improve a company's processes. They are mostly outsourced to external special-

Table 6.1. Expected position of megamarkets in global services by 2015.

Segments	Domestic	Emerging market	Advanced market
IT			
China	++	+	+
India	++	++	++
Russia	++	+	+
Banking			
China	++	+	−
India	++	+	−
Russia	++	+	−
Insurance			
China	++	+	−
India	++	+	−
Russia	++	++	−
Retailing			
China	++	++	−
India	++	+	−
Russia	++	++	+
Logistics			
China	++	++	++
India	+	+	−
Russia	++	++	+
Tourism			
China	++	++	++
India	++	++	++
Russia	++	+	+

++: leading position vis-a-vis AM rivals
+: competitive vis-à-vis AM rivals
−: not yet competitive vis-à-vis AM rivals

Table 6.2. Worldwide IT spending by verticals, 2006–2011.

	2006 (US$ bn)	2011 (US$ bn)	Annual growth (%)
Manufacturing	119.6	158.4	5.8
Banking and finance	107.4	144.9	6.2
Government	76.3	102.8	6.2
Telecommunication	40.2	57.0	7.2
Energy	25.4	35.4	6.8
Pharmaceuticals	16.8	22.7	6.2
Tourism, transport	14.4	18.5	5.1
Others	69.2	87.6	4.8
Total	469.3	627.3	6.0

Source: International Data Corporation (IDC). 2008.

ists. IT-specific tasks and back-office services are personnel-intensive and can be performed at a distance. The share of spending on in-house IT will drop from 45% of total expenditure in 2006 to 30%–35% by 2015; the bulk of the work will be outsourced to the low-cost economies of Eastern Europe and Asia.

Global IT spending (internal and external) amounted to US$470–500 billion in 2006; it is expected to increase at a compound annual rate of 6% to US$620–650 billion by 2010. In the mid to late 1990s, global banks were the first to adopt IT outsourcing as a business model.[1] This trend has gathered momentum ever since and now extends to many more industry verticals such as telecom, pharma and health care, travel, and manufacturing (see table 6.2). The horizontal service lines cover accounting, training, testing, infrastructure management, product development, advertising, engineering, BPO, legal services, and business intelligence. These functional areas have opened cross-selling potential across different verticals and geographies for frontline companies.

The global market for offshore spending on IT services for predominantly Western customers was around US$50 billion in 2007 and is growing in double digits. The BPO market was worth an additional US$25 billion. India has captured the bulk of this work (75%) both in IT and BPO, while China commands just about US$2–3 billion of the outsourced-services market. By 2010, India will export about US$80 billion worth of IT services compared with US$4 billion for China and US$2 billion for Russia (see table 6.3).

The big IT consultancies have opened offices and moved part of their operations including R&D units to the megamarkets. Accenture has fifteen thousand employees in India, China, and the Philippines. IBM has strengthened its position in Eastern Europe following targeted investments in Hungary, Czech Republic, Poland, and Latvia. In India, fifty-three thousand people work for IBM (2008), and further recruitment is planned. Other US IT leaders have announced plans to invest in India during 2007–2010 (Microsoft, US$1.7 billion; Cisco, US$1.2 billion; Intel,[2] US$1 billion) as growing numbers of their key accounts threaten to take their business to Indian IT firms to re-

Table 6.3. IT and BPO exports from the megamarkets, 2002–2010 (US$ bn).

	China	India	Russia
2002	0.5	9	0.2
2004	0.8	17	0.5
2006	1.0	30	0.9
2008	2.0	52	1.6
2010	6.0	80	3.0

Source: Gartner. Evaluserve. Business Week.

---

1. "IT Offshoring: Large Untapped Potential," *The Hindu Survey of Indian Industry* (2008): 150–151.
2. As a parallel measure, Intel will also build a US$2.5 billion integrated circuit manufacturing plant in Dalian, China, its first in an emerging economy. This way, it hopes to attain a tighter supply chain by getting closer to its customers (cell phone and laptop producers). See "From Low-cost to High-tech. Intel Investment Shows China Is Climbing the Value Chain," *Wall Street Journal*, March 26, 2007.

duce costs. The strategy of IBM needs to be closely watched; it aims at multiple synergies from three business lines:

- hardware: low- to medium-margin commodities, which face new competitors from countries such as China (IBM's PC business was sold to Lenovo in 2005)
- software: represents 40% of IBM's revenue (2003: 25%); IBM spent US$16 billion on the acquisitions of more than fifty specialized IT companies during 2003–2007

Table 6.4. Use of personal computers in leading economies, 2000–2010 (in mn).

	2000	2004	2010
USA	161	220	260
Japan	40	69	96
China	21	53	115
UK	20	36	45
South Korea	19	26	35
Russia	9	20	38
Brazil	9	19	32
India	5	13	40

Source: ITU World Telecom Indicators database.

- services: high value-added activities including business and IT consulting

IBM's objective is to secure key accounts—the large multinationals—through "automated" (standard) software, which generates license fees and can be reused by other customers in the same or related industries. But its rivals are pursuing a similar path. HCL, India's fifth biggest IT firm, has won contracts worth US$700 million for "infrastructure management" and "business transformation" from leading companies and banks in the EU since 2006.[3] Global IT consultancies like Accenture and EDS are concerned to see megamarket players pull the business toward them and improve their standing by developing new products in cooperation with Western customers.

Six powerful forces will drive megamarket growth in the IT industry in the years to come:
- highly educated mathematicians and engineers with advanced programming skills
- pressure on IT service suppliers to cut costs and outsource IT activities
- streamlining of business processes through innovative IT to increase competitiveness
- opening of unexplored market segments: government, public companies, SMEs, start-ups
- developed service culture
- wider spread of computer use, which correlates with the use of IT services (see table 6.4)

6.1.2. IT trends in the megamarkets

INDIA

India is the largest and fastest-growing provider of offshore IT-enabled services in the world. What started as a service for basic data entry now covers complex processes of rule-based decision-making and research. In the coming years, service industries (finance, retail, health care, legal, publishing) will spend large sums on IT. With the rise of inward FDI in industry, sophisticated IT products will also be required at the factory floor level and in administrative departments of companies.

---

3. "IBM and Globalization," *The Economist*, April 7, 2007, 65–67.

BPO will be driven by banking, insurance, health care, and general customer services. Legal process outsourcing (LPO) promises a vast potential, given that about US$250 billion is spent each year worldwide on legal services, about two-thirds of it in the United States. Again, India, with its English-language capability and common law tradition, is excellently placed to take a big slice of the business, including documentation, contracts, and patent applications. With US and EU lawyers costing US$300 an hour or more, Indian law firms can help cut bills by 75%,[4] particularly for medium-sized companies. More and more cutting-edge products are developed in India through knowledge process outsourcing (KPO), as seen from the growing number of patent filings; KPO will grow to be a US$10 billion industry by 2012.

Tata Consultancy Services (TCS)—India's leading IT company—generated sales worth US$4.2 billion and an EBIT margin of 33% in 2007. Wipro (US$3.5 billion) and Infosys (US$3.1 billion), the other two large players, also reported exponential business growth from outsourcing by AM companies. Their workforce grew four to five times to several tens of thousands compared with the year 2000. Indian IT companies aim higher still through increased value-addition and diversification to other geographies (including the home market) and expansion of the current client base of large multinationals (mainly from USA) to medium-sized customers in need of special solutions. India's IT companies view the financial crisis of 2008–2009 as an opportunity to improve efficiency and accelerate innovation.

To move closer to corporate decision-makers, Indian IT players open subsidiaries and sometimes acquire companies abroad. According to Infosys's Mentor Narayan Murthy, "The mindset of Indian firms is becoming increasingly globalised. It means the entire globe is our playground." Former CEO Nandan Nilekani adds, "Future IT giants must be able to combine development in low-cost environments with worldwide distribution and consulting."[5] Successful players will offer a combination of near-shore (immediate proximity of clients) and offshore (outsourced to India) projects. Near-shore countries for EU clients are Poland, Hungary, Czech Republic, Romania, the Baltics, and Russia. These are the countries Indian players are targeting for acquisitions. Before making this step, Indian companies assess a target's strengths in the following areas:

- client potential
- industry-specific know-how
- management and leadership style
- brand equity
- capability to offer turnkey and bespoke system solutions
- innovative strengths
- knowledge of culture and mentality in at least three to four EU countries
- personnel and career development schemes

If Indian companies want to compete with IT behemoths like IBM and EDS, acquisitions are the only way to grow rapidly in size. Infosys's targeting of UK-based Axon Group PLC for US$753 million will inspire other Indian IT majors to aim at big-ticket foreign companies.

---

4. "India's IT and Remote-service Industries Just Keep Growing," *The Economist*, December 17, 2005, 61–62.
5. "Infosys bläst zum angriff auf IBM und Accenture" [Infosys attacks IBM and Accenture], *Handelsblatt*, August 2, 2005.

Infosys generates 70% of its turnover in North America but is orienting itself more to the EU and the Asia-Pacific region. In China alone, it will create five thousand new jobs until 2010. Other players pursue an industry-focused strategy with a global orientation. TCS CEO Ramadorai summarizes this strategy as follows: "Besides classical IT services for banks and institutional clients, we see chances for the outsourcing of engineering services, especially for the automobile industry. We seek clients among the leading automobile and aerospace companies."[6] In 2005, ABN Amro granted TCS a landmark contract for providing the software and support services for its private banking operations in Brazil and the Netherlands. As a result, TCS won over other European banks as customers and launched an R&D-backed subsidiary in Hungary, which now generates 25% of its sales in Europe.[7] Wipro employs fifty R&D specialists in its German subsidiary. In 2006, it bought New Logic Technologies AG, the leading Austrian chip developer and specialist for wireless LAN and Bluetooth solutions, for US$47 million. Promising IT segments in the EU are software development, data bank management, computer and telecom system maintenance, office work outsourcing, and engineering services.

The three mainstays of India's IT business are booming exports, sales by foreign subsidiaries, and domestic sales. By 2015, domestic sales will account for one-third of IT revenue generated by Indian companies (15% in 2003). To get closer to the expanding Indian market, US companies that dominate the global IT scene (e.g., IBM, Accenture, EDS, Intel, Microsoft, Oracle, Google, AOL, GE, Motorola) have been invited to source and invest in R&D facilities in India. Siemens will allocate US$500 million to India in 2007–2010. The money will be used for expanding R&D centers and recruiting more software professionals. The German technology leader sees India as a regional R&D hub, but also as an export base. SAP from Germany is also expanding its operations systematically out of Bangalore.

About 850,000 people are employed by India's IT industry, but this figure will triple by 2010 (see table 6.5). Entry-level monthly salaries of up to Rs20,000 (US$500) attract young engineers. Yet, supply of talent is the biggest constraint. Experts predict a shortfall of 500,000 qualified IT personnel as the requirement far exceeds the number of students graduating from relevant disciplines. Young IT specialists from different AMs are nowadays recruited by Indian firms for their ability to communicate with non-English-speaking customers (e.g., German, French, Spanish, Japanese). These reverse *Gastarbeiter* are identified through specialized agencies in AMs or apply independently for positions in India. The current number of foreign staff employed by Indian IT companies is less than 3% of their total IT-BPO workforce of 1.3 million. The top five players (TCS, Infosys, Wipro, Satyam, HCL) plan to raise that percentage to 10%–20%.[8]

Table 6.5. India's outsourcing professionals, 2001–2010.

	IT	BPO
2001	120,000	150,000
2003	210,000	180,000
2005	360,000	450,000
2007	540,000	700,000
2010	1.3 mn	1 mn

Source: NASSCOM. India. 2007.

---

6. "TCS erhält grossauftrag von ABN Amro" [TCS acquires megaproject from ABN Amro], *Handelsblatt,* September 2, 2005.
7. "Indischer IT-dienstleister drängt nach Deutschland" [Indian IT company pushes into Germany], *Financial Times,* September 20, 2005.
8. "IT Majors to Up Foreign Hiring 10 to 20%," *Business Standard,* December 6, 2007.

To compete with the world's IT majors, Indian companies need to recruit the best talents so that they can shift from low-margin, low value-added maintenance and subcontracting projects to more demanding assignments. They are positioning themselves at the higher end of the value chain by upgrading to customized software and high-end consultancy. IBM Global Services, GE, and the big five US IT consultancies have an established brand equity, which helps them command premium fees. Moreover, operating from within India, these players can tap the same talent pool as their Indian rivals. Undoubtedly, as Indian firms move up the ladder and pitch for consulting projects in the EU and the United States, competition will get more intense.

The government supports the industry through tax and other incentives and the development of IT parks and IT SEZs, recently the creation of much larger information technology investment regions (ITIRs).

China

China is emerging as an IT and BPO back-office market. Not very long ago, the country's development strategy was focused on industrial advancement and rural reforms. Now policymakers, encouraged by the success stories of entrepreneurs returning from AMs, are turning their attention to services as the new engine of economic growth, which will help to better utilize the human potential. The software industry currently contributes modestly to national output (US$45 billion, or 1.7%), but it grows faster (+27% in 2006–2007) than the hardware segment (+10%). This trend will persist well into the 2020s as companies upgrade their IT systems and authorities try to attract FDI in this sector.

The city of Dalian, for example, has skillfully exploited its location advantages in China's northeast to form a BPO–call center cluster for multinationals intending to provide customer support services to their East Asian consumers based in Japan and South Korea. General Electric—through its Indian BPO subsidiary—intends to triple its staff in Dalian from 1,800 to more than 5,000 in 2008–2010. SAP, another example, opened an R&D center in Shanghai, which will employ 1,500 software specialists by 2009. A second IT platform was opened in Chengdu, Sichuan Province, where salaries are half those in Shanghai. In 2007, China replaced Israel as SAP's fourth-largest R&D platform after Germany, India, and the United States. A platform in China is essential for companies like SAP to offer customized solutions to local and foreign companies in China (e.g., German automotive components firms). SAP claims that 80% of its 1,500 clients in China are local firms. The advantages of SAP's Chinese IT location include the huge untapped market of large and medium-sized companies in second- and third-tier cities, affordable costs for engineers, a large pool of new recruits, high-class technical institutes, and government support. Similarly, Japan's NEC and Fujitsu employ several hundred people in R&D and software writing in China. The latest batch of companies to tap the Chinese market are Indian IT companies. TCS has its own campus in Hangzhou; it signed a triangular deal with the Chinese government and Microsoft to build China's first big software company. Infosys and Wipro opened offices and R&D facilities in Shanghai and Beijing, where they plan to increase their workforce from a few hundred to 5,000–6,000 each by 2012.

China is behind India in the business of outsourced services but intends to catch up. Young Chinese entrepreneurs—as happened with their Indian counterparts decades ago—inject fresh ideas and capital into newly opened back offices where people sitting at computer terminals process medical claims forms and car loan applications, or mark examinations for high school students. These IT/BPO start-ups benefit from government support in the form of modern facilities and infrastructure offered in high-tech parks (e.g., Shanghai, Dalian, Xian, Wuhan) and a network of premier engineering schools in the main cities.

But foreign investors also face risks. They must invest heavily in training engineers to become project managers or BPO staff and to be able to communicate fluently in English or in other languages. Foreign IT/BPO players indirectly subsidize the country's education system without having the guarantee that the engineer will stay. Intensive training can cost up to US$30,000 a year on top of the salary paid to a middle-level engineer.[9] Retention has to be therefore assured for at least five years to recover the cost.

Russia

Like China, Russia's government is determined to expand the national software base as part of an effort to make the country a truly high-tech country. The IT market, which in Russia also includes software development and hardware sales, topped US$27 billion in 2007. Hardware sales make up 67% of this market, but the software segment is growing at a much faster pace. By 2012, software and IT services are expected to draw even with hardware in terms of market share. By then, the overall market will be US$45 billion, corresponding to 0.4%–0.5% of GDP. This forecast is modest given that the government plans to channel millions of petrodollars into the creation of techno parks with all the facilities needed for establishing modern software and R&D centers.

The government's "Electronic Russia" master plan aims at the propagation of computers and to spread innovation across the country. It will translate into multimillion-dollar contracts for the IT and computer hardware industry. The plan is expected to achieve IT-supported scientific breakthroughs by 2025 in areas such as nanotechnology, bioelectronics, optoelectronics, and quantum computers. The government recognizes that oil and gas resources are limited while IT and electronics are based on a limitless, renewable resource—the human intellect.

Government bodies and Russian companies in many industries (see figure 6.1) will invest in more sophisticated IT systems, which is the reason why the world's leading IT players are expanding in Russia. USA-based Cadence Design Systems (CDS),[10] an electronic design company, opened its second Russian office for electronic design automation; its location in Zelenograd near Moscow puts CDS within close range of the leading Russian chips and semiconductor makers (e.g., Mikron, Sitronics). CDS, which was named one of the most innovative employers in 2007, leads in global electronic design innovation and can thus support the development of advanced semiconductors, consumer electronics, telecom equipment, and computer systems in Russia.

---

9. "Watch Out India," *The Economist,* May 6, 2006, 75–76.
10. Headquartered in San Jose, California, with sales offices, design centers, and research facilities around the world to serve the global electronics industry, Cadence reported 2007 revenues of approximately $1.6 billion and had 5,300 employees.

Figure 6.1. Main user segments for IT services in Russia, 2007.

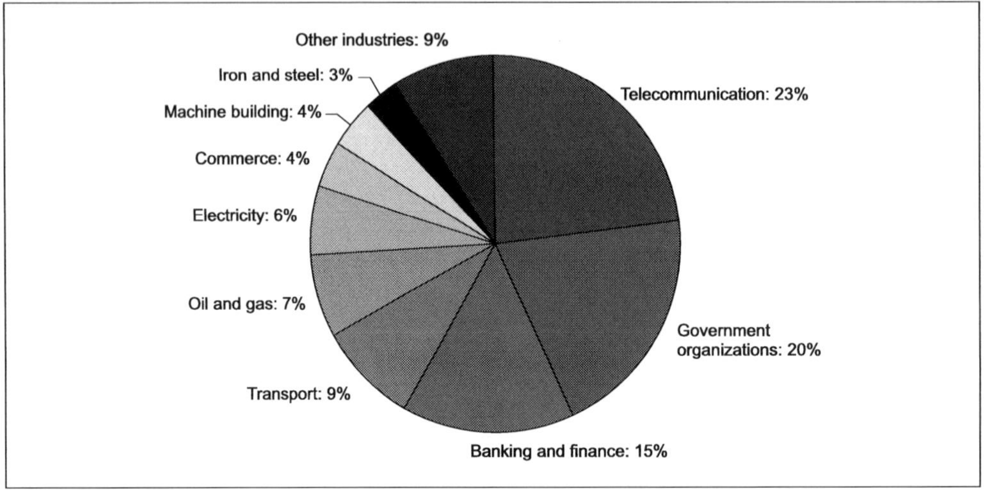

- Other industries: 9%
- Iron and steel: 3%
- Machine building: 4%
- Commerce: 4%
- Electricity: 6%
- Oil and gas: 7%
- Transport: 9%
- Banking and finance: 15%
- Government organizations: 20%
- Telecommunication: 23%

Source: Expert, 30 April 2007.

For Sun Microsystems from the United States, Russia has become the second-largest IT offshore development location after India. It employs three hundred programmers (2007) in its R&D center in St. Petersburg. Siemens and Microsoft also announced wide-ranging expansion plans. Similarly, Indian IT companies are opening subsidiaries in this new frontier market, which also covers Russian-speaking CIS countries.

Siemens and other EU suppliers of customized IT solutions (e.g., Efkon, Kapsch from Austria) are looking for solutions to decongest traffic in Moscow and St. Petersburg by installing intelligent transport systems (ITS) and satellite-radio communication. Russia's airports also require fail-safe traffic control and safety systems (e.g., supplied by Austria's Frequentis) that help minimize the risk of near misses against the backdrop of growing numbers of aircraft landings and departures. Local IT companies are scaling up their project managers, IT engineers, and hardware specialists to be able to offer their services as subcontractors.

Russia's advantage in IT and electronics lies in providing non-standard solutions for complex environments. The long tradition of science education, particularly in mathematics and physics, is a valuable asset. Russia's hardware experience in avionics, satellite systems, radar communications, and modern weaponry offers a good base for the design of advanced software packages with wide application potential in core industries (e.g., oil and gas, railways, transport). The Russian IT sector is characterized by many small and a few large players, such as Integrated Services Group, IBS Holding Group (including software developer Luxoft), Compulink, and Verysell. Turnover of the four biggest IT companies lies within the range of US$0.5–2 billion. Some of them, like IBS, have sold stakes to Western IT partners, including private equity funds and venture capitalists.

6.1.3. Challenges for foreign IT companies

A study carried out by Siemens Business Services (SBS) in Germany found that technically speaking 90% of IT and back-office services (e.g., billing, credit card applications, database management, toll-free customer service) can be externalized (see box 6.1). The biggest beneficiary will be India, where a software specialist costs ten times less than in Germany (€100/day against €1,000/day). The difference of a back-office person can be up to twenty times, depending on the level of social security contributions in the particular AM. India will remain the second leading player after the United States in global IT well into the 2020s. India outperforms all other AMs and is far ahead of China and Russia despite the wide-scale promotion programs of the governments of these two countries.

For EU companies, the choice between investing in the smaller new EU member states in Eastern Europe or the larger arena of China, India, or Russia can be a dilemma. While neighboring countries are easily accessible, the megamarkets offer two advantages: they can be used as a source of ideas (pool of specialists, joint venture partners) and simultaneously to increase sales (domestic customers, foreign investment community).

EU-based IT companies seek appropriate entry routes into the megamarkets by tying up with established locals. Some of them managed to accelerate market penetration via strategic partnerships. The stand-alone option is more complicated to put into practice except in customized IT applications where imitation is difficult. But partner spotting and selection has become a complex undertaking. India, for example, has thousands of IT boutiques, which are not easy to assess as they specialize in narrow niche markets (e.g., auto components, retailing, banking); many of them are located in Tier 1 and 2 cities.

Leading IT companies must apply strict selection criteria before engaging in collaborations or acquisitions in the megamarkets, including:

- high degree of specialization in determined verticals (e.g., banking, insurance)
- standardization of business models
- transparency of returns and costs
- consolidation of infrastructure and IT-based processes
- flexible and transparent contracts: clear definition of tasks and responsibilities
- business ethics
- quality orientation

Box 6.1. IT-enabled services that are increasingly externalized.
- Hardware installation and support
- Standard software installation and support
- Customized software applications
- Systems integration
- Network infrastructure management
- IT consultancy and training
- BPO/call centers: database administration (accounting, insurance, HR management), after-sales and engineering support, complaints management
- Business transformation and consulting

Competition for the best brains and cooperation partners is intense. In India, domestic companies offer very competitive salary packages to retain specialists or hire them away from competitors. In China and Russia, AM players are already challenged by Indian firms seeking to garner a larger share of the growing domestic IT markets.

6.2. Financial services

6.2.1. Global trends in financial services

Financial services—banking, insurance, as well as venture capital, private equity, and securities trading—have grown to great importance in the AMs, especially in the past twenty years. In the UK, financial intermediation accounts for about one-third of GDP, and it is thought that 30% of this figure is contributed by about 400,000 people in London working with IPOs, underwriting of insurance contracts, currency and commodity trading, and management of mutual funds, hedge funds, derivatives, and other financial instruments. Some of the capacity for these expanding and highly profitable activities[11] was created from the recasting of traditional clearing banks, building societies ("Savings & Loan" in USA), and brokerages into multinational financial trading houses.

Banks and other financial institutions in the megamarkets can at present only aspire to offer some of these advanced products and services. But they will learn from AM counterparts as they expand into these markets. Whether institutions in the megamarkets will be able to challenge the comparative advantage built up by London, New York, Tokyo, Paris, and Frankfurt in financial activities other than mainstream banking and insurance remains to be seen. So far, only two Chinese banks—Industrial and Commercial Bank of China (ICBC) and Bank of China—have made it into the list of the world's major banks. China, however, produced the highest number of new bank arrivals (seven) in the world's top one thousand. Meanwhile, AM banks, investment banks (e.g., Merrill Lynch), fund managers (e.g., Fidelity International), and charge card companies (e.g., American Express, Master Card, Visa) will strengthen their presence in the megamarkets to participate in the predicted fifteen to twenty years of growth in consumer and corporate finance.

EU banks have expanded far beyond their own local origins since the mid-1980s, but they face growing pressure from shareholders and regulators to cut costs and raise productivity. Some of them have enhanced their capitalization through mergers, minimizing redundancy, divestments, and acquisitions, followed by branch closures and staff cuts. The spectacular bid for ABN Amro by a consortium led by the Royal Bank of Scotland (helped by Hong Kong and Chinese investors) for an amount of over €100 billion in 2007 heralded what the *Sunday Times* (London) on December 16, 2007, called "the biggest financial services deal of all times." The 2006 acquisition of Germany's HypoVereinsbank by Unicredit, Italy, for €15.4 billion—at the time, the biggest cross-border deal in EU banking—already looks small in comparison. These and other expected spectacular transactions (e.g., possible merger of Unicredit and Société Générale) could stir Europe's mostly national banking structures into breaking down the barriers that block the single

---

11. Accounting in the US for 40% and in the UK for about 20% of all corporate profits. See "A Special Report on International Banking," *The Economist*, May 17, 2008, 22.

market for financial services. To play in the top league and overtake their US counterparts—Citigroup, Bank of America, and JP Morgan Chase—the leading EU banks (see table 6.6) must cross into new geographies and diversify away from the slow-growing, saturated Triad markets. Unicredit's interest in HBV is said to have been motivated mainly by the latter's control of Bank Austria, which has a wide branch network in Eastern Europe including Russia, a singular competitive advantage shared only by its Austrian rival, Raiffeisenbank. During 2006–2008, HSBC, BNP Paribas, Crédit Agricole, and Deutsche Bank grew mainly through acquisitions and operations in the emerging markets.

Table 6.6. The world's top fifteen banks, 1/1/2008.

	Sales (US$ bn)	Profits (US$ bn)
Citigroup, USA	159.2	3.6
HSBC Holdings, UK	146.5	19.1
BNP Paribas, France	140.7	10.7
Crédit Agricole, France	138.2	8.2
Deutsche Bank, Germany	122.6	8.9
Bank of America, USA	119.2	15.0
UBS, Switzerland	117.2	–3.7
JP Morgan Chase, USA	116.4	15.4
Royal Bank of Scotland, UK	108.4	15.1
Société Générale, France	103.4	1.3
Santander Group, Spain	89.3	12.4
Barclays, UK	80.3	8.8
Credit Suisse, Switzerland	78.2	6.5
Unicredit Group, Italy	77.0	8.2
Wachovia, USA	55.5	6.3

Source: Fortune 500. 2008. The Banker.

The increase in market capitalization of the large international banks, which made them attractive to stock markets and investors worldwide, came to a halt during 2007–2009 with the spread of the US subprime mortgage crisis. The high default rates on adjustable rate mortgages (ARM) granted to high-risk borrowers with lower income or less satisfactory credit history than "prime" borrowers[12] resulted in a global financial meltdown in the second half of 2008. By adopting "securitization" as a form of financial engineering, mortgage lenders had passed the rights to the mortgage payments and related credit/default risk to third-party investors via mortgage-based securities (MBS) and collateralized debt obligations (CDO). Corporate, individual, and institutional investors holding MBS or CDO suffered a contraction of liquidity as the value of the underlying mortgage assets declined with the falling home prices.

The dramatic repercussions of this crisis are poised to change the banking landscape across the world. Rising investor risk aversion, excessive exposure of bank balance sheets, and a general loss of confidence have led to bankruptcies in the industry and reduced lending to businesses and consumers. Even institutions formerly considered unshakable like Lehman Brothers, Merrill Lynch, AIG, Fannie Mae, and Freddie Mac have succumbed. Major banks, including heavyweights like Citigroup, Deutsche Bank, Royal Bank of Scotland, UBS and other financial institutions reported record losses of US$435 billion by August/September 2008, pulling down stock markets worldwide as well as economic growth.[13]

---

12. Loan incentives and a long-term trend of rising housing prices encouraged borrowers to assume mortgages, believing they would be able to refinance at more favorable terms later. However, once housing prices started to drop, refinancing became impossible, leading to defaults. In 2007, 1.3 million US housing properties were subject to foreclosures, up 75% from 2006 (see "US Foreclosure Activity Increases 79% in 2007." Realty Trac press release, www.realtytrac.com).

13. Economic growth figures were adjusted downward by 1–2 percentage points in the leading economies, some which (e.g. Spain, United Kingdom) are expected to even face negative growth in 2009–2010.

Many of the EU's major banks were unfortunately not spared. A survey conducted by the German Bundesbank revealed that Germany's 20 largest banks had "toxic securities" of €300 billion in their balance sheets at the end of 2008; just one-quarter of them had been written off. It is estimated that the exposure of all German banks taken together exceeds €1 trillion (€1000 billion), twenty times higher than the stimulus package approved by the federal government. Had there been a proactive policy to support more SMEs using only a fraction of these funds as loans, they would have been able to finance their investments in the emerging economies and generated better results.

Resource persons in the sector expect a long period of concentration into larger, diversified, or more specialized institutions that are less vulnerable to future crises while being tightly watched by regulators. Germany's expertise and competence in *Allfinanz*, a combination of universal banking (private and investment banking) and insurance, may offer models for creating diversified structures that offer varied financial products and are in a better position to overcome crises.[14] Some of the recent mergers combine banking and insurance interests to offer attractive *bancassurance* services. In Spain, for example, banks dominate the insurance market with 77% market share although prior to 1992 they were not allowed to distribute insurance products. In March 2007, HSBC acquired Erisa's life, property, and casualty operations in France. Consolidations from insurance toward banking seem to be less frequent than vice versa but may see a revival in the megamarkets. This model motivated Allianz's acquisition of a stake in China's ICBC bank although in Europe the insurer recently exited banking.[15] But there is also a reverse trend of shedding insurance interests by larger banking groups. In 2006, Crédit Suisse sold Winterthur Insurance to AXA for €7.9 billion so that it could concentrate on its core banking business. In a similar case, Banco Santander divested Abbey Life Insurance, which was taken over by Resolution for €5.2 billion. Many European banks appear to be moving away from ownership toward looser tie-ups with insurers aimed at enlarging the customer base and offering a wider product and service portfolio (e.g., Barclays-AEGON). In the wake of the financial crisis, banks started downsizing and specializing. In January 2009, Citigroup, after reporting a record fourth-quarter loss of almost US$10 billion, split into retail (Citicorp) and investment banking (Citi Holdings) that will hold the bank's riskier assets.[16]

Similar to banking, the global insurance industry is also witnessing a consolidation phase, which will be reinforced as a result of the financial crisis. Record volumes of M&As had already been reported during 2005–2007 (€25 billion in the EU alone). The continuing drive to develop competitive scale aims at consolidated portfolios, balanced earnings, benefits from diversified geographic presence, and enhanced capital and cash-flow strengths. Mono-line insurers (e.g., life, accident, health) will transform into diversified players offering the entire package. By merging, companies seek to expand distribution and achieve synergies outside their home markets. Tight margins and modest premium growth in

---

14. Germany has numerous public savings banks and large banks operating under the jurisdiction of the *Länder*; these *Sparkassen* and *Landesbanken* could well spearhead the creation of large European structures able to compete against the world's major banks.

15. Dresdner Bank was acquired by Allianz in 2004 but sold to Commerzbank in a transaction worth more than €10 billion in 2008.

16. "Citigroup loss raises anxiety over economy", *New York Times*, 16 January 2009.

established economies push operators into the uncharted territory of the megamarkets, where growing populations of cash-rich consumers and enterprises (foreign, local) promise high earnings. The potential for expansion in the megamarkets, and from there to other emerging economies is huge. In 2008, the world's top insurer Allianz realized only 5% of its total revenue in Asia, of which was not even 1% in China and 0.2% in India. Its competitors ING, AIG, AXA and Generali (see table 6.7) also still have a relatively weak presence in the megamarkets. On the other hand, megamarket insurers like China Life are acquiring know-how and climbing up the international rankings.

Table 6.7. The world's top fifteen insurance companies, 1/1/2008.

	Sales (US$ bn)	Profits (US$ bn)
ING, Netherlands	201.5	12.6
AXA, France	162.8	7.8
Allianz, Germany	140.6	10.9
Berkshire Hathaway, UK	118.2	13.2
Assicurazioni Generali, Italy	113.8	4.0
AIG, USA	110.0	6.2
Aviva, UK	81.3	2.7
Prudential, UK	66.4	2.0
Munich Re, Germany	64.8	5.3
Aegon, Netherlands	62.4	3.5
CNP Assurances, France	59.0	1.6
Nippon Life, Japan	57.9	2.3
Zurich Financial, Switzerland	55.2	5.6
Metlife, USA	53.2	4.3
China Life, China	43.4	2.9

Source: Forbes 500. 2008.

The large insurers, and particularly re-insurers, are the worst affected by climate change, whose catastrophic effects will adversely impact premium prices, reinsurance costs, and solvency requirements. Re-insurers such as Münchner Rück and Swiss Re will be in the frontline of any financial impact. With stock market liberalization and record savings, megamarkets offer new possibilities of local asset management, risk reduction, and securitization, especially through expanding pension schemes and life insurance policies.

6.2.2. Banking trends in the megamarkets

In all three megamarkets, deregulation in the banking sector is progressing at a fast pace. Authorities are opening the sector to foreign participation, but changes will be sequential, not abrupt, as banking and finance are considered a sensitive area where even minor shifts can destabilize capital markets and exchange rates, with negative effects for the national economy. The disastrous example of Russia, whose national currency collapsed in the late 1990s causing the government and major companies to default on all outstanding payments, was a warning to other emerging markets. Cooperation with the West is now viewed positively as a way to access the necessary know-how for reducing international financial risks and streamlining the sector. A parallel strategy consists in instructing central banks to amass foreign sufficient reserves so that authorities can inject liquidity into the banking sector in case of a crunch in the financial markets. While some Chinese banks are still cleaning up non-performing loans, a problem compounded by their recent exposure to the US subprime mortgage market,[17] Indian and Russian banks have lately been more cautious with their lending operations, also because supervision has been tightened and performance checked by authorities.

---

17. "Chinese Banks on a Gambling Expedition," *The Economist,* September 1, 2007, 62.

INDIA

India's banking sector grew at an average annual rate of about 20%–25% during 2002–2007. This rhythm is expected to be maintained until 2015 as the demand for banking and financial services from the growing middle class far exceeds the supply of banking institutions and outlets, particularly in rural India. The number of financially excluded households is around 135–150 million, second only after China; 15–20 million households are added to the bankable pool each year as potential customers of financial institutions.

According to figures released by Indian Banks Association, Indian banks generated revenues of US$82 billion during 2007–2008 (see table 6.8). This figure is poised to at least treble by 2015. State-owned banks account for 67% of deposits. The shares of private (e.g., ICICI, HDFC) and foreign banks are small at around 24% and 9%, respectively, but private banks have been gaining 1% market share on average each year since 1993. Off-balance sheet business is, however, dominated by foreign banks (70%).

India's banking industry is formed by 169 scheduled commercial banks including nationalized, private, foreign, regional, rural, and cooperative banks. The biggest bank is the State Bank of India (2008 revenue: US$12.8 billion), a bank with 10,000 branches (plus 5,100 branches of its associate banks), eighty-four international offices in thirty-two countries, and 180,000 employees. It is followed by ICICI Bank, which is the largest private sector bank (2008 revenue: US$8.7 billion). The largest of the twenty-nine foreign banks in India is Citibank with revenue in 2008 of US$1.8 billion, followed by Standard Chartered Bank and HSBC.

Personal finance and investment banking services are both in high demand. The most popular personal finance products are deposits, credit cards, mutual funds, mortgages, and consumer loans. In investment banking, which includes services for initial public offers (IPOs), there will be pressure on margins due to competition from M&A specialists (Goldman Sachs, consulting companies). SMEs form an important customer segment. Changes are expected in traditional corporate lending, which will be enhanced by off–balance sheet project finance and fee-based products such as cash management, forex (foreign exchange) services, and trade finance.

Despite progress, India remains one of the most underbanked markets among large economies, especially for modern retail products. Credit card holders represent only 8%

Table 6.8. Revenue of Indian banks, 2000–2010 (US$ bn, shares in %).

	2000	2004	2008	2010
State-owned banks	14.5 (84%)	24.5 (74%)	55 (67%)	74.0 (58%)
Private banking	2.8 (15%)	6.5 (20%)	19.5 (24%)	38.5 (30%)
Foreign banks	0.2 (1%)	2.5 (6%)	7.5 (9%)	15.5 (12%)
Total	17.5 (100%)	33.5 (100%)	82.0 (100%)	128.0 (100%)

Source: Indian Banks' Association. 2007.

of the bankable population[18] (2% of the total population), but their number is growing at 25%–30% annually. Consumer loans are well below international benchmarks, but they are growing at more than 20% annually, according to ICICI analysts, backed by high demand from a growing middle class with rising incomes, despite high interest rates.

The coming years for Indian banking will be characterized by:

- new products and services including credit cards, consumer finance, and wealth management in retail banking, and fee-based income and investment banking in corporate banking;
- higher interest rates, which will impact the weaker banks;
- increased interest in India from foreign banks and therefore more intense competition;
- demand for enhanced institutional capabilities and service levels of banks from more aware customers;
- fuller capital account convertibility requiring more vigilant risk management; and
- spread of e-banking and similar technologies, which will bring in new financial players as financial intermediaries and move transactions from the branch to Internet banking.

India's banking sector is regulated by the Reserve Bank of India (RBI), the country's central bank. Foreign banks can now hold up to 74% of an Indian bank (20% in the case of a public sector bank), provided any acquisition of shares exceeding 5% is notified to the RBI for approval. On February 28, 2005, the RBI issued a "Roadmap for Foreign Banks," together with "Guidelines on Ownership and Governance" of private banks in India. But various restrictions, including the number of branches foreign banks are allowed to add in a year (fifteen in 2007), are likely to be relaxed. Foreign banks will be granted full freedom of operation in April 2009, but the RBI will maintain its case-by-case discretionary powers so that it can extend the deadline if it deems that the Indian banking sector is still vulnerable. The government wants to give time to local banks so that they can consolidate their positions and scale up their operations before facing strong foreign competition. Meanwhile, the government and RBI are encouraging Indian banks to increase their size and efficiency through M&As. The opening up of the sector to foreign ownership and competition will have a far-reaching impact. A paradigm shift is expected over the next five to ten years as a result of the greater presence of international banks in India and the expansion of Indian banks into foreign markets.

The Indian system is more or less non-discriminatory vis-à-vis foreign and Indian banks. There are currently twenty-nine foreign banks operating in India, some for many decades; the five largest ones are Citigroup, Standard Chartered, HSBC, ABN Amro, and Deutsche Bank. They are issued a single class of banking license and do not have to upgrade from lower to higher class as in certain countries. In this way, they share the same level playing field as Indian banks. Foreign banks are allowed to establish non-banking financial subsidiaries. Prudential norms are the same as for Indian banks. No restriction is placed on the type of business routed through a foreign bank (e.g., FII business).

---

18. This could be because of the large undeclared cash part of the economy.

India's banking policies are benchmarked with international norms and best practices. Capital adequacy norms are now under the Basel II regime. The focus is on better corporate governance based on "fit and proper" criteria, on higher equity levels and integrated risk management systems, and on promoting market discipline through more transparent disclosure standards. The Board for Financial Supervision was constituted in 1994 to ensure a safe and robust banking system. Thanks to the multidimensional regulatory and supervisory measures taken by the Reserve Bank of India, prudential parameters have improved significantly, making India's banking system comparable to the best in the world—for example, India has among the lowest ratios of non-performing loans as a percentage of GDP.

These factors helped to cushion the impact of the 2008 financial crisis, which spread from the United States to Europe. "In India, we never had anything close to the subprime loan," said Chanda Kochhar, ICICI's CEO.[19] "All lending to individuals is based on their income. We never gave more money to a borrower because the value of the house had gone up. Our non-performing loans are less than 1%." Dr. Y. V. Reddy, former governor of the RBI, introduced stringent lending standards as early as 2006 to protect banks from a real estate bubble and leveraged lending. One of RBI's first moves was to ban the use of bank loans for purchasing raw land; developers could borrow only for construction and when they started building. Securitizations and derivatives were popular instruments elsewhere, but in India their use was sharply curtailed. The RBI also banned off-balance-sheet vehicles to hide debt, which incited banks to recover the loans. Risk weightings were increased on commercial buildings and shopping mall construction, doubling the amount of capital banks were required to hold in reserve. As a result, no Indian bank had to be bailed out during the financial crisis. Today, India has a healthy banking sector enjoying a comfortable capital base. The country's foreign debt and debt service is low; its foreign reserve cover and high domestic saving rate (34% of GDP) offer additional stability.

Russia

Stricter supervision and reforms in Russia's banking sector after the 1998 financial crisis have resulted in a much leaner and more transparent industry. The number of banks has decreased each year as undercapitalized institutions are forced to close down. Licenses are taken back from banks whose loan portfolios significantly exceed deposits held by corporate and private clients. In 2008, the number of banks dropped by 650 units compared with ten years earlier (see figure 6.2). Out of today's (2008) 1,050 registered banks, only 60% are traditional banks; the rest belong to either companies or investment funds. The reshuffling is expected to continue well into the 2010s.

The government is determined to have a competitive and stable banking sector. For this reason, it will maintain its stake in major banks such as Sberbank, VTB, Moscow Bank, and Gazprombank (see table 6.9). However, state participation in the banking sector has been reduced in recent years. The strategic objective of the Russian government and Central Bank is to ensure efficient banking services in a competitive environment consisting of large multidivisional (universal) banks, medium-sized specialists, and leading foreign

---

19. "How India avoided a crisis," *The New York Times,* December 19, 2008.

Figure 6.2. Number of banks in Russia, 1998–2010.

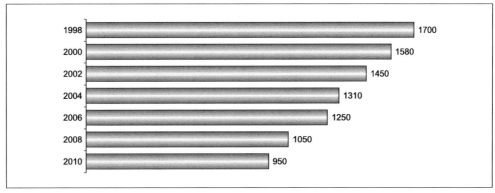

Source: Russian Central Bank. 2008.

institutions. In recent years, Russia's banking system has been progressively opened to foreign capital, which now represents 20%–25% of banking assets.

Russia's citizens are gradually regaining faith in the national banking system after the consecutive financial defaults and turmoil of the 1990s. But banks for them are still sources for loans and not custodians of their savings. It is estimated that only 35%–50% of Russians deposit their money in banks. On the other hand, the newfound predilection for spending has led to a steep rise in consumer loans: from Rbl16 billion in 2000 to Rbl4.5 trillion in 2007 (US$180 billion), or 35% more than in 2006. Credit offered to private households is expected to

Table 6.9. Russia's largest banks by assets and profits, 1/11/2008 (US$ bn).

	Assets	Profits
Sberbank	225.7	5.30
VTB-Vneshtorgbank	82.4	0.40
Gazprombank	44.5	0.30
Rosselchosbank	26.9	0.10
Bank Moskvy	26.0	0.25
Alfa Bank	23.1	0.46
Unicredit	21.7	0.40
VTB 24	20.3	0.26
Raiffeisenbank Austria	19.4	0.33
Rosbank	16.5	0.12
Uralsib	15.4	0.15
Promsvjazbank	14.5	0.20

Source: Profil, 22 December 2008.

reach a record volume of US$250 billion by 2010. According to data published by the Central Bank, 83% of consumer loans are granted in Greater Moscow, but significant increases have also been recorded in second-tier cities such as St. Petersburg, Yekaterinburg, Kazan, and Novosibirsk. The surge in consumption and lending in recent years prompts fears of a bubble, which Russia's optimistic bankers believe to be unjustified. According to an Alfabank director "Our loans have comfortable margins. Risk-related costs are included in our calculations. Russia's real estate market is unaffected by the US/UK subprime crisis, and our natural resources will secure us robust growth. Consumer finance and corporate banking will be our drivers."

Another trend for large banks is to strengthen their positions in near-abroad (CIS, Eastern Europe) and far-abroad (China, EU) regions. The main task of Ex-Economics Minister G. Gref since he took over as new chairman of Sberbank in 2007 will be to help Russia's biggest bank to internationalize its operations while raising efficiency levels. In February 2008, Russia's second-largest bank, VTB-Vneshtorgbank, opened its first branch in Shanghai, China.

Leading foreign banks are entering the Russian market now that it has become more predictable. In 2007, Austria's Raiffeisen took over Impeksbank and France's Société Générale acquired 10% of Rosbank. The combined value of these two deals amounted to roughly US$1 billion. Other banks, such as Deutsche Bank and Italy's Unicredit (the new owner of International Moscow Bank), are increasing their market shares by acquiring stakes in Russian entities while expanding their branch networks. Foreign banks plan to enhance investment banking (for corporates, IPOs) and private banking (consumer lending, mortgages) services. Switzerland's UBS, for example, is planning to extend its wealth management expertise, which it offers to rich Russian individuals abroad, to the local high-net-worth segment.

China

China's future economic stability will depend on the health of its financial institutions. Political leaders have shown a strong commitment to banking reform and transparency. Since 1998, the government has injected about US$280 billion into the top four banks so that they can shift bad debts into separate state-backed companies. China's leaders drew this lesson from the crises in Russia, South Korea, Thailand, and Japan. To prevent the long paralysis of Japan's indebted financial system, China has pumped in funds to avert a possible financial melt-down. China's banks have adopted Western accounting standards and work under regulatory and prudential requirements based on the norms for Western banks. During 2006–2008, the ceiling for compulsory reserves to be held by banks with the Central Bank was raised several times to attain 15% of all deposits in mid-2008. To supervise lending activities, the China Banking Regulatory Commission (CBRC) was carved out from China's Central Bank in 2003. The regulator is forcing banks to shift their focus from loan and deposit growth to preserving adequate capital and generating adequate returns on it. Starting from January 2008, lenders that cannot meet a capital ratio of 12%[20] of risk-weighted assets (Basel I standard) face sanctions, including the replacement of top management. CBRC also forced the top five banks to deny credits to some thirty energy-intensive, high-polluting enterprises in 2007.[21] The regulatory agency's 20,000 staff is ensuring compliance across the country. As a result, almost all of China's 128 commercial banks have introduced better governance, shareholding, and incentive structures. Many of them have hired independent directors onto their boards in an effort to change old practices, such as the negotiation and approval of loans by the same person, a practice that led to non-performing loans and corruption.

Overall business results of domestic banks were fueled by China's economic boom, which stimulated average annual loan growth to 16% and deposit growth to 18% during 2000–2007. Lending to consumers, which started only in 1997, increased 123-fold to more than US$420 billion in 2007. Corporate loans still dominate, but mortgages and automobile and education loans now make up 11% of the total and 26% of new lending (against 1.5% in 1999). Strong revenue growth and the offloading of bad debts onto the government in 2006–2007 made banks more profitable.[22] In 2007, the return on equity (ROE)

---

20. Twice the level it was in 2003.
21. "China's Top Banks Lend RMB 100 Billion in 2007 for Green Projects" *Xinhua Press*, February 26, 2008.
22. This practice seems to have inspired US authorities following the Wall Street crash on September 17, 2008.

of China's top thirteen banks was 12%. Banks reported record capitalization during 2006–2007. The largest Chinese bank, ICBC, has even made it into the world's top ten company rankings, together with PetroChina and China Mobile.[23] ICBC has 120 million private customers, 10 million corporate clients, and 22,500 branches across China.

Whether this model can be maintained in the future is questionable. Government efforts to check a lending boom and put a cap on exploding real estate prices since

Table 6.10. China's leading banks by assets, 2007 (US$ bn).

Industrial & Commercial Bank of China (ICBC)	685
Bank of China (BOC)	516
China Construction Bank (CCB)	472
Agricultural Bank of China (ABC)	455
Bank of Communication (BoComm)	138
China Merchants Bank	78
Shanghai Pudong Development Bank	61
China Minsheng Bank	58
Huaxia Bank	52
Shenzhen Development Bank	43

Source: China Banking Regulatory Commission (CBRC). 2008.

2006 have put significant pressure on Chinese banks. On their government-imposed reserves, banks receive a meager 2% interest. Typically, they earn 5% on loans, compared with 3% paid to depositors. The loan-to-deposit ratio for Chinese banks is a modest 68%, which restricts profitability in the long run. This poses a huge investment challenge, because lending should be their most lucrative business. Alternative assets are in short supply. The domestic bond market is thin, ironically because the Chinese government restricts competition for banks. The biggest of them (see table 6.10) thus began to hunt abroad for more lucrative assets, whose risks their management could not fully assess. On August 23, 2007, Bank of China revealed that it held US$9.6 billion (18% of shareholders' equity) exposure to securities backed by American subprime mortgages.[24] ICBC and CCB both disclosed exposures exceeding US$1 billion. Such losses may look small compared with the three banks' earnings and equity, but the financial loss could still be severe if larger amounts are to be written off or if there is more exposure in uncharted grounds in the future. Flush with cash from their public offers and from strong growth at home, Chinese banks have the chance to press into foreign markets, but they will need to tread cautiously.

FDI via M&As in China's banking sector is restricted to 25% of the capital. Hence, although foreign banks have started to invest significant amounts, their minority share in partnerships (see table 6.11) does not allow them to influence strategy or improve corporate governance. Bank of America paid US$3 billion for its 15% stake in CCB, China's third-largest bank. HSBC, Citigroup, BNP Paribas, and Deutsche Bank have all taken minority stakes in local banks totaling several billion US dollars. The Chinese government will gradually raise foreign ownership limits in line with WTO commitments, but it is unlikely to relinquish control of a major bank in the near future. The authorities still do not believe that by preventing foreign takeovers they may simply be delaying banking reform and that they will have to fund more costly bailouts in the future, as was done in Poland and the Czech Republic for several banks. The Chinese government optimistically believes that the Chinese banking system can be modernized without M&As from abroad. Banks are urged to streamline their operations and go public. The authorities believe that Chinese

---

23. "Chinese Companies," *The Economist*, September 1, 2007.
24. "Chinese Banks on a Gambling Expedition," *The Economist*, September 1, 2007.

Table 6.11. Banking participations in China, 2005–2007.

Foreign bank	Local bank in which stake was taken	Stake (%)	Transaction price (US$ mn)
Bank of America	China Construction Bank-CCB	15	3,000
HSBC	BoComm	20	1,750
Hangseng/IFC	Industrial Bank	25	326
ING/IFC	Bank of Beijing	20	215
HSBC/IFC	Bank of Shanghai	16	209
Newbridge Capital	Shenzhen Development Bank	18	145
Standard Chartered	Bohai Bank	19	120
Commonwealth Bank of Australia	Hangzhou Bank	20	77
Citigroup	Pudong Development Bank	5	72
BNP Paribas/IFC	Nanjing City Commercial Bank	15	26
Temasek Singapore/IFC	Minsheng Bank	5.55	23
DEG/KfW	Nanchong City Commercial Bank	13	4

Source: Handelsblatt, July 12, 2007.

bankers will gain experience also in complex cross-border asset-allocation decisions. The government is observing how other countries react to outward FDI from Chinese banks and will respond accordingly.[25]

Foreign banks kept on incorporating and expanding in China throughout 2008, but some of them had to sell part of their stakes in order to compensate for losses caused by the global financial meltdown.[26] Limited exposure to toxic financial derivatives has put Chinese banks in a better position than many of their Western counterparts to weather the financial crisis. The coming years will test the capacity of Chinese banks in internal risk management, crisis control and tighter checks of creditworthiness of borrowers.

6.2.3. Insurance trends in the megamarkets

The collapse and bailout of the world's largest insurance company, American Insurance General (AIG),[27] marks the start of a transformation of the insurance world, already shaken by natural catastrophes and terrorism. This world has been dominated by the United States (30% of world market), Japan, the United Kingdom, Germany, and other AMs, but the megamarkets are expanding fast and represent attractive new environments for AM insurers. World insurance premiums (life and non-life) totaled US$4.06 trillion in 2007, according to Swiss Re. By 2020, the megamarkets could together realistically capture at least 10% of the total world volume.

---

25. The US administration scrutinizes deals involving Chinese banks trying to acquire shares of US banks. It does so through the Fed, which must approve transactions in which a foreign investor takes more than a 5% stake in a US bank.
26. In January 2009, Bank of America sold a 13-percent stake in China Construction Bank at a profit for US$2.83 billion. See "BoA trims stake in Construction Bank," *China Daily*, January 8, 2009. The same month, Royal Bank of Scotland, one of the three banks bailed out by the UK government in October 2008, decided to sell its 4.3% stake (worth US$4.2 billion) in Bank of China as part of a review of its international assets.
27. AIG's capitalization dropped by 70% in September 2008.

CHINA

China will probably be the first emerging country to reach an insurance market size of US$100 billion by 2012 (2.5%–3% of world market). Interest in health, accident, and other types of insurance has surged in recent years. The removal of price controls for doctors, hospitals, and medicine has made many state health insurance schemes obsolete. Prospects for insurance specialists are promising as Chinese families need to plan better for "three fundamental pillars": children's education, health, and retirement. With a savings rate of 40% of GDP (the highest among large economies), China offers great promise for all kinds of insurance products. In 2007, less than 4% of the population was insured; only 10% had subscribed to a health insurance. Citizens subscribe to private health policies, often in combination with life, accident, or damage policies. With annual sales of €5 billion, China's health insurance market is five times smaller than Germany's (€27 billion). In 2007, China was already the eighth-largest life insurance market in the world with premiums amounting to US$38.5 billion (see table 6.12).

Table 6.12. China's insurance market, 2005, 2007.

	2005 (€ bn)	2007 (€ bn)
Total premiums	37.7	58.0
Life insurance	25.9	38.5
Accident/damage insurance	9.4	15.0
Health insurance	2.4	4.5

Source: Pin An. China. 2007.

Prospects for all insurance products will remain good in China for a number of reasons:

- The population is aging and already feeling the consequences of the one-child policy. By 2040, every third Chinese will be over sixty years of age. Thanks to medical progress, the 1-2-4 formula (1 child will have to look after 2 parents and 4 grandparents) will reverse the previous practice when 4 grandchildren looked after 2 parents and 1 grandparent. It has taken hardly two generations for China to reach the aging process that took around a century in Western Europe.

- Chinese citizens have few possibilities to invest their savings. Share markets are volatile, foreign assets are difficult to acquire, and the state-imposed interest of 2% on savings accounts is lower than the official inflation rate. Life insurance and private pension schemes provide alternatives.

- The rural areas, where several hundred million people are not covered by state insurance, represent a huge potential market.

- Health policies cover mainly hospitalization and surgical operation expenses, and, exceptionally, certain serious diseases. Service providers can fill other niches such as dental care.

- China's health infrastructure is hampered by the lack of good hospitals in the rural areas and of private doctors and clinics; cheating is also rampant (whole family is treated under one policy, wrong invoices are issued, long queues can be avoided through personal connections, etc.).[28]

---

28. "China schafft neuen Versicherungsmarkt" [China creates new insurance market], *Handelsblatt*, August 12, 2005, 20.

- Regulations have been relaxed. Previously, health and life insurance had to be offered by a single provider. Insurance products can now be sold separately, and consumers are getting used to selecting what they need.

The largest life insurers—China Life, Ping An, and China Pacific—are state-owned; they control 90% of the market. The twenty or so foreign life insurance companies present in China together account for only 3% of the market. In the big cities of Beijing and Shanghai, their share is higher, between 5% and 10%.[29] For foreign players, it is difficult to expand as their expansion is geographically restricted.[30] Acquisitions of controlling stakes in local companies are forbidden; even alliances are strictly regulated. Companies need permits from regional and local authorities to sell policies in their territories. Most foreign companies are compelled to accept minority stakes in Chinese insurers or large banks involved in insurance operations. Allianz, for example, bought a 2.5% stake in ICBC for US$1 billion and cooperates with Dazhong Life in developing life insurance. Its competitors, Prudential (UK), AIG (USA), Generali (Italy), and HSBC (UK) have similar arrangements with other mostly state-owned companies. Pressured by an overinsured home market, Japan's Mitsui Life, Sumitomo Life, Asahi Life, and Dai-Ichi Mutual Life also decided to participate in the growing Chinese market.

In health insurance, Germany's DKV has acquired a stake of 19% in China's state-owned PICC Health. This strategic partnership aims to develop innovative health-related insurance products specially suited to the Chinese consumer. PICC is one of the first five companies to be granted a license to offer private health policies by the state's insurance authority in 2005. PICC opened its regional branch offices in Beijing, Shanghai, Qingdao, and Shenzen. Foreign players base their strategies on two competitive advantages—their global spread and their long-standing expertise in asset management.

INDIA

The largest number of life insurance policies in force in the world is in India. As the average Indian's life insurance spending increases—it is already 5.4 times more than in 2000—the life insurance segment has the potential to reach US$100 billion by 2012. Insurance is a US$41 billion industry in India, which grew by 36% in 2007 over the previous year.[31] Insurance contributes around 4% to India's GDP. But penetration levels are low. India has an insurable population of 300 million, of which only 15% is insured, according to MetLife India. The penetration rate of both life and non-life insurance is only 4.1% and 0.6%, respectively. One of the reasons for the low rate for life insurance is that it was promoted mainly as a tax-saving option. This perception has changed as private players have linked it to family protection and added an interest-based savings dimension, which has proved to be popular.

---

29. "Chinesen müssen selbst für sich sorgen" [Chinese must take care of themselves], *Handelsblatt,* September 7, 2006.
30. Licenses are issued by the province and not the federal authorities, so any company needs to apply again and again to expand business.
31. Life insurance: US$35 billion; non-life insurance: US$5.6 billion (of which 56% is from motor and health segments). See Investment Commission of India: http://www.investmentcommission.in/insurance.htm.

Insurance expenses amount to US$6 per inhabitant, which is insignificant even when compared with countries like South Korea (US$1,400). Experts predict that market volume will double every four to five years, especially in the health, life, and pension segments. Although still smaller than the markets of South Korea or Thailand, India's insurance market, given the large population, will rise to third position in Asia after China and Japan, thus opening excellent prospects for EU players.

Until the sector was opened to private and foreign companies in 2000, India's insurance sector was dominated by the state-owned Life Insurance Corporation (LIC) for life and General Insurance Corporation (GIC) for non-life. LIC accounts for 75% of premiums in its segment; in non-life, the six state companies account for 66%. Since 2000, sixteen private players have entered the life segment and eleven private players, almost all joint ventures with foreign players, operate in the non-life segment (see table 6.13).

Table 6.13. India's largest insurers, 2007.

Company	Premiums (US$ mn)
a. Life insurance	
Public sector	
LIC	13,642
Private sector	
ICICI Prudential	1,281
Bajaj Allianz	1,041
HDFC Standard Life	395
Birla Sun Life	214
Tata AIG	156
b. Non-life insurance	
Public sector	
New India Assurance	1,222
National Insurance	929
Oriental Insurance	960
United India Insurance	855
Private sector	
ICICI Lombard	732
Bajaj Allianz	440
IFFCO Tokio	280
Reliance General Insurance	222
Tata AIG	180

Source: Insurance Regulatory and Development Authority (IRDA). 2008.

Foreign companies have reacted positively to the opening of the Indian insurance market. At present, the limit of their shareholding in a joint venture is 26%, but one of the priorities of the government is to raise this limit to 49%. The combination of local knowledge and foreign processes has created successes like Bajaj Allianz (Bajaj Finserve 74%, Allianz 26%). Created in 2001, Bajaj Allianz is today India's biggest private automobile insurer and is emerging as a strong player in the other segments. It has developed innovative products such as schemes for women and children. Bajaj Allianz's strength is its distribution network of 1,000 offices that can be found even in small towns and its 125,000 agents.[32] It is the largest private player, with a market share that more than doubled to 7.6% in 2006. Other companies like Prudential, Aviva (both UK), and Standard Life (USA) have selected strong Indian partners as well. Farsighted insurers are moving into Tier 2 and 3 cities to tap the large rural market.

RUSSIA

Russia's insurance sector, the fastest-growing in Europe, is also expanding at a fast pace. In 2006, policy revenue in Russia was already 2.5 times higher than in Poland and 4

---

32. In comparison, LIC has 1 million agents and ICICI Prudential has 100,000. See "Bajaj Allianz's Big Success Story," *Business Standard*, October 5, 2006.

Table 6.14. Insurance markets in Russia and Eastern Europe, 2007.

	Sales (US$ bn)	Density (US$/inhabitant)
Russia	16.0	75
Poland	7.0	148
Czech Republic	4.0	280
Hungary	3.0	195
Slovenia	2.0	570
Ukraine	1.5	17
Slovakia	1.3	160
Croatia	1.0	175
Romania	1.0	35

Source: Swiss Re. 2007.

Table 6.15. Russia's largest insurers, 2007.

	Premiums (US$ mn)	Share (%)
Rosgosstrach	1,200	21.6
Reso-Garantia	458	9.1
Ingostrach	417	8.4
Uralsib	237	4.7
Rosno/Allianz	175	3.5
Zurich Retail	154	3.1
NSG	142	2.8
Alfa Insurance	125	2.5
Standard Reserv	121	2.4
Soglasie	120	2.4
VSK	118	2.4
Slasskie Vorota	96	1.9
Renessans	84	1.7

Source: Expert. No. 19. May 12–18, 2008. Page 129. Insurance Panorama.

times that in the Czech Republic (see table 6.14). Russia's low insurance density (per capita revenue) makes it more attractive than the smaller markets of Eastern Europe, which have saturated. Unlike China, where life insurance policies are more in demand, Russians are more interested in non-life insurance products: motor, casualty, health, home and building, travel, as well as legal insurance for top managers. Russians are not accustomed to underwriting life insurance policies, but even this segment is expected to record double-digit growth during 2008–2015. In 2006, the average Russian spent only €5 on life insurance compared with more than €70 in Poland and above €2,000 in Switzerland. Motor insurance has benefited from the introduction of the statutory cover in 2005; it is expected to grow tenfold over the next ten years.

Apart from specialized insurance providers (see table 6.15), oil and gas majors such as Lukoil, Gazprom, and Surgutneftegaz have increased their stakes in this lucrative market. In the early 1990s, foreign insurers were only allowed to sell life and non-life policies as minority shareholders. The sector was liberalized in 2004, enabling foreign investors to acquire majority stakes or create new life insurance companies. In 2007, Germany's Allianz acquired a controlling stake in Rosno, the third-largest Russian insurer, for €1.5 billion from the Sistema Group; Allianz provides insurance-related know-how and capital while the Russian partner is responsible for marketing and expansion of the sales network (140 branches across Russia in 2007). Rosno is the market leader in private health insurance, which contributes more than one-third of its revenue. In a similar move, AXA acquired 36.7% of Reso-Garantia, Russia's second-largest insurer, for €810 million in early 2008. Other foreign players also plan to raise their stakes in the Russian market: AIG (USA),[33] Aviva (UK), Generali (Italy), ERGO (Germany), and Zurich Versicherungen (Switzerland). Russian insurance companies are valued at 1.8–2 times their gross written premiums, but the rate may rise as more foreign companies start prospecting for local partners.

---

33. This strategy will probably have to be revised against the backdrop of the 2008 financial crisis in the United States.

6.2.4. Challenges for foreign banks and insurance companies

Ever since the Russian government relaxed the rules for foreign companies, the number of M&As has increased. Looking beyond Moscow, foreign banks are buying into established branch networks across regional markets, where modern banking is underrepresented. Some banks have chosen the independent route of organic growth. For example, UK's HSBC—"the world's largest local bank"—will pump US$200 million into a network of newly opened retail subsidiaries starting in 2008.[34]

In China and India, the financial sector is expected to attract FDI despite restrictions. China imposes minority participation in both banking and insurance, India in insurance (but 74% is allowed in banking). Some foreign-Chinese alliances hardly expand because the Chinese partner engages in collaborations with various partners (e.g., Deutsche Bank and Credit Suisse with ICBC to develop investment banking and syndicated loans), which causes distrust that savoir-faire might trickle to a direct competitor. Lessons from other industries (e.g., cars) show that multi-partner joint ventures often fail. In India, foreign banks are overcoming the restriction on the number of branches to be opened in one year by appointing direct agents and exploring non-branch channels (rural fairs, association with retailers, etc.).

In insurance, Russia seems to be the most liberal, which explains the new wave of M&As led by the likes of Raiffeisen Bank, Société Générale, Unicredit, and Allianz. In their portfolios of acquisitions, dealmakers also include healthy regional banks with a good customer base and branch network. A key factor of success is the reputation, competence, and spread of the target. Foreign insurers and banks need to pay close attention to the choice of assets, appropriate structuring of the transaction, and related tax, accounting, and regulatory issues.

6.3. Retailing and commerce

6.3.1. Global retail trends

Retailing generates between 10% and 12% of national GDP and employment in the advanced economies and up to an average of 20%–25% in the emerging markets. Small enterprises remain numerically significant in both AMs and EMs. Single-store businesses account for 95% of all US retail establishments and generate about 47% of US retail sales. In Italy, the ratios are similar, while Germany and France both report much higher concentration levels. Powerful retail groups pursue their expansion by opening new stores in city agglomerations, launching new formats, and squeezing out small-scale independent shopkeepers, whose business prospects shrink, particularly in low-density residential areas in city suburbs. In the United Kingdom, Tesco has used this strategy to achieve a position in which its stores attract £1 in every £8 that British consumers spend. Competition is particularly fierce in AMs, so margins are low. In Germany, average sales margins of large

---

34. The company justifies its late entry compared with Austrian and German banks by highlighting that Russia's middle class is taking shape and now needs wider choices in retail banking and mortgage products. See "HSBC Foray into Russia: New CEO and US$200 Million," *The Moscow Times,* March 13, 2008.

grocery retailers have come down to below 1%. They need to keep generating higher volumes to compensate for low margins.

In many countries, large retailers have introduced their own brands ("private" or "distributor's" labels). They are thus in a position to enforce their recommended prices, quality, and delivery standards. Spurred by competition, retailers have to continually innovate their offers and improve customer relations. They have to streamline their supply chains to reduce costs, cut prices, and expand market share.

The life cycle of retail format innovations has dramatically shortened. For example, while department stores took more than one hundred years to reach maturity, warehouse clubs reached the end of their lifecycle in less than ten years. Retail companies have to keep churning out new concepts (e.g., Tesco's Fresh & Easy groceries in the US, Quick's tiny 24/7 convenience outlets in China), because competitors find ways to copy a model even before it reaches critical mass. "In retailing there aren't any barriers to entry," says Sir Terry Leahy, Tesco's CEO.[35] AM players also face stiff competition from the megamarkets, where innovations are copied, adapted, and brought to market quickly by dynamic local entrepreneurs.

Large retailers are compelled to stay in the vanguard and globalize their operations (sales, purchasing) by investing in high-profit locations. In its Global Retail Development Index (GRDI), AT Kearney, a consultancy monitoring the sector, considered Asia as the most attractive investment destination for retailing in 2005–2009. Central and Eastern European countries like Poland, Czech Republic, and Hungary, which topped the ranking up to the mid-2000s, are already facing high format density in most categories coupled with the saturation of domestic consumption, similar to Western Europe and America. Asia and Latin America as "young" continents offer new scopes for expansion.

Apart from Wal-Mart, US retailers[36] have been slower than their EU rivals in moving to the megamarkets and smaller high-growth emerging markets (e.g., Viet Nam, Chile, Argentina). While Europe's top seven retailers have all strengthened their presence in Russia, US retailers remain focused on domestic consumers and those living in neighboring NAFTA countries (Canada, Mexico), whose shopping habits are familiar to them. The share of turnover realized abroad is self-explanatory. Whereas 50%–55% of Metro's and Carrefour's sales are increasingly generated outside their home countries, Wal-Mart realizes only 22% of its turnover abroad. Presence, however, does not automatically fetch profits. Many Metro stores in China have apparently not yet broken even after many years of operation, although the company keeps expanding.

Thanks to its dominant position at home (4,100 stores), Wal-Mart is the world's largest retailer with sales exceeding US$379 billion in 2007. Wal-Mart employs 1.9 million people in the United States and more than 400,000 abroad. It sells 3.5 times more goods than the world's second-largest retailer, Carrefour. Even if Europe's three mega retailers, Carrefour, Tesco, and Metro, would merge, their sales would still be less than Wal-Mart's. Concentration moves can be observed worldwide. In 2007, Europe's top ten food retailers accounted

---

35. "Briefing Tesco. Fresh, but Far from Easy," *The Economist,* June 23, 2007, 77–79.
36. For example, Home Depot, Kroger, Target, Cosco, and Walgreens (pharmacy, drugstore).

for 42% of total sales, ten points more than in 1999 (see table 6.16). The 2008 financial crisis will accelerate the trend toward consolidation. Some well-known brands (Woolworth and Zavvi, UK; Circuit City, Mervyns, Levitz Furniture, USA) that were forced into bankruptcy protection or liquidation have to seek stronger partners.

The retail giants are expanding their purchasing operations as well and increasingly use supplier networks in the megamarkets. With their efficient logistics systems, major retailers control product and information flows, and can thus influence margins and prices of suppliers worldwide. Large retailers with long sourcing traditions in China are Wal-Mart, Karstadt-Quelle, Kingfisher/B&Q, and Toys"R"Us. Wal-Mart, due to its size, is the biggest buyer; it procures goods worth around US$10 billion in China for its local stores, and worth another US$8 billion for exports to the United States, Europe, and Japan. Wal-Mart's purchases of consumer and food products account for 25% of China's overall exports to the United States. The company established its subsidiary in India in 2001 for sourcing home textiles, apparel, fine jewelry, and household goods; currently at around US$600 million only, procurement will be scaled up fourfold in the coming years.

Table 6.16. Europe's top ten retail companies, 2007.

Company	Sales (€ bn)	Share (%)
Carrefour	98	7.9
Tesco	87	7.0
Metro	65	5.2
Rewe	53	4.3
Edeka	42	3.4
Schwarz Group[a]	41	3.3
Auchan	39	3.2
Aldi	37	3.1
Leclerc	32	2.6
Casino	27	2.2
Top ten	521	42.0
Others	720	—
Total	1,241	100.0

a. Including Kaufland, Lidl, Quelle, and Real.
Source: German Retail Association. 2008.

China and India are also major sourcing countries for IKEA. Twenty percent of the products seen in IKEA outlets are bought from Chinese suppliers, and this percentage will rise to 35%–40% by 2012–2015. The company sources 5% of its goods from India and employs 100,000 persons in its Indian supply chain; the company will also use India's expertise for its IT solutions. In Russia, IKEA has become a major buyer and producer of furniture.

JC Penney (sales 2007: US$19.9 billion) sources 55% of its global requirements of US$4 billion from China, 17% from India. The company has consolidated its sourcing base down from ninety to eighteen countries since 2000. KarstadtQuelle, the German department store and mail-order operator, has several purchasing offices in different parts of China.[37]

Urbanization has led to the emergence of supermarket chains and a series of other modern retail formats (specialty chains, catalogue/mail-order outlets, Internet retailing/e-shops, direct selling) in emerging economies. Better infrastructure has facilitated the establishment of large retail formats, including hypermarkets and malls, which provide an alternative shopping experience from small, round-the-corner stores. Megamarket consumers with

---

37. In 2006, the company purchased goods worth €250 million directly from Chinese suppliers, and goods worth another €300 million were transited through suppliers from Hong Kong. About two hundred containers leave Shanghai every week for Germany (mainly to Hamburg port).

their high disposable incomes have responded enthusiastically to the arrival of modern retail in the megamarkets. The positive impact of large retailers on production, imports, and packaging of goods is significant. These trends have opened opportunities for store design and equipment companies (e.g., Austria's Umdasch in Russia).

"Shoppertainment" is transforming the retail landscape. In large commercial complexes, the shopping experience is enhanced with the presence of food courts, multiplexes, and other forms of entertainment for leisure. Child-care centers, gyms, and clinics have also entered the traditional shopping space.

EU's leading retailers pursue three strategies:
- cost-cutting through concentration, consolidation, and mergers;
- innovation through IT, services, and new formats to reach specific target groups;
- internationalization and expansion into megamarkets and smaller emerging markets.

6.3.2. Retail trends in the megamarkets

Everyday shopping has undergone dramatic changes in the three megamarkets. As in Europe many decades back, retailing was the domain of small, family-run mom-and-pop stores. Traditional retailing is now challenged by powerful operators of chains and large-scale formats including hypermarkets, non-food specialty chains, department stores, and mail-order outlets. In third-tier cities and rural towns, however, traditional channels like grocery stores and open-air markets still retain a high market share of up to 70%. Penetration by larger chains is increasing, especially in China's coastal areas and Russia's central and southern regions. Although the retail revolution arrived only a few years ago in India, it has taken over all the large cities. Traditional shops are still omnipresent, but they are refashioning themselves, and modern retail formats are spreading in suburbs of metropolitan areas where easy access and parking can be offered to shoppers.

Federal and regional governments in the megamarkets are under pressure from the shopkeeper community, which forms a large vote bank, to protect their turf. Authorities are also under pressure from the large, homegrown retailers to restrict the sale of land (Russia, China) or postpone the opening of the sector (China, India) to foreigners so that they can reach critical size before large competitors like Wal-Mart, Metro, Tesco, Auchan, and Carrefour enter the scene. Retailers from the megamarkets have grown fast since 2003; they acquired financial clout and could step up their lobbying capabilities. According to a report released by Deloitte, six mega retailers from China and Russia have for the first time joined the list of the world's top 250 retailers in 2007.[38]

China

On December 11, 2004, China adopted the WTO ruling for full market opening in the retail sector. Overseas retailers are allowed to own 100% of their stores and can expand to the smaller towns as well (they were formerly restricted to big cities and provincial capitals of Beijing, Shanghai, Shenzhen, and Tianjin). Foreign investment in Chinese retailing shot

---

38. *2008 Global Powers of Retailing*, a Deloitte Consumer Business Industry report (January 2008).

up after the ruling. China's retail market is the largest among the three megamarkets. In 2007, sales attained around US$750 billion. Since 1998, retailing has grown faster than GDP, at 15% annually. Large formats (hypermarkets, giant supermarkets, mega specialty stores) have grown by 60%.

Adding stores is the main goal of the foreign retailers. Wal-Mart has opened forty-five outlets in twenty-four cities since its entry into China in 1996. The company plans to add another sixty stores by 2010, with the total rising to above one hundred. It will then draw even with its French rival Carrefour, currently the biggest foreign retailer in China in terms of number of outlets. Metro, Auchan, and Tesco also announced ambitious expansion plans. They buy land and property even in interior regions in anticipation of rising real estate costs, fueled by intense domestic competition. Tesco's management decided to add capacity through M&As (e.g., acquisition of the Hymall-Legou chain in 2007).

Table 6.17. Top retailers in selected Chinese cities, 2007.

Beijing	Shanghai	Dalian
Jingkelong	Shanghai Hualian	Parkson
Huapu	Lotus	Tesco-Hymall
Tiankelong	Hymall	Beijing Hualian
Wu-Mart	Nonggongshang	Wal-Mart
Carrefour	Lianhua	Lehana
Shuntianfu	Carrefour	Carrefour
Beijing Hualian	Jiadeli	Wangda
Chaoshifa	Trust-Mart	New-Mart
Meilianmei	RT-Mart	Dalian Shangchang
Shouhangguoli	Auchan	Quik
Share of local retailers: 80%	Share of local retailers: 70%	Share of local retailers: 85%

Source: Consumer Panel China. CTR Research. 2007.

But local chains still clearly dominate with a market share of 80%. They tend to form larger holdings, such as the Shanghai Bailian Group, which emanated from a merger of four retailers. In 2006, this conglomerate reported 6,200 stores and total sales of US$20 billion. In comparison, Wal-Mart, Carrefour, Metro, and Tesco together have less than 200 stores so far and combined sales of US$3.5 billion in China. Numerous local chains have reported excellent results and continuous growth since 2004 (see table 6.17). Some of them are in negotiations with Western partners to form alliances.

INDIA

Retail in India contributes more than 20% to the country's GDP. Valued currently at US$295 billion (2010: US$370 billion), it forms the backbone of the economy. The sector is dominated by small, owner-run stores, but the share of "organized" retail (retail chains) is growing rapidly (35%–40%) and will reach 15% of total retail by 2012 from only 4% in 2007. By 2013, organized retail will exceed US$100 billion. Overall retail will then be valued at a minimum of US$833 billion based on average annual growth rates of 10%.[39]

There are 12 million retail outlets in India, the highest in the world. The industry employs more people than any industry except agriculture.[40] However, these outlets are mostly owner-run mom-and-pop stores (*kirana* stores); only 4% are bigger than forty square meters. Indians do as much as 97% of their shopping in these kirana stores. But even these are changing as they face competition, but also learn, from organized retail. Hindustan Unilever, for example, is helping kirana stores get a facelift and become more efficient.

---

39. A.T. Kearney, *Emerging Opportunities for Global Retailers: The 2008 A.T. Kearney Global Retail Development Index*.
40. "Indian Retailing: Getting Cheaper and Better," *The Economist*, February 3, 2007.

Other FMCG companies, whose margins are under pressure from the retail chains, are also undertaking similar initiatives to help the kiranas. One of the main advantages offered by these small stores is the credit offered to large masses of low-income consumers. Some of the retailers are listed companies.

Organized retail, or retail chains, is a phenomenon that started in the early 1980s with the opening of Nilgiris, the first self-service supermarket, in Chennai. The retail revolution that started in the 1990s was pioneered by the RP Goenka Group when it acquired the century-old Spencer's store in Chennai; since then, it has grown into one of the largest retail chains. Development was faster in southern India, although now the mall and supermarket culture has spread across the country. New entrants—real estate companies or industrial houses—have grown rapidly; some are already listed companies (see table 6.18), and shares have appreciated significantly since they went public.

The top players include companies that started as regional chains. Subhiksha Trading Services, for example, runs 145 grocery and pharmacy stores in the southern state of

Table 6.18. Top players in India's retail sector, 2007–2008.

Name	Year of establishment	Formats	Brands
Nilgiris Group (Actis, UK investor)	1905	Convenience store	Nilgiri's
		Bakeries	Underway
K. Raheja Corp.	1991	Department store	Shopper's Stop
		Shopping mall	Inorbit
		Hypermarket	HyperCity
		Supermarket	Spencer's
		Specialty stores (books, apparel)	Crossword, Mothercare
		Home store	Home Stop
		Restaurants, cafés	Brio, Desi Café
		Airport shops	JV with Nuance AG
RPG Enterprises	1996	Hypermarket	Spencer's Hypermarkets
		Supermarket	Spencer's Super
		Convenience store	Spencer's Daily
		Neighborhood store	Spencer's Express
		Specialty stores (music, books, and stationery)	Music World, Books and Beyond
Pantaloon Retail (India) Ltd. (Future Group) JV with Etam	1997	Shopping malls	Central
		Hypermarkets	Big Bazaar
		Supermarkets	Food Bazaar
		Home stores	Home Town, Furniture Bazaar, Electronics Bazaar, Collection i, e Zone
		Eateries	Café Bollywood, Chamosa, Sport Bar, Brew Bar
		Specialty stores (apparel, jewelry, accessories, books)	Blue Sky, Brand Factory, Fashion Station, Lee Cooper, Navaras, Pantaloons, Replay, Shoe Factory, Top 10, Depot.
		E-tailing (portal)	Futurebazaar.com

Table 6.18. Top players in India's retail sector, 2007–2008 (cont'd).

Name	Year of establishment	Formats	Brands
Subhiksha	1997	Discounter	Subhiksha
		Specialty stores (telecom, pharmacy, consumer durables)	Subhiksha Mobile and others
		E-tailing	www.subhikhsha.in
Trent Ltd. (Tata Group)	1998	Department store	Westside
		Supermarkets	Star India Bazaar
		Specialty stores (books, electric and electronic goods)	Landmark, Croma
		Wholesale	Partnership with Tesco
Aditya Birla Retail (Aditya Birla Group)	2007	Supermarket	More. Acquisition of Trinethra Super Retail chain.
		Hypermarket	Underway
Bharti Retail (Bharti Enterprises) (underway)	2007	Hypermarket, supermarket, convenience store	Underway
		Cash and carry	JV with Wal-Mart
Indiabulls Retail Services (Indiabulls Group)	2007, following acquisition of majority stake in Piramyd Retail	Department stores	Indiabulls Megastores
		Supermarkets	Indiabulls Marts
		Wholesale	Indiabulls Wholesale
Reliance Retail Ltd. (Reliance Industries Ltd.)	2007	Supermarkets	Reliance Fresh
		Department store	Partnership with Marks & Spencers
		Specialty stores (consumer durables, apparel, wellness, footwear, jewelry, books, automotive, optical, electronics, office supplies, toys)	Reliance Digital, Reliance Trends, Reliance Wellness, Reliance Footprint, Reliance Jewels, Reliance Time-Out, Reliance AutoZone. Partnerships with Pearle, Apple, Office Depot, Hamleys
		Hypermarket	Reliance Mart
		Minimart	Reliance Super

Tamil Nadu; it plans to add another 650 stores across India by 2012. Some companies pursue multi-format strategies. RPG Enterprises (Mumbai) will invest US$100 million in bazaar-style shops, supermarkets, and convenience stores before getting into specialty outlets (furniture, DIY, sports chains). Another trend is to become a category specialist and expand in the main metros as downtown stand-alone stores or in suburban shopping malls. Traditional products like shoes, apparel, and sports goods are already marketed via specialized retail chains that are extending their reach nationwide (Metro, Liberty Shoes).

Non-retail players also scent the potential for future growth. Reliance, India's largest industrial conglomerate with stakes in petrochemicals, textiles, and telecoms, has defined retailing as a new priority business for the two decades to come. It plans to open five thousand supermarkets (Reliance Fresh), hypermarkets, and warehouse-like stores including in Tier 3 and 4 cities across India during 2007–2010, thus raising its investment in the sector to US$5.7 billion. Tata, India's second-largest company, will open one hundred Croma outlets for consumer electronics and computer hardware and software by 2012–2015 (up from eleven in 2007). Smaller players can also pursue a regional strategy before going national. Nilkamal, a family-owned plastics processor based in Mumbai, plans initially to expand its chain of furniture stores (@Home) in the state of Maharashtra during 2008–2010 before venturing further.

Malls develop alongside the retail chains. By 2007, 170 such malls were operational against four in 2001; another 400 malls will be added by 2015. The retail landscape has been completely transformed within only a few years. From urban to rural India, lifestyles and shopping patterns have adapted to the change, which will trigger a shopping boom never experienced before. Sophisticated advertising, promotion, and merchandising techniques are already applied shrewdly to incite consumers to spend, making retail groups more powerful.

The growth of the retail sector is quickly raising the entry barriers for foreign retailers. At present, FDI in retail is not permitted except for single-brand stores (e.g., luxury brands like Gucci, Louis Vuitton; producer's stores like Nike and Adidas), where the foreign investor can hold up to 51% in a local partnership. However, foreign wholesalers and cash-and-carry companies like Germany's Metro are allowed to set up wholly owned subsidiaries. Metro, which launched its first test store in 2003, faced teething trouble as it had to confront the wholesalers' lobby. Indian retail sector sounds particularly attractive to foreign players given its young customer base (52% under 25). Foreign retail giants recognize the opportunity and seek ways to overcome the restriction. Through its fifty-fifty joint venture with Bharti Enterprises (the group with the biggest mobile services company), Wal-Mart plans to open a dozen cash-and-carry stores by 2015, even though this is not its traditional format. It will provide back-end services (logistics) while Bharti will use its executive capability to handle the front end. Carrefour is contemplating a similar arrangement with Future Group after having prospected various local players. Tesco will enter the wholesale business with its own subsidiary; for retail, it has signed up with Trent to develop its discount hypermarket format. Marks & Spencer has entered into a joint venture with Reliance Retail.

Many more foreign retailers are waiting for a relaxation of FDI norms. Local players like Reliance lobby hard to temporarily check any move in this direction by the government until they reach a size that will allow them to compete with experienced and global players like Wal-Mart. The government, with an election year due in 2009, is anxious to preserve the loyalty of the large vote bank of kirana stores, who are also wary of local big chains, both domestic and foreign. But it is only a matter of time before the sector will be liberalized as the government is fully aware of the benefits to employment, manufacturing, logistics, and consumers that the entry of foreign companies will bring. The new guidelines released in February 2009 on the ownership pattern of retail companies allow foreign retailers to gain a majority through indirect holdings.

The main constraints are the rising real estate prices and the shortage of trained manpower. The issues of supply chain management, cold chain, and logistics are being addressed as Indian retail chains streamline back-end operations more and more efficiently and progress along the learning curve.

Russia

Rising affluence combined with a large population living in regions deprived of modern distribution systems offers great opportunities for domestic and foreign retail companies in Russia. During 2000–2007, roughly one-third of Russia's inward FDI flowed into trading and retailing. Growth has been more spectacular in Greater Moscow (25% during this period) than in China's booming Shanghai. A slowdown is expected starting from 2010–2012, but the sector will continue to grow at above-average rates compared with other Eastern European metropolises. Slower growth in Moscow will be compensated by growth in Russia's regional capitals, which are under-equipped with modern formats. Available retail space per inhabitant is much lower in Moscow (45 square meters per inhabitant) than in Budapest (164 square meters per inhabitant) and Warsaw (340 square meters per inhabitant). In Russia's regional capitals, it is less than half the retail space of Moscow.

Until 2003, the leading Russian retailers continued to expand their market shares. Perekrjostok, Sedmoi Kontinent (both supermarket and hypermarket operators), Kopeika, and Piatjorechka (both discounters) grew at 15%–20% each year since 1996; non-food chains like M-Video, Eldorado, Texnosila (all three, consumer electronics), and Chattabich (DIY) grew at the same pace. The only successful foreign operator at the time was Ramstor, a Turkish-invested hypermarket chain operator. Then in 2004, the sector witnessed the arrival of Western retail giants, headed by Metro, Auchan, IKEA (furniture), and Obi (DIY). To face foreign competition, domestic chains decided to pool their resources. Piatjorechka and Perekrjostok merged in 2005 with X5, a new company with sales of US$4.2 billion (2007). Russian retailers entered vacant segments such as high-end supermarkets and niche retailing (specialty stores for expectant mothers, secondhand outlets, optics chains, bookstores). Russian companies were very fast at expanding to other regions and managed to seize the best locations at reasonable costs before foreign rivals stepped in.

Consolidation will increase as smaller retailers are hampered in their expansion by a shortage of affordable retail premises in good locations. Rents in suburban malls have become expensive and can be recouped only if there is high frequency. The leading retailers (e.g., Sedmoi Kontinent, Magnit, Chattabich) have formed partnerships with developers and co-invest in the construction of new malls. This way, they can reserve the necessary space for themselves upon completion of the project.

Led by Metro and Auchan, EU retailers continue to step up their investments in land, commercial property, and warehouses in Russia. Metro (forty stores in Russia in 2007) plans to open eight to ten new stores every year. During 2001–2007, Metro invested €800 million, which makes Russia its most important project worldwide. According to Metro's country manager for Russia, "Growth would be even faster, if three obstacles could be removed: infrastructure bottlenecks, lack of local supply chains, inflexible labor code."[41] Smaller retailers from the EU (e.g., Billa/Spar, Edeka) who were hesitant a few years back are now also opening stores in Moscow suburbs (prime locations have been already taken),

---

41. "Russian Retailing," *American Chamber News*, no. 70 (March 2006): 12.

so far with mixed results. Many important discounters like Aldi, Lidl, and Casino missed the right timing to enter the Russian market. Local competitors such as Kopeika and Perekrjostok copied Aldi's discount model starting from the mid-1990s and secured the best locations in the larger cities. Some well-known non-food chains have also stayed out: Media Markt (consumer electronics), Marks & Spencer's (department store), and C&A (apparel, department store), just to name a few.

6.3.3. Challenges for foreign retail companies

Russia and China have become very attractive markets, whereas for many retailers India is still on the waiting list because of its restrictive legislation. Expansion for foreign retailers in China and Russia is possible through M&As and alliances, but asset prices have risen ten to twelve times today than in the early 2000s, which deters many companies (e.g., Praktiker from Germany) to use this route. Instead, they prefer nearby markets like Bulgaria, Romania, Serbia, and Turkey where investments remain affordable. At the same time, the leading megamarket operators will continue expanding in their home markets and from a position of strength gradually expand abroad. In the medium term, Western companies will have to enter into strategic alliances or cross-shareholding arrangements with them in order to preempt competition.

IKEA's popularity among Chinese and Russian consumers provides interesting lessons for foreign retailers:

- It offers a wide choice of products at competitive prices. It has a policy to keep reducing prices so that products become affordable to most consumer segments.
- It appeals to consumers who buy according to function and style. Customers are advised how to make the most of their living space and how to mix and match colors, designs, and concepts.
- It pursues a strategy of combining high product standards with locally adjusted advertising and promotional activities. It invests in image and branding. Goods can be replaced and defects corrected without discussions.
- It conducts regular intelligence on consumer preferences: focus groups, home visits, city visits, telephone surveys, and in-store promotions and surveys.
- It considers the three megamarkets as top priority and invests resources in understanding them. It is determined to lift the share of the megamarkets above 5% of total sales (1% today, or US$16 billion).

6.4. Logistics and transport

6.4.1. Global logistics trends

Globally, transport and logistics (T&L) is one of the fastest-growing sectors. According to a World Bank study, it accounts for about 10% of world GDP and up to 12% of employment.[42] Worldwide, T&L constituted a market of about US$2.8–3.0 trillion

---

42. Passenger and cargo transport plus handling.

in 2007 (see table 6.19), of which 30% were logistics services related primarily to the organized forwarding of goods (excluding passenger transport). The T&L sector is expanding at 20%–25% annually in the megamarkets, a trajectory that is expected to hold despite temporary contractions provoked by the global credit crisis in 2009. In the Asia-Pacific region, China and India—regional share of 40% and 16%, respectively—offer the best prospects because of the market potential determined by low rates of outsourcing (20%)[43] to category specialists or third-party logistics providers (3PLs) (see table 6.20). Improved transshipment links between port cities and interior regions make them more attractive. Category specialists include transport firms, warehouse operators, and customs brokers, while 3PLs are multitask firms offering a range of services under one roof,[44] thus relieving companies of the logistics burden. Third-party logistics providers coordinate and handle external service providers such as shipping lines, warehousing specialists, terminal/port authorities, export/free trade zones, and customs. Using IT, Web-enabling, and satellite technologies, 3PLs offer door-to-door services at a competitive price and speed. Shipments can be traced instantly, even along multiple transport modes (road, rail, sea, air).

The logistics sector is fragmented among tens of thousands of small and medium-sized players. The leading 3PLs (see table 6.21) have grown into global players with subsidiaries and alliances in key geographies. They have grown both organically

Table 6.19. Global logistics revenue by region, 2007–2015.

	Sales 2007 (US$ bn)	Annual growth 2008–2015 (%)
EU	175	5.0
North America	135	14.0
Asia-Pacific	120	15.0
Other	70	7.0
Total logistics	500	6.5
Transport[a] and logistics	2,500	

a. Including passenger transport.
Source: Datamonitor. 2008.

Table 6.20. Share of outsourced logistics expenditure, 2007, 2015.

	2007 (%)	2015 (%)
USA	80	90
EU	70	80
China	35	50
Russia	30	60
India	20	35

Source: Council of Logistics Management. 2008.

Table 6.21. The world's top ten logistics companies, 1/1/2008.

	Sales (US$ bn)	Profits (US$ bn)
Deutsche Post,[a] Germany	90.5	1.9
US Postal Service, USA	74.8	–5.1
Maersk, Denmark	52.4	3.3
UPS, USA	49.7	0.4
Deutsche Bahn,[b] Germany	42.9	2.3
FedEx, USA	35.2	2.0
La Poste, France	31.9	1.3
Poste Italiane, Italy	23.5	1.1
NYK, Japan	22.6	1.0
China Ocean Shipping, China	20.8	3.7

a. Including DHL, Danzas, Exel.
b. Including Schenker, Rhenus, BAX Global.
Source: Fortune. Global 500. 2008.

---

43. By comparison, outsourcing rates in North America and the EU are between 70% and 80%.
44. The slogan "do what you do best and outsource the rest" applies to more and more companies. Only multinationals with large handling volumes can afford to have their own transport and logistics subsidiaries (e.g., Volkswagen, Wal-Mart).

and through M&As.[45] They combine traditional services (warehousing, transportation, customs clearance, IT) with value-added activities such as packaging, assembly, repairs, customer service, and supply chain management (SCM). Deutsche Post, the world's largest logistics company with sales of US$90 billion in early 2008, acquired DHL (express services), Exel (US freight management and IT services), and Danzas (forwarding and warehousing) during 2006–2008.

Concentration is high in express services (UPS, FedEx, TNT) and sea cargo (Maersk, NYK, COSCO) where the required infrastructure (port facilities) and equipment (cargo ships) demand massive investments. The world's top five shipping companies[46] control 80% of seaborne traffic, while the top six terminals account for 50% of global cargo handling (see figure 6.3).[47] World container-port throughput is expected to rise by 50% from 400 million TEU[48] in 2006 to 600 million TEU in 2010. Big container ports such as Singapore, Shanghai, Hong Kong, Rotterdam, and Hamburg have posted record growth since 2000. In 2007, Hamburg port expanded ten times faster than the German economy thanks to well-organized feeder traffic across the Baltic Sea and transshipments by rail and road to Central Europe, Russia, and CIS. For the world shipping industry, 2003–2007 was a phenomenal period of full order books; but customers had to accept waiting periods along with high prices. The years 2008 and 2009 will be marked by growth slackened by a widespread drop in cargo demand (financial crisis); higher growth rates are expected after 2010. Shipping lines are investing in larger oil tankers, ferries, and container ships. A big container ship can carry up to nine thousand containers, but the growth in traffic requires mammoth vessels with double that capacity. Oil tankers and LNG (liquid natural

Figure 6.3. Share of top six container terminal operators,[a] 2007

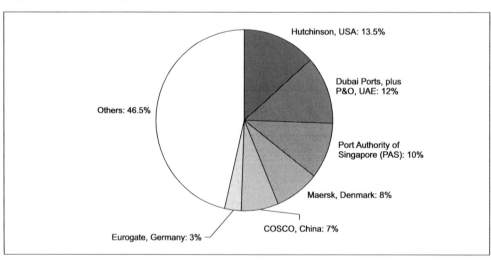

a. The six companies control more than 50% of global cargo handling.

Source: Singapore Port Authority. 2007.

---

45. Germany, for example, has sixty thousand transport operators; many of them are expected to merge into larger units or be sold off to logistics giants.
46. Maersk (DK), COSCO (China), Evergreen (Taiwan), Hapag Lloyd (Germany), Hanjin (South Korea).
47. Barenberg Bank, *Perspektiven für Maritime Wirtschaft und Logistik. Strategie 2030.* (HWWI, 2006).
48. Twenty-foot container equivalent.

gas) vessels are also becoming bigger, faster, and costlier. Sector insiders worry about a downturn in the AMs because of excess capacities and hope that China, India, and Russia will allow the industry to stay on a healthy growth path. The growing demand for logistics services will exercise a pull effect on transport equipment suppliers.

6.4.2. Logistics trends in the megamarkets

CHINA

According to the China Federation of Logistics and Purchasing (CFLP), T&L in China accounts for about 12% of GDP, or US$240 billion. Logistics represents a small fraction of this total (about 5%, or US$12 billion, in 2006). Express service providers account for about 50% of total logistics revenue (US$6 billion),[49] which leaves ample room for expansion in other segments (shipping, warehousing, forwarding, integrated, or 3PL services). The sector grew at an annual rate of 25%–30% during 2003–2007.[50] Three main drivers will determine future growth:

- Logistics is managed in-house by local producers, who will, however, outsource more of these services to specialists.
- Companies must become highly inventive to overcome transport bottlenecks. Overstretched ports and roads cry for solutions at the government level as well.[51] Toll fees collected by provincial authorities amount to 15%–20% of total transport costs, but if they are reinvested in infrastructure they can render logistics more effective in the long run.[52]
- FDI has burgeoned since the sector was liberalized in 2003 allowing 100% wholly owned subsidiaries as part of the country's WTO commitments. The experience and best practices of foreign players will help raise efficiency, although they have to struggle to introduce Western working standards. Wal-Mart China, for example, works with fifteen thousand suppliers who service its eighty or so stores, which also buy from other vendors. (In USA, by contrast, 3,800 stores are served by 6,100 suppliers.)

Foreign logistics companies that followed their AM clientele also canvass local clients. Large companies expand by acquiring local firms[53] or establishing greenfield operations,[54] while medium-sized firms prefer to take the alliance route.[55] Chinese logistics companies are smaller and specialize in one or two modes of transport (e.g., trucking, shipping, air

---

49. The four leaders, DHL (35% share), FedEx (20%), UPS (19%), and TNT (8%), all have joint ventures with Sinotrans, the largest domestic logistics provider.
50. This is a natural consequence of China's rise as the world's largest trader by 2010.
51. Paradoxically, reaching inland markets from a coastal city can take longer than exporting to the United States.
52. Because of tight profit margins, megamarket operators tend to overload trucks, causing many accidents. Deliveries are slow and goods are damaged because transport companies prefer to take toll-free but bad roads.
53. TNT acquired Hoau Logistics Group, which owns 1,100 depots and 56 hubs across all Tier 1 and Tier 2 cities. This adds to TNT's existing web of twenty-five wholly owned operating branches and presence in over five hundred cities and will turn the joint company into China's largest private transportation network for freight and parcels.
54. For example, FedEx's new US$150 million Asia-Pacific hub in Guangzhou.
55. Qingdao-based SITC Maritime, China's largest private shipper, merged with Beijing's New Times International Transport Service, the biggest airfreight forwarder, to form SITC Logistics.

cargo) and industry (e.g., food, electronics). According to the latest count by CFLP, there are more than 700,000 logistics enterprises registered in China, of which only 2%–3% have a turnover exceeding US$40 million. These large players are well established across the country in several provinces and represent attractive targets for Western, Japanese, or South Korean companies.

To improve logistics services, Chinese authorities are making every possible attempt to modernize the country's infrastructure (ports, airports, railways, roads, pipelines). China's ports are growing at breakneck speed. With third-party usage of logistics services moving from 30% today to 60% by 2015, the cargo-handling capacity of Chinese ports (see table 6.22) between 2007 and 2010 will rise from 3.8 billion metric tons to 5 billion metric tons, and coastal container throughput will rise from 75 million TEU to 130 million TEU. Shanghai overtook Singapore to become the world's largest port in 2006. It handled 443 million metric tons of cargo and 22 million TEU of containers in 2006, a 22% and 24% increase, respectively, over the previous year. At present growth rates, it will touch 40 million TEU by 2010–2012.

Table 6.22. China's main sea ports, 2005–2010 (mn tons).

a. Total cargo, mn t	2005	2007	2010
Shanghai	405	490	560
Ningbo	250	300	380
Tianjin	225	280	340
Guangzhou	220	265	310
Qingdao	170	195	230
Dalian	155	175	200
Qinhuangdao	155	170	190
Shenzhen	140	165	185
Zhoushan	85	100	130
b. Containers, mn TEU[a]	2000	2007	2010
Shanghai	5.6	21.7	39.0
Qingdao	2.1	7.7	12.0
Ningbo	0.9	7.1	14.0
Guangzhou	1.4	6.6	11.0
Tianjin	1.7	6.0	9.5
Xiamen	1.1	4.0	6.6
Dalian	1.0	3.2	4.8

a. Equivalent to 20-foot containers.
Source: Hong Kong Shipper's Council. 2008.

Major free trade zones (FTZs) have been turned into regional logistics hubs with attached port facilities and mandated to attract foreign shipping lines, terminal operators, warehouse providers, and 3PLs through tax exemptions, one-window customs and tax clearance, and co-financing benefits (access roads, facilities for repackaging and assembly). Dalian, Tianjin, and Shanghai FTZs were granted free port status by the central government; they can offer operators bonded storage and duty-free transshipment facilities. The growing need for logistics experts across major industries has prompted authorities to put more efforts into raising educational levels and promoting higher service standards. Logistics is a popular subject among college students, and many universities have opened logistics faculties and departments for transport management studies.

India

India's T&L industry is at an inflection point as growth in outsourced and contract services reaches double digits. Its T&L market is worth US$90 billion (2007) and is expected to reach US$125 billion by 2010.[56] Its share in GDP is 7%–8%, which will increase as the sector grows faster—by 12%–15%—than GDP. Growth could be even higher were it

---

56. Source: India Supply Chain Council and Datamonitor.

not for the country's infrastructure bottlenecks and long administrative formalities for interstate transport. As a result, transportation costs account for up to 40% of the total cost of production in certain industries. Third-party logistics providers represent less than 20% of the logistics market. At growth rates of 16%, 3PLs are forecast to reach a volume of US$30–35 billion in 2012 from less than US$15 billion today.[57]

India represents an extremely promising market for EU logistics companies. Many manufacturing and retail companies plan to outsource their logistic function to specialized service providers. The market for integrated 3PL services is therefore buoyant. The industry was pioneered in the early 2000s by global logistics majors (DHL, TNT), which gradually extended their services to Indian subsidiaries of multinationals. As a result, the number of local 3PLs grew to more than 420 in 2007. Three categories of players can be considered possible targets for acquisition or collaboration: domestic 3PL leaders with nationwide presence, regional 3PLs with strong presence in one to three regions, and small 3PLs focused on specific areas or locations.

Whereas in China, mainly retailing and consumer goods drive the logistics industry, India's 3PL services are pulled by the vehicle and auto component industries. TNCs like Fiat, Suzuki, Honda, BMW, and Ford will add capacity and expand distribution. Other sectors that will contribute to the growth of the 3PL market are consumer durables, electronics, and retailing (which will soon be opened to foreign investment). Large retailers seek more than just transportation of their products and expect logistics operators to offer customs clearance, forwarding, warehousing, labeling, packaging, fleet management, order picking, and inventory management. Another industry that will outsource logistics is textiles, which also has to meet the exacting delivery requirements of clients, often in multiple export markets.

Leading local players like Gati, Safe-Express, PILL, and TCIL have designed customized SCM packages geared to specific industries with a guarantee of cost savings to clients. Leading T&L companies have invested in IT and new-generation GSM scanners, which supply real-time information on shipments within fifteen minutes of pick-up or delivery. Similarly, at DHL, the thrust is on expansion; its first exclusive express handling unit was opened at Delhi airport, and it acquired a new fleet of more than three hundred vehicles from Mahindra & Mahindra, Maruti-Suzuki, and Tata Motors. Freight forwarders are acquiring assets to create container freight stations and inland container depots, in addition to container trains.

India's logistics industry is highly fragmented. Transportation is dominated by small trucking companies, while freight forwarding is handled by thousands of individual customs brokers and clearing houses. Very few service providers offer more than one service or cover all relevant logistics points to offer seamless door-to-door services. Indian companies tend to outsource individual logistics tasks to various service providers while retaining overall control of the logistics function in-house despite the heavy administrative and infrastructural costs involved. But things are changing as logistics becomes a strategic function. Large international logistics companies therefore plan to purchase stakes in local

---

57. According to information released by Frost & Sullivan.

Table 6.23. Acquisitions of Indian logistics companies, 2006–2008.

Acquirer	Country of origin	Indian target
DHL	Germany/USA	Blue Dart
FedEx	USA	Pafex
TNT	Australia	Speedage
Phoenix International	USA	Eastern Logistics
Kerry Logistics	Hong Kong	Reliable Freight Forwarders
CH Robinson	USA	Triune Freight and Logistics
Broekman Group	Netherlands	Courcan Cargo

Source: Business journals.

firms at different levels of the value chain to extend their presence in the country and to offer integrated services (see table 6.23). Logistics company valuations have gone up considerably since 2005 as a result of these acquisitions.

Infrastructure remains a concern for operators, who complain about congested roads and ports and inadequate warehousing facilities around major cities. Warehouses are being built in various parts of the country, contributing to the growth of the real estate sector. The Indian warehousing sector is growing at an annual rate of 35%–40% and will become a US$55 billion industry by 2010–2011, driven mostly by the surge in the commodities trading and retail sectors as well as the entry of 3PL operators.[58] By 2011, India will have more than 4 million square meters of warehousing space and more than a hundred logistics parks. Currently the turnover of the warehousing sector is US$20 billion (2007–2008), or 20% of the logistics industry. The potential is therefore very high for warehousing specialists (e.g., ProLogis of USA).

Five major decisions made by the government will drive the industry in the years to come:
- highway, port, and airport modernization programs[59]
- opening up of rail freight operations to private players (transportation by rail is cheaper and faster than by road) in 2007 to end the monopoly of the Container Corporation of India (CONCOR)
- completion of the two dedicated rail freight corridors by 2012 (cost: US$7.15 billion)
- further liberalization of FDI in client industries, which is expected to fuel the 3PL market
- phased introduction of VAT will simplify supply chain management

Russia

Like China and India, Russia is also experiencing a logistics boom. Initially focused on Moscow and St. Petersburg, logistics companies are setting up new storage and transport platforms at major junctions. Transit container traffic between Asia and Europe is expected to reach 145 million TEU annually by 2010, twice the 2001 figure. The trans-Siberian land route is much shorter and faster than the Pacific sea route, but the necessary

---

58. Cushman and Wakefield study on warehousing in India.
59. See 4.3.

infrastructure is not yet in place. The Eurasian land bridge[60] project, dubbed the New Silk Road, set a milestone in 2007 when a freight train loaded with containers left Beijing for Hamburg on a 10,000-kilometer journey. The route runs through China, Mongolia, along the Trans-Siberian railway, and then through Belarus and Poland to finally reach Germany. Six national railways took part; the total journey time was twenty days. The aim is to shorten it to twelve to fifteen days, which will be twice as fast as oceangoing vessels. Rail transportation will be cheaper than both ocean and airfreight for various types of cargoes. The six railway companies are keen on competitive offerings to gain market share from ocean and airfreight. But bottlenecks such as different rail gauges, outdated vehicle technology, and time-consuming customs formalities have still to be sorted out.

The Russian government is eager to play a developmental role in the country's logistics sector. It actively funds transport corridors (e.g., Trans-Asian Railways), new port projects (e.g., Novorossiysk[61]), as well as cross-border stations in the Far East (e.g., Zabaikalsk between Russia and China) to raise cargo-handling and container throughput. Port expansion programs are underway in the Moscow region, St. Petersburg, Novorossiysk, Murmansk, Yekaterinburg, Nakhodka, and Kaliningrad, Russia's only ice-free Baltic port. The annual capacity of the intermodal transport and logistics terminals to be completed by 2010 will exceed 100 million metric tons. The government will also initiate a vast modernization program for the Trans-Siberian Railway (Transsib), which is the shortest route connecting Asia and Europe and will give Russia indisputable competitive advantages, including:

- faster deliveries at competitive rates (fast trains can travel up to 1,500 km in a day);
- involvement of the private sector (30% of rolling stock will be renewed with investments by logistics companies amounting to US$6 billion by 2010);
- expansion of regional logistics hubs along the route (e.g., Krasnoyarsk, Novosibirsk, Yekaterinburg).

The government actively encourages the creation of vertically integrated transport holding companies that group all logistics services under one roof. Private players are allowed to take part in the modernization of logistics infrastructure, including investments in rolling stock, railway platforms, and road, port, and airport management. Foreign logistics multinationals and transport companies have responded positively to these measures. While EU logistics companies are involved in airport and port modernization projects (e.g., Hochtief) or want to expand into road management (Strabag), East Asian TNCs have set up logistics platforms along the Transsib route: Samsung, LG Electronics, Toyota, Green Logistics, Pantos Logistics, and Sinotrans.

Food and non-food retailers buy locally produced consumer goods that must be forwarded to the various stores. They will be driving supply chain developments in Russia. IKEA's Russian subsidiary sources 60% of its furniture from local suppliers, who are guided by IKEA for lifting their quality standards. They can use IKEA's global retail network to export their goods to foreign countries. Metro has a similar setup in the food segment. Manufacturers of food items and consumer goods will increasingly use the global hypermarket networks of large retailers to penetrate foreign markets.

---

60. See chapter 1.
61. The port's cargo-handling capacity will be increased by 50% to 120 million metric tons.

The leading Russian logistics players (e.g., Rewico, Armadillo, RLS, STS Logistics, Fesco) are trying to raise their competitiveness by moving up the value chain and offering comprehensive logistics services, including transport, warehousing, customs, and brokerage. With the trend toward containerization, they are investing in transport and storage hubs. Larger companies are turning into intermodal operators by combining the strengths of road, railway, and sea transport, often with investments in their own port infrastructure and terminal markets.[62]

6.4.3. Challenges for foreign logistics companies

Megamarkets offer a vast field of operation for EU logistics and 3PLs capable of supporting both international and local clients for in- and outbound logistics. Megamarket governments have opened logistics markets to foreign investors. Apart from strategic areas like ocean shipping and air cargo, 100% acquisitions are possible. Foreign investors can now hold a majority stake of up to 74% in air cargo companies in India; this decision was made in view of the interest of foreign companies (FedEx, Malaysian Airlines, HeavyLift Cargo Airlines) to establish bases in India. Given the development of the logistics sector and high expected growth in domestic and international air cargo, private airlines like Jet Airways and GoAir in India are planning to have their own cargo airlines.[63]

Logistics companies will need to enhance their services by investing in their own facilities/equipment or working closely with subcontractors. Most customers (retailers, manufacturers) want to be able to rely on a handful of reputed logistics companies that can offer integrated services. This is expected to drive consolidation in the market as logistics companies add services by acquiring existing operators in various segments. The industry will then be dominated by a handful of diversified companies who offer a full range of services in various geographies and to various industries in the megamarkets (see table 6.24). They will be supported by niche players in highly specialized areas such as hazardous materials and by numerous regional players. The advantage foreign entrants have over local players is experience in offering best practices in an end-to-end supply chain management system. Integrated services offer considerable savings to customers; this is a domain that domestic firms have so far been unable to manage efficiently.

Table 6.24. Segments targeted by 3PLs in the megamarkets.

Target segment	Motivation
Apparel/fashion goods	Speedy delivery
Food items	Freshness, time to market
Retailing	Speed, price
Energy	Pipeline monopoly
Minerals/raw materials	Access to source
Vehicles/components	Reliability, speed
Consumer goods	Availability
Industrial equipment	Technical service, advice
High-tech goods	Technology, speed

---

62. Fesco, for example, acquired 50% of the shares in National Container Company (NCC) in 2006. NCC was the leader in the terminal market; it owns the First Container Terminal in St. Petersburg (largest in Russia) and two modern terminals on the Black Sea (Novorossiysk, Ilyichevsk). Three new ground terminals in Moscow, Yekaterinburg, and Novosibirsk are under construction. Fesco comprises Transsiberian Intermodal Service (TIS), which ensures 30% of container traffic along the Transsib.
63. Experts predict air cargo services to grow at 14% annually during 2008–2010. Logistics services increasingly cover surrounding countries (Afghanistan, Bangladesh, Bhutan, Maldives, Nepal, Pakistan, Sri Lanka), which develop in the wake of the Indian subcontinent.

> **Box 6.2. Profile of ideal 3PL alliance partners.**
>
> - Wide contact network in the target market
> - Foreigners and locals in management positions
> - Own set-up and storage capacities in target market
> - Internal quality management
> - Experience and connections with customs
> - Used to working with all transport modes
> - Masters integrated supply chains: SCM, multimodal transport, consolidation/deconsolidation, warehousing, etc.

However, business expansion can be hampered by companies that imitate concepts. Overseas investors will need to protect their know-how, ensure a return before the competitive edge is eroded, and continue to reinvent their offers. A strategy of cooperation is risky as it can lead to theft of know-how; acquisitions may be a better tactic.

Competent logistics providers must have a certain profile to be able to participate in the global supply chain (see box 6.2). IT solutions are the key enablers for supply chain logistics. Most large corporations have invested in enterprise systems (ERP) and require their logistics partners to interface with them for seamless information flow throughout the supply chain. Third-party logistics providers have responded to this challenge by forming alliances with independent IT companies or by developing IT solutions internally. Software vendors, seeing the potential of this vertical, have responded with a series of supply chain execution (SCE) applications, including order management systems (OMS), warehouse management systems (WMS), and transportation management systems (TMS).

Megamarket governments will continue bolstering air-, sea-, and land-borne traffic by providing the necessary infrastructure and promoting a level playing field between domestic and foreign logistics companies.

6.5. Tourism and hospitality

6.5.1. Global tourism trends

Apart from being the showcase of an economy, tourism benefits many other sectors and is an important job creator, particularly in developing countries (e.g., Egypt, Tunisia, Turkey, Senegal, Thailand). But many advanced economies (e.g., Austria, France, Greece, Italy, Portugal, Spain) also depend heavily on this sector.[64] Developing countries, whose economic well-being is closely linked to tourism-related earnings, are aware that they must minimize the risk by balancing revenue generation with environmental concerns and the preservation of their cultural identity.

---

64. Europe represents a showcase of how cities, regions, and countries market their cultural heritage to attract tourists and corporate investors. For examples, refer to Ph. Kotler, D. Haider, Ch. Asplund and I. Rein, Marketing Places Europe (Prentice Hall Europe, 1998).

According to the World Travel and Tourism Council (WTTC), hospitality and tourism (H&T) are directly and indirectly responsible for generating 11% of the world's GDP or some 240 million jobs across the planet. A total of 860 million tourist arrivals were recorded worldwide in 2007, 12% more than in 2006; 2007 was the fourth year of consecutive growth. WTTC estimates total world personal travel and tourism expenditure at roughly US$3 trillion for 2007, with business travel accounting for an additional US$743 billion. The US market for personal travel is worth US$870 billion, about 30% of the world's total and more than three times that of the second-largest economy, Japan (US$287 billion). The US market also leads in business travel, with US$179 billion (24% of the world's total).

Continued growth in international tourism needs a robust global economy.[65] Until 2008, emerging destinations in Asia and the Pacific, Africa, and the Middle East reported healthy tourism growth. Some mature regions of Europe like Italy and Austria have regained momentum after years of stagnation. Germany reported record tourist arrivals and revenues (see tables 6.25 and 6.26), enhanced by the 2006 World Cup soccer championship. That same year, China, Mexico, and Russia entered the top ten ranking of major tourist destinations. India is also on a steady path toward becoming a major destination. China earned US$34 billion through tourism in 2006, a figure it hopes to double soon after the 2008 Olympics. WTTC has named India and China as the two fastest-growing tourism locations in the coming decade. Russia, too, has immense potential for expansion as it is still undiscovered by many tourists.

Travel-related expenditure continues to rise with the increase in international departures (outbound tourism). Fast-growing emerging economies are changing the world of travel both as destinations and as sources of newly affluent travelers. Strong growth in spending by outbound tourists comes from two large emerging megamarkets: Brazil (+33% in 2007) and Russia (+16%). Outbound travel from China has also increased, but the Chinese are more careful spenders. Top market destinations for emerging market tourists

Table 6.25. The world's top ten tourism destination countries, 2006–2007.

2007 rank	Country	Arrivals (mn) 2006	Arrivals (mn) 2007	Growth (%) 2007/2006	Share (%) 2007
1	France	75.9	79.1	4.2	9.2
2	Spain	55.9	58.5	4.5	6.8
3	USA	49.2	51.1	3.8	5.9
4	China	46.8	49.6	6.1	5.8
5	Italy	36.5	41.1	12.4	4.8
6	UK	28.0	30.7	9.3	3.6
7	Germany	21.5	23.6	9.6	2.7
8	Mexico	21.9	21.4	−2.6	2.5
9	Austria	20.0	20.3	1.5	2.4
10	Russia	19.9	20.2	1.3	2.4

Source: World Tourism Organization (WTO). 2008. www.world-tourism.org.

---

65. The 2008 financial crisis has led to a temporary contraction, which however should not affect medium-term growth.

in 2007 were Germany (+6%), the United States (+4%), and the United Kingdom (+4%). Hotels in these countries recorded high earnings in the past few years, with high occupancies and rising room charges as a result of strong demand from both business and leisure travelers.

Air carriers have been major beneficiaries. IATA, the association of the world's leading airlines, reports global commercial aviation revenues for 2007 to be US$473 billion (up from US$449 billion in 2006), of which 80% is passenger-related.[66] The price of aviation fuel remains a major constraint as it already constitutes 26% of operating expenses (compared with 10% in 2003). To cut costs, airlines and hotel chains offer online reservation systems. Direct electronic bookings that circumvent intermediaries (travel agents) reduce the cost for customers; purchasing tickets and tours online is also more convenient. The online travel market in India, for example, is expected to hit US$2 billion in 2008, up from US$750 million in 2006, or an increase of 270% in only three years.

Table 6.26. The world's top ten tourism earning countries, 2006–2007.

2007 rank	Country	US$ (bn) 2006	US$ (bn) 2007	Growth (%) 2007/2006
1	USA	81.8	85.7	4.8
2	Spain	48.0	51.1	6.6
3	France	42.3	42.9	1.5
4	Italy	35.4	38.1	7.7
5	China	29.3	33.9	15.9
6	UK	30.0	33.7	9.8
7	Germany	29.2	32.8	12.3
8	Australia	16.9	17.8	5.8
9	Turkey	18.2	16.9	–7.2
10	Austria	16.0	16.7	4.0

Source: World Tourism Organization (WTO). 2008. www.world-tourism.org.

Tour operators and organizers have reacted by developing new forms of tourism to attract the world's affluent including senior citizens: medical, adventure, recreational, educational, and ecotourism. Medical tourism, for example, has picked up strongly in India, China, and Russia, where AM patients can be treated with alternative therapies at lower costs. India's hospitals attract increasing numbers of dental patients for implants, crowns, and polishing from the United States, the United Kingdom, Australia, and the Middle East. Nearer to home, Hungary earned about €600 million in 2006 from 1 million European dental tourists. Hungary has also opened ayurvedic clinics, which are often co-managed by Indian owners. But prices for medical services have gone up steeply since the country joined the EU. Limited in size, Hungary has reached a saturation point and will not be able to compete with the megamarkets as more retirees and chronically sick seek relief. In 2006, over fifty thousand US citizens traveled abroad for medical consultation or surgery. The cost of a spinal fusion in India is US$5,500 against US$62,000 in the United States. In China, a heart bypass surgery costs US$11,000 against US$130,000 in the United States. As AM populations grow older and health-care costs surge, more people look for cosmetic and weight loss surgeries, heart treatments, hip replacement surgery, and liver transplants in emerging markets. Recognizing this opportunity, the Indian government has introduced a new category of visa for foreigners, the medical, or M, visa.

6.5.2. Tourism trends in the megamarkets

Tourism revenue has risen significantly in the megamarkets for both inbound and outbound tourism during the 2000s. Domestic tourism has also grown, owing to rising income

---

66. The remaining 20% is for freight services.

levels, vast geographic expanse, and the development of new resorts and attraction sites. Business travel has expanded with the inflow of foreign investment and high earnings of domestic enterprises. Luxury hotels have run at full capacity, and many new projects have been launched to meet the fast-growing demand, which has spread up to Tier 3 cities. During trade fairs, hotels in cities like Moscow, Mumbai, and Shanghai are fully booked, pushing room rates up to US$500–700 per night, beyond the reach of travelers of more modest means. The megamarkets are attracting the world's biggest H&T companies in the hotel, airline, and travel segments,[67] which want to grow with the economy.

Megamarket governments have declared tourism a priority sector because of its impact on employment and revenue generation. "For every job in a hotel, four new jobs are created around it in related services such as restaurants, cleaning, transport, museums, and guided tours," according to a speaker of the Russian Ministry of Tourism. Various incentives and promotional measures are offered by government-backed agencies including loans, marketing assistance, awards, media advertising (government-sponsored campaigns), and fair sponsorship. Financing, modernizing, and building new infrastructure have been taken up by governments.

INDIA

Compared with some of the smaller EMs (e.g., Malaysia, Morocco, Thailand), India's H&T sector plays a smaller role in the overall economy (3% of GDP), but it is set to grow. For many consecutive years, it has outperformed global tourism revenue growth. According to the Ministry of Tourism, India has the potential to create a US$80 billion industry by 2010, driven by increased spending power and the country's ongoing integration with the global economy. The current number of around 660 million domestic travelers will increase to 850 million by 2010. Outbound (abroad) and inbound tourism will also grow exponentially.

India used to be the country of choice for exotic budget tourism, but now the number of business travelers and affluent tourists is growing thanks to the buoyant economy. Around 5 million overseas visitors (+14%) spent US$9 billion in 2007, while 10 million Indians (+17%) traveled abroad (see table 6.27). There is significant room for expansion considering that the city of Singapore alone reports 8.5 million tourist arrivals a year.

As a subcontinent, India has more to offer than most other destinations in Asia.[68] Attractions range from sandy beaches in Goa and Kerala to thousands of famous historical sites and monuments spread across the subcontinent, not forgetting the new skiing resorts in the Himalayas and spas in Cochin. Tour operators now venture into

Table 6.27. India's hospitality and tourism sector, 2002–2008.

	2002	2005	2008
a. Number of travelers (mn)			
Domestic tourism	4.7	6.0	8
Inbound	2.8	4.9	6
Outbound	1.9	2.5	3
b. Spending (US$ bn)			
Domestic tourism	23	40.0	75
Inbound	5	6.0	9
Outbound	4	5.5	7

Source: McKinsey. 2007.

---

67. Germany's TUI set up a joint venture with Le Passage to India Ltd. in 2005. It had earlier created a similar joint venture with the Chinese partner CTS in 2003.
68. India has twenty-eight world heritage sites (2008).

entirely new market segments including alpine skiing, wild-water canoeing, glider flying, and cruises. Fifty international cruise lines called at Indian ports—mainly Mumbai, Goa, and Kochi—in 2008. Mumbai successfully floated tenders for building a US$50 million cruise terminal of international standard. India's rich wildlife can be seen in the 80 national parks, 440 sanctuaries, and 23 tiger reserves established by the government to conserve this vital resource. Tour operators offer special packages and incentives to the swelling numbers of inbound foreign and outbound Indian tourists.[69]

The government has earmarked US$9 billion for airport modernization and expansion during 2008–2012[70] to face soaring numbers of tourist and business travelers. The national fleet of aircraft will be doubled to above four hundred aircraft by 2012; private airlines are also adding capacity. To accelerate the development of tourism infrastructure, the government will speed up the authorization process for developers to build hotels across all categories. Visa formalities for foreign tourists are also being simplified; a new category—M visa—has been introduced to promote medical tourism. The government is also studying policies to ensure responsible tourism (protection of the environment and cultural identity). Budget allocations are made to create tourism facilities (reception centers, refurbishment of monuments, special tourist trains like the Palace on Wheels, cruise vessels) in addition to efforts to create more sports amenities and to clean cities. The Indian diaspora is a major source of tourism revenue because people of Indian origin (PIO) regularly visit their home country. Special tour packages (including pilgrimage packages) are designed to attract the second generation of PIOs. The most important and successful government initiative is the Incredible India campaign in major AMs as well as Russia and South Africa that uses various media to promote a positive image of India.

India has around 30,000 hotel rooms in the top categories, and another 30,000 are under construction.[71] In total, there are 110,000 rooms (1,975 hotels) across all categories, which is very low (New York alone has 74,000 rooms). The shortfall is around 150,000 rooms. Companies like Emaar MGF (collaboration with Accor), Ginger-Roots (owned by Taj), Sarovar, Choice Hotels, and Fortune Park–ITC are investing heavily in the promising budget segment.[72] India is well poised to become a major player in top-end luxury tourism as well. Chains like the Taj, the Trident (formerly Oberoi), and ITC Welcom, among the world's finest, are developing new properties in prime locations and heritage sites. Leading Hotels of the World, the international marketing company for luxury hotels, hopes to enroll more properties from India by 2010. It has currently ten members in India, including seven Taj properties.[73] There is no restriction to FDI in the hospitality sector: foreign investors are allowed to set up their own wholly owned subsidiaries; they can also benefit from tax incentives for developing properties in certain areas.

---

69. "Cruise Tourism Gains Momentum in India," *Hindustan Times,* December 11, 2007.
70. See 4.3.
71. Source: Knight Frank India study. 2008. "Ein lukrativer bettenmangel" [A lucrative shortage of beds], *Handelsblatt,* July 11–13, 2008, 44.
72. "Budget Hotels: Sector Report," *Business & Economy,* January 11–24, 2008, 33.
73. "Endorsing Luxury Hotel Brands," *Business Standard,* February 22, 2008.

China

China has attracted record numbers of foreign tourists each year since 1995. According to the China National Tourism Office, gross income generated by the H&T sector amounted to US$110 billion in 2007 (+16% compared with 2006), or 4% of GDP. Inbound tourism rose from 47 million to just under 50 million during 2006–2007. The cities of Guangzhou, Beijing, and Shanghai received most foreign tourists and reported the highest revenues. Outbound and domestic tourism has also surged: in 2007, 1.4 billion domestic travelers were counted, more than the country's total population. Of these, 580 million were urban (41.4%) and 820 million (58.6%) rural residents. With rising disposable income, domestic tourism peaks during national holidays such as the Spring Festival (Chinese New Year), Labor Day (May Day), and the Golden Week in October. The number of outbound Chinese tourists rose to 38 million in 2007, 80% of whom went overseas for personal reasons, 20% on business trips. The top ten destinations were Hong Kong, Macao, Japan, South Korea, Thailand, Russia, the United States, Singapore, Viet Nam, and Malaysia. According to WTTC forecasts, Chinese demand for travel and tourism will quadruple in value in the next ten years. By 2018, it will have closed the gap with the United States in terms of outbound demand.

The 2008 Olympic Games gave China's tourism fresh impetus. Attractive hotel complexes were constructed in Tier 1 cities, and beach resorts were developed along the coastline (Dalian, Qingdao, Xiamen) and on Hainan island off Viet Nam. As in India, the emergence of domestic mass tourism has led to the mushrooming of budget hotels in the countryside and along major highways. Operators such as Home Inns, JinJiang Inn, Motel 168, Super 8, Green Tree Inn, and Xinyu Inn are investing enormous sums. Home Inn operated around 130 hotels in 2007. In October 2006, the company went public on New York's NASDAQ to become the first Chinese hotel chain listed abroad. In 2007, the average occupancy rate of five-, four-, and three-star hotels in China was 69%, while the occupancy rate of budget hotels reached 92%. The proportion of commercial guests in five-, four-, and three-star and budget hotels was 48%, 49%, 40%, and 46%, respectively.

Geoparks as prime natural resorts are a new tourist segment meant to promote China's natural landscape. The Ministry of Land and Resources (MLR) uses this vehicle to protect geological heritage, disseminate scientific knowledge, and enhance cultural understanding and economic development of regional communities. Geoparks are located in scenic areas of scientific importance. By 2007, 142 national parks had been approved, of which 12 have been listed by UNESCO as world famous geoparks. Examples are:

- Jingpo Lake National Geopark in Mudanjiang, Heilongjiang;
- Mount Wangwu national geopark, Jiyuan county, Henan;
- Mount Daimei national geopark, Xin'an county, Henan; and
- Mount Taishan, Shandong.

Some of these parks are centers of Chinese religion and spirituality with Taoist, Confucian, and Buddhist temples. They serve as areas for conserving flora and fauna. Minorities are allowed to run their schools and institutes and open educational bases around these locations, which benefit from tourism-related revenue. Special areas at less visited locations are developed for ecotourism. Local governments understand the benefits of nature-based tourism and take many initiatives to protect and promote their cultural and natural heritage. China has three competitive advantages to develop all possible segments of the tourism market: ancient history, vast territory, and complex geographic and geological features.

RUSSIA

In Russia, the H&T sector has transformed beyond recognition compared with its condition in the 1990s. Following the breakup of the Soviet Union, a huge number of private travel agencies sprang up amid the ruins of the Soviet empire. There are today more than twenty-five thousand travel agencies registered in Russia. The largest ones have acquired long experience in both outbound and inbound tourism.[74] Russia's top fifty H&T operators managed to increase their revenue by 73% to more than US$5 billion in 2007 (they control slightly more than half of the H&T market) by selling more outbound trips and offering services to growing numbers of inbound tourists and business travelers.

According to the Federal Tourism Agency, direct spending on tourism, such as accommodations and tours, contributes 1.5% to GDP, about half the EU average. Tourism contribution has the potential to grow to 7%–8% of GDP (US$70–75 billion), which would have a favorable socioeconomic impact. Russians are active travelers and have replaced the Germans as tourism record holders in many countries. In 2007, 23 million Russians visited foreign destinations, especially Germany, the United Kingdom, Turkey, France, the Netherlands, Greece, and Egypt. India (Goa), Indonesia (Bali), Singapore, and China (Hainan) are favorite destinations in Asia.

About 20 million foreign tourists visited Russia in 2007. To attract more tourists, Russia's Federal Tourism Agency will in 2007–2008 treble its promotional budget, which is still low compared with other countries in Europe (€3 million against €8 million for Poland or €121 million for Greece).[75] But much remains to be done to improve the H&T infrastructure and reduce the shortage of hotels in all categories. Foreign visitors complain about the resulting high prices; the average price in the four- to five-star category, for example, rose to US$483 per night in 2007. To maintain the momentum, authorities and developers are developing much needed infrastructure in the more remote regions where many sightseeing places are located. Taking China as an example, the government decided to create six special tourism zones—Buryatia (Siberia-Baikal trail), Irkutsk (Baikal lake), Stawropol (thermal baths), Krasnodar (Black Sea), Altai (mountaineering), and Kaliningrad (Baltic Sea)—where investors are given tax and financial incentives and where the establishment of basic infrastructure will be funded by the government.[76]

Favorable investment conditions are attracting hotel operators from Asia, the European Union, and North America. The coming years will see the launch of several large new luxury venues in the centers of Moscow, St. Petersburg, and other tourist cities. There is a strong demand for boutique hotels as well. Around five hundred such properties were developed in

---

74. Examples are VAO Intourist, Akademservis DMS, KMP Group in Moscow, Arctur Travel, Baltic Travel Company, ISBA, and INEXCO Voyage in St. Petersburg.
75. "Tourism—Image Is Everything," *Business Week Russia,* December 19, 2006.
76. "Touristische Sonderwirtschaftszonen sollen mehr Besucher ins Land locken" [Tourist parks are supposed to attract more tourists to the country], *Moskauer Deutsche Zeitung,* May 2008.

St. Petersburg during 2002–2008. They are a direct response to both the lack of hotel space and the difficulties of converting historic buildings in central areas into hotels.

More than twenty cultural assets and nature preserves in Russia have been named UNESCO World Heritage Sites, adding to the country's attraction. Russia's provincial cities with long histories are also becoming popular tourist destinations: Novgorod, Pskov, Vladimir, Vologda, Yaroslavl, and the *kremlins* (fortresses) of Kazan, Nizhny Novgorod, and Siberian Tobolsk. Russia's vast expanses are ideal for adventure tourism. Affluent tourists from the West and Japan appreciate the helicopter outings in Siberia and the far north. The ultimate form of tourism is space travel, which is coordinated by Russia's Federal Space Agency. American Charles Simonyi became the world's fifth space tourist in 2007, describing his twenty-five-million-dollar trip as "terrific." Although very lucrative, this market is limited by the demand by Russia's own space program for higher launcher capacity.

6.5.3. Challenges for foreign tourism and hospitality companies

Growth in the tourism industry in the megamarkets will attract airlines, hotel chains, tour operators, and business consultants alike. Although FDI in civil aviation is restricted in the megamarkets, EU companies use other strategies to gain market share. Code sharing and participation in groupings like Star Alliance give better access to both the business and leisure travel segments.

The business segment is growing and becoming more influential. Lufthansa's direct Frankfurt–Pune (India) flight was sanctioned as part of the state's commitment to Volkswagen for selecting Pune as the location for its operation. Lufthansa's direct flight to Shenyang (via Seoul) is also linked to increased business travelers as a consequence of the investments made by German carmakers in the region (BMW in Shenyang, Volkswagen in Changchun and Dalian). This class of travelers is growing thanks to the intensification of business relations between the European Union and the megamarkets. Business travelers are more demanding customers for convenience, safety, reliability, and quality. The three national airlines Aeroflot, Air India, and Air China also compete for business travelers on major routes by offering better bargains.

Wealthy individuals and corporate executives who can afford it prefer private aviation to avoid the increasing hassle, inconvenience, and delays at congested hub airports and to increase executive productivity. The Lufthansa Private Jet service will offer a network of about a thousand airports in Europe, Russia, and the Middle East.[77] It has placed orders for at least nine executive jets for its most lucrative premium customers.

The leisure segment will polarize along two dimensions:
- luxury or premium segment with customers demanding top-class service, lifestyle, and exclusivity in secluded resorts (similar to the executive traveler segment);
- low-price or economy segment (e.g., budget hotels, last-minute flights, adventure tourism).

---

77. "Lufthansa to Launch Executive Fleet," *Financial Times,* March 9, 2008.

Hotel and tour operators will strongly benefit from these developments. They have made forays into the megamarkets through new investments and acquisitions. Similarly, EU consultancies can offer valuable know-how to megamarket governments for the conservation of heritage sites, improvement of museums, and development of infrastructure around these sites. These projects are usually coordinated by government agencies.

The megamarkets offer foreign investors ample opportunities as tourism infrastructure and services are still not commensurate with demand. All three countries are determined to make tourism a top earner and will deploy the necessary resources to support projects related to both budget and exclusive tourism.

PART II
SECURING LEADERSHIP IN THE NEW MEGAMARKETS

"In preparing for battle I have always found that plans are useless, but planning is indispensable."
—Dwight Eisenhower, former President of the United States

The preceding chapters highlighted business prospects in the megamarkets of China, India, and Russia and provided an insight into these countries' geostrategic weight as rising continental powers, their industrial assets, and their growing role as international providers of capital and know-how. This part will focus on how to approach the megamarkets in order to outflank competitors and make it into the top league.

To begin with, a company must set out with the idea of winning leadership in its business segment, and all its strategies must flow from this determining idea. To attain this objective in a megamarket, a company must achieve excellence at five levels through various measures:

- industry leadership: cultivating close relationships with strategic stakeholders; recruitment and retaining of best talents; reinvesting in R&D, environment-friendly practices, and corporate social responsibility;
- client leadership: privileged relations with key accounts at all levels; attentive ear to customers' most pressing problems; determination to provide solutions;
- product and brand leadership: incessant efforts to develop innovations in the product-service mix to stay ahead of imitators (a common risk in the megamarkets); imaginative brand management;
- process leadership: efficient measures for cost-saving and environment-friendly production without sacrificing quality; high labor productivity;
- financial leadership: profitability, without which supremacy in other functional areas is hollow; astute financial management and access to "smart finance" (private equity, venture capital, etc.).

A special six-step concept (see figure 7.0) has been elaborated for foreign companies in the Eurasian megamarkets. It is a proven and practical approach drawn from experience gained through actual implementation of megamarket entry and expansion projects with corporate clients in key industries over more than twenty years. These case studies (described in special boxes throughout the text) provide valuable insights not only into the mechanisms and forces that drive large emerging markets, but also about the responsiveness of the investor, independently of the sector of operation. The interesting revelation is that the second aspect, and not the first, has required more preparation as it has often lagged behind. Another important point to note is that although the concept was conceived for the megamarkets of Eurasia, it can easily be adjusted to accommodate strategies for

Figure 7.0. Six steps toward megamarket leadership.

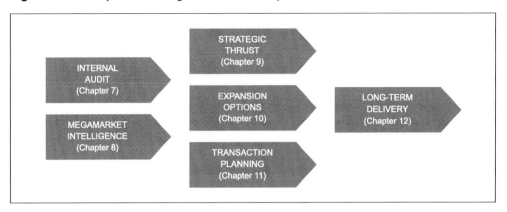

other emerging markets that are equally complex but at a much smaller scale in terms of geography and number of options.

The six steps aim to make preparatory work a systematic exercise that reduces to the extent possible the unknowns, which can jeopardize a venture. The first two steps (audit, intelligence) are analytical and environment-driven; they bring together the information and expose the opportunity (which context must we work in?), from which the other four flow (strategic thrust, expansion options, transaction planning, delivery).

The six steps are not a complex model, but simple as they may seem, they are often not applied. First, companies need to know if they have the required resources and competencies to face the respective megamarket (step 1); this is the internal audit. Western managers tend to ask if the market is good for them, but they do not ask if they are good for the market. Some companies carry out audits but focus them on internal resources such as staff and funding. They overlook the fact that the mindset and involvement of senior management and the recruitment of the most skilled specialists (including external experts) is the most decisive factor in making the megamarket venture work. Opportunity-seeking (as supplement to planning) and commitment to long-term investments (instead of exports only) are attitudes that will foster success. The megamarket team must be committed to profitability so that the venture does not become a permanent cost factor for headquarters.

Second, companies need to know their target market thoroughly before deciding how and where to invest (step 2). Megamarket intelligence is more than simple information gathering or going through market studies provided by research agencies. Data on GDP growth, inflation, the middle class, political risk, and so forth, hardly paint an accurate full picture. A new type of intelligence is required for the fast-moving megamarkets, which differs from that used in the familiar advanced markets. Business intelligence must zoom in from the sector down to the specific enterprise and people levels. The real source of information on real trends is the customer and the leading suppliers in the industry. Getting this information is a continuous exercise requiring intensive fieldwork, expeditionary marketing, and regular discussions with insiders in addition to statistical data collection and visits to the major exhibitions.

Conventional market research can help to refine marketing and distribution concepts in established markets but is of little use when a company must harness its innovative skills for emerging markets requiring special solutions for unspecified needs. Personal interviews with selected decision-makers can reveal more about demand patterns, competitive forces, and tomorrow's direction than expensive panel discussions and secondary research, which can be outdated by the time results are printed. What is the meaning of market share in markets that barely exist or with floating boundaries of industry and product classifications? Competition for leadership in the megamarkets is competition for opportunity share rather than fictitious market share. It is competition to maximize the share of future prospects (in terms of customers) a company could potentially access by preempting new entrants. Emerging markets require totally different abilities from chief executives, who must orchestrate their companies' core competencies to shape the future of yet unstructured industries by creating values and setting standards in virgin territories.

Third, a megamarket-specific strategy must be designed and put into operation. The interplay of the internal audit and megamarket intelligence yields various possible growth paths, entry/expansion options, and transaction challenges (steps 3–5). A strategy that brought success to one company may not work for another; the difference in size, corporate culture, or specialization (industry) in each case warrants a firm-specific master plan. In the same line of thought, a strategy developed for one megamarket cannot be symmetrically transposed to another. It is also wrong to duplicate strategies elaborated for mature markets (e.g., distributor-based expansion) and apply them to the megamarkets (which may demand FDI-intensive solutions). The strategy must include adjustment mechanisms for contexts where needs evolve rapidly but may not be clearly visible at the outset. It should match the capabilities of the company (managerial, human, technological, financial) and the receptivity of the market, including its various regional and sector dimensions. Above all, it should ensure the company profitability and not just presence. In the "gold rush" to China, how many companies can in all honesty state that their subsidiaries are truly successful and would be able to survive as independent profit centers without continuous support from the corporate head office?

Finally, in the megamarket strategy development process, delivery is the decisive factor (step 6). A well-thought-out concept has little scope if management lacks the mandate, skills, and determination to pursue its leadership concept against all odds. Resistance is mostly homemade: union pressure, shyness of shareholders, and personal interests of board members and middle managers. Chief executives and shareholders must speak with one voice and introduce adequate control mechanisms to succeed.

CHAPTER 7
Internal audit: Prepare for the venture

Before embarking on the megamarkets, a company should take an honest look at its motivation, offer, and resources to assess its preparedness. The reason is that not all companies are fit for this venture—they may be too small, financially vulnerable, their products not relevant to the market, or they may be targeting the megamarkets only because the "others are going there." The company should be clearly conscious about its position regarding these issues and the real advantages it can bring to the table of local business partners right from the outset. An internal audit is the best way of conducting this self-analysis. The audit revolves around three dimensions:

- the strategic motivation and vision of top management (What is the logic behind the decision to enter the megamarket?)
- internal resources to take up the challenge of the megamarket (Does the company have the necessary people, funds, and other essential assets?)
- distinct and relevant competencies for competitive advantage (Is the company's product and service portfolio relevant to the megamarket?)

Clarity of purpose, commitment, and a best-fit product or service is common to all successful European companies that have established themselves in the megamarkets.

Pause for thought

A medium-sized German producer of cleaning equipment invested in a joint venture with an Indian producer of smaller cleaning machines. The objective was to offer equipment ranging from the high-tech German machines to the mass-market manual road sweepers made in India. German and Indian engineers worked together to adapt German machines to Indian conditions and develop new upgraded versions, which were also included in the German company's international range. The joint venture is now showcased as a model for other German companies.

7.1. Adopting a new logic

To gain leadership, EU managers will need to adopt an unorthodox approach that is specifically conceived for the megamarkets. Unlike the more predictable, transparent, and culturally familiar advanced markets, megamarkets can throw up unforeseen opportunities and challenges. Megamarket strategies must therefore be tempered by patience and flexibility. Gestation periods can be long until a need converts to solvent demand. EU executives will need to exercise their judgment to follow new avenues uninfluenced by stereotypical myths about the market and to proactively seek opportunities. For this, companies must not only show flexibility in adapting their product range and adjusting their procedures, but they must also demonstrate their commitment by reinvesting earnings for the long term.

Recognition of the significance of the Eurasian megamarkets to a company's global operations must be supported by a strategic vision to steer the company toward sustainable leadership in these markets. The following questions will show how close corporate leaders are to this vision and what they still need to do to get there:

- Question 1: What drives the decision to expand in the megamarkets, reality or myths?
- Question 2: What is the company's strategic blueprint for its megamarket venture?
- Question 3: Is opportunity-seeking part of the corporate planning exercise?
- Question 4: Is the projected growth truly profitable?
- Question 5: What are the company's investment intentions for the megamarkets?
- Question 6: What role does senior management play in the megamarket venture?

These questions refer to basic principles (see figure 7.1) that constitute the building blocks for gaining sustainable leadership in the megamarkets. The challenge lies in adopting a balanced approach aimed at enhancing the company's competitiveness while taking away market share from principal rivals. Success implies a long-term positive impact of the company's operations on employees, external stakeholders, and the environment. There is thus a triple bottom line to sustainability that managers need to observe: people, planet, and profit.

Figure 7.1. Adopting a new megamarket logic (the six building blocks).

QUESTION 1:
WHAT DRIVES THE DECISION TO EXPAND IN THE MEGAMARKETS, REALITY OR MYTHS?

Long-term success in the megamarkets demands an innovative and intuitive approach. Corporate leaders must gain their own insight into market realities, which may differ strongly from myths propagated by third parties including the mass media. Various reasons can prompt a company to strengthen its presence in a megamarket. Some are realistic:

- strong demand for their product or service as highlighted by in-house preliminary research
- the need to uphold global leadership by expanding into a large market
- reduced growth in the home market
- the urgency to stem competition from megamarket companies by moving onto their turf
- the intention to continue supplying a big client who has moved to the megamarket

In these cases, a company can proactively increase its stakes in a megamarket with a clear game plan based on its own research.

But sometimes the motivation is ad hoc:

- a chance meeting at a trade fair with a megamarket company that proposes a collaboration
- fear of being left behind because other EU companies in the sector are moving eastwards
- media reports of megamarket El Dorados and similar myths

In such cases, the company should investigate further to identify a more valid reason.

At the same time, certain companies that would benefit from the megamarkets do not make the move. Common prejudices related to hearsay about Russia, India, and China (see table 7.1) for many years prevented many CEOs from regarding them as anything more than export targets. This attitude is now changing given the persisting economic recession in AMs and the economic rise of the megamarkets, which pushes the media and institutions (e.g., trade ministries, chambers of commerce, industry associations) to report in a more objective and in certain cases even overoptimistic way about certain developments. But at the same time, new myths are spread by companies eager to dissimulate their achievements in an attempt to keep rivals at bay. Policymakers and the media project a negative picture of human rights abuses (China), aggressive stances against neighbors (Russia), and ethnic and religious divides (India) to divert from problems at home (financial crises, poverty, immigration, education). In all this, Western CEOs gradually realize that megamarket companies are quickly moving up the value chain and are already on the verge of becoming formidable competitors in the global arena.

Instead, a company should conduct some basic investigation either in-house or through an external agency on the target market/industry to capture the reality in the field and to

Table 7.1a. Common megamarket myths—China.

Beliefs	Reality
China is the world's largest market with 1.3 billion consumers.	But not for all products! While almost everybody may buy a shampoo, only 30–40 million can afford luxury cars. For most consumer durables, the real market consists of 300–350 million consumers belonging to the middle class. Overall population figures hardly affect demand for high-tech and engineering goods.
China's growth rates will remain high for decades to come.	The 10% average growth rate of the past fifteen years will slow down to 5%–6% after 2010 as the base becomes larger. Rates will vary with the sector depending on the lifecycles.
Chinese are impenetrable partners and are ready to steal technology; therefore, wholly-owned subsidiaries are the best option.	The language barrier could feed this myth, although Chinese managers now speak English and have gained exposure. Besides, adding to excess capacity burdens the sector, and acquisitions or strategic alliances (based on mutual respect) may be a more viable option depending on the industry.
Government interference prevents foreign companies from growing. It is only government relations that count.	The Communist Party has been disengaging progressively from micromanagement and focusing on sociocultural and macroeconomic issues. The new constitution amended in 2005 welcomes entrepreneurs as party members. Most companies are nowadays run by private entrepreneurs.
China's oriental business culture and philosophy is not compatible with western business style. Key positions should be held by western expatriates.	Chinese who lived and studied overseas are gradually replacing western managers. Many Chinese managers have done their business studies abroad and significantly improved their foreign language skills over the past few years. In certain cases, local managers are more suitable than either expatriates or "returnees."
China is a corrupt country where bureaucrats wield absolute power.	Laws have been enacted to counter corruption, and there is visible impact at the federal level, although it is still rampant in some regions. The solution is to seek guidance from straight local persons for liaising with official bodies and avoiding the wrong steps. Chinese society is hierarchic, which means that officials can enact directives very quickly.

Table 7.1b. Common megamarket myths—India.

Beliefs	Reality
India is a poor and underdeveloped country.	India's middle class of 250–280 million is equal to the population of EU-15. India has 83,000 millionaires, and the number is growing by 10%–15% each year. Development indicators have been improving drastically. The number of business travelers visiting India has exploded.
India's Hinduism and its caste system are not conducive to economic growth.	Socialism and not Hinduism kept India back until economic liberalization in 1991. It is the same Hindus and their heirs who are notching 7%–8% growth rates today.
India is good at services, but not manufacturing.	Manufacturing accounts for a quarter of GDP, half of the exports, and three-quarters of FDI. Indian manufacturers are becoming global competitors and acquiring companies overseas.
India's infrastructure is inadequate and hampers economic activity.	The sector is growing at 15% per year. Many mega infrastructure projects are underway, mostly through public-private partnerships. In fact, the sector offers vast FDI opportunities to EU companies.
India is the world's largest democracy and a state of law, making contractual agreements easier.	True, but this does not obviate the need to carefully scrutinize contracts and partners, as in any other country.
India's colonial past makes it easier to adopt a Western approach.	True, Indian managers have been trained according to US and UK systems. But as any other country, it has its specificities, to which foreign investors should show sensitivity. Cultural and religious factors play a decisive role.

Table 7.1c. Common megamarket myths—Russia.

Beliefs	Reality
Russia's Communist past and its unbusinesslike attitudes cannot be easily wiped off.	The new generation of young managers has espoused international concepts and practices and is showing commendable performance. The new Russian is multilingual, dynamic, and has been exposed to foreign cultures.
Russia is controlled by the mafia, to whom all businesses have to pay "security fees."	The government's crackdown on such outfits has reduced their presence, even if they have not been completely wiped out. Risky activities are those where large sums of money are moved relatively quickly: trading, transport, construction, raw materials. Today, the rule of law prevails over organized crime, and enforcement of security organs and tribunals has improved significantly.
Russia's authorities institute arbitrary measures to extract unjustified taxes from companies.	Such measures mostly targeted oil companies such as Yukos, Sibneft, and recently TNK-BP. But regional authorities, who value foreign investors, are not as heavy-handed. SMEs are much less molested. The tax code allows any legal entity to seek recourse if it deems it was unfairly treated.
Russia has expertise in mainly oil and raw material extraction; its workforce has inadequate industrial skills.	Russia did lose its best engineers and scientists in the aftermath of the collapse of the Soviet Union. But the brain drain has been stemmed; economic growth is creating job opportunities for graduates in Russia itself. Russia's education system is on par with the European systems and produces high-quality engineers for industrial ventures, which benefit from investment inflows.
Russia is highly indebted and needs the West to survive.	Rising energy prices have yielded windfall profits to Russia. It has now practically paid off its entire debt to the Paris and London Clubs. The country's budget surplus amounted to 4% on average during 2002–2006. The balance has tilted, and it is now the EU that needs Russia more than ever to meet its energy requirements.
Russia was the core of the former Soviet Union. Now each independent former Soviet republic (today's CIS members) needs to be approached separately.	As Russia is the largest CIS market, it is more logical to radiate from it to the smaller republics than the other way about. The current customs union includes Belarus, Ukraine, and Kazakhstan. A Russian structure is useful for overcoming tariff and nontariff barriers.
Russia is an ideal location for companies in the raw material sector and their vendors.	Re-nationalization of energy assets has made this more difficult, particularly because Russian oil majors prefer indigenous products, whenever possible, unless they are high-technology products or are sold as a service component in the framework of a strategic alliance between vendor and buyer.

assess the potential for its products or services.[1] At least one visit—but not a whirlwind tour—by a senior executive should be undertaken, and the impressions should be reported and discussed among the team before making the decision. The visit should include discussions with potential customers, potential partners, local resource persons with domain knowledge, distribution and supply agents, service providers (audit and legal firms), and, if necessary, local authorities.

These two exercises—research and field visit—are a mark of the company's strategic interest in the market. They enable a company to quit the myths path and base decisions on hard facts rather than hearsay. Executives should be proactive and not linger with important decisions until it is too late.

---

1. See chapter 8.

Question 2:
What is the company's strategic blueprint for its megamarket venture?

In other words, how does a company approach the uncharted territory of a megamarket? Are tactical measures adequate to enforce implementation?

Strategy planners can adopt an approach that best suits their objectives and competencies:

- They can follow an "adaptive" approach, by which the company moves as effectively as possible and positions itself within the environmental context, keeping in mind the drivers of profitability in its business and market. This outside-in approach is basically context-driven and based on customer feedback.
- Or it can be "resource-driven," by which a strong and successful company believes that it needs to change the rules of the game in an industry through its offering (technology, know-how, patents). This approach[2] focuses on a company's own competencies and capabilities as the starting point for strategy development. It is particularly effective in nascent markets where the rules are still being written and Western know-how appreciated by megamarket business partners.
- Or it can adopt a "learning" mode, whereby strategy should not be prescribed but formed gradually through learning and project experience. This is particularly true for the megamarkets, where companies are constantly faced with new situations and compelled to readjust their focuses.

Prior macroeconomic and preliminary market investigations will have revealed five common traits of the emerging megamarkets:

- Although the customer base is immense, it is composed of mostly "value for money" customers, who are extremely cautious and fairly new to consumerism (low familiarity with the benefits of certain products, shopping behavior in transition).
- The customer base is highly fragmented and dispersed owing to cultural diversity and income differences. In certain cases, concrete needs cannot be formulated.
- The infrastructure and logistics variable is deficient, although it is developing fast.
- Labor costs are low but not necessarily labor productivity.
- Change is fast paced, even if bureaucracies are slow.

These factors must be kept in mind while formulating a strategy. But above all, the company should remember that it is in the target market for the long haul and that "fifty-two-week reports" are meaningless when developing or creating a market (converting need to solvent demand). Strategy makers should also aim for profitability right from the outset. Cross-subsidization from profits generated by other geographic areas should be avoided if the megamarket project is to become self-sustainable.

Often companies tend to formulate strategies that are vague and based on illusions rather than intelligence or too specific for a context that is still not fully known. In other cases,

---

2. G. Hamel and C. K. Prahalad, "Competing for the Future: Strategic Intent," *Harvard Business Review*, May–June 1989.

executives confuse the short-term measures of a budget document with the making of a sustainable strategy (formulation, implementation). Such measures propose a series of expenditures mostly based on assumed sales, profit, and cost projections, but they do not show the way to achieve market leadership. Another error foreign companies commit is to focus on temporary (tactical) advantages. They may pump large budgets into TV advertising, either "to prepare the market" or to counter competitors who are doing the same. Other companies spend huge sums on training local specialists, who afterwards join the competition. But such measures, which are visible for everybody (including competitors) and do not in any way guarantee lasting leadership, cannot be considered a strategy. China's ancient military commander Sun Tzu once stated: "All men can see the tactics whereby I conquer, but what none can see is the strategy out of which final victory is evolved."

A true megamarket strategy is unique; it addresses a range of issues in the light of its ultimate objective for the market (see box 7.1):

- Business format for entry and upscaling. This depends on the policies governing FDI and foreign businesses in the country. Although the economies have been liberalized, certain restrictions still remain, particularly for strategic sectors. The business can be scaled up—for example, from distribution to production, minority to majority share, or joint venture to wholly owned enterprise—as the company successfully climbs the learning curve.

- Product and service mix. Based on prior investigation, the company can determine which products from its portfolio will find the best acceptance or how it can modify them or develop new ones specifically for the market.

- Segmentation and regional dimension. The company will need to identify the emerging regional power centers in the megamarkets to pursue the best ways by which it can accelerate the different processes for developing its business in the most promising submarkets (segments, niches). Regional differences in these large countries can be as diverse as in the different nation-states of the EU.

- Envisaged sales and profitability. In industries marked by relationship management, complicated regulatory frameworks, overcapacity, and price wars, an alliance, acquisition, or combination thereof will allow the company to shorten lead time drastically compared with a stand-alone option.

Box 7.1. Dimensions of a megamarket strategy.

- Business format (model) for entry or expansion
- Product and service mix
- Segmentation and regional focus
- Sales and profitability targets
- Benchmarking and countering competition
- Resource allocation
- Processes
- Functional strategies
- Legal and administrative issues

- Benchmarking and countering competition. The company may find that it has to compete with not only its traditional rivals but also local players, who may have already set the rules of the game such that these deter new entrants. The company then needs to identify the gaps where it can place itself and then strengthen its position with tenacity while it keeps costs under control and observes the moves of possible new entrants (including producers of substitute products).
- Resource allocation. The company will need to determine the required competencies and resources—human, financial, and intellectual—it will need to allocate for developing its megamarket project, bearing in mind that it should factor in unforeseen opportunities (e.g., a partnership, an acquisition). This includes distribution of managerial responsibilities among the team members both at headquarters and on site.
- Processes. Infrastructure may be a constraint, so the company will need to determine how best its quality can be maintained in the circumstances. Labor costs are generally lower in the megamarkets, but high productivity levels need to be maintained. Investment in new equipment or manufacturing capacities may become a necessity. Investments should be tackled on time to take advantage of price levels and exchange rate differentials. Organizational processes must be streamlined and adjusted.
- Functional strategies. The company must design tactical measures for its business functions (e.g., marketing, human resources, R&D) that support its overall strategy in the megamarket. Transversal dimensions such as customer relationship, supply chain, and innovation management must be put in place.
- Legal and administrative issues. The company will need to spot changes in the political and legislative landscape, which can occur at central, provincial, and/or local levels. It should carefully monitor legislation and protect its intellectual property from the very beginning of an investment.

Employees in the field and also at the head office must be updated right from the outset so that they fully understand the implications for their own future of the proposed expansion into the megamarket. In this way, the company can count on their support for the project and avoid misunderstandings (e.g., about outsourcing). A successful strategy is one that marshals the company's various stakeholders (see figure 7.2) into a consensual community. Company staff, customers, and investors form the innermost circle that has a direct impact on the results. Surrounding them is the circle of suppliers, competitors, and authorities who can exert significant influence. The outermost circle is inhabited by the general and local public, the media, and, increasingly, politicians, who shape the general opinion on and image of the company.

A spin-off of this exercise is that it will coach strategy planners in building greater flexibility into the overall corporate strategy. They will then be better able to:
- balance strategic planning with strategic adjustment;
- search for non-linearity and creative breakthrough through self-analysis; and
- embrace risk, action, and acceptance of failure positively when confronted by unforeseen events.

Figure 7.2. The company's stakeholder universe.

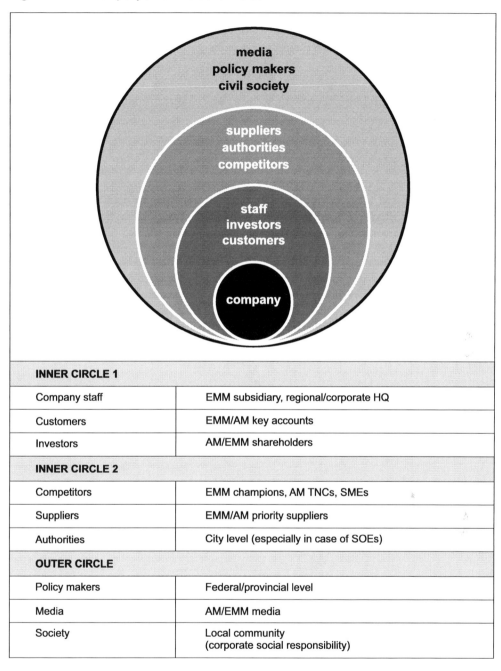

INNER CIRCLE 1	
Company staff	EMM subsidiary, regional/corporate HQ
Customers	EMM/AM key accounts
Investors	AM/EMM shareholders
INNER CIRCLE 2	
Competitors	EMM champions, AM TNCs, SMEs
Suppliers	EMM/AM priority suppliers
Authorities	City level (especially in case of SOEs)
OUTER CIRCLE	
Policy makers	Federal/provincial level
Media	AM/EMM media
Society	Local community (corporate social responsibility)

Preparation of a road map after the strategy formulation exercise takes the commitment further as the plan will reveal the human and financial inputs that the company must provide for. It requires thinking the project through. A typical plan should:
- lead to where the company aims to stand in three to five years in the target megamarket (realistic market share, turnover, profitability, etc.);
- propose concrete and prioritized actions with targets, budgets, schedules, and responsibilities;

- prepare a dashboard for information on relevant players (customers, competitors, suppliers, etc.) and policies (investment, labor, capital, etc.) that can be updated regularly so that the company has a complete overview of the local scenario at a glance; and
- involve senior management and future project managers from the start of the project.

The plan can be refined as more information is obtained on the unfolding situation in the market and the activities of local market leaders. Above all, it should factor in flexibility to allow for adjustments and midcourse corrections. Finally, a company can aspire for leadership only if (a) it manages to develop unique managerial and technical skills and (b) it succeeds in satisfying pressing customer needs by offering better and different solutions than its competitors. Market leaders fulfill both conditions and forcefully pursue investment-driven strategies. They reinvent their industries by anticipating trends and building competencies ahead of time.

QUESTION 3:
IS OPPORTUNITY-SEEKING PART OF THE CORPORATE PLANNING EXERCISE?

This question can also be broken down as follows: How does the planning exercise address the question of unforeseen opportunities (e.g., possibility of acquisition)? Is the annual budget flexible enough to allow a rapid response?

It is understandable that companies will not look at other markets until they face difficulties and declining sales in their own home markets. However, the rapidly changing global scenario calls for timely prospecting of opportunities elsewhere. Many EU/US companies have missed them for lack of foresight by family owners of SMEs as well as board members of multinationals who are unwilling to acknowledge this change or to recognize the megamarkets as priority countries for investment projects (and platforms for conquering adjacent economies) demanding top-class expertise that is not always available in-house. Companies with full order books and running at full capacity in Western markets are particularly vulnerable to complacency. Only now, when the rush is already on, have the mass of companies woken up to megamarket opportunities, and executives are pressed into taking quick action. Under such conditions, decision-makers have unfortunately little time for accurate strategy making, let alone a frank recognition that they lack the intercultural skills required for speedy implementation of crucial projects involving greenfield projects, acquisitions, and alliances.

The fast-evolving dynamic megamarkets throw up opportunities as they unfold:
- privatization of a state-owned company;
- divestment of equity, opening a chance for an outright acquisition or a participation in an IPO (initial public offering);
- interest in a co-investment shown by financial investors or venture capitalists;
- tenders for large public sector or industrial projects;
- management changes at a formerly inaccessible key account, which once again opens the doors for the company;
- change in government regulations in favor of the company's business.

Opportunities not foreseen in the business plan allow companies to leap beyond the planned objectives for gaining market share and increasing turnover. If such opportunities in an emerging market are not grasped in time and are seized instead by a competitor, the setback can cost a company many years of efforts to catch up. A megamarket strategy should be flexible enough to allow executives not only to respond to opportunities, but also to seek them proactively. A contingency budget that can be mobilized immediately when the need arises must therefore be provided for seeking and seizing opportunities in the three megamarkets simultaneously.

The probability of obtaining a complete picture on new opportunities increases with the right mindset and selection of right survey targets; it is not necessarily a consequence of increasing the sample population, which in any large market generates higher costs but not automatically good results. Successful businessmen are those who walk through the market themselves and know what to do and whom to talk to rather than be led by general opinions of, for example, journalists, politicians, compatriots, or distributors who may be based in these countries but may also see reality from a different angle or pursue their own agendas.

Once an acquisition target (company, brand), partner, or new client has been discovered, the top management should pursue the lead and think and act fast. In the megamarkets, it is considered an affront if senior executives from headquarters do not find the time to engage in high-level on-site visits and negotiations or if promises are not followed by real action.

Classical corporate planning, particularly by large corporations, tends to follow a sequential approach to business development in emerging markets due to risk aversion. SMEs are forced to do this due to budget constraints. But opportunities can arise simultaneously in different megamarkets. Success in emerging economies depends on a healthy mix of planning and opportunity-seeking (see figure 7.3).

Pause for thought

A French company carried out presentations in second-tier cities in China for introducing new waste management systems. Because of organizational changes at the head office, there was no follow-up of the project as promised by the field staff, and the company now has difficulties in repositioning itself with the same authorities.

Similarly, the failed promise by a German components company to hold regional workshops with engineers of a Russian key account led to negative reactions at the board level when the oil and gas major had to be contacted again after a few years.

***

Volkswagen's relative leadership in China was not accompanied by similarly aggressive and timely measures in India and Russia, where the company has fallen far behind its major competitors, with ultimately negative effects on its China and global business as well.

Figure 7.3. Planning and opportunity-seeking in the megamarkets.

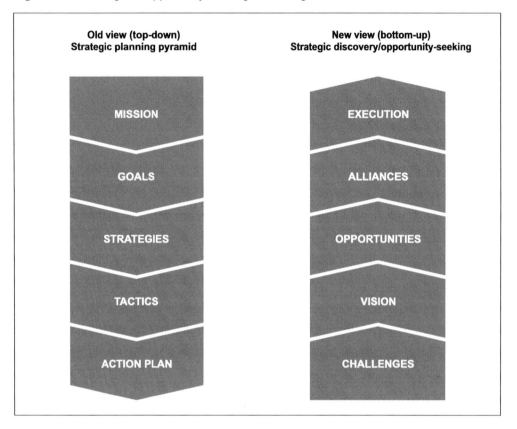

Question 4:
Is the projected growth truly profitable?

In other words, how soon will the company break even? "We are there for the long term," business executives often say, but can the company afford to wait years until it breaks even and moves on to profitability? Large multinationals with deep pockets could, but SMEs need quicker returns on their investments if they want to survive and grow. Eventually, low or no profitability forces even large companies to withdraw (e.g., Continental tires from Russia, Obi from China, Lafarge roofing from India). No company is large enough to subsidize activities that demand more and more funds just to keep the business afloat. Peer pressure will eventually usher in a retreat.

Higher contribution of the megamarket to a company's total turnover as well as higher business volume or higher market share do not automatically indicate profitability of the venture. According to studies conducted by the Sino-German Chamber of Commerce, about 70% of investments made by German companies in China cannot be considered profitable, some of them even after more than a decade. French, Italian, UK, and Scandinavian investors have similar problems. Executives admit this only reluctantly and mainly in private. However, presence in a megamarket, or even leadership, achieved at such cost cannot endure.

True success is achieved when each megamarket operation becomes a profit center by itself that can draw on its own resources to undertake the necessary investments for expansion. Cross-subsidization through profits generated in other markets gives megamarket managers a false sense of security. A cost-benefit analysis of each investment would protect companies from making the wrong choices, particularly in significantly large markets where viable investment projects can cost from €10 million upwards.

All too often, managers follow a growth logic that is concerned with size—and therefore prestige and image—more than with bottom-line profits. Once the operation is well underway, pressure is placed on expenditure (costs) to eke out a profit. But costs can only be reduced so far as they are already low in the megamarkets and thus cannot be reduced indefinitely. A true breakeven can be attained more effectively (i.e., faster) if the company satisfies its clients' needs by offering special competencies. At the same time, it would be equally unwise to pursue an aggressive profit-oriented approach based on Western shareholder value concepts whereby management aims at quarterly or biannual profit increases to satisfy faraway shareholders but at the expense of organic long-term business development. On the contrary, the megamarkets demand a long-term approach to profit-building where the interests of all major stakeholders, including society as a whole, and the environment are to be taken into consideration.

Western reporting systems demanding rigid profit calculations based on monthly assessments from local management often fail as the megamarket subsidiary is forced to act aggressively in the market without getting a chance to systematically build market share as a source of future profits. Some multinationals decided to change this practice.

Companies that are well established are networked with a series of clients and suppliers. This helps them to spot key factors of success, overcome bottlenecks, and achieve profitability. As a rule, they can act faster than new entrants who are at the very beginning of their marketing and lobbying efforts. But this rule cannot be generalized. Cases abound whereby established companies struggle for a very long time before they become profitable. Given little or no attention from the parent company—"the market is too small," "we just need to be there," "we shall act when the market grows"—local managers become complacent with the status quo and show scant motivation to strive for better results. In an emerging market, where information is scarce and cannot be double-checked, mismanagement

---

Pause for thought

Nestlé's success in the megamarkets can be attributed to its having adopted a long-term view, with the support of headquarters.

Similarly, many medium-sized "hidden champions" from the EU, such as Moulinex, Mapei, Delongi, Blum, Faber-Castell, Lapp Kabel, Pharmaplan, Ritter Sport, Schuler, Wurth, and Knauff, to cite just a few, continue expanding their market share by reinvesting in the megamarkets.

These companies have understood that the true source of profitability is a right strategy supported by talented management committed to the leadership principle in the megamarkets.

> **Box 7.2. Dimensions of excellence for the megamarkets.**
>
> - Highly qualified human resources
> - Production processes and technologies
> - Product quality and design
> - Superior service and advice
> - Speed in distribution and logistics
> - Tailor-made financial schemes
> - Innovative capability through advanced R&D

and low profitability can long persist. Lack of profitability is generally a sign of a wrong strategy and failure of management to take the right measures.

Time is an important factor in profitability. A profitable business can obviously not be built overnight in the megamarkets, which are enormous in size, culturally very different, and where business follows other rules. Just after Russia's financial crisis in 1998–1999, only very few foreign players saw the opportunity to take advantage of a low ruble for investing in local manufacturing. These companies have had the time to make their local base profitable, whereas their competitors who stayed away have to struggle to penetrate the market in changed circumstances.

CEOs must understand the rules of the game and spot entry barriers raised to protect existing players early enough to avoid unnecessary expenses. If entry barriers are too high, creative solutions need to be found. A stand-alone solution may have disadvantages over an alliance with a local sector leader who may have the required facilities (land, manufacturing platform). An alliance shortens penetration times and helps to save costs. In terms of investment, it is not necessarily more costly than a stand-alone greenfield solution. Unfortunately, many executives do not spend enough time studying the situation in the megamarkets (and the various investment options) as they are under pressure to solve more immediate problems at home. The profitability issue of the venture is neglected, which can have negative consequences for the company's global operations.

Profitability is determined by the ability to achieve singularity in the different business segments a company engages in. For megamarkets, this translates as the ability to impose price hikes on customers and/or to offer cost reductions, which both represent entry barriers for competitors. Entry barriers may differ from sector to sector, but in general they refer to certain dimensions in which a company must excel (see box 7.2).

QUESTION 5:
WHAT ARE THE COMPANY'S INVESTMENT INTENTIONS FOR THE MEGAMARKETS?

For many years, EU/US companies mostly exported to the megamarkets without any long-term plans of conquering these markets. These markets served as outlets for excess capacities that could not be absorbed by traditional markets. In most cases, this strategy failed, owing to high import duties and the absence of customer proximity expressed in

Figure 7.4. From export to FDI in the megamarkets.

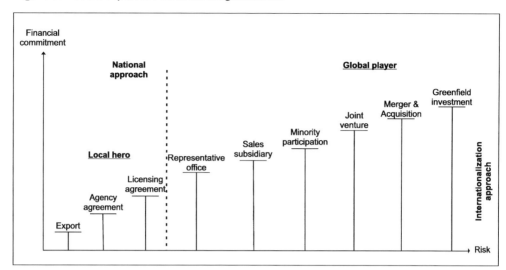

a high degree of client satisfaction and after-sales service. Nor could these companies bid for large contracts as they had no local structure that could lobby for the tender, invoice in local currency, and be held accountable.

Realizing that they are missing opportunities and motivated by above-average growth prospects, EU/US companies are now setting up more and more local offices for expanding their contact networks and preparing for more manufacturing investments. FDI already gives some of them a strong foothold in the local market and the chance to operate at the same level as local players (see figure 7.4). They can also benefit from the same low-cost advantages that their megamarket competitors are using to encroach on their territories.

A local structure is particularly important for those engaged in business-to-business (B2B) or business-to-government (B2G) activities. Through the local office, the company can offer services, lobby for its business, and be eligible for local contracts. Prices and margins become more predictable.

Medium-sized manufacturers that continue producing at high costs in the EU or the United States are taken aback when Western retail chains support their Asian competitors by opting for their lower-priced goods. Some retailers have set up buying offices and bought shares in local production units. Large operators like Wal-Mart, Carrefour, and Metro have become major players in logistics and transport activities from Asian

---
Pause for thought

Rather than be edged into niche markets, some of the leading Italian textile and footwear producers have set up manufacturing units in India and China, turning the tide on megamarket brands. Some, like Benetton, have been able to leverage their international image to increase their market share. The only way to be a leader is to first be an insider and investor.

> **Pause for thought**
>
> A leading dredging equipment producer from the EU selling through distributors in China could not reach breakeven and had to constantly readjust its sales forecasts downwards because customers were expecting direct involvement in sales and explanatory marketing of this manufacturer of technical goods.

countries. During 2000–2007, Wal-Mart alone accounted for 20%–35% of all Chinese exports to the United States. The only way out for the EU/US players is to produce in the megamarkets, beat local competitors at their own game, and participate directly in market growth through participations in local legal entities.[3]

The switch from export to FDI is per se not a guarantee for establishing leadership. Many companies tend to go to the other extreme once the FDI decision has been made. Being heavily involved in pushing forth prestige projects, they tend to overstate the investment aspect while neglecting the market and customers. A manufacturing base will by itself not generate a market. AM managers sometimes undervalue existing production (over)capacities and the aggressive marketing behavior of local rivals who are better positioned to shape future needs and outflank foreign players. Other AM companies fail to attain sales targets because they bank on indirect sales channels, which represent a "proven" marketing concept in advanced markets and were used when the company was exporting to the megamarkets.

Moreover, foreign companies must select an appropriate FDI mode that enables them to gain market share. Aggressive external growth through mergers, acquisitions, and alliances may be more effective than organic internal growth.

The FDI issue is drawing the attention of wider circles of politicians and union leaders, who are compelled to undergo a fundamental switch in thinking. The perception that national wealth can be created mainly by export stimulation as the ideal form of job preservation and possibly generation will have to make room for a broader standpoint including the acceptance that certain jobs will necessarily be relocated to emerging markets while others (the more qualified ones) can be retained provided that the country's competitive position is strengthened to face the challenge of globalization. FDI by leading companies in the megamarkets is necessary to overcome industrial rivalry on a global scale and ensure a durable export channel.

At the corporate level, the business model for FDI will depend on the capabilities of the company, market receptiveness, and the laws governing FDI in the particular megamarket. It should be such that it allows them to gain market share quickly and work their way to a dominant position. Closely linked to FDI is the issue of overcapacity, which can be circumvented by joining forces with the market leader.

Question 6:
What role does senior management play in the megamarket venture?

The degree of involvement of a company's senior management in the megamarket project reflects the commitment of the company to the venture. The strategic mindset and

---

3. See chapter 10.

authority of the top management is crucial for motivating the rest of the staff and designing and implementing the project. Senior executives alone can make the important decisions regarding, for example, equity participation or financial matters such as borrowing or lending. They must point at the business direction to be taken by encouraging the lower layers to conceive of something that the market really wants and that cannot be easily imitated by competitors. The real issue for top management is not simply "being in a business" but constantly reinventing it by actively motivating subordinates and shaping customer needs.

But many CEOs and board members even today labor under the impression that the megamarkets are "still emerging" or "one day heading for a crisis." They do not give the right responses and support to dynamic country managers faced with the need for quick and suitable decisions in the fast-moving and fast-changing environment of the megamarkets. These local managers lose precious time convincing headquarters to provide necessary support. CEOs must change this mindset, take the megamarkets seriously, and get involved in top-level recruitment while delegating more authority to the local structure. They must be committed to finding appropriate solutions with middle management and be convinced that competencies indispensable for each market should be developed.

The involvement of headquarters lends credibility to the local operation. In the protocol-sensitive business cultures of the megamarkets, the commitment of headquarters is important for gaining the trust of local customers and authorities, whose policy decisions can make or break the local subsidiary.

Timely visits by the CEO are not only highly publicized events, they serve to motivate local staff and to send positive signals to local authorities who can troubleshoot in case of problems. None of these benefits can be undervalued. Against the background of high attrition rates among staff in the megamarkets, such visits show commitment and ensure the loyalty of local staff. Regular interventions of CEOs can be crucial for acquiring stakes in local companies.

Pause for thought

A leading EU industrial component maker for many years approached key accounts in Russia through the local representative. Sales only started picking up when the vice president from the head office got directly involved in the initial but crucial marketing efforts.

In another case, a leading EU carmaker had to withdraw from India. The reason, apart from having chosen the wrong partner, was that headquarters lost interest once the joint venture was beset by difficulties, instead of trying tenaciously to find a way out of the problems. Expatriate managers sent to India were demotivated as their attempts to keep the joint venture floating met with slow responses from headquarters. The market cannot be faulted as other foreign carmakers are progressing well.

In contrast, DaimlerChrysler India was supported by headquarters throughout its early years when it was painstakingly building sales. India's luxury car market is a fraction of that in Germany, but headquarters remained convinced of its potential. The company's perseverance is paying off as the local subsidiary is expanding its operations and now even providing headquarters with valuable inputs on how to improve business in other emerging markets.

7.2. Empowering internal resources

Companies must make sure that they possess the internal resources needed to operate successfully in the megamarkets. Each resource, such as human talent, technology, know-how, and financial strength, needs to be carefully evaluated against market requirements. Resources must be employed sensibly for systematically generating a competence mix that distinguishes it from others and remains attractive to customers in the new markets. What a company is capable of doing in a megamarket eventually depends on the quantity and nature (quality) of its competencies that determine its competitive advantages.

A resource audit is meant to identify areas of competitiveness of an enterprise in supporting its megamarket strategy.[4] The study and planning of internal resources indicates how a company will be able to perform in its new environment, the analysis of which must also be given its due attention; it enables a company to translate intelligence into strategy and is therefore pivotal before engaging in costly operations in the megamarkets.

Internally available resources are related to the company's achievements, talents, and assets at corporate, functional, and regional levels. Megamarket business partners appreciate not only tangible assets but also soft factors such as a company's culture, its history, and reputation acquired in other markets. Indispensable resources for a megamarket project may be borrowed from the parent company, or they may already reside in the respective foreign subsidiary. For special interventions, there is an objective need to buy in talent and skills from external service providers, such as advisers, lobbyists, journalists, lawyers, and auditors. The qualification and experience of these outside specialists can decide the outcome of a marketing campaign, an M&A transaction, or a tender application. It is therefore essential to make the right choices, especially to understand the significance and timing of recruiting external help in critical situations. Many top managers of EU companies have difficulties in accepting that their previous job experience is of limited relevance for succeeding in new cultural contexts where business partners "tick" differently and other personal networks prevail.

Resources are made available, together with the respective skills, to a company through financial compensation (e.g., salaries, share options, fees). Farsighted companies allocate budgets on time to acquire indispensable skills and motivate specialists "to stay on board" until the operation is concluded. They constantly work toward refining vital competences and combining them into unique sales propositions (USPs) that are difficult for competitors to notice or imitate immediately. Internal resources fall into six categories, each of which must be honed for the megamarket venture (see figure 7.5). The resource audit enables management to identify their company's strengths and to remove gaps for building durable advantages. As long as a company does not dispose of indispensable assets (capital, people, know-how, soft skills) for the venture in the megamarkets or is too weak financially to

---

4. (a) D. J. Collis, "A Resource-based Analysis of Global Competition," *Strategic Management*, vol. 12 (1991): 49–68; (b) R. M. Grant, *Contemporary Strategy Analysis* (1991), 99ff; (c) Gerry Johnson and Kevan Scholes, *Exploring Corporate Strategy* (1993), 119.

Figure 7.5. Getting ready for the megamarkets (the six resources).

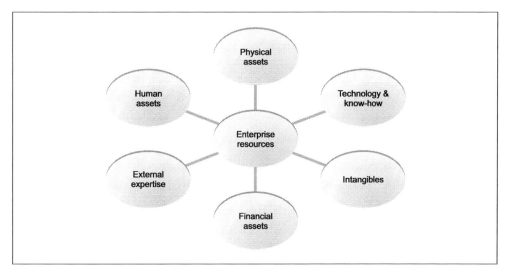

acquire them, it may seek cooperation with other partners as "facilitators" or postpone its decision to enter the megamarkets altogether.

Through a series of questions, a company will find out if it has the resources needed to penetrate the megamarkets:

- Question 1: Has the company assigned experienced management and support staff to the megamarket operation?
- Question 2: Are physical assets in line with the megamarket venture?
- Question 3: Does the company have leading-edge technology and protect its intellectual property?
- Question 4: Is the company's brand equity projected effectively?
- Question 5: Are financial resources adequate for expansion?
- Question 6: Does the company tap external expertise?

QUESTION 1:

HAS THE COMPANY ASSIGNED EXPERIENCED MANAGEMENT AND SUPPORT STAFF TO THE MEGAMARKET OPERATION?

Human resources constitute the decisive factor determining success or failure in a megamarket operation. Competent managers and motivated employees serve to steer a company in a context of regulatory unknowns, intense competition, and exacting customers. Companies that have established a leadership in megamarkets were all driven by managers with exceptional qualities:

- a strong belief in and enthusiasm about the megamarket(s)
- considerable adaptability to local customs and conditions (also for family members)
- curiosity and empathy for other cultures
- analytical and investigative mind to sift information and arrive at judgments

- knowledge of at least one megamarket language (Hindi for India; Russian for Russia; Chinese for China)
- diplomacy and ability to deal with business partners, local politicians, government officials, and subordinates

This combination of qualities, qualifications, and skills is not easy to find. Identifying such managers on the basis of careful and objective analysis is one of the most complex tasks facing a company in the megamarkets. High growth rates and intense competition for talents translate into many job opportunities and high fluctuation. The brightest and best trained staff is the quickest to leave if working conditions are considered no longer adequate. Western multinationals offer attractive employment packages, including performance- and seniority-based bonuses and training. These standards may be a selling point at the recruitment stage but are hardly a guarantee for retaining people once they have the job and start disagreeing with the working atmosphere or expect faster promotions.

Many multinationals in China have invested huge amounts in personnel development schemes including overseas stays, but they have not been able to stem the brain exodus from their main (Shanghai, Beijing) offices. Medium-sized players have had similar problems since they joined the race in competing for scarce talent. Having fewer financial means than transnationals, they hire young megamarket graduates. The "bearers of know-how" in the head office would become an unaffordable cost factor if they were sent overseas. Many technicians and other specialists are close to retirement and lack the enthusiasm for being stationed abroad. Successful companies attempt to take on the HR challenge at four levels: smart recruitment, performance-based compensation, fast-track promotion, and retention through training and international job rotations. Experience acquired in a megamarket should be considered by headquarters as an asset determining a manager's career path, similar to professional experience in the United States or any EU country.

QUESTION 2:

ARE PHYSICAL ASSETS IN LINE WITH THE MEGAMARKET VENTURE?

Physical resources consist of mobile and immobile assets related to essential business functions, such as general administration (office building, IT systems), production (plants, equipment), logistics (warehouse), and R&D (laboratories). Such facilities cannot be shifted that easily. Earlier, companies transferred secondhand equipment to developing markets. The Fiat 1100 and Ambassador car that dominated India's pre-liberalization market rolled out from complete Fiat and Austin platforms that were shipped to India. Plants made redundant due to surplus capacity are still being partly relocated (e.g., Volkswagen's engine plant from Hungary to China), but if the technology is obsolete or available on-site, the operation will become costly and not competitive with respect to new plants set up by local companies. State-of-the-art equipment, new factories, functional offices, and recreation centers (in-house restaurants, sports grounds) have become the pride of India's progressive IT giants (e.g., Infosys and Wipro) who show them to customers and use them as bait for hiring the best talents. Investments in top-notch greenfield units have been stepped up in the megamarkets since the early 2000s as companies are compelled to raise their standards to stay competitive. Production

> **Pause for thought**
>
> A world leader in refractories (fire-resistant materials) used in the steel, cement, and glass industries set up modern production units in Northern China. One of them is equipped with the latest state-of-the-art machinery, which makes the quality of its final products comparable to those manufactured in the company's US and EU plants. But the location advantage of being in a country with lower labor costs (China) is in a capital-intensive industry offset by costs related to investments, maintenance, spares, and depreciation. The prices of products sold by the company therefore remain above those of local competitors although the unit is based in China.
>
> ***
>
> The leading EU suppliers of printing machines and construction and office equipment have opened sales offices in the megamarkets, where they offer lower prices than in AMs to gain market share. Local equipment producers have improved in engineering, high-end functions, and after-sales, forcing EU producers to shift production and set up service/spare parts units. Many megamarket machinery makers have joined forces with foreign companies. These alliances often struggle with quality and financial problems when the local partner cannot meet Western quality standards.
>
> EU companies rarely purchase locally made equipment makers to restructure them. The reverse trend is very popular among megamarket companies, which increasingly buy EU companies. They can thus also benefit from other resources like R&D and testing laboratories.

in these units can be as expensive as in advanced markets if the investment is capital-intensive. In this case, all possible marketing and lobbying tools must be applied to gain competitive advantage.

Imported equipment is subject to customs duties (new) or quotas (secondhand) in the megamarkets. Local procurement can be less expensive.

Building excess capacity is fraught with risks. In China, many industries are marked by overcapacity. Despite state-of-the-art facilities, companies must cut their prices or increase exports aggressively, exposing entire industries to trade restrictions.[5] In a situation of excess capacity, the acquisition of existing assets or production sharing could be better options. The latter becomes precarious if know-how is transferred or the image tarnished due to the local partner using a foreign brand to promote its own products (e.g., Brilliance and BMW cars in China, MAZ and MAN trucks in Russia/Belarus, WBGC and SKF bearings in China).

QUESTION 3:

DOES THE COMPANY HAVE LEADING-EDGE TECHNOLOGY AND PROTECT ITS INTELLECTUAL PROPERTY?

Decades of inventiveness and innovation have earned EU companies a formidable reputation. New products and cost-effective processes, including IT and management

---

5. The EU introduced a 16% rise in tariffs to protect local industry from Chinese shoe imports on price-dumping allegations. The real cause of the problem is overcapacity in the industry.

systems, have given them a competitive edge. The technology and know-how package a company brings to the table must be valued and effectively leveraged in negotiations with future partners. Allocating values to relevant technology packages requires an understanding of customer needs in the target market.

However, technology leaks and copyright infringements undermine the value of a company's intellectual property (IP). Trade secrets may be disclosed by departing employees or former alliance partners despite non-competition clauses. Innovative capacity can be lost through formal (competition) and informal channels (counterfeiters). China and India are signatories to the WTO, including trade-related intellectual property rights (TRIPS). Russia's membership is expected by 2010, but the risk of counterfeiting is still significant in the three megamarkets. Chinese copies of the BMW blatantly exhibited at European car shows and of the Transrapid train are spectacular reminders of the risk of IP thefts. India's leading coffee shop chains (e.g., Barista, Coffee Day) are perfect blueprints of their Italian and US models, including the equipment sourced and franchising contracts used.

The vast territories, language barriers, and defensive networking make it difficult to identify the source of fakes, take illegal producers to court, or have their assets frozen. Outside the big cities, courts are slow, and the provincial and municipal authorities are ill-equipped or not motivated to enforce the law in such matters. Unemployment in backward regions plays into the underlying tolerance of IP rights infringement. Many counterfeiters are connected and protected. Counterfeiters may be forewarned or may shift production around many sites, which makes it difficult for the police to detect them and force them to close down. When caught, fines or penalties for them are hardly a deterrent against future violations. Infringers have thus become financially strong and more resourceful.

Companies must ensure that all patents, trademarks, and copyrights are properly registered in the destination country. Holding a patent or trademark in advanced markets does not automatically ensure protection in the megamarkets. Smaller companies often fail to register a trademark on time, only to find themselves unprotected and exposed to counterfeiting. Technology that is critical for long-term survival is not transferred to the megamarkets. In addition, various practical measures should be taken. If a key technology has to be introduced, management should guard it against unauthorized personnel. Sensitive information can be parceled out among different people so that no single person has access to the complete package. Multinationals work with IP security groups, detective agencies, and full-time monitors for protecting their intellectual property. Local alliance partners can be useful in tracking down illegal organizations as they are networked; it is also in their interest to protect their EU partner's IP (unless they are siphoning it off themselves). Conditional access software as well as solutions adopted by the IT industry can also be used.

Poor IP protection in the megamarkets influences decisions in R&D investments. At the same time, scientific talent in the megamarkets can compensate for the skills shortage in the EU. Co-development is an inclusive strategy that could enhance compliance; as ownership is shared with local developers, they also stand at a disadvantage from IP leaks. In recent years, megamarket companies have been registering their own patents and trademarks. IP protection is thus becoming a two-way street demanding increased awareness and appropriate countermeasures by the highest corporate echelons.

QUESTION 4:
IS THE COMPANY'S BRAND EQUITY PROJECTED EFFECTIVELY?

Western businessmen tend to view the megamarkets as places where cost considerations are the determining factor in a buying decision. While pricing is an important criterion, soft factors or intangibles like brand equity, reputation, and corporate culture (see figure 7.6) play an equal if not more decisive role. Intangibles are especially important to building business relationships given the higher comfort and confidence levels they help create between the seller and the buyer.

Brand equity, backed by a company's reputation, is one of the most valuable corporate assets. A famous brand normally represents a secure source of revenue as it warrants stable sales volumes and good margins (e.g., Coca-Cola, Louis Vuitton, Nestlé, Siemens). A medium-sized or small technology leader may not be as well-known as its big multinational clients in the megamarkets; these references should be used liberally. FMCG[6] multinationals spend huge sums of money on advertising and nationwide promotion to position and constantly recall their brands in the minds of consumers. Medium-sized players lack the financial resources for such measures and tend to adopt niche strategies by promoting their products in specific market segments (e.g., specialized instead of mass retailing) instead of going immediately for national coverage.

Goodwill acquired in advanced markets represents a valuable asset for building a strong reputation in the megamarkets. Megamarket consumers are brand conscious and ready to

Figure 7.6. The five intangibles for the megamarkets.

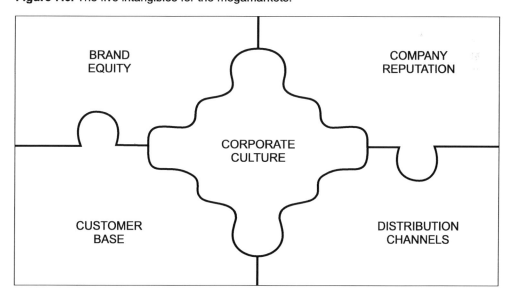

---

6. FMCG: fast-moving consumer goods.

spend more for status symbols. EU companies should, however, protect their trademarks before promoting a brand. There have been numerous cases where EU companies were denied the use of their trademarks in the megamarkets because local companies had anticipated their registration. Analogous problems arise due to preemptive squatting of Web site domain names by local companies.

Communication materials need to be adapted to the megamarket context. For China and Russia, they also need to be translated. Materials with a consistent design create a clear image of the company, particularly for a company or product still not known in the destination market. Samples (for FMCGs) and corporate gifts should not be forgotten while preparing the promotion budget. Medium-sized players, which lack the resources of the multinationals for ad spend, can adopt targeted promotion strategies aimed at specific market segments. A smaller company must be clear about its price points to avoid head-on confrontation with larger competitors. It will need to select a few channels and/or customers and seek close cooperation with them (staff training, merchandising assistance). Industrial goods, which fall typically in the B2B or B2G category, will require a program for lobbying, advice, training, and after-sales service.

Well-established brands can be used to reduce investment costs. Medium-sized players tend to underestimate or overlook the value of their brands when entering into negotiations with foreign alliance partners. Whenever EU companies seek to acquire stakes, they should assess the value of the brands that are bought along with the target. Brand equity valuation provides executives with the data needed to raise their bargaining position, to attract financial investors, and to reduce marketing expenses, which can run into several million US dollars. Good branding practice is now spreading to emerging markets where local players have grasped the relevance of brands to fend off foreign competition and to ensure customer loyalty. Governments try to protect domestic brands whenever their "holders" are threatened by a takeover that fails to include a clear commitment by the foreign side to preserve and develop the brand.

QUESTION 5:
ARE FINANCIAL RESOURCES ADEQUATE FOR EXPANSION?

A decision to move into the megamarkets is meaningless if adequate financial resources are not determined and allocated. What measures have been taken to set the budget? Does it allow purchasing assets, recruiting key employees, covering operational expenses (including for professionals, travel and stay), and so forth? How does the company handle eventualities such as unforeseen taxes, the need to replace a top manager, or the need to change the strategic course?

A company's financial health and architecture—i.e., the split between equity and different sorts of debt—have a direct impact on its investment capability. If the short-term versus long-term liability ratio is unfavorable and collateral deemed insufficient, banks may not fund a new undertaking in the megamarkets, where risks are considered higher than in the advanced markets. Issuing debt in the form of bonds legally obliges management of listed multinationals to pay interest and reimburse the sum borrowed on fixed dates. Equity from an ongoing and profitable company in the megamarkets can be used as collateral, but if a high debt burden is placed on local management, it will be demotivated. Long-term off-balance loan facilities, including project finance, require the approval of all shareholders and may delay an important project.

Corporate governance can impact resource allocation. The separation of ownership and control applies to most—listed and non-listed—companies in the EU and the United States. Top management has considerable discretion, sometimes at the expense of owner-shareholders who are not managing the business and less able to judge the significance of decisions. When dealing with new markets, "agency costs"—the financial loss to the "principals" (shareholders) due to the misuse of discretion by the "agent" (managers hired to run the company)—can have serious implications. Prior to deciding on an investment and setting the budget, all the decision-makers (owners, CEO) should therefore jointly take part in fact-finding missions so that they can correct, approve, or disapprove investment decisions to ensure that these create rather than destroy value.

The megamarkets nowadays host many financial institutions that are willing to provide venture capital, project finance, and general loans. Local banks can offer fair conditions due to competition among financial institutions although interests are usually higher than in the EU. Private equity has become a popular source of finance with the increase in the number of wealthy people who buy up stakes of companies, also by pooling their resources.

QUESTION 6:
DOES THE COMPANY TAP EXTERNAL EXPERTISE?

Large multinationals have significant in-house resources and expertise to cover most aspects of a foreign venture. But these in-house experts may not have adequate exposure to the megamarkets, their soft issues, and legal framework. They may be able to help run daily operations and execute orders but would have difficulties in countering wrong strategies from senior executives, facilitating decisions concerning acquisitions/investments, or lobbying government departments. No matter how competent or qualified the company's local management, it may not be able to obtain sensitive data for informed decision-making. Their line position in the company will hardly allow them to be "neutral" or "objective," or at least sector insiders and informants will have trouble seeing it that way. Moreover, many EU/US executives are not prepared to spend enough time in the megamarkets to oversee the establishment of the project and intervene in an adequate manner. Medium-sized companies cannot spare their human resources already involved in their traditional markets. In all these cases, external expertise can fill the gap.

External professionals have to be screened and delegated to precisely formulated tasks in the megamarkets, for example:
- entry and expansion strategy: international advisory firm with many years of hands-on project experience, capability to obtain sensitive information, and well-networked with local business community to spot trends, risks, and opportunities;
- company incorporation: local accounting firm;
- share purchasing and alliance agreements: law company with long contractual practice that is used to working with foreigners and understands their mindset and concerns;

> **Pause for thought**
>
> *After lengthy deliberations, an Austrian equipment maker eventually gave up a unique investment opportunity in China "for lack of managerial and technical resources" to accompany and supervise the project.*
>
> *The company's management would not rely on external expertise either and instead decided to "retrench" in Austria. Subconsciously, there was regret for the fact that its major Western competitors were stepping up operations in China and that in a few years Chinese competitors might be strong enough to sell and acquire companies in the EU.*
>
> ***
>
> *A family-owned Austrian multinational appointed two former partners of an international consulting company as general and financial managers for its Asia operations. Initially the motivation seemed plausible:*
>
> a. *in-house M&A/FDI expertise was not available;*
>
> b. *the company had previously made wrong decisions that prevented its timely entry into China and India; and*
>
> c. *fees of external consulting companies were considered excessive.*
>
> *After two years, senior executives realized they had been misled by their "advisers turned managers" who lacked true megamarket experience and, for fear of competition, blocked the inflow of additional expertise to select suitable alliance partners and solve problems with local authorities.*
>
> *In another case, a German car multinational hired a former department head who had just retired as "chief lobbyist" for their project in China. After four years of hard work, the company managed to get the approval of the relevant authorities and enter into an agreement with the selected joint venture partner. Meanwhile, the market had turned. Also, lobbying was not applied to obtain sensitive data on the real intentions and management background of the local company, which is today using the joint platform and quality reputation of the Western carmaker to push its own brand including in foreign markets.*

- real estate issues (industrial site, factory, office): local agents with contacts (e.g., architects, builders) and experience in vetting companies, ownership rights, and contracts;
- tax planning, statutory audit: international or local audit company;
- lobbying: individuals or small firms with high-level connections at the political level and knowledgeable of protocols and behavioral patterns in the "corridors of power;"
- promotion and public awareness: PR, media, and advertising agencies.

For top management used to a Western environment, it is difficult to judge whether they are picking the right adviser for a megamarket. Decisions are often based on reputation or brand from the viewpoint of a Western context: "A consulting or auditing company known back home will automatically do a good job in the megamarkets, or at least it will reduce my risk as manager in case something goes terribly wrong." Some companies recruit former managers as consultants in the belief that they have the time and the skills to take on any complex assignment. This prophecy often fails to come true. As emerging markets become more important for corporate success, project teams are measured according to achieved results. Selecting a well-known company is no longer an alibi if the financials (sales, cash flow) show little or negative performance. Some companies go further and recruit former consultants in order to capture their (external) expertise for an extended period of time and save consultancy costs (these people are paid monthly salaries instead of daily fees).

Local consultancies are often more affordable and better networked than their Western counterparts, which have set up offices in the megamarkets but recruit Westernized locals and apply Western methods. Most EU-based advisory companies connected to the megamarkets only from the early 2000s when it had become clear that these markets could add to their profits. Their motivation was to participate in markets that had suddenly become attractive rather than pursuing much earlier a vision to help their customers be first in anticipation of massive investments.

There is no recipe for selecting a good adviser; much of it will depend on the principal's intuition, courage, and ability to form a team. Advisers recruited by megamarket subsidiaries for significant issues with impact for the whole group should be screened by headquarters to ensure that their aims coincide with the mission set by headquarters, and not a conflicting agenda pursued by the subsidiary.

By integrating external professionals for milestone projects in the megamarkets and generating the relevant information they need, EU/US companies will be able to extract the best advice. Consultants can then serve as an extended arm in the megamarkets until the company's team is fully operational. The external professionals should be able to supplement internal teams and cover a combination of skills to help their principals succeed in the various project phases (see table 7.2). On the other hand, consulting companies operating at a group level on "transformation" or "restructuring" assignments can become a disturbing factor when implementing a megamarket strategy.

Pause for thought

As a result of an internal restructuring on the advice of a large consulting company, a French multinational decided to halt strategic entry into China, India, and Russia after a year of thorough intelligence and partner identification missions in the three megamarkets.

The consulting company had recommended refocusing on the advanced markets and only exports to the megamarkets. The megamarket project in India and China and the years of efforts were thus aborted just when it was on the verge of taking off.

Table 7.2. Essential skills for investment projects in the megamarkets.

	Intelligence phase	Transaction phase	Integration phase
Task-related skills	Market and trend assessment	Financial assessment	Legal assessment
	Strategy support	Legal assessment	Intercultural management
	Lobbying	Lobbying	Communication, PR and promotion
	Intelligence phase	**Transaction phase**	**Integration phase**
General skills	Negotiation tactics	Alliance models and options	Conflict resolution, HR policies
	Intercultural behavior	Valuation methods	Customer relations management
	Persuasiveness (to win over partners)	Accounting practices	Knowledge building

7.3. Mobilizing competencies for competitive advantage

Megamarkets have turned into sophisticated marketplaces where newcomers will find it increasingly difficult to fill residual gaps. Megamarket customers expect more than just a good core product that provides a solution to their needs. Local players and the leading multinationals therefore keep improving their selling propositions and cultivating good relations with customers, suppliers, and government. Penetrating these tightly woven, personalized networks demands meticulous preparation, intercultural talent, and, most important, a unique offer based on tangible competences.

Top performers build their strengths on resources and skills that are distinct and thus represent sources of sustainable competitive advantages (SCAs). Compared with key factors of success (KFS) that describe the basic skill sets needed to compete in an industry, SCAs based on company-specific attributes are the true profit drivers. Related to individual performance and perceived by customers as something valuable, rare, and inimitable (see figure 7.7), they can drive a company's efforts toward leadership. Like moving targets, SCAs must be constantly reviewed, adjusted, and benchmarked against those of competitors. If a brand can break even in those areas where its most formidable competitors are trying to find an advantage and can take the lead in new areas, its brand is in a strong—perhaps unbeatable—competitive position. Success in the megamarkets demands that special attention is paid to a third category of "soft factors" including personalized services, training, advice, and innovation management; they strengthen the vendor-customer relationship by contributing to the solution of concrete problems. The core product or hard factors are easier to imitate than the soft factors, which are embraced by the top management, employees, and corporate culture. SCAs can additionally be generated through the acquisition of stakes in first-class local companies, which bring to the venture more indispensable assets such as

Figure 7.7. Building sustainable competitive advantages in the megamarkets.

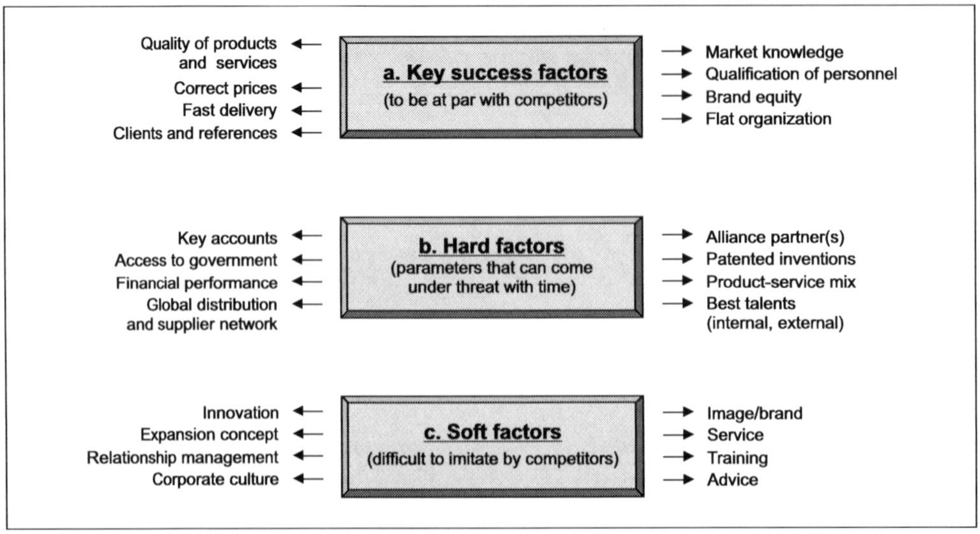

```
Quality of products          ←                                    → Market knowledge
   and services                    a. Key success factors         → Qualification of personnel
Correct prices               ←    (to be at par with competitors) → Brand equity
Fast delivery                ←                                    → Flat organization
Clients and references       ←

Key accounts                 ←                                    → Alliance partner(s)
Access to government         ←         b. Hard factors            → Patented inventions
Financial performance        ←    (parameters that can come       → Product-service mix
Global distribution          ←        under threat with time)     → Best talents
  and supplier network                                              (internal, external)

Innovation                   ←                                    → Image/brand
Expansion concept            ←         c. Soft factors            → Service
Relationship management      ←    (difficult to imitate by competitors) → Training
Corporate culture            ←                                    → Advice
```

Figure 7.8. Analytical tools for building competitive advantage in the megamarkets.

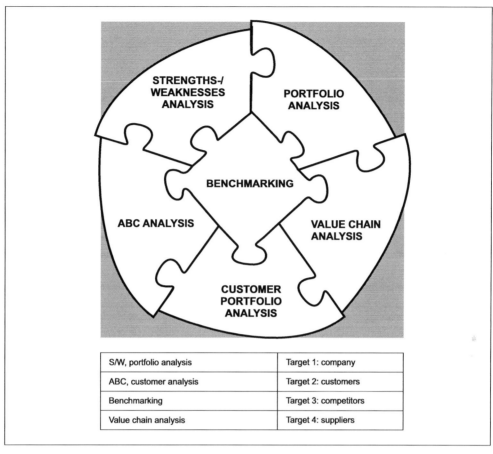

market share, local platforms, key accounts, distribution channels, supplier links, and access to authorities.

Articulating one's position in the market introduces discipline and clarity into the strategy development process, which can be accelerated by using management tools[7] (see figure 7.8). The six tools described below have been selected for their relevance to the megamarkets and the ease in implementation given that information in these markets is not as readily accessible as in the advanced markets. The tools require inputs from frontline specialists (sales and purchase personnel), advisers, and sector resource persons, especially business partners and industry participants (customers, buyers, suppliers, competitors), which at the same time represent vital targets for further analysis.

STRATEGIC TOOL 1:
STRENGTHS AND WEAKNESSES ANALYSIS

Building megamarket-specific competencies implies continuous questioning of the company's strengths (S) and weaknesses (W), which determine its possibilities and

---

7. K. Kerth and R. Puetmann, *Die besten Strategietools in der Praxis* [The Best Strategy Tools in Practice], (Carl Hanser, 2005).

limitations. Established companies use their broad knowledge and contact base to regularly evaluate their SW position and understand the attributes that lead to corporate success (see table 7.3). Management must focus on attributes that are particularly important to customers and where gaps may exist with competing offers. Clients may perceive these attributes differently in advanced markets and megamarkets. The company must find ways to transform them into SCAs by improving on what the competition does.

A SWOT analysis adds two new dimensions to an SW profile: perceived opportunities (O) and threats (T) in a specific industry or geography. Determining the OT balance is difficult for foreign companies in megamarkets with the consequence that threats are often overstated. Sector insiders should be involved in the process as they can contribute to a more objective assessment of the situation. Depending on the result of the assessment, the management has to pick the right investment/divestment option (see figure 7.9):

- SO strategies: The company can exploit a favorable situation by stressing internal strengths and investing in expansion.
- WO strategies: Management will need to curb weaknesses, for example, by restructuring a sales unit (to react more flexibly to market inquiries) or strengthening the company's innovative capability (R&D and engineering design department).
- ST strategies: The company's strengths (e.g., favorable equity/debt leverage) can help to anticipate threats, for example, by acquiring a growing rival and achieving scales effects.
- WT strategies: A company may try to improve its cost position by reengineering in order to survive in a declining market; if weaknesses cannot be removed and opportunities do not arise (for example, because of fierce competition), a company may opt out—i.e., divest from a particular market or submarket.

Figure 7.9. SWOT matrix for the megamarkets

	Opportunities - Reputation with users - Interest of partners - Government incentives - Environmental awareness	Threats - Strong competition - Price wars - Market saturation - Legislation
Strengths - Customer base - Innovative products - Know-how, technology - Sales force - Healthy cash position	SO strategies	ST strategies
Weaknesses - High-cost production - Product complexity - Low skills of staff - Corporate culture geared to other markets	WO strategies	WT strategies

Table 7.3. SW profile for corporate success in the megamarkets.

Area	Attributes	Own performance vs. competition (-2, -1, 0, 1, 2)	Area	Attributes	Own performance vs. competition (-2, -1, 0, 1, 2)
1. Company	History Values Reputation Brands Patents Customers		6. Production	Equipment Technology Location Productivity Quality management Capacity utilization Vertical integration Flexibility	
2. Management, leadership	Qualifications Career history International experience Intercultural skills Quality of decisions Leadership styles Team orientation Target setting		7. R&D	Innovation R&D budget (% of sales) Licensing Development potential	
3. Products	Product range/portfolio Service Quality Price-performance ratio Design		8. Human resources	Qualifications Training Age structure Incentives & motivation Salaries Learning culture Staff retention Image of employer	
4. Marketing and sales	Image Market share Distribution channels Advertising expenditure Customer fidelity Customer satisfaction Order processing Seasonal dependence Sales force Access to market data		9. Organization	Structure Processes Hierarchy Flexibility IT Project management Knowledge sharing	
5. Supply	Quality and stability of suppliers (foreign, local) Purchasing costs Warehousing and logistics Just-in-time delivery Raw materials access		10. Finance	Equity Indebtedness Financial health Profit growth Cash flow Investment plan	

The SWOT analysis provides a first assessment of whether the direction taken is viable or needs adjustment, in other words:

- if the company is doing the right things, but needs to do them better (higher efficiency route), or
- if the company needs to do new things (higher effectiveness route).

Strategic tool 2:
Portfolio analysis

Besides increasing the visibility of the company's product range in a single matrix, the portfolio analysis[8] (PA) helps to determine which products should be discontinued (poor dogs) or generate cash-flow and require additional investments to be promoted to stars and cash cows. Products (or technologies, SBUs—strategic business units) are presented in a two-dimensional matrix with four quadrants: cash cows, stars, question marks, and poor dogs. The company's competitive position (relative market share)—reflected on the x-axis—is compared to the industry's growth potential (sector attractiveness) on the y-axis. The relative market share—an indicator of competitive strength—is calculated as the ratio of a company's sales divided by the sales of its main competitor. For market leaders, the relative share is larger than 1; for non-market leaders, it is between 0 and 1. The company's products are positioned in one of the four quadrants depending on their market share and growth prospects, which are more or less determined by a product's life cycle. Products on the growth path of their life cycle appear on top, while those experiencing declining sales are positioned below. Besides the two axes, the matrix includes a third dimension, expressed by the size or diameter of each circle according to the contribution of each product to overall turnover (see figure 7.10).

The portfolio method aims to visualize the earnings capacity and capital or investment requirement of a company's product portfolio. The assessment is based on three market and financial parameters: growth, profitability, and relative market share. It is an effective monitoring instrument to channel corporate investments and ease decision-making. A series of implications for corporate behavior and strategy emerge from the financial indicators and the position of products/SBUs in the portfolio matrix.

The attractiveness of each product depends on the level of competitiveness of a company with regard to its major rivals. Healthily balanced portfolios consist of cash earners, future stars, and a few products that need to be phased out (poor dogs). A large number of companies direct their investments according to their product performance. Surveys conducted in the United States show that companies using this method have developed a strategic thrust for attaining long-term goals.[9] Rarely are

---

8. There are various types of portfolio matrices that can be used. The most famous is the market share/market growth portfolio developed by Boston Consulting Group (BCG) in the mid-1960s.
9. V. Markova and S. Kuznetsova, Strategicheski menedzment [Strategic management] (Moscow, Publisher Name: 1999), 91–124.

Figure 7.10. Portfolio matrix for the megamarkets.

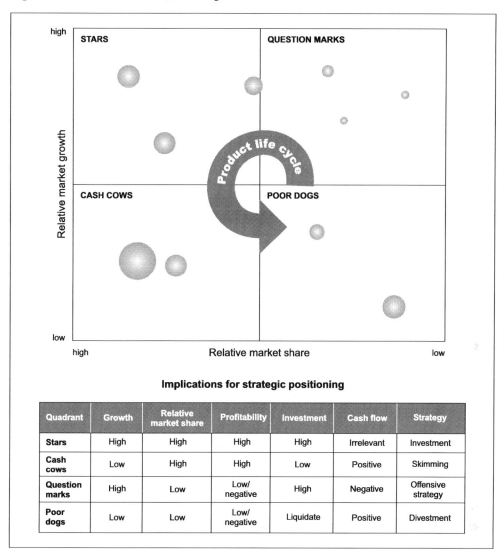

Quadrant	Growth	Relative market share	Profitability	Investment	Cash flow	Strategy
Stars	High	High	High	High	Irrelevant	Investment
Cash cows	Low	High	High	Low	Positive	Skimming
Question marks	High	Low	Low/negative	High	Negative	Offensive strategy
Poor dogs	Low	Low	Low/negative	Liquidate	Positive	Divestment

such product-focused exercises conducted in the megamarkets, even less so for pre- and after-sales services, which are becoming an indispensable element of a company's USP (see box 7.3).

A dynamic function can be introduced especially for the megamarkets to overcome the weakness of the traditional PA, which describes a company's present situation rather than its possible future position in a market. For this purpose, expected sales of products/services are compared with market growth in the coming five years (see figure 7.11). Products/services positioned on the diagonal grow as fast as the market, while those below/above the diagonal are expected to grow faster/slower than the market. Thus, a product/service that by Western standards is developing fast may be a "poor dog" in a megamarket, where competition grows much faster.

Box 7.3. Service portfolio for the megamarkets.

- Information
- Training
- Finance/leasing
- Guarantees
- Repair
- Replacement
- Logistics
- Packaging
- Technical advice

Figure 7.11. Dynamic portfolio analysis.

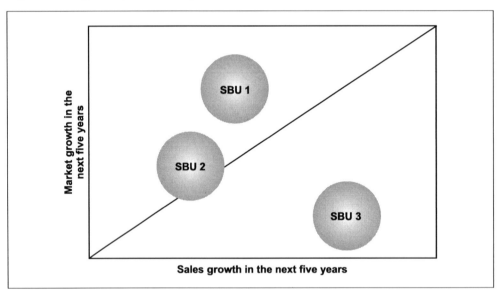

SBU = strategic business unit

Strategic tool 3:
Value chain analysis

A company planning to extend its reach to a new geography is well advised to study, for that particular market, its value chain (see figure 7.12) and the costs related to each step in the process of procuring, manufacturing, and distributing a product. It must detect activities that underpin its competitive advantage or where external partners show better performance parameters. Originally designed to determine areas of cost improvements or added value, value chain analysis (VCA) is mainly utilized to define areas of competitiveness[10] while helping management to decide on where

---

10. M. Porter, *Competitive Advantage* (Free Press, 1985).

Figure 7.12. Market value chain.

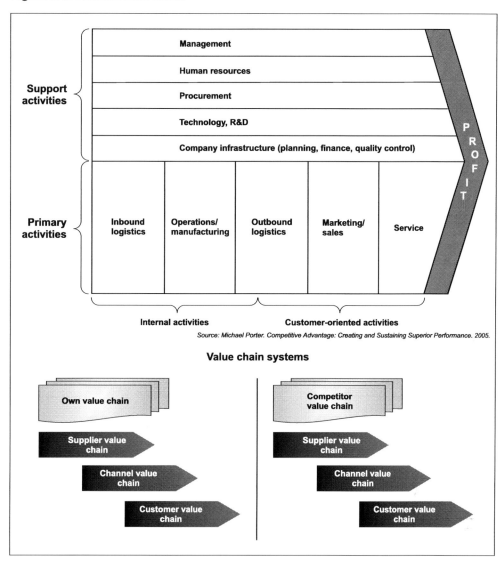

to operate more efficiently (cost-cutting) and whether to "make or buy"—i.e., to determine which activity should remain within the company's scope or be outsourced. VCA illustrates areas of internal growth by strengthening core competences and areas of external expansion through acquisitions or alliances (upstream/downstream suppliers/customers). Companies offering more than one product category need to break down the analysis at the product group level.

Value chains are broken down into two types of activities:
- primary activities: inbound logistics, operations/manufacturing, outbound logistics, marketing and sales, services
- support activities: management, human resources, procurement, technology/R&D, infrastructure (planning, finance, quality control)

The combination of primary and support activities determines whether a company operates at lower/higher cost than the competition and (eventually) whether it generates higher/lower satisfaction levels for customers. Analysts at the corporate office will have to rely on information provided by their megamarket subsidiary for conducting a megamarket-based VCA. A company is usually part of a wider system of value creation involving the value chains of its suppliers, distributors (channel members), and customers. Value system analysis depicts the main activities within and outside the company and aims for its linkages with business partners within the same cluster. Globalization of markets translates into value systems involving many companies from many countries linked through contracts and partnerships. In industries marked by fierce competition, value systems based around lead companies dominating other cluster participants are moving toward networks based on tight connections between compatible players. Globalization has enabled megamarket players to become vital links in such global networks or value systems (textiles, auto components, pharmaceuticals).

Leadership implies cost savings at various levels of the value chain. Once the cost factors and value drivers are known, a company can exert pressure on other chain members (suppliers, intermediaries, clients) and negotiate favorable terms. Knowledge of the value chains of competitors can reveal:

- activities where the company already has a distinct advantage;
- activities that competitors have the potential to optimize; and
- possible synergies for converting a competitor into a partner.

Sector participants are the best sources of information on competitor behavior. Competitors must be preempted and outperformed through a better sales proposition. Otherwise, they must be won over as potential partners ("coopetition") or takeover candidates to consolidate the value chain system in the industry.

Strategic tool 4:
Benchmarking

This instrument allows showcasing a company's performance (e.g., product/service quality, innovation, production processes, organizational efficiency, and profitability) with that of its competitors. Benchmarking is a derived competitive analysis, but additionally, it covers best practices of companies belonging to other industries. The *leitmotiv* of benchmarking is "striving to become better than the best," first in the same industry and later among best-practice companies across industries. Benchmarking is instrumental for setting ambitious goals after understanding the company's real position in the market. It shows where competitors are heading and charts a scenario of the future.

Japanese companies have always been masters of benchmarking, which eventually enabled them to do better than their Western competitors. Chinese and Indian businesses

Figure 7.13. Benchmarking categories and phases for the megamarkets.

Internal benchmarking (Group benchmarking)	a. Builds on experience available within the company/group. b. Compares performance of factories/subsidiaries to generate learning effects.	Example: In 2006, following a serious drop in its revenue, General Motors benchmarked its Opel plant in Germany with that of its second European subsidiary Saab in Sweden before deciding where to retain staff or divest.
External benchmarking (Industry benchmarking)	a. Aims to learn from top performers in same industry (best-in-class). b. methods: reverse engineering, competitive shopping.	Example: Tata as industry leader for cars in India serves as a yardstick for rivals eager to catch up.
Lateral benchmarking (Best-in-practice benchmarking)	a. Analyzes the best-of-best companies across the industry spectrum. b. Important for companies, which in terms of cost position, profitability and customer share, dominate an industry.	Example: Famous turnarounds at GE or IBM are studied as guidelines to increase the competitive edge.

The five phases of benchmarking

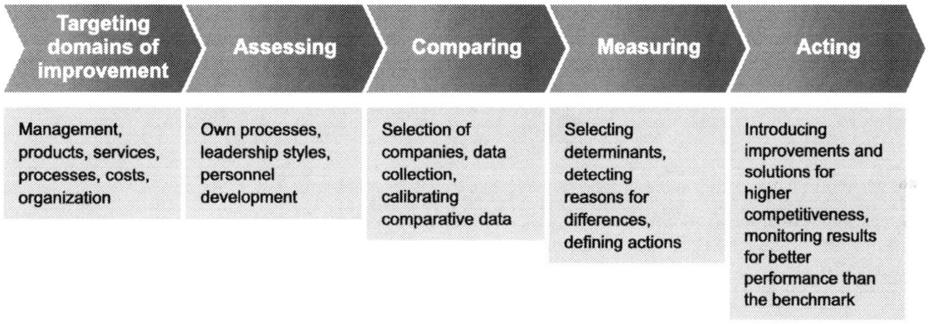

Targeting domains of improvement	Assessing	Comparing	Measuring	Acting
Management, products, services, processes, costs, organization	Own processes, leadership styles, personnel development	Selection of companies, data collection, calibrating comparative data	Selecting determinants, detecting reasons for differences, defining actions	Introducing improvements and solutions for higher competitiveness, monitoring results for better performance than the benchmark

are also pushing into international markets where they must comply with higher standards. They study the strategies of industry leaders to improve their own performance. Benchmarking takes several forms and can be subdivided into five phases (see figure 7.13).[11] Best-practice orientation stimulates improvement, creativity, and networking for better results.

Benchmarks in the megamarkets can be foreign or domestic players holding visible market shares. The success factors of foreign players may be easier to assess than those of local companies, whose relationships with customers and performance metrics are not readily accessible. Selecting the right benchmark and finding data collectors are fundamental to undertaking a thorough benchmarking. The exercise should be entrusted to one or two executives of confidence who have an open mind and the requisite investigative skills as well as a reliable contact network in the market, or to an external agency having thorough knowledge of the particular industry. Establishing a competitive portfolio helps to position the company in relation to its competitors and to take action for a strategic approach (see figure 7.14).

---

11. C. Gerberich, *Benchmarking* (STS, 1998).

Figure 7.14. Industry benchmarking with direct competitors.

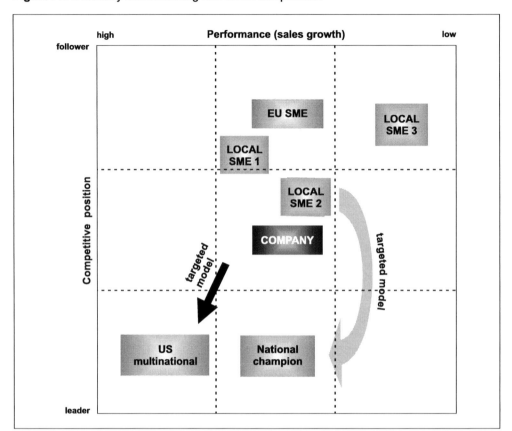

Strategic tool 5:
Customer portfolio analysis

More and more EU/US companies are obliged to follow their clients to the megamarkets to stay in the business. Megamarket customers are also approached and represent a growing share of the business. The customer portfolio (CP) analysis helps to screen and group various types of customers so that the company knows where it can direct its efforts profitably. According to the 80/20 rule, a company should invest in those key customers (20% in number) who represent the bulk of orders (80% of sales). A CP analysis is meant to identify the key accounts and profile their requirements. However, companies exporting to the megamarkets through independent agents (importers, distributors) may not know their final clients, their wishes, and their price expectations, and the margins are earned mainly by intermediaries.

Decision-makers should be in a position to list customers by importance (order volumes, margins, growth, prices, satisfaction levels, reputation) and the company's relative supplier position/share (purchasing volumes or value) with respect to competitors. Key account strategies depend on where the client is located in the client portfolio quadrant (see figure 7.15). The approach is similar to establishing a product portfolio; it leads to four types of clients with specific strategic implications: cash cow, star, question mark, and poor dog clients.

Figure 7.15. Client portfolio mix and strategic implications.

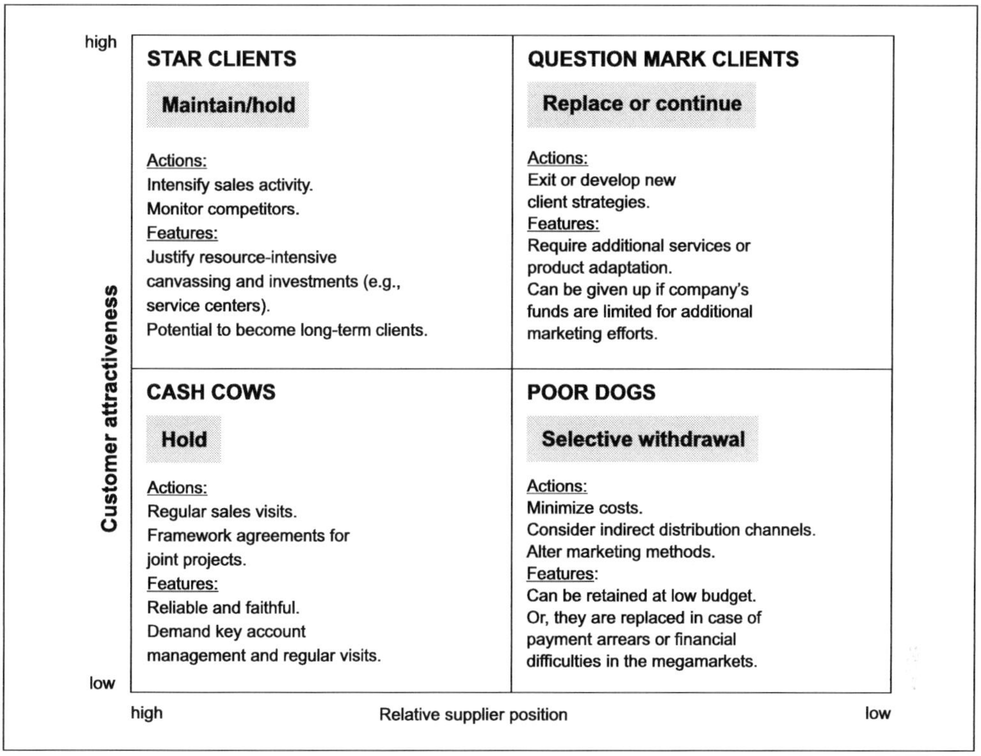

	Relative supplier position	
Customer attractiveness (high)	**STAR CLIENTS — Maintain/hold** Actions: Intensify sales activity. Monitor competitors. Features: Justify resource-intensive canvassing and investments (e.g., service centers). Potential to become long-term clients.	**QUESTION MARK CLIENTS — Replace or continue** Actions: Exit or develop new client strategies. Features: Require additional services or product adaptation. Can be given up if company's funds are limited for additional marketing efforts.
Customer attractiveness (low)	**CASH COWS — Hold** Actions: Regular sales visits. Framework agreements for joint projects. Features: Reliable and faithful. Demand key account management and regular visits.	**POOR DOGS — Selective withdrawal** Actions: Minimize costs. Consider indirect distribution channels. Alter marketing methods. Features: Can be retained at low budget. Or, they are replaced in case of payment arrears or financial difficulties in the megamarkets.

STRATEGIC TOOL 6:
ABC ANALYSIS

The CP can be refined by the ABC analysis, which is equally customer-centered and straightforward to be easily applied to megamarkets (see figure 7.16). Clients are classified as:

- A clients (highest share of current turnover);
- B clients (good future prospects); and
- C clients (less important clients).

To determine the category a client belongs to, a company will need to collect as much information as possible on annual order volumes, technical/service preferences, and other indicators that enable management to make a correct assessment.

The ABC analysis attempts to answer the following questions:
- Is the company approaching the right clients?
- Is there a healthy relationship between marketing efforts and sales (regular, high-value orders or only small, sporadic orders)?
- Can more customers be converted into key accounts with significant and steady order volumes?
- Which client segments are worth investing in to improve the company's market position?
- How does the regional dimension (e.g., distance) impact customer canvassing?

Figure 7.16. Megamarket ABC analysis.

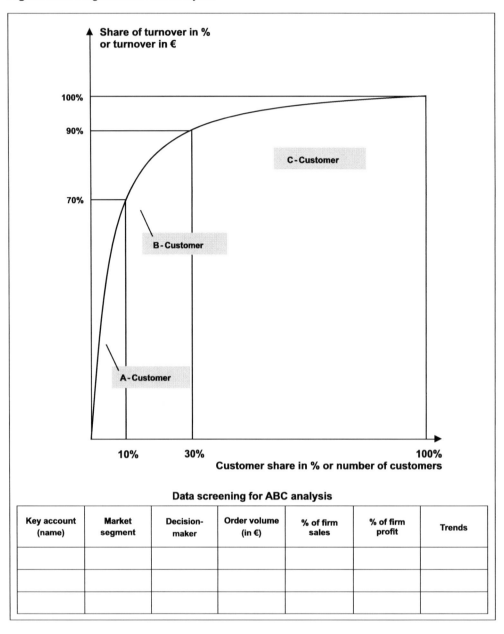

Both CP and ABC analyses improve customer intelligence; they are escalated as the company gains market share. Once key megamarket customers have been spotted, senior executives should get personally involved and if necessary attend important meetings to win them over with engagement and special incentives (e.g., discounts, events, preferential treatment). They should be cultivated and "coddled" in the same way as advanced markets key accounts. Megamarket customers are sensitive to protocol and prefer to transact with the ultimate decision-makers in the supplier/partner company, with whom they will share sensitive and confidential information. Lower echelons should therefore not be assigned for important regular interactions with decision-makers at leading local companies.

CHAPTER 8
Megamarket intelligence: Scan before the venture

Every executive knows how important it is to monitor the external environment in which the company operates. Only a few, however, know the mechanisms for managing intelligence or how to allocate the resources for setting up such a system. Marketing and market research need to be rethought in many companies, especially with respect to emerging economies. Business development departments must be headed by visionary thinkers who absorb external knowledge and accept the challenge of new opportunities (which demand constant research and analysis). This is the only way a firm will be able to influence market trends actively instead of passively responding to them.

Business intelligence is essential for:
- obtaining a comprehensive and realistic picture of macro and sector trends;
- examining the fit between internal capabilities and external realities;
- spotting business segments and target customers that ensure rapid returns;
- choosing suitable partners and entry options for expansion in the selected megamarket;
- preempting competitors by being there first, positioning the company firmly in the market, and occupying all available segments;
- implementing a consistent strategy and action plan for the selected megamarket and regional submarkets; and
- designing marketing, communication, and image- and brand-building campaigns with long-term impact.

The strategies of all companies, no matter their size, sector of activity, or country of origin, are affected by macro parameters related to the overall business environment as well as the micro context shaped by the behavior of market actors in a specific industry. A careful evaluation of the conditions and opportunities at macro and micro levels will highlight paths to profitable growth. Management can make informed decisions and minimize risk, particularly when faced with several options for moving forward.

For successful expansion, a company needs to achieve transparency at three levels—macro, industry, and enterprise (see figure 8.1)—through a combination of desk research and field investigations.

General information on the megamarkets is not difficult to obtain as there is no dearth of macroeconomic data (Level I) and much of it is posted on Web sites of the World Bank

Figure 8.1. The three levels of megamarket intelligence.

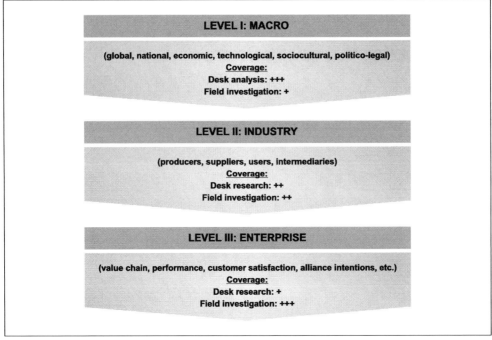

+: relatively important
++: important
+++: very important

and other UN agencies, OECD, CIA Factbook, and similar international organizations. Information coverage has improved since these economies have moved to the spotlight of international politics, business, and finance. Level II information on specific industries (e.g., steel, energy, construction, automotive, luxury goods, etc.) can also be obtained through desk research. Several organizations (e.g., Economic Intelligence Unit, BfAI) offer sector reports against payment, although their prices can be quite high; national trade commissions (e.g., of Australia, Canada, UK, USA) produce sector studies to promote exports. But the statistics are often outdated, fixed, and not comparable between countries. Information brokers, like SVP in France, Euromonitor in the UK, or GfK in Germany, can also be approached for obtaining preliminary information for a fee.

Intelligence on enterprises (Level III) is more difficult to obtain and verify in the megamarkets, and yet it is decisive for a new entrant seeking partners and clients. Apart from established agencies like Kompass, Dun & Bradstreet, or Creditreform, other reliable

---

Pause for thought

In China and India, medium-sized and small enterprises (SMEs) represent 80% of the enterprise population and about 40%–50% of sales.

Even in Russia, where until ten years ago the economy was dominated by large industrial and financial groups, small entrepreneurship is thriving and already represents a significant part of the enterprise population.

Table 8.1. Dos and don'ts for intelligence in the megamarkets.	
Dos	Don'ts
Investigate at all three levels for full transparency: macroeconomic, industry, and company. Check secondary sources and available sector studies to avoid duplication of work and unnecessary expenses. Supplement desk research with regular field visits. Cross-check information on companies by interviewing various sources (their suppliers, distributors, end-users, competitors). Approach competitors as potential partners so that information is exchanged.	Listen to hearsay about expected trends, which is not reliable and should be double-checked to avoid being misled by competition. Seek comprehensiveness by covering the whole territory, which overstretches the research budget; it is better to focus on representative targets and selected market segments. Conduct research based on Western standards aimed at the highest degree of precision; this is not useful, and such information may not be available. Some degree of intuition should be used for speedy decision-making. Delegate intelligence work entirely to external consultants; the company must also get involved in fact-finding itself.

sources of information need to be tapped to get a full picture. Listed companies can be investigated more easily as they are legally obliged to publish their annual results. But attractive opportunities—in terms of outlets, supplies, and partnerships—can be found also among non-listed, often family-owned, businesses.

For EU/US managers, the first port of call is often their country's embassy or the bilateral chamber of commerce. These specialize in general information rather than reality checks on specific business segments and companies, which would overburden these institutions' limited resources. The next option is to address a query to the local trade associations. While these compile data on their specific sectors (production and market), they do not always have updated and detailed information on their members. Moreover, the information that they have is that disclosed by the members. As business intelligence is not the main mission of these two agencies, which focus on lobbying the interests of their members with the government, the information obtained from them can at best cover Level I and to a limited extent Level II. Trade fairs, another frequently used source of contacts and information, offer a fairly good idea of the general situation in the sector, but not all key players may participate, and those that do may not be represented by their decision-makers.

The wide spread and diversity of the mega-economies defy standard in-depth market surveys for the entire territory (see table 8.1). Investigations have to be limited to regions and to representative players with the highest potential in a given industry. Given the quick pace of change in the megamarkets, data are short-lived and need to be frequently validated through targeted field visits and renewed desk research.

8.1. Understanding the macro drivers

Managers of AM companies tend to be overconfident in their assessment of external driving forces at the macro level. Their decisions to invest further or withdraw from a market are inspired by subjective assumptions—based on media reporting or hearsay—rather than objective analysis. Managers can be more easily influenced by opinionated journalism than by objective data based on independent analysis. Medium-sized companies, in particular, lack the resources, or are not willing to allocate budgets, for continuous market monitoring. Progressive companies are run by chief executives or owner-entrepreneurs who recognize the value of careful intelligence-gathering and analysis at all levels in informing their own intuitions.

Systematic surveillance of decisive macro events, such as legislative changes, economic policies, and socioeconomic improvements (employment, inflation, consumption, trade balance, etc.), can provide an objective basis for decision-making. A macro intelligence methodology that covers diverse parameters can present the whole context for the new venture. Carefully chosen parameters allow executives to track long-term trends of the economy without being distracted by current events with short-term impact.

During the 1998–1999 financial default in Russia, the withdrawal of many foreign companies was strongly influenced by credit rating and news agencies, which issued alarming reports on the economic prospects of the country. Few executives expected that this crisis would be immediately followed by a spectacular economic revival. On their corporate radar screens, they hardly noticed that the country's economy had reached the very bottom of a downturn in terms of private consumption, industrial production, and corporate profits, from where it could only recover. The country's oil and gas deposits and other raw materials resources had been ignored. Nor had managers in faraway headquarters grasped the role of the intellectual capital Russia possessed to prepare it for the next economic cycle. Had these parameters been tracked, many more executives would have understood that Russia was on the verge of consolidating its position as a major energy and raw materials supplier, given the rising energy needs and phenomenal potential demand of Europe and the East Asian economies. After 2002, they still failed to correctly interpret the real intentions of the newly appointed President Putin and his ministerial team, who were determined to build a modern, economically powerful Russia. Most companies waited for another four to five years until they decided to invest. By then, prices for real estate and corporate assets had risen fivefold and the Russian ruble had gained 40% vis-à-vis the US dollar. Some companies that stayed on and are successful today may have overstated the risks of an engagement in Russia during seminars and conferences as an effective tactic to keep competitors at bay. They were only too happy that decision-makers of competing enterprises decided to pay their first visits to the country in 2007–2008, when the next crisis was in the making.

An almost identical situation occurred in India, which on July 1, 1991, had to sell part of its gold reserves to the Bank of England as collateral for a US$400 million loan to correct its balance of payments and to prevent the country from sliding into a default. Subsequently, India has experienced healthy growth, accumulated foreign reserves, and posted one of the world's most spectacular stock exchange rallies (500% during 2002–2007). For many years, Western managers—mostly influenced by the media—avoided investments in an apparently poor country without prospect of closing the gap with industrialized nations. Such prejudices seemed almost anachronistic to India's entrepreneurs who took immediate advantage of economic liberalization following the 1991 crisis. Most EU companies waited almost fifteen years, until 2005–2006, to realize that India had become a major economy and a megamarket. But by then, other, more perspicacious players from within India, Asia, and North America had occupied entire market segments and raised the cost of market entry. To buy a company in India today costs about ten times what it did in the late 1990s. Property prices have increased by the same token; in the main cities, offices and flats are higher than in Europe's capitals.

China provides yet another example of the wrong interpretation of facts. While India and Russia were not really discovered as important new markets until the mid-2000s, China kept attracting Western companies throughout the 1990s. The general belief in the long-standing myth of the China market, consisting of 1.3 billion consumers,[1] has made companies forget the risks and difficulties of a venture in China (including during the SARS outbreak in 2002). Even today, few managers seem to be worried about operating profits; according to a survey conducted by the DIHT[2] in 2006, over two-thirds of German companies that invested in China are not profitable today. The main objective is apparently to show business partners that the company also has a presence in China. By the mid-2000s, following major investments, many companies had finally realized that all they had done was to add surplus capacity to market segments already saturated by cutthroat price competition.

There are three macro forces acting upon companies: politico-legal (P), techno-economic (E), and sociocultural (S). An interdependent analysis of the key parameters of these forces (see box 8.1) is meaningful only if it is conducted regularly and over a longer period of time so that major events and crises in a country can be compared objectively for corporate decision-making.

8.1.1. Politico-legal forces

Governments exert significant influence on business activity through their macro policies, which are backed by legislation in a number of areas. The overall policy framework is based on the political agenda of the ruling formation, which yields more or less power depending on the political system.

Advanced markets adopted democracy much earlier and have honed the system. India is the world's largest democracy, with a bicameral parliamentary and multiparty system based on the British model. The prime minister, who heads the government, may sometimes have to depend on coalition partners when the ruling party does not have a clear majority. This may slow down decision-making, but it also rules out the risk of abrupt fundamental reversals in policy following a change in government. Russia's leader, Vladimir Putin, wields considerable personal power to implement his vision for the country, unconstrained by any political allegiance. China is governed by the Communist Party, and its leader, President Hu Jintao, is also a powerful political figure, although important decisions are decided collectively in the Central Committee. Important decisions concerning foreign policy and defense are made fairly quickly in China, but other acts must take their prescribed course in the legislature, as in other countries.

The degree of interaction between the political and business elites is extremely well developed in the three megamarkets. As soon as a foreign player plans an important

---

1. See 7.1.
2. Deutscher Industrie- und Handelstag: coordinating body of German chambers of commerce abroad.

Box 8.1. The three macro forces.

a. Politico-legal forces (P)

These are not always easy to encapsulate, let alone quantify. Perhaps the nearest to doing so are the league tables of national political environments published from time to time by the international business weekly *The Economist*. These are based on work carried out mainly by NGOs such as Amnesty International, the Stockholm Peace Research Institute, and international election monitors.

They typically cover such things as:
- Political parties and ideologies
- Political significance of armed forces and other special interest groups
- Political interference and politico-business nexus
- Economic policies (foreign trade and investment, domestic trade and investment)
- Compliance with multilateral agreements (e.g., WTO, Kyoto Protocol)
- Freedom of the press and other media
- Legal environment
  - Independence of and respect for judiciary
  - Taxation and social legislation
  - Foreign exchange regulations
  - Foreign trade and customs regulations
  - FDI laws
  - IPR laws and enforcement
  - Labor laws and enforcement
  - Environmental laws, enforcement and compliance

b. Techno-economic forces (E)
- Macro trends: GDP, economic growth, inflation, exchange rates
- Socioeconomics: population, age groups, employment
- Domestic consumption and investment
- Foreign trade (import, export, balance)
- FDI inflows and outflows
- Human resource availability and costs
- Infrastructure (e.g., roads, buildings, other physical assets)
- Industrial capacity
- Raw material availability and prices
- Foreign currency reserves and budget deficit/surplus
- Triangular exchange between Eurasian megamarkets
- R&D and innovation potential (institutes, engineers, etc.)
- Patent applications
- Breakthrough technologies generated in the country

c. Sociocultural forces (S)
- Influence of political regime
- Influence of religion
- Official languages (spoken, written)
- Minorities and human rights records
- Income and wealth distributions
- Social structure and mobility

investment or acquisition, domestic enterprises—often represented by their industry associations—contact government officials to highlight possible negative consequences for national industry. The takeover of a significant megamarket enterprise requires not only tact and diplomacy but also knowledge of decision-making mechanisms and direct contacts with key personalities in the politico-business nexus.

A policy issue of major importance is the role granted to mass media with their influence on political decision-making. In Russia, their role has been curbed under Mr. Putin, at least regarding news and opinions on the overall direction in foreign policy (e.g., nuclear cooperation with Iran) and economic ideology (e.g., renationalization of leading energy companies such as Yukos). In China, the media is also controlled, and no direct criticism of the Communist Party is allowed publicly. China and Russia have both embarked on a high-growth trajectory, and their leaderships do not accept any diversion from this. India has a free press, but journalists abstain from aggressive criticism of the government on TV.

Economic policies can hamper or encourage business development by both domestic and foreign investors. In the past, overactive legislation (e.g., on taxation and customs, labor and investments, etc.) in the name of socialism or communism curtailed private enterprise. Economic liberalization has ushered in a new era of stable economic growth buttressed by reasonably predictable policies and legislation. International credit ratings have been upgraded significantly for the three economies, which is a sign of growing investor confidence. But FDI and foreign trade, particularly inward-bound, still face many barriers. Protectionist tendencies in the EU and North America directed at outbound investments from the megamarkets may lead to countermeasures by megamarket governments.[3] The setting up of a trading company, a procedure that has been more or less liberalized in China following WTO accession, still requires good contacts and knowledge of rules and standards to speed up procedures and registrations (e.g., articles of incorporation, sales license, work contracts for foreign managers).

Pause for thought

Food imports into China, for example, are subject to restrictive measures, which are imposed without prior notice by the authorities who may use a health warning (e.g., risk of bird flu) to retaliate against protectionist barriers imposed by other trading partners (e.g., EU food import restrictions, textile and toy anti-dumping legislation).

A German canned and packed sausage producer who had worked for a year to appoint distributors in China, obtain all the necessary permits, and prepare a marketing strategy had to abandon its plans following a sudden embargo by China on German meats. It could only resume its sales into China once the embargo was lifted, just before the August 2008 Olympics. Today the company is selling well, but the worry of a "pending embargo" remains. Starting with local production may reduce this risk in the long-term.

Non-tariff barriers can also hamper business in India and Russia and are a major reason for companies to choose the FDI route once a certain business volume can be anticipated.

---

3. In March 2007, the Russian government warned the EU that it will retaliate for attempts from Brussels to restrict Gazprom from investing in national gas distribution networks.

Another example refers to the location of a production site. China successfully introduced the concept of special economic zones (SEZs) in the mid-1980s. They served as an example for similar zones in India and Russia, which are also governed by investor-friendly legislation. Policies related to industrial zones, free-trade areas, and technology parks can influence investment decisions. Numerous foreign firms launched operations in such zones because they were promised incentives such as tax holidays and other support measures including low-cost office space and warehousing. Unfortunately, when preferential treatment is discontinued after some time, it is too late to rectify the neglect of other more important factors such as proximity to consumers and cost of logistics. Terms and conditions also vary with the type of zone (e.g., high-tech zones, free-trade areas, industrial development zones, technoparks, etc.). Also, the same name does not indicate the same conditions in the three megamarkets; for example, India's SEZs offer tax benefits but are exclusively export-oriented unlike the Chinese ones.

Adapting to foreign laws is not easy and may require changes in business procedures for the megamarket venture (see box 8.2). Fortunately, India's laws are written in English and are based on British common law. A company that follows the rules carefully can avoid expensive and time-consuming litigation. Laws must be studied not only for their impact on the business but also on its target market.

Interestingly, all three megamarkets have adopted a pro-foreign-investor stance. Authorities are keen on keeping a high profile among the foreign investment community. In case of legal conflicts between local and AM companies, compromises and solutions can be

---

Box 8.2. Laws and policies influencing business in the megamarkets.

- Administrative acts
- Labor/employment
- Taxation
- Environmental protection
- Antimonopoly rules to enhance competition, prohibit cartels, and protect strategic industries
- Foreign trade and investment
- Intellectual property: patents and copyright
- Property law
- Bankruptcy/corporate law
- Contract law
- Foreign exchange law
- Legal enforcement through the national court system
- Arbitration
- Research & development
- Balance of power between federal, regional, and local authorities (including tax-sharing arrangements)

> **Pause for thought**
>
> *The reduction of excise duty on beer in certain Indian states increased demand by 500%. Beer companies decided to immediately step up their investments, which induced EU suppliers of equipment to expedite their entry into the Indian market.*
>
> *Several alliances and greenfield projects were hammered out as a consequence of these policy changes in 2007–2008. This led to a significant rise in capacity in the industry. Latecomers will face price increases for land and buildings and a constraint in finding adequate managers.*

negotiated that take into consideration the worries of the foreign investor, provided management has always cultivated good relations with local bodies.[4]

8.1.2. Techno-economic forces

A country's statistical system serves as an economic barometer. The national statistical offices of the three megamarkets provide comprehensive macro data on economic achievements and future trends.[5] Entrepreneurs can use the historical time series of key macro indicators to follow developments over the years and compare parameters for the three countries, provided the definitions for these indicators are similar. Macro aggregates such as GDP, price indices, and foreign trade are often internationally comparable, given that all three countries collect these data according to UN conventions on classifications, collection, processing, and dissemination systems. Employment and industry statistics, for which significant differences existed in the past, are now mostly compiled to internationally accepted standards, making comparisons possible even with AMs. Official statistics can be an excellent source of information for studying economic influences (see box 8.3).

Besides the national statistical services, there are numerous economic research organizations and institutions that interpret official data and publish their own analyses. Certain chambers of commerce and trade associations of G7 countries associate with their counterparts in the megamarkets. While they generally lack the resources to carry out individual projects for companies, their macro analyses are often very useful. International organizations (e.g., UNIDO, World Bank, IMF, EBRD) and international banks also regularly publish economic reports and statistical overviews.

Most managers tend to limit their studies to key economic indicators but often lack the skills to look deeper and interpret the data correctly. Here is an example. Individual purchasing power in the three megamarkets has shot up spectacularly in the new millennium. But this will not be reflected in data converted into dollars or euros as the exchange rates are still low despite the recent appreciation of local currencies. Hence, data in purchasing power parity (PPP) rather than US dollars or euros creates a more realistic picture of the parameter. This is particularly true for parameters such as per capita income and salaries, which must be considered in combination with expenditure levels in the country. Moreover, even these

---

4. Knauff's connections in Russia are said to have been the major reason why this leading German building materials producer has won so many legal cases even in remote regions.
5. For macro data on the megamarkets, see chapters 2 and 3.

> **Box 8.3. Statistical indicators for techno-economic forces.**
> - GDP trends and business cycles
> - Inflation rates
> - Employment and unemployment figures
> - Disposable incomes of households
> - Industrial production and employment
> - Construction and infrastructure statistics
> - Agricultural and forestry statistics
> - Transport, retail, and service statistics
> - Investment activities
> - Interest rates and money supply
> - Foreign trade and investment
> - Regional differences in per capita income and industrial development
> - Energy demand and supply
> - R&D statistics
> - International comparisons

statistics may not tell the whole story. According to official statistics, the average annual income of a Russian is US$3,500, which by itself is unimpressive. However, the fact that 85% of Russians became owners of their flats during privatization in the mid-1990s has greatly increased their effective purchasing power.

PPP can also be used for comparing sector-related information or company turnover. Thus, in the case of an acquisition, a Chinese company with sales of RMB600 million is comparable to a German company generating a PPP-denominated turnover of €180–200 million, although at the official euro/RMB exchange rate, the Chinese company's turnover would be only around €60 million. If the German company seeks to acquire the Chinese company to strengthen the combined company's position in the Chinese and surrounding Asian markets, then it should base its evaluation on PPP and consider the expected continuous rise of the local currency. The same rules apply to India and Russia, where similar trends exist. PPP data in the form of adjustments to market exchange rates for foreign currencies has been published from time to time by various international agencies, especially the World Bank, which commissioned the original work on the subject

> **Pause for thought**
>
> *The following statement was made by Sun Interbrew's CEO about India: "The Indian beer market is still quite small (only 3% of people are beer drinkers), but our group will not only watch closely but make all possible efforts to establish a strong presence. For us three factors count: India's annual growth rate of 7%–8%, a middle class of 250–300 million consumers, and the relatively small share of beer among alcoholic beverages, which we see as a big opportunity to shape a new market."*

> **Box 8.4. Technological indicators.**
> - Government and private sector spending on R&D
> - Innovative capability expressed by patent and trademark registrations
> - Enrolled technical/engineering students
> - Number of working scientists by main discipline
> - Competitive position of country in key basic and applied technologies
> - Innovation and substitute technologies (e.g., new telecom standards)
> - Trade-off between environmental standards and performance

by Professor Irving Kravis. Probably the best-known and most readily accessible series are the "Big Mac Indices," published regularly by *The Economist* magazine, which are based on prices of the eponymous hamburger in outlets around the world.

What counts are the economic macro fundamentals and the future market potential, which are often overlooked.

Leading AM players have understood that it would be wrong to judge the megamarkets by the current situation in an industry; instead, they check whether the overall economic fundamentals form a good base for future development.

The technological gap between the AMs and the megamarkets is narrowing, which can be seen from the main indicators (see box 8.4). The megamarkets are opening markets in return for technology by inviting multinationals to set up R&D centers. Future technological innovations are most likely to emanate from the megamarkets. China's US$30 billion investment in public R&D places it sixth in OCDE's world ranking. It now needs to improve access to finance by private and medium-sized enterprises as until now the large banks fund R&D mainly by state-owned companies; at the same time, China needs to strengthen intellectual property protection. When Jack Welch was CEO of General Electric, he said that India "is a developed country as far as its intellectual infrastructure is concerned. We get the highest intellectual capital per dollar here." Russia has a long and distinguished history in science and technology, which it is capitalizing upon to become an R&D powerhouse for global companies.

All three countries educate millions of young engineering students each year in various disciplines. More than 2 million people work in over 4,500 R&D centers throughout Russia, of which at least 1 million are researchers and scientists, which is far more than in any other country in the world. India has the third-largest scientific and technical manpower in the world; each year, its 162 universities award 4,000 doctorates and 35,000 postgraduate degrees. National institutes and universities are strong in both fundamental and applied sciences.[6] For EU/US companies, it is extremely important not only to make market-oriented or cost-related investments in the megamarkets, but to also study

---

6. See 3.1.3.

possibilities of setting up research platforms linked to national R&D networks in order to stay in the vanguard of technological progress.

Generally speaking, new technologies enable businesses to use a broad spectrum of new options to craft their strategies. A recent study by McKinsey[7] summarizes eight technology-enabled trends that will transform new markets and businesses. Three of them, if applied to the megamarkets and referring to managing relationships, promise to spark new ways of cooperation and alliance building with megamarket enterprises in the coming decade.

Trend 1: Innovation outsourcing to business partners who work together in networks. A university-based R&D lab from Germany, which may not be an ideal partner to a Western company, can now team up with an Indian pharma company to form a competitive "center of excellence" developing new nature-based molecules for later marketing in EMs and AMs. Advances in open-standards-based computing are making it easier to co-create physical goods for more complex value chains between, for example, a Chinese auto parts supplier and its French key account. Specialists expect that this form of networked and co-shared innovation may contribute to the elimination of some important R&D work in companies. Intellectual property rights issues become more relevant, hence the need to engage in cross-investments and to avoid loose cooperation where know-how may drift away.

Trend 2: Using consumers (mass products) and users (technical products) as innovators. New Web 2.0 technologies make it possible for companies to tap this new form of "buyer engagement" by setting up permanent question-and-answer platforms with key accounts/consumer segments in the megamarkets. This will enable a firm to design adapted products and to develop new competences.

Trend 3: Tapping the world of (external) talent. This is already happening in IT but will certainly spread to other services (legal, advisory, advertising, real estate) where EMM companies are gaining ground for both domestic and global use. EU service providers will have to increase their stakes in megamarket companies in order to compete on a global scale.

8.1.3. Sociocultural forces

The macro view of a specific economy would be incomplete without information on the country's social situation, which covers demographics, age groups, gender issues, social structure and mobility, income and wealth distributions, and so forth. Cultural factors including the value system, history, and religious beliefs are also determinants. Knowledge of these "soft" factors of the macro environment (see box 8.5) greatly facilitates confidence building and relationship management with business partners in the megamarket.

Given their territorial expanse, all three Eurasian megamarkets can be compared to complex organisms consisting of many sub-regional community networks, each following its own rules and patterns.

Religion[8] greatly influences business behavior in India, where almost all the main world religions are found. Although India is officially a secular state, respect for all religions is

---

7. J. Manyika et al., *Eight Business Technology Trends to Watch* (McKinsey, December 2007).
8. See 1.1.1.

> **Box 8.5. Soft factors of the megamarket macro environment.**
>
> - History
> - Language
> - Culture
> - Religion
> - Social attitudes
> - Lifestyles
> - Business attitude and etiquette
> - Negotiation styles
> - Educational attainments
> - Work ethics
> - Leisure choices

enshrined in its constitution. China officially has no national religion and looks racially homogeneous: about 90% of Chinese are Hans of Sino descent. But China also hosts various minorities with their own languages and religions (Huis, Uighur Muslims, etc.). Russia is also a huge melting pot of different minorities. The majority are Orthodox Christians. Protestant and Catholic Christians only represent about 5% of the population. Tatarstan and Chechnya are semi-autonomous republics with a Muslim majority, whereas Kalmutyia in southeastern Russia along the Caspian Sea is Buddhist. Minorities express their distinction mainly through their attitude related to four dimensions: religion, language, food habits, and customs (e.g., respect for the elderly, observance of social hierarchies).

Megamarket governments are often criticized by humanitarian groups for not respecting human and minority rights (e.g., China and Tibet, Russia and Chechnya, India and Kashmir). They counter by pointing to abuses and social distress in AMs as well: United States and its history of racial segregation and lasting human rights abuses in Guantanamo Bay prison camps since 9/11, France and its Muslim ghettos, and Italy's problems with its Roma and Albanian immigrants. The human development index compiled by the UN covers issues like education, health, and other factors that determine the quality of human resources and prospects for inhabitants including immigrants. It can be applied to all countries.

The comprehensive study of macro forces, or PEST analysis, is a combined study of political, legal, economic, social, and technological factors influencing corporate decisions in the megamarkets. Depending on the risk or opportunity, market leaders can move swiftly along with the main drivers of change or vice versa. The macro forces of each economy are themselves interacting with those in other economies. Global competitive forces will impact more on enterprises as more countries cooperate after opting for open trading regimes, which—contrary to popular belief—will reinforce their national companies. The macro analysis can be applied to competitors and their reaction to external influences. Competitors may respond differently to these challenges depending on their managerial farsightedness and strategic preferences (i.e., as pioneers, leaders, followers). Macro forces influencing economic development can be analyzed on the basis of secondary data available from official sources. These need to be validated and supplemented by regular field visits, during which discussions with customers and suppliers will enlighten executives on happenings behind the scenes.

8.2. Aiming at sector transparency

A clear insight into the architecture and mechanisms of an industry, its main actors (including suppliers and customers) in the value chain, and their position and bargaining power makes the strategy more effective. Such industry scans help executives detect suppliers, customers, and potential partners as well as opportunities for strategic alliances and acquisitions.

Sector forces are shaped mainly by the economic actors operating within a given industry. Dominant players can, through their behavior and strategy, determine the rules of the game and even impose conditions (e.g., norms, technologies, price policies) on smaller, financially more dependent actors. Foreign companies have a chance to gain leadership if they understand these mechanisms and manage to tilt them in their favor. However, the rapid strides made by national champions in the megamarkets, often with the help of politicians, make this increasingly difficult, hence the significance of the first-mover advantage.

If budget and time constraints do not allow a detailed industry scan, EU/US companies should acquire at least a snapshot covering industry structure, trends, main actors and their significance, and competitive forces (see box 8.6). Although not detailed, a snapshot reveals the main trends used to determine current and future market potential, the cost of market entry, and key factors of success. The industry scan starts with desk research using data from secondary sources. Aggregate indicators for respective industries according to UN classifications depict structural features and trends. Such background information can be useful for later calibrating field surveys. Future potential is what the

---

Box 8.6. Indicators for megamarket industry scan.
- Industry classification, product categories
- Size of industry in terms of output and employment
- Annual growth rates of industry
- Company size classes/categories
- Regional dimension: output, turnover, company distribution
- Imports vs. local production
- Exports by product categories and destination countries
- Investment activity of leading players
- Cost structure in the sector
- Rules and regulations affecting the sector

senior executive needs to spot, like the perspicacious entrepreneurs who entered at low cost during Russia's 1998 financial crisis and who now reap rich benefits. Entry costs and the pay-back periods rise as the sector develops. Late investments take at least five years, usually longer, to fructify.

To obtain additional parameters for appropriate decision-making, the preliminary analysis then needs to be deepened to the next level of detail to understand the forces that impact the industry and their interactions.

8.2.1. Market actor analysis[9]

Besides general industry statistics, an investor should obtain background information on major forces or actors impacting an industry and the way they interrelate with one another. If the constellation of these actors is favorable, the payback period of an investment can be shorter as the company can impose its terms and standards on other market actors and command higher margins before competitors gain strength. Focusing on the main actors allows a firm to understand the fundamental structural conditions of the industry and makes it possible for management to work out how it can be more profitable and less vulnerable to attack. Even when the forces are apparently intense, as they are in such industries as textiles, consumer electronics, and cars, leaders always identify niches or segments used to break into the market or expand market share.

Five actors determine industry dynamics and attractiveness regardless of the country, region, and sector (see figure 8.2).

- **Customers.** They can be located anywhere in the industrial value chain depending on the product or technology in question:
  - raw materials or industrial clients in the case of technical products and equipment
  - retail chains and wholesalers in the case of consumer goods

Figure 8.2. The five actors impacting on megamarket investors.

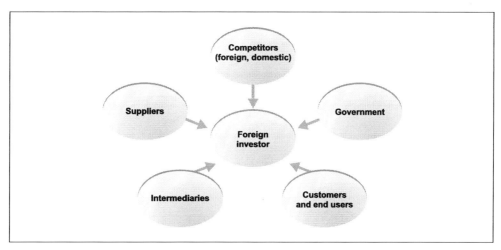

---

9. See also Michael Porter's five competitive forces in *Competitive Strategy* (1980).

- manufacturers or distributors of consumer goods
- manufacturers or independent wholesalers and distributors of industrial goods
- municipalities and public utility companies for environment-related and other technologies
- service providers in the case of equipment manufacturers
- infrastructure companies in the case of both equipment and service providers

- **Competitors.** They can be:
  - local companies
  - established foreign companies
  - newcomers to the megamarkets
  - manufacturers of substitutes breaking into the industry

  An understanding of competitive forces (for example, the weight of leaders in a particular industry) helps to determine whether it is necessary to set up new capacities, to enter into an alliance with a local player, or to acquire a local business.

- **Suppliers:**
  - suppliers of raw materials
  - producers of intermediaries and components
  - outsourcing companies
  - service providers

- **Intermediaries:**
  - dealers
  - importers
  - retailers
  - wholesalers providing indispensable distribution and logistics services

- **Government.** In megamarkets, strategic industries are monitored by public bodies or dominated by state enterprises. Examples are:
  - steel (China, India),
  - oil and gas (China, India, Russia),
  - aerospace (China, India, Russia),
  - machine-tools (China),
  - automobiles (China, Russia),
  - shipbuilding (China, India), and
  - insurance and banking (China, India, Russia).

  Acquiring a controlling stake in national champions belonging to strategic industries requires aggressive lobbying at central, regional, and city levels. Although megamarket governments acknowledge that FDI is an important driver for growth, they impose sectoral restrictions either to protect local players (e.g., retail trade in India, banking in China and Russia) or for security (e.g., arms industry). Among the measures used are preferential duties (for favored industries) or non-tariff trade barriers (for less favored industries).

The configuration of market actors in the five categories is an indicator of profitability levels in an industry. Many foreign companies are incurring losses in the megamarkets because management underestimated competition, customer behavior, and the role of government while selecting their investment option. In each of the five categories, existing players will try by all means to raise entry barriers for newcomers. The intensity of competition is higher when there are many players in a specific industrial segment. Industries with high-technology and knowledge content tend to be sellers' markets whereby selected manufacturers control distribution and can act upon their suppliers. In most consumer goods industries, which have switched from seller to buyer markets, many companies compete in an environment marked by thin market shares.

The model works very well also for newcomers in the megamarkets who may just use the threat of entry—not whether and when entry actually occurs—as a bargaining power. Local players know that new competition based on higher technology levels will eventually squeeze their profitability as it forces them to invest simply to reinforce the barriers of entry. Knowing exactly the situation in an industry gives the investor an information edge, which allows him to negotiate a favorable alliance or even convince local entrepreneurs to merge and sell a majority share.

Each of the five actors must be treated as a separate field of intelligence, the three major ones being customers, competition, and suppliers in descending order of importance. Discussions with resource managers within the industry will provide answers on the functioning of the industry:

- What is the relationship between the key actors of a specific industrial cluster?
- What are the rules of the game?
- What are the key factors of success (KFS) in the industry?
- How strong is government intervention?
- Which unique selling proposition (USP) can be submitted to customers? And how?
- Does the new investor's USP have a competitive edge? How long will it take for the market and competition to catch up? When does innovation become the decisive factor?
- Can the company's know-how and technology help erect entry barriers for other competitors?

In a second step, background information is collected on the leading companies in each of the categories. It generally includes data on assets, strengths, management, financials, international experience, ongoing alliances, and so forth. This type of information can be obtained from financial Web sites and interviews with decision-makers of the companies or executives in charge of business development.[10]

Initially, megamarket industry scenarios appear opaque due to the size of the megamarkets and the number of possible targets. Sometimes many large and small players compete aggressively for market share, and it takes time to determine who is a category leader and to understand the bargaining power and reasons for success of the main players.

---

10. See 8.3.

> **Box 8.7. Issues underlying the megamarket actor analysis.**
>
> - Bargaining power of players belonging to each of the five categories depending on size and standing
> - Market share of top five players in each category
> - Distribution channel analysis (layers of intermediaries)
> - Protection of sector by government bodies
> - Role of state enterprises
> - Importance of foreign investors
> - Technology levels
> - Key factors of success
> - Entry barriers for newcomers

Intelligence on the five actors should therefore be conducted methodically and cover a range of megamarket-specific issues (see box 8.7).

The actor analysis helps management to grasp the KFS and on that basis refocus corporate strategy. KFS are sector-specific and evolve constantly with changes in the demand and supply patterns. They refer to strengths demonstrated by market leaders in an industry, such as:

- high customer satisfaction and market share;
- high engineering skills;
- cost-effective production;
- effective marketing;
- corporate reputation and brand image.

> **Pause for thought**
>
> *How an actor analysis helps refocus an entry strategy is seen in an example from the brewery equipment business. Until 2006 the Chinese market was dominated by a successful local company that had started to quote for international turnkey projects. The five actors analysis showed strong personal connections between the company and its customers and that it would be virtually impossible for a new supplier to enter this tight circle. The analysis also showed dominance of the local company vis-à-vis suppliers and intermediaries. Moreover, there would be no government interference even at the local level should the newcomer attempt to acquire the local player (e.g., through the bargaining power of state-owned client companies). This information was crucial to the European competitor changing its initial idea of setting up a greenfield operation.*
>
> *In another case in Russia, the actors analysis revealed to a European supplier of turnkey plants for manufacturing concrete roof tiles that the best strategy was to team up with a downstream player (i.e., a customer). The Russian roofing market was dominated by suppliers of other types of roofing materials (e.g., metal- and bitumen-based roofing systems), which meant creating a demand for cement roof tiles.*

Table 8.2. Entry barriers raised by megamarket actors.

	High entry barriers (low sector profitability)	Low entry barriers (high sector profitability)
Customers	Stagnating market Buyers already order from a few established firms (local/foreign) High brand awareness High price sensitivity High switching costs Different customer preferences	Growing market Buyers need new products and technology for their own progress Low brand loyalty Low price sensitivity Low switching costs Similar customer preferences
Competitors	Intense competition Low capacity utilization Protection of product and process know-how (intellectual property) through patents Standards and price lines already set by existing players	Moderate competition High capacity utilization No patent protection (e.g., pharmaceuticals) Absence of restrictive standards and flexible price lines
Suppliers	Risk of forward integration by big suppliers Absence of suitable suppliers Low order volumes	Many small specialized suppliers with limited resources Presence of several suppliers High order volumes
Intermediaries	Limited access to national distribution network Multi-layer channels	Easy access to intermediary sales channels Availability of direct channels
Government	Sector considered sensitive by authorities Market controlled by prominent state-owned players	No direct government involvement (production, distribution) Few state-owned enterprises

Future profits of an investor are affected by entry barriers, which can originate from any of the five actors. Barriers can be higher or lower depending on the degree of competition and the bargaining power of buyers, suppliers, and government. Profitability is usually higher in industries where competitors have set up high barriers for newcomers (see table 8.2). These should then seek entry by offering a winning concept or—if this is not possible—stay out of the industry as the investor will not be able to carve a share of the profitable market. The financial strength and other capabilities of the investor also count. There have been cases where companies providing advanced process and product technologies or competitive services have managed to successfully penetrate industries in the megamarkets that were controlled by local players.

8.2.2. Megamarket segmentation

One of the actors, the megamarket customer, requires deeper study through precise market segmentation. A market segment consists of customer clusters sharing similar sets of requirements and seeking a specific mix of comparable benefits. It helps to group homogeneous targets that can be approached independently. Each target segment should:

- be big enough to justify allocation of resources;
- show a genuine need for the product and service mix offered by the company; and
- have potential for growth and increase in value.

The segmentation process helps to:
- identify and analyze current and future customers;

- qualify the company's actual and feasible market share;
- check a company's own strengths and weaknesses; and
- determine marketing objectives and the strategies and investments required for implementing them.

A company may enter with its flagship product, but it may also start with other lines depending on the target or readiness of the market to absorb a certain product. Segmentation implies insight into the type of product applications that might interest market participants in the industrial value chain. A diversified company should not overlook new possible applications in a megamarket context.

With increasing consolidation among customers, in most industries the three to four leading players account for a large share of the demand for a specific product, service, or technology. However, the fragmented "long tail" should not be neglected. Much interest is being shown in the "bottom and middle of the pyramid"[11] as a huge potential market for all sorts of consumer products and services, ranging from shampoo sachets to micro finance and insurance. Some technologies have not yet reached the emerging markets. But that does not signify the absence of demand. Potential customers should also be targeted to translate their need into a demand.

Because of the inherent differences between consumer and business markets, marketers cannot use exactly the same variables to segment both, although a certain convergence can be observed. There are, however, important lessons to be drawn from emerging markets given that sales of both consumer and industrial goods underlie similar rules. Imports of both categories, for example, face intense competition from local producers and demand fast decisions concerning the relocation of manufacturing or local assembly. In addition

---

Pause for thought

A European packaging company surveying the Chinese market found out that its main folding-box line geared to the cosmetics industry (90% of sales in the EU/USA) would have taken very long to launch. The market was not yet mature as the main customers, the Western and Japanese cosmetics multinationals, were still bringing in the ready-packed products from abroad.

Having identified a qualified alliance partner, it therefore decided that it would be best first to approach other segments such as pharmaceuticals, premium foods, and gift wraps. It could thus prepare for entry into its core market, which was expected to grow as Chinese and Japanese cosmetics companies were gradually switching to local suppliers.

***

In India, clay bricks are produced by micro-enterprises in open-air kilns in the proximity of construction sites. But they are polluting, and their quality is not suited to modern constructions. There are very few clay-brick factories, the assumption being that the cost of production and transport will be uncompetitive.

But a European company with the right strategy can ally itself with real estate groups that are ready for backward integration of businesses that ensure quality supplies.

---

11. See 9.2.2.

> **Pause for thought**
>
> *In India, Toyota's multi-utility vehicle Qualis was intended as a personal car but was snatched up by taxi fleet operators. Toyota therefore expected Qualis's successor, Innova, to also appeal to these operators. But it is the personal car owner segment that is pushing sales of the luxury variants of the model, while the fleet operators have not been as forthcoming as expected for the basic Innova model.*
>
> *In another high-growth business, a diversified European producer of packaging materials will have to study accurately both the traditional paper-based and film-based (including BOPP) packaging segments in India in order to position its products.*

to general variables that apply to all product categories, those specific to the business are used as segmentation criteria (see box 8.8).

The most important segmentation criteria refer to market actor targets, industries/applications, and geographic coverage, which for certain industries are usually national (e.g., alternative energies, steel, pharmaceuticals), whereas in others (e.g., building materials, logistics services) it can be regional. A company may initially apply the segmentation criteria it is familiar with in AMs. But in an emerging market, still low in specialization, customers can be found in non-conventional sectors.

Customers or users may belong to both the private and public sectors depending on the products/technology and services offered. With exploding budgets owing to healthy growth coupled with foreign exchange inflows and high tax income, public entities in the megamarkets have become large clients for environmental technologies, construction/infrastructure projects, health care, education, and tourism. They float even global tenders to attract the most advanced technologies at the best possible price.

8.2.3. Megamarket potential analysis

Allocation of human and financial resources will depend on profitable business development in the megamarkets, which should preferably be run as separate profit centers.[12] No industry analysis will be complete without concrete figures on the sales that can be realistically attained within the next five years. Market potential analysis (MPA) evaluates, on the basis of selected indicators, whether and to what extent a true market exists at present and in the future for a given product or service. It indicates estimated proceeds through turnover and sold quantities to potential customers in light of competition. MPA helps to clarify if and within which time frame an offer will find an acceptable number of buyers in the target market and what they would be ready to pay (price point). The sales potential needs to be assessed at both industry and geographic levels for the main customer segments or niches targeted by the company. Market surveys of key accounts, and if possible detailed market research based on a wide customer sample, are useful tools for approximating the market potential. Accurate selection of the key accounts among a sample of companies in the main segments will yield reliable results as they usually account for at least two-thirds of projected sales.

---

12. See 12.2.

Box 8.8. Segmentation criteria for megamarket expansion.

Criterion 1: Market actors in the value chain

- Industrial users (for engineering goods), different categories of companies depending on applications
- Wholesale and/or retail customers (for consumer goods), different categories of companies depending on applications
- Suppliers, different categories depending on delivered parts, components, and OEM products
- Same-category producers/competitors
- Manufacturers of substitutes

Criterion 2: Industries/applications

- User cluster 1
- User cluster 2
- User cluster 3
- User cluster 4
- Foreign subsidiaries
- State-owned companies

Criterion 3: Geography

- National coverage
- Coverage of selected regions or provinces
- Coverage of selected cities
- Coverage of non-city markets (rural areas)

Criterion 4: Company size classes (by sales or/and employees)

- Target companies
- Medium-sized companies
- Small companies
- Micro enterprises

Criterion 5: Socio-demographic and psychographic factors (end consumers)

- Gender
- Age
- Education
- Income groups
- Family status
- Social status
- Residential category (e.g., house-owner, flat-dweller)
- Behavioral features (lifestyle, occupation, purchasing motivations)

Six analytical steps are suggested:
- Define market segments according to types of users by application and/or geographic location (market segment table).
- Identify the name and location of possible key accounts that control the largest market share in specific segments.
- Survey a representative sample of possible customers.
- Quantify order volumes and price levels.
- Value competitors' market share as well as their strengths and weaknesses.
- Calculate possible relative market share for the company based on its USP.

An MPA prevents over- or underestimation of the market as it is carried out in the field and is not only based on criteria used in the traditional advanced markets. Theoretical sales volumes are different from real market potential. The time and resources required to counter any existing customer relations network established by local competitors should also be factored into the analysis. If this network is too strong, the European company could consider a takeover to shorten lead time. MPA facilitates the evaluation of three focal points: market size, demand, and trends (see figure 8.3). The art is to predict the future and create a market from an almost invisible demand, which represents a constant challenge in emerging economies. Even if the MPA shows limited sales in the first few years, the company should look at latent demand patterns and devise strategies to tap its hidden potential.

8.3. Screening business partners

Before venturing into a megamarket, it is necessary to refine industry analysis with a more in-depth study of individual customers, competitors, and distribution companies that have been preselected as possible business partners. This task, referred to as a "reality check," demands strict confidentiality and unique skills to obtain confidential information on management intentions and financial performance of the target and its related entities. Various sources can be tapped:
- existing business partners (customers, suppliers, competitors, channel members);
- industry associations;
- resource persons from the industry (suppliers, customers, associates, etc.);
- banks;
- public authorities;
- confidential discussions with the target.

The main purpose of "enterprise reality checks" is to find out:
- at the customer level, if key accounts are financially stable, well managed, and ethically clean for building a lasting business relation (megamarket customers attach great importance to personal contacts and generally reject vendor-client relationships not based on mutual trust and not involving senior executives from headquarters; they

Figure 8.3. Market potential analysis.

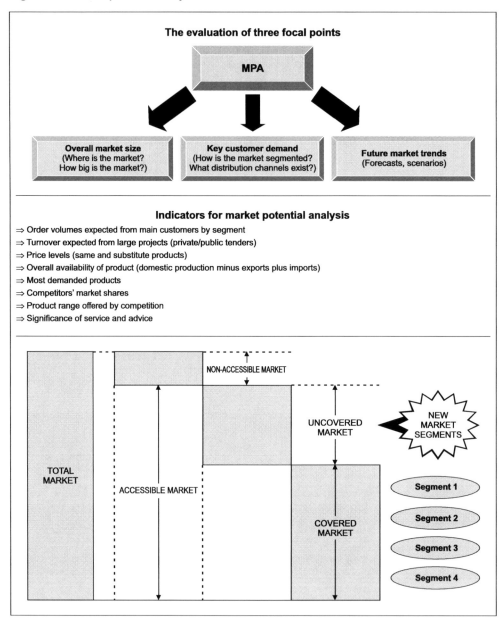

must be financially healthy and have high moral standards in paying their bills and not disclosing sensitive information to competitors (customer reality check);

- at the competitor level, how far firmly established rivals are open to a strategic alliance or takeover proposals and whether they have committed management and financial resources to put such projects into practice on the condition of "goal congruence" (competitor or potential partner reality check); and
- at the channel level, which players add real value and invest resources for promoting the company's products and acquiring new customers as compared to gaining flat commissions for simple mediation (channel reality check).

A company may also decide to invest in related industries. In this case, a partner check is not equivalent to a competitor check as the target is not yet directly competing with the investor. Suppliers can also be selected as "upstream" (input providers) or "lateral" (service providers) partners, in which case the reality check can be extended to them as well. In this section, we shall limit ourselves to the first three categories.

Although for large and listed companies information is available in the public domain, there is little or no published information on smaller, closely held family businesses. In India, the Registrar of Companies can supply some data, but they are of a very general nature. In China and Russia, too, information is scarce on family-held, non-listed companies. The market (suppliers, vendors, clients, end users, banks, public bodies) still remains the best source of information. Resource managers within the industry usually possess more updated information on trends and pending shifts in the industry than databases. As market insiders, they are valuable for providing insight on how companies function and operate in their clusters. They should be consulted when vetting business partners before the final cooperation or share-purchasing agreement is signed. Absolute discretion, confidence-building, and integrity in the country or industry in question are indispensable qualities of the informant and the receiver of information who both must act according to strict ethical principles and standards.

8.3.1. Customer reality check

Reality checks of customers or key accounts deal with a series of issues:
- identification of non-satisfied needs and requirements;
- motivation for purchase;
- buying patterns, volumes, and behavior;
- decision-making and organizational structures;
- financial and business credentials;
- history and reputation.

For consumer goods, purchases are triggered by culture-based preferences, customs, and traditions. Prestige and fashion as well as comfort, mobility, and security are additional drivers. Purchase motivations and the "psyche" of potential buyers are important determinants of price levels. The growing middle class in the megamarkets is prepared to pay a higher price if it can associate a product with superior quality and experience a certain lifestyle. For industrial goods, purchases are motivated by cost/energy savings, speed of delivery (e.g., hot-strip rolls for a steel plant, just-in-time components for the car industry), security (e.g., scaffoldings for the construction sector), and environmental considerations.

Customer or key account analysis helps to determine the indispensable mix of products and services to be sold. Management tools can help standardize essential information for carrying the investigation further.[13] There are five dimensions: price, quality, value, volume, and time. Each of these elements is reflected in every product or service, but it

---

13. See 7.3 (strategic tools): "Customer portfolio analysis" and "ABC analysis."

can vary from one industry to another. Quality is product-intrinsic (resistance, durability, customer-friendly use, etc.), whereas value is a function of customer expectations (e.g., distinctive style, color scheme and mix, comfort, fashion, etc.). Generally speaking, people will not buy, use, or consume a product or service if an essential element is missing. Timing has become a critical factor in the mix. No matter whether products bear in them the advantage of low price or exclusivity, they must be provided when the market is ready for them.

For most foreign companies in the megamarkets, the rules of the game in their industry become clearer with time. The learning period can be reduced if the investor networks skillfully with important business circles and receives regular updates from industry insiders: decision-makers of leading players, retired top managers, advisers, directors of sector associations, and highly placed government officials.

Customer reality checks need to be carried out in-depth whenever the vendor (supplier) intends to buy a stake in or invest together with a key account. There will be a far greater understanding of exact requirements, concerns, and possible conflict areas if customer surveys are conducted on a regular basis in important industries as preparatory steps for future joint investments. Such surveys are able to determine satisfaction levels, value drivers, and essential parameters in a business relationship, which is the basis of a solution-based approach aimed at supporting customers in generating better results (e.g., cost cuts, environmental issues, image). Megamarket customers are known to be price-sensitive, but they also base their decisions on quality, reliability, and partnership aspects. The "emotional factor," which triggers the buying decision, is related to good functioning of human relations, which can take years of effort to solidify. Knowledge of the customer and personal contacts with key decision-makers will help to anticipate trends and time investments in the megamarkets, no matter whether it is with one of the key accounts or other market participants attempting to cater to the same customers.

8.3.2. Competitor reality check

Initially, competition always represents a disturbing factor, although it helps to bring down prices for users and spurs innovation. The study of leading competitors should give the company all the elements to decide:

- if it is worth entering the market head-on;
- if it is better to adopt a "guerilla" strategy by attacking still unoccupied segments and/or regions (e.g., in Russia's European regions, Western and Eastern Siberia, China's interior territories, India's Tier 2 and 3 cities);
- which are the distinctive features that competitors cannot or do not offer (this presupposes regular observation of a competitor's value proposition and performance of its main corporate functions, especially marketing, HR, finance, operations, and R&D);
- when the company should enter the market or expand further;
- which talent can be headhunted from a competitor; and
- if and when a competitor can be turned into an ally.

The last point is worth a more thorough analysis. Reality checks of competitors are meaningful if the investor intends to forge an alliance with an established player. As part of the division of labor and rationalization efforts prompted by more intense competition in global markets, a growing number of companies have opened up to the idea of engaging in a win-win "coopetition" (cooperative arrangement with rivals) instead of head-on competition leading to destructive confrontation and losses on both sides.

Foreign companies face five types of rivals, who may have a strategic interest in an alliance:
- national champions or market leaders with an established brand (state-owned or privately held);
- local medium-sized privately held companies;
- foreign multinationals;
- foreign family-controlled, mostly small and medium-sized companies;
- companies external to an industry that offer substitute technologies.

Having developed in a protected context, megamarket companies are more apprehensive of competition, particularly from new entrants. Information-gathering on possibilities to cooperate becomes easier once confidence is built. If a competitor senses a chance of becoming more successful by joining forces with a strong partner, sensitive data on profitability, market shares, sales by key accounts, cost structures, and so forth, is shared more easily. If there is serious interest, a letter of intent (LOI) can be signed followed by a technical evaluation and legal and financial due diligence (data room) as major milestones toward an alliance.[14]

It is not recommended to engage in outright industrial espionage or enter binding arrangements with several parties simultaneously under the pretext of forging alliances. Informal networks work extremely well in the megamarkets, and such an attitude may have adverse effects for the future business. Western companies should avoid criticizing Western rivals and proposing alliances to defy them openly and aggressively. The ethical code in the three Eurasian megamarkets imposes discretion and respect for one's fellow countrymen (including competitors), and any lack thereof might jeopardize confidence-building with the local business community, which is essential for long-term partnerships to develop.

For most foreign companies, the rules of the game in an industry become clear only with time. The learning period can be reduced if the foreign company is well networked in relevant business circles. It must be willing to share information about itself and others with industry insiders if it wants to receive intelligence on competitor moves. Permanent observation of market developments will allow updating competitor checklists at regular intervals (see box 8.9). It is important that this analysis not only covers financial data and performance-related information on competitors, but also offers a broader picture of the corporate culture and identity of potential targets so that top management can sense whether a competitor would be an appropriate fit for an acquisition or alliance. These soft factors become of particular relevance when conducting competitor reality checks in non-familiar sociocultural contexts.

---

14. See chapter 11.

Box 8.9. Competitor checklist.

- Ownership
- Profile of management
- Organization
- Product and service portfolio
- Corporate goals
- Manufacturing and technology
- Sales and distribution
- Cost structure
- Financial data
- Overall strategy
- Future plans
- Strengths and weaknesses
- Culture: customer-orientation, attitude toward staff, technology, innovation, performance, cost management
- Corporate identity

8.3.3. Channel reality check

Distribution channel checks are a third important area of analysis at the enterprise level in the megamarkets. They enable a company to get a detailed overview of the present distribution system, how it will evolve in the future, the ideal number of layers/partners, and information on individual priority players for possible long-term alliances demanding greater financial commitment. In consumer goods markets in China, India, and Russia, traditional structures (e.g., corner grocery stores, open-air markets) are being challenged, but not yet replaced, by more modern formats (e.g., hypermarkets, malls, e-commerce). Unlike in Western environments, modern and traditional channels have a tendency to coexist, which can make reality checks more complex. There are many reasons for this symbiosis in the megamarkets: government regulation, importance of rural areas where tradition prevails, convenience, and the low penetration level of modern food and non-food formats, which will take time to build a regional presence in vast territorial markets.

Because of their territorial size, megamarkets are characterized by multi-layer channel systems. Depending on the distance from major cities (e.g., Tibet for China) and the product category (e.g., FMCG, industrial components), distribution channels can attain up to four or even more layers, with each intermediary earning a margin for warehousing, moving, and distributing the merchandise to the next level in the value chain. Direct channels (e.g., door-to-door, Internet) are also growing fast to reduce costs related to mediation. For technical goods, many foreign multinationals still use independent agents

> **Box 8.10. Elements of a megamarket channel check.**
> - Overview of distribution system (types, including Internet) and channel dynamics (forecasts)
> - Information about average margins for each channel
> - Distribution strategies of competitors (vacant and occupied channels)
> - Channel matrix: contact/client data of dealers and brands listed
> - Staff, infrastructure (warehousing, logistics), and reach (domestic local, regional, national, overseas)
> - Perception and decision factors for purchasing from specific vendors/suppliers (get to know what dealers think about the firm)
> - Strategies for more effective selling and channel management

although many companies now understand the advantage of having their own sales teams who can explain the product and provide individual advice and service to the customer.

Similar to competitor and customer reality checks, channel checks should be based on surveys. The leading dealers and distributors in the industry need to be identified and interviewed. Their statements will have to be cross-checked with the opinions of manufacturers using these channels and other distribution experts (see box 8.10).

To devise an appropriate strategy, management must understand which channels should be used at what time and for what purpose. The best way is to chart hierarchies and layers as well as inter-linkages stating the percentage of flows each channel (by type/format or player, in the case of key accounts) commands. Channel members may be categorized on the basis of their margins (to get an idea of where cost-cutting is indispensable) and satisfaction levels (with the company with respect to its direct competitors). Margins can be increased by minimizing transport and reducing logistics and warehousing costs.

The main satisfaction parameters for channel checks (see table 8.3) should be studied on a regular basis through telephone and field surveys: margins, warranty times, delivery time, product quality, product variety, service quality, marketing support, and sales support.

Pause for thought

A German producer of high-quality food exporting several containers a month to China gradually realized that the local partner (importer-distributor) was selling at a high margin to finance its sales force and "privileged" intermediaries, which were earning the bulk of the revenue generated.

Had the foreign company performed a thorough reality check of the main wholesale and retail channels, it would have been able to understand the margin structure at each distribution level and to adjust its price policy accordingly.

Table 8.3. Megamarket channel typology and analysis.

Examples of channels	Products distributed	Buying volumes	Margins in past three years	Satisfaction levels
a. For consumer goods:				
Small grocery stores				
Super-, hypermarkets				
Discounters				
Convenience stores				
Department stores				
Specialized retailers				
Cash & carry				
Mail-order house				
Franchises				
Distributors				
Wholesalers				
Direct vendors				
b. For industrial goods:				
Importers				
Technical wholesalers				
Distributors				
Suppliers				

CHAPTER 9
Strategic thrust: Get the fundamentals right

In the previous two chapters, we have seen how companies can improve their internal readiness and external surveillance. These analytical exercises are essential to minimize risks and evaluate a company's real chances in the megamarkets. They also provide the necessary inputs for determining possible approaches, options, and measures that enable management to reach out to megamarket partners and customers (chapters 9–12).

Many foreign companies struggle to make inroads into the megamarkets and to recover the cost of the invested capital. They are not clear about their strategic intent—i.e., the vision of what they want to or should achieve for long-term business expansion and survival in these new markets. Strategic intent involves stretching or overhauling the company's current design (structure, organization) and operation (practices, planning) to fit them into a futuristic paradigm and ecosystem.[1] This will be easier if management acknowledges that success or failure in the megamarkets will determine the company's global position and thrust in the next decade. A successful concept rests on three cornerstones of strategic thrust: project management, expansion principles, and growth path (see figure 9.1).

Figure 9.1. Cornerstones of strategic thrust in megamarkets.

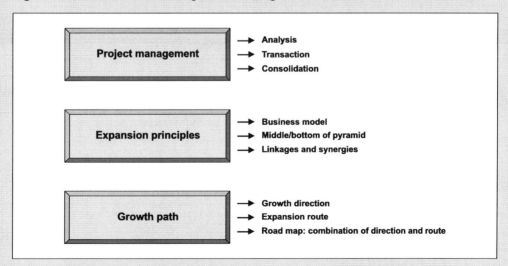

---

1. See 7.1.

> **Pause for thought**
>
> In a landmark case, a family-controlled food company from Europe bought a majority stake in a Russian brand for a few million US dollars. Since its investment, it has enjoyed much higher growth than its main rival, a large US food multinational, which invested several hundred million US dollars to acquire assets of a gigantic Russian enterprise. The key success factor was the focus on identifying the best possible target from the outset, followed by assiduous execution of the transaction.
>
> In another case, a Russian manufacturer of baby food successfully entered the Chinese market through incremental investments. At each step, the situation was reviewed to minimize risks by closing information gaps on market segments, competition, and logistics. The Russian owner traveled intensively to understand the supply chain. One of his trips took him up to New Zealand, where he signed long-term contracts with producers of essential milk-based ingredients. The successful concept had been thought through and adapted to the local situation; it thus enabled the decision-makers to move forward cautiously but with determination until visible results were achieved.

Opportunities are lost when companies follow export and trading strategies or ad hoc FDI, while the megamarkets call for deeper engagement and judicious investment. This conceptual mismatch can ensnare them in a value trap—the more resources they allocate, the more money they lose. Good results in traditional markets are used to offset losses or low returns in the megamarkets. Overheads are charged to headquarters so that the megamarket subsidiary can keep going and looks healthier than it actually is. Payback periods of investments are extended to wave through projects that would otherwise never qualify or lose approval. These expedients are not sustainable in the long term and impact the survival of both the megamarket subsidiary and headquarters.

Experience shows that a coherent approach and the right choice of projects are more effective than large cash positions or half-hearted decisions. Nor is size a guarantee or an obstacle as is evidenced by the success of certain medium-sized players vis-à-vis large ones.

9.1. Project management

True global players are present in all three megamarkets as this also gives them the scale that brings attention to their brand name. Depending on its capacity, a company's management can initiate and coordinate projects in one or more megamarkets either simultaneously or consecutively (see figure 9.2). A systematic approach based on a hierarchy of priority projects allows companies to coordinate interdivisional efforts and attain a higher market share within a shorter time span. The paradox of orderly planning with opportunity-seeking seems to be difficult for managers to blend and handle, but project management is the most important methodological tool distinguishing a market leader from non-visionary followers driven by reactive and dispersed behavior. Successful companies cultivate a project culture and realize breakthrough projects, which enable them to attain leadership.

Project management outlines the way forward toward a specific objective, which could be the acquisition of a local competitor, a technology alliance with a large customer, the identification of a site for a new plant, or a distribution/logistics center. Long-term goals may include the integration of an acquired target or the establishment of a financial holding company to consolidate stakes bought in various entities. This exercise finds its

Figure 9.2. The megamarket project and its subprojects (example of a chemical company).

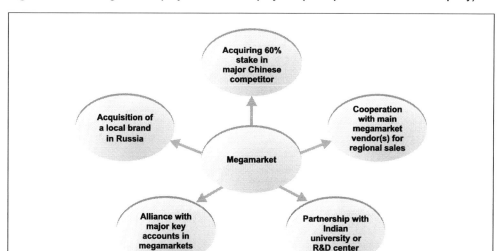

culmination in transaction planning, which will be covered later.[2] Control mechanisms are installed so that the management or board can intervene if need be. The megamarket project team drawn from across functions is appointed to carry out the tasks.

The number of specialists required depends on the scope of work and entry strategy. Greenfield investments require the initial support of the functional departments (see table 9.1). This may be the case, albeit to a lesser extent, in M&A and alliance-oriented

Table 9.1. Composition of a megamarket project management team (example of a greenfield project in India).

Function/division	At the start of the project	On establishment of megamarket operation
Top management, board	Entry strategy, allocation of resources	Expansion strategy, allocation of resources
Marketing	Megamarket intelligence on market size, user needs, competitors	Brand management, integration of megamarket in global operations
Human resources	Coaching headquarters staff on megamarket specificities	Recruitment, skill enhancement of middle managers and local staff
Product divisions, R&D	Product adaptations	Product development for megamarket based on information from the marketing division
Legal division	Company formation, intellectual property implications	Further acquisitions
Production division	Adaptation of process to local conditions, including procurement of local equipment and components, alignment with processes at headquarters	Improvement of local process using efficiency benchmarks from headquarters
Finance division	Capital input for megamarket subsidiary	Financial engineering for expansion, ERP implementation, assessment of initial public offering (IPO)
IT division	Installation of IT system (hard- and software) aligned to headquarters	Regular upgrading of IT system

---

2. See chapter 11.

> **Box 9.1. Project terms of reference (TORs).**
> - Background information
> - Project objectives
> - Expected results
> - Links with other projects
> - Definition of tasks (actions) with detailed work plan
> - Timeframe and deadlines for the various actions
> - Budget for each phase
> - Project team with responsibilities
> - Fees for external consultants
> - Reporting
> - Coordination and control

projects during integration when the local partner "needs to be brought to level." During megamarket intelligence-gathering, project teams are generally much smaller, consisting of a coordinator, a country specialist, external advisers, and, intermittently, top managers at the group level for important exploratory visits where their presence is required to get the information or convince the contacts.

Megamarket projects need to be performed and delivered under certain constraints related to scope, costs (budget), and time. They must be defined in terms of reference (TOR), which should also lay out the responsibility of each "internal" and "external" (advisers) team member (see box 9.1). At each project milestone, progress is measured against the set objectives and reported to top management. Investments are made judiciously after assessing the market and competitive situation. Top management monitors revenue growth and bottom-line profitability. The personal involvement of the CEO at important crossroads of the project/venture is decisive for execution.[3]

A project-based approach is meaningful if the methodology is applied rigorously throughout the strategy-making cycle from pre-analysis (intelligence) to transaction and consolidation (see figure 9.3). These three steps enable a company to carry out any sort of expansion assignment in the megamarkets, independently of the chosen path (non-equity, FDI-based[4]) and difficulty level (large-size vs. small-size investment; clear-cut vs. combined option).

Interestingly, many companies conduct breakthrough projects and adopt a disciplined, project-based approach in advanced markets but not in emerging markets. As in Western markets, business expansion projects should aim to trigger a virtuous circle by increasing revenue streams for funding higher market penetration in the long run (see figure 9.4). Cost-effective project management is a prerequisite for achieving such results. In the

---

3. See chapter 12.
4. See chapter 10.

Figure 9.3. Project management in the megamarkets.

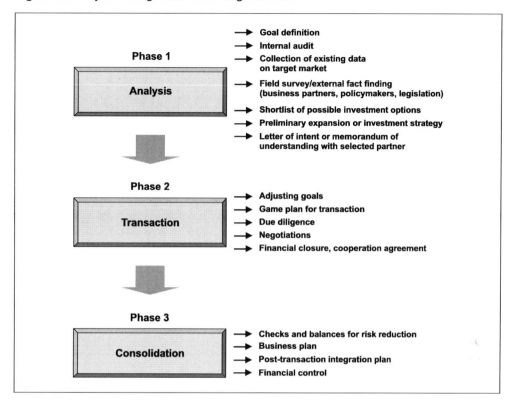

Figure 9.4. Virtuous circle of revenue streams and FDI.

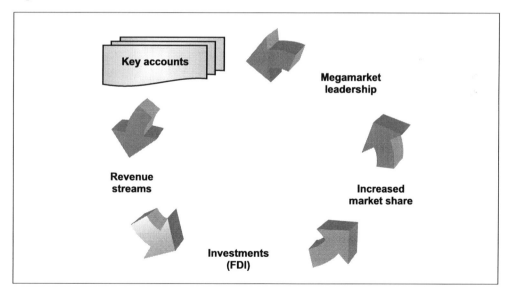

megamarkets, EU companies tend to adopt a project approach when a "stand-alone (greenfield)" decision has been approved by shareholders. But all the work related to other entry modes (M&A, alliance) or activities prior to the investment during the study phase

> **Pause for thought**
>
> A German industrial components producer selected a site for a new assembly and service unit in Russia following recommendations from a subsidiary of the group. The site was not systematically benchmarked against other locations and options available through alliances. At a very advanced stage of the project—when the building plans had been finalized—the management learned from key customers that the location was geographically remote for just-in-time deliveries and cost-effective after-sales service. Had the company conducted a user survey before making its investment decision, it could have gotten clues for a better site.
>
> In another case, a German construction materials manufacturer spent eighteen months negotiating an agreement with a Russian joint venture partner without studying other options. Negotiations were first complicated and then suddenly halted upon the recommendation of an international law firm. The board decided to go ahead with the "only viable alternative left," a greenfield project (coordinated by the same law firm). Once the land had been bought, the management realized that it would take two to three years before the new factory would become operational. Senior executives underestimated the difficulties of hiring local staff from scratch and obtaining all the government permissions. Russian rivals had meanwhile strengthened their brands in the booming construction sector of Greater Moscow and secured market share.
>
> Careful partner screening before market entry (there were five leading players at the time) would have revealed a window of opportunity at a time when reputed companies were still ready to sell a majority stake in exchange for know-how and capital from a European technology leader.

(sector trend analysis, screening of strategic partners) tends to be ad hoc. Under pressure to act fast and to save costs, managers cut budgets for the crucial pre-deal analysis that determines the outcome of the final project.

Efficient project management strongly depends on how much effort is spent on intelligence.[5] Philip Kotler, a leading US marketing professor, exhorts managers to start any business-related action with research (R) so that promising market segments (S) can be identified and targeted (T), thus opening the way for a leadership position (P). Kotler's marketing focus has absolute validity for megamarket expansion (see figure 9.5). As a general rule, markets and customers should be at center stage when a company decides to invest in a

Figure 9.5. Kotler's five steps of market expansion.

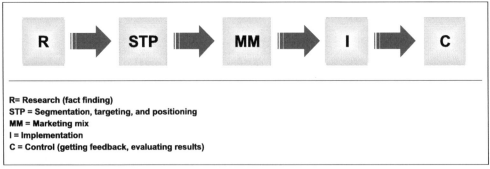

R = Research (fact finding)
STP = Segmentation, targeting, and positioning
MM = Marketing mix
I = Implementation
C = Control (getting feedback, evaluating results)

Source: Philip Kotler. 2001. Kotler on Marketing. USA: Simon & Schuster. Page 30.

---

5. See chapter 8.

megamarket; their opinion counts the most. Client or user needs combined with available opportunities determine the direction of growth as well as the entry and expansion modes.[6] Pre-expansion analysis demands extra time, effort, and money, but it pays off as it increases chances of success throughout the transaction and integration of a megamarket project.

9.2. Expansion principles

Newly recruited or reassigned managers in charge of market development or with a responsibility to turn around a failed investment in the megamarkets need to unlearn certain Western management theories or case studies if they want to succeed. The megamarkets have their own rules of the game. Even large corporations have to bow down to the local business principles and mentalities. While certain rules are determined by the balance of power among sector participants—producers, suppliers, users, and intermediaries—others are drawn from the country's history and culture, which inspire the local business mindset.

Many large companies in China or Russia, for example, are said to be governed by the "rule of man" rather than the "rule of statutes" or other contract-backed formalities. Rights derive from hierarchical power expressed by the position of a highly placed individual who will not easily empower his lower ranks to make fundamental decisions. When initiating an alliance with or an acquisition of a megamarket family enterprise, chances are that the owner is a self-made man or is from a family that has built an industrial empire that has grown over time. Such patriarch-owners are very powerful and have the ultimate say on the outcome of a deal. In the case of SOEs, such hierarchies are extended to highly placed party members in the city where the company is located. Although laws cover almost all business issues in megamarkets, enforcement is weak. A company's or an individual's status can influence application or non-application of a law, hence the weight given to personal connections. Strong contacts with decision-makers can lead to favorable outcomes of business dealings, including lawsuits.

Foreign companies are well advised to observe three essential principles when preparing for expansion in the megamarkets (see box 9.2):

- They should design a business model distinct from the one used in Western markets.
- They should offer value to consumer segments at the middle and bottom of the pyramid, which represent the fastest-growing and largest markets.
- They should exploit strategic inter-linkages and synergies between the megamarkets.

Box 9.2. Megamarket expansion principles.

- Megamarket business model (MBM)
- Middle and bottom of pyramid (M/BOP)
- Integrated megamarket strategy (IMS)

---

6. See chapter 10.

9.2.1. Business model for the megamarkets

A business model is a conceptual tool that expresses the logic behind a company's intentions in a given market. More specifically, it embodies the value (products, services) a company decides to create for its customers as well as the architecture (organizational design, distribution system, alliance network) it will use for delivering that value. A business model is made up of building blocks that together determine the company's value proposition (offer) and thus its revenue and profit streams (see figure 9.6). Business models need to be in tune with the megamarkets, which are culturally sensitive and at a different stage of development than AMs.

Many foreign executives believe that the easiest way to penetrate a megamarket is to sell brands, products, services or technologies already introduced elsewhere. In many segments, however, the demand for typically Western products is still limited in the megamarkets, compelling foreign companies to add new features or new products to their traditional range. Industrial goods and high-tech companies add services such as training and advisory support to build a demand for their products, particularly when the concept or technology is new to the market. Client education enlightens customers on the need and advantages of the product, while training demonstrates how it can be used beneficially.

When preparing for market entry, many foreign companies tend to look at price points and ignore costs. Lower costs allow price adjustments while maintaining or even increasing margins. Conversely, higher costs push a firm to sell at a higher price in order to stay profitable (but not competitive). Whenever a company depends on imports of finished

Figure 9.6. Elements of a megamarket business model.

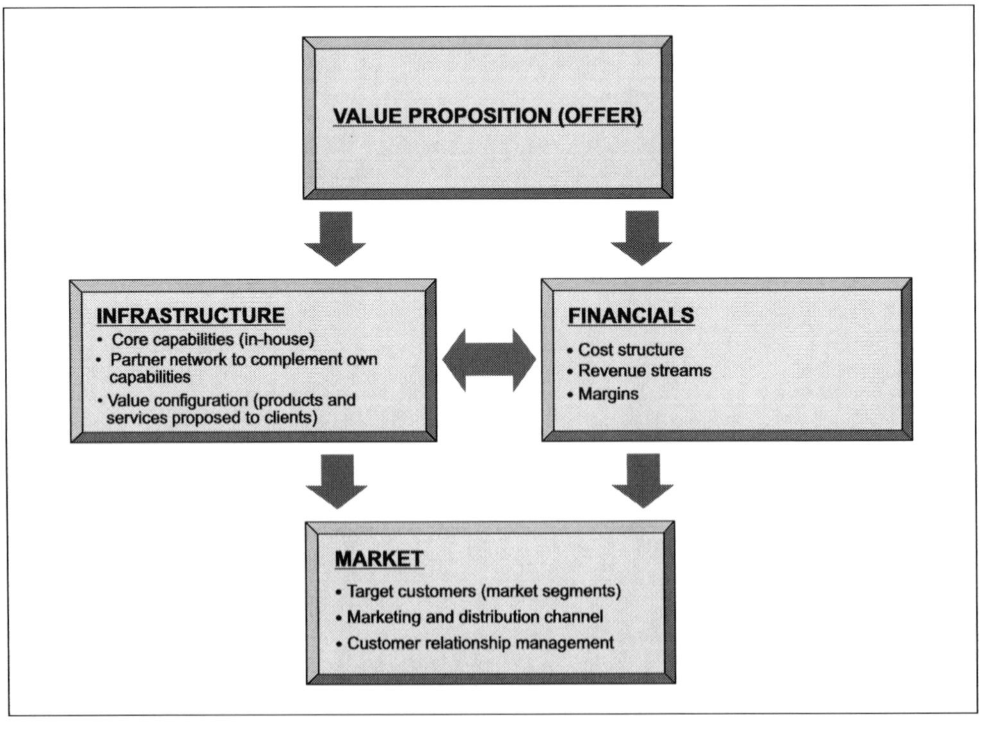

```
                    ┌─────────────────────────────┐
                    │   VALUE PROPOSITION (OFFER) │
                    └─────────────────────────────┘
                         ↓                  ↓
   ┌──────────────────────────────┐   ┌──────────────────────┐
   │ INFRASTRUCTURE               │   │ FINANCIALS           │
   │ • Core capabilities (in-house)│ ↔ │ • Cost structure     │
   │ • Partner network to          │   │ • Revenue streams    │
   │   complement own capabilities │   │ • Margins            │
   │ • Value configuration         │   │                      │
   │   (products and services      │   │                      │
   │   proposed to clients)        │   │                      │
   └──────────────────────────────┘   └──────────────────────┘
                         ↓                  ↓
               ┌──────────────────────────────────┐
               │ MARKET                           │
               │ • Target customers (market       │
               │   segments)                      │
               │ • Marketing and distribution     │
               │   channel                        │
               │ • Customer relationship          │
               │   management                     │
               └──────────────────────────────────┘
```

> **Pause for thought**
>
> Kellogg's, a US food giant, entered the Indian market with its flagship cornflakes in 1995. After initial success, it faltered because it did not realize that Indians like cereal with warm milk, which made Kellogg's cornflakes soggy. A local company gained ground when it created cornflakes that remained crisp even in warm milk. Kellogg's other constraint was its high price, which limited sales to the upper tier of the social pyramid. However, it should be given credit for learning from its mistakes and lately creating a breakfast cereal market that is growing by 30% per annum and now caters to both the urbanized rich and middle-class families who value time and convenience.
>
> Nestlé, on the other hand, introduced variants of its Maggi instant noodles: one that appealed to the spice-loving Indian palate and another made from whole wheat that reassured the health-conscious. Nestlé has a complete experimental kitchen and sensory laboratory at the corporate headquarters of Nestlé India, which is the first of its kind in India. Its target is to achieve a preference ratio of 60:40 for every Nestlé product as opposed to competition. While Kellogg's has limited itself to a narrow niche (its foray into biscuits failed in India), Nestlé adapted its products fully to local taste and offered a wide range. This is demand-driven innovation at its best and is more sustainable than competitive advantage assumed because of success in Western countries.
>
> Here are other examples of companies that succeeded by radically changing their business models in the megamarkets:
>
> - In China, B&Q, the UK's leading DIY chain operator, diversified into design and refurbishing services for home owners, an experience enabling it to take over the operation from Germany's OBI (which was not successful because it imposed the German/European DIY business model on reluctant Chinese consumers) and now expand into other Asian emerging markets.
> - In Russia, Knauff, a German company initially producing gypsum, extended its range to become the leading all-around supplier of construction products.
>
> ***
>
> A French maker of plastic waste containers that only tried to export and distribute its products failed to achieve a breakthrough as it did not advise clients on waste collection, which would have allowed it to establish a close relationship with municipalities for winning subsequent tenders.
>
> A UK-based oilfield services and equipment provider was compelled to adjust the product range and design special pre- and after-sales services to promote its products with key accounts in the Russian market.

products or essential components, its offer automatically moves to the upper price category owing to duties, transport, and higher production costs abroad; this strategy can work only if the higher cost can be set off against quality, innovation, and brand. Calculations of sales potential based on these higher price points do not give a realistic view of the market potential, which can be much higher. This can be seen by benchmarking the calculation with the market share of similar, locally produced products.

Farsighted companies pursue mixed strategies combining imported with locally produced parts, products, or brands to reduce costs. They set up assembly units or share sales offices with reliable local partners and then attack the market under different premises. Their trick consists in recalculating costs by bearing in mind a future local operation, which enables them to attain acceptable price points, expand market share, and recover the investment. If products are only sold at a premium, volumes will remain constantly low and never justify the investment in the business plan. A multi-brand policy can also contribute to higher sales volumes. The premium brand can, for example, be imported from a traditional AM, whereas the lower-priced brand can be produced locally or in a low-cost country. In this case, the low-cost unit can be either a greenfield unit or an acquisition. Companies increasingly acquire lower-priced local brands to complete their range. Local brands should cover different price points so that they do not "cannibalize" the premium brand's business away from it.

High performers have to backtrack sometimes on their normal business practices when they take on the megamarket challenge. They have to grow a new market, reinvent their business, and do things never imagined before.

Market leaders have discovered the importance of alliances and acquisitions for growing in the megamarkets. This is particularly true for B2B and B2G companies. It also makes them more cost-competitive. Distribution channel set-up and customer relationship management are two areas where cooperation is increasingly used for extending reach and constitute important elements of the megamarket business model. When the product or technology is new, the vendor's support is enlisted to ensure that specifications and quality standards are met. Carmakers routinely involve their tier-one component suppliers in the

---

Pause for thought

Microsoft, one of the world's largest companies in terms of capitalization, had to finally accept market realities in China. In the mid-1990s, its software was sold through Taiwan under the same conditions as in Western economies. That model did not work, not because of lack of brand acceptance (everyone was using cheap pirated copies of Windows) but because no one was willing to pay Microsoft's high prices. The company had a virtual market but little revenue. For many years, Microsoft fought bitterly to protect its intellectual property but lost regularly in court. The strategy proved to be counterproductive, preventing the company from expanding in the world's fastest-growing software market.

In 2006, the company hired a new CEO for China, who turned the situation around by involving influential stakeholders: state bodies, universities, and IT players. The company reacted in a more relaxed way to pirating. Instead of suing infringers, it developed a mainstream market for its products (at lower prices with slightly reduced margins) among that very segment that had used its products but denied Microsoft its rightful revenue. The company also appeased the authorities by opening a research center, thus demonstrating to them that its software was not a secret tool of the US government and that it was helping China develop its own software culture. Ever since, Microsoft's annual sales in China have climbed to two-digit levels.

***

A UK producer of specialty chemicals was not satisfied with its export strategy to Russia via importer-distributors. It decided to approach Russian key accounts to sound out their interest in setting up joint service, laboratories, and training centers.

As Russian client companies were switching to higher value-added and environmentally friendly manufacturing, this business model proved to be a success, paving the way for long-term penetration based on lasting relations with selected partner-clients. The company is now envisaging an acquisition or strategic alliance to further strengthen its market position.

design and engineering processes. Backward integration through the acquisition of a stake in a major vendor is a strategy that ensures quality and timely delivery. In specific B2B or B2G markets, it is expedient to focus on special projects with key accounts.

In mature economies, market development is planned differently in that the estimated sales potential determines the size of the investment. The sales potential can be gauged with near accuracy because of access to data and system stability. But in emerging economies, companies face a dilemma because it is practically impossible to predict sales for new products. Successful local entrepreneurs operate under a different logic: they invest to create a market based on the perception of a need (e.g., QQ's mini car for city ride and parks) or to anticipate competitors (e.g., retail chains in India). For EU companies, the only chance to become a leader is to grow the market and then expand with it. By adjusting its business model, a company will satisfy latent needs in the target market. Imagination and creativity must be used to predict a future scenario and consistently work toward it. This latent need must hold promise of sufficient volume and value of business to ensure a reasonably rapid return on investment.

9.2.2. The bottom and middle of the pyramid [7]

Consumers in the megamarkets are structured like a pyramid, at the base of which are people with limited purchasing power; in the middle, a fast-expanding middle class; and on top, a dynamic layer of a small but equally fast-growing number of rich people (see figure 9.7).

A wide-based pyramid is typical for many emerging markets.[8] Managers of Western companies hold on to the view that they should focus on the top layer, which mainly lives in large cities and shares features with the middle/upper class they are familiar with in Western economies. This bias that permeates decisions regarding the megamarkets often skews product, sales, and innovation strategies. Corporate executives mistakenly ignore the sharp drop in discretionary incomes in Western countries over the past ten years and the fast growth and changing patterns in consumption in the emerging economies in both urban and rural areas:

- Bottom-layer consumers have become upwardly mobile thanks to better education, health care, and job opportunities; each year millions of people move upwards into the category of middle-income households.
- Middle-layer consumers become more numerous each year, especially in the cities, where the middle class is expanding very fast and, with it, average national incomes. Over the next ten to fifteen years, these consumers will draw even with the middle classes in advanced economies in terms of purchasing power.
- Top-layer consumers are extremely rich, even by Western standards. Differences between the rich in the megamarkets and their EU/US peers have vanished, but this category of consumers is growing much faster in the emerging than in the advanced markets. It is

---

7. C. K. Prahalad, *The Fortune at the Bottom of the Pyramid* (Wharton School, 2006).
8. According to World Bank projections, the world's population in the lower layers of the pyramid could swell to more than 6 billion over the next forty years.

Figure 9.7. The megamarket consumer pyramid, 2010.

Annual per capita income	Tier	Share (%)	Population in millions
More than US$ 20,000	1	20	520
US$1500-20,000	2	65	1690
Below US$ 1,500	3	15	390
Total			2600[a]

Consumer segments (tiers):
1. Upper middle and above (similar to western middle-class consumers)
2. "Next billion consumers"
3. Low-income groups

a. China: 1300 million, India: 1160 million, Russia: 140 million.

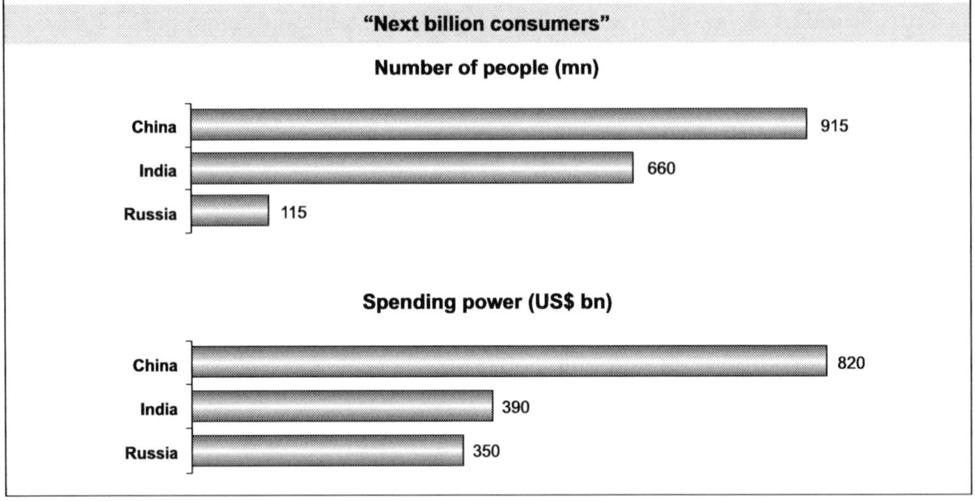

"Next billion consumers"

Number of people (mn)
- China: 915
- India: 660
- Russia: 115

Spending power (US$ bn)
- China: 820
- India: 390
- Russia: 350

Source: Own calculations based on World Bank statistics.

totally anachronistic to make direct comparisons between rich megamarket consumers and middle-class households in AMs whose incomes are correlating downwards toward middle-class consumers in EMs.

Relying on official data, Western managers mistakenly neglect the bottom and middle layers as worthwhile targets for their products. Classical market research hardly reveals the reality behind lower-strata consumers supposedly living on a few dollars a day. True living standards are not disclosed by statistics but rather by knowledge of lifestyle and culture. For example, many migrant laborers in India live in shanty towns close to city centers. They pay little rent, earn mostly undeclared income, and save for their return to the rural areas. Their shanties contain color televisions, refrigerators, and food processors, and they own mobile phones and other electronic gadgets, motorcycles, and even cars. They are gradually offered good-quality housing by business-minded developers who help them swap their precious land for new flats in city suburbs. The middle layer includes small entrepreneurs, government officials, and lower-rung employees, whose consumption patterns resemble those of Europe's middle classes in the 1960s; they are fast catching up. Favorable tax policies and lower price levels have given the megamarket consumers a real purchasing power that in many instances already exceeds that of average consumers (including pensioners) in Western markets. In most cases, all family members participate in the purchase of cars, durables, and apartments by providing interest-free loans or making straightaway gifts. It is the purchasing power of these consumers that is responsible for the shopping and construction boom in the megamarket cities and their suburbs.

The perception that the middle and bottom of the pyramid is not yet a viable market fails to take into account the importance of the informal, underground economy, which amounts to 20%–30% of GDP. Moreover, as the Peruvian economist Hernando de Soto has repeatedly pointed out, conventional GDP measurement ignores the existence in many developing countries of substantial property held without legally registered title by lower income groups. Much like an iceberg with only its tip in plain view, these huge segments of the megamarket population, along with their massive market opportunities, have not yet hit the radar screen of many foreign companies. Domestic firms have, on the other hand, pushed into these segments much earlier and established their brands. These consumers may be harder to reach via conventional distribution, credit, and communication channels, but the quality and quantity of products and services available to them is constantly rising.

To appreciate the potential, EU companies must re-examine a set of assumptions on the lower and middle classes that color their orthodox views of newly emerging markets:

- Assumption 1: They cannot be a promising target because current cost structures in these segments compress profit margins.
- Assumption 2: They cannot afford and have little use for products and services sold in advanced markets.
- Assumption 3: They are content with the previous generation of technology as they do not have the means to pay for new technologies demanded in advanced economies.
- Assumption 4: The bottom and middle of the pyramid in emerging markets is not vital to the company's long-term expansion.
- Assumption 5: Redesigning products for these segments is time-consuming, and the return on investment is low.

Each of these assumptions obscures the true value to be generated at the middle and bottom of the pyramid, which defies conventional logic but still represents a large and unexplored territory to be tapped for profitable growth. Decisions based on wrong assumptions can impede future sales.

The total count for the first two categories (low- and middle-income groups) in the three megamarkets alone is around 2.1 billion people (80% of their combined population), which represents a huge market. The combined purchasing power of these consumers is significant. For EU companies, this market poses a new challenge: how to combine low cost, good quality, sustainability, and profitability. They need to harness the power of new technology, their abundant know-how, deep knowledge of their products, and long experience to adapt costs, marketing, and delivery (see table 9.2). EU companies have the wherewithal but often lack ambition and determination.

Table 9.2. Strategies for the bottom and middle of the pyramid.	
Products	Develop robust products resistant to harsh conditions and rough use, with simple features; avoid over-engineering (consumer durables, equipment). Localize content to the extent possible to reduce cost (consumer durables, equipment). Design new packaging: smaller sizes for lower price points (consumer products). Consider local tastes and habits (food, clothes, personal care). Consider local production or at least local repackaging (commodity foods). Imagine new distribution concepts (consumer goods). Conceive resource-saving, recyclable products. Add client education and training, advisory services.
Profitability	Avoid overpricing. Reduce margins. Aim at high volumes.
Marketing	Invest in rural distribution channels. Expand brand visibility in urban areas. Establish personal relations with key accounts.

It would be wrong to believe that only large global companies have the technological, managerial, and financial edge to dip into the well of innovations. Medium-sized enterprises have more flexibility to dramatically reinvent cost structures. In certain segments (e.g., fast-moving consumer goods, packaging), costs must be reduced by at least one-third. This can be achieved by rethinking business and production processes, including the option of local assembly and production.

Profits from the middle and lower levels of the pyramid are generated through volume and capital efficiency, instead of high margins. Managers who focus only on gross margins lose long-term opportunities to acquire customers and gain market share. The middle- and lower-level consumer categories offer new chances of growth for EU companies that are ready to introduce innovative solutions, which may in a second step also be used for other emerging markets as they open up. Few EU companies are willing to adjust their offers to these market segments.

Consumer goods companies in particular have no alternative but to target the emerging middle class in the megamarkets. Access to these segments requires analysis and imagination; it is not as impossible as it appears to be. These consumers are well informed and connected by mobile phones, TV, and increasingly the Internet, which raises brand awareness and loyalty. The mushrooming shopping malls have given a new dimension to consumerism; here, producers can showcase novelties, which the consumers are ever willing to try and adopt if they are affordable. To reach this market, companies must multiply and train their channel partners, suppliers, and financial institutions (for personal loans).

As the Unilever example makes clear (see facing page), serving the mass segments (the future middle classes) involves bringing together the best of technology and a global resource base to address local market conditions. In the industrial goods segment in the megamarkets, users of equipment and process technologies are still very price conscious. They look for flexible solutions to meet their immediate constraints. By focusing on low- to medium-price segments, Japanese, South Korean, and Taiwanese machine-tool companies have garnered market share and from there gradually expanded into higher-margin segments. However, the goal of competitive price without compromising on

> **Pause for thought**
>
> *A joint venture between a European manufacturer of cleaning equipment and an Indian engineering company illustrates how this strategy can succeed. The high-end ride-on machines are imported from the EU; at the same time, the Indian partner developed a non-electric walk-behind version, which is now marketed by the EU company in its other markets.*
>
> *On the other side of the strategy spectrum was a European pasta company that expected to export as many tons of pasta to India as it did to its Eastern European markets. The pasta is a popular food in Europe, and if the country is a new EU member there are no customs duties, whereas in India the logistics situation is different, and pasta is only beginning to penetrate the market. The EU company did not learn the lesson from another EU pasta company whose market share has been eroded by local companies who have improved their quality and now offer new versions of pasta at very competitive prices. The EU company would not even consider local repackaging of bulk exports; their market will be limited to a few exclusive food outlets and five-star hotels.*
>
> ***
>
> *In the 1990s, the Indian company Nirma started selling detergent products for the country's middle-income and poor consumers, mostly in rural areas. The company created a new business model that included a new product formulation, special packaging for daily consumption, low-cost manufacturing processes, a wide distribution network, and value pricing.*
>
> *Hindustan Lever Ltd. (HLL), the Indian subsidiary of the Anglo-Dutch multinational Unilever, initially dismissed this strategy but soon realized that its local competitor was winning market share in a segment it had disregarded. HLL responded with its own offering after drastically altering its traditional business model. HLL's new detergent, called Wheel, was formulated to substantially reduce the ratio of oil to water in the product, responding to the fact that low-income groups often wash their clothes by hand. HLL decentralized production and marketing and created sales channels in city suburbs and the countryside to reach thousands of small outlets that serve consumers at the middle and bottom of the pyramid. HLL also changed the cost structure to introduce Wheel at a low price point. By 2007, HLL (renamed Hindustan Unilever) had overtaken Nirma and registered a market share of almost 40% in the detergents sector. The parent company, Unilever, transported HLL's business concept to create a new detergent market for the low-income groups in other emerging markets. In Brazil, the Ala brand has been a big success. More importantly, Unilever has adopted the bottom-and-middle-of-the-pyramid concept as a strategic priority for expansion into the emerging markets. Managers with emerging market experience are promoted within the group.*

quality demands innovation in technology, business models, and management processes. Business leaders must be willing to experiment, collaborate, empower locals, and create new sources of competitive advantage and wealth. For EU companies, the best approach is to marry local capabilities and market knowledge with global best practices.

9.2.3. Megamarket synergies and linkages

Since the early 2000s, interrelations and cooperation between China, India, and Russia have improved in many areas: politics, economics, business, science, culture, military, and so forth. Political framework agreements, partially aimed at forming a counterweight to US dominance, provide a strong basis for business exchange and alliances. Advanced

IT hardware and software clusters are, for example, being formed between India and China. Russian nuclear power and civil engineering specialists are linking up with general contractors and equipment producers from China and India. Software engineers from India are taking technological innovations developed in Eurasia's new geostrategic triangle to a global scale. In the years to come, the three emerging mega powers will move closer, and this will have serious geostrategic implications for investors and enterprises in any sector of activity. Travel—the first step toward a rapprochement—has risen dramatically since 2004 among the Eurasian countries; visa formalities have been simplified considerably. This has boosted trade, FDI, and capital flows.

EU players are well advised to participate directly in the growth of these economies (e.g., through their own legal entities) and thus leverage improved ties among Eurasia's three megamarkets to their advantage. EU companies have encountered difficulties in transferring high-level managers to China, India, or Russia. These talents are mostly needed at headquarters or in the established markets for their technical qualities and leadership skills. As a result, young middle managers are shifted to the megamarkets, or—another recent trend—managing directors and chief engineers are recruited locally. The cost for the company may in this way be lower than sending senior-level expatriates with their families, but the internal/external networking capabilities and perception of strategic interlinkages among the megamarkets may well be lost in both cases. This would be a typical responsibility of highly placed executives at headquarters whose horizon would enable them to connect far-reaching decisions from a global perspective. Locally recruited management is primarily measured by how it succeeds in developing the business in the market it operates. Some multinationals operate through regional headquarters, but even these entities are mostly run by "rotating" executives without project experience in at least two megamarkets. Most expatriates, including those belonging to the generation of the 1960s and 1970s, have primarily US- and/or EU-based professional experience. Their thinking is marked by issues related to "transatlantic relations" and skills acquired in familiar Western universities. They lack the megamarket language capabilities (Chinese, Russian) and knowledge of different Eurasian cultures and mentalities, which are indispensable "door openers" for exploiting sector, technology, and cultural linkages on the Eurasian continent.

To benefit from the business potential and synergies among the three megamarkets, EU companies must pursue a holistic strategy to raise effectiveness. This demands competent and broad-minded executives, who are extremely difficult to find; once identified, they must be motivated to stay with the employer. The leading megamarket companies seem to be more aware of interlinkages in the megamarket triangle, primarily because geographic proximity and similar cost and price levels expose them to constant travel, analysis, and competition from other megamarket counterparts. They understand better the importance for their companies to invest and strive for leadership in other megamarkets than their EU rivals. Examples are India's family-owned auto components companies that are establishing themselves in Russia and China to serve the growing automobile sectors there, Russia's oil (e.g., Rosneft) and aluminum (e.g., RusAl) majors that are investing in China and India, and China's electronics giants Haier and Lenovo, who are expanding aggressively in India and Russia. These moves draw other companies (suppliers, peers) and will result in much stronger economic ties among businesses in

Figure 9.8. Exploiting geostrategic linkages between megamarkets.

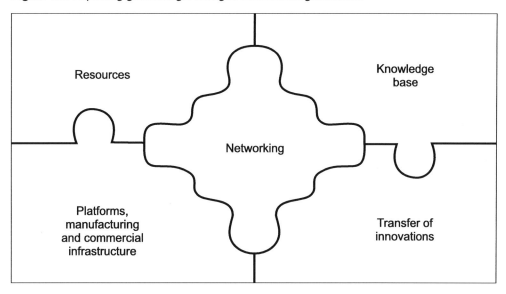

the emerging Eurasian triangle, making it all the more important for EU companies to take part as suppliers, customers, and investors in the expanding trade, investment, and technology flows among these fast-growing mega-economies. Rather than consider the three markets individually, EU companies must encompass them in an integrated strategy based on location advantages.

Size can be important if a company aims to fully exploit inter-megamarket linkages (see figure 9.8). The knowledge base and managerial, technological, and financial assets must allow the establishment of a viable infrastructure. However, it is not only large multinationals that can undertake such ventures; dynamic and nimble-footed SMEs can succeed as well. Certain conditions must, however, be fulfilled for a company, independently of its size, to be able to benefit from geostrategic linkages:

- Resources. Building viable distribution channels and communication networks in each megamarket is a resource- and management-intensive task. In the long run, they must be financed through reinvested profits fed by growing sales in promising market segments. A cost-effective business concept aimed at leadership and making its product-service package indispensable to clients allows a company to spend less and optimize its inputs.
- Knowledge base. Only professionally managed, committed, and performing companies are in a position to transfer knowledge from one market to another and have a panoramic view of different location advantages. A unique knowledge base cannot be easily imitated by rivals.
- Platforms. Financially strong players can be nodes for building the required manufacturing and commercial infrastructure and providing access to knowledge, managerial imagination, and financial resources to partner firms. Established players can offer "piggyback" platforms for suppliers that cannot afford to set up their own infrastructure.

> **Pause for thought**
>
> A German supplier of industrial seals for the oil and gas industry lost an opportunity in Russia because it did not integrate its Indian subsidiary in the sales and marketing efforts. The Indian unit was producing exactly the type of product that Russian customers were seeking in terms of price-quality ratio and after-sales requirements. Instead, German executives focused on products from their Western market portfolio, which for local customers was overpriced and over-engineered but apparently "secured jobs at the main production sites." They did not accept the fact that Russian oil and gas companies, in spite of their strong financials, preferred simple, cold-resistant, robust, and lower-priced solutions.
>
> In another case, a car multinational recognized only very late that it could have exploited synergies in supply chains among Brazil, China, and Russia, with positive repercussions on logistics, transport, and distribution costs for both exports and imports of key components. The same multinational is now studying the possibility of importing components from Western Europe into China via Russia (by using the Transsiberian rail network) and re-exporting them to other emerging markets. The aim is to save logistics costs and speed up just-in-time deliveries. Its recently launched Russian subsidiary serves a double purpose: to increase the company's market share in Russia and to exploit synergies in the value chain of its Russian and Chinese operations. The Russian experience (factory layout, processing system, IT integration, phased approach) will also serve as an example for the planned investment in India.

- Transfer. Strong companies have the capability to transfer innovations from advanced markets to megamarkets and from higher to lower consumer categories within the megamarkets. They can also transfer innovations developed in the more frugal megamarkets to the developed world, where resources are also growing scarce. Multinationals are therefore setting up R&D facilities across the megamarkets.
- Networking. Competition and cooperation are interdependent attitudes. High performers cooperate with partners in the value chain and with local and international rivals. Partnerships are screened carefully as they represent both opportunities and risks. Reliable alliances enable a firm to expand its knowledge base, to anticipate trends, and to reach a market position it could not have attained alone.

9.3. Growth path

EU technology leaders have established bridgeheads in China, lately also in India and Russia. But having a structure does not necessarily imply having a good strategy or an attractive offer that ensures stable profits. EU investors cannot afford to miss "windows of opportunity," which appear ever more rarely and remain open for a limited period of time. Latecomers who do not seize such opportunities must put up with below-average returns, which sooner or later overstretch the payback period of their investments.

To count among the successful, a company needs a winning expansion concept, which it may implement alone or via alliances with best-in-the-class partners. Top management needs to make major strategy decisions on (a) the overall direction of growth and (b) the investment mode or expansion route (see table 9.3). The final strategy depends on the market context; there is no single path valid for all companies. At each intersection, examples of both successful and unsuccessful companies can be found. Many combinations are possible between growth directions (e.g., consolidation and subsequent globalization)

Table 9.3. Growth path in the megamarkets.

		Growth direction			
		Consolidation	Integration	Diversification	Globalization
Expansion route	Sales/sourcing				
	Greenfield				
	Alliances				
	M&A				

and expansion/investment modes (e.g., greenfield project through an alliance). The possible growth path must be in line with the company's culture, inclinations, resources, and competitive position. There are general trends, such as the focus on core competences (as opposed to diversification), that began in advanced markets many years ago and can now be observed in the megamarkets as well. Another trend is the creation of wholly owned subsidiaries, which has become the preferred route of foreign investors in the megamarkets. The search for the ideal expansion route or FDI option is a challenge in itself for decision-makers[9] as much as the choice of the ultimate growth direction, the pros and cons of which need to be understood by the top management in the light of competition and demand prospects (see next sections).

Advanced market players must be creative in order to confront their megamarket competitors who launch guerrilla tactics from other emerging market bases (e.g., Huawei's entry into northern Africa and the Middle East as bridgeheads for penetrating EU markets). By adopting this strategy, which includes the whole spectrum of possible expansion combinations (e.g., consolidation via M&A, diversification via alliances), many megamarket companies have come out stronger and earned global respect and recognition: steel (Mittal, Tata), cement (Cemex), beer (SAB Miller), oil (Lukoil), and gas (Gazprom).

9.3.1. Consolidation

Consolidation is the act of concentrating forces and merging many entities into one. It is mainly directed at ridding the market of competitors. This horizontal orientation involves acquiring and integrating other units into larger entities, a trend formerly observed mainly in advanced countries but which is now gradually shifting also to emerging economies. Consolidation is aimed at achieving higher revenue and margins through greater market power vis-à-vis suppliers and customers. Three motivations press companies toward consolidation: (a) more favorable cost position through economies of scale, (b) solution to overcapacity and price wars, and (c) need to placate shareholders dissatisfied with the company's financial performance. The challenge for companies opting for consolidation is to identify sources of revenue or savings so that the investment is paid off within a short time after the transaction. As a rule, large groups swallow their smaller rivals, but cases abound whereby a lower-ranked firm acquires a larger rival through financial leverage (e.g., Sanofi vs. Aventis). Banks or financial investors may

---

9. See chapter 10.

take stakes and participate in the restructuring of consolidated groups, but they usually exit within three to five years.

Waves of mergers and acquisitions, the most visible type of consolidation, have swept almost every industry in the advanced markets. Concentration movements mostly start in countries where companies have reached a certain maturity level and from there spread globally. The movement started in the West in the 1980s; the sights soon turned on megamarket companies, although in most cases they were protected by restrictive FDI laws. M&A projects have not been very successful in the megamarkets, owing to a mismatch between partners, the time pressure to reach critical mass, and government interference. Now, megamarket companies, strengthened by high growth, are treading the consolidation path as well. They find it easier to acquire in the West, where many companies are ripe for the plucking. EU players must re-dynamize themselves if they want to remain in the race and not just be reduced to acquisition targets.

The quickest route is to target industry leaders as "going concerns" (companies in operation) rather than opting for greenfield FDI or joint ventures, which are not immediately operational, hence the importance of selecting the best target. Many EU market leaders wake up too late to this strategy; by then, interesting targets have appreciated to a point at which they are almost unattainable or the owners are not willing to sell.

Successful consolidation allows timely responses and better management of supply-and-demand volatility. As players become stronger and smaller in number, they are able to synchronize trends. They ensure that markets are not flooded at times of weak demand. Price fluctuations are lower. Economies of scale and scope can be achieved across key areas, including purchasing, marketing, and capital expenditure. On the

---

Pause for thought

The best consolidation story comes from ArcelorMittal. The prime reason for Mittal's eagerness to consolidate the steel industry was to raise the group's bargaining power vis-à-vis potent raw materials suppliers. Backward integration was impossible with oligopolists dominating the iron ore market. Mittal built an almost impregnable group by acquiring sick steel mills in developing countries (Latin America, Eastern Europe, and Asia) and then turning them around. Assets in the advanced countries were initially avoided out of cost considerations and to lull competitors. Once sufficient capital was accumulated, the strategy changed. The new tenets were "to press forward with the necessary restructuring should ensure a more stable, less volatile future by using two-digit operating margins, independently of the target country" and "avoid complacency and sitting back and letting profits roll in during good times." Mittal completed a total of twenty acquisitions during 2000–2007 in both advanced and emerging markets. ArcelorMittal accounts for 12% of global steel production (110 million t).

Other large steelmakers followed suit: Russia's Evraz took over Oregon Steel (USA) and Delong (Singapore-China), and India's Tata Steel acquired Corus (UK). The steel industry remains fragmented in China, where consolidation is expected to gain speed. Similar trends are to be expected in India and Russia.

Consolidation will also have serious consequences for equipment and iron ore suppliers, who will have to consolidate as well in order to be able to face much larger steel customers. Similar trends are to be expected in many other strategic industries in the megamarkets (e.g., energy, raw materials, telecommunication, automotive).

> **Pause for thought**
>
> *A leading EU producer of truck and railway components opted for a joint venture in China in the early 2000s. The partnership failed to yield the expected results, forcing the company to look for export markets as the domestic market had turned out to be very price sensitive. The company's management now admits that had the company acquired a major Chinese player right at the outset it could have controlled price levels in the industry. The chosen investment mode (joint venture) was not conducive to realizing the required direction (consolidation) in order to grow.*
>
> *Two Chinese competitors meanwhile strengthened their positions thanks to economies of scale achieved in the domestic market and with the acquisition of smaller local firms. One of them has opened a liaison office in Europe, which represents an additional threat for the EU company.*
>
> ***
>
> *Knauff, a leading German construction materials company, has a market share of 70% in Russia, which has become the firm's dominant market. The biggest push came when the company acquired depreciated assets of local players during the financial crisis of 1998–1999. The company took its chance and continued investing in the early 2000s, backed by a strong euro. Since 2004, the euro has appreciated by 50% against the US dollar and megamarket currencies, which are partly tied to the US dollar.*
>
> *Unfortunately, EU companies have not always been quick to seize this foreign exchange–related opportunity, which may not last very long as megamarket currencies have started appreciating.*

other hand, consolidation can be a problem for policymakers as there is a risk of cartelization.

Using the megamarket momentum to build critical size and then exercising the acquired financial clout to spread backwards in the advanced markets—the Mittal model—is an option that even SMEs in the EU or the United States can envisage. Megamarkets enable them to attain larger dimensions much faster, but this strategy can also fail.

Acquisitions are becoming more competitive with the growing number of entrepreneurs following the consolidation route. This is a positive step, even if it does mean that acquisitions are becoming dearer. Consolidation efforts are more complex abroad than at home. In the megamarkets, there are very few industries dominated by foreign companies who now play a key role in consolidating their industries.

Table 9.4. Pros and cons of consolidation.

Pros of consolidation	Cons of consolidation
Removes competitors.	Constrained by antimonopoly rules.
Raises margins.	Leads to cartelization of prices.
Checks overcapacities.	Creates oversized entities that stretch managerial resources and breed bureaucracy.
Increases up- and downstream bargaining power.	Incites up- and downstream players to consolidate as well.

9.3.2. Integration

Integration is a special form of vertical consolidation that is also visible in the megamarkets. An integrated company controls upstream supply chains of inputs and/or downstream distribution channels of its output. Business expansion via integration happens by acquiring a supplier (backward integration) and/or a buyer/distributor (forward integration). A company may also decide to expand upstream or downstream by setting up entirely new structures (greenfield plants, warehouses, retail outlets). The ultimate goal of this strategy is to control the value chain.

Powerful buyer groups can substitute suppliers and are in a position to force down input prices and to demand better service, including just-in-time deliveries. Retail giants, for example, demand significant promotional budgets and listing money for items from their suppliers; automotive multinationals negotiate razor-thin margins with a limited number of components makers. Conversely, a few powerful suppliers may also exert pressure on downstream customers by dictating high prices, long deliveries, and reduced service. The world's iron ore supplies are dominated by three conglomerates located in Australia and Brazil, which regularly increase their prices, provoking concentration moves in the steel industry.

A foreign player faces barriers when pursuing an integration strategy in an emerging market. It is usually more difficult to investigate and understand the game rules in upstream and/or downstream industries.

The risk of vertical integration involving a majority acquisition of up- or downstream assets by a foreign company is that it is venturing out of its core area and that, too, in a foreign context. The target should be a segment leader whose management has the strategic and cultural fit to the acquirer. As with all suppliers, the target may also be furnishing inputs to the acquirer's competitor. Vertical FDI would allow the acquirer to gain control over the supplier and exclude other players from a strategic source of procurement. The intention of a European drilling company, for example, to buy into suppliers of rigs and other crucial components in China was driven by similar motivations.

In the megamarkets, the value chain in core sectors such as steel and automotives has historically been controlled by large domestic corporations, similar to Japan's *zaibatsus* and

---

Pause for thought

Leading EU companies were obliged to secure supplies and/or distribution abroad in order to grow. Some of them have been successful with this strategy, for example in:

- *Consumer goods. Downstream FDI into retailing: Germany's WMF opened its own stores for its entire cutlery range in the three megamarkets; the same applies to Austria's Swarovski and many French and Italian luxury goods brands.*
- *Electricity. Upstream FDI into power generation: Italy's ENEL alliance with RAO UES, Russia.*
- *Oil. Downstream FDI into gasoline retailing: Italian ENI's AGIP filling stations in Russia.*
- *Do-it-yourself furniture. Upstream FDI into furniture manufacturing: Sweden's IKEA acquired majority stakes in local furniture makers in Russia and China.*

> **Pause for thought**
>
> *Oil companies in the megamarkets maintain vertically integrated structures along the entire supply chain from exploration through locating oil deposits, drilling, crude extraction, transport, and refining to distribution; they own their own filling station chains for retailing to the end consumer.*
>
> *A well-known UK-based drilling company had to give up hopes of acquiring a drilling unit from Russia's oil majors even after years of being a subcontractor. None of the country's six publicly and privately held oil majors were willing to lose ownership over their strategic drilling divisions or subsidiaries. The top management was unwilling to consider the outsourcing of this service, a practice common in Western countries. As early as the 1970s, Western oil majors began to spin off non-core businesses and to subcontract services to independent external specialists for drilling, rig management, installation, warehousing, transport logistics, and so forth. That is how companies like Schlumberger and Halliburton grew into global oil service multinationals.*
>
> *Another example is the steel industry. While Western steel plants work closely with equipment suppliers and engineering companies (e.g., SMS Demag, Danieli for turnkey plants), megamarket steel majors tend to keep their suppliers (e.g., rolls) within their fold.*

Korea's *chaebols*. These companies remain under the influence of the state even if they have been corporatized or partially privatized. State representatives still influence ownership and governance. In China, even restructured state-owned enterprises are still directly or indirectly controlled by state bodies and political organizations. In India and Russia, such controls are limited to companies belonging to strategic sectors (raw materials, aerospace, defense, energy). In the advanced markets, large enterprises outsource important tasks to specialists out of efficiency and cost considerations. In China, for example, conservative views prevail, giving rise to unwieldy conglomerates, from which it is difficult for Western investors to pry away supplier/distributor units, especially in sensitive industries.

Integration movements are sometimes triggered by the market and government regulations. Meat processing and distribution in China is a fragmented cluster of many private enterprises. Many local meat and sausage distributors were compelled to open restaurants to survive because of a prolonged government embargo on imports of meat products. Some distributors diversified upstream into livestock farms to overcome shortages and secure timely supplies of raw meat for their restaurant chains. Forward integration, however, can reap competitive advantage and growth given that economic clout is moving downstream, closer to the customer. Western pharmaceutical, cosmetics, and luxury goods manufacturers are investing downstream in franchise distribution, thus reducing layers in the value chain and moving toward direct distribution. Their megamarket competitors are following suit. Conversely, large retail chains are securing upstream supplies by investing in food and non-food production units that sell under the distributor's brand (backward integration). Instead of running and controlling supplier and customer companies, which are not its core competences, a company may opt for minority investments in selected competitors and partners along the value chain to keep a finger on the pulse, a strategy followed by brewery multinationals in China.

Upstream and downstream integration is quite popular among megamarket entrepreneurs as it ensures their independence vis-à-vis competitors, suppliers, and government. An

> **Pause for thought**
>
> IKEA's two stores in Russia were taking losses in the mid-1990s. Supplies were not coming on time and were not of consistent quality. The company managed to improve its market position only after it decided to acquire a local plant. Since then, the company has gained a visible competitive advantage. It is now applying a similar concept in other emerging economies.

integration strategy can be capital-intensive and difficult to manage as each business in the value chain requires special know-how and technologies. Management in Western companies is accountable to shareholders who expect companies to focus on core competencies. Megamarket companies may come around to the same viewpoint once they are fully integrated in the world economy. Outsourcing allows companies to focus on activities that are the source of their competitive advantage. It increases flexibility, but it also increases dependence and must therefore rely on a good logistics chain. There are limits to how much can be outsourced. It is very important to decide in which direction an integration policy, which worked in the past, should in fact be reduced. Worldwide, companies are redeploying from backward integration. Automotive companies are moving ever greater responsibility to their tier-one suppliers. The strong manufacturing bases in the megamarkets stand to benefit and become privileged suppliers of Western multinationals.

In the megamarkets, young managers returning from overseas and implementing concepts learned in MBA courses or through work experiences gained in Western multinationals adopt rigorous supply chain management and favor outsourcing in their "make or buy" decisions.

Table 9.5. Pros and cons of integration.

Pros of integration	Cons of integration
Allows economies of scale and scope.	Adds cost of developing new competences and control functions.
Reduces cost.	Upstream capacity needs may not be in line with downstream operations.
Improves competitiveness by capturing upstream or downstream profit margins.	Decreases flexibility to buy from other, more competitive suppliers.
Gains autonomy from powerful suppliers and customers.	Requires managerial and technical expertise, which may not be locally available.
Ensures stricter control over the value chain.	The state may block the endeavor or impose unfavorable conditions (e.g., personnel cuts after limited period).
Raises entry barriers against potential competitors.	Requires additional organizational and managerial inputs.

9.3.3. Diversification

Diversification, another possible direction of growth, aims to increase profits through higher sales obtained from new businesses in new market segments. Diversification is akin to "not putting all one's eggs in one basket." The rationale behind such a strategy is to spread the risk of market contraction for the existing product portfolio by conquering positions in new, promising growth areas. Diversification can be achieved through organic (internal) growth, mergers, acquisitions, alliances, licensing, and distribution of new product lines. Many small and medium-sized businesses grow through diversification.

Venturing into unknown territory with new products or markets stretches a company's human, financial, and technical resources while it turns focus and investments away from the core business. Companies should choose this option when they observe deceleration in their current products or markets. Needless to say, the idea must be thoroughly investigated before it is implemented; many attempts by companies to diversify have led to disastrous losses, especially in unknown territories.

In the megamarkets, the earlier diversification in all azimuths is being disciplined. India's big industrial houses entered into a vast array of businesses before 1991 because the government did not allow foreign investments and a gap had to be filled, and because of the regime of industrial licensing. Since the mid-1990s, the groups have streamlined their structures by hiving off the smaller, non-core businesses. At the same time, they have used their renewed strength to diversify into very promising emerging businesses, like insurance, telecommunication, and retail distribution, in which FDI is still restricted. In China, former SOEs have been trimmed, converted into joint stock companies, and packaged to attract foreign financial and direct investors. Large divisions have been converted into separate legal entities that are accountable to independent boards and professional managers. As business develops, capital is raised on the stock exchange. Diversified groups have converted the megamarkets into highly attractive places for initial public offerings.

Capital-intensive industries such as energy, steel, aerospace, automotive, railways, and shipbuilding are still dominated by large, diversified groups (India) or state-owned enterprises (China, Russia) for three main reasons: political influence (strategic sectors), management talent, and financial clout enabling funding through banks and the capital markets. As these factors change, the role of diversified megaplayers will be reviewed and probably decrease in the future. As part of extended efforts to privatize and convert conglomerates into listed holdings in order to increase managerial accountability while reducing the role of the state, conglomerates will come under scrutiny. As major success stories are found among focused companies, the pressure to concentrate on a few businesses will mount even more in the years to come.

The real issue in diversification is whether and how synergies can be exploited. The problem is that top managers plot diversification strategies based on synergies that must be actually achieved by middle managers working in different parts of the organization following investments in new market segments. Large companies are mostly organized like

---

Pause for thought

Sistema, Russia's largest telecom and electronics holding company, has raised its capitalization to US$20 billion in just ten years. It started as a merger of several former state-owned companies, including Intourist in the hospitality sector and Detski Mir in retailing, which were subsequently restructured and converted into listed companies.

During 2006–2008, Sistema invested US$850 million to buy up companies in its main business areas, which it then supports to raise profitability levels. Its latest investments include the acquisition of majority stakes in an Indian mobile operator (geographic diversification) and in an Austrian engine and drive manufacturer (diversification into mechatronics).

Pause for thought

A Russian flexible packaging company decided to create a holding company with controlling stakes in family-owned Indian firms that specialize in paper-based packaging (horizontal diversification).

It also planned to move into packaging machinery (lateral diversification) in order to create an integrated packaging group "under one roof," in the same way as it had already done in Russia. It hoped the Indian platform would offer it Eurasian leadership (exports to the EU, Middle East, and China) in combination with the possibilities offered by Russia as a market and resource base.

***

A famous Chinese beer producer was faced with high competition, price wars, and overcapacity in its core business. It had grown by expanding its product line from one original brand to an umbrella of more than fifty regional brands, covering all imaginable price points. The company was compelled to reduce this wide-ranging portfolio by shedding non-profitable brands. The question was where to grow the company.

The management opted for cross-industry diversification into pharmaceuticals, packaging, printing, and transportation, as well as a more closely related endeavor in fruit-wine cultivation. The owners wanted to join the ranks of the country's top companies by adding all possible businesses to the initial activity. They were forced to rethink their strategy after incurring losses in the non-related areas where they lacked competence.

***

Reliance Industries, which started out as an oil refinery company, has grown to become India's largest conglomerate following successful investments in high-growth segments such as alternative energies, telecom, insurance, and retailing.

An Indian manufacturer of cleaning equipment had built a strong customer base and distribution network. It entered into joint ventures and technical collaborations with EU producers of different types of equipment so that it could offer a range of solutions to its customers. On its own, it could not have developed the range.

To build market share, a brewery may contemplate producing and marketing different types of beverages, including liquor, wine, soft drinks, fruit juices, bottled water, and so forth. The world's largest soft drink producers have moved into other types of beverages via acquisitions and alliances; earlier, the required know-how was developed through greenfield investments. Food companies may also diversify into beverages, which can be put through the same sales channels.

This category management is considered a safer path to growth than jumping, for example, from beverages to packaging or bottling equipment, which are not bound by linkages in markets and technology.

***

SMS Demag, a German equipment and turnkey solution provider to the world's steel plants, had to dispose of its plastics equipment division in 2007 after a series of unrelated acquisitions in familiar markets (USA, UK).

The risks would have probably been even higher if the diversification strategy had been adopted in unfamiliar markets.

silos, with few horizontal linkages at lower levels, which makes it impossible to achieve any synergy whatsoever. Medium-sized players are often in a better position to recognize possible synergies and put them into practice following an investment.

Chinese managers are slanted toward large-scale entities, especially in state-owned enterprises, which has not always been very successful in the past.

A company fares better when it attacks new growth industries, where the playing field is still level and the company has time to develop the required special competence.

Companies should use one or more of their strengths in related segments as a starting point for diversification. This is the path followed by customer-driven solution providers.

Foreign companies must have a clear goal in sight before embarking on diversification ventures in the megamarkets. The earlier example of the brewery highlighted the difference between a product line, a category, and a lateral diversification. Beer is a product line; beverages is a category; and packaging and printing are lateral diversifications for an alcoholic beverages producer. When contemplating a diversification, the company should ask two key questions: "Who is the customer?" and "What is the customer's buying behavior?" The same consumer will drink a variety of beverages. However, the customer for packaging and printing is an industrial user. End consumers and business users are entirely different buyer categories. Category dominance, on the other hand, works, as evidenced by many category giants: Siemens in equipment, Nestlé in processed foods, and Daimler in vehicles.

Table 9.6. Pros and cons of diversification.

Pros of diversification	Cons of diversification
New market segments can be targeted.	Developing new core competences involves additional costs.
Risk can be spread.	Cross-subsidization provokes internal friction between SBU heads.
New avenues of growth can be explored.	Antimonopoly laws may thwart efforts to build diversified conglomerates.
Diversified conglomerates have the financial clout vis-à-vis the government.	Specialists compete against a conglomerate's parts by focusing on USPs.

9.3.4. Globalization

Globalization is a form of geographic diversification encapsulating all possible market options. It is the growth strategy espoused by a growing number of companies today. It is often seen in combination with consolidation efforts to achieve bigger scale and market dominance. Large multinationals—but also medium-sized, family-run businesses—want to benefit from the global economy, which is characterized by greater connectivity and integration. The megamarkets will play a greater role in corporate decisions on globalization owing to their growing economic weight and the wealth generated by megamarket companies.

EU companies have a long tradition of trading with other countries. The first phase of internationalization from the 1960s to the 1980s was exclusively export-driven. Investments were undertaken in the West (Western Europe, North America). The end of the Cold War opened new markets, and companies intensified their investments in Eastern Europe,

Asia, and Latin America. Since the early 2000s, the three Eurasian megamarkets have hit the radar of corporate executives moved by different motivations for FDI:

- market development: first phase, large agglomerations in the megamarkets; second phase, second- and third-tier cities and rural markets in the megamarkets; third phase, neighboring economies; fourth phase, other emerging markets (e.g., Africa);
- resource security: first phase, inputs for factories within the megamarkets; second phase, inputs for factories worldwide;
- cost reduction: first phase, local production for exports to advanced markets; second phase, local production for sales in megamarkets;
- preemptive strikes at competitors: first phase, strategic presence as a deterrent; second phase, encroaching on a competitor's home turf.

Once a company has established its presence in a megamarket, its strategy may have to undergo a midcourse correction to ensure further expansion.

Efforts to globalize business activities by using the megamarkets as a platform revolve around four assumptions:

- possibility to reduce unit prices because of lower cost levels (step 1);
- opportunity to exploit economies of scale because of huge domestic markets (step 2);
- chance of increasing exports to other high-growth emerging markets with similar needs (step 3);
- integration of megamarket operations in the company's global supplier and client network (step 4).

Megamarkets are targeted for their size, which—many managers believe—makes them excellent candidates for quick business expansion through fairly standardized offers. This, they believe, reduces the risk in case of a downturn in the volatile emerging markets. This perception also applies to companies that had originally set up export-oriented operations and are now shifting their attention to domestic consumers/users. These companies see globalization as a means of taking a tried and tested standard business model and extending it geographically, with minimum modifications, to maximize economies of scale. From this perspective, the key strategic challenge is to determine how much of the value proposition should be standardized or localized to respond to specific market characteristics. In other words, should the company's global strategy optimize scale or exploit differences? Most companies prefer to focus on similarities across countries and the potential for the scale economies that such commonalities unlock. This is seen as the primary source of added value. Differences between markets, in contrast, are viewed as obstacles that need to be overcome with minimum adjustment.

The lessons drawn from successful players are revealing. In numerous industries where multinationals entered by pushing for standardization, and thus economies of scale, one can see a move in the other direction, toward more localization. High-performers adopt "glocalization" when they step beyond their cultural and geographic boundaries. Roland Robertson, the sociologist who coined the word *glocal*, explained it as "the tempering effects of local conditions on global pressures." Companies that practice "glocalization"

> **Pause for thought**
>
> *A leading EU manufacturer of brake systems for trucks set up a manufacturing platform in China. After its first joint venture, top management had to recognize that sales targets could hardly be met in the domestic market. The company decided to increase exports to the company's global subsidiaries and to customers in neighboring South Korea and Japan.*
>
> *In another case, also in China, an EU manufacturer of dredging and mining equipment set up a production unit in the early 2000s out of cost considerations. Input costs eventually turned out to be higher than in Europe because of the low local content. Essential parts had to be imported from the company's production units abroad, which weighed heavily on the Chinese subsidiary's performance. The company had to devise a new strategy for linking up the Chinese subsidiary to its global procurement system.*
>
> ***
>
> *Nestlé has two hundred blends of its instant coffee, which shows a degree of localization.*
>
> *Another FMCG company, L'Oréal, was perspicacious in understanding the Indian consumer. When its professional products division entered India in 1997, the hairdressing industry was unstructured, without organized education and training; hairdressers did not use professional products, and if they did, the products were prohibitively expensive imports. L'Oréal had the vision to realize that with initial localized efforts it could tap a huge virgin market for hair color. It invested heavily in hairdressing education and training. Thanks to these efforts, L'Oréal's professional products—Professionnel and Kerastase—are leaders in the Indian market. Price has been also seriously considered. By increasing the number of products and setting up a production unit in India, L'Oréal has been able to control its prices effectively. It followed a similar path in China and Russia.*
>
> ***
>
> *Acer, one of the world's largest computer manufacturers, started with contract manufacturing of personal computers, operating out of low-wage Taiwan. In the early 1990s, its management started pushing Acer as a global brand, particularly in the advanced markets. This two-track approach turned out to be problematic. The branded business grew to significant volumes but continued to generate losses because the competitive environment was particularly tough for a late mover.*
>
> *Meanwhile, customers for Acer's contract manufacturing arm like IBM started to worry that their business secrets would be leaked to Acer's competing line of business. They cancelled their orders, fearing that Acer could cross-subsidize its own brand and undercut their own prices by using profits generated from the contract manufacturing operation.*
>
> *Acer responded by making some hard choices. Contract manufacturing was spun off into a separate company, and it remained focused on customers from developed countries. Meanwhile, sales of its own branded products were redirected to emerging markets, particularly China, India, and Russia, where contract customers could not sell at a price low enough to compete with Acer's product. With this logic of localization, Acer managed to build a strong brand, which was later globalized. Meanwhile, IBM's computer division had ceased to exist after being sold to China's Lenovo, today Acer's major competitor.*

are customer-focused, market-oriented, and innovative in their ways of using their global principles to create local adaptations. The relevance of a "think global, market local" attitude holds across all contexts and kinds of companies, be they big or small, product manufacturers or service providers.

"Glocalization" also means that different customer segments must be approached with distinct strategies depending on their needs and location.

The degree of localization can vary with the business function and the time of entry. Whereas product development, marketing, procurement, and human resources have to be localized early in the venture, other functions like leadership, organization, and R&D can start as standardized functions that are localized as business grows. Marketing in particular must address itself directly to the local audience. A brand may be global, but its advertising campaign must be steeped in local color. In India, Coca-Cola uses Hinglish (Hindi + English) to capture the attention of its young consumers. Interestingly, finance, which has always been considered as a typically centralized (and therefore standardized) function, is being gradually localized by progressive players keen on tapping local sources of finance. EU companies can turn to cash-rich domestic banks, private equity, and the stock markets to finance expansion in the megamarkets.

Foreign companies that participate in local communities by indigenizing their approach can reduce risk considerably. Consumers will be less intimidated by foreign ownership if the company merges in the milieu and becomes a good corporate citizen. In China, for example, all divisions of Siemens are regularly involved in community activities, skill development, cultural exchange, and sponsorships of local events, institutions, and environmental initiatives. Nestlé, with roughly half of its factories and people located in emerging markets, invests millions in educating local employees and developing community partnerships, tailoring its programs to the respective country.

Building networks and partnerships with reputed and powerful local firms accelerates "glocalization." For this, the foreign company must put forward valid arguments to attract a leading local company into its fold. Globalization today is far less about leveraging economies of scale than about leveraging economies of expertise and knowledge. It is about building advantage by tapping local expertise and sharing globally available knowledge. A company can never localize its roots, but it can build strong national and regional companies in the megamarkets, which should enable it to assemble, produce, distribute, package, brand, and communicate locally.

Internationalization of deliveries through exports is only the very first step toward globalization. EU companies must go one step further and fully integrate their megamarket operations in their global supply, sales, and R&D systems so that they can retain the markets that have been conquered through sales. The future challenge is to find the right switch from the earlier solely Triad-oriented global strategy to one encompassing a full-fledged presence in both the Triad economies and the emerging megamarket triangle of Eurasia as an additional pillar of growth and profit maximization.

This is the globalization strategy implemented by the rising stars from the megamarkets. Companies such as Bharat Forge, CNOOC, Dr. Reddy's, Haier, Huawei, Infosys, Lenovo, Ranbaxy, Sistema, Tata, and Wipro are appearing on the global stage, starting from another home base, where they have learned how to leverage engineering talent, low costs, and market access. Less capitalized than the multinationals, these companies have taken up the global challenge, and after initial snags, these successful megamarket players can serve as examples also for Western multinationals (see box 9.3).

> **Box 9.3. Two megamarket examples of successful glocalization.**
>
> a. Haier's five globalization strategies
>
> - Globalization of design: to maintain the competitive edge in the international market, Haier has set up eighteen design centers worldwide.
>
> - Globalization of manufacturing: to innovate and produce according to local standards and best practices, Haier has set up ten industrial parks and twenty-two plants overseas.
>
> - Globalization of marketing: to satisfy customer demand and build a world-class brand based on interaction and exchange, Haier sells through more than five thousand overseas retail outlets and has invested in over ten thousand service centers.
>
> - Globalization of purchasing: strategic partnerships have been established with leading global suppliers who participate in the front-end design of Haier products. On-line links enable bidding for public tenders and e-ordering.
>
> - Globalization of financial operations: Haier has invested in banking, securities, and insurance. By listing its shares on the Hong Kong Stock Exchange, it can finance its expansion through the international capital markets.
>
> Source: www.haier.com. Section « Corporate Culture, Values & Philosophy, VIII.
>
> b. Infosys's four operational shifts for succeeding in the "flat world."
>
> - From building loyalty through good service to building loyalty through innovation at operating process, business unit, corporate, and business partner levels.
>
> - From spending money on information to making money from information: the financial and operational information it generates is useful for finding slacks in the deployment of its resources (people, support activities, business units).
>
> - From dreading the "China price" to being the "China price": cost effectiveness by employing talent on a global scale wherever it is available, sourcing from wherever it is cost-effective, selling where it is most profitable.
>
> - From winning in the straight way to winning in the turns. Addressing volatility and uncertainty in global markets by developing capabilities (recruitment of best talent, motivation, incubating new services) required to win in both upturns and downturns.
>
> Source: http://www.infosys.com/flat-world/business/perspectives/john-hagel-case-study.pdf

Globalization can be a double-edged sword (see table 9.7). The globalizing firm has the potential to reap several types of benefits, such as the vast potential of a much larger market arena, opportunities to capture scale- and location-based cost efficiencies, and exposure to a multiplicity of new product and process ideas. However, globalization also exposes the firm to numerous strategic and organizational challenges emanating from a dramatic increase in diversity, complexity, and uncertainty—external as well as internal to the firm. How managers address these challenges determines whether globalization yields competitive advantage or disadvantage and makes the company stronger or weaker. "Smart" globalization is the ability to capture the benefits and minimize the costs and risks. Top management must, for example, give its newly acquired megamarket subsidiary sufficient leeway to operate in international markets while avoiding head-on competition with other subsidiaries by ensuring tight coordination and rational product/market concentration.

Table 9.7. Pros and cons of globalization.

Pros of globalization	Cons of globalization
Choice in terms of supply chains, distribution channels, and finance can be extended to a global scale.	Costs and complexity of operations are higher.
Global brands bring in additional revenue.	The company is exposed to risks in foreign markets: exchange rates, import barriers, government interference, other unknowns.
Local inputs can be obtained for innovations and knowledge.	Interests at home are opposed to and exert pressure against outsourcing and relocation.
Local competition can be handled better.	Adopting the right mix of standardization and localization can be difficult.
Challenge of intercultural exchange can be converted into a strength.	Finding managerial talent with a global mindset can be difficult.

CHAPTER 10
Expansion options: Select a road map

China, India, and Russia offer foreign companies many alternatives for entry strategies, alliance partners, and geographic destination. A winning concept emerges from the detailed study of the different value-maximizing options derived from two basic strategic choices: non-equity- and equity-based expansion modes.

Non-equity-based expansion is mainly sales- and/or procurement-driven, but at a later stage a company may invest in a representative office, the incorporation of a sales/purchasing subsidiary, the setting up of a logistics and service center, or even establishing an alliance with a supplier/customer to consolidate its position. Equity-based expansion is capital-intensive as it implies an FDI operation either through an acquisition of an existing undertaking (minority, majority) or the creation of a new entity (solely or in partnership). Each basic strategic choice (BSC) consists of sub-choices and their combinations (see figure 10.1).

Switching from non-equity- to equity-based modes is quite common, whereas converting an equity-based venture to a non-equity-based one is rare. Medium-sized newcomers to the megamarkets tend to appoint importer-distributors for their products or to open a sales

Figure 10.1. Strategic choices for megamarket expansion.

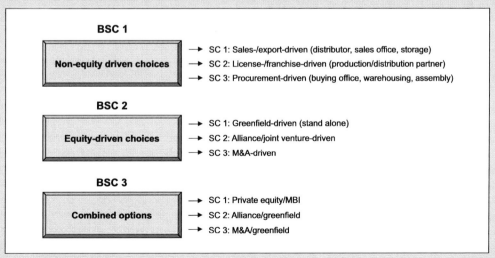

BSC: basic strategic choices
SC: sub-choices.

> **Pause for thought**
>
> In India, customers are willing to pay a higher price for office chairs from a well-known German company, but at the time of placing the order, they are told that they have to wait for almost two months for the goods to be shipped from Germany, which the customers are not prepared to do.

office before engaging in capital-intensive FDI routes. It is a low-risk, low-commitment option; its results are therefore proportionately low. This strategy has no lasting impact and fails to produce durable results. Pricing and customer proximity cannot be satisfied through imports alone. The high import duties imposed in megamarkets artificially raise the price of the goods. Nor are customers ready to wait for goods to be shipped from the EU.

Gradual penetration starting with exports and culminating in FDI is therefore not always effective. With service becoming an important differentiator, it is important to build confidence with key accounts by showing an immediate commitment to invest locally.

Companies aiming at leadership will have to directly opt for a high-involvement strategy including immediate investment in local assembly or manufacturing. This way, they can grow the market by reaching the bottom and middle of the pyramid (for consumer goods) or price-conscious users (for technical goods). Seeding the market used to be a judicious strategy, but it is too slow for penetrating the emerging megamarkets. Even the sphere of exceptions to this rule—pure export strategies for high-tech goods and advanced equipment—is shrinking as megamarket players are catching up even in these knowledge-rich segments. The best way to counter them is by showing a strong presence through R&D-rich investments coupled with a controlled transfer of technology and know-how from headquarters to local units (legal entities). With services becoming an important differentiator, it is impossible to build relations of confidence with key customers without a strong local presence.

Because of the higher investment and risk involved, equity-driven options need to be evaluated and benchmarked, not only against other variants but also existing local undertakings in the same business. Resource persons with deep knowledge of local markets, industries, and mentalities can help EU/US companies understand the situation and elaborate viable options. The chosen path depends on the company's objectives—basically if it wants to be a pioneer or prefers a more cautious follower approach. However, leadership and success beckon those with a lasting commitment to the local market, regardless of the sector of activity.

Moreover, megamarket authorities are very supportive of knowledge-intensive projects. They vie with others to attract foreign investors from all over the world by luring them with market size, tax incentives, and state support. Smart EU/US companies have learned how to play this game by negotiating land prices, tax exemptions, infrastructure, and so forth. They win over local authorities with the employment and know-how advantages of their undertakings while pursuing their own agendas to generate and repatriate the required profits. Even an export-led strategy is in fact initially often "sold" as a "full-commitment strategy" by making non-manufacturing investments such as the establishment of a subsidiary, the opening of a warehouse or service center, and the possible purchase of stakes in local suppliers. There is no limit to a company's creativity for convincing partners and the authorities and determining the ideal expansion route based on a winning concept. The main thing is to see beyond the immediate plan and draw a picture of a possible long-term strategy.

10.1. Non-equity-based expansion

Non-equity-driven choices are still very popular modes, especially among smaller players. They consist of three main sub-choices: export-based sales, licensing/franchising arrangements, and procurement. They are expansion modes with much lower capital requirements than investments in manufacturing or innovation. With time, non-equity modes can be converted into investments in the form of M&As (e.g., purchase of stake in a local supplier) or alliances (e.g., opening of a service center together with a key account). These options will be covered in the next section.

10.1.1. Export-/sales-driven choices

Exports simply aim to increase turnover by utilizing excess capacity at home and winning megamarket customers through shipments from home or any other production site controlled by the company. These measures are not based on a long-term game plan to gain leadership against established competitors who employ local platforms, allowing them a cost, information, and responsiveness advantage. Exports can help a company maintain a competitive position only if its products or technology are inherently superior to those available in the target market. In a growing number of industries, EU/US exporters face tremendous technological challenges from within the megamarkets. Competitive advantages for external technology providers will gradually be eroded if they refuse to become domestic players through FDI. Large orders placed by the leading private or state-owned industrial groupings are increasingly linked to local content rules and accessibility.

Pause for thought

Airbus's offices in Russia and China have large training centers and customer support units; in addition, the offices are involved in material procurement, product manufacturing, and component delivery, conditions laid by the host governments for orders of aircraft.

Airbus and Boeing are in a race in India to use it not only as a market but also as a destination for outsourcing and software development.

***

In the late 1990s, a German premium carmaker set up a US$25 million warehouse for spare parts on the outskirts of Moscow to support its exports and sales. Prior to this, essential parts had to be brought in by truck and by air and taken through long customs procedures, which all adversely impacted repairs and the company's image, especially when cars of VIP customers (ministers) remained stranded for weeks. These cost savings enabled the company to subsequently set up an assembly unit and expand the dealer network across major regions.

> **Box 10.1. Export segments for EU companies.**
>
> - Aeronautics and space technologies
> - Premium cars
> - Machine-tools and special equipment
> - Fine and specialty chemicals
> - Pharmaceuticals, including biotechnologies
> - Communication technologies
> - Medical equipment
> - Fashion and luxury goods

Intense global competition forces EU exporters to buttress traditional non-equity modes with higher investments in non-manufacturing structures (offices, sales subsidiaries, services, spare parts platforms, storage, packaging units) and up- and downstream partnerships. Capital outlays in such cases can be significant and comparable to equity-related modes.

A sales-focused approach becomes relevant for companies or players possessing advanced products and state-of-the-art technologies that are unique and difficult to imitate. EU players have acquired leadership positions in numerous such segments (see box 10.1). Current trends confirm that, in these formerly export-oriented industries, leading players strive to get a foothold in the megamarkets through more active involvement. This attitude is compounded by intense triangular US–Japan–EU competition, which plays into the hands of megamarket governments and enterprises.

Growing export volumes automatically lead to higher complexity in distribution and logistics. Total dependence on third-party agents (distributors) for these services bears a high risk. The company can hardly assess at what price products are eventually sold and if end users are really satisfied with the offer. The exporter may not sense when the

> **Pause for thought**
>
> *Aerospace provides a good example. To preempt Boeing, Airbus announced new assembly/manufacturing projects in the megamarkets. Airbus managers were not entirely ready for such a move and would have preferred to continue exporting aircraft out of Europe. However, they were forced into this move to secure sales of the new A380, which faces infrastructure problems in most airports.*
>
> *A similar situation can be observed in another high-tech application: high-speed hot strip working and support rolls for steel mills. This heavy equipment produced out of special alloys was imported for many years into the megamarkets, including China, the world's largest user of equipment for steel plants. In the mid-2000s, large steel equipment multinationals began investing in local manufacturing, obliging medium-sized players from the EU to look for alliance partners to strengthen their local presence.*
>
> *Megamarket governments played a vital role in stimulating, in both industries (aerospace, steel), inward investments by imposing local content rules and linking higher incentives, including government orders (direct B2G or through state-owned companies).*

time is ripe for a strategic switch to a deeper engagement. Interestingly, many companies eventually change to an FDI mode because they start feeling the competitive pressure but continue their privileged relationship with their distributors even after they have made the investment. Or they may acquire a stake in the distributing companies. Smaller firms are reluctant to finance their own sales team out of cost considerations.

Selecting a local agent for distribution is not an easy task. Distributors and dealers work for a host of principals, sometimes even competing companies, and therefore lack the strategic focus to promote one principal. Megamarket distributors face difficulties in selling highly engineered products with deep technical and service content as they lack the knowledge of the product's advantages and trained manpower.

In this context, marketing should be seen as an investment and not a cost as it enables the company to assess needs, to measure their extent and intensity, and to determine whether a profitable opportunity exists. This way, a company can create markets instead of just serving them. In many cases, only exporting exposes companies to unexpected risks. Local authorities can suddenly ban imports of the item for a variety of reasons, including retaliatory measures against particular governments.

To succeed and prepare the way to FDI, EU exporters must focus on acquiring megamarket key accounts (MKAs) for the long term. Only following EU customers to the megamarkets through piggyback arrangements is not sufficient to ensure sustainable order volumes and capacity utilization. Local MKAs expect their suppliers to have their own sales offices or subsidiaries so that they are always accessible. MKAs are more powerful today; they know what they need and have a wide choice of suppliers, which

---

Pause for thought

A famous dredging and earthmoving equipment maker from the EU had this experience after launching its greenfield site in China. Independent distributors whom the company had used before the investment decided to turn to fast-moving and more profitable products (supplied by competitors) as they continuously missed the high sales targets required by the company's new investment.

At the time of this writing, the board was in the midst of rethinking its strategy in view of the circumstances, which were totally different from those in its traditional advanced markets, where distributors are well trained and there is no need to deploy marketing and sales teams to support independent agents.

***

A Belgian meat and sausage producer had registered its products for distribution in China but had to stop all its activities and write off its investment after the Chinese government imposed a ban on meat imports coming from the EU in late 2006, supposedly because of avian flu outbreaks in the EU but actually as a countermeasure to EU anti-dumping procedures against Chinese footwear. Incidentally, meat imports from the United States, Australia, and New Zealand faced no restrictions.

When the ban was lifted and the chance to boost market share increased, it became obvious that the products had to be adjusted to the taste of Chinese consumers and to meet the channel requirements (supermarkets, cash-and-carry, hotels), which demanded additional investments.

allows them to negotiate and, in most cases, dictate their terms. A few principles must be taken into consideration to succeed:

- Core competences must be promoted aggressively.
- The offer must be needs-focused and solution-oriented.
- Products and technologies must be distinctive from what is already available.
- No compromise should be made on quality or on any other factors that built the brand.
- Success in other markets breeds success in the megamarkets; good references are a door-opener.
- Regular visits and events cement customer relations.

Certain EU/US companies procrastinate when switching from sales to manufacturing in the megamarkets as they believe they have to have built a worldwide reputation based on Western quality standards. Luxury goods and certain fashion labels may be justified as they can command a premium on this basis. Dior lost its luxury tag by indiscriminate outsourcing and merchandising. But as the number of high-net-worth individuals increases, luxury brands are no longer the sovereign right of an exclusive group. A new class of "affordable luxury" brands has therefore started producing some of their brands in the megamarkets.[1] Mass consumer goods brands, however, cannot leverage the equity of premium-end luxury brands. L'Oréal understood this and opened production units in the megamarkets. The same applies to fashion goods. Some of the goods are produced locally but are under tight control by the foreign brand owners, which also invest in merchandising, promotion, PR of their brand, and their own retail outlets.

The other question is whether megamarket consumers will remain faithful to foreign brands. Brand awareness among young people has weakened and is not as relevant anymore as other factors, such as price, product design, and special discounts. With the growing success of megamarket companies, brand prioritization will change, giving more weight to local brands. Many young Chinese females under thirty years of age follow Asian trends and consider Japanese and Korean brands as fashion leaders. Similar trends can be observed for cosmetics, pharmaceuticals, and consumer goods. EU market leaders are compelled to enlarge their range by acquiring local companies and introducing second-tier brands for medium-quality products only for EMs.

10.1.2. Licensing and franchising

Two expansion routes—franchising and licensing—are still popular among new entrants, especially SMEs keen on capitalizing on their existing know-how. Whereas licensing is mostly oriented toward one partner per geographic region (country or region), the rationale behind franchising is to widen penetration by multiplying the number of units (franchise partners).

Franchising is catching on very fast in the megamarkets.[2] It represents a long-term relationship in which the franchisor (the owner of the brand) assigns to independent

---

1. See 4.7.2.
2. According to the World Franchise Council, there are about 16,000 franchise systems in operation around the world, and the number of franchisees exceeds 1.6 million. The global franchise industry generated sales of over US$1 trillion in 2007 and created more than 20 million job opportunities.

partners (the franchisees) the right to market its goods or services and to use the business name for a fixed period of time in return for a fee paid on the basis of the turnover generated. The franchisor provides assistance in training, merchandising, procurement, quality checks, finance, planning, and management systems. Franchising consists of a number of business models. These include:

- manufacturer–retailer, where the retailer as franchisee sells the franchisor's product directly to the public (e.g., passenger car dealerships);
- manufacturer–wholesaler, where the wholesaler as franchisee under license manufactures and distributes the franchisor's product (e.g., soft drink bottling arrangements);
- wholesaler–retailer, where the retailer as franchisee purchases products for retail sale from a franchisor wholesaler (frequently a cooperative of franchisee retailers who have formed a wholesaling company through which they are contractually obliged to purchase, as in hardware and automotive product stores);
- retailer–retailer, where the franchisor markets a service or a product, under a common name and standardized system, through a network of franchisees; this is the classic franchise business format (e.g., fast-food chains).

This arrangement between the owner of the system (franchisor) and the owner of the individual outlet (franchisee) has spread to virtually every service sector of the economy in the megamarkets: fast food, tourism, food and non-food retail, health care, fitness, entertainment, filling stations, and automotive, just to name a few. Many EU/US franchisors have established a win-win relationship where as franchisors they expanded their market presence without eroding their own capital, and the local franchisees have gained access to proven business systems and international brands at lower risk and to their own commercial advantage. The scheme provides small businesses (franchisees) with the tools of big business (provided by the franchisor). Franchising is a legal relationship, with the obligations and responsibilities of both parties outlined in a franchise agreement, which can vary in length and conditions.

Similar to franchising, licensing arrangements aim at reducing the capital exposure for the foreign company (licensor), which intends to transfer know-how—usually a limited technology package compared with a more comprehensive package in equity transactions—to the local company (licensee). Licensing was a popular entry mode throughout the 1970s, 1980s, and 1990s, but it has gradually become a risk factor for EU/US players who underestimated the strong ambition of megamarket companies to learn, grow, and compete. In the 2000s, many licensees raised their technology standards and gained competitive advantage. These companies managed to raise the capital to engage in strategic partnerships and eventually even acquire equity of Western players.

Pause for thought

In India, where FDI in retailing is restricted to single-brand stores, the franchise route has been used by companies like McDonald's (US fast-food chain) and Lavazza (Italian coffee chain) to enter the market.

Depending on new policy measures, it may be used by international retail groups to launch operations in food and non-food retailing.

> **Pause for thought**
>
> *Russia accused Bulgaria and other NATO countries of counterfeiting Russian weapons and resorting to intellectual piracy at dumping prices without paying license fees to Russian manufacturers, which resulted in annual losses of about US$2 billion.**
>
> *In 2007, the Russian government also threw a punch at Microsoft, claiming the software giant's overly strict and costly licensing regime is to blame for the high rates of piracy in the country. Low average incomes and underfunded state universities would indeed lead to the relatively widespread use of cheaper pirated copies of the software.*
>
> * Statement issued in Russia by First Deputy Prime Minister Ivanov in March 2007 (RIA Novosti).

Licensing has been a major driver for China and India to strengthen their industrial bases and has helped them leapfrog in many industries (e.g., generics, machine building, wind energy). The governments of both countries impose strict rules, which have to be followed by companies. Special laws, such as the Law on Chinese-Foreign Contractual Joint Ventures, regulate approvals, royalty payments, and tax-related issues of licensing arrangements between foreign and local partners. India's *licensing raj* forced many foreign companies to sign similar agreements with local joint venture partners (they were not allowed to set up their own units). Now that agreements have expired, Indian licensees have emerged as competitors in many industries, ranging from auto components, plastics, and machinery to chemicals, steel equipment, and semiconductors.

Licensing agreements have lost their flair as sources of know-how for progressive megamarket companies, which prefer cooperation or shareholding schemes enabling them to learn and eventually acquire the know-how. They are more discerning about the technology to be obtained through licensing because of high royalty payments. Strong local companies have started developing their own technologies and filing patents. Infringement accusations are now being vocalized in the other direction.

Given the higher technology levels in the megamarkets and the widespread reach of their companies, EU/US licensors need to first assess the license-worthiness of their technology. This route can no longer be used for extracting more revenue from a technology at the end of its life cycle. Once license-worthiness has been established, all efforts should be made to protect the technology and to avoid a backlash (the licensee turns competitor). This is not easy as it is difficult to control the use made by the licensee and R&D investments in future developments.

10.1.3. Procurement-driven choices

Supply-oriented strategies focus on cost, quality, and speed optimization in procurement. China and India have turned into dominant sourcing regions for industrial, retail, and trading companies; they host a large number of factories that can engage in mass production or customized solutions by using much cheaper labor and, sometimes, raw materials than in the West. The low-cost supply strategy has been pursued by EU/US companies engaged in both consumer and industrial goods (apparel, textiles, footwear, toys, machinery parts, tools, bulk drugs, active pharmaceutical ingredients, etc.).

Western retailers are the biggest importers. Although EU retail chains have started looking for even cheaper sourcing markets in ASEAN countries, Bangladesh, and Sri Lanka, they maintain large buying and design centers in China and India. China is the world's number-one sourcing market for home appliances, DIY products, car components, and sanitary equipment. India has caught up in sportswear, tools, gardening instruments, furniture, and metal parts. However, the lower cost of labor is, in many engineering-intensive industries (e.g., automotive supplies, machine-tools), compensated by the high cost of imported materials and parts, which weighs on margins.

The sourcing of components and products becomes risky whenever know-how has to be supplied in the form of drawings and training. Megamarket industrial suppliers are swift at imitating and competing with similar offers in foreign markets. Many Italian SMEs have lost their international position after shifting part of their production to Chinese suppliers without reinforcing control by acquiring stakes or without protecting their core technologies. With hindsight, it would have been better to bear higher costs at home and not lose their business. Often, too many EU/US companies chase a few megamarket suppliers, who become powerful and can then impose higher prices. A supplier may also suddenly turn into an ally of a competitor and stop delivering goods. Risks can be reduced by acquiring equity in leading vendors with good track records and customer referrals (upstream investment). To gain confidence, EU/US companies should work with suppliers for some time in product planning and development before engaging in a joint operation. Vendors and buyers should share the same concern for quality, ensure just-in-time deliveries, and update each other regularly on new rules and regulations.

Another common mistake to be avoided is to use megamarkets only as a source of products for the advanced markets while missing out on opportunities in the domestic megamarket. Companies can win more easily by adopting a combined supply and sales strategy with a future objective of gradually moving toward local assembly, production, and R&D. High performers have localized their main business functions (sales, purchasing, production, R&D, and finance). Companies can design different sourcing strategies in the megamarkets. Success depends on the option selected (see box 10.2) and a series of other factors:

- accurate assessment of a company's current spending and of the local supply market;
- analysis of logistics and the supply chain for main products, including those that should later be produced locally;

> **Box 10.2. Procurement-driven choices.**
> - Loose purchasing agreement with supplier
> - Opening or buying office to reach out to suppliers
> - Strategic alliance with supplier for FDI in assembly/warehousing, repacking, labeling
> - Joint venture with supplier for procurement and logistics
> - Equity participation in supplier for integration in global supply chain

> **Pause for thought**
>
> Volkswagen will increase its purchase volume in China from US$250 million to US$1 billion during 2007–2009. It has already signed binding long-term agreements with suppliers. It announced it will invest heavily in logistics platforms including buying stakes of local companies.
>
> Austria's RHI, the world's leading supplier of refractory products for industrial high-temperature processes, bought 80% of the shares of Liaoning Jinding Magnesite Group (LJMG) to gain access to the company's magnesite mines in Liaoning province in China's northeast, where one-fifth of the world's magnesite reserves are concentrated. LJMG also operates plants for the processing of magnesite, which is an important input for the production of refractory materials. RHI invested several million US dollars to expand and modernize its production facilities in northeastern China.
>
> ***
>
> Nutritek, a Russian baby food producer, entered the Chinese market via a preliminary investment in a supplier from New Zealand. Once the supply source had been secured, the company started building a factory in China.
>
> This is a perfect example of a switch from a mere procurement mode to an FDI-based strategy in order to reduce the risk of disruption of a vital supply line.

- comparison of procurement conditions for purchases required by production units in Europe and plants in other markets;
- selection of vendors with a long track record of international supply chain management;
- purchasing from more than one source to reduce risks of dependence and discontinuity;
- determine required warehousing capacity to avoid disruptions in deliveries;
- explore possibilities offered by B2B e-purchasing, which is picking up in the megamarkets;
- introduce high transport efficiencies through alliances to optimize supply management;
- use of sourcing tools such as reverse auction, contract management modules, and spend intelligence;
- continually track results and benefits from outsourcing.

Larger EU/US companies increasingly contemplate buying into local supplier networks to control the supply chain and reduce the risk of bottlenecks.

Megamarket managers are themselves studying carefully the supply chain to identify profit areas.

10.2. FDI-/equity-based expansion

There are several reasons why companies choose to set up a manufacturing unit or engage in any other sort of direct investment in the megamarkets (see box 10.3).

At first sight, local manufacturing helps to overcome import barriers (quotas, tariffs, embargoes) and importer–distributor defections, but this should not be the sole driver.

Box 10.3. Reasons for selecting the FDI route.

Market considerations

- Proximity and better understanding of the market
- Continued service to international customers
- Relations with new local customers
- Fast delivery and service
- Creation of demand
- Stronger influence on distribution channels

Cost considerations

- Access to qualified manpower at lower cost
- Cheaper use of inputs
- Larger supply of raw materials
- Proximity to suppliers
- Lower taxes
- No import duties
- No impact of import bans (embargoes)
- Reduced transport and coordination costs

Strategic reasons

- Presence of competitors
- Local content requirements imposed by authorities
- Capacity bottlenecks in mature markets
- Access to indigenous technology
- Possibility to improve market observation and intelligence
- Networking with authorities

The promise of an emerging megamarket as a production site, however alluring, should be carefully evaluated in terms of potential pitfalls, risks, and revenue expectations.[3]

Finance is a major issue for EU/US companies given that Western banks are rather reluctant to fund operations in emerging markets; these companies therefore have to fund the megamarket venture through internal accruals of equity. With a few exceptions (e.g., Austrian holdings), investments by EU/US companies in the megamarkets are not tax-deductible. However, innovative expansion algorithms probed in Western environments, including hedge fund–backed or private equity–backed takeovers, vertical integrations, and management buy-outs (MBOs) and management buy-ins (MBIs), can now be availed

---

3. For practical examples, refer to Hualin Pu and Ying Que, "Why Have Some Transnational Corporations Failed in China?" *China and the World Economy*, vol. 12, no. 5 (2004): 67–79.

in megamarkets as well. Rising price/earning (P/E) ratios have incited many companies to turn to the stock markets for raising capital through IPOs. As a rule though, local industrial partners lack experience in putting such financial schemes into practice and therefore prefer to have a foreign partner with a brand to convince authorities that the foreign investment in their company is creating jobs in advanced technology sectors; in such cases, approvals are granted more easily.

Procedures and rules differ substantially from those in the advanced markets. In China, a state-owned joint venture partner may suddenly fall under the protective umbrella of a city or provincial government. Or a local minority partner may not be willing to sell out and can hinder business expansion if local laws (e.g., blocking minority) or the articles of association contain a provision in favor of the minority partner. Similarly, greenfield projects need to be planned carefully on the basis of facts rather than managerial optimism.

A decade back, FDI into China, India, and Russia consisted mainly of joint ventures with local partners. These schemes consisted in creating separate legal entities in which both parties usually held equal parts, the risk being that both parties continued to operate their original companies which drew most financial and managerial resources. Restrictive FDI regulations did not allow greenfield projects and acquisitions. Attitudes toward FDI have changed since then; megamarket governments have now more FDI-friendly laws. Nowadays, there are no limits to creativity in conceiving models and structuring deals in the megamarkets. Even seemingly risky innovative moves can improve the position of a foreign player, provided each step is carried out diligently and with the personal commitment of top management.

Today, a foreign player can operate almost autonomously in the megamarkets, which has opened many more opportunities and combinations, including:

- its own production units for exports-cum-domestic-sales;
- greenfield with a joint venture partner;
- production in combination with company-controlled retail outlets;
- acquisition of local partners who stay in the business with a minority share;
- strategic alliances with key accounts (e.g., service centers, production units);
- MBOs of existing management with or without the support of external managers (MBIs) or venture capital providers;
- restructuring of a brownfield plant belonging to a supplier;
- cross-shareholding between foreign and local entities;

> **Pause for thought**
>
> A French advertising agency was on the verge of losing one of its biggest key accounts because it did not have a presence in India. For almost a year, it scouted for a partner among local agencies. But these were already aligned with other international agencies or held competing key accounts, raising the issue of conflict of interest.
>
> It finally poached a rising star who was appointed managing director for the parent company's wholly owned subsidiary.
>
> Since then, the Indian subsidiary has added many local key accounts and is today a money-making company able to repatriate profits to headquarters.

- R&D and global sales alliances;
- production-cum-R&D investment.

A growing number of EU/US companies are conscious that they must strengthen their presence in the megamarkets to attain leadership. Production-oriented options may be time-consuming and resource-intensive in the beginning but are justified by the significant expansion of the company's footprint in the megamarket. Local production allows the EU player to customize solutions and align products to local specifications, deliver on time, and provide individualized after-sales support and on-site engineering. EU/US companies can avoid over-engineering their products after their local teams assess the real needs and buying preferences of customers.

There are many forms of penetration through FDI (see box 10.4). The final choice depends on expected profitability, which is determined by market forces and the company's core competences.

Box 10.4. FDI modes for megamarket expansion.

- Assembly
- New production site (greenfield)
- Refurbishing of existing production site (brownfield)
- Strategic alliance in a functional area
- Joint venture as a separate legal entity
- Acquisition of a majority or minority stake
- 100% takeover
- Merger

Pause for thought

Famous EU brands such as Grundig (consumer electronics), Zündapp (motorcycles), Grohe (sanitary equipment), Fendt (tractors), and Walter Bau (construction) have ceased to exist or have been acquired as they failed to understand the requirements of customers including those in newly emerging large markets.

***

An Austrian building materials producer planned to enter the Indian market through a greenfield investment. Neither an acquisition nor an alliance was realistic as the industry was populated by only micro players. The company opted for a greenfield solution, but the team of young expatriates could not set up the first factory within the planned time frame; the entire plan to set up new plants in the main regions, as announced by the board, was compromised.

An innovative option to partner with companies in related sectors (other building materials, construction companies, developers) that were willing to enter a new field of business was dismissed. These companies would have brought to the table their contacts, and, very important, their human resources (the industry is handicapped by a shortage of engineers and skilled operatives).

Many investments in the megamarkets fail to take off because senior management lacks creativity and the time to study and compare alternative options.

A greenfield investment, for example, can become a doubtful choice in an industry controlled by oligopolistic supply structures. The acquisition of a competitor is then a better choice, provided the target's management shares the same philosophy and represents a strategic fit.

10.2.1. The strategic alliance route

Strategic alliances can take many forms (see box 10.5), ranging from cooperation in a specific functional area (sales, after-sales service) to the creation of a newly incorporated joint enterprise with varying degrees of participation (minority, fifty-fifty, majority). Alliances can start with a low investment (loose collaboration) and become more intense as business expands and the partners gain confidence in each other. Companies may first forge an alliance and then switch to other investment modes such as greenfield plants and other acquisitions in a joint effort. Strategic alliances can involve partners at the same level (competitors) or different levels in the value chain (producers in identical or related markets, suppliers, customers, distributors). Cooperation resulting from the sale of shares in an existing company also leads to joint activities, but by definition, this type of transaction is considered an acquisition rather than an alliance (see the next section).

Megamarket complexities prompt EU/US executives to look for cooperation partners before opting for stand-alone solutions or acquisitions. When choosing between M&A and alliances, some companies prefer alliances because post-merger integrations in the megamarkets are considered an insurmountable challenge. This may be shortsighted as alliances often have as many coordination issues as integration, yet control and decision-making are frequently less clear. Nevertheless, the decision to enter into an alliance instead of an outright acquisition may be appropriate when the investor only needs a specific function, product, or other capability of the local partner firm. This entry route may be a way of "testing the waters," assessing how well the two sides can work together before engaging in a merger.

To function well, alliances must be based on complementary competences of the two partners, which guarantee future synergies. They imply the coexistence of two separate identities without either of the partners losing its independence whilst jointly running a separate joint venture company. The objective is not to integrate the partner into a formal frame (enterprise or group) or to subjugate its identity, as is the case of majority acquisitions. Strategic alliances are long-term in nature, which distinguishes them from financial participations where the investor's main concern is its exit once profitability has reached a target level.

Box 10.5. Types of strategic alliances.
- Partnerships (to optimize specific business functions)
- Minority joint ventures
- 50:50 joint ventures
- Majority joint ventures

Different motivations drive companies to form alliances:
- risk reduction through shared costs in complex markets;
- economies of scale, synergies, and learning effect;
- technology swaps;
- greater market weight to withstand competition;
- overcoming of administrative/political barriers;
- long-term cooperation to achieve common goals.

Strategic alliances with megamarket enterprises, particularly collaborative and equity joint ventures, have been a popular entry route into remote markets where local support is useful for lobbying a company's interests with public bodies and for adjusting marketing efforts. Until the mid-1990s, foreign investors faced strict licensing procedures to manufacture goods (India) or were forced into joint ventures with local players in key industries (China, Soviet Union). Megamarket industrial policies were aimed at restricting the influence of multinationals and protecting domestic players who enjoyed infant industry status. China's political establishment distinguishes between cooperative joint ventures (CJV, or loose collaborations without financial participation of the foreign partner, usually accompanied by licensing arrangements) and equity joint ventures (EJV, or alliances with financial participation). These policies were more or less abandoned with the rising competitiveness of domestic enterprises, market opening, and global integration of factors of production starting from the early 2000s, but also owing to WTO regulations. Today, all possible FDI routes, including the creation of wholly owned subsidiaries, are permitted, with the exception of strategic industries (e.g., automobile sector in China, insurance in India, banking in Russia), which are governed by the joint venture rule obliging foreigners to take local partners, and of sectors of national interest (e.g., energy, natural resources, space, defense), which are closed altogether to foreign influence.

Many joint ventures are motivated by the need, mostly of medium-sized companies, to reduce costs and risk. A joint venture is generally less costly and the payback period is shorter than with other forms of FDI; but long-term expansion can be hampered by a partner which pursues its own agenda. A few rules apply to successful strategic alliances with megamarket players:
- The combined strength gives the coalition a competitive advantage that neither partner would have gained by itself.
- The two partners are of similar size and bring equal strengths (e.g., financial/technological strength against market knowledge); neither partner dominates.
- The probability that any partner becomes a future competitor should be low.
- The commitment of decision-makers and mutual trust are essential attributes for both sides.
- Both partners must ensure that there is a young generation of managers to continue the cooperation.
- Reciprocal sources of knowledge, skills, and learning can be tapped.
- Both sides show cultural sensitivity to prevent mentality clashes.

But joint ventures can also break up. Back in the early 2000s, many managers had proudly stated that their companies were on a growth trajectory only to admit a few years later that they had separated from local partners who had set up competing units.

Joint ventures are difficult to manage and control in the megamarkets, especially when one of the partners is not willing to commit the required resources or pursues other goals. In India, the joint venture partner can establish a separate subsidiary in the same industry provided the Indian partners submit a no-objection certificate. The goal of partnerships is to use synergies to make $1 + 1 = 3$, but the reality is that they mostly produce less than 2, often because of cultural conflict at the management level rather than faulty business logic. Personal factors play a greater role than contractual arrangements. Cultural undercurrents—i.e., the soft side of the business, which can easily derail partnerships—must be managed tactfully. There should be a match of philosophy and value systems among top management of both sides, including their attitude toward employees, customers, innovation, and future generations. The

---

Pause for thought

Danone, France's food giant, filed a lawsuit against its former Chinese partner Wahaha, who operates eleven plants producing identical products, for using the same brand name in violation of the exclusivity agreement with Danone. In 2007, when all mediation efforts failed, the Chinese partner's CEO resigned in the midst of confusing statements by the Chinese side. In December 2007, the two partners agreed to settle the issue out of court through negotiations.

MAN, a leading German truck maker, has failed to build strong partnerships in Belarus/Russia and China where it thought joint ventures would make market entry smoother and less costly.

BMW's experiences in the megamarkets are almost identical. Know-how leakage from its joint manufacturing platforms with Chinese competitors has resulted in a copy being exhibited at European car shows. Or put simply, the local partner will push its own products and not those of the foreign company.

In another case, a famous German truck components producer ended up being one among many partners baited by a powerful Chinese entrepreneur whose hidden agenda was to build an advanced automotive supply cluster based on foreign technology through a series of joint ventures. The joint venture became a black hole for management's time and resources.

Strangely, all foreign JV partners accepted three unfavorable conditions imposed by their Chinese partners (they would probably never have done so in a Western context): (a) minority or equal shareholding although the technology came from the Germans, (b) investment in a local company devoted to many foreign partners at the same time, and (c) investment in a legal entity where part of the ownership is held by "non-active" employee-shareholders, with the consequence that idle partners share the control without contributing to the JV. This situation allowed the Chinese company to play off the different foreign partners against one another. With time, the Chinese side's bargaining power had become so strong that it managed to extract continuously more funding for expansion projects, making it even more powerful.

There are numerous such joint ventures also in India, where local players have altogether come out stronger than their European counterparts, who now increasingly resort to the wholly owned subsidiary route by buying out their partners.

diplomacy of intermediaries knowing both sides and their respective cultures and priorities can facilitate overcoming misunderstandings, but eventually the two sides must be able and willing to establish friendly relations and meet the main requirements that can reduce the risk of failure (see box 10.6).

In earlier days, foreign partners provided capital, knowledge, jobs, and access to international markets. Local partners opened the doors to the labor market, customers, and regulatory authorities in a fast-growing economy. Nowadays, neither side of this bargain is as attractive as it was, for four reasons:

- Megamarket companies have outperformed their Western rivals in many industries. They have become financially strong and have their own technology base or have found other ways of acquiring it (e.g., manufacturers of equipment and capital goods).
- Investor-friendly policies of megamarket governments obviate the need for a local partner, especially if the foreign investor has deep pockets and has the staying power to carve out its own market share.

Box 10.6. Risk minimization in megamarket joint ventures.

Requirement No. 1: COMMON VISION

- The two sides must share the same goals, aspirations, and priorities, which should not only aim at good financial performance, but should include intangibles such as good corporate citizenship and high morale of management and employees.
- Their priorities (acceptable, desirable, nonnegotiable) for the issues at stake should also match.

Requirement No. 2: COMPLEMENTARY STRENGTHS

- There should be little overlap in products, technologies, and applications.
- The synergies in terms of product portfolios, technical know-how, finance, and markets that mutually reinforce competences should be noticed by the competition.
- An alliance is successful if the combined force of both partners leads to a new positioning in the industry.

Requirement No. 3: SENIOR MANAGEMENT DEVOTION

- Senior executives of the two companies should devote their efforts to the success of the joint venture (third company), rather than the interests of their individual companies.
- The management team of the joint venture must be empowered by both sides. Its loyalty should be first to the joint operation, rather than the parent organizations.
- The management should concentrate on increasing the size of the pie, rather than dispute over the parents' shares of the pie.

Requirement 4: CONTROL MECHANISMS

- Progress of the venture should be tracked regularly in terms of financial, technical, and commercial performance indicators.
- There should be regular exchange of people and views to ensure that the initial enthusiasm is not lost and that differences and misunderstandings are timely removed.

> **Pause for thought**
>
> *A European mechanical components maker had formed a joint venture with a Chinese enterprise in the same field of business. The foreign investor realized after many years that profits were being siphoned off to the Chinese parent company, which was operating under a newly created holding. The foreign company had no possibility of influencing decisions by these superimposed structures and stopped transferring know-how to the joint venture for fear that it would be used against it by the holding, which was becoming a fierce competitor in the market.*

- Megamarket companies have become nationalistic and not willing to share their local contacts and markets; they prefer to pursue their own global ambitions.
- Foreign investors are also wary of sharing knowledge and international markets with local partners for fear of creating competitors.

However, if certain principles or prerequisites are taken into account, the chances of success can be increased (see table 10.1). Better results are achieved if the foreign partner keeps at least a slight majority in the venture and the board of directors. Each partner may appoint either the managing director or the financial director, who acts as vice managing director. Both partners should together select and supervise the directors for marketing and sales, purchasing, finance, and human resources. Certain caveats need to be taken into consideration when undertaking alliances in the megamarkets (see table 10.2).

In China, state-owned companies are at times subject to opaque decision-making mechanisms and government interference. Complex structures of holdings and sub-companies must be vetted carefully before any investment is made.

Similar problems can arise with private companies. Russia and India saw the rise of diversified family empires. These structures ventured into new and promising businesses, and one of the ways of shortening the learning curve was to form alliances with foreign partners who possessed the required know-how. Before Indian companies ventured into acquiring companies abroad as a direct route to know-how, many had multiplied alliances

Table 10.1. Prerequisites for successful alliances in megamarkets.

Western partner	Megamarket partner
Technological leadership in processes including robotics, systems, IT.	Good standing in local market.
Experienced and open-minded management.	Distribution network in megamarket.
Qualified employees.	Quality production premises and modern equipment.
Product innovation, R&D.	Ability to absorb new technology and ideas.
Service philosophy.	Service orientation.
Customer base and sales network in Western markets (opportunity for exports from megamarkets).	Financial strength.
High market share in home country.	Qualified managers and staff.
Good financial performance.	Transparent structure and ownership.
Logistics systems.	Support of local administration.
Understanding of local customs and traditions.	Openness and experience in foreign collaboration.

Table 10.2. Dos and don'ts in implementing strategic alliances in the megamarkets.

Dos	Don'ts
Define the goals for the venture, the legal set-up, organization, and market side.	Make the overall framework one-sided.
Conduct a thorough check of the partner and its assets.	Believe in secondary sources and rumors.
Consult an experienced auditor on profit repatriation, double taxation, royalty payment, and similar issues.	Save on commercial, legal, and financial due diligence.
Select lawyers and auditors independently.	Use lawyers and auditors associated with or suggested by the partner.
Include in the JV contract: an exit clause, right of first refusal, definition of sales territories, appointment of key executives, rights and responsibilities.	Underestimate time for management to study the contract and build a personal relationship with the partner.
Determine required future capital outlays, project financing, and profit distribution in consultation with the partner.	Leave decisions on crucial decisions for a later stage.
Invest in a high-caliber managing director who represents the investor's interests.	Recruit without background checks and several rounds of interviews.
Protect trademarks and patents (technology transfer can be paid via royalties from JV).	Hope that worldwide registration of intellectual property is automatically recognized and accepted by megamarket players.
Engage in the supervision of the venture. Agree with partner on the establishment and content of a performance monitoring system.	Leave the operation of the venture to the megamarket partner.
Accept that all knowledge and relevant contacts are not available in-house no matter how qualified the managers are.	Reject without deeper study the expertise of external specialists; neglect to screen advisers.

at home with different foreign partners. The risk for the foreign company was that it became one among many, and the local company was too dispersed to devote time and resources to the venture.

This also happens with many SOEs in China. Frictions arise once the Western firm understands that its intentions (e.g., retention and reinvestment of earnings in the venture) are not shared by the local counterpart. The biggest danger occurs when the financial performance, track record, intentions, and business practices of the alliance partner are not checked carefully before the start of the venture (see box 10.7).

> **Box 10.7. Alliance valuation criteria.**
> - Strategic, technological, and cultural fit
> - Congruence of objectives
> - Level and nature of contribution expected
> - Clear idea of promising pilot project
> - Structure and size
> - Matching financial strength
> - Complementary market reach
> - Willingness to develop new products for the megamarket
> - Viable exit formula

10.2.2. The greenfield/brownfield route

Since the late 1990s, megamarket governments have allowed the establishment of wholly owned enterprises (WOEs) and accepted majority acquisitions by foreign players in most industries. This has resulted in numerous new plants, corporate restructurings, and technology transfers. Moreover, China and India have established special economic zones (SEZs) that attract important investments through tax incentives and administrative support.[4] Russia will soon launch a dozen or so SEZs starting from 2007.

Investing in plants can take two forms:
- greenfield: new plant construction on land purchased or leased by the foreign investor;
- brownfield: purchase and restructuring of a secondhand plant formerly owned and run by another manufacturer (seller), usually but not necessarily in the same or similar sphere of business.

Decisions concerning greenfield projects follow the same pattern as other forms of investment (alliances, M&A). The first rule is to compare several options for site selection, preferably after surveying potential customers. A detailed study supplies information on location advantages, land prices, ownership laws, zoning plans, building sites, ownership issues, infrastructure (roads, water, gas and power supply), taxation, labor laws, availability of workers and specialists, supplier proximity, and possible financial support from the local authorities.

Real estate agents can help with the preselection, but the company's project team must ensure that it gives detailed specifications for the company's requirements. Future business partners or hired executives alone cannot judge the suitability of a location; they may also have subjective preferences (e.g., location close to their residences) or may not be able to visualize the project as viewed by the investor (e.g., low cost versus quality).

Government authorities can also skew decisions on site selection. The Chinese government wants to narrow the development gap between different regions, and it has announced a series of incentives to encourage foreign investment in central and western China. However,

---

Pause for thought

The Mumbai-Pune axis in western India has become a magnet for industrial investments, particularly for engineering goods. A European engineering company seeking a suitable location for its factory was first misled by the partner it was negotiating with, who preferred a low-priced location close to his "part of the town"; later, it had to contend with its country manager, who had to be convinced that the company preferred to pay a higher price to be in a prime industrial belt along the main highway as it would be easier to transport the voluminous equipment.

A Spanish building materials producer faced a similar problem in Russia. Eventually, it found an appropriate industrial site, which now gives it better prospects for future expansion.

---

4. Tax incentives for foreign investors will gradually be abolished in China following a new initiative by Commerce Minister Bo Xilai to create a level playing field and introduce a uniform tax rate of 25% for both foreign (formerly 15%) and domestic (formerly 33%) enterprises. See "China kassiert mehr von Investoren" [China expects more from investors], *Handlesblatt,* March 16–18, 2007.

the foreign investors find themselves isolated from ports, suppliers, and customers, which adds to their costs. There have been cases also in India where foreign investors were lured into earmarked areas run by the regional "Industrial Development Corporations" through apparent tax benefits and other incentives, but in the end found themselves in unfavorable locations with respect to customer proximity, availability of specialists, and land ownership (lease vs. freehold).

Land ownership and zoning should be carefully considered. In India, a foreign investor can own land to build a factory, office, guest house, and residences for its employees. But zoning laws must be respected: factories cannot be built on what is purported to be agricultural land. To increase industrial space, the government is converting agricultural land to industrial land. In China, on the other hand, landholders do not actually own the land; rather, they hold the right to use the land. This right is either allocated or granted. Allocated rights are not transferable or leasable, but the period of use is not limited. Granted rights can be mortgaged, but they are limited to a certain period of time. It is therefore important to scrutinize the contract with the land administration department. In Russia, with its wide territory, well-negotiated leases (which are less costly than bought land) give a company practically the same rights and security as direct ownership, especially if the factory/warehouse buildings belong to the investor.

There can be steep differences in land prices depending on the location. Ideally, an investor should purchase land where the prices are still low, for example, by anticipating strong demand in and around high-growth cities. If an opportunity arises, the investor should buy a bigger plot than required to secure space for future expansion. Across the three megamarkets, land prices have skyrocketed in the main agglomerations since 2000 and will continue to do so in the coming years. In China, for example, they have already gone up three- to fourfold in all the leading SEZs as a result of massive FDI inflows. In attractive second-tier coastal cities like Dalian, Qingdao, Ningbo, and Xiamen, prices per square meter touched US$45 in 2008, which corresponds to a 220% increase compared with four years earlier. Information obtained from existing investors will indicate the bargaining margin with the authorities. In Dalian, Ningbo, Suzhou, or Tianjin SEZs, the price paid can differ by a factor of 1 to 2.5 depending on the foreign investor's weight, its connections, and its negotiating skills. Large investors even manage to get land for free because of the promise of large-scale employment (e.g., Volkswagen engine factory in Dalian DDA). Outside organized zones in China, square meter prices can range from US$10 to US$25. Coastal areas are, in general, far more expensive than interior regions.

In Russia, too, the steep price hikes in and around Moscow and St. Petersburg have now spread to second-tier cities (e.g., Kazan, Nizhni Novgorod, Rostov, Samara, Volgograd, Yekaterinburg). The Moscow region, where a growing number of plants are being transferred, has a total area of 47,000 square kilometers, with roughly 7 million inhabitants living in a dozen or so medium-sized cities whose populations range from 100,000 to 300,000 inhabitants. In these cities (e.g., Yegorevsk, Zelenograd, Krasnagorsk, Dmitrov), prices for secondhand plants have shot up by 300%–500% during 2003–2008. Land prices have also risen dramatically. Moreover, sellers are switching from US dollars to euros in search of exchange-related windfall profits, thus increasing the burden for investors. Having local guidance can help an investor save money. A German investor bought

Table 10.3. Office leases in megamarket capitals, 2002, 2008.

	Medium (US$ per m²/year)	Premium (US$ per m²/year)
Beijing	2002: 150 2008: 320	2002: 350 2008: 800
Delhi	2002: 100 2008: 340	2002: 300 2008: 760
Moscow	2002: 100 2008: 400	2002: 350 2008: 1,100

Source: Knight Frank.

a majority stake in a local food-processing company. When the partners had to decide on an expansion plan, the Russian team negotiated a very low lease with the local authorities for a period of ten years with automatic extension. Buying additional land would have cost much more.

India is facing an identical situation fueled by a real estate boom, which has reached all the major cities. Previously much cheaper than the other two megamarkets, India is now closing the gap and gradually approaching the price levels in China and Russia. In first-tier cities Mumbai, Delhi, Kolkata, Bangalore, and Chennai, it is almost impossible to find a good location at a reasonable price, compelling companies to invest in more remote areas up to 100 kilometers away. Prices for office space, warehouses, and assembly units are already higher in second-tier cities like Pune and Hyderabad than in many European capitals. These price levels are gradually spreading to third-tier cities like Indore, Nashik, and Aurangabad, which are being connected with express highways. Office space is also becoming scarce in the Tier 2 and 3 cities, which are unprepared and overwhelmed by the sudden influx of foreign investors. True, in cities like Pune, Nanjing, and Kazan, prices for offices have risen faster than in the capital cities, but this is also because the latter have reached such record levels that they have started beating all expectations (and financial possibilities) of many foreign investors (see table 10.3).

Price and state incentives are not the only factors to be considered for site selection. The geographic location of customers in relation to the proposed site will impact on logistics costs. The company should be able to attract qualified key executives and skilled workers to the selected site. The biggest mistake very often made by Western managers is to focus on tax incentives and neglect market acceptance and access. Attracted by tax holidays, they select a location without being assured of business from a single customer. Or they may choose a site only because another affiliated company or a compatriot company has also invested in the area. "Me-too" decisions are the root cause for errors in greenfield investments. Few enterprises are guided by managers who take a route distinct from the mainstream. Unique strategies carried out by pioneers are often rewarded in the megamarkets.

A crucial element in the selection of a suitable location is the availability of managerial and other staff. Key executives will not relocate to remote locations with a low quality of life. Expatriate managers, who may be needed in the initial phases to set up a new operation,

---

Pause for thought

Smaller companies allow themselves to be led by peer experiences and their large Western customers. A large EU aeronautics company insisted that its suppliers all locate their offices on its large campus. But for security reasons, the suppliers were not allowed to carry out work for other clients at these offices. A small EU service provider therefore had to set up a separate office for its other work, which was an additional cost burden. While piggybacking on large customers can help surmount initial hurdles, it is hardly a guarantee for future business expansion.

usually come with their families. They must be certain that the new work environment offers good schools for their children and other facilities (shopping, domestic help) as well as entertainment, including sports and club life for the spouses.

While the real estate boom in the megamarkets reflects an optimistic outlook against the backdrop of a booming economy and a bullish stock market, costly greenfield investments can also bear a significant risk for an investor, especially if:

- the sector is dominated by two to three well-established players who can defend their positions through price dumping, sales cartels, or other methods;
- the project has not been planned carefully and drags on longer than expected, entailing consecutive cost overruns for building materials, leases, import logistics, equipment, IT systems, and personnel; in fast-growing economies, rapidly changing market conditions can turn a promising venture into an unprofitable one;
- the company is not networked to recruit qualified key executives or lobbyists with negotiation skills for promoting the project with the different authorities, who may hamper its progress; and
- the location has not been carefully selected; clients might be dissatisfied because the facilities are too far to ensure immediate customer service, and/or the site may be too small to allow for future expansion.

The brownfield option involves leasing or purchasing and then refurbishing existing facilities (plants, warehouses, assembly sites, stores, etc.); it has become a popular entry route for EU companies in Russia. In recent years, many local producers have developed successfully and reorganized their production; some of them are ready to sell their assets as they move on to bigger locations. Similar situations can be encountered in China and India. Asset deals can be less risky than share deals if hidden liabilities are an issue and the local brand is not significant for business expansion. On the other hand, asset deals can be subject to higher tax rates than share deals (e.g., in Russia). In India, a lump sale (fixed assets, current assets, liabilities) attracts a lower tax rate than an itemized sale.

A brownfield is worth considering if the building is in a good state, meets the technical specifications, and does not require much refurbishing. Such brownfields can reduce lead time considerably. In China, brownfield sites located outside SEZs but close to motorways can be much cheaper than setting up new units in SEZs, where costs for water, electricity, and heating have risen faster than in sites outside the zones. Brownfield sites can also be an interesting option for retailers who cannot find good premises for their stores. One advantage of brownfields is that they do not add to the existing overcapacity, especially in China.

In Russia, certain local administrations[5] assist investors in identifying free areas (greenfield) and existing production facilities (brownfield). In China and India, authorities also help but mainly in well-defined areas (e.g., SEZ, state-owned industrial parks). Otherwise, investors usually rely on real estate agents. There are no fixed rules as small agents may come up with better options than international chains (e.g., Knight Frank, Colliers, etc.). In India, some "showcase communities" (e.g., Metlakatla, AK) have started to promote sustainable economic development through brownfield clean-ups and redevelopment while restoring

---

5. Example: Yaroslavl Region, www.adm.yar.ru/english.

and protecting the community's natural resources. But their sphere of operation is limited to smaller geographical areas, which reduces the chance of attracting reputed foreign investors. At the same time, some enlightened farmers have formed "land cooperatives" that control entire clusters of land. Site development is outsourced to construction companies. The plots or built-up premises are sold, but the cooperatives, like other promoters, prefer to lease office space to ensure regular income for the future against the backdrop of steeply rising prices.

Interestingly, outward investment from the megamarkets is dominated by brownfield investments linked to the purchase of entire companies (legal entities) together with their trademarks and production facilities. Whether it is FDI in larger (e.g., Corus by Tata, Rover by SAIC) or medium-sized investments (e.g., Betapharm by Dr. Reddy), megamarket companies rarely add a greenfield capacity but rather use an existing brownfield through which they immediately start expanding. A major reason for this is that brownfield sites in AMs, no matter whether they belong to an ongoing business or a company in the process of closing down, are in a much better state than similar plants in the megamarkets. There is an overcapacity of well-kept plants, which obviates the need to set up new facilities.

10.2.3. The M&A route

When seeking a lasting presence in the megamarkets, there are a number of reasons why EU investors prefer acquisitions, takeovers, and mergers. For financially sound players, buying a local enterprise assures an immediate presence, through which they can control and use locally available resources, brands, goodwill, sales channels, and so forth. They avoid the risk of being handicapped by an incompatible joint venture partner. In industries marked by high entry barriers, the M&A route can accelerate penetration as it removes a serious competitor from the market. There are other, not less important reasons for the M&A option:

- to gain access to industries and regional markets closed to newcomers;
- to acquire managerial, engineering, and scientific talent;
- to acquire products, services, distribution, and logistics platforms in specific user segments and geographic areas;
- to acquire a local brand with a good reputation and potential;
- to gain immediate market share and, possibly, sector dominance;
- to gain control of sources of raw materials and semi-manufactures (supplier base);
- to win local tenders for the B2G and B2B markets;
- to facilitate penetration into adjacent markets.

The period between 2003 and 2007 saw a surge in M&A deals in industrialized countries; flush with new capital, companies felt the pressure to enhance shareholder value by embracing globalization to achieve economies of scale. M&A transactions reached a new high in 2007 when cross-border deals reached US$1 trillion. However, for most companies, integrating the newly acquired organizations with their distinct processes, systems, and cultural dynamics became a daunting challenge. Many deals in the megamarkets have not yielded the desired results. In the future, greater attention must be directed at:

- improvement of the M&A methodology and transaction processes[6] independent of whether the target is large or small, private or state-owned;
- verification before the transaction of the cultural and strategic fit of the two organizations, particularly of the personal characters of the owners, their perceptions, values, goals, management systems, and leadership styles, which may be accentuated by the legacy of the two companies;
- constant improvements by the acquirer following the transaction to achieve greater market strength, technological leadership, greater process efficiency, and higher profitability;
- human resource development and talent-building in both companies; and
- larger market share and long-term stability rather than short-term benefits for shareholders.

M&As in the megamarkets can be initiated by the buyer or the seller. The five most frequent types of transactions involving EU investors are:

- the EU company initiates a search and identifies and selects a suitable candidate in the megamarket;
- a state-owned enterprise in a megamarket invites global bids for a planned privatization;
- a private megamarket company looks for a buyer as it cannot compete in an industry dominated by larger rivals;
- MBOs and MBIs are initiated whereby existing managers (buy-out) or an external team (buy-in) acquire a controlling stake in a megamarket company, possibly with the support of a foreign strategic/financial partner;
- a hostile takeover attempt by a foreign buyer; this approach can provoke the intervention of public authorities to protect a target of national interest.

Depending on the degree of control, acquisitions can be grouped under six categories (see table 10.4). Control in the first five categories can also be scaled up gradually and each phase linked to performance criteria (sales, profits, achievements).

Acquisitions bear a number of dangers, which can be minimized by widening the analysis to all leading players in the industry without limiting the investigation to one or two random targets known by chance to the acquiring company's management. When approaching possible candidates in megamarkets, the EU/US company should be cautious and observe a few important rules:

- Decision-makers. Executives from the acquiring company must be experienced and exhibit a good understanding of how the target will react to integration.

Table 10.4. Types of M&As in the megamarkets.

Minority, non-blocking	<25%
Minority, with own blocking right	>25% up to 50%
Parity	50%
Majority, simple	51%–74%
Majority, with limited blocking right of local partner	>75%
Outright acquisition	100%

---

6. See chapter 11.

Top management of the target company should be approached discreetly by neutral persons with direct access to decision-makers and familiar with the corporate culture and mentality of both sides. Various stakeholders (banks, suppliers, customers) and even public bodies should be interviewed to understand the target's true motivations to sell, interests to stay in the business, and possible successors. The owner of a privately owned target may have little interest in staying on once a good price is negotiated, or the owner may prefer to keep a minority stake and continue managing the company. Whether these attitudes are advantageous will depend on the acquirer's game plan and management resources. A state-owned target may focus on social and political aspects as well as the future position of the company's CEO.

- Strategic rationale. A strategic concept to combine two companies should state how the merged enterprise will be able to accomplish what neither company could achieve alone. Unfortunately, a strategic rationale is often drawn up after the fact. Extra care should be taken to analyze the rationale when a deal is initiated by an intermediary (investment bank, auditor, consultant, political figure). Intermediaries may attempt to initiate and push through deals that benefit them more than the acquirer. An acquisition will succeed if the strategic concept mobilizes synergies for long-term expansion in terms of employment, technology input, financial support, and markets. The concept must accommodate the vision of the target.

- Value orientation. The biggest hurdle is the question of who will be in charge after the transaction. Many deals promote the interests of previous owners and the careers of executives rather than raise the value of the combined companies to provide a future for the employees and stakeholders. Acquisition projects differ depending on the ownership and legal form of the company to be acquired. Acquiring a state-owned enterprise can be a time-consuming exercise, demanding political lobbying to accelerate the process. Both local and federal authorities must be kept in the loop. The legacy of the enterprise must be handled carefully when reforms are introduced post acquisition.

- Role of competition. The acquirer must be aware of the different roles and motivations of strategic and financial investors. Financial investors can outbid their rivals with cash, especially when the target company is highly profitable and has the potential to be consecutively listed on the stock exchange via an IPO. Conversely, strategic investors are keen on long-term business development as they understand the industry and can help to fill management, technology, and knowledge gaps. Strategic investors can be less than ideal partners if their policies are not clearly documented or if they hesitate to make commitments on how the acquired company/brand will be supported following a deal. There have been cases where strategic investors (especially large multinationals) have acquired targets with the objective to remove a local competitor, resulting in large-scale layoffs and the closing of research centers to cut costs and improve short-term results. Because of such cases, megamarket authorities are careful before granting permissions, which are again checked by anti-monopoly bodies in the three countries.

- Post-acquisition integration. Acquirers either prefer to completely and quickly assimilate a target (to avoid a lengthy integration) or to leave the acquired unit autonomous (to avoid disrupting existing systems and processes). While both strategies bypass severe integration tensions, they also hamper value creation. Some form of blending has to take place to create a new entity. It would be a mistake to remove well-connected managers of the acquired firm immediately, unless they have a bad track record.

Table 10.5. Benefits and risks of megamarket M&As.	
Benefits of M&A	**Risks of M&A**
Advantage of immediately operating an ongoing business with management, staff, organizational set-up, physical plant, facilities, customer base.	Legacy of target company, challenge of integration; negative reaction of employees and other stakeholders if the foreign investor does not present a convincing expansion plan; possible restrictions by authorities.
Fast market penetration because of existing distribution network and customers.	High failure rate due to misreading of intercultural and language factors during transaction and integration.
Immediate use of reputation, brand, and goodwill of acquired company.	Negative reaction to the foreign acquirer's brand equity.
Removal of a competitor, who becomes a partner once the transaction and integration have been completed.	Difficult post-merger integration, if the partner has different views on the way forward.

The most successful acquisitions are those where the investor has a profound knowledge of and respect for the target country, industry, main players, legal systems, and political entities.[7] Such "strategic" acquisitions can offer significant benefits over other types of FDI, but they are not without risks (see table 10.5), which, however, can be handled with the right mindset and approach by the acquirer.

A majority acquisition signifies the purchase of more than 50% of the shares of the target. For medium-sized players, it may be advantageous to keep the previous owners plus important managers in the business as minority partners with a shareholding of 20%–45% (of which, 5%–10% for managers) depending on the transaction value and the involvement of the owner of the target company. Local partners understand the business context and customer expectations much better, also in other emerging markets. They can ensure a smooth integration of local staff and the retaining of valuable customer, supplier, and logistics networks. Whenever the previous owner stays on as a partner, the following points should be taken into consideration to reduce conflicts:

- The EU investor, as the stronger partner, should not hide behind a smaller local target with restricted financial and technological possibilities. If the partners are more or less equal in size, the foreign company should strive for either a simple majority (51%) or a majority offering the target a minority blocking right.
- If the owners of the acquired entity stay on to run the business for some time, they should be treated with respect and dignity, not as mere "executors of orders" from headquarters. Conflicts are inevitable when managers of the acquiring company treat the acquired entity as a mere supplier without offering it a growth perspective.
- If the acquisition is not an outright (100%) purchase but an equity participation, the agreement with the remaining local partner should include an exit clause, and the EU investor should ensure that it has the right of first refusal.
- The EU investor should stress proper governance based on a well-conceived and equitable code of conduct.
- The EU investor, as majority shareholder, should show commitment through timely allocation of funds for additional investments (e.g., plant expansion, equipment) and the recruitment of fresh talent.

---

7. China, India, and Russia have FDI laws that regulate the activities of foreign investors in respective industries.

- There should be strict financial control by the majority investor through the board of directors (which should convene more often than stipulated at least during the initial period) and by assigning a full-time coordinator, controller, or financial director for introducing checks and balances; this should be stipulated in the bylaws (articles of association).
- The foreign investor should gain full insight into marketing, sales, and distribution activities and not leave them entirely to the local management.
- The revised bylaws should highlight the rights and duties of the shareholders, provided these are not covered already by the country's respective company laws; important issues are the approach on international markets (splitting, central coordination; joint marketing and sales), the future use of the two companies' brands (two-brand, one-brand, or combined-brand policy), and reporting mechanisms (to ensure that shareholders receive quarterly financials according to international norms).
- A neutral person who enjoys the trust of both parties should be appointed to the board of directors; this person can serve as mediator and coach for a turnaround.

A foreign investor may also prefer or be compelled to enter with a minority share at first and scale up its stake as the relationship develops and financial results of the merged entity improve. This option can be agreed upon contractually if the owners of a family business on the seller's side want to see the new partner's commitment (new clients, transfer of technology, contribution to fresh investments) and performance before ceding further equity. This situation may occur also if a foreign investor decides to acquire a state-owned company in a sensitive area that enjoys special protection by local authorities. Here, the share purchase agreement (SPA) can stipulate that know-how from the investor will be transferred proportionately with the level of its shareholding until it reaches a majority stake of at least 51%. In case of incremental investment, continuity in leadership, as well as supplier and customer relations should always be maintained. Shareholders should ensure that professional management is in place before major changes in the share structure are undertaken. Mutual trust between the foreign and local partners and congruity of objectives and strategy[8] are key factors of success during and after the joint enterprise. Once shares have been entirely transferred, former partners may stay in the board to guarantee smooth transition.

Many combinations are possible in terms of initial and final stakes. Investors who plan a rapid integration of the target in their global sales and supply networks should negotiate a majority stake straightaway as changes may be difficult to impose at a later stage. The recent case of a European cement producer who acquired 26% (with a 49% option

> **Pause for thought**
>
> *When a Russian technology concern became a majority stakeholder in an Austrian SME, it was agreed that the founder would stay with the company as managing director for at least five more years. The Russian foreign investor thus ensured continuity and reassured the employees of its good intentions (no layoffs, expansion, global ambition).*

---

8. The megamarket partner may pursue a strategy of profit maximization for his local enterprise (despite a minority stake) while the foreign investor seeks to eliminate a former competitor and preserve jobs at headquarters.

within four years) of a listed company in China bears three risks: (a) crucial know-how may be transferred too early, reducing the motivation for the Chinese side to sell additional stakes, (b) numerous shareholders may have to be convinced to adopt the future strategy, which is even more difficult when a company is listed (to avoid such a situation, public bodies or tycoons may buy up a significant number of shares in a hostile takeover), and (c) the local management could switch from an entrepreneurial to an employee mode as the former founders gradually dispose of their shares and responsibilities. Similar minority investments in the beer and financial sectors in China did not bring good results either. That is why many large Western and Russian companies have a strict policy not to engage in M&A negotiations if they cannot acquire a majority or once the target has filed an IPO.

If the foreign investor is obliged to accept a minority stake, it should know the implications, especially the minimum stake necessary to ensure oneself a blocking minority right (26% in Russia, 26% in India, 30% in China). Financial investors accept minority acquisitions more easily as they envisage an exit within five years or once the target has reached a predetermined level of profitability. Minority stakes can have benefits and risks for the investor (see table 10.6). Normally, a minority investment can be considered a strategic partnership if the contract stipulates that the acquirer has the possibility of raising its stake toward parity or majority on certain conditions (good financial results, transfer of knowledge).

Table 10.6. Majority vs. minority acquisitions: Pros and cons.

a. Pros of majority acquisitions	a. Cons of majority acquisitions
Acquisition of a controlling stake in a reputed company with high brand visibility.	Partner stays in the company and blocks decisions without bearing the bulk of the investment (minority blocking right).
High return on investment if the target company is profitable.	Partner may have different views of profit distribution and capital injection as these may dilute the partner's share.
Easier to integrate a target or turn it around if the investor has a majority stake.	Integration mismanaged by investor's managers or blocked by minority shareholder.
Lower risk of knowledge leaks and misuse because of majority or full control.	In case of blocking minority, risk of knowledge misuse by partner for its own interests.
Preferable if previous owners stay and continue their success story.	Difficulties in replacing management, if former owners have a firm standing in the market and investor lacks connections.
b. Pros of minority acquisitions	**b. Cons of minority acquisitions**
Acquisition of stakes in a reputed foreign company with a relatively low investment.	No possibility of influencing strategic decisions.
High return on a low investment, if the target posts good results.	A minority stake does not protect from intellectual property rights (IPR) infringement and the disclosure of business secrets.
Possibility of checking out target company with a low investment before committing a high investment.	The minority partner is considered as a mere financial investor, of no consequence and weight, unlike a strategic investor who acquires a majority because it understands the business.
Entry barriers can be raised for competitors by acquiring a minority share at first with the option to increase the stake at a later stage.	Competitors outstrip the investor by acquiring a majority stake of a local competitor.
Low involvement and commitment of scarce human resources.	The investor does not have the power to bring about changes.
Possibility of entering restricted sectors with foreign investment caps.	Policy changes for removal of caps may take time and require aggressive lobbying; meanwhile the investor will have to part with intellectual property to compete with local companies.

Market leaders prefer to take over seriously run companies with sound leadership principles and corporate culture. Good results are achieved when acquisitions happen after a long and close cooperation between partners who know each other well already. As a rule, smaller firms are more easily integrated than large conglomerates, especially if they formerly belonged to the state. Generally speaking, negotiations are easier with strategic investors as they understand the business and how to lift it to new levels in partnership with a local firm. As a result of the financial crisis, which hit the major economies in 2008–2009, financial investors suffered a serious setback in the megamarkets in terms of funding (owing to sharply reduced credit lines from banks) and image.

10.3. Options for combined FDI

Megamarkets offer a vast range of possibilities to foreign investors. A winning expansion concept may consist of an inventive mix of M&As and other investment modes, which can be implemented sequentially or simultaneously, depending on available opportunities and the investor's financial clout. Examples are aplenty. Successful organic growth, for example, through a series of greenfield projects can result in additional partnerships and acquisitions because of regular peer contacts in the industry. A state-owned company may wish to divest from a smaller unit whose management team decides to merge with an experienced foreign player and together acquire the assets of the SOE. Leveraged buy-outs (LBOs), either investor-led or management-initiated, are often used by local or overseas Chinese investors to acquire "mainland" companies. Indian and Russian investors have also been involved in such transactions by utilizing a high level of debt to buy the target company, in most cases the cash they borrowed using the target's assets (asset-based lending) and cash flows. LBOs have been more popular in capital-intensive industries that have assets that can be used as collateral for debt; they haven't taken place as often in project-based (e.g. IT, construction) or service industries where there are fewer fixed assets. Western participation in such deals depends on the confidence levels acquired with local managers who can be useful in studying local conditions and organizing permits and funding. In high-tech industries (pharmaceuticals, specialty chemicals, telecom) investors may appoint importer-distributors while simultaneously invest in their own local R&D and logistics facilities to get closer to megamarket key accounts.

Many "hybrid" FDI options are possible, and there is no limit to creativity when conceiving a suitable combination of investment modes (see box 10.8).

Project work in the megamarkets shows that many FDI-based deals and transactions fail to create any additional value. The premium paid for shares and/or assets is very often much higher than the value generated by the transaction. FDI projects in the megamarkets can be very complex, and even insiders find it difficult to assess the real prospects and to determine if a deal will add value. Failures are mostly due to people-related issues and the strong egos of managers on both sides. Lack of vision by chief coordinators at headquarters, loss of key personnel, culture shock, poor communication, and limited readiness to share knowledge and information are common reasons for disaster.

True market leaders demonstrate organizational flexibility and respect for the other culture. They pursue, together with their local partners, coherent goals based on a vision to exploit

> **Box 10.8. Options for combined FDI.**
> - Alliance followed by greenfield
> - Greenfield (manufacturing, logistics, R&D facilities) in combination with M&A
> - Alliance (JV) and successive M&A
> - Brownfield combined with greenfield investment
> - M&A in combination with MBI after divestment of SOE
> - Simultaneous M&As in suppliers and competitors
> - Minority M&A with gradual build-up toward majority M&A
> - Minority M&As in rivals coupled with greenfield investments
> - Combined leveraged buyout (LBO): financial investor with internal management (MBI) and/or external management (MBO)
> - External management LBO
> - Triangular M&A with megamarket partners in selected markets
> - Cross-shareholding M&A

synergies and attain leadership. When implementing FDI/M&A projects, progressive companies look at content—i.e., complementary markets, customers, distribution channels, product lines, technologies—rather than additional sales. Totally new business areas where the company has no core competence are left aside.

The secret of well-planned investments and acquisitions is to avoid common traps (see box 10.9), to keep to essential milestones, and to make all decisions about people and the organization within a short time following a merger or takeover. The acquisition process itself is a critical factor in the deal's ultimate fate. Surprisingly, many companies destroy value not as a result of inattention to detail during the transaction but through excessive zeal in their integration efforts after the deal is completed.[9] Dragging over important decisions affecting people in the targeted company and technologies to be transferred must be avoided. Lack of direction will dishearten employees, leading to low productivity with a correlating loss in competitiveness and profitability for the acquirer.

> **Pause for thought**
>
> *The general manager of a leading German multinational recently made the following statement concerning acquisitions: "If we don't understand the market and the technology, our success rate is zero. If we understand only one aspect, either technology or market, our chance rises to 30%. If both aspects are covered, our chance is 50%. Only if we can additionally gain a competitive advantage can our chance exceed 50%.*
>
> *"FDI through M&A, alliances, and greenfield is a means to an end—not an end in itself. It must be embedded in the company's overall mission and help promote its strategic goals and objectives."*

---

9. See 11.3.

Box 10.9. Common FDI/M&A errors in the megamarkets.

- Wrong selection of due diligence team (lawyers, auditors, strategists)
- Poor negotiation of favorable terms
- Open-ended contracts with loopholes
- Neglect of local management and employees during integration
- Failure to adopt a logical, sequential approach when confronted with different mindset of the target
- Inability to understand complex taxation issues
- Lack of lobbying skills by the acquiring team
- Weak contact network in the target market
- Failure to interview key customers and suppliers about the envisaged investment
- Inability to perceive the newly created or acquired unit as an independent platform for expanding business into markets not covered by headquarters

CHAPTER 11

Transaction plan: Acquire and integrate

Investments in new markets always bear a risk, and their implications must be studied in all details. A large number of projects in the megamarkets end up with disappointing results because managers underestimate the importance of getting each step right throughout the entire FDI process—from pre-deal analysis to deal-making (transaction) and target integration. The transaction process passes through three distinct phases (see figure 11.1) regardless of the selected entry or expansion mode (M&A, alliance, stand-alone). The outcome of megamarket investment projects will depend on proper execution in each phase:

- The pre-deal assessment (intelligence) phase involves mostly analysis of the different components of the transaction to ensure that what is contemplated brings value to the investor. The challenge at this stage is the right project design, the identification of the best target and investment option, and determining the value drivers in terms of synergy and added benefits. Market leaders continuously scan important markets and can draw on this experience for evaluating possible targets across industries that are likely to converge and open new options for the FDI/M&A process.

- In the deal-making (transaction) phase, negotiations get more intense as the target is evaluated. The transaction price is determined after financial and legal due diligence of the target, including tax implications. The challenge here is to reconcile different accounting systems although stock-listed companies do follow international accounting norms. However, private limited companies and sole proprietorships—the bulk of companies in the megamarkets—may be difficult to assess. Certain parameters (goodwill, brand equity, accounts payable and receivable, inventory) may not be easy to define. Commercial and management due diligence helps to uncover hidden values and pitfalls. Negotiations revolve around what each party considers a realistic price and management for the new entity after the contemplated transaction. The most challenging parts of this phase are mentality-related issues, which further complicate the usual power play for board composition, voting rights, governance, and management control. In the case of state-owned targets, the foreign investor is confronted with superimposed authorities that may tie the sale to strict conditions in terms of know-how transfer, opening of new international markets, branding, and pricing policies.

- The post-deal integration phase starts with the closure of the transaction. Immense flexibility is required to integrate the new entity in the group. Legacy is an important factor, and human sensitivities can play a larger role as megamarket targets are often successful companies and do not accept majority shareholding and advanced market success as the sole reasons for changes in corporate practices and cultures.

Figure 11.1. The three phases of successful transactions in the megamarkets.

Type of transaction / The three phases	M&A	Strategic alliance, joint venture	Greenfield, brownfield
INTELLIGENCE (pre-deal assessment)	a. Target screening b. Identification of synergies, value drivers, deal stoppers; determination of strategic fit c. preliminary pricing ⇒ Non-disclosure or confidentiality agreement, LOI	a. Partner screening and assessment b. Study of objectives, rationale, and feasibility; defining scope of collaboration c. Preliminary investment ⇒ Non-disclosure agreement, LOI	a. Site/location screening, comparing of land prices b. Asset evaluation in case of brownfield c. purchase or lease in case of greenfield ⇒ Non-binding offer
TRANSACTION (deal making)	a. Due diligence; valuation structuring of transaction (shares, control, taxation) ⇒ Purchase offer b. Terms and conditions, price negotiation ⇒ Final agreements (share purchase agreement, statutes, management contracts) ⇒ Financial plan c. Regulatory filings including antimonopoly procedure d. Payment and share transfer	a. Due diligence; technical assessment; structuring of alliance (governance, control, taxation) ⇒ Alliance offer b. Structuring of alliance, business plan ⇒ Final agreements (JV agreement, statutes, management contracts) ⇒ Financial plan c. Government permissions d. Payment of equity, incorporation, share ownership	a. Due diligence environmental check tax planning ⇒ Purchase offer b. Title clearance ⇒ Agreement (e.g. land purchase or lease agreement, business transfer agreement in case of existing venture) ⇒ Financial plan c. Local permissions for construction d. Payment
INTEGRATION (post-deal consolidation)	a. Planning of life after acquisition b. Coordination team c. Integration plan	a. Post-alliance planning b. Joint strategy formulation and execution c. Coordination of JV activities	a. Upgrading of brownfield b. Construction at greenfield c. HR policy

Technically, these steps correspond to transactions in advanced markets, but market, sociocultural, legal, and fiscal specifics can change the nature of valuations and negotiations. Each step has deal-stoppers that have to be handled with sensitivity, soft skills, and tact at the highest decision-making levels.

Equity-based investments have an underlying algorithm that needs to be reviewed post-deal based on the steps detailed below. This feeds organizational learning so that similar risks can be reduced in future investment projects. Each deal must hinge on a strategic logic developed over time through proactive use of business intelligence. Potential new targets and FDI opportunities must be constantly monitored and observed. Such reviews also ensure that the investment project is still "on track" in delivering targeted shareholder returns.

Of the different options for EU/US companies in the megamarkets, M&As have become particularly important expansion modes in China, India, and Russia, where strong domestic players dominate entire industries and would immediately oppose any stand-alone solution from a newcomer. Multinationals that have been successful in acquiring or forging alliances with local players, and in integrating the new entity seamlessly, have a competitive edge over those who decided on mainly organic growth. Any transaction must be deeply rooted in the company's long-term strategy for that particular market and be considered as a means to attain a goal, not an end in itself. The phases elaborated below relate in particular to alliances and M&As, although transactions for greenfields or brownfields follow a similar pattern, including the indispensable post-deal integration work (e.g., management coaching, staff training).

11.1. Pre-deal assessment

Careful planning is needed for the five important milestones in this phase:
- Milestone 1: Nomination of a transaction team
- Milestone 2: Target/partner screening
- Milestone 3: Determining value drivers
- Milestone 4: Preliminary pricing
- Milestone 5: Signing of initial agreements

MILESTONE 1:
NOMINATION OF A TRANSACTION TEAM

The transaction team should be composed of specialists who understand the business mentality and socio-market context of the target. Spearhead persons should be in charge of "opening doors," i.e. establishing personal relations at a high level based on mutual trust through competence, experience and reliability. In addition to expertise in the core areas of strategy, finance, international law, taxation, and technology, the team should be knowledgeable about the language, culture, history, economics, and geopolitics of the target country. Seminars on doing business with Russia, India, and China are now quite common; some organizations also offer individual coaching in soft factors. Such familiarization will help the team greatly, especially at critical moments of the transaction. Small companies that do not have enough people can recruit external coordinators for the project, and the owners can confer with senior executives and division chiefs on the negotiation strategy.

Milestone 2:
Target/partner screening

While it is easier to identify targets in established markets and industries, for new business activities another approach must be adopted. The target in this case will in all probability be a player from a related sector who wants to diversify (toward the business that is of interest to the investor). Information on such prospects can only be obtained through skillful interviews of resource persons within the sector.

This step will require assiduous study, or else the remaining milestones will be jeopardized as they will be based on second-best options. Various investment alternatives (e.g., M&A, stand-alone) should be explored before zeroing in on the best possible option. The company should also consider what it is itself capable of achieving based on available resources (including financial means to acquire a target), what the competition is doing, and where the market is moving.

The typical ratio of viable targets to investments in China is 40–50 to 1 in consumer mass markets marked by large enterprise populations (e.g., household goods, electrical tools) and 15–20 to 1 in equipment-related industries (e.g., electrical motors, instruments). In India, it would be 20%–30% less in consumer goods and generally significantly lower in equipment-related industries. In Russia, the ratios are much lower as key industry segments are dominated by a few players.

Megamarket industry structures can be quite different from those in advanced markets. Some industries are controlled by conglomerates operating in multifarious businesses. Even family-owned SMEs may be in various types of businesses. This puzzling scenario may prompt an EU/US senior executive to pick the first possible target identified casually at a trade fair or a seminar. This would be a sure recipe for disaster because the choice is made without studying the particular business ecosystem and determining which investment alternative is the most appropriate.

The momentum of transactions in the megamarkets can be too fast for an EU/US player, particularly a small one, to pause and reflect on the choice, leaving it with a wrong partner. The same applies to greenfields. Investors are carried away by the sops offered by local governments to attract investors to second-tier areas only to find that the location is unsuitable for the business. To avoid such pitfalls, foreign companies should work with local

> **Pause for thought**
>
> *Brick-making is a micro-enterprise in India, so when a European producer of clay bricks looks for a partner, it may also have to sound out large construction companies or promoters interested in backward integration.*
>
> *The search for a bottling equipment target (an established industry) in China should cover producers catering to various segments of the market—brewery, soft drinks, dairy products, liquid cosmetics (e.g., shampoos)—and propose different types of equipment (filling, pasteurizing, washing, packaging, labeling).*

advisers who can ferret out the hidden facts through their networks and help management obtain the intelligence required for making informed decisions.

MILESTONE 3:
DETERMINING VALUE DRIVERS

In a megamarket alliance, value-drivers can remain mere concepts and declarations of "win-win" intentions if the aspirations of the other party are not correctly assessed. In China, most companies now want knowledge and access to international markets, whereas the EU/US investor seeks a local market and a low-cost production base. Very often these aspirations cannot be matched as the potential partners are not willing to share their main assets. Value in this case can be derived only if the Chinese partner opens the local market for the EU/US partner, who then shares proprietary knowledge against a guarantee that it will not be used to compete against the EU/US company in other markets. The EU/US company can use a series of proven indicators to determine the value drivers and fit of potential megamarket candidates, which have to be later confirmed through discussions with and valuation of the target (see figure 11.2).

Figure 11.2. Candidate selection based on "fits" and value drivers.

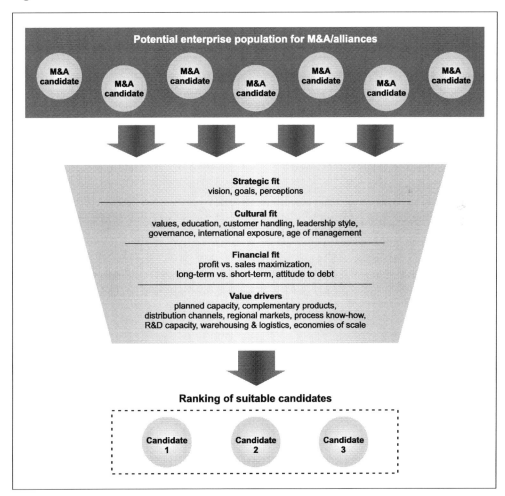

Milestone 4:
Preliminary pricing

Preliminary pricing is based on information disclosed by the other party at the outset of the project. Data sources for an assessment are the balance sheets and loss and profit accounts for the current year and the past two years, as well as forecasts for the two subsequent years, provided the company is listed or the owners agree to disclose the information prior to negotiations. If not, the value has to be determined through discussions with resource persons in the industry, upstream suppliers, or downstream distributors. In China and Russia (not in India), many non-listed firms have two sets of financial statements, one depicting the official version that is submitted to the tax authorities, the other reflecting the real situation based on unofficial accounts. Interpretation of financial statements from megamarket companies is not always accurate as the three countries have yet to implement International Financial Reporting Standards (IFRS); India will do so by 2011.

An approximate value can be calculated on the basis of actual profits generated and realistic forecasts by adopting EBITDA/EBIT and sales multipliers common to the industry (comparison with peer groups). If the target is negotiating with banks and equity partners or preparing for an IPO, the task of preliminary pricing becomes easier for the foreign investor as an evaluation usually already exists.

Milestone 5:
Signing of initial agreements

Before any exchange of confidential information, the two parties as a rule sign a non-disclosure agreement (NDA), which protects them from the disclosure of important documents to third parties but does not state any definite intentions or price ranges. If the first discussions are successful, the parties then move on to sign a letter of intent (LOI) or a memorandum of understanding (MOU) stating that they consider working toward an alliance by agreeing to common goals and certain conditions and deal parameters (see box 11.1). In case the target is on the verge of another transaction that needs to be prevented (e.g., IPO, private equity investor), the foreign buyer can submit a confirmation of interest letter or a non-binding offer (NBO), which expresses the investor's commitment, including an approximate purchase price, and ensures a period of exclusivity for carrying out the due diligence and negotiations. The substance of an NBO is more concrete than an LOI.

These initial documents normally have no direct legal implications; they set the transaction framework for future negotiations and the drafting of the definitive agreements. The text should be acceptable to both sides, inspire trust between the partners, and set the timelines and milestones until transaction closure. The documents can include an exclusivity provision with a timeline and an exit clause should the negotiations fail. An LOI describes and paves the way for subsequent steps including the due diligence, a technical evaluation if required, a value assessment of the brand, and further negotiations. The document is submitted to the boards of the two companies for approval and signature.

> **Box 11.1. Structure of an LOI for a strategic alliance.**
> 1. Background: market position and financials (sales, profits)
> 2. Declaration of intent: strategic intentions, action plan
> 3. Provisions for investment or shareholding
>   3.1 Type of preferred equity participation
>   3.2 Preliminary purchase price subject to due diligence
>   3.3 Management and governance
> 4. Further steps
>   4.1. Due diligence: start, deadline, and payment
>   4.2. Offer by acquirer and transaction closure (deadlines)
>   4.3. Expenses: who should bear the cost of the due diligence?
> 5. Exclusivity of negotiations
> 6. Confidentiality clause
> 7. Duration of LOI with exit clause
> 8. Liability
> 9. Governing law
> 10. Signatures and seal

In exceptional situations when an official evaluation report already exists, a preliminary price can be quoted in the LOI or NBO; in this case, the price should, however, be non-committal and made subject to the results of separate financial and legal due diligences conducted by independent auditors hired by the investor. Not all business partners in the megamarkets are prepared to sign detailed LOIs with tight schedules for completing the subsequent steps of the transaction. They may be afraid of not being able to meet the obligations and may interpret certain passages of the LOI as binding—i.e., having legal consequences in case of non-fulfillment. The approval of a mutually acceptable text can, in such cases, take long and nullify the effect of or delay actual negotiations. Certain companies therefore may prefer to sign only an NDA and move directly to the due diligence.

The LOI should be simple and focus on the underlying principles and ultimate goal of the venture. Procedural and other details should be consigned to a term-sheet. It is very important to explore and reach a basic understanding on the deal structure right at the outset. This includes items like:

- future management of the company;
- use of the company's brand and logo;
- products, technologies and markets;
- governance issues (existing and superseded board of directors); and
- share in equity between new and old owners as well as possible put or call options on remaining shares by the majority shareholder.

> **Pause for thought**
>
> A transaction between a Russian packaging company intending to acquire a brownfield in India and the Indian party came to a grinding halt because of serious errors in the translation into Russian.
>
> The owner of the Russian company (investor) thus misinterpreted the scope of the due diligence proposed by the Indian auditors and lawyers. A list was proposed based on practice common in Russia but not applicable to India.
>
> Further delays were caused because of misunderstandings related to the requirement imposed by responsible public bodies to clear essential equipment of the local factory from typically Indian export promotion schemes, which the Russian side interpreted as a sign of non-compliance by the seller.

These structural issues can be as decisive as price ranges. An entrepreneur-owner used to working independently and without outside interference may, for example, not like to continue working under a larger concern following an acquisition. His options may be a significant/outright sale (75%–100%) and/or the disposal of the remaining stake within a given transition period for transferring management. With certain projects involving megamarket buyers or sellers, it is expedient to agree to a scaled approach. The investor enters with a minority participation that is increased within a period of one to three years until it attains a majority, provided that certain conditions are fulfilled, such as:

- new orders, in the form of number of projects, absolute sales figure, or percentage increase in sales (with respect to the stand-alone scenario);
- continuity of core management, which should stay on for a minimum period of three to five years;
- retirement provision for CEO in case he/she has reached a certain age;
- use of investor's international sales channels and creation of joint marketing teams;
- phases of financial integration and reporting;
- dispatch of specialists in engineering, sales, finance, and general coordination to the megamarket entity, and vice versa, transferring megamarket specialists to headquarters;
- transfer of technology and set-up of joint R&D teams.

The official version of the legal documents for transnational transactions is mostly in English. This does not pose a problem in India, where English is the business language, but in Russia and China, the drafting and translation of the documents can be a long, drawn-out process given that business partners consider the LOI as a prelude to the final contract. The foreign company should check the translation to ensure there is no misinterpretation, which can lead to misunderstandings and disrupt subsequent negotiations. In China and Russia, LOIs must bear the company seal next to the signature to make them official documents.

11.2. Deal-making

The following milestones need to be covered during this phase:
- Milestone 6: Conducting the due diligence in strategic areas

- Milestone 7: Selecting a valuation method to determine a price range
- Milestone 8: Submitting a purchase offer
- Milestone 9: Drafting the agreements
- Milestone 10: Ensuring funding and approval

Milestone 6:
Conducting the due diligence in strategic areas

The due diligence is an indispensable step in a transaction. It helps to check the veracity of the legal and financial information supplied by the target, the authenticity of legal documents, as well as compatibility in terms of philosophy, identity, and goals. The scrutiny reveals the fair value (price) for the target firm or part of it. If the megamarket target has gone through a due diligence procedure earlier (e.g., to launch an IPO, privatization, competing offer), the existing report can be taken as a reference, but it must nevertheless be updated/supplemented by an independent auditing team commissioned by the buyer in compliance with international standards. The due diligence should be completed before submitting a firm and binding offer or signing a purchase agreement. Access to a data room given after signing an LOI is bound by stringent restrictions in the megamarkets, particularly if the foreign buyer is a competitor. In India, for example, the target's financials are not made available electronically unless the buyer signs a binding offer, which can have some legal implications.

Reputed international auditing and law firms are often recruited by M&A departments at headquarters for the due diligences, which must take into account both contexts. These external professionals must be briefed by the foreign investor on the objectives of the transaction, the envisaged synergies, and possible deal-breakers. The project coordinating team needs to select legal and auditing firms that are also trusted and accepted by the target, which has to disclose sensitive information.

Pause for thought

A Chinese or Russian target may reject a German auditing firm if the acquirer is also a German company, for fear that the two German entities may connive to lower the final price.

Chinese and Russian targets prefer that the buyers use the services of local rather than EU/US or international professionals, which is not reassuring to EU/US companies.

An Indian company accepted an unknown Russian buyer for its hived-off unit primarily because the Russian company appointed reputed international and local firms for the due diligences.

***

In a project in India, the due diligence team had to make sure that the local entrepreneur understood the advantages of building an alliance with a bigger European partner and was willing to make compromises on the stake to be acquired and future governance issues. The local partner's enterprise value expectations were much higher because they were based on an assumption that future sales had indefinite expansion potential but without considering the investment costs for an expansion nor the competition factor, which, should the alliance not have taken place, would have implied sharply reduced cash flows.

Intercultural issues and psychological factors play a significant role throughout the due diligence process.

A due diligence exercise consists of several steps. Most companies focus on financial and tax due diligence, which generally parallels or precedes the legal due diligence. Scrutinizing financial statements (balance sheets, profit and loss accounts, cash flow statements) reveals the target's profitability, assets, and liabilities; it may indicate the reasons why a company wishes to sell. The legal due diligence revolves around the vetting of contracts and legal documents (see box 11.2). There is always some overlapping between the two, for example, in general issues (corporate records, organization, strategy) and taxation matters.

Due diligences are time-consuming, expensive exercises and should be undertaken with a tight schedule in mind and only if prior assessments of the target indicate a real potential. The first assessment of the target should be market-driven and based on information gathered from outside the target to obtain an objective perspective on its markets, future prospects, and competitive position (commercial due diligence). In the megamarkets, a target's customers, suppliers, competitors, joint venture partners, and employees should not be ignored as sources of data, information, and insight because of the lack of formal and reliable data. This lowers the risk of selecting targets not having the operational or strategic fit or the capacity to meet the EU/US purchaser's revenue and profit targets.

Market-related analysis determines if the company operates in an expanding market where the investor can add superior value to the acquired target following the transaction by making use of all possible synergies. This part of the evaluation also helps to determine an appropriate EBIT or sales multiplier following financial due diligence. EBIT multipliers can be higher if sales expectations and profits point upwards, which is mostly the case in expanding markets and when targets enjoy excellent brand equity.

> **Box 11.2. Legal due diligence issues in the megamarkets.**
> - Corporate records (including structure, subsidiaries, rules)
> - Agreements between shareholders
> - Partnership agreements
> - Employment agreements (including pensions, union issues)
> - Loans and credit lines
> - Land and real estate issues (including mortgages)
> - Intellectual property rights (patents and trademarks)
> - Marketing and distribution agreements
> - Litigations (commercial, labor)
> - Insurance policies
> - Taxation issues
> - Government notices

The management and people due diligence supplements the findings by examining the integrity of senior leaders and middle managers, their leadership skills, and acceptance levels by local staff. Focused on the individuals themselves, this type of intelligence should include background checks and exhaustive interviews with individual managers and concerned partners and/or employees. The management team—its attitude and stability—is a determining factor for success or failure of a megamarket venture.

Another factor of strategic relevance is the company's contribution to the local community expressed as part of corporate social responsibility (CSR), which extends beyond customers and immediate shareholders to embrace all the stakeholders (local communities, environment, civil society, government, etc.). Partnering with a local company that contributes to the investor's CSR will enhance the foreign company's brand equity significantly. Examples are:

- Microsoft, which focuses on building digitally connected societies in China and India by sponsoring IT literacy measures in educational curricula.[1]
- Essilor from France, which is conducting free eye tests and dispensing spectacles at subsidized rates in rural India (and also Africa). The strategy is part of the company's rural marketing program geared to raising health standards in the countryside, thus contributing to society at large.[2]

Time is a crucial factor in a due diligence in fast-expanding megamarkets. Normally a company has a window of opportunity of a couple of months to complete the pre-deal formalities, including the evaluation of the target and brand. During that time, it must seriously engage with the senior executives of the target so that they maintain the momentum and keep to time frames. When the transaction is protracted, local partners tend to lose interest or else strive to renegotiate the price, especially when the target develops positively and shows improving financial results. Price hikes are common also with land and corporate premises (logistics centers, buildings, offices), which can seriously

---

Pause for thought

A German company that planned to acquire a Russian food company found through its management due diligence that the Russian owners wanted to continue running the business after the sale of a majority stake. They had successfully managed the company and grown it from a small enterprise into a major brand.

Detailed discussions with them showed that they were committed to their brand, and they acknowledged that the participation of the new owners would technically and financially help them realize their expansion plans.

They were given management control by the German company, which recognized the advantage of retaining them rather than recruiting other managers who would not be as committed.

Their interest in developing new markets further east, such as China and South Korea, added to the list of plus points for selecting the target.

---

1. "The strategy behind corporate virtue," *Indian Management*, May 2006.
2. "Essilor's India's Rural Project," *The Hindu*, June 13, 2006.

Table 11.1. Due diligence categories for megamarket target evaluation.

Due diligence categories	Contents	Responsibility
Business or market DD	Understanding of market trends, products, regulations, competition, customers and users, channels, suppliers. Evaluating the reputation of the target, its competitive position, its rank, whether it serves growing markets, its perceived future.	In cooperation with strategy and intelligence consultants, research teams based on information from various stakeholders (suppliers, customers, employees, etc.).
Legal DD	Employment/labor contracts, land/building use contracts, land ownership, trademarks, bank loans, intellectual property rights (IPR) and other ownership rights, insurance policies.	Outsourced to law firm.
Financial and tax DD	Understanding of value drivers and main financials of corporate performance: assets, liabilities, equity positions, sales, EBIT/ cash-flow/equity ratios.	Outsourced to audit firm.
Management and people DD	Integrity of senior management, leadership qualities, type of organization, corporate culture and philosophy, code of conduct, HR policies, team culture, training, personnel retention and development policies. Ethical issues including corporate social responsibility (CRS) activities.	Internal or in cooperation with HR consultants and intercultural trainers.
Technical/environmental DD	Compliance with international norms across the value chain, application of ISO norms.	Internal, in close cooperation with specialized engineering consultants.

affect greenfield projects. The different parts of the due diligence can be carried out in parallel by separate teams to gain time, preferably under the supervision of the project leader (see table 11.1). The detail level will depend on the size and nature of the target and the degree of rapprochement required for the alliance.

Following the due diligence, senior management will have to decide whether it intends to go ahead with the project and, if yes, if it prefers a share deal or an asset deal. A share deal enables an investor to acquire stakes in an existing company, its brand, and its reputation. While the continuity of the business is ensured under such a deal, it involves a certain number of risks related to hidden liabilities that may come to the fore later (taxes, pension-related liabilities, letters of exchange, claims by former shareholders, suppliers and managers, unresolved legal proceedings, image problems). An asset deal is preferable when the investor is not interested in the company (going concern) and its intangibles such as goodwill, brand, knowledge, and so forth, but in its human resources and part of its material property (plant, equipment, office building, warehouses, etc.). If the investor is not interested in the material assets of the target company either, a third option is to acquire only a part of the management and the most qualified engineers, salespeople, and support staff into a new structure.

Due diligence is often seen as the bidder's responsibility. It may be just as important—in the case of reverse FDI from the megamarkets to the advanced markets or from one megamarket to another—for the target to conduct a due diligence of the bidder so as to determine whether the offer is bona fide and legitimate and, most important, whether the bidder has the financial capacity to complete the transaction. The deal team leader must be provided with the power to make an informed recommendation to other board members and shareholders as to whether to accept the offer.

> **Pause for thought**
>
> *In Russia, a major European consumer goods company rejected a share deal after finding out through due diligence that the shares of some of the target's shareholders had not been registered in due form with the state registrar.*
>
> *The analysis of relevant tax returns and legal documents revealed inconsistencies that could lead to claims by the authorities and other creditors in the future.*
>
> *The EU company therefore switched to an asset deal for a brownfield site (including office buildings and equipment) that enabled it to set up a local production unit managed by newly recruited local managers. The value of the unit rose fourfold during 2003–2007 as land prices had meanwhile skyrocketed in the Moscow region.*
>
> ***
>
> *A Russian investor in India decided to curtail the terms of reference of the financial due diligence that were submitted by an international audit firm supposed to carry out the assignment based on Indian minimum standards. The audit firm agreed (under pressure to please the customer), but eventually the work was not complete and items had to be added in order to make an accurate assessment of the investment.*

Saving on acquisition costs by skipping the due diligence step or by reducing the items in the terms of reference for the professional service firms is counterproductive. It is certainly important to study the contents and methodology of the work for cost considerations, but common standards applicable in the country should eventually be accepted. In the long run, the financial burden of litigations and the destruction of shareholder value (through a failed investment) may prove to be far more costly.

Milestone 7:

Selecting a valuation method to determine a price range

Considering the plethora of elements to be validated in an FDI project, the valuation or value assessment exercise of a target in a megamarket can become a complicated undertaking. Valuations are a challenge as they require an understanding of unfamiliar accounting definitions and methods. Moreover, the unofficial portion of the financial statements is usually much larger. During this exercise, which involves the use of appropriate multipliers, exchange rate mechanisms, and a combination of valuation methods, the company must be guided by M&A professionals with experience in this field.

The valuation of private companies—the majority of cases—is far more complex than determining a value for listed public companies (determined by the stock price multiplied by the number of shares outstanding). Financial reporting by private companies does not have to meet the stringent standards imposed on listed companies; their financial statements are often not properly audited and reflect higher costs for the purpose of reducing taxes. The intermingling of personal and business expenses also complicates the task. As salary and dividend both return to the owner, they cannot be easily distinguished. A private company's value is not entirely objective; it is partly subjective, and it is this part that challenges valuation experts.

The first result of a valuation is an arithmetic price, which, however, may not reflect the full picture. Owner-managers stress "value" more than just "price." They feel a sentimental attachment to the company they have created and are proud of its results and image in the market. The perception of what is valuable thus differs between the buyer and seller. The acquiring company is usually more led by facts and figures. Many factors influence the ultimate value (and price) of an investment in a megamarket, including:

- a co-shared vision, making the target more attractive;
- high industry and sector growth rates, translating into filled order books;
- privatization of the target through auctions, tenders, and bids, raising its price;
- financial health of the target company (not always easy to determine in a volatile megamarket context);
- intangibles such as quality of management, corporate culture, brands, and distribution;
- synergy with the existing business of the investor;
- liabilities such as tax claims, off-balance-sheet debts (e.g., pension plans), and environmental damage factors, all of which are arguments for lowering the price.

Far too often, emphasis is placed on the abstract strategic value of the target without specifying how this value will translate into future benefits through combined efforts after the transaction. The value drivers and value destroyers (deal breakers) both need to be assessed (see also Milestone 3).

As value can be quite different from price, the results of the financial and legal due diligences can only be a first attempt at value determination. Experience shows that business/market factors and people-related soft factors are the most precious value creators. They are the foundation on which a company's long-term stability, and hence its ultimate value, depends. Four sets of value drivers are considered in an acquisition or transaction:

- basic price;
- synergy value (determinant of greater efficiency);
- strategic value (with respect to market and competitive forces in the industry);
- management control premium (in case of 100% takeover).

Several internationally accepted valuation techniques can be used for evaluating a company or investment (see table 11.2). In a megamarket context, some of these methods should be combined for arriving at a realistic price range for the target before engaging in actual negotiations. For completeness, analysts can run different scenarios regarding the expected

---

Pause for thought

An Austrian entrepreneur was positively surprised to strike a deal within a fairly short time frame with an Indian investor based on a company evaluation about four times higher than average market value in Western Europe.

The high "premium" was justifiable with the target's know-how and technology, which would allow the investor to secure long-term government contracts back home.

Table 11.2. Valuation methods.

Valuation methods	Measure	Megamarket suitability
Enterprise multiples	Multiple of profits / Multiple of revenue/sales	Relatively easy to calculate as it concerns results attained in the past and forecasts. Should be based on actual, not fiscally adjusted accounting figures. Convenient to compare both measures (profits and sales).
Discounted cash flow (DCF)	Based on future profit or earnings flows discounted to the current day	Dependent on business plan assumptions and forecasts. Values can swing significantly depending on the assessment of the future earnings scenario.
Equity multiples	Price-earnings ratio	Enables cross-sector comparisons between large players. Does not capture the full business reality if the stock market is under- or overvalued.
Asset valuation	Value of fixed and current assets	Important to take market value, not balance sheet value of fixed assets. Vital to measure value of intangibles such as brands, intellectual property, people, and goodwill.
Accretion analysis	Measures the impact of acquisition/FDI value on the company's overall earnings	Based on realistic market assumptions. Difficult to assess accurate long-term business developments.
Sum of parts approach	Independent value of each business unit or segment to arrive at the total business value	Interesting for diversified companies. Results should be compared with those of other methods.

future performance of the company, typically consisting of three types: optimistic, most likely, and pessimistic.

Most large and medium-sized megamarket companies are familiar with these valuation methods, but the data underlying them are often based on local accounting methods that need to be made compatible with internationally recognized standards with the help of experienced auditors.

The process of concentration is well underway in the megamarkets. The ongoing consolidation into larger entities pushes up transaction values. Multiples are generally higher in the megamarkets than in advanced markets, owing to the enormous future market potential of these countries—for example, up to 12 in megamarkets for food companies against 4–5 in advanced markets (see table 11.3). Large-cap EBIT multiples for bigger companies can be 50%–100% higher than for small caps (medium-sized enterprises). The sales multiple can range from 1.2 to above 10 depending on the business.

Similarly, increased reverse FDI from the megamarkets raised share prices and company valuations in the EU. Earlier, outward Chinese and Indian investors were US-focused, but they now see EU targets as valuable sources of synergies and often accept prices Western competitors would reject. The drop in share prices caused by the global financial crisis from mid-2008 offers more opportunities for acquisitions and equity-based alliances.

Multipliers are determined through negotiations and bargaining between the parties.[3] Values derived from valuation methods are a good starting point for negotiations. The

---

3. The value of corporate assets and shares came down in a few megamarket industries during the 2008–2009 financial crisis. Eventually, multipliers depend on the industry structure, the owners' intentions and the target company's market position and performance.

Table 11.3. Multiples in advanced and megamarkets for selected industries, 2008.

	Small caps[a]				Mid/Large caps[b]			
	EBIT multiple		Sales multiple		EBIT multiple		Sales multiple	
	AM	EMM	AM	EMM	AM	EMM	AM	EMM
Food	4–7	8–10	0.5–1	1–2	6–9	9–12	0.5–1	1–2
Light industry	3–5	6–8	0.3–0.5	0.5–1	4–7	5–7	0.3–0.7	1–1.5
Machinery	4.5–6	5–6	0.4–0.7	0.8–1.5	5–9	5–9	0.4–0.8	0.7–1.5
Chemicals	5.5–8	7–12	0.4–1	1–2	6–10	7–12	0.6–1.2	1–2
Automotive	6–8	5–7	0.5–0.7	0.4–0.7	5.5–8.5	5–7	0.5–0.8	0.5–1
Pharmaceuticals	6.5–8	7–11	0.6–1.5	1–2	8–12	6–11	0.8–2.4	1–2.5
Construction	2.8–5	4–9	0.3–0.5	1–2.5	3–9	5–11	0.4–1.1	1.5–2.5
Utilities	5–8	6–10	0.7–1.3	1–2	7.5–10	8–10	0.9–1.4	1–2.5
Environment	4.5–6	5–7	0.5–1	0.5–1	5–8	6–9	0.7–1.2	0.7–1
Transport, logistics	4–7	4–7	0.4–0.7	1–1.5	7–10	6–8	0.5–1.1	0.8–1.5
Retailing	4–8	6–12	0.4–0.9	1.2–2.4	5–8	6–12	0.5–0.9	
IT, software	6–9	6–11	0.8–1.6	1.2–3	6–9	6–9	1.1–1.8	1.4–2.5

a. Small caps: enterprises with annual sales up to € 50 million.
b. Mid/Large caps: enterprises with annual sales above € 50 million.
Sources: Finance journals.

final price will depend on the seller's expectations, additional investments that need to be made (e.g., restructuring, new equipment, new plant), debts, future market, company perception of the buyer, and the overall importance of the deal for the buyer and seller. The seller must take into consideration the "competition factor" in case a powerful investor intends to enter the market via stand-alone or an alliance; selling at a "reasonable" price may be a better option than accepting market share and value erosion because of more intense competition to come. The investor will have to evaluate the risks involved if the business does not develop as expected. The most common risks that have an impact on final pricing with respect to emerging markets are:

- economic risks: drop in growth rates, weakening of overall demand, high energy costs, currency-related risks, sudden regulations with adverse effects;
- market/industry risks: competitive pressure, price drop, new demand patterns (a company can limit this risk and influence it positively through innovation, diversification, internationalization, higher efficiency in the value chain, and key account management);
- technology risks: every company must incessantly continue developing its technology base by improving its knowledge and information management;
- supply risks: price changes in supply markets can be compensated by long-term agreements with suppliers; effective supply chain management depends on careful selection of suppliers and reduction of their bargaining power;
- production risks: these are related to possible overcapacities or inefficient production processes; optimization of stocking capacities, just-in-time systems, and lean production reduce this risk;

- personnel risks: special programs must be designed to retain management and key staff in the company including attractive compensation schemes and personnel advancement programs; and
- credit risks: customers in emerging markets are not all trustworthy, and some of them have bad payment morale.

Western companies have a tendency to overstate the risks and undervalue the opportunities; decision-making is also slow. The real risks are that the price of the megamarket target will rise rapidly, buoyed by economic growth, or that the target receives a competitive bid from a less risk-averse company. During 2003–2008, the price of corporate assets rose more than five times in the megamarkets across industries, but began to level off in 2009 as stock markets fell.

A growing number of foreign companies are looking for popular brands in the megamarkets, especially in food and other consumer goods industries. The obvious advantage of such acquisitions is that they offer immediate market share by entering into an established business with secure earnings; this shortens the expected payback period. According to the US GAAP (Generally Accepted Accounting Principles) and IFRS (International Financial Reporting Standards), which most EU/US companies nowadays follow, brands must be balanced separately from the company's value (goodwill) in the balance sheet. Brand evaluation should take into account the actions envisaged by the target company to enhance the value of its brands (e.g., promotion, listings, fresh capital injection). A common indicator is the future revenue-generating capacity of a brand (see box 11.3). Legislation in China and Russia forbids foreign companies from acquiring controlling stakes in local companies owning famous "live" brands. The authorities also forbid foreign investors from overvaluing their know-how component including immaterial goodwill, which also includes the investor's brand, when acquiring shares of well-known local players.

Box 11.3. Parameters for brand valuation.
- Market (number of units) and market growth
- Market share
- Volume
- Price and price change
- Sales
- Cost of sales
- Marketing costs
- Depreciation
- Central cost allocation
- Capital and working capital
- Earnings/profits from brand
- Brand discount rate

Milestone 8:
Submitting a purchase offer

Based on the due diligence and valuation findings, the two parties arrive at a fair market price through preliminary negotiations. Megamarket entrepreneurs are adept at bargaining, and negotiations can be inordinately protracted for foreign companies. Proud of their achievements, ambitious, and self-confident, these entrepreneurs are buoyed by a booming economy and growing numbers of international clients "knocking at their doors." Selling shares or assets to a foreign investor is just one of the options for them. Many prefer to continue growing their businesses and, unlike in Western countries, do not face the problem of succession. These entrepreneurs generally demand the highest possible price using large multiples for future profits; they forecast exponential sales growth without factoring in possible downturns or rising costs of expansion. In such situations, it may be advisable for the EU/US investor to opt for a greenfield operation and recruit its own local staff.

In long, drawn-out negotiations, the company's value may rise due to market-related factors (strong growth, emergence of other buyers with competing offers). The local partner can insist on renegotiating the price or else back out of the deal. Foreign investors must be ready for such surprises. They must be skillful, swift, and at the same time patient during negotiations before submitting a final purchase offer, which is binding for both sides.

The purchase offer or nonbinding offer (NBO) marks the culmination of the valuation phase. It is made in writing even if certain megamarket companies, particularly state-owned enterprises, prefer verbal communication to avoid any commitment. The offer is followed by a formal acceptance, in writing, of the offer by the local partner. Further negotiations are held on the moot points raised in the acceptance letter.

The most important element of a purchase offer is the price the buyer is willing to pay for the target. The offer will reiterate the advantages for both sides and state options including majority/minority stakes. It sets the framework for the definitive agreements and highlights the issues that need to be addressed and completed (e.g., title deeds, government clearances) before these agreements are signed. It also ensures a period of exclusivity for the two parties. Typically, the NBO is drafted by the buyer's legal advisers, either a local law firm or an international firm with a local presence for a full understanding of local laws.

Price negotiations can be difficult with both private and state-owned enterprises. The socio-political context of the latter only adds to the complexity. The restructuring process of a Chinese SOE and tender procedure, for example, can take several months. If a foreign company wants to win, it must present a convincing concept which appeals to the Chinese side. Factors such as retaining existing managers (often Party members), employment generation, learning effects, technology transfer, and personal interaction between CEOs of both sides are often as important as the financial factor. China has been very successful in protecting national interests and preventing foreign companies, including large multinationals, from winning controlling stakes of leading national enterprises without a viable concept of securing employment and protecting important national brands. Sometimes it is literally impossible to acquire a majority no matter how much effort is put into the matter by the investor's managers. In such cases, it is vital to work with insiders who can help judge when to back out of a deal so as not to commit unnecessarily further managerial and financial resources.

Milestone 9:
Drafting the agreements

At the end of the negotiations, the partners sign a legally binding document containing all the provisions and stipulations related to the deal (see box 11.4). The definitive agreement can have different forms and include several term-sheets and related documents to be signed by both parties:

- share purchase agreement (SPA), in the case of an acquisition of a stake in a local firm (minority, majority);
- business transfer agreement (BTA), in the case of a business or division transferring to the buyer by a megamarket group divesting its unit;
- JV contract, in the case of the creation of a separate joint venture;
- sales and distribution agreement;
- agreement for land purchase or lease agreement in the case of a greenfield operation.

In addition, other documents have to be filed for integrating the new unit:

- bylaws or articles of association for any new company to be created by the two parties or an amendment of bylaws of an existing company that has been acquired
- employment agreements, including management contracts, in case some of the partners/managers continue working for the company on behalf of the new owner (investor)

Once there has been a general agreement on the final purchase/sale price, the legal advisers of the two parties can start drafting the final agreement. Although the legal teams take over from this point, the foreign company must keep up the dialogue with the seller

---

Box 11.4. Important provisions of a megamarket transaction agreement.

- Purchase price
- Share distribution
- Composition of board
- Establishment of supervisory board
- Export markets
- Use of brand(s)
- Assignment of supervisory and coordinating personnel by the acquirer
- Financial reporting
- Rules for replacement of managing director
- Mechanism for shareholders to back out and sell their shares
- Criteria for the majority shareholder to top up his stake (e.g., under circumstances of material breach by the minority shareholder which endangers the future of the company)

> **Box 11.5. Caveats when negotiating a megamarket transaction agreement.**
> - Base assumptions on realistic expansion concepts and evaluation methods.
> - Analyze financials and forecasts accurately (neither over-optimistic nor over-pessimistic).
> - Use specialists who understand etiquette, hierarchy, and behavioral rules.
> - Avoid rupture of communication flow during the entire process.
> - Assure constant and creative involvement by top management.
> - Speed up transaction phase.
> - Keep communicating to shareholders and stakeholders.
> - Prepare in time for regulatory approval including approval from antitrust bodies.

at all levels, particularly the highest. In fact, negotiations continue until a consensus is reached on all the finer points that emerge during drafting. An open communication line helps to sort out these issues, which could otherwise destabilize the project (see caveats in box 11.5). It also helps to understand with time the hidden agendas and personal aspirations of the local, particularly minority, partners, who will insist on being able to exercise as many blocking rights as possible to stall key decisions (e.g., capital increase, which will dilute their stake; sale of stake or brand; acquisition of other companies).

Sometimes the legal advisers double up as intermediaries as they try to find a mutually acceptable solution for the two parties. For this, they need an unbiased view to produce a balanced document that takes the interests of both parties into account. A one-sided document will lead to problems at the time of integration.

For an ongoing concern, the time lag between closing (signing of the formal agreements) and the actual transfer of shares or ownership becomes significant. A cutoff date has to be set for valuation of the current assets, inventory, stock, and similar items, and these have to be once again updated on the day the actual transfer takes place.

Regarding payments, the agreements specify the mode and schedule of payments. These days, buyers opt for staggered payments according to the fulfillment of certain obligations (provision of official documents, share transfer, performance, etc.) by the seller.

Until the final signature is put on the agreement by both sides, there is an inherent risk of failure. Western businessmen should not underestimate underlying difficulties, often related to different mentalities, which can have an impact until the very last moment of the negotiations. Megamarket entrepreneurs who sell stakes to a Western investor are extremely sensitive about future command lines and government rules. They want to be part of strategic decisions concerning the future development of the very same company they have taken years to grow. Often, the SPA goes through smoothly, but negotiations on management employment contracts can be a stumbling block. Former entrepreneurs (in the case of an acquisition) react in a different way than locally recruited managing directors (in the case of a greenfield). A foreign investor must understand these nuances and provide the right incentives (e.g., blocking rights for the minority shareholder whenever decisions can affect the company's future, such as capital increases, sale of shares to third parties, crucial investments, and bank loans; stock options to former board members) but also impose the necessary checks and balances (e.g., recruit managers other than those suggested by a previous shareholder or a newly appointed managing director) to protect its own interests.

For many Western executives, a signed contract is a proof of success. They are fast at publicizing a success story around a "waterproof" legal document checked and approved by their legal advisers. After that event, they return to their routine tasks back at headquarters. They forget that post-deal integration is as important as all the efforts made before and during the deal (see 11.3). Provisions that encourage the two parties to work closely together in order to consolidate their relationship with time are easily drafted—e.g., appointment of permanent joint coordination teams, an investor's on-site representative, or regular board meetings. Joint efforts to exchange knowledge, train personnel, and invest in promising projects demand more time and effort. Intense interaction between management and specialists should therefore be cultivated long before closure to facilitate subsequent joint work.

Milestone 10:
Ensuring funding and approval

Although this is not specified in most transaction agreements, both parties are expected to have already ensured that funds are available for the transaction. Many transactions fail because at the last minute the buyer cannot obtain the credit line to finance the purchase. Before spending valuable time on meetings, negotiations, or costly evaluations, the investors must complete their financial planning exercise. The party to be acquired should stay within the agreed price range and not exploit changes in the scenario to repeatedly raise the price. But this is sometimes beyond the control of the acquirer and its professional advisers, and surprises are always possible.

Companies with favorable equity-to-debt ratios are in a stronger position to finance an investment project in megamarkets than companies with high financial exposure and dependence on external banks and creditors. Venture capital and private equity are possible in the megamarkets, especially for new start-ups in high-growth sectors, but this source of finance is not readily available for projects in traditional industries. Syndicated loans by several banks are granted for large-scale projects involving large multinationals, sometimes with the participation of an international institution like the World Bank, Asian Development Bank/ADB (e.g., infrastructure projects in China and India), and the EBRD (e.g., FDI projects in manufacturing, banking, and other service industries in Russia).

Two new forms of finance have become popular in the megamarkets: project finance and leasing. Project finance is attractive to investors who have exhausted other credit lines but come up with an interesting investment project backed by a solid business plan. Leasing is popular in real estate–backed projects (e.g., office buildings, distribution and logistics centers, factories, equipment). Most Western banks limit their leasing finance to existing buildings and not to "construction projects in progress." They have each object checked very carefully regarding future revenue streams (e.g., tenant lists, duration of rental contracts). Megamarket partners can also help to tap additional funds from local banks, which have raised their financial clout over the past five years.

> **Pause for thought**
>
> *The leasing subsidiary of a leading European bank with a branch network spanning across Eastern Europe took almost two years to assess an office park project in the outskirts of Moscow. When the bank's risk department eventually produced the final documents for approval by the board, an internal policy change obliged the investor to shift the project application to the real estate (not leasing) subsidiary within the same group. Lack of coordination between subsidiaries led to unforeseen delays, which adversely affected the outcome of the project.*
>
> *Investors should tap many sources of finance among Western and megamarket institutions so as to reduce the risk of sudden policy changes or last-minute rejections.*

Most investment projects must obtain a special government approval. Project screening and an antitrust review by authorities in charge may take longer than expected and require some lobbying effort by auditors and lawyers representing the investor's interests. In China, acquisitions of domestic enterprises, including private ones, must be filed with the Ministry of Commerce whenever the acquisition (a) involves important industries, (b) affects national economic safety, or (c) causes a change of control of a domestic enterprise that owns a traditional Chinese brand and its trademark. In India, 100% FDI is allowed in all except strategic sectors (e.g., defense industry) through the automatic route; the investor needs to only inform the Reserve Bank of India when the capital is transferred. For those sectors where there is a limit to FDI in a project (e.g., insurance), investments above the limit require clearance from the Foreign Investment Promotion Bureau (FIPB). In Russia, the Antimonopoly Commission has to approve all investments with combined asset values exceeding 1 billion rubles (about US$40 million). Medium-sized companies that fall within this category must have their transactions cleared before starting operations with local partners. The commission has offices in most large cities of Russia. Antitrust clearance takes a few weeks after submitting all the required forms and documents, preferably through established law firms experienced in these formalities. Moreover, a new FDI law that passed Parliament in 2008 defines strategic industries where FDI is heavily restricted and requires the explicit approval by the respective state organs.

11.3. Post-deal integration

Few acquisitions and alliances create long-term value to investors. One reason is that management overlooks the importance of careful post-merger integration. According to the CEO of a Swiss multinational that realized many successful acquisitions in the megamarkets, "The period after the deal contributes as much, if not more, to success than the period before a deal." The real work in an acquisition therefore starts after the transaction. Much of the EU/US senior management's attention must be directed at developing a workable post-transaction integration plan that will generate the expected revenue drivers and cost savings and open the path to other investment projects.

An integration team composed of representatives from both companies should be formed to quickly and effectively implement the stipulations of the agreement and carry out the integration process. Its duration depends on organizational adjustments and the speed

Figure 11.3. Post-deal integration options.

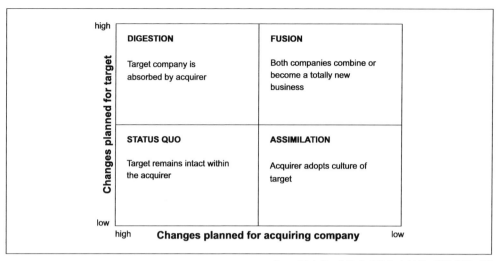

Source: Adapted from S. Moeller & Ch. Brady. Intelligent M&A. 2007. p. 231.

of communication at different managerial levels across geographic borders. If in Western economies only three out of ten M&A and joint venture deals can be termed successful, this ratio is certainly much lower in the megamarkets, especially when foreign entities are involved. In AMs, post-deal integration is often an exercise in cost-cutting, staff reduction, facilities rationalization, and the force-fitting of one company into the template of another.

In a megamarket context, success is more likely if the investor understands what the acquired company has to offer and learns what it should teach. Post-deal integration can be compared to a change in the management process for a company given that top management must decide on the desired way forward, establish clear leadership, communicate effectively, maintain customer focus, and take appropriate action against internal and external resistance. It usually involves changes for both the acquiring and acquired companies (see figure 11.3).

Post-acquisition integration delivers the expected benefits when four critical areas are brought in line after the transaction:
- human resources
- finance and accounting
- marketing and sales
- integration plan

These aspects will be covered below and elaborated in the next chapter on delivery.

Milestone 11:

Human resources alignment

Human resources, including managerial and support staff, is probably the biggest challenge in an acquisition or alliance project in the megamarkets. New roles have to be carved out, while others have to be aligned (salaries and designations, recruiting and

> **Pause for thought**
>
> In a transaction involving a Russian listed company and a European family-owned business, the European owner, who remained minority shareholder with a blocking stake, failed to inform his executives on time of the new ownership structure and the contractual agreement, by which three Russian directors had to be appointed to the board.
>
> The Russian majority owner's attempt to appoint its members therefore met with resistance and suspicion, which spoiled the cordial relations that had reigned throughout the negotiations before the transaction.

retrenchment, organization charts, IT systems, etc.). Duplication of employees and roles is an unavoidable result of an acquisition (especially when the investor already owns a unit in the same market); redundancy can affect the morale of staff across all positions in both organizations. While some level of reduction is inevitable, experienced personnel should be retained. A seasoned CEO of an acquired company can become the country head reporting to the EU/US board to ensure continuity during the initial period of three to five years. Good-performance companies sometimes offer the CEO of the acquired company a board position at headquarters to demonstrate the importance of the megamarket for the group.

Personnel-related challenges must be taken seriously also in the case of greenfield investments. The positions of managing, technical, marketing, purchase, and finance directors must be filled with experienced professionals, appointed, if possible, by a recruiting team consisting of senior executives representing the interest of the investor. The recommendations of the seller or a newly appointed managing director, who may be tempted to build his own empire, should be avoided to prevent the formation of a local nexus.

Communication is the key during integration. Employees of the buyer and seller must be informed of the acquisition before the news becomes public. Thus they become integrators and change agents. The owners or CEOs of both the buyer and seller should spearhead the exercise of direct communication (e.g., meetings, e-mails, newsletters, frequently asked questions to employees, etc.) with all stakeholders, and information channels should be opened for feedback from them. These responses will help to better execute the integration process. The integration team should be geared for rapid responsiveness during this crucial period of transition.

There should be regular meetings between representatives of the buyer and seller after a successful transaction. Informal encounters should supplement official board meetings. Integration can be smoothened through reciprocal stays of key personnel (e.g., financial accounting, human resources, marketing), which demonstrates the interest of both parties to make the venture grow.

Milestone 12:

Financial management and accounting

The existence of different accounting systems is one of the first hurdles to be crossed when integrating two different entities. Logically, it is the system of the acquirer or the majority owner that prevails, especially if it is a listed company that must comply with international accounting standards. The change in accounting standards also requires software integration and workforce training to align the support systems to the new standards. While EU companies follow the International Financial Recording Standards, large megamarket companies, listed on national or foreign stock exchanges, have adopted mostly US GAAP. Smaller companies, however, follow national systems. In China and Russia, companies may also have double bookkeeping (official and non-official).

It is very important to keep a check on the acquired company's financial performance following an acquisition. There are two basic types of acquisitions in megamarkets: (a) "bargain acquisitions," whereby non-performing firms are acquired at a reasonable price, and (b) "high-stake acquisitions"—this type is becoming much more frequent—involving excellent performers who are targets because they have become serious competitors for foreign companies in national and foreign markets. While it would be unrealistic for an acquired non-performer (variant "a") to show results immediately, it would also be a mistake to overextend the break-even period. On the other hand, top performers can easily slip down a downward spiral if key staff cannot be retained due to disagreements with the new owners about the future direction of the company or following the appointment of expatriates with a different management philosophy or branding and pricing policies.

Banking and borrowing also need to be aligned. The acquirer and its target will invariably have arrangements with different banks. Rather than change these long-term arrangements, the acquirer should continue with the target's bank and ensure that the same or more favorable loan conditions are offered to the new entity (this may be possible when a financially strong Western partner appears on the scene). Otherwise, the foreign investor may bring to the table its own contacts, provided its banks extend their credit lines to the megamarkets under the same conditions as in the advanced markets (refinancing rates; strategic, long-term loans; project finance; leasing; etc.). Local banks can be used if:

- they are large enough or are correspondents of the international bank(s) of the acquirer;
- the acquired company has a good and long relationship with its bank;
- the local bank can offer innovative forms of finance including mezzanine, project-related, and consortium-supported borrowing schemes.

MILESTONE 13:
MARKETING AND SALES

After the transaction, the acquisition team is instantly confronted with the issue of integrating marketing and sales activities to eliminate duplication and better satisfy customer needs. The work of two sets of sales teams and brand managers has to be coordinated, especially if they used to approach similar customers. If two brands are maintained, there is a danger of cannibalization of one brand by the other if activities are not properly coordinated, including in third markets. But, very often structural issues take precedence over marketing issues.

> **Pause for thought**
>
> A leading European equipment manufacturer faced competition from a Chinese company in which it had acquired a majority stake. The lawyers had in fact failed to highlight areas of probable conflict between the partners: use of brands, exports to international markets, project coordination, key account management, after-service support, and image. Moreover, key passages in the contracts had different interpretations in English and Chinese.
>
> The problem could only be defused once the majority owner (European company) offered to increase its stakes to almost total majority.

In consumer goods industries, investors prefer to buy brands, not companies. Brands have a support infrastructure consisting of distributors, salespersons, sales antennas, listings with retailers, warehouses, logistics agents, and so on, which must be understood. Pricing, product, and packaging features should not be changed until the brand and its distribution are fully understood.

Competitors can take advantage of the fluid situation after an acquisition to poach customers and key employees in charge of sales. Likewise, supplier relationships are at risk as well. The acquirer should visit key customers and suppliers together with the existing customer relationship managers so that their trust is not lost.[4]

Milestone 14:
Integration plan

Post-deal integration demands advanced analytical and practical work as well as social and behavioral competence by top management and the integration team. The success rate of deals can be improved if top management pursues a structured approach and follows through on a series of actions that must be embedded in major milestones (see table 11.4).

Generally speaking, foreign investors in the megamarkets should take certain lessons to heart:

- Top management plays a key role; if the figureheads on both sides are not willing to compromise, it is difficult to come up with win-win solutions.
- Transactions that retain the main focus of the company produce better results.
- Alliances between companies of equal size are easier to implement than acquisitions.
- Integration is easier if the companies belong to the same industry but their products do not compete directly.
- Early planning of the integration of the new human and physical assets improves the chances of success.
- Fast-paced integration and early pursuit of cost savings improves the outcome.
- Managers must designate an integration team and provide appropriate incentives for the team leader.

---

4. See 12.3.1.

Table 11.4. Milestones of successful integration in the megamarkets.

Milestones	Actions
Constitution of integration team	Involvement of visionary leaders and devoted staff.
Road map document	Documenting and communicating an integration plan and performance milestones based on the original rationale for the transaction, independently of issues surrounding hierarchy and turf battles.
Communications plan	Announcement of the transaction details to key stakeholders (investors, employees, customers, suppliers, media, and industry analysts).
Human resources plan	Personnel retention, integration, and development initiatives (key executives, technical staff, etc.). Transparency in reduction initiatives to achieve cost savings (redundant personnel).
Organizational alignment plan	Definition of optimal organizational design based on revised business objectives, including creation of new organization charts, benefits, and compensation schemes.
Product and technology integration plan	Identification of synergies in the product portfolio, setting of priorities for new product development, feedback mechanism to track progress and obstacles.
Operations and IT integration plan	Forum for issue identification and resolution in main functional areas: marketing, sales, distribution, engineering, manufacturing, and purchasing. Merging and adjusting technological systems related to reporting and accounting standards.

- Integration managers must be cognizant of cultural differences between organizations and avoid conflicts by frequently communicating with employees, customers, and other stakeholders.
- Particularly in transactions involving technology and human capital, managers must retain the talent that resides in the acquired firm.
- Customer and sales force attrition must be minimized.
- Advisers and insiders can accelerate the process.

CHAPTER 12
Long-term delivery: Join the top league

High-performing companies are driven by a vision of operational excellence at all levels of the organization. Shareholders, senior executives, and line managers share an unflagging determination to count among market leaders. They develop a bespoke concept and execute it with diligence. Inspired by a brilliant concept, they can roll out a strategy that will make the company unique among its peers. Ultimately, however, success depends on how effective the company's leaders are at executing the strategy. Timing and speed are crucial factors.

Megamarket investors fall into one of three categories:

- Type 1: companies that operate without a clear megamarket vision; they are mostly export- and sales-oriented, follow their (Western) customers, and wait for peers to move first.
- Type 2: companies that dispose of all the information but fail to implement an aggressive megamarket strategy for lack of drive or vision at the top.
- Type 3: companies that aim at leadership in the megamarkets by allocating the resources required for improving competences and preempting competition; these companies have done most of the groundwork, intentionally or instinctively, as described in the preceding three chapters.

Throughout the 1990s, EU/US companies had practically no megamarket strategy. Then, starting from the early 2000s, the megamarkets started to draw the attention of managers. Most entrants belonged to the first two types; they may have generated additional sales but eventually failed to develop the skills required to attain enduring leadership. The third type is the only one that brings lasting value to shareholders, and its population is increasing as more EU/US companies now have a plan and allocate budgets for focused actions to improve their positions in these geographies.

The pressure to perform lies heavily on senior executives, who have to steer clear of possible execution failure (see box 12.1). This chapter dwells on three areas of execution excellence—corporate governance, organization, and operational performance—and how these processes need to be adapted to the specific situation of the megamarkets.

> **Box 12.1. Causes of execution failure in the megamarkets.**
> - Shareholders do not recognize the promise of the megamarket and refuse to back the venture as suggested by top management.
> - Senior executives focus on the wrong entry/expansion option in the megamarket.
> - Middle managers (including heads of megamarket subsidiaries) lack the exposure or the open-mindedness and flexibility to learn from ground realities and act accordingly.
> - Talent retention is not given sufficient attention to motivate young recruits both at headquarters and in the megamarket subsidiary.
> - Organizational misalignment impedes quick response to growth opportunities.
> - Headquarters and the megamarket subsidiary disagree in their assessment of the path to be taken.
> - Divisional and subsidiary performance metrics are not in line with corporate strategy requirements.
> - Functional strategies are not adjusted to the megamarket context.

12.1. The governance factor

A company's ability to complete megamarket projects or transactions depends on good governance at all levels (see figure 12.1). The decisive factor is the conviction, determination, and charisma of headquarters leaders who provide direction and oversight to the megamarket project and its organization. Shareholders, who may or may not be part of management, need to support executives not only by approving the resources needed for strategic investments, but also by monitoring and reviewing actions and ensuring ethical conduct and regulatory compliance. The group's figureheads must be ready to contribute personally and directly to the success of canvassing efforts with key local customers and the realization of milestone projects aimed at consolidation and expansion (alliances, M&As).

Top leaders (owners, CEOs, and senior executives) of well-run corporations usually share a compelling dream, a feeling of stretch or challenge that energizes the entire organization and provides the emotional framework for optimizing processes and supply chains. A feeling of strong strategic intent to count among the winners lies at the heart of their breakthrough decisions defining the company's sense of discovery and direction. High performers observe basic rules of implementation, which gradually enable them to understand and unlock the "magic code" of their industries in the megamarkets.

Absence of delivery power by the owners or the headquarters executive team is a major obstacle to successful expansion. In owner-led companies, execution can be faster as decision-making and managerial responsibilities are concentrated in the same person(s). However, they need to undertake regular on-site exploratory visits with their division heads to form their own opinions rather than rely on background and feasibility reports prepared by others who may not fully grasp the local requirements or the leader's vision.

Figure 12.1. The four leadership levels of effective execution.

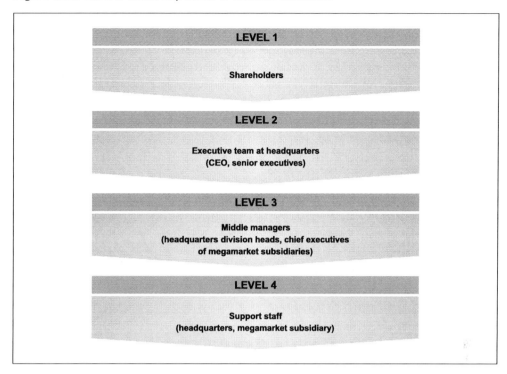

12.1.1. Top-echelon engagement

Rule No. 1:

The board should exercise control

Strategy execution starts with the board of directors—the highest instance representing the interests of the shareholders. Market leaders are cautious about the board composition and the interaction of its members. While preparing for a new venture in China, the CEO of a German company uttered the following tenet: "The higher the integrity, experience, and commitment of senior board members, the larger the chances of success." Megamarket projects are increasingly considered priority agenda items in multinational boards after decades of neglect in the 1980s and 1990s. Once the megamarket operations are on stream, certain companies invite megamarket nationals to join their executive teams.

Most transnational corporations operate in the megamarkets through their own subsidiaries rather than joint ventures or import agents (distributors). Group board members also sit on the boards of these subsidiaries. But in many instances, these second-level boards convene less frequently, often as a mere formality, and thus do not exercise adequate control on the megamarket team. Local partners or the subsidiary executive team (managing directors, directors of finance, marketing, R&D, etc.), particularly of medium-sized EU companies, are often given more leeway than is judicious. Without checks and balances and multichannel feedback to headquarters, this is fertile ground for abuse of the power vested in the local team.

Headquarters boards can exercise control through independent audit committees appointed by them for specific agendas (e.g., finance, human resources, strategy) to supervise local implementation. Independent experts can include retired CEOs, auditors, and consultants known to the company; they can ensure on-site control, mentor the local executive team, and report to the group board to give a balanced view so that corrections, if any, can be made in time. Needless to say, these independent experts should be selected by the group board or its executives and not on the recommendation of the subsidiary's chief. Consistent reporting and regular visits by the group's functional and strategy chiefs represent other important control mechanisms.

Rule No. 2:
The group CEO should lead the project

The personality, professionalism, and involvement of the CEO in milestone projects are crucial elements in megamarket project execution.[1] While most Western CEOs

> **Pause for thought**
>
> Thanks to the frequent visits of its CEO and other members of the executive team, an EU equipment manufacturer was able to set up an operational Indian manufacturing unit in a record nine months: company incorporation, purchase of industrial site, leasing of office space, and selection of key service providers (bank, auditors, lawyers, architects) and core subsidiary team (managing, technical, purchasing, and finance directors, project managers). In this way, they established the groundwork and set the direction that the company would follow. Once the embryo operation was in place, the EU division chiefs took over to mentor the subsidiary team.
>
> ***
>
> After acquiring a majority stake of a local equipment manufacturer, the same EU company—this time in China—was shocked to hear that the local minority partner wanted to override the partnership contract and participate autonomously in global tenders. The contract included a provision whereby the EU majority partner would take over the coordination of global sales but left some room for interpretation. The Chinese side was unhappy with the way it was treated after the share transfer and was determined to compete independently for international projects and be allowed to participate in overseas sales efforts as an equal partner. The situation was defused when the CEO mediated between the group board member responsible for sales and the minority Chinese owner (who had stayed on as minority shareholder and managing director of the acquired Chinese company). The CEO implemented a master plan for passing additional orders to the Chinese subsidiary and made the decision to meet with the Chinese side every six weeks to discuss important international projects. Relations became friendlier and solidified over time, which gave new impetus to the alliance.
>
> In contrast, what happened to a Scandinavian multinational attempting to acquire shares of a Chinese SOE is revealing. This top priority project received the personal attention of the group's CEO but later flagged when the company's China chief overrode the CEO's decisions to push his own ideas. Lobbying activities with political institutions and high-level contacts were abruptly halted; as a result, two years of intense negotiations were wasted as the project did not come to fruition.

---

1. See 7.1.

graduated and worked in North America or the EU, they are still on the learning curve for the megamarkets. Lack of understanding of and experience in these countries could result in prejudice, suspicion, and wrong behavior. There is an attitudinal change among CEOs as they grow acutely aware that the company's future will depend heavily on the megamarkets. Investment projects in the megamarkets place a heavy demand on the CEO's time and commitment.

In the beginning, the CEO will have to devote a substantial amount of time to formulating strategy and monitoring results. Showing up intermittently on short courtesy stints is insufficient to signal interest, motivate local staff, and secure long-term business.

An important role of the CEO is that of a mediator.

A CEO's role does not end with the establishment of a megamarket subsidiary. CEOs must spend more time developing and cultivating a network of local stakeholders (employees, customers, government agencies, present and future partners, etc.) after establishment of the subsidiary. As CEOs of the parent company, they are held in high esteem, and this card should be played to help promote the subsidiary with key accounts and government officials and, most important, to motivate the subsidiary's employees at all levels so that they feel integrated in the global group.

Many multinationals like Bayer, Cadbury, Daimler, IBM, Kraft, Sony, Siemens, and Unilever have integrated well with the communities in the megamarkets, earning them precious goodwill, thanks to the commitment of the successive CEOs of these companies and their farsightedness. The first CEOs understood cultural sensibilities and passed on this knowledge to the following generations of managers. Over the years, the companies thus built strong brand equity and expanded early in "tomorrow's markets."

CEOs must first of all recognize the importance of the emerging mega-economies. They must act as visionaries and charismatic leaders if they want their teams to win. Decisions of successful leaders are based on entrepreneurial, not just managerial, judgments (see table 12.1). These leaders bring about change by spurring others to take initiatives and come up with new ideas. They are not afraid of upsetting the organizational balance by interacting directly with all ranks to achieve a goal.

Table 12.1. "Entrepreneur" CEO vs. "manager" CEO.		
Attributes	**Manager CEO**	**Entrepreneur CEO**
Goals	Based on what is required	Based on what is possible
Initiative	Reacts to external influences	Is him-/herself proactive
Focus	Administers the business	Realizes a vision
Style	Accepts given orders	Provokes continuous changes
Customers	Are to be satisfied	Are to be newly shaped
Debates	Are to be defused	Are to be stimulated
Risks	Are to be avoided	Are considered a new challenge
Belonging	Respects existing order	Questions structures and rules
Empathy	Low personal emotions	High feeling for others
Ideas	Works in existing framework	Initiates problem solution

Conversely, CEOs who, for lack of time or interest, delegate the execution of crucial tasks to others down the line or do not take the advice of experts seriously are very likely to lose opportunities or misjudge risks.

Rule No. 3:
Senior executives should adapt to the project

Senior executives must possess eight qualities to succeed in the megamarkets (see box 12.2). Western executives stepping out of the Judeo-Christian sphere are confronted with unfamiliar behavior patterns and value systems: Chinese pragmatism, Indian argumentativeness, and Russian patriotism, to mention a few oversimplifications. Avoiding culture-caused misinterpretations is a complex juggling act requiring prudence and new tactics to avoid impasses.

The executive team should find a balance between implementation of the company's guiding principles and adaptation of the means to implement them. The purchase of industrial, real estate, or financial assets for the launch of an alliance in a megamarket is a strategic matter that requires competent handling.

Pause for thought

Laxmi Mittal's handling of the merger with Arcelor in a reverse situation is enlightening. Arcelor's European executives strongly opposed an alliance with Mittal Steel, mainly because they could not accept being acquired by an Indian entrepreneur "who has made money but has neither a Western culture nor brand awareness," as one senior executive of Arcelor put it before the transaction. Mittal Steel approached the delicate cultural issue by offering concrete advantages that showed the Indian entrepreneur to be as caring as an EU businessperson. Mittal won the battle of hearts by offering Arcelor shareholders a higher price plus a job conservation scheme and promising career prospects for employees, in addition to faster integration and consolidation that would vastly improve Arcelor's position, particularly vis-à-vis large suppliers.

***

In a recent case, an EU food producer acquired a 75% share in a Russian enterprise that owns a highly visible brand, particularly with the country's top retail chains. After initial euphoria, the executive team distanced itself from the project and tried to send assistants for important negotiations, with the result that the Russian side did not take the intention seriously. The deal was delayed by almost two years with disastrous consequences for the buyer: 50% increase in the share price, a missed opportunity to acquire a secondhand factory site, and lost market share of 5%–10% because competitors had meanwhile captured market niches.

In another case, the vice president of a German industrial components manufacturer gave carte blanche to the newly recruited managing director of the Russian subsidiary. The company had established high-level contacts in Russia's energy sector. These would have preferred a customer-vendor partnership with co-investments in assembly and service. But the Russian subsidiary's managing director preferred to hard-sell components imported from Germany. As the vice president was close to retirement, he wanted to avoid a conflict although initially he did not agree with the managing director's strategy. The rest of the executive team did not want to confront the vice president, and the German company finally could not win over a single key user in Russia's booming oil and gas sector. Key accounts were lost to competing suppliers who were willing to invest in ancillary structures for increasing local content as that assured stable order volumes.

> **Box 12.2. Eight qualities of senior executives for the megamarkets.**
>
> - International experience
> - Intercultural sensitivity
> - Transparency and integrity
> - Accessibility
> - Empathy
> - Strategic thinking
> - Financial expertise
> - Customer-driven mindset

> **Box 12.3. Middle management to be supervised by the CEO and board.**
>
> - Area managers at headquarters or regional office in charge of megamarket
> - Functional managers at headquarters responsible for cross-sectional departments: business development, personnel, legal, finance, IT, R&D
> - Managers responsible for products, services, technologies at headquarters
> - Managing directors and directors of regional headquarters (e.g., Singapore/Hong Kong for Asia)
> - Managing directors and directors at megamarket subsidiary level (e.g., China, India, Russia operations)

12.1.2. Middle management performance

By middle management, we mean headquarters division heads (area, function, product), regional heads, and chiefs of megamarket subsidiaries (see box 12.3). Whereas senior executives should take part in milestone activities (e.g., lobbying, recruitment of core local team, etc.), frontline managers, including the subsidiary's executive team, have the task of translating strategies into tactical moves on a day-to-day basis. The working style and reliability of this echelon reflects directly on the company's image in the megamarkets and determines how the company is perceived by the local business community.

RULE NO. 4:
SELECTION AND RECRUITMENT OF MIDDLE MANAGERS MUST BE DONE CAREFULLY

Recruiting candidates for the top positions at the megamarket subsidiary requires sharper judgment and a more stringent screening process than in the advanced markets because of the geographical distance and cultural differences. Candidates for such positions can be expatriates, local managers, or returnees (non-resident Chinese, Indians, and Russians returning after a stay in an advanced market). Although there is a trend to localize management, many advanced market companies prefer to entrust their megamarket subsidiaries to expatriates, especially middle managers from headquarters who know the company well and are therefore in a position to transfer the company's guiding principles to the subsidiary and get the necessary support from headquarters. They are useful in the initial stages for transferring valuable skills (technical directors) or controlling key functions (finance directors) before responsibilities are handed over to a local manager.

But expatriates who consider megamarket postings as career killers or lack the support of family members for the new assignment should be avoided just as should those who regard the posting as a reward for past performance or a refuge from strife at headquarters. These candidates tend to rule with the power of their office, which they put above principle, instead of serving as examples by means of their convictions, personality, and competence. Given the high level of education of local staff in the megamarkets, the question of expatriates will revolve around the identification of areas where the individual can bring in the knowledge acquired in the parent company. This is sometimes easier to define for technical functions: technical director, chief engineer, technical expert on a short-term visit, and so forth. Sending expatriates for non-technical functions (marketing, purchasing, communications, human resources, general administration) will require more convincing of the local management of the expatriate's comparative advantage over locally recruited professionals, who can be as competent and speak the local language to build a contact network.

When recruiting local senior executives, the best practice is to undertake background checks (with former employers, customers, suppliers, bankers, auditors, legal advisers, etc.) before signing the employment contract. The report will reveal if the candidate has the required talent mix (see figure 12.2) and shares the same values, philosophy, and goals of the foreign company.[2] A mismatch at this level can result in anything from an underperforming megamarket subsidiary to its closure. However excellent a company may be in its home market, this excellence will not flow into the megamarket subsidiary if the locally recruited chief executive does not offer a suitable conduit. In the megamarkets where people networks are of overriding importance, selecting a candidate from a mediocre network will entrench the subsidiary in that network (suppliers, service providers, employees, customer contacts, government agencies, etc.). It is advisable to test a candidate's skills and character by including six months' probation time in the contract.

The cost factor sometimes prompts medium-sized players from Europe to recruit returnees as local managing directors because it is assumed they have international experience combined with an understanding of the local language and mentality. This choice may

---

Pause for thought

An Internet survey of German companies mentioned on the India Brand Equity Web site* revealed that growing numbers of subsidiaries are headed by Indian nationals. The reasons for this trend are: medium size of the EU company, non-availability of EU company staff prepared to move to India, and joint venture with a local partner. The EU company in such cases exercises control through its directors on the board or an expatriate finance director transferred to the subsidiary.

At the same time, in an interesting reversal of trend, large Indian companies are recruiting foreign executives. They aim to get the best managerial, technical, and scientific talents. However, purchasing, marketing, and sales as well as HR managers are mostly recruited locally as these functions require a wide-ranging contact base and good knowledge of local language(s) and the Indian business mentality.

* *Interesting case studies of German companies in India can be found at http://ibef.org.*

---

2. Inviting the candidates with their spouses to a restaurant can reveal a lot about their true personalities. As is often the case in India, men may acquire a global veneer while their core remains ultraconservative, if not fiercely anti-Western (colonial backlash), which can be seen from the spouse's behavior and expectations from a new employer.

Figure 12.2. Required talent mix for middle managers.

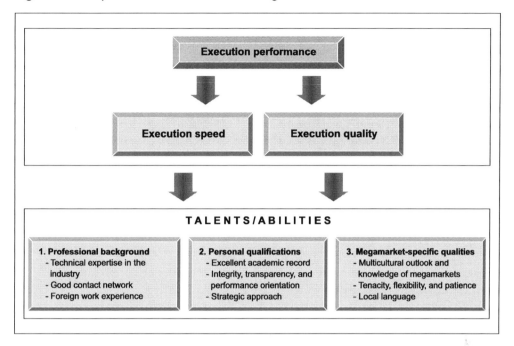

bear a risk, especially if the returnee has adopted a Western lifestyle and now disrespects local traditions, making the person unacceptable to compatriots.

The chief executive of the megamarket subsidiary is the crucial link between the foreign headquarters and its local subsidiary. Much depends on this kingpin, who can either make or break the relationship between the two sides. To be avoided in particular in the megamarkets is a chief executive or managing director with a neo-colonial (expatriate, returnee) or anti-colonial (local recruit) attitude. The "them-us" divide that such individuals can create will have disastrous consequences for the company. Recruiting the core local team should therefore be given due attention and time. A combination of headhunting, advertisements, and contact networks should be used and followed up with a thorough background check on the candidates before the employment contract is signed.

Successful companies never rely on one person—managing director or permanent representative—but lean on a core team of talented managers and people who are recruited directly by headquarters and not by a single individual (e.g., subsidiary chief, regional head), who could use this freedom to surround himself with like-minded subordinates from the same social community or weak characters who will follow orders.

Pause for thought

A German machine-tool producer hired through a recruitment agency a Chinese based in Germany to help integrate a majority acquisition in China and after some time become the local managing director. But the Chinese germanophile's derision of things Chinese did not gain him any friends when he returned to his home country. The Chinese minority partner was therefore not willing to introduce the returnee to key customers and suppliers. It did not help that the returnee was sent without a clear mandate or explanation for his possible contribution to an already well-managed company.

> **Pause for thought**
>
> *A European auto components supplier put its venture in India at risk after recruiting a managing director who created a nexus of acquiescent employees and suppliers, resulting in project delays and loss of image to the company.*

This applies to the core subsidiary team as well. In India, the team should represent a regional mix (people from northern, southern, eastern, and western India) to avoid a communal bias, which could be a serious handicap. Prior experience with a multinational in India or abroad and knowledge of the EU/US company's language are more than just assets as they shape the mindset and business practices of the individuals. Similar situations can arise in China where southerners may encounter difficulties when approaching partner networks or customers in the center or north and vice versa. In Russia, business development in Greater Moscow may be quite different from orchestrating networks in St Petersburg or other city markets.

Rule No. 5:
Checks and balances must be put in place prior to recruitment

Controls and multi-channel reporting ensure that existing and recruited middle managers—independent of their location (group headquarters, megamarket subsidiary) and origin (expatriates, locals, returnees)—remain transparent in their dealings with headquarters and local business partners, pass on relevant information, and are not tempted to deviate from the road map for market leadership.

EU/US chiefs should lend an ear to information from different sources (customers, suppliers, local advisers, and well-wishers) for early warning signals about goal deviations, unethical behavior, or attitudes that may hamper expansion or harm the image of the company. While US and Japanese companies tend to set up such systems right at the start of their operations, many EU companies give full rein to subsidiary chiefs without testing them until mistakes or irregularities are uncovered, when it may be too late. A system of checks and balances put in place at the outset will allow headquarters to guide and control middle management teams.

Some transnational corporations recruit a permanent representative to monitor activities and report to headquarters. The relationship between such a person and the subsidiary requires careful handling to avoid friction with the subsidiary's executives, particularly the local management. Reporting lines must be clearly defined, and the role of the representative must be accepted by local staff; otherwise, the individual will find it difficult to accomplish the stipulated duties. The representative will face distrust and suspicion if he/she is perceived as a "mole" of the parent company.

Rule No. 6:
Skill development of managers must be an ongoing effort

Speed and quality of execution depend on the middle managers' talents and experience. Not all managers have the requisite and specific skills and knowledge at the start of their

> **Pause for thought**
>
> *Sitting in front of an impassive Indian government official (representing a huge potential key account) was an enthusiastic young export manager from a leading EU company participating in a tender: "We are number one in Europe for …" he started. The official was unimpressed and wanted to know what the name of his company meant, how long it had been in the business, what the core competencies were, and how much more expensive his product would be compared with the local ones. The EU manager, hurt by these "disparaging remarks," advised his superiors back home to abandon all canvassing efforts and to revert to other markets. Soon after, he quit the organization. Three years later, a new team of managers returned to find out that "the Indian market offers far better prospects than was originally thought." The company had to step up its investments in skill development to prepare managers for new challenges.*

assignment. Training and experience hone professional skills. Executive coaching programs are increasingly offered to improve personality traits and adjust them to the demands of the job. Megamarket-specific skills are acquired through extended stays and work experience in the target market. Experience in one megamarket is useful but not sufficient to run operations in other megamarkets. In the case of local employees, knowledge of best practices and experience in the advanced markets will help them better understand the thought process underlying decisions from headquarters.

Development of soft skills is important for managers dealing with the megamarkets. The most difficult truth to swallow for managers making their first steps into these markets is the reversal of status and the need to behave with humility and modesty.

The biggest challenge, especially for SMEs, is grooming talented, culture-sensitive managers who can reliably assume positions of responsibility in the megamarkets. The candidates can be "true fits" or "stretch fits." The second category refers to managers who are upgraded to top positions in the megamarket subsidiaries without any previous experience in that position. They are not ready for the job and should work under the tutelage of an external coach or mentor (e.g., retired former managing director, HR consultant) for some time. The mentor is mandated by the board to give authority and legitimacy. The mentor may meet the managing director periodically (weekly or fortnightly) to discuss issues of strategic relevance. The board may thus detect deficiencies and introduce corrective measures, including the replacement of the managing director in the case of non-performance.

12.1.3. Staff retention

Personnel-related issues determine long-term planning and execution in the megamarkets. The management team must be supported by the best human talents available. There is nothing more damaging to strategy realization than discouraged employees. Execution quality and speed depends on the company's talent portfolio, which must be superior to that of competitors. Selecting professionals for exacting projects demands balancing today's and tomorrow's agendas.

Rule No. 7:
Young talent must be motivated and retained

Young talents must be recruited, groomed, and motivated to remain with the company and carry their work forward. High performers attract the best talents. Wise managers look for specialists who are better than they are in finding solutions in their respective area of work. To cultivate this philosophy, executives do not shun personnel shake-ups, which have an educational effect on other team members. Most leading players went through numerous changes, even if it implied replacing or shifting persons because they were hampering developments in fast-growing markets. At the same time, it is important to create a culture where mistakes are permissible, knowing that if people don't make mistakes, they will hardly generate any success.

Winning the battle for such talents is all about meeting the aspirations of employees. It requires a shift in perception of the role of megamarket employees, who would like their operation to be central rather than peripheral to the parent company's global business. They expect the employer to offer them the same career opportunities in the company's global operations as talented young individuals from other countries. They would like to see that the flow of knowledge, capabilities, and people runs not just from the Triad—EU, Japan, USA—to the megamarkets, but also in the reverse direction. Leading multinationals rotate their best talents across the global organization regardless of nationality and level of responsibility.

The importance of training and retention cannot be stressed enough given that talents are scarce and attrition rates are high (see figure 12.3). This appears paradoxical in countries like China and India with their high populations. But the education systems in the megamarkets are still not geared to produce enough employable graduates; those produced are immediately absorbed by fast economic growth. In China and Russia, employees in their forties and fifties trained under the former regime lack the entrepreneurial spirit that

---

Pause for thought

SAP, Germany's leading software company, has launched a series of initiatives to ensure lifelong learning, specific skill development, and other programs to nurture talent. The company is successfully adopting some of these concepts in the megamarkets by integrating megamarket specialists in the global programs, which include:

- *high potential program: young managers with great potential are trained and encouraged to improve their skills so that they can be promoted to higher positions*
- *succession planning program: talented candidates with visible leadership skills are spotted early in their careers and systematically prepared for top jobs at headquarters and foreign subsidiaries*
- *special training courses: offered to both senior executives and middle managers keen on proving their qualifications in general management and at the functional level*
- *SAP University: special courses, workshops, and online training for staff members interested in acquiring a degree and improving their knowledge for rising within the company's hierarchy*

Figure 12.3. Attrition rates in the advanced markets and emerging megamarkets, 2008.

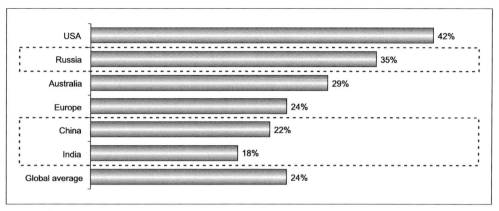

a. Moscow/St Petersburg.

Source: Times News. New York, 2008.

the young ones are fast acquiring. Foreign companies therefore face a shortage of qualified middle managers with eight to ten years of job experience.

Job hopping to wring a higher pay and poaching by competitors are common in the three megamarkets, where job opportunities exceed the supply of professionals. Staff turnover rates can be as high as 15%–20% in the bigger cities. Attrition is high across all functions. In India, the average attrition rate in the BPO sector is around 30%–35%, even if it is lower than the 70% attrition rate in the United States in the same sector.

Scarcity leads to above-average increases in salaries of managers in the megamarkets. They started from a much lower base than in the advanced markets and, for certain high positions, have almost caught up. On average, salaries have been rising by 8%–10% annually since 2002; for lower positions, increases were even higher. The challenge of job attrition in their megamarket subsidiaries is new to HR managers at headquarters of multinationals. They usually deal with the inverse situation of layoffs in the advanced markets. They need to re-program themselves to find ways of filling the talent gap and retaining staff they have recruited in the megamarkets (see box 12.4). Some companies offer long tenures to build trust, while others manage to induce job satisfaction through the careful establishment of shared values, objectives, experiences, and rewards.

One of the points in box 12.4 mentions "imparting a sense of adventure." For HR directors at headquarters, this may clash with the low morale of employees in advanced markets who face the threat of job losses. But HR can create osmosis between the optimistic megamarket employees and the pessimistic advanced market employees through employee exchange programs and knowledge sharing. The intention is a transfer of the enthusiasm of the megamarket and the skills of the advanced markets. Interestingly, high performers use external specialists to speed up the execution of paramount projects. They understand that such experts can complement the firm's in-house talent pool and observe basic rules of ethical conduct. They try to retain them like qualified employees.

Box 12.4. Basic rules for retaining specialists in the megamarkets.

- Note that pay raises work only up to a point; afterward it is job satisfaction that counts.
- Understand the deep sources of job satisfaction and address them: treat employees as the "first customers."
- Offer opportunities for staff to work in the group's foreign subsidiaries.
- Impart a sense of adventure to the young recruits from the megamarkets who are ready to relocate and learn new things.
- Accept and implement megamarket concepts in other subsidiaries; recognize employee's ownership of the idea.
- Help motivated recruits gain more skills through targeted training programs.
- Learn from best practices of local companies (e.g., Tata in India).
- Remember that local employees expect the foreign company to bring its know-how and best practices into the megamarket.
- Headquarters HR should get involved in formulating HR practices that combine both global and local elements.

RULE NO. 8:

PERSONNEL DEVELOPMENT AND REWARDS

Campus recruitment alone will not help to fill the talent gap. Once the novelty of a highly paid job wears off, the fresh graduates wake up to the realities of work pressure. The toughness of a job and the responsibilities it entails are not adequately conveyed at the outset. Apart from the induction and project training, not much investment is made in motivational coaching and a continuous training program to help new recruits and their spouses adjust to the real world. Large multinationals are responding by investing heavily in personnel development schemes that comprise training, job rotation, stays abroad, and special bonus awards. They tailor their talent development strategy and offer attractive packages of monetary and nonmonetary rewards to outstanding individuals, regardless of their nationality.

Compensation packages (see box 12.5) are intensely negotiated by megamarket managers. In addition to salary, incentives, and perquisites, they expect the package to be tax efficient. Certain managers in the larger cities are already better paid than their Western counterparts once lower income tax and living costs are factored in. The yearly take-home pay adjusted for spending power of top executives in China, India, and Russia can reach US$180,000–200,000, about twice as much as their counterparts in France, Germany, Japan, or the United Kingdom (see table 12.2), according to Hay Group, an international HR consultancy.[3]

Table 12.2. Annual salary brackets of managers in the megamarkets, 2008 (US$).

	China	India	Russia
Office support staff	12,000–20,000	8,000–15,000	24,000–36,000
Middle managers	27,000–32,000	20,000–28,000	48,000–60,000
Senior managers	46,000–54,000	32,000–40,000	72,000–90,000
Top executives	90,000–110,000	65,000–90,000	130,000–200,000

Source: Korn Ferry.

---

3. "Executive Pay," *The Economist*, July 28, 2007, 90. See also www.haygroup.com.

Box 12.5. Elements of a compensation package for local managers.

- Basic salary
- House rent allowance
- Children's education allowance
- Leave travel allowance
- Special allowance (e.g., club membership, car + chauffeur, phone)
- Annual bonus for outstanding results
- Retirement benefits
- Insurance (health, personal accident, critical illness)
- Coaching and training
- Stock options

Pause for thought

- *BASF, a world leader in chemicals, attracts and retains young talents through its professional development program (PDP). It formulated a catalogue of values and principles, including a leadership compass, so that unity is preserved despite a growing cultural diversity within the group. BASF fosters the creation of internal communities between like-minded people to make it difficult for headhunters to poach specialists from the company. These measures, which also concern managerial staff, are supplemented by "horizontal" procedures promoting transparency via team building, multichannel information flow, and senior executive accessibility. Human resources specialists promote a positive employer-employee atmosphere as a starting point for overcoming personnel gaps.*

- *Multinational headquarters can sometimes learn from their megamarket subsidiaries. At Procter & Gamble, which is rated among India's top five employers because of its "sizzling young atmosphere" and "focus on knowledge-enhancement," the two biggest attractions for recruits are early responsibility and the ability to chart out a rapid career path through the provided global opportunities. As one employee put it, "Right from day one, P&G gives you the feeling that you are in charge. And your career path isn't restricted by geographical limits." The company is not driven by hierarchies and protocol. It seeks to provide shareholder value by keeping employees' interest at the forefront.*

- *Similarly, Hewlett-Packard India stresses transparency, empowerment, and equality at work. Its founder-CEO Suresh Rajpal openly claims that employee satisfaction is the first goal on his business agenda, followed by customer satisfaction. He institutionalized employee satisfaction surveys, which are conducted at regular eighteen-month intervals, covering nineteen areas relating to leadership, work environment, job content, pay, and benefits. Similar concepts are now being tested in HP's US headquarters.*

- *Claas, a leading German agricultural equipment producer, created Claas Mitarbeitergesellschaft (CMG), a special "employee investment company." The idea of converting employees into shareholders interested in the future health and long-term survival of the company has so far worked out well. The shares of CMG were valued at roughly US$20 million in 2007.*

- *The Tata Steel Web site features an "employee community" so that all employees of Tata Steel across all branches stay connected: "Whether you are a part of the Tata family or have separated in pursuit of newer ventures—you can still seek out a friend, build your community and share your thoughts here."*

Apart from compensation and personal development, what do megamarket employees seek? Bonding is important in the megamarkets.

Megamarket senior executives are also status-oriented and do not accept differential treatment of expatriate and local staff. Although, ironically, local senior executives want to be differentiated from compatriot lower cadres and bargain hard for additional perquisites (including the model of the car) that set them apart.

Rule No. 9:

Leadership styles

The expatriate CEO of a megamarket subsidiary knows that the Western leadership style has to be adapted to the local context but does not know how to do this. The CEO can start by studying the most admired business leaders in the country: Narayan Murthy (Infosys) and Azim Premji (Wipro) in India; Li Ka-Shing (Hutchison Whampoa) and Wang Chuanfu (BYD) in China; and Alexei Miller (Gazprom) and Vladimir Evtushenkov (Sistema) in Russia. However, most megamarket companies are not mentored by such iconic leaders whose leadership styles may not always be appropriate to manage smaller entities. In China and India, owner-managers run their companies like business empires. This looks authoritarian to outsiders, but internally it fosters respect and accelerates execution. As patriarchs, owner-entrepreneurs wield great power over their staff, but at the same time, they have a moral obligation to care for their employees and their personal problems. Meanwhile, many Russian managers have been shedding the leadership style of the erstwhile hierarchical command economy. As the context of leadership is changing, the historical emphasis on hard power is becoming outdated. The "global Russian" stresses charismatic and democratic management based on information-sharing and networking. Modern Russian leaders rely on their entrepreneurial spirit but also take into consideration the views of core managers and advisers who form the inner decision-making circle of the company.

Clear-cut methods focused on individual accountability and bottom-line results are ineffective in the context of Asian governance where the emphasis is on hierarchy, social competence, and relationship management (networking). In the megamarkets, business partners attach great value to personal relations and invest time in getting to know the other side. Another difference is related to time management. EU/US companies planning well ahead and showing patience are more successful than those pursuing a short-term approach. Democratic versus autocratic style is another choice for a company's leadership to make. The shift toward more liberal or democratic methods observed in Russia should not conceal that in traditionally run companies (the bulk of players) employees are not supposed to jump hierarchical levels and talk to top decision-makers directly. Often, a mix of participative and directive styles can be observed depending on the situation. The clash of cultures and leadership styles following an acquisition can lead to delays in the execution of important projects. It is crucial to sensitize staff to the new owners and evaluate which healthy mix of leadership styles can accelerate success (see box 12.6). In reverse situations, too, leadership styles take an unexpected turn when, after a merger, a Western employee-focused family enterprise becomes an integral part of a listed megamarket group with formalized rules and business-centered management aimed at quarterly results.

> **Box 12.6. Leadership styles for the megamarkets.**
> - Democratic vs. autocratic
> - Participative vs. directive
> - Results-oriented vs. relations-based
> - Employee-centered vs. business-centered
> - Short-term results vs. sustainable market share

Korn Ferry's study on leadership styles in Asia on "*The Dream Team: Delivering Leadership in Asia*" mentions the following as the leadership styles Western companies should adopt to be successful in Asia:

- establishing strong local networks
- consensus building
- loyalty to company
- focus on execution
- care for staff
- emphasis on profitability
- reliance on family and friends

Among the qualities of the expatriate CEO, the study cites the ability to understand, respect, and empathize with local cultures. Asia is not homogenous. An expatriate CEO who believes, for example, that China and India are "Chindia" has not understood the nuances of their rivalry and will not succeed. In return, the Western practices that Asian (and also Russian) businesses will need to adopt to go global include:

- focus on strategic vision;
- empowering employees to take initiatives and act independently;
- promotion of an innovation culture;
- emphasis on customer service;
- communication and presentations; and
- respect of international practices and standards (e.g., when undertaking M&As abroad).

The leadership style of the future is more likely to be a combination of Western and Asian practices. In modern companies, power is increasingly diffused and traditional hierarchies are being undermined, making soft power more important. But that does not mean that coercion takes a back seat to persuasion. The best approach is "smart power," a combination of soft and hard power, and an inherent flexibility to adapt the leadership as circumstances change. Charismatic and team-oriented leaders will allow local staff to participate in the goal-setting and decision-making processes. As a rule, these leaders are more accepted worldwide as cultural convergence grows with globalization.

Senior executives and managers of megamarket subsidiaries need to follow basic leadership principles if they want to achieve execution excellence (see figure 12.4):

- active participation in execution to set a good example as a role model (charisma);

Figure 12.4. Leadership principles for the megamarkets.

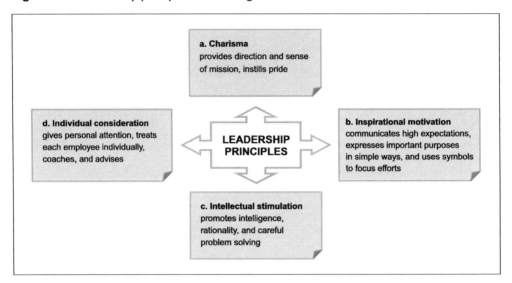

- formulation of clear and challenging goals (inspirational motivation);
- creation of an engaging and stimulating environment for personal development (intellectual stimulation);
- preparation of the next generation of leaders (personal consideration).

A new generation of managers is moving up the career ladder in megamarket companies. Having studied and lived abroad, they can very well make out a true leader, whose decisions are led by vision, from simple, middle-level managers (with a "compartmentalized" view of results) and/or administrators (in charge of rules and procedures).

12.2. Organizational alignment

Companies that push the boundaries in emerging markets will encounter significant organizational resistance, mainly because rules, incentives, and reward systems are not aligned to encourage expansion. Its legacy does not allow the company to meet the demands of megamarket customers and partners. Decision-making mechanisms, in particular, are not coordinated and clearly defined. Overcoming these constraints places an additional burden on senior executives in direct confrontation with reticent middle managers at the center and in the frontline. It is frequently not clear where best to locate the critical decision (e.g., about operating expenses, capital expenditure, project budgets, new recruits) that should govern the allocation of scarce resources. Too often such decisions are made in uncoordinated ways and not based on an analysis of the situation.

Relying on traditional organization models is not always conducive to effective project execution in the megamarkets. Adjusting the typical organizational architecture can therefore help seize new opportunities and preempt competition. Medium-sized companies—the bulk of Western players—sometimes respond faster to challenges than larger TNCs through informal networks and flat structures, in which the owner is the sole decision-maker. But these smaller companies do not have the human resources to spare for undertaking a megamarket project in addition to their normal responsibilities. In SME organization charts, megamarkets are grouped along with other markets served by the international or export divisions at headquarters. Larger companies have more people who can be assigned to projects, but managers may lack the authority to make decisions or be hampered by hierarchical incompatibilities and internal politics.

12.2.1. Traditional organizations: Functional, divisional, and matrix models

TNCs organize their megamarket operations by function, region/area, or business unit/product groups. Each of these models represents an equally common organizing principle for companies independent of their size, sector of activity, or long-term objectives. Medium-sized players offering a limited range of products are mostly organized by five major functional domains:

- general export;
- operations (production-technical, procurement);
- marketing (distribution, sales, after-sales);
- support services (HR, finance, IT);
- R&D (which is supposed to secure the future).

The functional model has its limitations when approaching the megamarkets. Inter-functional conflicts occur when executives at headquarters pursue a different agenda through proxies in the megamarket subsidiary.

Larger companies covering many market segments with a wide range of products use divisional structures along major product/technology lines and geographic areas. Each division has its own functional departments and acts as a profit center (see figure 12.5). Budgets for large-scale projects or investments with wider implications are approved by the group, where key strategic functions such as intelligence, corporate planning, finance, and R&D are concentrated. The "division" or "strategic business unit" structure has produced good

---

Pause for thought

Take the example of the China marketing chief of a leading German construction equipment maker based in Shanghai who for many years forecasted overoptimistic sales figures that served as the basis for output targets by the China production chief running a greenfield unit in another city. Overproduction resulted in higher stocks as the equipment could not be sold as expected. The two functional chiefs for China, both expatriates, could not agree on a strategy and called upon the group's board for mediation. The production chief, whose functional superior (board member for global operations) had in the meantime lost influence on the marketing board, was eventually called back to Germany to defuse tensions. The root cause of the problem—an indirect sales policy via independent agents—remained, leading to further losses in market share. Chinese clients demanded technical service, advice, and direct contact with their vendors, which only a well-trained, in-house sales force, and not agents, can guarantee.

Figure 12.5. Functional and divisional organizations.

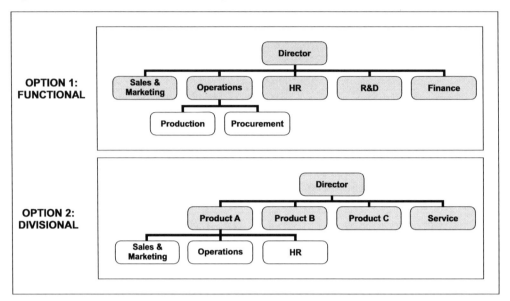

results with companies operating in mature markets, but it can create overlaps in emerging economies where interdivisional resources need to be merged for speeding up expansion.

Large multinationals like Cisco[4] have created special "emerging markets" teams or even "BRICs" units to react to their rising importance. With time and as business expands, it is expected that separate units will be established for each of the megamarkets so that sales propositions can be adjusted even more to local conditions, which can differ significantly according to regional markets.

Matrix structures intend to combine two divisional dimensions to leverage the benefits of both (see figure 12.6):

- The product division exploits global economies of scale (purchasing, sales) for a given product family, technology, or application.
- The geographic or area division adds value by generating knowledge related to individual markets and the needs of local clients.

Matrix organizations offer the advantage of centralized coordination, functional expertise, and economies of scale for individual product families while maintaining autonomy in marketing and sales. But a product line–geographic (area) matrix can lead to confusion when middle managers have to report to two bosses: the country executive (e.g., head of the megamarket subsidiary) and the global product line director at headquarters. The "dual-boss reporting dilemma" can slow down the execution of important tasks or projects because of a possible divergence in views between senior executives responsible for the row or column of the matrix. This impacts accountability. Conflicts programmed inherently in this structure come to the fore when the megamarket subsidiary becomes of strategic importance to the group. The product line head is away at headquarters while the country

---

4. See www.cisco.com.

Figure 12.6. Matrix organization for global product groups and geographies.

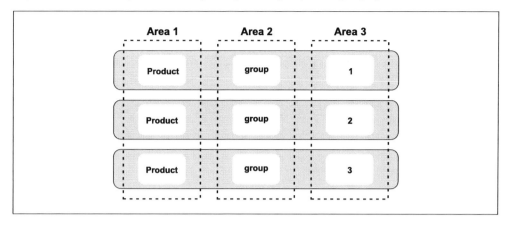

Pause for thought

In Russia, three divisional units of the same German multinational opened independent sales offices in different locations. Their activities were not bundled, which prevented the company from pooling resources, lobbying important projects with local governments, and promoting the umbrella group brand. Worse still, after a few years of operation, one unit decided to launch a manufacturing plant, but alone it lacked the weight to negotiate favorable terms with the local authorities, and the investment cost the group 40%–50% more than what it would have paid had the units stayed united.

***

A German multinational set up a new Asia holding in Hong Kong with control functions over all the companies owned by the group in China, Japan, and South Korea. The group's two major divisions have manufacturing units in China as well as control over a recently acquired medium-sized European SME with headquarters in Germany. Owing to the matrix structure, profit and loss (P&L) responsibility lies with the Hong Kong holding, not with the (acquired) German head office of the Chinese unit. The head office therefore decided to bill its Chinese unit (daughter company) for each delivery and service as if it were an external supplier. For the group, the German company represents a profit center that should maximize its results instead of supporting its (own) faraway unit, which organizationally (not technically) belongs to the Asia holding. As a consequence of high pricing of inputs from Europe, the Chinese unit gradually lost its competitiveness in the local market, obliging it to look for sales opportunities in other markets. Moreover, the organizational structure so far has not allowed for a design of an M&A strategy in China, which would be a more effective way to remove competitors from the market. The holding in Hong Kong pursues other financial priorities.

---

head (megamarket CEO or managing director) is on-site and can impose his standpoint, which may not be in the best interest of a particular product division. Project team leaders, stuck at matrix intersections, struggle to coordinate between the preferences of "row" and "column" heads, which can lead to delays or loss of quality. While matrix organizations help to improve financial control, they may entail dysfunctions that hinder growth of newly established subsidiaries.

Large multinationals grant special decision-making powers to individual megamarket subsidiaries that operate as separate legal entities with their own CEOs and boards of

Figure 12.7. Holding structure for megamarket operations.

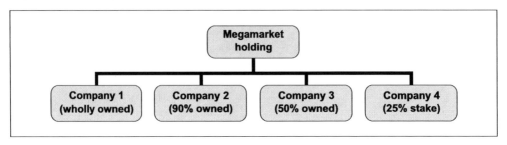

directors. In multinationals like Siemens, activities are coordinated by a central executive committee comprising the senior executives of the parent company. This committee examines the overall strategy, suggests potential business opportunities, and reviews performance against targets. Megamarkets like China and Russia are gradually being treated at par with major advanced markets. A local holding structure is created that is headed by a CEO who is responsible for all the activities in the country, including those of independent local companies and joint ventures. The holding entity has service-level agreements with the local companies held by it to provide corporate support in finance, accounting, sales, marketing, and R&D (see figure 12.7). Such structures also optimize taxes and spread the risk. This is a complex issue involving double-taxation treaties, transfer pricing, interdivisional sales, and local taxes at both headquarters and the megamarket subsidiary. It can be affected by decisions to float the company on the stock exchange via an IPO.

12.2.2. Intrapreneurial organizations

High-performing companies grant various degrees of decision-making rights to their divisional (single or matrix) structure, except for strategic issues, which are approved by the corporate board. While combining two divisional levels, innovative structures adopt a project-oriented approach involving the relevant divisions. Selected specialists are assigned to cross-functional teams while administratively they still belong to their original division (product or geographic area) or functional unit (e.g., engineering, marketing, R&D) and to which they return when the project is completed. Team members report to their project coordinator or team leader, but also to their respective divisional and functional leaders. By superimposing a project orientation upon the divisional (product and geographic) structure, the company is in a better position to identify and seize new opportunities in the megamarkets.

Companies can go even further and grant project managers equal power as the division or functional chiefs for the implementation of important projects. Project managers report directly to the corporate board and have the power to decide on measures to achieve goals set for specific projects (e.g., acquiring a stake in a megamarket company), while divisional and area managers provide the required support and review performance. "Virtual or networked structures" operate across traditional boundaries and can be dismantled or reassembled in response to changing opportunities (see figure 12.8). They are called "intrapreneurial" as they represent decentralized management, encourage team building, and enhance knowledge and innovation management. Such models are not restrained by horizontally or vertically rigid structures. Cross-functional teams dissolve horizontal barriers and enable the organization to respond quickly to contextual changes as they

Figure 12.8. Virtual organisation.

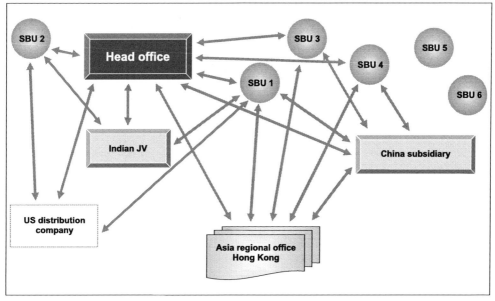

SBU = strategic business unit

have direct contact with board members and local business partners. While organizations based on the intrapreneurial concept relinquish a degree of control, they ensure better communication and faster execution.

In the context of global competition, companies must select an organizational structure that improves reporting and accelerates decision-making. They must function smoothly like networks and delegate responsibilities. Leading companies operating simultaneously in many markets set up core centers of gravity in important geographies. CEOs are connected virtually with multicultural executives and project teams around the globe (see box 12.7).

Box 12.7. Operating principles of networked organizations.[a]

- Few hierarchical levels
- High sharing of information
- Close to users/customers
- More people in the market
- Slim headquarters and overheads
- Global presence
- Use of Internet
- Fast decisions
- Structured approach

a. Example of www.booksurge.com.

> **Pause for thought**
>
> *Accenture, for example, has no headquarters but several "core" centers based on industry groups. One such center will be opened in either India or China.*
>
> *IBM has consolidated global functions such as procurement in China, finance in the United States, and accounting in the Philippines.**
>
> *Medium-sized players can learn useful lessons in organizational design and corporate culture from these initiatives.*
>
> * *"Globalisation: The Way Forward," The Economic Times, February 16, 2008.*

12.2.3. Coordination and communication

Implementing a megamarket project raises the issue of interaction between headquarters and the megamarket subsidiaries. For headquarters to add value, the benefits from its strategic thinking, decision-making, resource allocation, and monitoring must exceed the cost of its functioning. Value is destroyed when decisions are delayed, responses are slow, and resources are wrongly allocated. Chief executives of subsidiaries, on their part, must keep headquarters informed. Communication between the two should overcome constraints of:

- geographic distance (including time difference);
- informational distance (lack of awareness and knowledge about megamarkets at headquarters; misunderstanding of headquarters' intentions by megamarket chiefs); and
- cultural and psychological distance (mentality-related aspects, soft factors).

Support from headquarters will also depend on how well megamarket chiefs "sell" their territory to the board to claim the appropriate share of resources and attention.

Problems occur when resources are concentrated in central functions and jobs at headquarters are perceived as better career platforms than field assignments. Ideally, top management will encourage megamarket assignments by offering promotions to returning staff. Talents are quickly identified by reducing the chain of command, enabling megamarket managers to report directly to the corporate board (instead of division or regional headquarters). Senior management needs to find a balance between the principles of autonomy (ensuring efficient operations) and interdependence (ensuring that the megamarkets are synchronized with the company's global strategy).

Information sharing, knowledge transfer, and effective communication must underpin execution at all organizational levels. Accountability for key decisions and actions must be the guiding principle. A series of critical success factors affect the relationship between headquarters and megamarket subsidiaries:

- headquarters' commitment to the megamarkets;
- clout of megamarket chief with board members;
- creation of megamarket awareness at all levels at headquarters (VIP visits, orientation programs);
- shift in power and budgetary authority to megamarket operations.

Multi-layer hierarchies are to be avoided to foster better interpersonal relations between headquarters and the group's subsidiaries. Point persons can be designated at headquarters for various functions and divisions so that the megamarket executives have access to information rapidly. To reduce hierarchies and accelerate information flows, it is advisable to convert megamarket subsidiaries into regional headquarters rather than manage megamarket operations from external locations (e.g., Singapore for China, Dubai for India, Poland for Russia).

Execution fails when leaders do not align people and processes to the strategy. The more people involved in shaping the course of action, the greater their support. The more information leaders get from the front line, the faster execution will be. An enabling organization will facilitate execution, not hinder it. For this, it must communicate and promote its business intent and strategy clearly to the different divisions. Strategies often lean heavily on financials (sales growth, ROI, EBIT margin, market share) as the final outcome without specifying the road map and mid-term objectives that will lead to the expected results. Senior executives may declare that they want their company to be number one or number two by doubling revenue in three to five years but without providing executing staff with an insight into what value proposition, customer segment, geography, product, or channel will distinguish the company from other market participants. Without clarification of connections among the drivers, actions, outcomes, and rewards, a strategy loses its force.

Companies are transforming into globally integrated enterprises to improve synergy and handle scale with fewer people. Modern companies are shifting away from hierarchical management structures to empowered systems with less directive and more democratic systems based on collaborative and collegial operating principles. The megamarkets will be the main drivers for triggering a new thinking process in corporate boardrooms.

12.3. Operational excellence

Foreign investors operate semi-autonomous megamarket subsidiaries as full-fledged legal entities that integrate major business functions for developing their local business. These divisions are basically replicas of the functional units at the corporate office: marketing and sales, operations (production and purchasing), human resources, administration, and sometimes R&D. But the megamarkets require additional leverage to strengthen a company's external relations and knowledge base, which are significant selling arguments for local business partners.

Three fundamental domains[5] or transversal tasks relating to customers, suppliers, and knowledge/innovation could be considered (see figure 12.9). They can reinforce the work of the traditional functional divisions and thus help optimize operations. These domains can be embedded within existing divisions or act as supportive domains staffed with specialists enjoying direct reporting lines to the corporate board. In advanced markets, consultants and IT firms offer applied software for customer relationship management (CRM), supply

---

5. The fourth important domain is "support services," comprising personnel, accounts, finance, legal, and IT.

Figure 12.9. Transversal domains for higher functional performance in the megamarkets.

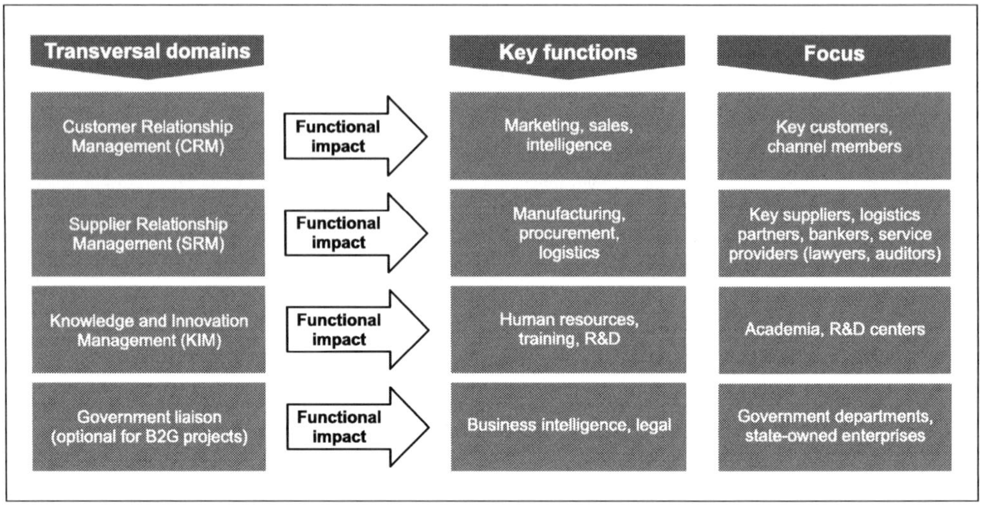

Transversal domains		Key functions	Focus
Customer Relationship Management (CRM)	Functional impact →	Marketing, sales, intelligence	Key customers, channel members
Supplier Relationship Management (SRM)	Functional impact →	Manufacturing, procurement, logistics	Key suppliers, logistics partners, bankers, service providers (lawyers, auditors)
Knowledge and Innovation Management (KIM)	Functional impact →	Human resources, training, R&D	Academia, R&D centers
Government liaison (optional for B2G projects)	Functional impact →	Business intelligence, legal	Government departments, state-owned enterprises

chain management (SCM), and innovation management; these concepts are gradually being introduced in the megamarkets. When companies are heavily involved in public tenders and/or B2G projects, they may consider "government liaison and lobbying" as a transversal function cooperating closely with the business intelligence and/or legal departments.

12.3.1. Customer relationship management

Rule No. 10:

Customer focus and proximity

The biggest threat for EU/US companies is their own complacency, while competitors, particularly those from the megamarkets, strive to snatch away large clients (key accounts), first in the megamarkets and then at the global level. Managers should follow the example of leading players, who base their decisions on regular feedback from clients and staff to hone their "corporate memory."[6] Successful companies don't go after everyone; they identify the best prospects and interact with them to customize the offer and build stronger relationships.

The challenge for foreign businesses in the megamarkets is the vast territorial expanse, consumer diversity, and difficult access to the "next billion" consumers in the rural areas. To reach these markets, distribution systems have to be rethought and set up anew as Unilever or Nestlé did in China and India. Bajaj Allianz, the Indo-German car insurer, thinks that more than half of its turnover will be generated in India's rural areas after 2015. For marketing its insurance policies, it has created a special grassroots distribution system that integrates small kiosks, telephone card vendors, and door-to-door salespersons.

A CRM specialist effectively supports the marketing (research-oriented) and sales (turnover-driven) teams by sharpening customer focus through effective key account management

---

6. For examples of successful businesses in the megamarkets, refer to H. Sirkin, J. Hemerling, and A. Bhattacharya, *Globality: Competing with Everyone from Everywhere for Everything* (2008).

> **Box 12.8. CRM tasks.**
> - KAM: key account management
> - CPA: customer portfolio analysis
> - Marketing mix: the four Ps

(KAM), competitive positioning, and marketing mix of four Ps (see box 12.8). KAM cultivates and serves major buyers in B2B, business-to-consumer (B2C), and B2G areas. Independent of the geography, key accounts are extremely important as they can represent the bulk of the business.[7] International alignments can be very useful for gaining that first crucial contract to start off in a megamarket. An auto components producer who wants to launch its products in a megamarket should start with its international car company clients who are already present in the megamarket; a big contract from one of them for their megamarket subsidiary will give the auto components manufacturer a good foothold and a solid reference.

Megamarket customers seeking technology from EU/US vendors fall into the "key account" category if they contribute to a company's effort to extend its global/Eurasian reach. Data show that in advanced markets both the biggest and smallest customers are often the least profitable. Large buyers of equipment (e.g., steel makers) or consumer goods (e.g., retail chains) are notorious for negotiating low prices, thus squeezing vendors, while smaller buyers may drag on with payments or sometimes even default on their commitments. Financially strong megamarket customers can help compensate such losses and improve the firm's overall margin, although their bargaining power has grown significantly as well over the years.

CRM includes customer portfolio analysis (first-time, one-time, repeat, or regular buyers) and efforts aimed at retaining/rewarding customers (via loyalty programs, awards, discounts) and/or winning back "defectors" (through product extras, post-purchase service, customized solutions). Being customer-centric, CRM provides the framework for executing tailor-made marketing strategies for narrow segments of the market or even individual customers if they are of strategic relevance to the firm. CRM treats each key customer individually and uniquely by applying one-to-one marketing. Because of cultural affinities, US companies often use their German subsidiaries for developing special relations with their Russian customers. In such cases, effective CRM systems are not confined to partnerships among marketing, sales, and IT departments but are likely to span divisional boundaries to include functions such as finance, operations, and human resources.

Active involvement of senior management is also vital for addressing key customers and establishing relationships with the top decision-makers in the megamarkets. Apart from customized presentations that address the client's concern, visits can be organized to headquarters or workshops held in resorts with division heads. Such events are useful to get firsthand information, and at the same time, it fosters a team spirit across divisions of the EU/US supplier. This is quite common for large B2B or B2G transactions. Customer advisory boards can be formed to turn customers into permanent advisers and ambassadors; this approach is practiced by some of the EU's leading cosmetics companies.

---

7. G. Shainesh and J. Sheth, *Customer Relationship Management* (MacMillan, 2006), 96.

Box 12.9. Efficiency test for CRM/KAM in the megamarkets.

- Can management classify customers according to ownership, business health, buying volumes, and industry segment?
- Are executives informed about customer share and satisfaction levels?
- Are mechanisms in place to check if sales objectives are in line with market potential?
- Are field surveys carried out to update management on trends and changes in the industry?
- Is information on strengths and weaknesses of major competitors (domestic, foreign) available? Why do certain customers prefer them?
- Do headquarters executives visit megamarket key accounts regularly?
- Is the work coordinated between marketing and sales specialists?
- Have priority products/services been defined for specific customer segments and regions?
- Are price levels adjusted to react to price sensitivities?
- Does the marketing concept encompass a service and advisory component to leverage products and technologies?
- Are the best distribution channels being used?
- Has communication material been adjusted to the megamarket requirements (not just translations)? What is the impact of advertising and promotion efforts on sales?

There is a link between satisfied and loyal employees and good customer relations. If the team does a good job, customers will help it build a profit chain. They will not just stay (retention), but they will give an additional share of their wallet by buying more products/services (related sales), and they will tell other customers about the company (referrals). Without professional CRM/KAM (see box 12.9), it will be difficult to identify main megamarket customers, assess their needs, and devise appropriate strategies to intensify the relationship.

RULE NO. 11:

AIM AT CUSTOMER SHARE, NOT JUST MARKET SHARE

Marketing and sales departments of subsidiaries are usually instructed by the EU/US headquarters to meet aggressive sales targets aimed at boosting market share. To this end, expenses and profits are budgeted once a year, but without reference to specific projects, clients, or channel members and without regard to long-term profitability and sustainable leadership. Aggression invariably translates as price wars, which do not improve profit margins in the industry.

In the competitive and volatile environment of an emerging market, it is better to maximize the output-to-input or revenue-to-cost ratio for individual clients through an appropriate CRM program. Customer share or "one-to-one" marketing—increasing the amount of business each customer does with the company—is more profitable than seeking high overall market share, which can overstretch resources and squeeze margins. Profitability can be disconnected from market share. In industries dominated by one to three players,

Table 12.3. Market share and profit margins determine profitability.

Players	Market size (US$ mn)	Market share (%)	Profit margin (%)	Net profits (US$ mn)
TNC 1	10,000	33	5	1,650
TNC 2	10,000	25	10	2,500
SME	10,000	20	15	3,000

TNC: transnational corporation; SME: small and medium-sized enterprise.
Source: Project examples, India.

the market leaders report good profitability, but so do well-managed medium-sized players operating in profitable niches[8] (see table 12.3), where they bring in above-average pre-tax earnings by focusing on potent customers commanding higher margins. Market share and profitability should therefore be balanced. Executives pushing aggressively for volumes by selling at a low price will erode profit margins. Business leaders only aiming at profit will lose market share because of high pricing. A certain market share is required for visibility and to maintain sales momentum.

Each key account has a lifetime value that companies must assess (see box 12.10). High-profit customers should be retained throughout the lifetime of a product by providing spares and additional services. This approach has proved to be effective in both B2B and B2C markets. In India and China, a car owner does not change a model for six to seven years. The initial purchase price represents only around one-third of total lifetime expenses of a car; the rest is made up of after-purchase expenses. CRM should target the remaining two-thirds of the expenses to increase customer share by providing car loans, insurance, maintenance service, parts, and so forth. In B2B, vendors of equipment or industrial goods can assess their individual clients' needs for spare parts by offering after-sales service and technical advice. Service and spare part deliveries can represent a large share of turnover

Box 12.10. Lifetime value of a key account.

- Acquisition costs: cost of cultivating a customer including travel, samples, test runs, pilot projects, and promotional expenses; keeping existing clients is usually far less costly than finding new ones, while losing a key account dents profit margins.
- Base profit: regular orders by a customer contribute directly to profit.
- Additional revenue: usage levels rise as the customer gets used to a product/service and generates additional revenue streams.
- Cost savings: once the customer understands a product/service, support costs decrease.
- Referrals: a satisfied customer is more inclined to recommend the product/service, at little cost to the company.
- Price premiums: loyal customers continue their patronage even when competitors enter the market with cheaper propositions.

---

8. Studies show that companies with market shares exceeding 35%–40% can earn average ROIs of 25%–30%, or three times that of those with market shares under 10%. In the megamarkets, the profitability threshold is reached at a market share of 20%–30%. Few EU companies fall into that category.

as they prolong the relationship between the seller and buyer for very long after the initial purchase of the equipment. Interdependence can become so intense that it can result in joint investments (service centers, merchandising). The art lies in switching from a single transaction at the beginning to repeat sales spread over time with one customer. Many satisfied customers will result in higher market share.

Cross-selling is one way of increasing customer share. Valuable lessons can be learned from megamarket players.

Customer share is determined by correct positioning. In the megamarkets, where demand often has to be created for new products, positioning on superior competence has to be substantiated with facts (see box 12.11 a). General statements on a company's history, reliability, and reputation in advanced markets do not automatically trigger sales as the context of these statements is sometimes alien to megamarket customers. Megamarkets are often not familiar with brand names known in the West, particularly for consumer goods. Stripped of its brand support, the newcomer has to re-present the value proposition of its products, particularly if it is new.

Low price is not the argument on which a durable customer relationship can be established, even in the megamarkets. The strategy will backfire if the company does not address the real concerns of its customers, who are prepared to pay a reasonably higher price if the company pays attention to their needs and offers the appropriate product and guidance. This is why around 40% of railway bearings sold in China consist of more expensive imports; the Ministry of Railways (MOR) is concerned that domestic suppliers will not match the quality and security requirements for high-speed passenger trains. Megamarket buyers expect products to have "minimum" attributes, or else the supplier would not be in the business. Unfortunately, sales personnel tend to fix on competitors, trying to outstrip them in price and delivery to strike a deal. They fail to anticipate the motivations of key customers and are unprepared to answer typically asked questions and strike the deal (see box 12.11 b).

Pause for thought

India's two largest retail banks, State Bank of India (SBI) and ICICI Bank, are data mining their vast customer bases (more than 25 million) to sell them insurance products, a variety of loans, and credit cards. The advantage is that parameters such as credit rating can be checked quickly as customer data are already available in the bank's database. SBI target is that 50% of its loan customers are covered by its insurance products. Almost 60% of ICICI's credit cards sales and 35% of its home loans are generated from its own customers.

***

When a German construction chemicals manufacturer established its operation in India, the construction industry was still using traditional materials. Although the company has production sites in ten countries, in India it was relatively unknown. The Indian subsidiary undertook an intense customer education program including around fifty conferences dedicated to special construction materials, renovation, repair, and so forth. It also published more than seventy-five articles in various journals. The company now has two production sites in India. It is an important sponsor of the Indian Concrete Institute, where it has instituted an award for the Outstanding Concrete Structure.

> **Box 12.11. Competitive positioning in the megamarkets.**
>
> a. Examples of sales arguments for the megamarkets
>
> - If you encounter any problem with our equipment or product, our customer service staff will be at your site within two hours (customer service).
> - This year, less than 1% of our customers have returned our products (quality).
> - We guarantee that our team will finish the task within one month, much faster than any of our competitors (responsiveness).
> - Over 80% of our business is from referrals (reputation).
> - After switching to our technology, our clients reported cost savings and productivity increases of 25% (good results).
> - Our professionals have a minimum of fifteen years' experience, twice that of our nearest competitor (competence).
> - Personnel turnover rate is not even 2% (good management).
> - Customer retention rate is 98%, which is much higher than the competition (trust).
>
> b. Typical questions asked by megamarket buyers
>
> - Why should we buy from you? Which features distinguish your offer from competing ones? Where is the uniqueness, what are the marks of distinction?
> - Which concrete advantages can we expect? Is the business algorithm proposed based on insights into our present worries and future needs?
> - In which technology, industry, or geography has your firm attained a position of excellence? What are your most important achievements and reference projects?
> - How serious are senior managers about investing and sharing knowledge? Is there an action plan for strengthening your firm's presence in our market? Who are the decision-makers that can be contacted locally?

RULE NO. 12:
ADAPT THE FOUR PS TO THE MEGAMARKET

CRM helps to synchronize the four Ps of the marketing mix—product, price, place, promotion—and gear them to the needs of local clients. Usually, megamarket customers expect adaptations of the product-service package (first P) toward more service and advice (see figure 12.10). Pricing, promotion, and distribution need to equally be attuned to the megamarket context and may in their combination differ significantly from what the central marketing department is used to proposing for other markets.

Pricing, the second P, impacts margins but also determines at which price point the company can position itself in the megamarkets. Typically, managers try to cut overall costs while aiming to boost the number of units sold in a particular market. Price—the essential variable besides costs and units sold that determines profitability and customer share—reflects whether the company has paid attention to customers' needs; a company has four leverage points impacting turnover and costs to determine profit (see figure 12.11). Prices are high if the product is manufactured in the high-cost advanced markets. The target megamarket price can be derived from competitors' prices and can be achieved

Figure 12.10. The four Ps of the marketing mix in the megamarkets.

PRODUCT	PRICE
Features Quality Packaging Brand image Guarantees Service Advice	Level Policy Sensitivity Discounts Payment terms
PROMOTION	**PLACE**
Advertising Client education Sales promotions Public relations Merchandising Selling	Customer location Distribution channels Outlet location Logistics Deliveries by agents Cities and regions

Figure 12.11. The pricing variable: Four leverage points for profit making.

Turnover = units sold x price

Profit = turnover (units sold x price) - costs (variable costs + fixed costs)

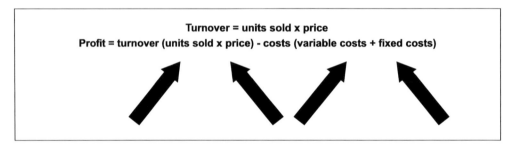

through local assembly or production and effective supplier management, which enables the company to cut costs. Prices of Japanese and South Korean companies are lower during launch because they phase out cost recovery: initially only variable costs and then, as sales volumes grow, the fixed costs. Margins in the megamarkets can be generally higher because of the importance of status in combination with lower manufacturing and related costs (in the case of local production). European brands can command a high premium, particularly for luxury and semi-luxury goods.

Promotion (third P) has become a costly investment in the megamarkets since the mid-1990s. It therefore needs to be refocused and its effects carefully studied. In B2C markets, producers, in particular, have to choose the appropriate combination of general media advertising, investment in personalized customer promotion, direct selling, and training. Too much of one (e.g., media advertising) could in the long-term harm the company's standing if other, more direct actions are neglected in markets where business partners demand explanations, support, and advice. Three direct promotional activities stand out as they can have a lasting impact on megamarket success: regular client workshops, image building with the authorities, and training of channel partners. The most effective promotional measures are summarized in box 12.12.

Box 12.12. Promotional mix for the megamarkets.

- Client workshops
- Public relations campaigns and event marketing (including corporate social responsibility actions) to strengthen brand equity
- Image building with government agencies (to build corporate reputation)
- Training of channel partners
- Participation in local trade fairs
- Technical articles in newspapers, magazines, and trade journals
- Advertising in print and electronic media
- Direct sales promotion
- In-store, point-of-sale advertising (for consumer goods)
- Internet Web sites

Pause for thought

A famous brand of German chocolates refused to spend for even point-of-sale advertising, let alone media advertising in India. Meanwhile, another European brand increased shelf space in the supermarkets and later set up a production unit. In another case, a European SME was set to introduce high-quality shoe-care products in India but without making the required local investment to position, at an acceptable retail price, its products against lower-quality brands from the large multinationals or even to set up shoe-care kiosks, which would have been winners.

B2G markets may have similar requirements if the product addresses a general need. A famous waste disposal company was not prepared to invest in public education campaigns and informational workshops and conferences in India to explain the advantage of a modern sorting and collection system, which was so successful in its EU home markets. Valuable opportunities were lost, and local competitors entered this niche. The company lost a potential market of several hundred million US dollars because it was hesitant to create a market.

Selecting effective distribution channels—the fourth P—is yet another challenge facing foreign investors. Distribution systems for consumer goods in the megamarkets can be a maze of multi-layer networks,[9] owing to the large geographical reach and the spread into regional markets, and the lack of logistics management, organized distribution channels, and modern retail formats. Conversely, selling industrial goods demands heavy investments in training external agents and in-house sales engineers. The decision before the company is the balance between its own sales force and external distributors who may represent various principals. Many EU companies, particularly those with small teams at headquarters, rely heavily on agents (distributors) or joint venture partners, who may not be as committed to the company's brand and may prevent them from spotting and retaining key clients. Nor is the subsidiary's own sales force a guarantee of success; it must be trained and coordinated by capable local managers.

---

9. See 8.3.3.

12.3.2. Supplier relationship management

Consumer fickleness has resulted in intense competition. To stay cost and price competitive, Western companies are compelled to procure standard products and components from lower-cost countries. Industry leaders have linked up the megamarkets to their global supply chains; their efforts are directed at orchestrating selected procurement partners for higher efficiency compared with rival supply lines. The megamarkets are increasingly used as hubs to coordinate suppliers located within them and in adjacent markets (mainly Asia).

Supplier-based production beachheads are established in a market when:
- products have high transport costs relative to their value;
- products are exposed to extreme demand volatility or short lead times;
- trade barriers are significant; and
- being "local" offers a valid selling proposition.

While in certain cases it is advisable for companies to strive for co-ownership of supplier structures (e.g., by buying stakes in companies) in an effort to reduce delivery or quality risks, in most other instances supplier networking based on minimum orders, information exchange, and financial support is sufficient (see box 12.13). Supplier orchestration as an "asset-light" model has proven successful when the customer purchases 30%–70% of the output of the supplier's factory, allowing for flexibility while ensuring a continuous learning effect for vendors from interactions with other customers.[10]

Box 12.13. Decisions related to SRM.

- Set up a megamarket purchasing platform once business exceeds a certain volume (e.g., € 5–10 million of orders per year).
- Build in-house capability at headquarters or megamarket subsidiary for quality control, engineering, logistics, and legal aspects, including intellectual property rights (IPR).
- Form professional SRM teams knowledgeable in process and product engineering to inspect megamarket factories
- Conduct regular tests and due diligence of key suppliers.
- Use local advisors for top contacts and preliminary supplier checks.
- Check possibility of joint purchasing with other companies.
- Invest in suppliers and finance joint activities (joint research, presentations, training).
- Tie suppliers to the company by acquiring stakes, thus avoiding imitations and IPR-related disputes.
- Develop triangular supply networks for parts and components deliveries between megamarkets (Russia–India, Russia–China, India–China).

---

10. V. Fung et al., *Competing in a Flat World*, 131–142.

> **Pause for thought**
>
> *Salamander has all its shoes produced in Asia; the German headquarters has been reduced to a design center with a coordinating function for promoting the brand. Quality engineers travel regularly to check emerging market suppliers.*
>
> *Many industries, like apparel, toys, appliances, auto components, machine parts, bulk chemicals, and packaging, follow similar patterns.*
>
> *In today's "flat world," the buttons for men's shorts may come from China and the zippers from Japan; the yarn is spun in Pakistan and woven into fabric and dyed in China; the garment is sewn together in Bangladesh or India.* Yet each pair of shorts will look as if it were made in one factory when it reaches the retailer in the EU or North America.*
>
> *In such a radically transformed business environment, a single firm will find it difficult to stand against competitors who belong to an orchestrated network.*
>
> * V. Fung et al., Competing in a Flat World (Pearson Education, 2008), 10.

Rule No. 13:

The megamarkets should be tapped as sourcing platforms

"Make or buy" decisions are strategic for increasing the competitiveness of a company's products. Burdened by high production costs at home, multinationals have been relocating factories to low-cost destinations, including the megamarkets. They outsource goods and services to the megamarkets for their global operations. Their megamarket subsidiaries will also need to localize supplies, not only to reduce costs but also to comply with local-content stipulations. These vary with the country and the products. Buying from independent suppliers is a common practice for medium-sized EU/US companies to overcome manpower, time, and resource limitations. Their purchase managers are turning to the megamarkets.

Globalization has accustomed companies to dealing with distant suppliers and finding ways to increase control over the vendors so that the components reach dispersed production sites on time and with the requested quality specifications so that processes can be optimized for timely dispatch of finished goods. According to a recent study, India and China will remain the key outsourcing hubs for consumer and semi-finished goods and services in the coming years. Their low costs, number of supply options (competitive offers), pent-up demand, and export facilities (e.g., special economic zones, duty-free export-oriented zones) make them preferred sourcing platforms. This trend is being accelerated by local contents rules forcing vendors to produce in the megamarkets (e.g., car components in Russia).

In certain industries, it took long to design and implement a consistent supplier relations management (SRM) strategy. In India, for example, automobile multinationals faced for many years serious difficulties with their vendors because of quality inconsistencies and capacity constraints. Quality problems and logistics costs continue to be an impediment when suppliers are located far inland away from principal agglomerations and cannot be reached or visited that often. With improvements in infrastructure, components can now be shipped freely among the megamarkets and the smaller emerging markets, allowing multinationals to establish scale-effective plants. China and India will continue to be the major outsourcing hubs, particularly for consumer and semi-finished (e.g., components) goods, for years to come. Cost used to be the primary concern; however, as competitors also source from the same countries, low cost is no longer a differentiator. Companies will need to accurately track their cost savings by accounting for logistics, duties, and insurance (obvious measures), as well as opportunity costs of interrupted supply, late delivery, product rejects, and non-compliance to norms. Costs of taxes are the most complex measure to compute.

While quality has been improving in the megamarkets—thirteen of the twenty foreign recipients of the Demings Prize were from India—product safety and environmental concerns remain. Another hidden cost is that of monitoring and coordinating production in the megamarket as well as the cost of inspection and certification. All these procedures need to be factored into a detailed planning process to avoid delays in delivery. Contracts have to be vetted by local legal firms to ensure that the vendor complies with all the requirements. Legal fees therefore need to be included in the final cost.

The leading EU/US players will need to gain a permanent foothold in each of the megamarkets. For this, they must form industrial micro-clusters with their main suppliers. Quality is a decisive criterion; it must be handled carefully and consistently. Suppliers thus co-determine the company's long-term image in the megamarkets.

Pause for thought

An EU company that wanted to offer a mix of imported critical components and locally manufactured lower-cost and voluminous (to save on transport) components to a buyer of their turnkey plant in India invited their auditors as well as those of their clients to compute the tax factor as it was too complex for the in-house accounting departments. After months of analysis and calculations, the company's financial department came up with a solution that helped the company save 40% in duties and taxes.

***

Unlike the Japanese, European carmakers (except Mercedes) did not consider India a strategic market until now. BMW and Audi-Volkswagen now realize that local manufacturing with corresponding supplier networks is the only way to grow in the expanding but highly competitive Indian context.

Affluent Indians already accustomed to Japanese engineering and efficiency expect much more from the value proposition offered by the Germans. BMW and Audi will have to not only lower manufacturing costs by increasing local content but also keep the cost of spares and after-sales on par with the Japanese. Moreover, in India, Japanese cars are not viewed with a certain contempt as in Germany and therefore compete equally with BMW and Audi.

Nor should the internecine rivalry between Volkswagen, Audi, and Skoda be allowed to spill into the Indian market; instead, they should create a common cause against their competitors.

Rule No. 14:
Integrate purchasing in the megamarket strategy via alliances

Globalized companies recognize the complexity of the purchase function and its contribution to competitiveness and profitability. The erstwhile buyer–vendor relationship is being transformed into a partnership so that the two companies cooperate to design and manufacture a quality and cost-effective product. This cooperation can take the form of an "orchestrated alliance" or equity participation (ownership) in the immediate supplier company through backward integration.

When companies with a large supplier base—like car manufacturers, turnkey project companies—set up operations in the megamarkets, they encourage their vendors to be present in these countries as well. Sometimes, the multinational will also try to broker alliances between its preferred suppliers and local companies. In this way, it ensures continuity of high quality standards and timely delivery as in its home base.

Work on the SRM strategy has to start in parallel with the megamarket project as it will ultimately impact on the subsidiary's profitability. Key suppliers should be given the same status as key accounts. Similar to CRM with its focus on customers, this second transversal task (SRM) is meant to tighten relations with upstream partners. Long-term relationships with well-selected vendors ensure better compliance, commitment, and inputs from suppliers. Key vendors are also often involved in the co-designing of components (particularly for vehicles). Greater involvement of suppliers in the manufacturing process is thus a strategic decision to be debated and made by the company's top management.

Megamarket purchasing, supported by SRM, is fast becoming a key element of a company's global supply chain management. Critical areas need to be monitored and decisions made accordingly (see box 12.14).

The example of a European producer of electrical motors (see figure 12.12) describes the constraints management faces when establishing and maintaining a functional supply line that increasingly presupposes a global approach covering also the megamarkets. The company guarantees steady order volumes to its immediate Tier 1 suppliers (Chinese producers of electronic controls) but equally tries to ensure a smooth flow of raw materials in the right price-quality configuration all along its value chain;[11] it could, for example, spot a strategic source of metals for its supplier in Russia. On the market side, it should identify its immediate customers but also needs to map potential end users at the very end of the chain, all of

---

Box 12.14. SRM tasks.
- Identify and screen suppliers regularly
- Design business models for collaboration with key suppliers
- Monitor performance of suppliers
- Integrate business processes and partnering (alliance, equity participation)

---

11. For value chain analysis, see 7.3 (strategic tool number three).

Figure 12.12. Integrated supply chain (example of an electrical motor company).

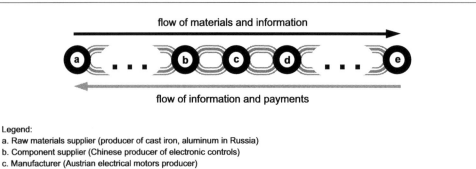

Legend:
a. Raw materials supplier (producer of cast iron, aluminum in Russia)
b. Component supplier (Chinese producer of electronic controls)
c. Manufacturer (Austrian electrical motors producer)
d. Customer (German/Swiss equipment manufacturer)
e. End user (US bottling plant operator in Russia)

> **Pause for thought**
>
> A German company set up a greenfield plant in China in 2004. Initially, many parts had to be imported from overseas. The purchase department at headquarters was responsible for handling these activities, and it worked closely with the technical department at the Chinese subsidiary. But the Chinese parts manufacturers could not deliver the required quality and design.
>
> In a visionary move, top management decided to appoint an SRM chief in charge of optimizing procurement in the subsidiary rather than blindly follow local content rules. The adoption of SRM-related tasks by the department enabled it to spot areas of cost savings by signing long-term delivery contracts and joint parts development projects with strategic suppliers. The company managed to outpace its rivals as it had secured the loyalty of its upstream business partners.

whom have distinct requirements depending on the industry and the location (geography). Segmenting[12] the value chain with its specific customer and supplier systems is a crucial exercise in strategy making and execution. It enables top management to exploit the linkages between CRM and SRM. Companies that succeed as "SRM team leaders" can skillfully leverage the information advantage to cultivate strategic partnerships with other chain members.

Recognizing that the purchase function plays a significant role in the overall corporate strategy, some companies also appoint chief purchase officers (CPOs) with megamarket experience to the board. They get personally involved in joint projects with key suppliers that may lead to strategic alliances. They place SRM specialists in their megamarket subsidiaries when business exceeds a certain volume.

Rule No. 15:
Innovate the supply chain

Market leaders are able to change a whole industry through supply chain innovation (e.g., Dell, Amazon.com). The car industry provides excellent examples of supply chain innovation as first components, then assemblies, and now integrated systems are outsourced.

---

12. See chapter 8.

Pause for thought

From India, Renault will triple the value of sourced auto components from €100 million to €300 million over the next two years; GM has announced a target of US$1 billion value of sourced components by 2010.

These and other car companies will invest significant resources in training and joint product development projects with key suppliers in the megamarkets.

Figure 12.13. Supplier portfolio for the megamarkets.

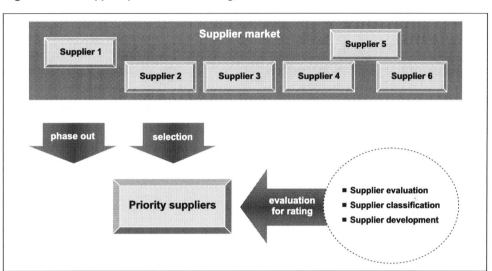

These innovations trickle down from Tier 1 to Tier 3 suppliers. Only 28% of the manufacturing cost is controlled by the car company, whereas 45% is controlled by the dealers. The megamarkets will figure increasingly in the supply chain.

SRM is concerned with the smooth functioning of buyer–supplier relations based on reliability and trust. Its tasks are similar to CRM (see figure 12.13). Apart from the organizational aspects, SRM has the responsibility of bringing innovation into the buyer–supplier relationship by diversifying the supplier base across locations and devising a new model for the relationship. EU managers tend to maintain the status quo by procuring components from their traditional Western suppliers, who are requested to set up manufacturing and logistics units in the new markets. Challenging the status quo involves conducting quality checks and assuming responsibility for a wrong selection, which few managers are prepared or instructed to do. But in the process they may overlook suppliers who are better and more competitive. The company also needs to exercise greater control in the new environment (fierce competition, risk of technology leakage as more critical parts are outsourced). To achieve this, relationships with key suppliers have to be cemented through new business models.

SCM software[13] can optimize work flows, eliminate redundancy, and thus help companies to take products and services to market faster and in a more cost-effective way without

---

13. For example, SAP or Epicor software.

compromise on quality. Each company in the value chain can thus focus on its core competences. But SCM cannot replace regular inspections, support, and personal interactions to foster voluntary behavior and responsiveness of the suppliers.

To ensure that by outsourcing the company does not slip on quality and timeliness standards, better tests have to be devised before it endorses a megamarket supplier. While megamarket vendors are improving on their standards, they are often not at par with EU standards. As environment norms in the megamarkets are not strictly enforced, suppliers will have to be educated on the need to comply with EU environment norms (e.g., azo dyes). Awareness of the inhuman conditions in sweatshops and the use of child labor is growing in the megamarkets thanks to efforts by NGOs and "ethical investment" movements, which exposed multinationals and made them answerable for both product and process when they sell their products in the advanced markets.

SRM and purchase managers have to devise appropriate audits of and stringent qualification criteria for their megamarket vendors. It takes, for example, up to one year to qualify a supplier of Germany's SMS Demag, the world's leading turnkey steel plant producer. The best suppliers are audited and invited to participate in concrete projects, whereas non-successful candidates are phased out. Audits are based on procurement and financial requirements as well as process quality aspects, similar to an ISO 9001 norm.

Banking, another crucial issue, will be increasingly localized. Megamarkets offer many options to finance the initial investment in capital goods or expansion, ranging from banks, venture capital, and private equity providers to leasing companies. But compliance criteria are becoming as stringent as in Western economies. In India, it is mandatory for banks to fill in a detailed "know your customer" (KYC) form before opening an account for any large transaction. Private equity firms in the megamarkets may sometimes offer more favorable conditions, including an average tenure duration of the investment of seven to eight years. Privileged relations with selected service providers—similar to essential components suppliers—can enhance a company's overall position and help it reduce the time required.

12.3.3. Knowledge and innovation management

The megamarkets have grown into economic powerhouses; they already challenge the industrialized world in sectors with high-technology and services contents. Many companies are compelled to integrate them into their global knowledge and technology networks. Setting up production, procurement, and sales facilities is no longer enough to secure sustainable leadership. Lasting competitiveness depends on constantly developing unique products and processes through better knowledge and innovation management (KIM), the third transversal dimension affecting functional performance in the megamarkets. Technological leadership is possible if the company manages to fuse intellectual capabilities and organizational learning. This will create a progressive R&D function in the megamarkets. In today's information- and knowledge-driven markets, companies derive value from intellectual rather than physical and financial assets.

Rule No. 16:
Assess and share knowledge

KIM draws on human competence, intuition, ideas, and motivations to generate value. KIM comprises a range of practices used by companies to identify, create, and distribute information and knowledge. What staff, managers, and advisers know is codified and shared across the organization and with external partners (e.g., suppliers, customers). KIM contributes to higher productivity and revenue streams by enabling:

- better, more informed decisions;
- innovation through the free expression of opinions and ideas;
- higher customer satisfaction and revenues;
- employee retention by acknowledging their knowledge and experience; and
- lower costs by streamlining operations.

Knowledge can be explicit or tacit. Explicit knowledge (e.g., patents, business plans, customer lists, market trends) can be documented, archived, and codified, often with the help of IT. However, knowledge management is more than software and systems, even though they can be important aspects of it. Much harder to grasp, share, and manage is tacit knowledge—i.e., the know-how contained in people's minds and reflected in their experience. The cultural context plays an important role in finding ways to harness and distribute this knowledge. Successful globalized companies capitalize on their multicultural talent base, which is a rich source of ideas and innovations. They build lasting knowledge pools across geographies and set new ideas in motion by encouraging a virtuous knowledge-building cycle (see figure 12.14).

Particularly among larger firms, knowledge management has become an accepted part of the corporate agenda.[14] Specialist roles have emerged such as chief knowledge officers (CKO), knowledge managers, or directors of intellectual capital. The knowledge management strategy of these firms, often through board-level engagement, is to combat information overload, lack of time for sharing knowledge, and the inability to use knowledge effectively, the ultimate aim being the "systematic development of intellectual capital in a learning organization." With the emergence of the megamarkets and their potential as new sources of know-how and innovation, companies will need

---
Pause for thought

Novartis's mission statement reads as follows: "Our success in building a high performance organization will be substantially based on the capability of sharing and exploiting our professional knowledge better and faster than our competition." The company's organizational structure and corporate culture across all geographies must be geared to the goal of using its knowledge effectively. Knowledge goals must be integrated into corporate strategy and project planning. Knowledge management therefore requires the commitment of the company's top executives.

---

14. For more information on the subject, see Ashok Jashapara, *Knowledge Management: An Integrated Approach* (Prentice Hall, 2004).

Figure 12.14. Knowledge-building cycle for the megamarkets.

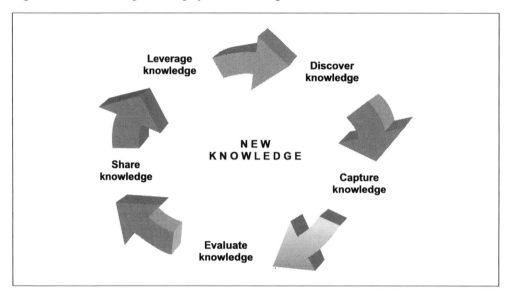

to integrate megamarket specialists and build competitive advantage through adequate interpretation of qualitative and quantitative data gathered from these fast-changing environments.

Rule No. 17:
Recognize and exploit the knowledge potential of the megamarkets

Companies that formerly regarded the megamarkets as low-cost environments for producing standard products now recognize that these markets have moved up the knowledge chain and are themselves using skills to create value. EU and US companies are therefore shifting their knowledge-intensive products and services to the megamarkets. China, India, and Russia offer the ingredients for conducting knowledge-based research: a talent pool of qualified engineers, specialists in relevant areas at moderate cost, top-class R&D facilities, and institutes of higher learning. Leading multinationals are establishing R&D labs and centers of excellence in the megamarkets for a number of reasons:

- As technology companies, they need both the market and local talent.
- They seize opportunities offered by new inventions on a global scale.
- They need the scale of the megamarkets to recover investments in future innovation and R&D.
- They seek to exploit synergies (e.g., Indian IT companies setting up shop in China and Russia).

This trend will intensify as the megamarkets churn out increasing numbers of engineers and researchers aided by an unimaginable youth bulge[15] and proactive education policies. High

---
15. See 3.1.1.

> **Pause for thought**
>
> BASF's network of R&D centers (total of 8,300 employees) has cooperation agreements with 1,400 universities, research institutes, partner firms, and business start-ups all over the world, also in the megamarkets.
>
> In addition to doing its own R&D, Procter & Gamble is focusing on what it calls C&D (connect and develop).* The idea of this "open innovation circuit" is to identify and connect to new ideas wherever they are in the world. P&G shifted from building on the work of 7,500 R&D people inside the company to joining these resources with 1.5 million people outside the company (many of them in China and India), with a permeable boundary between them. This has accelerated learning and led to the rapid introduction of innovations.
>
> Taking a similar course of action, BP's R&D department cooperates with megamarket universities like the University of Technology in Dalian, China, to carry out fundamental research related to crude composition and geological exploration.
>
> L. Huston and N. Sakhab, "Connect and Develop inside Procter & Gamble's New Model for Innovation," Harvard Business Review 84, no. 3 (2006): 58–66.

performers cooperate with strategic partners, including research institutes, engineering bureaus, and universities. Such alliances serve to:

- cut costs and development time;
- generate synergies through sharing knowledge, equipment, personnel, and finance;
- access regional markets with different consumer needs;
- share the burden of rising expenses;
- create an information pool for the exchange of thoughts and ideas; and
- overcome the innovation deficit by developing targeted solutions.

Medium-sized firms are more reluctant to shift their R&D; some simply cannot afford it. At the most, they shift part of the applied research but without making compromises on fundamental research, which as a core activity should stay at headquarters. But even these companies recognize that technologies cannot be divided because of process interdependence involving megamarket suppliers and EU/US buyers. Local customers are also becoming important sources of ideas and innovation, thus helping companies to shorten the payback period of inventions, provided R&D is driven by market needs and the lead time between idea generation and product marketability is reduced. Each company must decide how a cooperation based on joint R&D efforts with a local partner will supplement internal research activities. The intellectual capital of a company counts as much as its financial clout. SMEs with a solid knowledge base can suddenly raise their bargaining barrier when negotiating alliances, including with larger partners.

What is most interesting about the megamarkets is their emphasis on many areas of knowledge simultaneously. Broad-based schooling, widespread interest in obtaining degrees, and the strong will to learn and succeed even at an advanced age have turned these markets into an unlimited pool of know-how and skills for many years to come. Megamarket subsidiaries should therefore be integrated into any effort to generate, evaluate, and leverage knowledge in the overall interest of the company. The strength and challenge of KIM in the megamarkets comes from its interdisciplinary potential encom-

> **Pause for thought**
>
> A family-owned EU generics company was invited to use the laboratories and related facilities of a large Chinese pharmaceutical player. Interestingly, the smaller foreign company was allowed to hold a majority stake in the newly created joint venture because of its superior know-how.
>
> This cooperation was later extended to the city's main research institutes and technical universities.

passing many interrelated subjects. This knowledge can be discovered and harnessed by boundary-spanning individuals who are able to see beyond the narrow margins of their own discipline and geography and recognize the value of dialogue and debate at all levels of the organization.

Rule 18:

Be aware of the risks, but never stop learning

Managing manufacturing and R&D operations simultaneously can become a daunting task in the megamarkets. To drive revenue growth, companies are ought to innovate to meet the needs of these growing new markets. Western players are caught in a dilemma. They are compelled to set up R&D facilities or cooperate with external R&D centers in order to adapt products to local needs and to take advantage of these countries' research base. Yet know-how is leaked when skilled staff is poached by local competitors wanting to acquire it.

Before shifting to more sophisticated activities, companies must assess the potential risks of the operation. One of the threats facing businesses operating in emerging markets is intellectual property and technology theft. This risk is compounded when manufacturers, encouraged by governments, relocate higher-value activities with complex production, R&D, and sophisticated service operations, or part with know-how in a bid to win a high-value contract. Germany's ThyssenKrupp and Siemens had to share proprietary knowledge of their Transrapid train to win the Shanghai Maglev contract. Later, China offered similar trains to other buyers. The country has now embarked on one of the most ambitious railway expansion plans in history. The country has the financial clout to buy, dismantle, and disseminate knowledge so that national companies become privileged suppliers. China's State Council encourages its engineers to "learn and absorb foreign advanced technologies while making further innovations." In the three megamarkets, governments aim high and would like their countries to join the world's top ranks in terms of knowledge generation and innovation. The problem starts when the "absorbed" foreign technology is repackaged and sold in competition with the original inventor. Blatant copying of cars—Chery QQ based on Daewoo's Matiz, Geely Merrie 300 based on Mercedes C, Zonda A liner bus based on Neoplan's Starliner, and so forth—is causing serious concern and threatens the voluntary spread of knowledge.

Knowledge management becomes a crucial issue when dealing with alliance partners or integrating local management following an acquisition. Many megamarket companies are run by entrepreneurs who want to stay in the business, often by keeping a share even after an acquisition. They learn continuously, even if it means borrowing from others. "Any good leader looks at what works elsewhere and then interprets what he sees for his/

her own business model," says the owner of a Chinese metallurgy group who believes that "there is nothing wrong with that, and it should be everyone's priority to know what the rest of the industry is doing and to improve on that."

EU/US companies must counter their megamarket competitors on innovation through a combination of inventiveness and market success. Whereas inventions can be bought from the patent holders, each company must realize its own market success through hard work and unique products. EU/US companies must be best-in-class at innovation for four areas:

- premium products for middle- and high-income groups, which command a high margin and for which consumers seek the "Made in the EU/USA" stamp (e.g., luxury goods)
- smart products, which leverage innovative production technology and know-how to achieve the price points accessible to lower-income and rural customers; these products help to build brand equity in rural areas (e.g., Nano car, single-dose sachets of shampoo)
- new products not yet known in the megamarkets (e.g., clay-based construction materials)
- product-service combinations with high advisory content to customize the offer and optimize customer relationships (e.g., bottling equipment and after-sales maintenance)

Western TNCs have no other choice but to become more proactive and initiate technological change. High performers leap ahead by creating a change culture-centered on the customer and innovation. Continuous improvement, cooperation with academia, and research institutes along with talent grooming is the only effective way to stay ahead of megamarket rivals, who are increasing their investments in R&D to secure future business. The best arm against know-how drifts is satisfied employees who remain loyal to the company. Open organizations, imbibed with entrepreneurial spirit from the top, encourage a learning culture by promoting information sharing, creativity, and collective intelligence (see box 12.15). Continuous learning is a huge stimulant for megamarket employees who value education and knowledge.

Box 12.15. Collective and continuous learning.

- Invest in employee education to infuse new ideas.
- Encourage employees to share knowledge.
- Create online and offline "lending libraries" that focus on international subjects and best practices.
- Bring in external speakers to introduce new concepts.
- Benchmark with other companies, especially competitors. Visit their clients, plants, and facilities whenever possible.
- Celebrate success of group and individual contributions.
- Encourage impromptu meetings and discussions involving employees and managers.
- Openly address problems, ideas, opportunities, and success stories.
- Adjust reward systems to honor contributions to project results.
- Engage high-level executives in benchmarking and organizational learning.

Specialists in the advanced markets will increasingly compete with young talents from the emerging markets, who offer the same or even higher skills at lower cost. In a knowledge-driven world, a university degree and fluency in one foreign language (mostly English) is only the first step of a lifelong learning curve. Occasional seminars need to be supplemented with study courses and work stays in other countries where new knowledge can be absorbed. Owing to the demographic shift in the advanced markets, the forty-five-to-fifty-five-year-old group (the "Best Agers") will within ten years represent the highest share of the workforce. In the EU, this category of employees will have to accept that their retirement age will be raised and that they have to keep pace with developments.

EPILOGUE

Eurasia's three megamarkets represent a challenge for Western players, both multinationals and SMEs. Companies with experience in China, India, or Russia can testify to the difficulties encountered there, from frustrations with local administrations and weak law enforcement to problems with partners. Western managers report fastidious language, administrative, and cultural barriers as frequent causes for misinterpretations of contracts and misunderstandings between parties that often culminate in deteriorating business relations and breakups of partnerships.

Because of these problems, many foreign companies have not been able to build profitable businesses in the megamarkets. Top management is, however, coming under pressure to perform. In their assessment of the return on investment in megamarkets, shareholders increasingly scrutinize their managers' ability, empathy and leadership style; they wish to know the total cost of the operation, including product recalls due to quality problems, training of local staff, and transport and logistics-related expenses. Is it worth investing in the megamarkets without a clear concept based on thorough intelligence of where customers, competitors, and suppliers are moving?

A 2008 study by the Confederation of German Industry (VDI) suggests that some German SMEs have moved back their production after unsuccessful forays into China and other emerging markets. The main reasons for such decisions are technology theft, patent infringements, departure of key personnel, goal incompatibility, and legal hassles with joint venture partners. But there is little evidence to suggest that this is a general trend, and companies therefore quit China and other emerging markets in large numbers. On the contrary, most EU technology leaders aim to increase their market share by expanding and taking on competitors on their home turf. According to a survey conducted by the German Chamber of Commerce in 2008, only 3% of eight thousand German companies contemplate returning home while more than a third has clear plans to grow in China. "It is absolutely normal that some companies fail and give up while others carry on and prosper," states a senior executive, pointing to the success story of Germany's automakers in China. Germany's Machine Builders' Association (VDMA) regularly interviews its member companies and found out that China, India, and Russia have all three been on top of the list of preferred destinations for outward investments since 2003.

Some megamarket success stories are worth studying and emulating. A closer look explains how individual companies managed to hone their abilities and thrive in complex settings through concerted effort and by executing a structured approach and recruiting the best talents. Their strategies were driven by the pursuit of clear goals and the determination of both the shareholders and top management at headquarters to lead after focusing on unique competences, if necessary by adapting or reinventing them. The best strategies are only as good as their execution. High performers catalyze change and emphasize long-term commitment to the megamarket through direct investment rather than mere trading, outsourcing, quick profit-taking, and opportunistic relations. They manage to stay ahead of the change curve and provoke transformation from a position of knowledge and financial strength. Top performers like to play in the "ivy league" by assiduously converting hurdles into long-term success (see table).

In the 1990s, China, India, and Russia were just emerging, and the main challenge for multinationals was to organize a presence for selling their goods. Today, most Fortune 500 companies and the leading listed companies from Europe have operations in China and Russia; they are stepping up their presence in India, the last frontier megamarket. Meanwhile, homegrown competition has risen rapidly, and foreign companies have come under pressure to optimize processes and raise profitability. They need to enhance their capabilities and match them to the growing potential while generating higher profits, which is more difficult in highly complex emerging markets belonging to a different sociocultural context. Chief executives also need to see the broader picture: that the three economies are increasingly interwoven economically and politically. Market leadership in one of them can only be sustained if a company is successful in the other two as well.

The fast pace of economic and technological transformation will compel enterprises to adjust, decide, and execute fast. Timeliness has turned into a competitive force, similar to product and service quality, leading-edge technology, and managerial experience. Managing change by growing with the megamarkets, or even outgrowing them, presupposes an open mind, a readiness to learn, and humility and respect toward local partners and staff so that each link in the value chain provides intellectual input in a winning process based on sharing knowledge and improving execution. Many Western managers are aware of

Megamarket hurdles and success factors in the 2010s.	
Hurdles	**Success factors**
Lack of megamarket exposure of top executives	Understanding and clear perception of importance of megamarkets among the top executives
Inadequate resource allocation for the venture	Constant competence building, contingency budgets for seizing opportunities
Opportunistic approach	Proactive goal achievement based on observation and intelligence
Tactical reaction to competitor moves	Systematic quest for milestone projects to ensure first mover advantage
Standardization of offer to cut costs	Differentiation of business model
Exports and sales orientation	FDI-oriented expansion via M&A and alliances
Ad-hoc selection of partners and managers	Targeting of best-in-class candidates
Organizational status quo	Alignment of structure and procedures to context
Standard business functions	"Transversal" management to optimize functional performance

what needs to be done; they require the attitude and courage to put it into action while monitoring their megamarket operations to stay on track.

The coming years will show how many more EU and US companies will succeed in this demanding but exciting venture and how many will lose their advantages and fall behind. Even economic downturns (e.g., 2008–2009 financial crisis) can open new avenues and unexpected opportunities to gain competitive advantage in the megamarkets.

If this book can contribute to more success stories by providing management with the skills, enthusiasm, and stimulus to act effectively, it will have served its purpose.

BIBLIOGRAPHY

Books

Aaker, D., Strategic Market Management (John Wiley & Sons, 2005).

Agtmael, A., The Emerging Markets Century (The Free Press/Simon & Schuster, 2007).

Arenkov, I., and Marov, V., Strategicheskoie Upravlenie Rossiskimi Kompaniami (St Petersburg University, 2004).

Balz, U., and Arlinghaus, O., Das Praxisbuch Mergers & Acquisitions (Verlag Moderrne Industrie, 2003).

Berezin, I., Marketingovi Analiz (Eksmo, 2002).

Broadman, H., Africa's Silk Road—China and India's New Economic Frontier (The World Bank, 2007).

Brzezinski, Z., The Grand Chessboard: American Primacy and Its Geostrategic Imperatives (Basic Books,1997).

Chanda, N., Bound Together: How Traders, Preachers, Adventurers and Warriors Shaped Globalization (Caravan, 2007).

Child, J., et al., Cooperative Strategy—Managing Alliances, Networks and Joint Ventures (Oxford University Press, 2005).

Collier, P., The Bottom Billion (Oxford University Press, 2007).

Crosetto, M., Project Design (Il Sole 24 Ore, 2003).

Czerniawska, F., Management Consultancy—What Next? (Palgrave MacMillan, 2002).

Daniel, M., Strategy—A Step-by-step Approach (Palgrave MacMillan, 2004).

Delios, A., and Singh, K., Mastering Business in Asia (John Wiley & Sons, 2005).

Faber, M., Zukunftsmarkt Asien (FinanzBuch Verlag, 2004).

Fischer, P., FDI in Russia: A Strategy for Industrial Recovery (MacMillan/Palgrave, 2000).

Fischer, P., Foreign Direct Investment into Russia: Five Steps toward Success (Flinta, 2004).

Franke, R., et al., "Cultural Roots of Economic Performance: A Research Note," *Strategic Management Journal* 12 (1991): 165–173.

Friend, G., and Zehle, S., Guide to Business Planning (The Economist Newspaper Ltd., 2008).

Fung, V., et al., Competing in a Flat World (Pearson Education, 2008), 10.

Gagnon, M., and Lexchin, J., More Money for Advertising than for Research (Plos Medecine, 2007).

Gardner, H., Comparative Economic Systems (Dryden Press, 1998).

Garten, J. E., The Big 10: The Big Emerging Markets and How They Will Change Our Lives (Basic Books, 1998).

Gesteland, R., Cross-cultural Business Behaviour (Handelshøjskolen, 1997).

Gordon, S., When Asia Was the World (Da Capo Press, 2008).

Gösche, A., Mergers & Acquisitions im Mittelstand (Gabler, 1991).

Hamel, G., and Prahalad, C. K., "Competing for the Future: Strategic Intent," *Harvard Business Review*, May–June 1989.

Handfield, R., and Nichols, E., Supply Chain Redesign (Financial Times Prentice Hall, 2002).

Heinsohn, G., Soehne und Weltmacht (Orell Füssli, 2003).

Hickson, D., and Pugh, D., Management Worldwide (Penguin Business, 1995), 25.

Higgins, R., Analysis for Financial Management (Irwin/McGraw-Hill, 2000).

Hirn, W., Angriff aus Asien, (S. Fischer Verlag, 2007).

Huston, L., and Sakhab, N., "Connect and Develop inside Procter & Gamble's New Model for Innovation," *Harvard Business Review* 84, no. 3 (2006): 58–66.

Izraeliewicz, E., Quand la Chine Change le Monde (Editions Grosset & Fasquelle, 2005).

Jarillo, C., Strategic Logic (Palgrave MacMillan, 2003).

Jashapara, A., Knowledge Management: An Integrated Approach (Prentice Hall, 2004).

Johnson, G., and Scholes, K., Exploring Corporate Strategy (Prentice Hall, 1993).

Kalam, A., Envisioning an Empowered Nation (Tata McGraw-Hill, 2004).

Kalam, A., Wings of Fire (University Press, 2007).

Kaplan, R. and Norton, D., Alignment (Harvard Business School, 2006)

Kerth, K., and Pütmann, R., Die Besten Strategietools in der Praxis, (Carl Hanser, 2005).

Khann, T., Billions Entrepreneurs—How China and India are Reshaping Their Futures and Yours (Penguin Books, 2007).

Koch, W., and Wegmann, J., Praktiker Handbuch Due Diligence (Schaeffer-Poeschel, 1998).

Kotler, Ph., Kotler on Marketing: How to Create, Win and Dominate Markets (Simon & Schuster, 2001).

Kotler, Ph., The Marketing of Nations (The Free Press/Simon & Schuster, 1997).

Kotler, Ph., Haider, D., Asplund, Ch., and Rein, I., Marketing Places: Europe (Prentice Hall Europe, 1998).

Kotler, Ph., and Keller, K., A Framework for Marketing Management (Pearson Prentice Hall, 2007).

Kumar, N., Globalization and the Quality of Foreign Direct Investment (Oxford University Press, 2002).

Lewis, R. D., The Cultural Imperative: Global Trends in the 21st Century (Intercultural Press, 2003).

Lodge, G., et al., Ideology and National Competitiveness: An Analysis of Nine Countries (Harvard University Press, 1987), 9–10.

Manyika, J., et al., "Eight Business Technology Trends to Watch", *The McKinsey Quarterly*, December 2007.

Mariotti, S., and Mutinelli, M., La Crescita Internazionale per le PMI (Il Sole 24 Ore, 2003).

Markova, V., and Kuznetsova, S., Strategicheski Menedzment (1999), 91–124.

Mazzei, F., and Volpi, V., Asia al Centro (EGEA, Bocconi University, 2006).

Moeller, S., and Brady, Ch., Intelligent M&A (John Wiley & Sons, 2007).

Myasnikov, The Strategic Triangle of Russia, China and India: The Eurasian Aspect (Russian Academy of Science, 2003).

OECD, Staying Competitive in the Global Value Chain (OECD, 2007).

Peerenboom, R., China modernizes (Oxford University Press, 2007).

Prahalad, C. K., The Fortune at the Bottom of the Pyramid (Wharton School, 2006).

Popkin, J., and Iyengar, P., IT and the East (Harvard University Press, 2007).

Porter, M., Competitive Advantage (The Free Press, 1985).

Porter, M., The Competitive Advantage of Nations (MacMillan, 1990).

Pu, H., and Que, Y., "Why Have Some Transnational Corporations Failed in China?" *China and the World Economy*, vol. 12, no. 5 (2004): 67–79.

Rasgotra, M, and Chopra, V., India's Relations with Russia and China (Gyan Publishing House, 1997).

Savona, P., et al., Geoeconomia—Il Dominio dello Spazio Economico (FrancoAngeli, 1995).

Shainesh, G., and Sheth, J., Customer Relationship Management (MacMillan, 2006), 96.

Siegwart, H., et al., Mergers & Acquisitions (Schaeffer Verlag, 1990).

Simon, H., 33 Sofortmassnahmen gegen die Krise (Campus Verlag, 2009).

Sinn, H.-W., Die Basar-Ökonomie, Deutschland: Exportweltmeister oder Schlusslicht? (Ullstein Buchverlage, 2005).

Sirkin, H., Hemerling, J., and Bhattacharya, A., Globality: Competing with Everyone from Everywhere for Everything (Business Plus, 2008).

Sunter, C., The New Century—Quest for the High Road (Human & Rousseau Publishers, 1992).

Töpfer, A., Das Management der Werttreiber (Frankfurter Allgemeine, 2000).

Turnheim, G., Chaos und Management (Gabler Verlag, 1993).

Warner, M., and Joynt, P., eds., Managing across Cultures: Issues and Perspectives (Thomson, 2002).

Weber, G., "Top Languages," *Language Monthly* 3 (1997): 12–18.

Weissman, A., Die Grossen Strategien für den Mittelstand (Campus Verlag, 2006).

Weule, H., Integriertes Forschungs- und Entwicklungsmanagement (Carl Hanser Verlag, 2002)

Wilson, D., and Purushothaman, R., "Dreaming with BRICs, The Path to 2050," *Global Economics Paper*, no. 99 (GS Global Economics Web site, 2003).

Reports and studies

A.T. Kearney, Emerging Opportunities for Global Retailers: The 2008 A.T. Kearney Global Retail Development Index.

Barenberg Bank, Perspektiven für Maritime Wirtschaft und Logistik. Strategie 2030 (HWWI, 2006).

BP Statistical Review of World Energy, June 2007.

CIA World Factbook.

Deloitte, 2008 Global Powers of Retailing, a Consumer Business Industry report (January 2008).
Economist Intelligence Unit, Foresight 2020: Economic, Industry and Corporate Trends
Euromoney, Country Risk Survey.
Euromonitor, Asian Marketing Data and Statistics.
Euromonitor, European Marketing Data and Statistics.
Freedom House, Survey of Freedom in the World.
Food and Agriculture Organization, Global Forest Resources Assessment (2005).
Heritage Foundation, The Index of Economic Freedom.
IIF, Capital Flows to Emerging Market Economies.
International Energy Agency (IEA), Annual Energy Outlook.
International Energy Agency (IEA), Key World Energy Statistics (2007).
International Monetary Fund, World Economic Outlook, April 2008.
International Telecommunication Union, ICT Indicators.
Merrill Lynch and Cap Gemini, The World Wealth Report.
The Hindu Survey of Indian Industry (2008).
US Census Bureau Foreign Trade Division, Country Data.
US Energy Information Administration, International Energy Annual.
World Bank, World Development Indicators.

Periodicals

American Chamber News
BBC Business Report
Beijing Review
Business & Economy
Business Standard
Business Today
Business Week Russia
China Business Weekly
China Daily
China International Business
China Today
El Pais
Expert
Financial Times
Financial Times Deutschland
Handelsblatt
Hindustan Times
India Now
Indian Management
Moskauer Deutsche Zeitung
New Scientist
Profil
RBK Daily
The Economist
The Hindu
The Hindu Business Line
The Indian Express
The Moscow Times
The New York Times
The Wall Street Journal
Vesti
Wall Street Journal
Wirtschaftsblatt
Wirtschaftswoche
Xinhua Press

Made in the USA
Charleston, SC
03 December 2009